Status, Network, and Structure

STATUS, NETWORK, AND STRUCTURE

Theory Development in Group Processes

EDITED BY

Jacek Szmatka, John Skvoretz, and Joseph Berger

STANFORD UNIVERSITY PRESS
STANFORD, CALIFORNIA
1997

Stanford University Press
Stanford, California
© 1997 by the Board of Trustees of the
Leland Stanford Junior University
Printed in the United States of America

CIP data appear at the end of the book

Contents

PART II
Status, Sentiments, and Comparison Processes

PART III
Structure, Social Networks, and Rational Choice

Contributors

RICHARD BELL is Associate Professor of Sociology at the University of South Carolina at Sumter. He received his Ph.D. in 1986 from the University of Maryland. His research includes work on the role of charisma as a type of illegitimate authority, on state formation in early modern Europe, on gender roles and female crime participation, and on the ideologies of correctional reform in the United States. He is currently involved in a project that attempts to employ a unified approach to the examination of power, influence, and legitimacy in bureaucracies.

JOSEPH BERGER is Professor of Sociology at Stanford University and Senior Fellow (By Courtesy) at the Hoover Institution. He was chairman of the Department of Sociology at Stanford University from 1976 to 1983 and 1985 to 1989. He received the 1991 Cooley-Mead Award. His current research interests are status processes and expectation states, reward expectations and distributive justice, and problems in the development of cumulative theory in sociology. He has coauthored and co-edited many publications, including *Expectation States Theory: A Theoretical Research Program*; *Status Characteristics and Social Interaction*; *Status, Rewards, and Influence: How Expectations Organize Behavior*, *Types of Formalization in Small Groups Research*; and *Sociological Theories in Progress*, Volumes I, II, and III.

ELISA JAYNE BIENENSTOCK is Assistant Professor of Sociology at Stanford University. She received her Ph.D. in Sociology from UCLA in 1992. Her primary research interests focus on the relations between sociology, economics, and social networks. Her current research is on power in social networks, agricultural privatization in Hungary, and urban inequality.

PHILLIP BONACICH is Professor of Sociology at the University of California, Los Angeles. He received his Ph.D. in Sociology from Harvard University in 1967.

His primary research interests are in the mathematical analysis of social structure and in the uses of game theory for sociology. His current work focuses on coalitions within exchange networks.

BERNARD P. COHEN is Professor Emeritus of Sociology at Stanford University. His principal interests are in social psychology and methodology. He is the author of *Developing Sociological Knowledge*, which deals with problem formulation, operationalization, and theory construction. He is completing a monograph analyzing the effects of group structure on group interaction and group productivity that is based on a large-scale study of 224 research and development teams drawn from 30 large corporations. He is also planning a project dealing with the relationship between group support and cardiac rehabilitation.

ELIZABETH G. COHEN, Ph.D., is Professor of Education and Sociology, and Director of the Program for Complex Instruction at Stanford University. For many years, she has directed a program of applied research using Expectation States Theory to produce equal status interaction in heterogeneous classrooms. Based on this work, many teachers in the United States and around the world use strategies for status equalization and for the achievement of equity in the classroom.

KAREN S. COOK is the James B. Duke Professor of Sociology at Duke University and Director of the Sociological Laboratory. She has served as editor of *Social Psychology Quarterly* and was Chair of the Social Psychology Section of the American Sociological Association. Her publications focus on issues of social exchange, power relations in networks, justice, and trust. She edited *Social Exchange Theory* (1987) and co-edited *The Limits of Rationality* (1990) with M. Levi. She was previously at the University of Washington, where she served as Chair (1993–95).

SHAWN DONNELLY is a graduate student at the University of Washington in the Department of Sociology, where she received her M.A. She participated in conducting research in the Laboratory for Social Exchange Research at the University of Washington for several years and has studied social exchange relations and the interplay between distributive and procedural justice. She has collaborated with Cook and Yamagishi on other research projects.

JAMES E. DRISKELL is president of Florida Maxima Corporation, a behavioral science research firm, and also serves as an adjunct professor of psychology at Rollins College, Winter Park, Florida. Although he has maintained a long-term interest in basic research topics such as status and group processes, he has devoted recent attention to research on group performance in applied settings. This work includes research on dynamics of air-crew interaction and group decision making in complex and demanding environments, funded by the Federal Aviation Administration, Army Research Institute for the Social and Behavioral Sciences, and others. Recent work includes research on task and dominance cues (*Journal of Applied Psychology*, 1993), cohesiveness and decision making (*Small Group Research*, 1994), and a book (edited with E. Salas, 1996) entitled *Stress and Human Performance*.

THOMAS J. FARARO is Professor of Sociology at the University of Pittsburgh. His primary research interests concern the formalization and unification of theoretical frameworks in sociology. His published work includes *Mathematical Sociology* (Wiley, 1973) and *The Meaning of General Sociological Theory* (Cambridge, 1989).

MARTHA FOSCHI is Professor of Sociology at the University of British Columbia. She received her Ph.D. in Sociology from Stanford University in 1970. Her primary research interests are the theoretical analysis and experimental study of group processes, particularly those involving status, power, affect, and influence. She has recently completed a series of experiments on the activation and use of gender-based double standards for competence in task settings. Her publications include *Status Generalization: New Theory and Research*, co-edited with Murray Webster, Jr. (Stanford University Press, 1988), and *Group Processes: Sociological Analyses*, co-edited with Edward J. Lawler (Nelson-Hall, 1994).

M. HAMIT FISEK is currently Professor of Sociology at Boğazici University in Istanbul and a principal member of the Turkish Academy of Sciences. He received his Ph.D. from Stanford University in 1969. His substantive interests are in status and justice processes in groups, and his methodological interests are in the construction and testing of mathematical models of behavior.

GUILLERMINA JASSO is Professor of Sociology at New York University. Recent work includes: "Exploring the Reciprocal Relations between Theoretical and Empirical Work" (*Sociological Methods and Research*, 1996); "Deriving Implications of Comparison Theory for Demographic Phenomena: A First Step in the Analysis of Migration" (*Sociological Quarterly*, 1996); and "The Common Mathematical Structure of Disparate Sociological Questions" (*Sociological Forum*, in press).

J. DAVID KNOTTNERUS is Professor of Sociology at Oklahoma State University. His interests include theory, social structure and inequality, social psychology, and group processes. He is working on a theory of structural ritualization and is engaged in research on the plantation slave system in the United States and the educational system of early modern France. He is co-editor (with Christopher

Prendergast) of *Recent Developments in the Theory of Social Structure* (JAI Press, 1994).

EDWARD J. LAWLER is a Professor in the School of Industrial and Labor Relations at Cornell University. He received his Ph.D. in Sociology from the University of Wisconsin (Madison) in 1972. He is series editor of the annual JAI series, *Advances in Group Processes*, and he was the editor of *Social Psychology Quarterly* from 1993 to 1996. Power processes are the central theme of his theorizing and research, from his early work on revolutionary coalitions to his most recent research on commitment in exchange relations. A key theme of his current work is to incorporate the role of emotion more explicitly into social exchange theory and into theories of organizational commitment and solidarity.

ROBERT K. LEIK is Professor of Sociology and Associate Dean of the Graduate School at the University of Minnesota, Twin Cities. His areas of interest include mathematical sociology, statistics and methods, social psychology, and sociology of the family. Current projects include a longitudinal study of families first interviewed when they had a child in Head Start, a series of computer simulations of interaction processes, analyses of nonlinear structural models, and investigation of the social consequences of structures like the European Union and NAFTA.

RACHEL A. LOTAN, Ph.D., is Senior Research Scholar and Co-Director of the Program for Complex Instruction at the Stanford University School of Education. She received her Ph.D. in Education and her master's in Sociology from Stanford University. Her research interests are sociology of the classroom and the social organization of schools. At present, she is formulating the sociological principles of curriculum design for heterogeneous classrooms.

MICHAEL J. LOVAGLIA is Assistant Professor of Sociology at the University of Iowa and editor of the peer-reviewed, electronic journal, *Current Research in Social Psychology* ⟨http://www.uiowa.edu/~grpproc⟩. He currently investigates group process effects on IQ and continues a research program that investigates power in exchange networks. He also publishes on the sociology of science.

BARRY MARKOVSKY is Professor of Sociology at the University of Iowa. He is Director of the Center for the Study of Group Processes, co-editor of the annual *Advances in Group Processes*, and associate editor of *Current Research in Social Psychology*. His research and writing have been in the areas of status, power, justice, decision making, solidarity, social networks, social judgment, social perceptions, social psychophysiology, computer simulations, and theoretical methods.

BARBARA F. MEEKER is Professor of Sociology at the University of Maryland, College Park. Her research areas include mathematical sociology, social psychology of equity and social exchange, formal theory and the use of computer simulation for theory construction. Current research projects include studies of allocation norms using vignette techniques, a series of computer simulations of interaction processes, and analyses of nonlinear structural models.

CECILIA L. RIDGEWAY is Professor of Sociology at Stanford University. Her research focuses on status processes, affect, and legitimation, with emphasis on the role of status hierarchies in gender inequality. Recent work includes *Gender, Interaction, and Inequality* (1992), special issues of *Social Psychology Quarterly* on "Conceptualizing Structure in Social Psychology" (1994) and on "Gender and Social Interaction" (with L. Smith-Lovin, 1996), and "Interaction and the Conservation of Gender Inequality" (*American Sociological Review*, 1997).

JOHN SKVORETZ is a Carolina Distinguished Professor of Sociology at the University of South Carolina. Current research projects concern formal models of social networks, status and participation in discussion groups, power in exchange networks, and theoretical studies of action structures. He is the editor of *Connections*, the bulletin of the International Network for Social Network Analysis, and an associate editor of the *Journal of Mathematical Sociology*. He was recently elected to membership in the Sociological Research Association.

TADEUSZ SOZAŃSKI is Assistant Professor of Sociology at Jagiellonian University, Krakow, Poland. His Ph.D. thesis (1982) deals with applications of graph theory in sociology, since then the main area of his interests. He has published several papers in mathematical sociology and co-edited the volume *Structure, Exchange and Power: Studies in Theoretical Sociology* (1993, in Polish). His current research is focused on formalizing network exchange theory and game-theoretic models of social interaction.

JACEK SZMATKA (Ph.D., Jagiellonian University) is Professor of Sociology at Jagiellonian University, Krakow, Poland, and Adjunct Professor of Sociology at the University of South Carolina. He is currently working on the extension of Elementary Theory to conflict relations and networks, on status-related effects on power distribution in exchange networks, on the intersection of learning processes and network structures, and on mechanisms of theory growth in the social sciences. His work published in Polish includes *Individual and Society: On the Dependency of Individual Phenomena on Social Phenomena* and *Small Social Structures: Introduction to Structural Microsociology*. He has co-edited many publications, including *Structure, Exchange, and Power: Studies in Theoretical Sociology* and *Contemporary Social Exchange Theories*.

MURRAY WEBSTER, JR., is professor of sociology at the University of North Carolina, Charlotte. Previously, he was Director of the Sociology Program at the

National Science Foundation, and a faculty member at Johns Hopkins University, University of South Carolina, and San Jose State University. With Robert K. Shelly he continues work on sentiment and other group structuring processes. With Joseph Whitmeyer and John Skvoretz, he is collecting data to extend the Skvoretz-Fararo model of group differentiation, and with Stuart J. Hysom he is working to extend Ridgeway's theory of ways that group processes create status characteristics.

DAVID WILLER is Professor of Sociology at the University of South Carolina and Director of the Carolina Laboratory for Sociological Research. His work contributes to extending and formalizing Elementary Theory. That theory seeks to relate structure to activity. His research focuses on testing the theory experimentally and applying it to historical and institutional cases. Current work includes the study of countervailing power and the development of a new, flexible experimental system called ExNet II.

TOSHIO YAMAGISHI is Professor of Behavioral Science and Sociology at Hokkaido University in Sapporo, Japan, where he directs the Laboratory for Social Research. He has published widely on social networks, social trust in cross-cultural perspective, social exchange, and social dilemmas. His publications appear in *Journal of Personality and Social Psychology, Journal of Experimental Social Psychology, Social Psychology Quarterly, American Sociological Review*, and in various Japanese journals. He previously was on the faculty of the University of Washington, where he received his Ph.D.

MORRIS ZELDITCH, JR., is Professor of Sociology at Stanford University and was chairman of the Department of Sociology at Stanford from 1964 to 1968 and 1989 to 1993. He was editor of the *American Sociological Review* from 1975 to 1978. He has coauthored and co-edited many publications, including *Status, Rewards, and Influence: How Expectations Organize Behavior, Status Characteristics and Expectation States; Types of Formalization in Small Groups Research;* and *Sociological Theories in Progress*, Volumes I, II, and III. He is currently at work on a book with Henry Walker on the politics of redistributive agendas.

Status, Network, and Structure

Introduction

Jacek Szmatka, John Skvoretz, and Joseph Berger

Recently, a special issue of *Sociological Forum* on the scientific health of sociology finds the patient grievously ill. To diagnose the ailment and perhaps offer a remedy, *Forum* assembles several learned "physicians," Stephen Cole, Randall Collins, James Davis, Harvey Molotoch, and Arthur Stinchcombe, among others. Their diagnoses vary—some offer remedies, and others none. But all agree that the patient is in critical condition.

Cole (1994) takes it for granted that sociology does not make progress like the natural sciences and proceeds to explain why. He offers two reasons: sociologists choose topics of study based on non-cognitive criteria, and the phenomena studied are inherently mutable, that is, the basic cause and effect schemes are historically and culturally bound. Collins (1994) identifies the ailment with the absence of research technology/hardware that enable the discovery of new phenomena. Davis (1994) suggests sociology's disease is willfully systemic, displaying a truly depressing array of symptoms: it is incoherent in subject matter and more content to study how and why it learns things rather than what it learns, worships non-existent theory, refuses to study those phenomena (social psychological phenomena, in fact) for which it has developed the best methods, accepts ideological cant as legitimate academic sociology, and, finally, examines intractable problems because they are socially important, rather than tractable, if socially unimportant problems. Molotoch (1994) sees the problem not as one of too much openness, but one of too little. Sociologists lacking the confidence to express themselves in their own voices mimic the scientism of natural science and stay inside writing for each other. Finally, Stinchcombe (1994) agrees that sociology lacks integration in the sense that there are many different and incompatible standards for good work. This operates against the prestige of the field among academic administrators (they do not know whom to hire, since no one agrees on who the best sociologists are). It creates endemic conflict between colleagues over what should be taught even in the introductory course. Worse yet, there is no remedy.

Against this Greek chorus of woe, we offer the papers collected in this volume. The authors have struggled with these problems of sociology as a field. Individually, none of the papers offers a "magic bullet," a prescription that if followed would cure sociology: make its subject matter coherent, reduce standards to a few compatible ones, eliminate scientism, improve problem selection, identify the nonmutable aspects of social phenomena, and increase the field's prestige among academic administrators. Collectively, however, the papers offer a counterpoint to *Forum*'s gloom. By example, they show that in subareas, sociology can make progress, identify nonmutable aspects of social phenomena, select problems appropriately, and cumulate an integrated and coherent set of findings and theoretical understandings. Skeptics, of course, will not be convinced because, as the proverb has it, "example is not proof." That parts of sociology's corpus can be healed is no guarantee that the entire body can be restored to health. The challenge is great, but it is overwhelming when practitioners abandon hope.

The papers belong to one of the most active and successful traditions in sociology, the group process tradition. This tradition has roots in the "small groups" research tradition of the 1940's and 1950's. This intellectual ancestor includes both classics of field research (Whyte 1943) and classics of experimental research, such as the jury studies by Strodtbeck and colleagues (Strodtbeck, James, and Hawkins 1957; Strodtbeck and Mann 1956) and the discussion group studies by Bales and colleagues (Bales, Strodtbeck, Mills, and Rosenborough 1951; Bales 1953). In relation to classical theory in sociology, the small groups tradition ranges widely from the W. I. Thomas concept of the definition of the situation to Simmel's conception of formal sociology as the study of abstract forms of interaction that transcend the particularities of a given social mileau. This heritage influences research programs in the contemporary group process field: some refine ideas in these classic studies while others react to their theoretical failures.

A research tradition encompasses a set of research programs, which share presuppositions about their subject matters. Each program, in turn, is composed of an evolving set of specific theoretical models. In the group process tradition, these models are not discursive but formal, a basic presupposition about how to best understand relevant phenomena. Postulates are set out to describe the fundamental character of a form of interaction, and the properties of the interaction form are deduced from the axioms. Simulation is often used to explore a model's properties when analytical complexity is great. A second basic presupposition in the group process tradition is the commitment to account for the properties of relevant bodies of empirical data. Experiments explicitly designed to test theoretical models are often the research method of choice.

Finally, Foschi and Lawler (1994: vii) note that in contrast to experimental psychology, group process research programs focus on "social structures, how they emerge and change, and how they affect and are affected by individuals."

The theoretical models operate at the level of the actor in a social situation, the "person-in-a-context." As Lawler, Ridgeway, and Markovsky (1993) point out, usually simple actors with minimal abilities are presumed, the easier to see how the social structural "givens" of the situation play themselves out and determine individual and collective outcomes.

The group process research programs paddle upstream against the river of failure lamented by *Sociological Forum*'s contributors. Davis would say it is because they examine tractable problems posed by (social psychological) phenomena for which sociology has the best methods of study. Collins would point out that the field is one of the few areas in sociology where there is the (sometimes actualized) potential for a hardware-based, technological research front that discovers new phenomena. The potential lies in the field's commitment to experiment and observation and the need to continually develop more precise research instruments. Even Cole might grant that of all fields in sociology, the group process one comes closest to using cognitive criteria in the choice of problems and nearest to studying immutable phenomena. Our hope is that the papers in this book provide models for researchers struggling to develop, integrate, and make coherent sociological theory and knowledge. They may join our authors in their canoes or build their own for the journey upstream.

The papers in the first part are concerned with problems related to theory construction, theory growth, and theory testing in sociology. The first three papers discuss the notions of "theory" and "theoretical research programs." Markovsky sets out criteria for theory in sociology and discusses issues related to theory testing as well. Berger and Zelditch propose an improved multidimensional model of theory growth by refining the concept of a theoretical research program, and Meeker and Leik show how computer simulations contribute to the process of theory development. The remaining three papers discuss, from different angles, issues of theory testing: Cohen argues that current methodology based on comparing experiment and control groups using random assignment does not solve the problem of rationally using evidence for theory choice; Szmatka tests elementary theory for universality by applying it in two contrasting settings and proposes cross-national replication experiments for testing theory for universality. Finally, Fisek shows some benefits of what he calls the test by derivation of implications from the model (or an informal test through mathematical analysis) as compared with a standard empirical theory test.

The debates over the meaning of "theory" in sociology have a long tradition, almost as long as the history of sociology itself. Recently, with the emergence of theoretical research programs (Wagner and Berger 1985; Berger and Zelditch 1993; see also Berger and Zelditch, this volume) allowing cumulative growth of sociological knowledge (Wagner and Berger 1985, 1986), the issue of criteria for determining whether or not a given argument is a theory became even more critical. Markovsky's paper is located within a tradition of methods of theorizing

in sociology that aims at establishing transparent and physics-like criteria for a
theory (see also Freese 1980b, Freese and Sell 1980, Willer 1984, Jasso 1988,
Cohen 1989). He distinguishes theories from "quasi-theories" (empirical generalizations, ideological positions, general perspectives, and the like) and offers a
set of conditions for the existence of well-formed, ever-improving theories.
Also, Markovsky discusses and enumerates problems and issues that can arise in
testing theories with a focus on multilevel theories in sociology.

Wagner and Berger (1985) uncovered a good deal of growth in sociological
theory by distinguishing orienting strategies and unit theories from their concept of a theoretical research program. Berger and Zelditch (this volume) refine
their multidimensional model of theory growth in three ways. They differentiate
elements of orienting strategies with respect to roles in, rates of, and reasons for
growth. Next, Berger and Zelditch refine and elaborate the notion of theory-
theory relations, especially with respect to theory integration. Finally, they differentiate theory-based empirical models from both theories and the empirical
outcomes of theoretical and applied research. Based on philosophical programs
of Hempel, Popper, and Lakatos, Berger and Zelditch's concept of a theoretical
research program explains the mechanism of intraprogrammatic, cumulative
theory growth.

Meeker and Leik (this volume) relate computer simulations to the process of
theory construction. They argue that computer simulations are an increasingly
important tool in sociological theory construction, especially as applied to issues
of how social structure, networks, and decisions develop. After reviewing several
theoretical simulations developed in sociology, from Axelrod's model of cooperation to exchange network simulations, Meeker and Leik offer an analysis of a
model capturing abstract properties of cooperation, competition, and interdependence characteristic of several different social situations (interaction between
spouses, authority relations, international conflicts) and a variety of units of
analysis (dyads, small groups, organizations). They compare computer simulations of Richardson's original model of the international arms race—with fixed
values of parameters—with their own "additive" model in which they manipulate values of the parameters for reciprocity, fatigue, and justice. The results of
their simulations support the view that normative processes such as equity or
conformity to role requirements are important factors in the development and
maintenance of a stable social exchange. However, they warn against mixing
empirical data and simulation-generated data, arguing that only empirical data
qualify to test theories.

Cohen's work focuses on problems related to development of rational criteria
for theory choice. He argues that current methodology based on "Mill's methods" does not solve the problem. As Mill's canons or Fisher's factor designs are
still associated with experiment in general in research method sociology textbooks, Cohen's criticism is actually directed against the entire tradition of ex-

perimentation in sociology and social psychology. In seeking an alternative, he proposes, after Laudan, to substitute "problem solving success" for truth-falsity ideas. Establishing a foundation for a new methodology, Cohen develops the idea of the Cumulative Research Program, which is akin to Berger and Zelditch's Theoretical Research Program idea discussed in this volume. According to Cohen, programs are cumulative in their ability to solve conceptual and empirical problems at a later stage that were not solvable at earlier stages. The examination of Cumulative Research Programs supports the view that comparative assessment of problem-solving success provides a way to use of evidence rationally to assess theories and families of theories.

Szmatka (this volume) tests elementary theory for universality by applying it in two contrasting settings, the United States and Poland. He also offers a method of theory testing for universality that he calls cross-national replication experiments. The structures investigated by Szmatka include the "T-shaped" profit point network, strong and weak exchange networks, and strong and weak coercive networks. The theory predicts differing rates of exchange and of coercion for these networks, predictions intended to be independent of time and place. To evaluate the effects of structure and setting, Szmatka applies a two-way analysis of variance to data from experiments in the United States and Poland investigating the same array of networks. In all cases he found that the effect of structure is significant and the effect of setting is not. The results of Szmatka's tests support the universality of elementary theory by showing that predictions hold independent from the particulars of time and place.

In his paper, which concludes the first part, Fisek offers a method that he labels implication test. His test derives general properties from a formal, mathematical model and asks whether these general properties fit the commonsense understanding of the phenomena being modeled. For illustrative purposes he uses the model embedded in the 1977 formulation of the theory of status characteristics and expectation states. In conclusion, he says that although an informal test of the model cannot have the same weight as the rigorous empirical test, as a procedure it should not be ignored.

Each of the papers in Part II is concerned with extending and elaborating existing theories of group processes. Building on recently developed research programs, they tackle critical problems in the study of status, sentiments, and comparison processes.

Expectation states theory assumes that all action occurs within a social framework whose enduring elements consist of cultural, interpersonal, and formal elements (Berger 1992). But how do these structural elements shape social interaction and what are transsituational outcomes of such interaction? Knottnerus (this volume) analyzes status characteristics theory from this perspective. He examines, among other issues, how beliefs about the distribution of status positions in the society affect the legitimation of power and prestige orders in groups, how status expectations formed in one situation transfer to a second situation, and recent theoretical work on how cultural elements can arise out of group processes. Knottnerus also describes new theoretical links between expectation states theory, the "new institutionalism" (Powell and DiMaggio 1991), and exchange theory (Willer and Anderson 1981; Emerson 1972a,b; Cook 1987) that promise to further the development of structural analysis.

Ridgeway is also concerned with relations between the level of interaction and that of the enduring social framework. Assuming conditions where individuals possess states of culturally distinguished categories and greater or lesser amounts of material resources and that the possession of resources and states are correlated, she describes processes by which the category states acquire different status evaluations and expectations and thereby become status characteristics. As status characteristics, they are enduring elements in the actor's social framework and are used (when activated) in structuring behavior on the level of interaction. A crucial component of this theory deals with the issue of how constructed status characteristics become consensually objectified (Ridgeway 1991, Ridgeway and Balkwell 1992). In her paper (this volume), Ridgeway presents her most recent results which document the powerful role of small groups in the formation of status beliefs and which suggest the existence of asymmetry in the diffusion of negative as against positive status evaluations. Her research also demonstrates how processes that are significant on different social levels can be combined in formulating a theory on the construction of status characteristics.

Sociologists have long understood that sentiment and affect processes can dampen the differentiating effects of status (Strodtbeck, James, and Hawkins 1957; Berger, Fisek, Norman, and Zelditch 1977). But are there conditions under which sentiments and affect processes can also intensify the differentiation produced by status? To answer this question, we need to understand how status and sentiments organize interaction (Shelly 1993). Lovaglia (this volume) formulates conditions under which positive and negative emotional reactions increase status differentiation as well as conditions in which they decrease status differentiation, and he demonstrates these effects in a set of experiments.

Driskell and Webster are concerned with related issues, and they show through their experiments that differences in status lead to sentiment differences, but that differences in sentiments (without status information) do not lead to differences in the ascriptions of capacity. However, they also show (as does Lovaglia) that when status and sentiment differences operate simultaneously, they have a combined effect on behavior. As Driskell and Webster argue, such studies direct us to the same fundamental theoretical question: if status, sentiments, and affect elements combine, what are the processes by which this occurs?

Martha Foschi and Margaret Foddy have pioneered in developing a research program in which a major focus has been on the operation of multiple standards in status situations (Foschi, Warriner, and Hart 1985; Foschi and Foddy 1988;

Foschi 1992). In this volume, Foschi argues that the activation of a diffuse status characteristic—say, gender—leads to biased evaluations and that, under certain conditions, different standards (strict or lenient) are used to assess the same performances of men and women. As a result, expectations of differing strengths are formed which act to maintain the status quo. Foschi reviews recent research that is relevant to her formulation, and then proceeds to extend her theory to deal with sentiments and affect processes. She argues that differences in sentiments (likes and dislikes) can also result in the activation of multiple standards. This extension (like the related research in papers by Lovaglia and by Driskell and Webster) opens up new avenues of research on the interrelations of status and sentiments.

Research on the application of status characteristics theory to institutional settings such as schools and to major status distinctions such as gender, race, and ethnicity has evolved parallel with the development of the theory (Entwisle and Webster 1974; and E. G. Cohen 1982, 1993). In their report of field research on status processes in middle-grades classrooms, Cohen and Lotan (this volume) show that "local" status characteristics—that is, academic and peer status distinctions—have a direct effect on classroom interaction and that classroom interaction has a direct effect on the educational gains of the student. In addition, they present the provocative finding that status problems are less severe in incongruent classrooms—those in which there is a negative or no correlation between peer and academic status—than in congruent classrooms. Their research also addresses the problems involved in relating societal wide status distinctions to those that operate in formalized institutional settings.

Guillermina Jasso has played a major role in the development of a sociological theory of distributive justice. Her earliest work was concerned with integrating theoretical elements from the exchange-equity approach of Homans (1961); Adams (1965); and Walster, Berscheid, and Walster (1976) and the competing balance-theoretic approach of Berger, Zelditch, and Anderson (1972); Cook (1975); and Webster and Smith (1978). In this research Jasso first formulated the concept of a justice evaluation function which she incorporated into her theory of distributive justice (Jasso 1978, 1980). This theory has been intensively developed and has been extended to comparison processes generally (for a review of its development, see Jasso 1993). In this volume, she further elaborates this research program, describing in detail how derivations and important quantitites can be obtained from the postulates of her theory. She also illustrates how, by using her results, one can analyze and obtain answers to such questions as the effect of inequality on a collectivity's well-being, on the public benefit of the cloister, and on the severity of subgroup conflicts. The paper exhibits both the analytic and explanatory power of this theory.

The papers in Part III address theoretical issues at the intersection of social structure, the pattern of connection in social networks, and the process of ratio-

nal choice. Four of the papers depart from the body of studies that examine
exchange in networks and how the distribution of power is determined by the
structure of the network. The papers, however, go in different directions: Willer
and Szmatka describe how theory resolves three general problems created by the
"actor-in-network" perspective; Cook, Yamagishi, and Donnelly refine an existing measure of structural power; Sozański formalizes the notion of an exchange network and the general problem of power distribution; and Bonacich
and Bienenstock address the rationality of actors in such networks by examining
the consequences of different decision strategies. Two of the remaining papers
deploy rational choice premises to analyze fundamental social phenomena: Fararo and Skvoretz develop a rational choice model of deviance, and Lawler focuses on the formation of commitment and solidarity as by-products of instrumental decision making. The final paper, by Bell, looks at social structures with
a concern for their legitimation.

Willer and Szmatka focus attention on three general problematics at the intersection of actors in networks: the joint action of individuals within ties to
distribute valued resources, how the structure of ties between actors impacts
their solutions to joint action problems, and the effectiveness of different types
of ties—exchange ties versus ties of coercion—in producing unequal distributions of the valued resources. Elementary theory, a body of ideas that models
relations between rational actors in terms of sanction flows, forms the theoretical
framework for the discussion of these problematics. Willer and Szmatka demonstrate how the principles of elementary theory (1) generate solutions to the
joint action problem for an isolated pair of actors, (2) explain the changes in
solutions that occur when the pair is embedded in a larger network of connections, and (3) allow the direct comparison of coercive structures and exchange
structures with respect to the creation of resource differentials.

Cook, Yamagishi, and Donnelly review various measures of power in exchange networks that have been proposed by various research groups active in
this area. They focus particularly on measures that develop from the conceptualization of power as related to an actor's dependence on another for valued outcomes. They introduce and evaluate a measure that refines the logic of an earlier
approach. In this refinement, an actor's comparison level for the share of resources available from a particular partner takes explicitly into account the likelihood that an exchange can be concluded with some alternative partner. The
preliminary empirical results they describe support the predictions of this new
refined measure of power.

Sozański tackles the important problem of unifying the various theoretical
proposals to identify the structural bases of power in network exchange research.
His effort is one of integration rather than refinement and rests heavily on
generalized formalization of the objects of study. In this general framework, exchange networks widely studied fall into one particular type, profit pool net-

works. Sozański's rich formal structure enables him to derive significant theoretical propositions for these types of networks. In particular, he offers a formal basis for the systematic comparison of the orderings of positions by their structural power generated by the two dominant theoretical proposals, power dependence and GPI-resistance approach. The comparison will enable future research to undertake critical tests of the two approaches by selecting for study those networks where the predicted orderings differ the most.

Bonacich and Bienenstock use simulation to explore the effectiveness of different negotiation strategies in exchange networks. They examine variants of two basic types of strategies, accommodative and exploitative. Positions using accommodative strategies try to maximize the chance that they are included in an exchange, whereas positions using exploitative strategies try to maximize the earnings from exchange. Each strategy is a different algorithmic specification of the sense in which actors behave "rationally." The simulations show that the effectiveness of different strategies depends on the kinds of positions occupied by the strategy users.

Fararo and Skvoretz review various theories of deviance and control and show how they can be embedded in the framework of a dynamic sociocultural network model. Their analysis incorporates elements of balance theory into a rational choice representation of an actor's decision to conform or deviate. This rational choice representation provides the micro-logic of the model. The mechanism that leads from the micro-level of actor choice to the macro-level of rates of deviance is termed a dynamic sociocultural network with parallelism. In this conceptualization, actors make choices in a socio-moral environment defined by orientations to particular and generalized others. The element of parallelism inheres in the fact that choices made change other actors' situation of action in a recursive manner. In this paper, Fararo and Skvoretz concentrate on the formal development of the micro-level component as a necessary step toward a fully dynamic model.

Lawler's work focuses on an important and unintended consequence of rational choice processes, the formation of affective, emotional attachments to an actor's social groups. His theory assumes that persons become emotionally tied to groups that give them a generalized sense of control. Social structures generate greater or lesser opportunities for choice, that is, opportunities for actors to deliberate over alternatives. Greater and more repetitive opportunities produce stronger perceptions of generalized control and thus stronger attachments to those groups perceived to be responsible for the choice opportunities. Furthermore, Lawler argues that strong attachments condition the metaframework used by persons to evaluate alternatives, biasing it toward evaluations based on group and subgroup welfare rather than merely individual and personal well-being. Lawler shows how this theory applies to an impressive range of phenomena, from macro-level differences in worker commitment between primary and secondary labor markets to the stabilization of exchange relations in micro-level network exchange structures.

Bell considers the conditions under which a social structure of nonlegitimate domination can be stable, although it has neither validity, that is, a general acknowledgment as an accepted and objective fact of social life, nor propriety, that is, a general perception that a normative structure is just and fair. In particular, he deploys the idea of endorsement, as developed in the experimental research on legitimation by Walker, Thomas, and Zelditch (1986), to Weber's observations on the history of governance structures in cities. Those structures of political domination could not be validated by the existing feudal order, nor could the feudal system of hierarchical obligations provide city regimes with a sense of propriety. Bell's reexamination of this history highlights the importance of endorsement by key political constituencies to the stability of the governance structure of medieval cities. Legitimation of these structures was achieved not by appeal to a superordinate set of values but by the mutual endorsement of the structure by the peers of key political actors.

PART I

Theory Construction, Tests, and Strategies

Building and Testing
Multilevel Theories

▶▼◀

Barry Markovsky

In the last decade or so, accelerating numbers of sociologists have climbed aboard the "micro-macro" bandwagon. Broad interest in building theoretical bridges between person-centered and group-centered phenomena has been stirred by an influx of monographs and collections on or relating to the subject (Roberts and Burstein 1980; Knorr-Cetina and Cicourel 1981; Hechter 1983, 1987; Eisenstadt and Helle 1985; Alexander, Giesen, Münch, and Smelser 1987; Coleman 1990; Huber 1991), and by prominent journal publications using "micro-macro" terminology (e.g., Collins 1981; Coleman 1986c; Kalleberg 1989). The micro-macro "problem" has also served as the theme for major conferences, and is even appearing in introductory theory texts (e.g., Collins 1988; Ritzer 1991, 1992; Turner 1991). Beyond the fact that some social theorists prefer *individualist* explanations and others like *structuralist* or *collectivist* approaches, the precise nature of the "problem" is usually not discussed very explicitly.

Sometimes those who write about micro-macro issues refer to a "problem" or "debate," and the question is asked: "which level of analysis is more important?" (e.g., Collins 1988; Zelditch 1991a). Other times, the issue is framed as a "gap," and the question becomes how best to fill it (Turner 1991). By one very different view, the abstractness of well-constructed theories precludes their being micro, macro, or both (Berger, Eyre, and Zelditch 1989). Instead, only particular interpretations or applications of a theory may be deemed micro or macro, relative to some other level of analysis.

In other sciences, the topic of multilevel theorizing per se has not been the focus of much attention, despite an abundance of multilevel theories. Cosmological theories span levels of analysis whose elements range from the smallest conceivable to the very largest (e.g., Spergel and Turok 1992: 54). Evolutionary biology spans the biochemistry of genetics to the dynamics of ecosystems (e.g., Monod 1971). Some economic theories link consumers, firms, markets, and economies in seamless formalized expressions (e.g., Hadar 1971). Neural network models (e.g., Caudill and Butler 1990) computer-simulate systems of richly interconnected decision units, with the behavior of each unit conditioned on patterns of input signals from other units. At a higher level of analysis, trained neural networks exhibit such properties and capacities as pattern recognition, generalization, associative memorization, fault tolerance, and, perhaps most remarkably, self-organization. Many social scientists interested in forging micro-macro linkages crave the appearance of such *emergent properties* in their formulations (Hechter 1987).

This is but a tiny sample of the ways that multilevel theorizing has developed in other sciences, and the way such theories are accomplished should serve as a lesson for us. They are rigorous and concise, and they only evolve through concerted and collective efforts. In sociology, *few discussions of multilevel theory actually attempt to develop multilevel theories.* They are for the most part descriptive or strategic. They are descriptive when they summarize theories that in one way or another seem to link ideas about individuals—behaviors, decisions, cognitions, emotions, and so on—with ideas about sets of individuals—group solidarity, class conflict, mobility, and so on. The discussions are strategic when they suggest particular substantive bridges between micro- and macro-level theories as a means to resolve debates or to fill gaps. Sometimes these take the form of new terms or typologies, and sometimes they entail new changes in old theories. Rarely, however, are such discussions methodological, either in the sense of providing logical criteria that must be satisfied by micro-macro or "multilevel" theories, or procedures for establishing empirical tests of such theories.

This is not to say that sociology lacks multilevel theories. It has several, and at varying stages of development. For example, social network theories can model causal interactions bridging across structures, substructures, positions, and sometimes actors in positions (Marsden 1983; Markovsky et al. 1993). Burt (1982, 1993), Coleman (1990), and Fararo (1989) are notably rigorous in their integration of models of the interests and judgments of humans in relational structures, in organizations, stratification systems, or institutions. A second area in sociology that exhibits multilevel theoretical activity relates to the so-called problem of collective action. Such theories address the question of why self-interested actors would invest resources for public goods, rather than refuse to contribute and just enjoy the benefits. They are specifically directed at problems of explaining emergent group phenomena based on mutually contingent choices of actors in those groups. The most rigorous of this research uses computer simulations to precisely express theoretical assumptions and to capture dynamics too complex for intuitive approaches. (See Oliver, Marwell, and Teixeira 1985; Oliver and Marwell 1988a,b; Heckathorn 1988, 1989, 1990; Macy 1990, 1991a,b.)

Ironically, in the several volumes on micro-macro linkages in sociology that have appeared in the past decade, such multilevel theories are scarcely noted. Most of the talk concerns strategies for theorizing rather than actual theorizing.

There is much debate about what conceptual linkages are best, for example, without concomitant efforts to develop theories that utilize those concepts and linkages. This paper is methodological in both senses. The first part establishes criteria for determining whether or not a given argument is a theory, and whether a given theory is a multilevel theory. The second section enumerates some of the special problems and issues that can arise in testing multilevel theories.

Criteria for Theories

A theory is, among other things, an intellectual tool that serves as a repository for knowledge and insights pertaining to a class of worldly phenomena. The more accurate a theory's explanations—the greater the congruence between its predictions and relevant observations—the better. Judgments of accuracy are relative and depend on available measurement technologies, the theorist's purposes, and comparisons to the predictions of alternative theories. In each case, however, accuracy is assessed through testing. Comparisons are drawn between hypotheses generated by the theory and observations of empirical events.[1] It may seem trivial to say so, but it is absolutely essential to establish that the formulation to be tested is actually a theory *prior* to conducting any tests.[2]

Surely some verbal formulations must be more theory-like than others. The problem is that standards for theory construction are rarely discussed in sociology, and there is no agreed-upon notion of what it means for a formulation to be theory-like. Actually, to say that there is a lack of agreement may be somewhat deceptive. It is not the case that the field as a whole is embroiled in disagreements over the nature of theory. It is more the case that most sociologists are not concerned with the formal properties of their claims. To the extent that any standards are employed, they are generally idiosyncratic—for example, whether the formulation "rings true" or whether it seems to explain particular cases of interest. To the extent that a formulation is not a well-formed theory, so-called tests do not verify anything, and generalizations springing from those tests are invalid. Unless one adopts strict criteria for constructing and evaluating theories, it is most likely that the product of one's efforts will be something less than theoretical—something that does not serve its purpose as a repository for sound knowledge and insights.

In the following sections, I will first distinguish theories from "quasi-theories,"

[1] To be precise, a "hypothesis" is a statement that conditionally relates two or more empirical phenomena at a particular location and time (past, present, or future). Strictly speaking, theories do not contain hypotheses. Rather, they contain small numbers of general, abstract, conditional statements that may be transformed into large numbers of hypotheses by substituting operational terms for theoretical terms, as guided by the defining properties of the theoretical terms.

[2] The term "formulation" is used to indicate any argument, whether or not it satisfies the definitional criteria for "theory" given below.

the latter being a residual category that captures much of what passes for theorizing in sociology. Second, I will summarize criteria that establish conditions that promote the evolution of ever-improving theories. Third, I will suggest a set of necessary and sufficient conditions for the existence of a well-formed theory. Last, these conditions will be extended to provide necessary and sufficient conditions for well-formed multilevel theories.

Theory versus Quasi-Theory

Much of what passes for "sociological theory" is really *quasi-theory*: empirical generalizations, free-floating conjectures, ideological positions, general perspectives, interpretive schemes, metatheories, methodological preferences, agendas, and so on. Granted those generalizations may be highly accurate; those conjectures, perspectives, and schemes may be insightful and creative; those agendas and ideologies may be socially beneficial and morally sound. Quasi-theory may even be extremely useful in the theory-building process; perhaps indispensable. Nevertheless, quasi-theorizing falls well short of any ideal for theory construction for the simple reason that it has no standards. Quasi-theories are virtually immune to systematic analysis through logical or empirical methods, and are thus resistant to progressive development. For example, structural functionalism, an approach once dominant in sociology, was in no sense disproved. Its proponents simply went on to other endeavors or passed away. In this sense, quasi-theories are much like Kuhn's (1970) scientific *paradigms*. Unlike Kuhnian paradigms, however, quasi-theories do not collapse under the weight of accumulated falsifying evidence. They are, in essence, unfalsifiable.

An evolutionary epistemology seems a fitting prescription if a research field is to have the capacity to generate theories that are ever-improving in terms of their accuracy and breadth: *Theories must be formulated in a way that promotes the application of selection pressures* (Markovsky 1993). Scientific theories exist both in intellectual and in empirical environments, and they must vie for superiority in both worlds. To implement this epistemology, a theory must have enhanced survival chances when, relative to its competitors, it is semantically and logically coherent in its intellectual realm, and it is well-corroborated in its empirical realm. The former ensures that different people who use the theory will derive knowledge from it in identical ways. The latter ensures that the knowledge is valid and reliable.

In sociology, formulations are often buffered from selection pressures through a variety of means. For example, (1) the truthfulness of the theory is asserted by reference to authorities rather than to data; (2) the language of the theory defies operationalization by non-initiates; (3) a verificationist approach is taken whereby confirmations are amassed and disconfirmations are either discredited, explained away post hoc, or altogether ignored. Each of these short-circuits mechanisms that would otherwise force theorists to seek improvements for their theories. Such is the fate of quasi-theories. Although the illusion of progress (with respect to accuracy and breadth) may be created through a variety of rhetorical shucks and jives, any progress that occurs does so only to the extent that selection pressures, however weak, are brought to bear on arguments within the quasi-theory.

Quasi-theories serve us best when they inspire us to theorize. They are pointless when we mistake them for theories and argue over their truthfulness. This is why I think it is useful to reserve the term "theory" for a more restricted class of objects: harshly tested sets of logically related statements composed of well-defined terms. It so happens that to date, most of the micro-macro "theorizing" in sociology is quasi-theorizing. What is true of quasi-theorizing is true of multi-level quasi-theories. Moreover, what ought to be true of theories—the standards to which they are held—ought to be equally true of multilevel theories. Next we consider those standards.

Fostering Evolutionary Progress: Criteria for Semantic and Logical Coherence

Earlier it was stated that to foster evolutionary progress, theories must be subjected to selection pressures in two realms: the intellectual and the empirical. Selection pressures in the intellectual realm cull theories on the basis of their relative degrees of semantic and logical coherence. For the remainder of this part, we will focus on eight selection criteria that foster the emergence of these properties.[3] Associated with each is a *ceteris paribus* clause—given two theories that satisfy seven of the criteria equally well, the one that better satisfies the eighth is preferred.[4]

Communicability. The terms of a theory must be meaningful to its intended audience. To the degree that the meanings of any terms in the theory are ambiguous, vague, obscure, or otherwise unavailable to the analyst, its communicability is compromised. Communicability is essential for scientific theories: because any theory that cannot be subjected to peer evaluation is outside the purview of science. Theories must be available for critical analysis by those qualified to do so.

Theories need not communicate to everyone. In fact, they are perfectly justified in containing terms that are unlike any used in everyday discourse. If the terms are well chosen and defined, this can be a great asset, for theories are supposed to provide insights that transcend everyday conceptions. To be comprehensible, however, such terms must form a *conceptual system* in which (1) the meanings of some terms are *primitive*, that is, they are assumed to be already

[3] Cohen's (1989) book *Developing Sociological Knowledge* covers some of these in more detail.

[4] There looms a much larger problem, however: the relative importance of different criteria. Here I will only make the provisional suggestion that we attach import to a theoretical criterion in proportion to the objectivity with which it may be determined. Thus, to mention two of the criteria to follow, it is more important that a theory be completely free of contradictions than that it be extremely abstract.

shared by the theorist and audience, and (2) the meanings of all remaining terms are defined in such a way that their definitions contain only primitive terms and/ or previously defined terms. If primitive terms are chosen judiciously vis-à-vis the theory's intended audience, and if definitions for defined terms contain only primitive terms and previously defined terms, then the meanings of all terms in the theory become intersubjective, that is, understood in the same way by the theorist and the audience members.

It is not uncommon for social theorists to commit the so-called *error of reification*—a conflation of the terms of their arguments with the "reality" to which they purportedly apply. Related to this is the *essentialist fallacy*, whereby scholars will debate what they believe to be the "true meanings" of the terms they employ. In fact, theoretical terms are most useful and clear when they are assumed (by theorist and audience) to possess *only* the properties explicitly assigned to them by the theorist. Problems arise when one assumes that the terms of a theory do more than this, that they holistically describe empirical phenomena or capture their essences. However, the burden is on the theorist to build his or her theory's conceptual system with great care, for everything that the theory is to say, and none of what it is not to say, must be communicated to others through its terms. The benefit is protection against misinterpretations, misapplications, and inappropriate tests.

Parsimony. The semantic coherence of a given theory is also facilitated by the use of as few terms and statements as possible to express the theory's claims and to define its terms. All else being equal, simple theories are preferable to complex theories. The chances of misunderstanding rise each time an undefined synonym substitutes for a theoretical term, or the same theoretical assertion is restated using different terms. Misunderstanding is virtually guaranteed if the *real* theoretical term or assertion is never distinguished from others intended to provide amplification or clarification. Moreover, the power or efficiency of a theory is related to its ability to explain as much as possible using as few expressions as possible. Obviously, in addition to accurate communication, these functions are also served by parsimony.

Freedom from contradiction. A theory containing a *contradiction* loses explanatory power. Consider the statements (1) If x increases then y increases, and (2) If x increases then y decreases. Each statement implies that the other is false, yet their presence in the theory implies that both are assumed to be true. As a result, a theory containing both of these statements must always be *logically false*, whatever the substantive meaning of x and y. In logic, the Law of Contradiction states that it is false to assert that a statement is both true and false. Relaxing this restriction would, among other problems, result in self-falsifying theories. That is because any observation that supports one side of the contradiction would automatically refute the other side. If x and y both increase and (1) is thereby corroborated, (2) is automatically falsified.

Freedom from ambivalence. Theories that contain ambivalent statements such as "Increases in A may cause increases in B" are ineffectual because they are always *logically true* regardless of their content. The theory would have no predictive power because it is unable to anticipate when or how B can be predicted by A. Despite this problem, sociological arguments are almost always filled with such slippery assertions.

Precision. In the present context, precision is the capacity of a theory to articulate fine-grained (as opposed to crude) hypotheses. Although a theory may generate predictions that are highly precise, the *accuracy* of those predictions— their correspondence to empirical observations—may vary. Thus, adding ambivalent statements to a theory may greatly increase its accuracy (by covering all possible empirical outcomes), but that also diminishes the theory's precision and so undermines its explanatory power.

Abstractness. This is the quality of not being bound to specific objects, times, and places. Theories must be applicable to real events and phenomena, but they must not be wedded to a closed set of specific cases. They should be capable of transcending particular cases so that they remain applicable whenever and wherever the appropriate conditions arise. This is accomplished through expressing the claims of the theory in abstract terms, as opposed to concrete terms. In this way, multiple and varied empirical circumstances will fall under the purview of the theory.

Generality. Abstractness promotes broad applicability of theories, but does not ensure it. A theory is general to the extent that it applies to a relatively large number and wide range of empirical instances, and its predictions for those instances are accurate.

Conditionality. Cohen (1989) suggested three ways that theories are conditional. First, they contain chains of logically related *conditional statements* that predicate the state or level of one term on that of another. "If x then y" is an example, as is "Increases in x cause increases in y." Without such statements, the theory would give us nothing to test. Second, *initial conditions* use definitions of the theory's terms to apply the theory to empirical phenomena; they allow us to derive hypotheses. Third, *scope conditions* provide abstract, provisional guidelines describing the sorts of contexts in which the theory is deemed applicable by the theorist (for example, "capitalist societies," "task-oriented groups," "rational actors"). These protect the theory from being tested inappropriately.

In sum, by promoting logical and semantic integrity, the eight criteria help to ensure that theories will be self-correcting and ever-improving with time. Further, attending to these criteria focuses attention where it is most needed: *on the theory.* When members of a research field agree that the terms and statements of a theory are to be the focus of debate and research, then it no longer matters who wrote them, what someone thinks the theorist *really* meant, whether it solves pressing social problems, or even who cares or does not care about the theory. As Donald Campbell (1974) points out, even if a research tradition is working with a "trivial" topic, if strong theoretical criteria are applied, then knowledge will advance more rapidly than research focused on a more "important" problem whose researchers lack a sharp and consistent selection system. Over time, the strong theories—even if trivial at the outset—will grow in strength and comprehensiveness, and ultimately overtake the weak.

Criteria for Multilevel Theories

The above points lay foundational criteria for theories, but it is not the case that *only* theories can satisfy them. In this section, we thus consider some additional criteria to determine whether or not a set of claims constitutes a theory. In the following section, several further criteria will determine whether or not a given theory is multilevel. All these criteria are expressed in set theoretic terms;[5] however, here I will only sketch them briefly and informally. In this scheme, *multilevel theories* consist of *theories* that are combined in certain specified ways. In turn, theories are composed of building blocks called *theory units*. And finally, in turn, a theory unit has the four elements described next.

Theory Units. The theory unit (TU) is a *knowledge* unit. It brings together a minimal set of terms, a theoretical assertion, and a domain specification.[6] It has four subsets: operators, terms, one assumption, and one or more scope conditions. (1) Operators include mathematical functions (for example, addition, exponentiation) and/or logical connectives (for example, "if," "then," "therefore") whose meanings are established in an analytic system exogenous to the theory. (2) The terms of a TU include primitive (undefined) terms whose meanings are also given exogenously, and defined terms whose meanings are established in the theory through definitions that consist of only primitive terms or previously defined terms. (3) The assumption conditionalizes one statement on another—that is, it is (or can be put) in the form "If ⟨antecedent⟩ then ⟨consequent⟩." For instance, assuming the following terms have been established as primitive or defined, the antecedent may be a statement such as "A task group is densely connected" and the consequent could be "Members of the task group will become friends." (4) Scope conditions express the domain of the assumption's applicability—for example, "The assumption applies only to newly formed groups." To help serve the criteria for semantic coherence, the assumption and scope condition should contain only terms and operators, every term and opera-

---

[5] At this writing, the latest version of this definitional system is in a manuscript-in-progress. The relevant sections are completed, however, and available from the author upon request. A less refined version is provided in Markovsky (1988b).

[6] This is similar to Cohen's (1989) "simple knowledge structure" (SKS). However, in addition to requiring observation statements which are not needed for TU's, the SKS serves mainly a pedagogical function, whereas TU's are a component of a larger system that defines theories and multilevel theories.

tor should appear in the assumption and/or scope conditions, and there should be no redundancies among terms. The idea of a TU is useful in that it provides a fundamental building block for theories. Its explicitness and limited size make it simple to analyze. However, if it is problematic—its scope conditions too comprehensive, its terms ill-defined, its assumption ambivalent—then its problems will infect any theory of which it is a component. On the other hand, TU's are of limited value in that they have limited capacity to generate knowledge. The restriction to a single assumption inhibits the derivation of new general implications from existing knowledge. This function is in the province of theories.

Theories. In addition to satisfying the eight general criteria given earlier, theories must possess certain structural properties. First, a theory includes two or more linked TU's. The locations for these links are the subsets of the TU's. Specifically, given two or more TU's, their union forms a theory if and only if (1) the terms of each TU intersect with those of at least one other TU, (2) their scope conditions intersect, and (3) each TU connects logically to at least one other. For two TU's to connect logically to each other, one must have an antecedent that appears as a consequent in the other. The result of this logical connection is that the theory is able to generate new logical consequences or *derivations* that were not available from any of its TU's. Thus, theories have the capacity to synthesize prior knowledge and produce new knowledge.

Multilevel theories. Multilevel theories compose a special class of theories that span levels of analysis. They require two sets of criteria beyond those for theories: containment conditions and bridging conditions. Containment conditions ensure that the theory refers to at least two distinct entities or *units*, one of which is fully contained in the other. Examples could be group/members, network/bonds, person/cognitions. More formally, (1) statements in the theory refer to units at two or more levels of analysis, and (2) any higher-level unit contains multiple lower-level units.

Containment conditions exclude theories whose units of analysis are not formulated in such a way that one contains the other, *even if it may seem "obvious" that they are or may be so related*. For example, suppose a theory asserts

> Assumption: If an individual is exposed to a culture of criminality then he or she is more likely to engage in criminal acts than one not exposed to such a culture.

To determine whether containment conditions are satisfied, we would consider the relationship between "culture"—a seemingly "macro" entity—and the "individual" who may commit criminal acts—an apparently "micro" entity. In spite of appearances, the containment conditions are not necessarily satisfied. For condition (1), a theory may contain the terms "culture" and "individual" without requiring that these different *units* of analysis exist at different *levels* of analysis.[7] In other words, the theorist may choose to define culture in such a way that, despite its being in a sense "larger" than any individual, it may nevertheless be assumed to impinge directly upon an individual (like a warm breeze) without being *composed* of individuals. Some combination of circumstance and history may cause individuals to experience certain cognitions or make certain judgments, without the individual's necessarily being part of those circumstances or that history. Alternatively, the definition of culture may be given explicitly in terms of individuals—that is, the culture cannot exist without the presence of individuals to inhabit and maintain it. In this case, criterion (1) would be satisfied. The assumption would then also satisfy criterion (2) because its antecedent statement and consequent statement are at different levels of analysis.

In addition to the containment conditions, multilevel theories must also satisfy bridging conditions. These ensure that there will be at least one statement asserting something at one level of analysis which is predicated on something at another level of analysis. This may be accomplished in either of two ways: (1) there is an assumption "If x then y" in which the level of the subject of statement x differs from that of the subject of y, or (2) the subject of one of the theory's statements is a higher-level unit that is defined in terms of a lower-level unit that serves as the subject of another statement.

The bridging conditions thus establish the cross-level linkage in one of two ways. The first allows a conditional statement to link two levels of analysis. Two examples, assuming our terms satisfy containment (and all other) conditions: "If actors make only short-run self-interested judgments, then their social system will disintegrate at an accelerating rate." "If a kidney is removed, the organism will die." If properly formulated, such statements would not be true by definition. A social system may contain multiple actors, but not be defined in terms of them for a given theoretical purpose. An organism may fully contain multiple kidneys without being defined in terms of them. The asserted relationships between actors' judgments and social disintegration, kidney removal, and death are testable and not true by definition.

The second type of bridge may be constructed through a definition. For example: "A class system exists if and only if socioeconomic strata form a transitive hierarchy." Here, the relationship between system and strata is established by fiat and is not testable. Anything that does not possess transitively ordered strata cannot be a class system, so the relationship cannot possibly be tested.

Having asserted these provisional criteria for theory units, theories, and multilevel theories, I will next review some considerations that arise in the search for empirical confirmations.

[7] Note that this assumes the theorist may define a term in a way that may or may not accord with common sense or other notions of that term's meaning. Definitions, in this view, are formulated to give meaning to terms that are useful in testable assumptions. They are not formulated with the intent of capturing "essential" properties of a phenomenon, and thus committing the error of reification.

Issues in Testing Multilevel Theories

There are some special issues that arise when multilevel theories are tested. The discussion of these issues in this section is organized by the stages of the research process. These include operationalizing terms of the theory, designing research, and analyzing data.

Operationalizing Multilevel Theories

To test a theory, operational terms—those having specific, concrete referents—are substituted for the terms of an abstract and general assumption or derivation. The resulting statement is a hypothesis, which asserts the coincidence of two or more empirical phenomena. Hypotheses provide feedback to the theory, operating in a manner analogous to the senses. It is through hypotheses that a theory responds and adapts to the surrounding world. Hypotheses press the theory's implications into the empirical fray, and the theory is strengthened to the degree that it survives a battering. Theories protected from empirical challenges can only become weak and flaccid. Thus, the careful linking of abstract terms to the concrete world is a necessary and critical step for the multilevel theorist.

Errors of reification have especially pernicious effects when it comes to operationalizing multilevel theories. It is well documented that people have great difficulty suspending their ontological preconceptions. There is little or nothing to be gained (for most people) by "seeing" a wooden table at the level of its cellulose structure or of its planks and joinery, or by noticing the way that networks or ecological forces affect our behavioral options and opportunities. Notoriously, even while transcending the biases of common sense, social theorists are also reluctant to stray very far from their adopted perspectives—as if theirs were the *only* way to transcend common sense. This merely replaces one type of reification with another.

At the same time, the micro-interactionist need not always account for the impact of broader contextual spheres, nor the macro-organizationalist always feel the need to bring people back in. As long as theorists of a given stripe are using their perspectives in service of formulating explicit, testable theories, there is no problem with donning such blinders. If the theorist is not shielding the theory from critical testing, then data will eventually reveal its flaws. However, when perspectives are religions, and those religions become the theorist's reality, and when so-called tests are nothing more than well-chosen and filtered verifications of loosely interpreted scripture, the benefits of the scientific method are subverted, and the process of developing objective knowledge dies. Such failings occur at any level of analysis.

To be sure, not all theories need be multilevel. However, multilevel theory-building renders transparent some of the pitfalls of reification. In the process of conceptualizing multilevel phenomena—positions in social networks, for example—one soon realizes that the very same object in nature can be usefully understood in different ways *simultaneously* and without conflict. Sometimes it may be more useful to think very holistically of the table in the earlier example, treating it as a culturally determined and historically specific artifact. For other purposes it may be useful to focus on the design and arrangement of its components. And for still other purposes, the molecular structure of its wood may be of interest. A functional theory of bird anatomy may similarly attend to one or more levels of analysis: interactions among internal organs, and/or aerodynamic properties, and/or population dynamics and adaptation over numerous generations. A theory of social influence may also consider one or more levels of analysis: intrapersonal arrangements of cognitions as they determine attitude changes regarding issue X; the impact of the ratio of pro-X to anti-X contacts in one's social network; the broader diffusion process whereby issue X enters the network to start with. A macro theory may focus on diffusion; a micro theory may focus on cognitions. *Diffusion* is a potentially useful concept; *cognition* is a potentially useful concept. Theorizing about diffusion does not necessarily assume the nonexistence of cognition; theorizing about cognition does not obviate diffusion. *Diffusion* and *cognition*, as concepts, provide two different lenses by which social reality may be viewed at two different scales. They are not mutually exclusive. They are not even incompatible. They may serve well in tests of a given multilevel theory.

The process of operationalization, or *instantiation* (Cohen 1989), or what logicians call *interpretation*, identifies empirical instances of theoretical terms. Because abstract terms are not the same thing as empirical instances, there is opportunity for slippage when connections are made between the empirical and the abstract realms. The more rigorous the specification of defining properties for the theoretical term, the less chance for slippage in its operationalization. The narrower the specification of a term's defining properties, however, the narrower the range of empirical instances.

In multilevel theory construction, a greater than usual opportunity for slippage exists because many traditional concepts are loosely defined and can be associated with empirical units at several levels. For instance, we can speak of a person as being guided by a norm as easily as we can speak of a group being so guided. For most people, the actual "thing" doing the guiding probably differs for these different levels of analysis. One implicit definition of the individual-level norm is something like "a set of expectations held by an individual linking social sanction probabilities to behaviors." Clearly, a group does not "hold expectations" in the same way that individuals do, and so this definition of norm is inappropriate for use at the group level. By the same token, thinking metaphorically about the concept of "group expectation" could inspire one to devise a very useful group-level concept. Thus, "group norm" may be defined, for example, as the existence of an expectation, *shared by a majority of members*, that particular punishments will follow certain behaviors, coupled with the belief *on the part of those members* that a majority of other members also share this expectation. A less reductionistic version might simply specify the condition that a group norm is a rule created and enforced by a group's governing body. Clearly this conceptualization of group norm does not entail the definition of individual norm. Importantly, a given theory may contain a cross-level assumption that treats one type of norm as a determinant of the other.

In general, operationalizing multilevel theories demands the same attention as unilevel theories to the a priori specification of defining properties for theoretical terms. Each theorist must presume that all the key terms of his or her theories will be understood only by, and exactly by, the definitions that he or she supplies for them. This will facilitate communication, though perhaps not perfect it. Further, when defining terms for multilevel theories, one must take special care to avoid reification errors and the misapplication of terms developed for units at one level to units at another level. To the degree that there are ambiguities in the criteria that compose the definitions of any theory, multilevel or otherwise, the ability for observations to corroborate or falsify the theory is compromised. The test becomes less of a test to the extent that the relevance of the data is questionable.

Designing Research

Definitions narrow the range of potential operationalizations for the terms to which they give meaning. So do the exigencies of empirical reality: The choice or availability of research settings and methods further restricts the number of ways to instantiate terms. Thus, it makes most sense, whenever possible, to let the theory guide the choice of research settings, indicators, and analytic methods, as opposed to choosing a setting or a pet method and trying to adapt the theory to it. This point may seem obvious. However, it is often the case that empirical research is not firmly coupled to rigorous, explicit theorizing, which thereby allows rhetorical dynamism to widen the range of empirical findings that *appear* to lend support to the theory. The greater the degree to which data are open to interpretation, the greater the likelihood that their support for any particular theory will not be exclusive. That is, the data may also be interpreted in ways that support other theories.

Hypotheses derived from multilevel theories may or may not span levels of analysis, depending on (1) the particular derivations from the theory that one wishes to test, and (2) how the bridging conditions are satisfied. Regarding (1), the conditions for the content of multilevel theories do not require that all statements of the theory build multilevel bridges. Thus, to thoroughly test a multi-level theory, it will generally be necessary to design research that tests at least some hypotheses that relate units at the same level of analysis. As for the second point, the two types of bridges between levels of analysis have important impli-cations for research design. Recall that the first bridging condition can be satisfied by a conditional statement in which the level of analysis of the subject of the antecedent differs from that of the consequent. In such a case, the theoretical statement could only be tested by a hypothesis that also links two different levels of analysis which correspond to those from the theoretical statement. The other type of bridge allows a higher-level unit to be defined in terms of the lower-level unit. Where such "definitional bridges" exist, *there is no multilevel hypothesis to test*. If by definition a group must have more than one person, then one cannot hypothesize that "if there is a group in the laboratory then there are at least two people present." This hypothesis cannot be falsified and thus cannot be tested.

Given that one has derived multilevel hypotheses around which to design research, there are no special concerns introduced, save for the fact that there must be sufficient numbers and variation among cases at all relevant levels. What is "sufficient" is an issue of statistical power. If one hypothesizes that a group will not survive without a critical mass, c, of zealous members, then one will need to measure zealousness for all individuals in not just a single group (as well as whether or not the group survives), but in a sampling of multiple groups that satisfy the theory's scope conditions. Survival is the group property, and knowing only that a particular group survived with c zealous members does not allow us to attach much confidence to the hypothesis. Nor, obviously, would a sample of N groups help us much if all N groups have c zealots and survive.

There is also no a priori restriction on the research method to be used. Any method that may be used to test unilevel hypotheses may be adapted for multi-level hypotheses. Of course, the fact that there will be units within units will require special care in drawing representative samples of sufficient size, in the case of survey research, or in randomizing across units at both levels, in the case of experimental designs.

Analyzing Data

Multilevel data-analytic methods have far surpassed multilevel theoretical methods in their level of development. Therefore, I need not provide much information here beyond a brief summary of approaches, and citations to meth-odologists who address the benefits and costs of such methods in more detail.

Hannan's *Aggregation and Disaggregation in the Social Sciences* (1991) focuses pri-marily on how and when "grouping microobservations tends to produce changes in correlation and (in special cases) regression coefficients" (1991: 59), thereby distorting conclusions drawn from aggregated data. The book was first published in 1971, and so thorough was the original treatment that not much new material appears in the revised edition. Hannan examined mathematical relationships between statistical models operating on the same data but at different levels of aggregation—for example, using individuals' education levels to predict their occupational attainments, versus testing the relationship by using means for education and attainment across counties. The mathematical analyses allowed Hannan to show, among other things, how and when parameter estimates for the two approaches will differ, what conclusions may be drawn, and the potential for biases introduced through model misspecifications.

Some of the problems that Hannan identified are circumvented by the use of explicit theorizing. For example, a researcher working with an explicitly individual-level theory that links frustration to aggression should be less likely to make capricious use of group-level data (such as mean incomes and strike propensities for workers in different industries) than the researcher doing atheoretical exploratory analyses. The group-level measures quite obviously fail to pertain to the theorized units. Such problems frequently occur when researchers have only aggregate data at their disposal and succumb to the temptation of making inferences about lower-level units based on their results. By the same token, we have seen far too many papers by micro-sociologists in which the behaviors of individuals interacting in laboratory settings are extrapolated without constraint to the behaviors of large-scale groups. Such inferences are just as fallacious as those extending from the macro- to the micro-level.

From a strictly pragmatic standpoint, contextual analysis provides an attractive approach to the analysis of multilevel data. Boyd and Iverson (1979), for instance, show how standard multiple regression techniques can be modified so that an individual-level variable is predicted by other individual-level variables and also by group-level variables. The idea is that such a model may be misspecified if not for the presence of the group variable—the contextual effect. Thus, the technique allows us to test the hypothesis that workers' productivity levels are determined by their individual levels of satisfaction and also by the mean satisfaction level in their immediate groups. From the other direction, the relationship between group-level independent and dependent variables may be informed by the proper specification of relationships between corresponding individual-level variables. Boyd and Iverson also discuss a number of other methods for making cross-level inferences.

Conclusion

Fully two-thirds of this paper is about *building* multilevel theories, and only the last third is on *testing* them. This reflects my contention that, in our field, a better understanding of the nature of theories is needed before the results of our sophisticated empirical tests can make contributions to knowledge. This is even more critical for the case of multilevel research. Bringing multiple levels of analysis into the picture only multiplies the number of ways that the picture can be obscured. On the other hand, with remarkably small logical and empirical tool kits, elegant and sophisticated multilevel theories are possible. Without those tools, all the promise of multilevel bridges currently discussed in the meta-theoretical literature will remain just talk.

Theoretical Research Programs: A Reformulation

◥◤

Joseph Berger and Morris Zelditch, Jr.

The purpose of the present paper is to reformulate the concept of a *theoretical research program* in light of recent developments in understanding of theoretical growth. Building on the pioneering work of Imre Lakatos (1968, 1970), we have argued in a series of previous formulations that the theoretical research program is the most appropriate unit for the analysis of the growth of theory (Berger 1974; Berger and Zelditch 1993; Wagner 1984; Wagner and Berger 1985, 1986). A *theoretical research program* was defined by Berger (1974) and Wagner and Berger (1985) as a set of interrelated theories, together with a body of theoretical research that tests, refines, and extends these theories and a body of applied research grounded in them. Theoretical research programs are a distinct level of theoretical analysis. They differ both from individual theoretical arguments, such as Emerson's theory of power-dependence relations (Emerson 1962, 1972a,b) or Davis and Moore's theory of stratification (Davis and Moore 1945), which Wagner and Berger called *unit theories*, and from overarching metatheoretical structures, such as Parsons' theory of action (Parsons 1951) or Alexander and Colomy's neofunctionalism (Alexander and Colomy 1990), which Wagner and Berger called *orienting strategies*. The distinction was made for the purpose of understanding differences in roles in and rates of growth. Orienting strategies appear to be relatively stable. If one is looking for growth of theory, to focus on such strategies obscures the amount of growth taking place in a field. Unit theories do change, but attention to growth at this level focuses largely on theory-data relations. Growth occurs at this level, but it is only one kind of growth. There are other kinds of growth that arise from theory-theory relations. Furthermore, even at the theory-data level it is widely understood that changes depend on theoretical alternatives (Popper 1959; Lakatos 1968, 1970). That is, growth again depends

We gratefully acknowledge research support to J. Berger by the Hoover Institution, Stanford University.

on a context of theory-theory as much as theory-data relations. For both reasons, theory-theory relations are important to understanding growth. But Wagner and Berger (1985) pointed out that there are several different kinds of theory-theory relations that grow in different ways. Hence, they proposed a multidimensional model of growth. It is this multidimensional model of growth that is formulated by the concept of a theoretical research program. It differs both from the unidimensional, cumulative model of growth of positivism (for example, Hempel 1965; Nagel 1961; Popper 1959) and models of discontinuous change by such postpositivists as Kuhn (1962, 1970).

But the multidimensional model of growth has itself evolved since originally formulated. First, there have been substantial changes in understanding orienting strategies and their relation to theory growth (Berger, Wagner, and Zelditch 1989, 1992; Berger and Zelditch 1993; Zelditch 1991, 1992). Second, there have been refinements in understanding theory-theory relations (Berger and Zelditch 1993). Third, there have been changes in understanding the relation of theories to relevant bodies of theoretical and applied research (Berger and Zelditch 1985; together with new work in the section entitled "Models" of the present paper). Refinements in understanding theory-theory relations, while significant enough, fit adequately within the existing conceptualization of the theoretical research program. But changes in understanding of metatheory-theory and theory-research relations do not, motivating reformulation of the concept.

The section "Theories" of the present paper briefly reviews the core element of theoretical research programs, its multidimensional model of theory-theory relations. This section, though it incorporates refinements made since Wagner and Berger (1985), is not fundamentally different from it. It will, however, be useful for readers unfamiliar with the original model. The following two sections motivate the reformulation described in the present paper. "Strategies" reviews how understanding of metatheory-theory relations has changed since Wagner and Berger (1985), drawing on Berger, Wagner, and Zelditch (1989, 1992), Berger and Zelditch (1993), and Zelditch (1991, 1992). "Models" describes how understanding of the relation of theory to theoretical and applied research has changed since Wagner and Berger (1985), drawing on previously unpublished material. The final section reformulates the concept of a theoretical research program in light of these developments.

Throughout, we use examples from expectation states theory. This is not intended to suggest that the theories of this program are either the only or even the best examples of a theoretical research program. They are merely the example we understand most thoroughly. We in fact want to argue that the concept of a theoretical research program is perfectly general in its conceptualization of theoretical growth. Many of the changes we describe are based on analysis of other programs—for example, those analyzed (by their original authors) in the volume to which Berger and Zelditch (1993) is the introduction.

Theories

The core component of a theoretical research program is a set of interrelated theories. Theories within and between programs are interrelated in many ways. But which kinds of interrelations represent growth and development? This is the problem which Wagner and Berger addressed in their paper, "Do Sociological Theories Grow?" (1985). On the basis of their analysis of the anatomy of a number of ongoing theoretical research programs, they proposed that we distinguish five types of relations within and between programs—elaboration, proliferation, variation, competition, and integration—that represent different types of theory growth. It is extremely important to recognize that they also represent different types of goals and strategies that are available to the theorist in developing research programs.

Elaboration

We say of two theories, T_1 and T_2, that T_2 is an *elaboration* of T_1 if T_2 is more comprehensive or has greater analytic power or has greater empirical grounding than T_1 provided that T_1 and T_2 share the same family of concepts and principles and that they are addressed to the same general explanatory domains.

T_2 may become more comprehensive than T_1 by either an expansion of the scope conditions of T_1 or an expansion of the explanatory domain dealt with by T_1. Both types of growth are to be found in the status characteristics branch of the expectation states program. The scope conditions of the initial status characteristics theory (Berger, Cohen, and Zelditch 1966, 1972) was restricted to two actors discriminated by a single status characteristic. Subsequent formulations (Berger and Fisek 1974; Berger, Fisek, Norman, and Zelditch 1977) extended the scope of the theory to multi-actor situations in which actors may possess any number of discrimination or equating characteristics or sets of characteristics. Similarly, although the explanatory focus of these theories was originally restricted to the development and organization of power and prestige behaviors, more recent work has extended the explanatory focus to include processes of legitimation and delegitimation and dominating and propitiating behaviors associated with these processes (Ridgeway and Berger 1986).

Increases in the analytic power of the theories in a program are most often realized through formalization of the theory. While the original status characteristics theory was not formalized, for subsequent versions a graph theoretical formulation has been developed. This allows the analysis of an extremely large number of different types of status situations, the derivation of general theorems about these status situations, and with the estimation of relevant parameters the generation of interval ordering behavioral predictions in specific status situations (Berger, Fisek, Norman, and Zelditch 1977; Humphreys and Berger 1981). It is also the case that after the initial formulation, each subsequent formulation has been able to account for an increasing body of empirical results.

Elaboration is a basic form of growth in research programs and is driven by a *combination* of goals. These include theoretical—expanding the explanatory domain of a theory and enlarging its scope of application; analytical—formalizing a theoretical structure and developing models; and empirical—increasing the empirical consequences of a theory and its corroboration.

Proliferation

We say of two theories, T_1 and T_2, that T_2 is a proliferant of T_1 if T_2 enlarges the range of application of the ideas and principles in T_1 to social phenomena beyond the original domain or the original set of problems (within a domain) addressed by T_1. Through proliferations, concepts and theoretical principles from T_1 are carried over to T_2, often with significant modifications. In addition, new and auxiliary concepts and principles typically are introduced to deal with the specific issues of the new domain and the new set of problems. Thus while sharing major concepts and principles, proliferants will also differ in the concepts and principles that they employ. Unlike the situation where T_2 is an elaboration of T_1 and where T_2 may be used to predict what T_1 predicts and more, in the case where T_2 is a proliferant of T_1, T_2 may make few if any specific predictions about the problems dealt with by T_1. In this sense, the status characteristics theory and the status value theory of distributive justice (Berger, Zelditch, Anderson, and Cohen 1972) are proliferants. In both theories the notion of expectation is central, and while the former is concerned with the formation of expectations for performance, the latter is concerned with the formation of expectations for rewards. Key concepts of the distributive justice theory are identical to those in the status characteristics theory including the ideas of the possession, association, and relevance of status elements and the concept of a diffuse status characteristic. But the explanatory focus of the status value theory of distributive justice, which is on how actors can determine that the allocation of rewards is just and unjust, is different from that of the status characteristics theory. And there are concepts and principles in the former but not in the latter that have been introduced to deal with the unique concerns of the justice theory.

Proliferants may evolve in different ways—with one theory spinning off from a second (or two theories spinning off from each other), as is the case of the status value theory of distributive justice and the status characteristics theory, or with two or more theories differentiating from some common formulation, as is true of the exchange networks branch and the behavioral structure branch (Cook, Molm, and Yamagishi 1993) in Emerson's power and dependence program (Emerson 1962, 1972a,b).

Proliferants represent "theoretical leaps" in the growth of a program. By these theoretical leaps, existing concepts and principles in combination with new and auxiliary concepts and principles are used to extend the range of the program in terms of scope and domain.

Variants

We say that two theories, T_1 and T_2, are variants of each other if they employ concepts and principles from the same family of concepts and principles and if they are addressed to similar explanatory problems. Variant theories are closely related and often apply to similar if not identical scope conditions. They differ, however, in that they make use of one or more different mechanisms to describe how the relevant process operates. In the expectations states program, a set of status theories developed by Freese and Cohen (1973), Hembroff (1982), and Hembroff, Martin, and Sell (1981) are theoretical variants of status characteristics theories. They use concepts and principles similar to those of the status characteristics theory. They have similar scope conditions, and they have the identical explanatory focus—both are concerned with how power and prestige orders evolve and are organized in interpersonal situations. These theories differ from the status characteristics theory in that they propose a balancing mechanism in the processing of multiple items of status information. By a *balancing* mechanism, actors eliminate status information so that they are confronted with univalent information when they form self-other expectation states (see also Lenski 1966). In contrast, the status characteristics theory proposes that actors combine multiple items of status information in a manner described by the "principle of organized subsets" when they form their expectations (Berger, Fisek, Norman, and Zelditch 1977).

Variants are often constructed by theorists in an effort to get more precise knowledge of how a process works. This strategy involves constructing theories so that, for specified conditions, they generate conflicting predictions. This has occurred in the case of the controversy over whether status information is combined or balanced. (See Webster and Driskell 1979; Hembroff 1982; Berger, Norman, Balkwell, and Smith 1992. For a general analysis and assessment of these variant status theories, see Balkwell 1991b.)

The outcome of research on variant theories may be that one theory displaces the other, or an integration is formulated that describes the conditions under which each holds. In either case, there is an advance in theoretical knowledge. Thus, variants contribute to theory growth by providing precise knowledge on alternative conceptions of a specific process that are formulated within a single family of concepts and principles.

Competitors

We say two theories T_1 and T_2 are competitors if their structures involve different concepts and theoretical principles and if at some point they address the same explanatory problems.

Competitors may differ in fundamental ways, focusing on different behaviors, different explanatory factors, and being addressed to distinct explanatory phenomena. However, if for some particular explanatory problems they confront each other with conflicting predictions, their relations to each other can be important to theory growth. Within the expectation states program, competition with status characteristics theories has appeared in a number of cases. This is particularly true in the competition between dominance theories represented by Mazur (1985; see also Mazur et al. 1980) and Lee and Ofshe (1981) and the status characteristic theory dealing with status cues (Berger, Webster, Ridgeway, and Rosenholtz 1986) and that dealing with legitimation processes (Ridgeway and Berger 1986). These theories differ in concepts and principles: the former focuses on mechanisms of competition, stress, and deference-demanding behaviors, while the latter focuses on the role of expectation and status value processes in accounting for the attainment of power and prestige positions.

Conflicts between competitors normally are more difficult to resolve than those between variants, and competitors can exist side by side for long periods of time. This is due not only to their differences in conceptual structure but also to the fact that they often address disparate problems in addition to those they have in common. Nevertheless, resolutions can occur. For specific explanatory problems, one theory may come to dominate the second, and it is also possible that concepts and principles from each theory are rendered into some third formulation as part of a theoretical integration (see below). Thus, competitors contribute to growth of theory by providing knowledge on alternative conceptions of some specific process or of some specific set of theoretical problems where these conceptions are drawn from different families of concepts and principles.

Integration

Integration is a relation between three theories, T_1, T_2, and T_3, where T_3 "consolidates many of the ideas found in T_1 and T_2 in a single formulation, usually suggesting interrelationships between these ideas" (Wagner and Berger 1985).

We can distinguish different types of integration. To begin with, there are integrations of variants and integrations of proliferants where in both cases the theories are from the same family of concepts and principles. In the case of variants a common mode of relating the theories to each other is through *conditionalization*, which involves specifying conditions under which the process described by each variant operates. While no such formulation currently exists within the expectation states program, it is reasonable to imagine that one can be constructed which integrates the variant balancing and combining status theories by stipulating conditions under which actors balance multiple items of status information, for example, those involving high levels of social-emotional activity, and conditions under which actors combine such information, for example, those involving strong emphasis on task- and goal-oriented activities.

A common mode of integrating proliferants is to describe the *interrelation* of the different processes described by each of the theories involved. In the expectation states program, this is done in the theory of reward expectations (Berger, Fisek, Norman, and Wagner 1985), which partially integrates status characteristics theories and the status value theory of distributive justice by describing how both expectations for performances and expectations for rewards are formed simultaneously in status situations.

We also distinguish integration of competitors and, following the analysis of Fararo and Skvoretz (1993), what we may call the integration of "independents," where in both cases the theories differ in their basic conceptual structures. In the former case, the two theories also compete on common explanatory problems; in the latter case, the explanatory problems of the theories are fully distinct, and they do not compete on common problems. Since competitors and independents employ concepts and principles from different conceptual families, a major task in the integration of such theories is to render ideas and principles from the two different theories into the common language of still a third theory. Just this type of rendering of ideas from *competing* theories takes place in Jasso's integration of equity theory (Adams 1965; Homans 1961) and the status value theory of distributive justice (Berger, Zelditch, Anderson, and Cohen 1972) that leads to her formulation of a specific justice evaluation function (Jasso 1978). Using a similar strategy that involves *independent* theories, Fararo and Skvoretz (1987) have integrated Granovetter's (1973) theory of weak ties and Blau's (1977b) theory of differentiation in terms of biased net theory (see also Fararo and Skvoretz 1986).

Integrations represent major steps in theory growth. However, it is important to recognize that they may also entail losses, in that ideas and principles in T_1 or T_2 may not be captured in T_3 but may yet be useful for other purposes. Thus, the reward expectations theory (Berger, Fisek, Norman, and Wagner 1985) in the expectation states program, though it integrates some ideas from the theory of status characteristics and the theory of distributive justice, does not incorporate ideas on the "spread of status value" which are an important part of the latter theory. (The same is true of Jasso's integration of equity theory and status value theory of distributive justice.) As a consequence, the status value theory of distributive justice is not fully replaced by the theory of reward expectations. More generally, this suggests that there may not always be "strict replaceability" when later theories build on earlier theories in the growth of a research program (Laudan 1976, 1977). In turn, this fact stresses the importance of treating the theoretical research program as the unit of analysis in understanding growth.

Strategies

Orienting strategies, such as functionalism, social behaviorism, rational choice theory, or postmodernism, are sets of metatheoretical concepts, presuppositions, and directives that guide the construction of theory and conduct of inquiry. The elements of orienting strategies range from very broad, general presuppositions such as ontologies and epistemologies to specific, concrete prescriptions such as Durkheim's doctrine of emergence (Durkheim 1951) or the Hempel-Oppenheim-Popper paradigm of explanation (Hempel and Oppenheim 1948; Hempel 1965; Popper 1959). Although they are fundamental frames of reference in terms of which specific theories are constructed, Wagner and Berger (1985) did not include orienting strategies in theoretical research programs. Wagner and Berger's goal was to analyze growth. Orienting strategies appeared to be very stable. In particular, ontologies, epistemologies, and such other elements as the fundamental aims of inquiry seemed to change only very slowly, if at all. Wagner and Berger argued that to include orienting strategies in theoretical research programs obscured the amount and nature of theoretical growth in a field.

But closer study of the elements of which orienting strategies are made up suggests that they differ in nature, function, and rates of growth (Berger, Wagner, and Zelditch 1989, 1992; Berger and Zelditch 1993; Zelditch 1991, 1992). Some are quite stable, as the fundamental aims of inquiry, ontologies, and epistemologies appear to be. But some change frequently, even grow, as the concept of a "state organizing process" grew with the evolution of expectation states theory (Berger, Wagner, and Zelditch 1989, 1992), or as the concept of a theoretical research program itself has grown (Berger 1974; Wagner and Berger 1985; Berger and Zelditch 1993).

Anatomy

What are these elements? From the point of view of their nature, function, and rates of growth, it seems most useful to distinguish the very broad, abstract presuppositions that constitute the *foundations* of orienting strategies from the specific, concrete directives of the *working strategy* that more immediately guides the actual construction of theory, conduct of inquiry, and theory growth.

The foundations of a strategy include its fundamental aims and its most abstract and general methodological and substantive presuppositions. The *aims* of a strategy include its substantive objectives, for example, the focus of expectation states theory on basic social processes (Berger, Eyre, and Zelditch 1989), and its methodological objectives, for example, expectation states theory's generalizing orientation (Berger, Zelditch, and Anderson 1972). Particular methodological presuppositions are a strategy's *methodological foundation positions*. They typically consist of basic assumptions about what there is, that is, ontology, and how we know what there is, that is, epistemology. *Substantive foundation positions* are the strategy's most abstract and general substantive presuppositions. They typically consist of basic assumptions about the nature of the actor, of action, and of social order, such as the agency of the actor, the rationality of action, and the relation between consensus and coercion.

Working strategies, on the other hand, are much more specific and concrete. *Methodological working strategies* are more specific, concrete concepts and principles dealing with the nature of theory and of empirical inquiry, the logic of explanation, criteria for assessing theory, and the nature of theoretical growth. The Hempel-Oppenheim-Popper paradigm of explanation (Hempel and Oppenheim 1948; Hempel 1965; Popper 1959) is a methodological working strategy, as is Blumer's naturalistic method of symbolic interactionism (Blumer 1969). So is the methodological strategy underlying expectation states theory: ideas such as the importance of abstraction (from diverse, particular instances); the search for unitary processes through simplifying the complexity of concrete particulars in order to achieve the regularity desired by a generalizing orientation; the use of formalization to increase the analytic power of theory; and the use of experiment to increase the power of theoretical research to test, refine, and generalize theories.

Finally, *substantive working strategies* are more specific, concrete concepts and principles dealing with the what, rather than the how-to, of theories. They conceptualize the basic nature of actors, action, and society in more concrete terms and direct the investigator to solvable problems and the concepts and principles that will solve them. Fararo and Skvoretz's (1986) E-state structuralism, Merton's (1949) paradigm of functionalism, Lawler, Ridgeway, and Markovsky's (1993) program for a structural social psychology, and expectation states theory's "state organizing processes" (Berger, Wagner, and Zelditch 1989, 1992) are all substantive working strategies of this kind. (See the papers in Berger and Zelditch 1993, for illustrations of the use of both substantive and methodological working strategies in the development of major theoretical research programs.)

Roles in Growth

The elements of orienting strategies differ not only in nature but in function. Working strategies direct in a more immediate sense than foundations do. It is substantive working strategies that generate theoretical questions. The specific answers to these questions constitute the different theories of a program. Methodological working strategies shape the nature of the theories a program constructs and the specific methods of observation and inference used to test, refine, and extend them.

Thus, the substantive working strategy underlying expectation states theories conceptualizes social interaction as a state organizing process (Berger, Wagner, and Zelditch 1989, 1992). Because interaction is a process, the strategy directs an investigator using it to ask how and under what conditions a process is activated. In status characteristics theory, for example, a valued, collective task is one of several features that activates the status generalization process (Berger, Cohen, and Zelditch 1966; Berger, Fisek, Norman, and Zelditch 1977). The task or goal of co-oriented action is thus thought of as a critical element defining the situation of action. But the state organizing strategy also distinguishes the situation of action, such as goals, from the larger social framework, that is, enduring, trans-situational, consensual elements, such as pregiven norms, values, beliefs, social networks, and social categories, within which situations of action occur. By this distinction, theorists using this kind of working strategy are also directed to ask what elements of the pregiven social framework enter into the particular process in question and how and under what conditions the elements of the social framework are accessed. For example, diffuse status characteristics constitute the social framework in the theory of status characteristics. Referential structures are the social framework in the theory of distributive justice. How they are accessed is described by salience principles in the theory of status characteristics (Berger, Fisek, Norman, and Zelditch 1977), by spread of status value principles in the theory of justice (Berger, Zelditch, Anderson, and Cohen 1972). Additional directives derive from the fact that behavior in state organizing processes is governed by situationally stable states that evolve in the course of interaction but, once evolved, are relatively stable so long as the conditions of the situation do not change. Hence, a theorist using the working strategy is also directed to ask what behaviors are and are not determined by the states and how the states, once formed, are translated into observable behavior. In the status characteristics theory, the states are self-other expectation states, and the behaviors are the action opportunities, performances, reward actions, and influence that make up the observed power prestige order. The theory formulates principles such as that of organized subsets to describe how information about status-valued characteristics of actors in the situation combine to define expectation states and principles such as the basic expectation assumption to describe how states are translated into behavior (Berger, Fisek, Norman, and Zelditch 1977).

Foundations play a less immediate role in the construction of theory. What they do is provide the premises that justify working strategies, which, in turn, realize these premises at a more concrete level. Thus, the experimental methods of expectation states theory are justified by premises derived from the aims and presuppositions of a generalizing orientation to sociology. The aim is lawlike understanding of social behavior. It is presupposed that such lawlike understanding is general. This implies that a status characteristic created in the laboratory, if it satisfies the same criteria of definition as race, gender, and occupation, should behave in the same way as race, gender, and occupation. Therefore, it should not matter to understanding the principles of the theory of status characteristics what status characteristic one studies. A choice of a situation in which to test the principles of the theory is therefore a pragmatic question of how to achieve the most control and most precise measurement conditions. Experimental methods would be difficult to justify without the aims of a generalizing strategy or the presupposition that abstract knowledge is possible, or that wholes are dissoluble into parts that are relevant and parts that are not, or the presupposition that in tests of theories it is general principles that are important rather than particular, concrete effects (Berger, Zelditch, and Anderson 1972).

Rates of Growth

But from the point of view of understanding the growth of theory, the most important way in which foundations differ from working strategies is their respective rates of and reasons for change. Foundations seem to change very, very slowly, if at all. It is true that new ones appear all the time—for example, postpositivism (Kuhn 1962), poststructuralism (Foucault 1972), and postmodernism (Lyotard 1984; Rorty 1979). But often they do not seem to displace or even modify old ones. And such changes as do take place do not seem to be responses to the assessment of theories. Working strategies, on the other hand, change relatively rapidly, and their changes seem to respond to the assessment of theories.

Thus, the state organizing conception of a social framework, and its distinction of the social framework from the situation of action itself, only gradually emerged in expectation states theory. The concept was in fact present in even the earliest expectation states theory, but in a very simple form (among the conditions defining the scope of the theory) and without any recognition of how general an idea it was. In the theory of status characteristics (Berger, Cohen, and Zelditch 1966; Berger, Fisek, Norman, and Zelditch 1977), a social framework, the diffuse status characteristic, was the most important concept of the theory, but still without recognition that some form of social framework defines *any* state organizing process. A social framework appears again, in the form of the referential structure, in the theory of distributive justice (Berger, Zelditch, Anderson, and Cohen 1972), but again without explicit recognition of how general the concept of a social framework is. It was relatively late reflection on these three theories in the course of further extension of the strategy of the program to other phenomena that led to the abstraction, generalization, and explication of the idea of a social framework as a constitutive element of any state organizing process (Berger, Eyre, and Zelditch 1989; Berger, Wagner, and Zelditch 1992).

Nor did we begin with a concept of a theoretical research program anything like the present concept. In fact, expectation states theory as a program began with the goal of cumulative growth as it was commonly understood in the 1950's. It had a rather simple linear model of growth in mind in which a sequence of theoretical arguments grows ever more empirically adequate and ever more comprehensive in scope with later theories displacing earlier theories. But this model was consistent neither with our own experience of theory growth nor with our reading of the experience of other sociologists. Our model of growth therefore began itself to undergo growth. The first change was to recognize that "expectation states theory" was not *a* theory, but a theory program consisting of a number of interrelated theories (Berger 1974). But this first reformulation focused attention only on the anatomy of programs, without distin-

guishing different patterns of growth. A multidimensional model of growth did
not emerge until Wagner and Berger (1985), undergoing further change ever
since (Berger, Wagner, and Zelditch 1989, 1992; Berger and Zelditch 1993;
Zelditch 1991, 1992).

But "growth" may include changes in the use of, as well as the reformulation
of, a strategy. A notable case of a strategy that has been widely quoted but seldom
used is Merton's paradigm of functionalism (Merton 1949). Possibly this is because it is difficult to realize empirically Merton's directive to formulate the net
balance of functions. (There are functional theories, such as Davis and Moore
[1945], but they do not realize Merton's directive.) Contemporary functional-
isms, such as Alexander's neofunctionalism, seem altogether to have abandoned
Merton's paradigm (for example, Alexander and Colomy 1990). But abandoning
a working strategy because it cannot be realized in actual theoretical products is
a form of growth.

It is important not to be misled by the fact that some elements of metatheory
do change in response to assessments of theory. We do not argue that the relation
of working strategies to data is like the relation of theories to data. Working
strategies are as metatheoretical, and hence as irrefutable, as foundation positions
are. They do not change and grow because they are directly assessed by such criteria as corroboration, precision, generality, and analytic or instrumental power.
Such criteria are used to assess theories, not strategies. Working strategies grow
because they are more or less fertile and their use in the construction of theories
is more or less fruitful. They can be assessed indirectly, in terms of their utility as
directives in constructing theories. It is because they are used to construct theories, and because theories can be assessed by criteria like corroboration, precision, generality, and power, that working strategies change and grow. The experience of using them affects but is also reciprocally affected by the successes
and failures of the theories they are used to construct.

That foundation positions and working strategies differ in roles in, rates of,
and grounds for change suggests a need to rethink Wagner and Berger's (1985)
sharp separation of orienting strategies from programs. Their purpose was to
define a unit most appropriate for understanding the growth of theory. For this
purpose, foundation positions do in fact appear unsuited. The broadest, most
general aims, concepts, and presuppositions of orienting strategies, though they
play a fundamental role as the foundations of all inquiry, play a much less immediate role in the growth of particular theories. They change very slowly, if
they change at all, and such changes as do occur do not seem to be in response
to assessments of theory. On the other hand, working strategies play an immediate, directive role in, and grow reciprocally with, the growth of theory. One
would therefore like to conclude that foundation positions should be excluded
but working strategies included in a unit defined for the purpose of understand-

ing growth. But this more differentiated treatment of orienting strategies would not be feasible if orienting strategies were tightly integrated systems of thought. We therefore need to consider the nature of the relations among the elements that make up orienting strategies.

Compatible and Incompatible Elements

Because of the diversity of elements in an orienting strategy, one should not expect strategies to be tightly integrated systems, and they are not. Some meta-theoretical positions do entail others. For example, if one is committed to the aim of general knowledge of social behavior, one is at the same time committed to abstraction, because wholes are unique; to dissolubility of wholes, without which abstraction is not possible; and to the search for regularities, without which lawlike phenomena and hence general knowledge do not exist. But more often, an orienting strategy's position on one foundation question is compatible with more than one position on other foundation questions, and more than one working strategy realizes it in specific directives. For example, a commitment to a generalizing orientation commits one to nothing about the agency of the actor. It is compatible with agents, with structural actors whose behavior emanates from institutional scripts, or with dispositional actors whose behavior emanates from early socialization. And both experimental and nonexperimental working strategies can be specific realizations of a generalizing orientation.

There are limits to compatibility. Two elements are *incompatible* if they make or imply contradictory claims. For example, a commitment to objective empirical inquiry requires that one believe that there is a reality independent of the social position of the observer, however veiled one's knowledge of it. Any such strategy is incompatible with a radical relativism such as that of Maines and Molseed (1986), where the observer's values are seen to create theories and theories are seen to create their data. Furthermore, working strategies that realize incompatible foundation positions will themselves be incompatible. Thus, a structuralism that realizes a strategy without agency is incompatible with a state organizing strategy, which presupposes agency.

But the relation among the elements of an orienting strategy is more often one-to-many than one-to-one. Such one-to-many relations admit several possible combinations of theoretical elements. Thus, eclectic combinations of strategies are common, such as Parsons' (1951) synthesis of functionalism and the theory of action. Fission of strategies is also common—that is, the division of a strategy into competing variants that differ over a particular foundation position while remaining very similar in other respects. For example, rational choice and behavioral exchange theories differ largely over the status of theoretical unobservables, but they share many other foundations (compare Coleman 1990 or Hechter 1987 to Emerson 1972a,b or Homans 1961). Working strategies also may differ with respect to one directive but have many other directives in common, for example, Chicago versus Iowa interactionisms (compare Blumer 1969 to Kuhn and McPartland 1954).

Thus, closer study of orienting strategies suggests a need to differentiate foundation positions from working strategies. Working strategies play so immediate a role in growth and grow so reciprocally with the growth of theory that they should be thought of as elements of theoretical research programs. On the other hand, because they play a less immediate role in growth, change so slowly, and change for reasons that are less responsive to assessments of theories, foundation positions should be differentiated from the concept of a theoretical research program. It would not be possible to reformulate the concept of a theoretical research program in this way if orienting strategies were tightly integrated systems of thought, but they are in fact very loosely integrated.

Models

Wagner and Berger (1985) did not distinguish between empirical models based on the theories in a program and the results of empirical research involving these models. One of the ways in which programs are evaluated is on the basis of their theory-based models. Therefore to understand their growth (or nongrowth), it is necessary to conceptualize these models as distinctive components of programs. The empirical outcomes of research involving these models, however, have significance across different programs and therefore are not distinctive components of a program.

The theories in a program are often abstract and general in nature, and simple in structure. Theory-based empirical models are constructed to apply these abstract and general theories to describe and explain specific events and phenomena in specific situations.

Typically, the construction of theory-based empirical models involves a number of critical identifications and stipulations. To begin with, their construction involves the identification or *instantiation* of abstract elements in the different theories of the program with particular aspects of the situation and phenomena that is being modeled, for example, gender as a diffuse status characteristic. Second, their construction involves the *specification* of theoretically relevant special conditions, under which the model holds, for example, the nature of prior expectations in the situation. Third, their construction involves the *identification* of one or more sets of observational techniques and procedures that will provide information that is necessary in the application of the model. A fourth feature of such models, which is of interest to us, is that their construction often involves the *interrelation* of theoretical elements from different parts of a research program (or from parts of different programs), because of the complexity of particular situations.

A Model for Power and Status Processes

We illustrate these features of a theoretically based empirical model by considering one that is based on the expectation states program that has recently been formulated by Michael Lovaglia (1992). Lovaglia was interested in how power and exchange behaviors are transformed into status relations in interpersonal situations. The interrelation of power and status is of course an old and very general problem in sociology. Lovaglia, however, restricted his research to a set of highly specific contexts. This he did by formulating the problem as that of describing how power and exchange behaviors as studied in the standardized Cook-Emerson situation (Cook, Emerson, Gillmore, and Yamagishi 1983) are transformed into status relations as these are studied in the standardized experimental situation developed within the expectation states program (Berger, Fisek, Norman, and Zelditch 1977).

Lovaglia argued, putting it most briefly, that a pattern of power exchange behaviors, in the Cook-Emerson situation, that is consistent in its outcomes over a given number of decision trials and that is consistent with initial differences in power positions will lead to the formation of performance expectations which coincide with these power differences. These performance expectations in turn are transferred across task situations and become the basis of status relations as studied in the standardized experimental situation.

To describe a process by which this occurs, Lovaglia constructs a theoretically based model that makes use of three different formulations in the expectation states program. First, he identifies the power and exchange behavior in the Cook-Emerson situation with the abstract concept of behavioral interchange pattern as it appears in the behavior status theory developed by Fisek, Berger, and Norman (1991). *Behavioral interchange patterns*, as described by Fisek and his colleagues, emerge from consistent sequences of interaction and lead to status typifications which are behavior-based performance expectations. Second, Lovaglia identifies high and low bonuses which are allocated in his study to actors in high and low power positions with the notions of high and low reward levels as they appear in the reward expectation states theory (Berger, Fisek, Norman, and Wagner 1985). By arguments described in that formulation, the allocation of such rewards in themselves leads to the formation of high and low performance expectations. Since these reward allocations are consistent with the exchange outcomes, they serve as additional bases for the formation of performance expectations that coincide with the differences in power positions in the situation. Finally, using the theory of the evolution of status expectations (Berger, Fisek, and Norman 1989), one can argue that once formed, these performance expectations are transferred to a subsequent task situation and become the basis of a status order in that situation.

It is also to be observed that the model which Lovaglia constructs takes into account some of the special conditions in the situation under which this process is occurring, as, for example, that the actors start with no prior history and therefore that they hold no prior performance expectations. The model also identifies observational techniques and procedures, those used in the Cook-Emerson situation and in the standardized experimental situation and in the procedures of the semantic differential, which provide information on behaviors and reactions that are relevant to the model.

Status Models of Gender

The Lovaglia research illustrates the construction of a model to describe specific events in specific situations. Other types of models have been constructed that focus on particular phenomena as these phenomena manifest themselves across different types of situations. This is particularly true of status characteristic models that have been formulated to deal with race, ethnic, and gender behavior in interpersonal situations.

In a recent examination of status characteristic applications to gender, Wagner and Berger (1993b) have shown that these applications consist of distinct theoretical accounts of how status operates to structure gender behavior. Since the focus of this research is to account for a particular type of phenomenon, that is, variations in gender behavior in interpersonal situations, these accounts are in effect a *set* of interrelated models with each of the models providing explanations of gender behavior in a different situation. Thus, there is a model to describe the emergence of performer and reactor interaction profiles in mixed gender groups (Wagner and Berger 1993b) and a model that describes the construction of social types such as "dominating" and "expressive" persons on the basis of such status-based behavioral profiles (Gerber 1992, 1993). There is a model that describes how the gender typing of tasks determines the different status positions that men and women achieve in problem-solving status situations (Wagner and Berger 1993b; Dovidio et al. 1988). There is also a model that describes how men and women form different expectations for rewards in distributive justice situations (Wagner 1992a,b) and a model, among still others, that describes the differences in the behavior of men and women in situations where their power and prestige order is legitimated as compared to situations in which it is not legitimated (Ridgeway and Berger 1986; Ridgeway 1988).

Several additional things are worth noting about this type of theory-based modeling and related model building. First, as was true in the case of Lovaglia's model, the construction of this set of interrelated models involves the simultaneous use of a number of different formulations in the theoretical research program. In the case of the gender models, these have included, aside from the core status characteristics theory, the theory of reward expectations (Berger, Fisek, Norman, and Wagner 1985), the theory of status cues (Berger et al. 1986), and the theory of the legitimation of status structures (Ridgeway and Berger 1986), among others. This highlights an important feature that these models have in common. The different parts of a research program provide the *theoretical resources* that are used in the construction of these theory-based models.

Second, as is true of single unit models that are constructed for specific events in specific situations, the individual models in the interrelated set can be evaluated for their empirical adequacy. However, the existence of an interrelated set of models permits additional evaluations. Specifically, it allows us to assess the extent to which the set of interrelated models encompasses the *full* range of situations that is of interest to us in studying the particular phenomenon. Since these models are based on theory, this criterion also serves as an important basis for evaluating the program within which they are constructed.

Tests and Applications

Theory-based models also differ along other important dimensions. Among these is the consideration of how abstract or how concrete are the terms of the theory-based model. The terms in a model of power and exchange behavior such as the one we described above are fairly abstract, whereas the terms used to construct a model—say, of mixed gender behavior in a jury setting—would tend to be more concrete. Models also differ in the simplicity and complexity of the situations they represent, and whether these situations are highly controlled or involve little or no control. What is of particular interest is that models that are abstract, and that are of relatively simple and highly controlled situations ("artificial" situations), traditionally tend to be those that are used in *tests* of the theoretical formulations in a program. On the other hand, models that are concrete, and that are of situations that are highly complex and involve little or no control ("natural" situations), traditionally tend to be those that are designated as *applications* of the theories in the programs. Without questioning the value of this distinction, our analysis suggests that insofar as these different types of models are based on the theoretical arguments of the program, they each contribute, albeit in different measure, to the empirical grounding of the program.

Programs can be assessed through their models which can be evaluated in terms of different criteria. Among these is their empirical adequacy in representing a specific situation; the range of situations, events, and phenomena to which they can be applied; and their instrumental utility—how useful they are as a basis for social interventions. Such assessments are an important basis of program growth.

However, our analysis strongly suggests that it is not the only basis and that in fact there are multiple sources of program growth. Changes in its working strategies through the articulation and refinement of these strategies; attempts to realize its theoretical goals through the formulation of elaborations, proliferations, and integrations; as well as assessments of the empirical adequacy and instrumental utility of its theory-based models are each involved in determining the growth of a theoretical research program.

A Reformulation

Developments in understanding strategy-theory and theory-research relations call for a reconceptualization of theoretical research programs. They suggest that a *theoretical research program is a set of substantive and methodological working strategies, a set of interrelated theories that embody these working strategies, and a set of empirical models based on these theories.* This definition differs from earlier definitions (Berger 1974; Wagner and Berger 1985; Berger and Zelditch 1993) in two ways. First, it explicitly incorporates some elements of orienting strategies, though it excludes others. Having differentiated working strategies from foundation positions, we need to incorporate working strategies into our concept of a theoretical research program if we are to construct a concept appropriate as a unit for analysis of theoretical growth. Working strategies play an immediate, directive role in growth and grow reciprocally with the growth of theories. On the other hand, the definition still excludes fundamental aims and substantive and methodological foundation positions because their role is less direct; they change slowly, if at all; and the changes that do take place do not seem responsive to the assessment of theories. Second, it incorporates theory-based empirical models employed in theoretical and applied reasoning while excluding the empirical outcomes of such research. Theory-based empirical models are needed to understand growth because it is through them that the theories of a program are linked to empirical outcomes. On the other hand, the outcomes themselves are excluded because they are not distinguishing features of theoretical research programs. Both modifications of our definition of a theoretical research program are motivated by the objective of defining a unit of analysis most appropriate to understanding the growth of theory. These changes in the conception of a theoretical research program should make it a more powerful instrument for understanding the considerable growth of theories that is currently taking place in our field.

Uses of Computer Simulation for Theory Development: An Evolving Component of Sociological Research Programs

Barbara F. Meeker and Robert K. Leik

In this paper we discuss integrating computer simulations into theoretical research programs. As with most techniques in science, computer simulation has both costs and benefits, and we suggest ways in which computer simulation can be well used, and some cautions. We do not argue that computer simulation is the only way to construct theories. We do argue, however, that computer simulations are increasingly common, that they are useful adjuncts to the development of theories, and that we need to pay attention to issues of standards for techniques and presentation, rationales for interpretation, and possible sources of error from artifacts or unstated assumptions. We also argue that there are some theoretical questions for which computer simulations can provide uniquely useful answers. These include questions about how complex social structures develop from simple social processes, questions about the relationship between levels of actors ("micro-macro" questions), questions about how the logic of social situations can place constraints on the kinds of structures that can develop, questions about the causes of instability in social structures, and speculations about what resources or actions would be required to produce certain structures.

Simulations and Theories

For purposes of this discussion, we are defining a *computer simulation* as a computer program that moves through a set of steps or choice-points in accordance with an algorithm that reflects assumptions about some real process. (One can also have a computer "simulation" program that incorporates assumptions about a nonreal world, such as the popular "dungeons and dragons" type of computer game.) Its output, thus, is a prediction about how some object or entity will appear or behave if the assumptions are correct. Computer simulations appear regularly in journals such as *Simulations and Games*; the *Journal of Mathematical Sociology* had a special issue devoted to computer simulations in 1990 (vol. 15,

48 MEEKER AND LEIK

no. 2). Simulations may also be conducted without computers; for example, one of the original research publications in the study of small group processes, Bales (1951), reports a Monte Carlo simulation conducted by hand.[1]

As defined above, a computer simulation is a kind of theory. Much of the work in sociology that emphasizes theory growth and theory cumulation has been influenced by philosophical concepts introduced by the mathematician and philosopher of science Lakatos (for example, Lakatos 1968; Lakatos and Musgrave 1970). Lakatos proposed that scientific research proceeds within a "research programme" which contains both a "negative heuristic" (core assumptions that cannot be questioned) and a "positive heuristic" (accepted ways of developing, modifying, and elaborating the program). He states, "The positive heuristic sets out a programme which lists a chain of ever more complicated *models* simulating reality; the scientist's attention is riveted on building his model following instructions which are laid down in the positive part of his programme" (1968: 171). In other words, a computer simulation uses the tools of the computer to engage in an activity that is already at the center of scientific research—the development of theoretical models that simulate reality and that are of increasing complexity. Furthermore, although the predictions produced by these models are to be compared with empirical reality, the actual construction of the models follows guidelines established in the *theory* of the research program.

Some Types of Computer Simulations

Several quite distinct types of computer simulations can be found in the social sciences. Although we are focusing on one particular type (type 3, below), it may be helpful to distinguish this type from others which are also useful at different points in the construction and application of a research program.

Computer Simulations That Extrapolate from Well-Established Principles and Known Trends to the Near Future

This is probably what most often comes to mind when people think of "computer simulation"; an example is an economic model of the national or local economy that tells us when we can expect to pull out of a recession. These require very well established principles and good quality input data. They are often extremely complex, and they tend to work best in the short term. They can also be used to suggest the probable consequences of social policy (for example, raising the taxes on gasoline) or the "costs" of some phenomenon (for example, the economic costs of lack of health insurance). Simulations that use

[1] In a Monte Carlo simulation, the algorithm requires that at each choice point the process consult a probabilistic device, such as tossing a coin or using a table of random numbers, to decide which of two or more paths will be taken.

well-established principles are also used as training devices; for example, a variety of teaching "games" for such things as business decision-making exist. Something like a flight simulator also uses well-established scientific principles to train a student by demonstrating what the consequences would be of certain actions without forcing him or her to experience the actual disasters those consequences might entail.

The extrapolation type of simulation appears much less often in sociology than in economics. (Prediction of the outcomes of elections based on models of voting behavior is one exception.) It is tempting to say this is because sociologists have fewer well-established principles and less good-quality input data. However, we suspect we do have enough information, both theoretical and empirical, about many social phenomena (for example, birth, marriage, divorce, and death rates; geographic and social mobility; changes in households over the life course; patterns of job change or of switching among religious denominations; and so on), and could produce more extrapolations than we do.

Computer Simulations as Part of a Data Analysis Project

It is increasingly common to encounter a computer simulation along with a set of empirical results, presented as a kind of "control condition" or "baseline" against which to compare the data. These can be of several types.

Describing a random distribution. In one type, the researcher assumes that processes occur randomly and uses the simulation as an equivalent of a t-distribution or other random distribution when the phenomenon does not adequately meet the assumptions of one of these distributions. An example of this is a study by Clawson, Neustadtl, and Bearden (1986), part of a research program examining the network structure of American corporate political action committees. They used a computer simulation to answer the question of what a network of PAC's would look like if there were only random connections among them, in order to test the hypothesis that there is some unity (nonrandom connections) among businesses in attempts to exercise political influence.

Estimating parameters. In another type of data-related simulation, the results of an empirical study are fed into a simulation as values of parameters, with the assumption that the process works as theorized, and the results compared with the original distribution of data. Examples of this can be found in the research program on affect control by Heise, Smith-Lovin, and others (an early example is Heise 1979; for a recent review of this research program see MacKinnon and Heise 1993).

Computer Simulations That Expand or Cumulate Theories Within Research Programs

This is the type of simulation that concerns us. It is the closest to the type of activity described by Lakatos as activity within the positive heuristic of a progressive research program. In seeking examples for analysis, we tried to locate reports of simulations that were published recently and in which simulation is the main activity reported, but which are part of a research program in which empirical data[2] collection and analysis are or could be relevant. We also looked for reports of simulations that appeared in journals or books that are *not* primarily devoted to mathematical or computer work; since part of our argument is that computer simulation has become a widespread tool for constructing theories in sociology.

The first examples discussed below meet all these criteria. Apart from that, they do not represent a systematic "survey" of computer simulations; they are articles we came across in the normal course of our own professional reading and found interesting, well presented, and theoretically useful. The fact that it was easy to find them is an indication that simulations appear routinely in general research outlets, and as parts of research programs that are of general interest to sociologists. Most of these are Monte Carlo simulations, based on an assumption that the process being simulated is a probability process.

Examples of Theoretical Simulations

Axelrod's Model

First is a well-known and interesting example of the use of computer simulations to answer a theoretical question. This is Axelrod's (1984) examination of strategies for dealing with Prisoner's Dilemma situations. He conducted a tournament in which contestants could submit computer programs that had as algorithms strategies for "winning" at a repeated Prisoner's Dilemma, and ran them all against each other. Although many of the programs submitted were based on complex strategies, it turned out that the simplest, the "tit for tat" (respond on the next trial with exactly what the opponent did on this trial), came out ahead over the course of a number of games.

An Example by Macy

Macy (1991b) uses computer simulations to explore some additional questions posed by the logic of Prisoner's Dilemma situations, or, more generally, "social traps."[3] Macy's model compares a stochastic learning theory with a rational choice model for the underlying process of individual behavior. That is, he assumes that actors "adapt" their behavior in response to immediate past outcomes rather than rationally calculating future outcomes. He concludes that "adaptive actors are led into a social trap more readily than are fully rational

---

[2]Normally, we object to the phrase "empirical data" as redundant (aren't all data empirical?). However, one of the paradoxes of computer simulations is that they produce data that look just like "empirical data" but are not. Thus, in talking about computer simulations, one does need to distinguish between empirical and computer-generated "data."

[3]These, like the Prisoner's Dilemma, are situations in which individually rational choices are in the long run mutually undesirable.

actors, but they are also better at finding their way out" (p. 808). Parameters representing size and severity of sanctions, size of payoffs, and degree of temptation to defect are varied. An extension to N-player games suggests some intriguing consequences of having to keep track of more than one other player, with applications to network analysis. In the conclusions, a set of hypotheses is suggested that could be tested with laboratory studies using real subjects. This is part of a research program applying stochastic learning theory to problems of collective action (Macy 1989, 1990).

Marwell and Oliver's Simulation Program

Problems of "collective action"[4] are logically similar to social traps. In collective action problems, a "good" (such as a public park, or a successful lobbying campaign on a local political issue) may be created by action by a few persons and then benefit many more. Thus, it is in the short-run self-interest of members of the public to wait for someone else to contribute to the collective good and then benefit cost-free from its existence. However, unless a minimum number of actors overcome this self-interest and contribute, the collective good is not created. Marwell and Oliver (1993) use a set of computer simulations to examine several related theoretical questions about such situations. Their basic question is, under what conditions can we predict that a sufficient number of actors will contribute a sufficient number of resources to create a collective good? Among the factors they are able to examine using simulations are group size, the distribution of resources and interests among the public, network connections among possible interested actors, and organizers' strategies for recruitment of participants. They reach some conclusions that are counterintuitive (for example, that under some conditions it may be most effective to recruit actors with the *lowest* level of interest in the issue first), as well as some that are intuitive (such as showing how successful social movements tend to move away from promoting the issue that first recruited participants and toward promoting the interests of the contributors with the most resources).

Some of these results may have practical uses for organizers of political and social movements; however, Marwell and Oliver (1993) are careful to point out that the assumptions of their models, while plausible, may not represent the facts of a real setting, and that it is important to consider the assumptions of the models before using the results.

An Example by Heckathorn

As part of a research program examining the sources and consequences of norms and sanctions in collective action situations, Heckathorn (1990) presents a simulation of a formal model that assumes that actors can be punished for other

---

[4] These are also variously called collective goods problems, free-rider problems, and "the tragedy of the commons"; they appear in current research and theory in several social science disciplines.

actors' violations of norms and hence are rationally motivated to monitor each other's actions. He concludes that "group responses to sanctions depend on the strength of sanctions, monitoring capacities, and the efficacy and cost of intragroup control." Other reports from this research program include Heckathorn (1988, 1989).

Simulation Work by Carley

In a different theoretical area, Carley (1991) presents a Monte Carlo simulation model of a "society" (a group such as a formal organization with either one or two subgroups). On each trial the outcome is either (1) an interaction between actor i and actor j in which fact k is transmitted from i to j or (2) no such transmission. The model's basic assumptions are that actors interact more often the more they already share information, and information is more likely to be transmitted if they interact. New actors and new information may enter from another group if there is one. "Perfect stability" is achieved when all members of the "society" know all the facts. Among Carley's conclusions are that group size and complexity of information are important factors in the time to stability, that most simulated groups experienced oscillations on the way to stability, and the "groups that are stable in the short run do not necessarily retain their distinctiveness in the long run as new members enter or new ideas are discovered" (p. 331). For other reports in this research program, see Carley (1986, 1990).

The Feinberg and Johnson Program

Several simulations have been applied to crowd behavior. One such phenomenon, the transformation of an assemblage of individuals into an acting crowd through "milling," is simulated by Feinberg and Johnson (1989; for other reports from this research program, see Feinberg and Johnson 1988; Johnson and Feinberg 1977). They posit three processes in a crowd: intragroup influence (spread of opinion about a course of action among members of a small group who are close to each other in physical space and who will act as a unit if they achieve consensus); intergroup influence (spread of opinion from a small group that has achieved consensus to other groups); and movement through physical space (groups move toward others with whom they share opinions and away from those with whom they do not, and groups nearer the center of the crowd have more influence).

The question of whether crowds should be viewed as assemblages of isolated individuals or as collections of small groups is an important theoretical issue in the study of collective behavior. The simulation allows the researchers to compare a situation with small groups and one in which persons assemble as individuals, which have outcomes such as whether consensus on crowd action is achieved, time until consensus is achieved, final distribution of participants into centrally located actors and peripherally located onlookers, and so on.

They conclude that "crowds in which participants assembled individually were more likely to reach consensus than were those assembled in small groups," that "when participants were sorted in such a way that those with action-choices that had considerable support within the crowd were in a location in which they had special opportunities to influence other crowd members, consensus at or near their position was likely," and that "more time is required to achieve a high consensus value, suggesting that long periods of milling are necessary for radical crowd action to occur" (Feinberg and Johnson 1989: 77).

Exchange Network Simulations

Examples of the use of computer simulation by several researchers in a theoretical research program can be found in the work on exchange networks by Cook, Emerson, Gillmore, and Yamagishi (1983), Marsden (1983), and Markovsky (1987). For a recent review of this program, see Cook, Molm, and Yamagishi (1993). It has been shown in laboratory studies with real subjects that positions in exchange networks may have unequal power; specifically, that persons with more choice of bargaining partners enjoy structural advantages. In the computer simulations by Cook, Emerson, Gillmore, and Yamagishi (1983) and Marsden (1983) this effect is replicated in simulations that assume individually rational actors and vary the network connections. Markovsky (1987) does the reverse, holding the network constant and introducing varying assumptions about the behavior of the actors, especially about bargaining strategies that might be used by actors in disadvantaged positions. Some of his conclusions are counterintuitive; for example, some simulations indicate that united stubbornness in refusing exchanges on the part of disadvantaged actors may help equalize the exchange, while stubbornness on the part of the advantaged actor reduces that actor's advantage. Markovsky (1987) remarks on the usefulness of computer simulation in combining assumptions about processes at different analytical levels.

Some Comments on These Examples

Reporting Technical Details

The first set of comments that occurs to us after looking at these examples is that there is a lot of variation in what in presented about simulations. Some tell us exactly what computer language was used, what system the simulation ran on, and provide a copy of the program. In at least one other case, it is not even clear that a computer was used to do the simulation. Likewise, there is a lot of variation in the details presented about the algorithms: a flow chart, a set of equations, a brief verbal description. This is a relatively new technology, and the discipline does not seem to have developed standards for what should be presented and how, so as to ensure adequate communication and the ability to spot errors if they exist. We suggest that every presentation of a simulation should at least tell the reader what computer language and system are used, and enough information about the algorithm, including equations, to allow a reader to go through one cycle. More exercises like Axelrod's Prisoner's Dilemma tournament might be useful.

Second, there is a lot of variation in what is included about why certain decisions were made: for example, how many iterations, and how many runs; why certain values for parameters; why certain assumptions about starting values; what constraints on outcomes or parameters; why this number of "actors"; and others. Sometimes these make a theoretical difference—sometimes they may introduce artifacts that affect the results; sometimes they are purely pragmatic. Simulations are often described as being useful because they force the simulator to be clear about assumptions and to specify processes. However, sometimes they also force decisions for which there exists no good theoretical rationale. It is important in interpreting the results to make clear which decisions did and which did not reflect theoretical rationales. It would be helpful to have more discussion of such "methodological" issues in published literature.

Interpreting the Results

There also seems to be a lack of agreement about appropriate standards for interpreting results of simulations. One problem is that the results look very much like empirical results; they can be counted and added up, they have means and variances, they have meaningful labels such as "cooperation," "conformity," and "learning." In fact, since simulations can produce massive amounts of output, they require data reduction and summary just as empirical observations do. It is easy to slip into a fallacy of misplaced concreteness and start talking about them as if they really were people or groups taking actions. In interpreting the results of a simulation, one should distinguish between "empirical data" and "simulated data"; after all, from the point of view of the computer program these are electrical signals, not human beings, and they might as well represent bumblebees or raindrops. To put this another way, the results of a simulation are not a "test" of a theory; computer simulations *are* theories, and the results are derivations from theories, not empirical observations. This point is made in several of the examples we discussed (see especially Marwell and Oliver 1993: 192; Markovsky 1987: 113).

As with other theories, computer simulations may be used either deductively or inductively. Used deductively, the results are predictions and may appropriately be called "hypotheses," which are available for test by comparison with empirical data in research designed to test these hypotheses. (Macy's paper described above ends with a set of hypotheses.) Used inductively, a simulation is explanatory; it answers the question, what set of assumptions is required to produce a (previously observed) phenomenon? The Johnson and Feinberg article is an example, as they address the question of what set of assumptions can produce a "crowd" ready to "act." Marwell and Oliver's simulations have both inductive and deductive goals—deductive in seeking to understand the consequences of assuming variations in crucial features of a collective action situation, and inductive in seeking to answer the question, what combinations of factors produce sufficient contributions to produce a collective good? Markovsky's (1987) simulation is primarily deductive, seeking to examine the consequences of different assumptions about actors' strategies.

It is clear from these examples that interpretations of the results of simulations can be both quantitative and qualitative. Quantitative interpretations may use data reduction and statistical techniques that are commonly used with empirical data. Qualitative results include the appearance of patterns such as oscillations (noted by Carley in her "societies"), polarization (noted in some cases by Feinberg and Johnson in their "crowds"), or possibly other things such as differentiation versus equality (noted by Markovsky 1987), stability versus instability, or threshold effects (seen in Marwell and Oliver 1993). Although it is tempting to emphasize the quantitative interpretations (these being most familiar from empirical data analysis), the qualitative could be the most useful for construction of theories, especially for inductive or explanatory theory construction.

Simulation and Theory Growth

These examples show some of the ways in which computer simulations are useful in developing more abstract and complex theoretical models. First, they derive consequences of assumptions that may not be derivable from examination of a set of equations. This is especially relevant to theories about processes that occur many times. Repetition can be either through many iterations over time, or through the application of a set of assumptions to many actors. The examples above all use many iterations over time, in which the result of actions or choices at one time feed into the actions at the next time. The results of such a process carried out over and over again may not be easily seen without a simulation, as the pattern may take a long time to develop (all these simulations demonstrate this). This is especially the case when a random element is involved at some choice-points. They all show that a rather simple set of assumptions can produce complex patterns and changes over time if allowed to run through a large number of iterations.

Another way in which simulations can help make theories both more abstract and more complex is through allowing the integration of theories from two or more different research programs. For example, in Macy's models, an assumption from behavioral learning theory (that individuals adapt based on results of their last action) is combined with assumptions from game theory. In both the Carley simulation and the Feinberg and Johnson model, assumptions from models of cognitive and social structure are combined. Carley and Feinberg and Johnson assume that individuals become more like those they interact with, and interact more with those to whom they are similar, and also assume that new "information" can come in from other actors. These processes are reciprocal and deal with relations between actions at the individual level and changes at the structural level. Combining assumptions from several theories expands the range and complexity of all the theories and may well suggest new empirical observations that are relevant to all of them.

A Nonprobabilistic Model of Interdependence

In the final section of this paper, we present in more detail some examples from a computer simulation project on which we are currently working (Leik and Meeker 1993, 1995; Meeker and Leik 1994). The general project explores the theoretical applicability of a set of models to describe competition and outcome interdependence. At a more abstract level the processes described by these models are very similar to processes that can plausibly be hypothesized to affect interpersonal behavior. Unlike the previous examples, ours is not a probabilistic model. Social processes have usually been pictured as probabilistic in part because it is desirable to have a model in which outcomes are not predictable. This type of nondeterminism reflects the actual unpredictability of much human behavior and also seems to incorporate the possibility of "free will" or individual choice. Deterministic models, on the other hand, are seen as oversimplified and not allowing for variability in behavior or outcomes. Although this is true of many deterministic models, there do exist models that, while using very simple deterministic equations for processes, produce several kinds of variability and/or unpredictability in outcome. This type of model is the precursor of "chaos" models. Although the results we report here are not "chaotic," they do, like chaos models, demonstrate that rather simple assumptions about interdependent processes, if reiterated a sufficient number of times, may result in predictions of long-run instability.

Our project examines the underlying abstract properties of cooperation, competition, and interdependence that characterize many types of social situations, and a variety of units of analysis. Thus, although we can picture our results as representing something like the number of acts in a discussion group or amount of contribution to a group task, we could also picture them as authority relations in an organization, international conflicts, interaction between spouses over the years of a marriage, and so on.

Elements of the Leik-Meeker Simulation of Interaction

Our models involve the following basic elements:

—two actors, #1 and #2
—a series of time points, t = 0,1, . . . t
—each actor's "output" at each time point, and

—the assumption that each actor's output is a function of three things: the other actor's previous output; the actor's own previous output; and factors specific to the situation but independent of either own or other's previous level of output.

We have been exploring variants of two models from quite different empirical areas: an additive model based on Richardson's (1960) international arms race model, and a model of species competition from population ecology (for example, Volterra 1931; Boyce and Diprima 1986). Although the models were originally continuous differential equations models, we have modified them to be discrete time-difference equations models. Our simulation is written in PASCAL and runs on IBM PC's.

We focus here on some results from our work with the Richardson model. Richardson based his model on both theoretical considerations (how do nations decide what level of arms is necessary for self-protection in a hostile international environment?) and on historical data from numerous sources about actual international conflicts. He proposed that the level of armaments (number of weapons stockpiled in a given time period) for each of two rival nations X and Y can be described by two equations:

$$\text{Arms}_{1,t+1} = \text{Arms}_{1,t} + S_1 * \text{Arms}_{2,t} - F_1 * \text{Arms}_{1,t} + G_1 \qquad (1a)$$

$$\text{Arms}_{2,t+1} = \text{Arms}_{2,t} + S_2 * \text{Arms}_{1,t} - F_2 * \text{Arms}_{2,t} + G_2 \qquad (1b)$$

In words, in each time period, the total amount of arms each nation has is the sum of the previous accumulation plus an increase or decrease. At each time period, each nation *increases* its arms by an amount equal to a parameter (which Richardson called "sensitivity," denoted by the letter "S" in equation 1) times the level of arms of the other nation in the previous time period, and *decreases* level of arms by an amount equal to a parameter (which Richardson called "fatigue," denoted by the letter "F" in equation 1) times the nation's own level of arms in the previous time period. Richardson also assumed that each nation would increase its level of arms by an amount independent of the level of own and other's actual level of arms, which he called "Grievance" (denoted by the letter "G" in equation 1). Richardson pointed out that this system is unstable (that is, level of arms of both nations expands infinitely) if

$$S_1 * S_2 > F_1 * F_2 \qquad (2a)$$

Also, the system is stable (the arms level of both nations reaches an asymptote) if

$$S_1 * S_2 < F_1 * F_2 \qquad (2b)$$

Richardson's model is one of a general class of differential equation models of iterative, interdependent processes in which the outcome of the process is entirely different depending on whether parameters meet condition 2a or 2b. These models are mathematically described as having "sensitivity to initial conditions." Although the equations for a single iteration are simple and deterministic, the outcomes over a long series of iterations can be complex, and a small difference in initial values for parameters can produce different results in the long run.

Adapting the Richardson Model to Social Exchange

Models in this class have a general applicability: it is easy to think of many social interactions between two actors in which the actions of each are affected by actions of the other, actions of self, and factors independent of actions of self and other. The labels used by Richardson tend to limit our thinking to situations of conflict, in which the "output" is some negative action such as arms buildup. If we relabel sensitivity "reciprocity," we can see that it is a parameter that reflects actor's response to other's actions. If this parameter is 1, there is exact reciprocity; if it is 0, there is no effect of other's action on actor's behavior. This can apply to cooperative as well as competitive interactions. We continue to use the label "fatigue" for the parameter that decreases output with accumulation of own past output, although the underlying process is theorized to be satiation. We relabel grievance "justice," as it conceptually represents the amount an actor finds fair or proper to contribute regardless of actions of self or other.[5]

We thus restate Equations 1a and 1b as:

$$O_{1,t+1} = O_{1,t} + R_1*O_{2,t} - F_1*O_{1,t} + J_1 \tag{3a}$$

$$O_{2,t+1} = O_{2,t} + R_2*O_{1,t} - F_2*O_{2,t} + J_2 \tag{3b}$$

Where 1 and 2 are the actors, O is Output, R is Reciprocity, F is Fatigue, J is Justice, and t is a particular cycle.

The Concept of Reciprocity

In sociology, Gouldner (1960) introduced the idea of a "norm of reciprocity" which requires that an individual return both rewards and punishments received from others. Gouldner hypothesized that the existence of a norm requiring such returns acts as a "starting mechanism" for social exchanges by ensuring that individuals know that an initial favor will be returned, and also that reciprocity should produce rough equality between actors.

In anthropological exchange models, norms of reciprocity play an important theoretical role. These range from the early theory of Mauss (1954), that in many primitive societies being "in debt" for a gift places a person in a perceived state of magical vulnerability, to Malinowski's (1922) model of the Kula ring and Lévi-Strauss's (1949) model of marriage systems. In both Malinowski's and Lévi-

---

[5] As our work has progressed, it has become clear that "justice" may not be a good label for this parameter, because other processes also contribute to the amount an actor feels is fair or proper to contribute independently of a history of own or other's contributions. In one of our later applications, it has appeared that this is *negative*. This illustrates both the advantages and disadvantages of trying to tie abstract mathematical objects to specific empirical contexts.

Strauss's theories, reciprocity is indirect rather than direct. That is, individuals or groups are integrated into a larger social structure by the fact that they must send their gifts or daughters to one recipient and receive gifts or daughters-in-law from another source. In these models, too, equality of both participation and outcome is produced by the operation of reciprocity. Rather little empirical research has examined processes of reciprocity as distinct from other interpersonal exchange processes. In one example, Meeker (1984) reported some experimental evidence that positive reciprocity is associated with having a cooperative orientation to an exchange.

Equity and Satiation

In introducing behavioral models into sociological social exchange theory, Homans (1961 [1974]) paid less explicit attention to normative aspects of reciprocity, preferring to explain the maintenance of stable rates of exchange by mutual reinforcement. He did, however, feel the need to introduce a type of equilibrating or balancing mechanism in the form of "distributive justice." According to this, if a person is not receiving the amount of reward he or she expects or considers "fair" or "just," both emotional distress and actions to change the situation will result. Homans also pointed out that the behavioral psychology concept of "satiation" should also apply to interpersonal social exchanges. Satiation is the phenomenon of decreasing response to reinforcement: the more recently an act has been reinforced, the less a given amount of reward preserves the act's propensity. It is satiation that keeps exchanges (positive or negative) from escalating to ever-increasing levels of activity. This makes satiation theoretically important in explaining the development and maintenance of stable exchanges. In spite of this, few empirical or theoretical studies have been done on satiation as a contribution to interpersonal processes.

Much more attention, both theoretical and empirical, has been paid to the processes by which a sense of fairness or distributive justice is developed. Such processes include both the formation and implementation of social norms (for example, Berger, Zelditch, Anderson, and Cohen 1972; Berger, Fisek, Norman, and Wagner 1985; Meeker 1971; Stolte 1988) and cognitive or emotional processes (for example, Anderson 1976; Harris 1983; Markovsky 1988a; Jasso, 1980, 1990a; Hegtvedt 1988, 1990). Although a variety of different theoretical viewpoints exists, most posit a social comparison process in which own and others' inputs or contributions and outcomes or rewards are compared according to some normative standard such as equity, equality, need, or expectations for role and status. General reviews of research on justice, equity, fairness, and allocation may be found in Deutsch (1985); Greenberg and Cohen (1982); Cook and Hegtvedt (1983).

One result of the large amount of work on these topics is a lack of standardization about terminology. Here, we will use the term "distributive justice" to refer to the subjective sense of participants in an exchange that outcomes are fair, and "equity" to refer to one of several possible standards by which such fairness may be judged—namely, that outcomes to participants in an exchange should be proportional to inputs in the exchange. When the participants are status equals, equity also specifies that inputs should be equal. Reciprocity and equity are theoretically related in that a standard of equity provides a way of determining how much reciprocity is required.

Effects of Social Comparison

In our simulation, we address these theoretical questions about reciprocity and equity by incorporating an assumption about social comparison. We assume that the degree to which an actor reciprocates acts of the other is a function of the comparison of the two actors' outputs using a standard of equity. Inequity can be conceptualized in a variety of ways, including normative, cognitive, personality, and perceptual dimensions. For our purposes, it is a "cognitive balance" phenomenon, that is, when contributions to an exchange are inequitable, actors are motivated to change either their rate of contribution or their reactions to others' contributions. When equity prevails, no changes in rates or reactions will appear. We focus initially on homogeneous groups in which the standard for fairness should be equality. Thus, we assume that when rates of participation depart from equality, some change in rate of participation or response will occur.

If the standard for fairness is equality of participation, so that if there are unequal rates of participation a sense of tension or discomfort, and consequent motivation to change, exist, the question arises: is this stronger when the individual is behind others (competitive disadvantage), ahead of others (guilt), or merely different (failure of equality)? We shall compare these three possibilities.

Translating the Theoretical Concepts into the Simulation

We introduce these assumptions into our model by means of an additional set of equations for each iteration, by which the value of the parameters for reciprocity, fatigue, and justice increase or decrease on each cycle by an amount determined by the ratio between #1's and #2's output on the previous iteration. As noted above, departure from equality can mean being ahead of the other or being behind. Our model examines several different assumptions relevant to this question.

On each trial the value of the parameters R, F, and J will change as a result of the outcomes of the previous trials. The algorithm for this applied to R is as follows (algorithms for S and J are similar except that J is not constrained to be between -1 and $+1$):

    a. Set the minimum value of R to 0 or to -1, maximum $+1$.

    b. Calculate a factor $d = (1-R_{i,t})(R_{i,t})$ which creates an asymptotic change in R (i.e., smaller d as R approaches either maximum or minimum).

c. Calculate the ratio of 1's to 2's Output,

$Rel_{i,t} = O_{i,t} / (O_{1,t} + O_{2,t})$ for i = #1, #2

and where O_t = Output at time t.

d. For condition FX: $R_{i,t+1} = R_{i,t}$

UP: $R_{i,t+1} = R_{i,t} + d (Rel_{i,t} - 0.5)$

DN: $R_{i,t+1} = R_{i,t} + d (0.5 - Rel_{i,t})$

In analyzing and interpreting our results, we focused initially on qualitative analysis—that is, on whether the simulations produced patterns of instability or equilibrium, of equality or differentiation, of oscillation or monotonic change, and of gradual or abrupt change.

A Methodological Application

One immediate result of the simulation's attempt (Leik and Meeker 1995) is a realization of the large number of decisions that must be made about details of the model. Many of these have consequences for the results of the simulation, and also theoretical meaning, but they are not theoretical issues that would necessarily have come up without our having to think through the steps of constructing the simulation. For example, we have constrained the parameter R so it never gets larger than 1 or smaller than 0 in some applications but allow it to be as small as −1 in others. The amount R changes is smaller as it approaches either limit. If we conceptualize R as "reciprocity," this makes some theoretical sense. Other choices have less theoretical meaning for this application. We have assumed that the recent past has more impact than the distant past, and that the initial output for both #1 and #2 is 1 (but we can vary these factors). We have been forced to consider what it means to "add to" an exchange, whether it makes sense to have negative contributions, and whether a negative output makes sense.

A Deductive Application

When we turn to theoretical applications, there are a very large number of possible combinations of parameter values that can be investigated. We now present in some detail one of these applications. This is in a deductive mode, as we investigate what the consequences are of assuming (1) that social comparison has no effect, (2) that social comparison is an effective force when the actor is behind the other (DOWN), and (3) that social comparison is an effective force when the actor is ahead of the other (UP). Figures 1, 2, and 3 show a sample of results from the "additive" (Richardson) model. These are run under the assumption that the parameters, when they vary, are constrained to be between .01 and .99; that the recent past is more important than distant past (each iteration "discounts" past iterations by a factor of .05); and that both actors begin with output of 1.0 on the first iteration.

```
1000 cycles   tau = 0.010    discount = 0.950   #1,t0 = 1,  #2,t0 = 1
                             Additive

      PARAM FORM                                      PARAM VALUE
   for #1           for #2                         for #1        for #2
                                               Init   Min    Init   Min
       Fx              Fx       RECIPROCITY     0.10    0     0.10    0
       Fx              Fx       FATIGUE         0.05    0     0.05    0
       Fx              Fx       JUSTICE         0.20    0     0.20    0
#1<=10001.00,#2<=10001.00,                   #1_____  #2_____
```

```
                          #1 =    9721.129
                          #2 =    9973.604
                          t  =        148

Output



#1>= 1.00,#2>= 1.00,
    time 1                                              time 1000
```

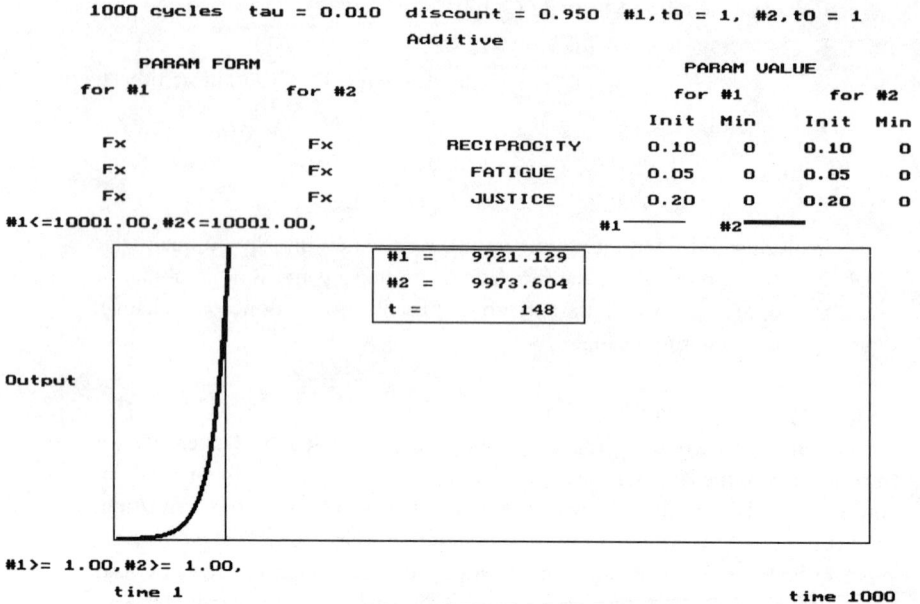

Fig. 1a. Richardson (additive) model, all parameters Fixed, parameter values leading to stability

Figures 1a and 1b show simulation of the original Richardson model, with fixed values of the parameters. This is the assumption that social comparison has no effect on the parameters. Figure 1a shows an unstable system, with parameters Reciprocity and Fatigue meeting condition 2a, and Figure 1b shows a stable system, in which these parameters meet condition 2b. They are run for 1000 cycles, but the simulation is ended if output level reaches 10000. (In Figures 1a and 1b, the maximum and minimum values for Output are shown at the bottom; the inset box shows values of Output for #1 and #2 at a particular time designated by t. Entries above the graph show the starting values for the parameters.) In Figures 1a and 1b, the parameters are Fixed—indicated by FX—meaning they have the same values through all 1000 cycles.

The results shown in Figures 1a and 1b constitute a kind of "control condition" for our exploration of the role of equity in exchange processes: they show what happens when the tendency to reciprocate, to satiate, or to adjust "justice" does not change. When we assume that these tendencies do change, and that the change is a function of amount of departure from equality of Output, the results are shown in Figures 2 and 3. Figures 2 and 3 should be compared to Figure 1b; here the initial values of Reciprocity and Fatigue are set to meet the conditions of Equation 2b, stability. In Figures 2a, 2b, and 2c we see the results of assuming that one or both of the actors have parameters that change according to the

```
   1000 cycles    tau = 0.010    discount = 0.950   #1,t0 = 1,  #2,t0 = 1
                                  Additive
              PARAM FORM                                   PARAM VALUE
      for #1              for #2                      for #1           for #2
                                                   Init   Min       Init   Min
        Fx                  Fx        RECIPROCITY   0.05    0        0.05    0
        Fx                  Fx        FATIGUE       0.10    0        0.10    0
        Fx                  Fx        JUSTICE       0.20    0        0.20    0
  #1<=  4.00,#2<=  4.00,                            #1━━━━━ #2━━━━━
```

```
                        #1 =      3.985
                        #2 =      3.985
                        t  =      101

Output



  #1>=  1.00,#2>=  1.00,
       time 1                                              time 1000
```

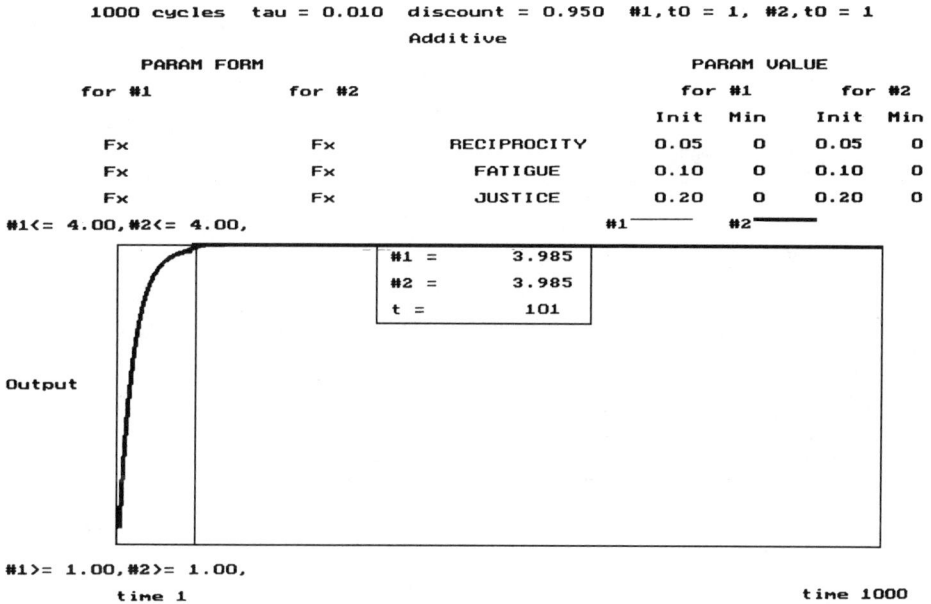

Fig. 1b. Richardson (additive) model, all parameters Fixed, parameter values leading to escalation

assumption that equity is activated when the actor is *behind* the other in output (DN, for short). Look first at Figures 2a and 2b, at the top and in the middle. These show simulations under the assumption that only one actor has changing parameters and the other's parameters are fixed. Both show a pattern like that in Figure 1b: output is stable at the same level and in the same number of iterations. However, when *both* actors are assumed to have parameters that change (Fig. 2c), the system shows a different pattern; output declines quickly, then rises slowly and is still rising by the end of 1000 iterations.

Figures 3a, 3b, and 3c show the results of a simulation in which the starting values meet the conditions for stability,[6] but the parameters for the actors change on each cycle according to the assumption that being *ahead* of the other (UP, for short) causes the actor to increase reciprocity, fatigue, and justice. When both actors have changing parameters (Fig. 3c), the parameters quickly move into the unstable combination. When only one actor has changing parameters, very strange things happen; if #1 has changing parameters and #2 has fixed (Fig. 3a), the output eventually achieves stability, but after an initial gradual increase

[6] The reader is doubtless wondering what happens in the simulations in Figures 2 and 3 if the initial parameter values are in the *unstable* range. The answer is that all results are unstable; whether the assumption is that inequity means being ahead or behind, and whether only one or both actors have changing parameters, the results look much like Figure 1a.

	PARAM FORM			PARAM VALUE			
for #1		for #2		for #1		for #2	
				Init	Min	Init	Min
Dn		Fx	RECIPROCITY	0.05	0	0.05	0
Dn		Fx	FATIGUE	0.10	0	0.10	0
Dn		Fx	JUSTICE	0.20	0	0.20	0

#1<= 3.98,#2<= 3.99,   #1 ———   #2 ▬▬

#1 =	3.965
#2 =	3.976
t =	101

Output

#1>= 1.00,#2>= 1.00,

time 1   time 1000

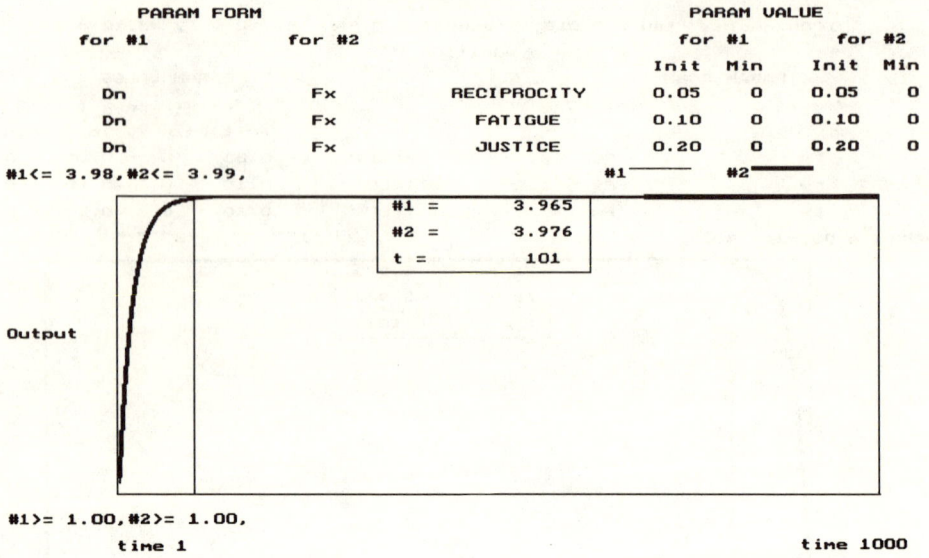

Fig. 2a. Additive model, initial parameter values leading to stability, all parameters for #1 are Down, for #2 Fixed

	PARAM FORM			PARAM VALUE			
for #1		for #2		for #1		for #2	
				Init	Min	Init	Min
Fx		Dn	RECIPROCITY	0.05	0	0.05	0
Fx		Dn	FATIGUE	0.10	0	0.10	0
Fx		Dn	JUSTICE	0.20	0	0.20	0

#1<= 3.99,#2<= 3.98,   #1 ———   #2 ▬▬

#1 =	3.972
#2 =	3.961
t =	101

Output

#1>= 1.00,#2>= 1.00,

time 1   time 1000

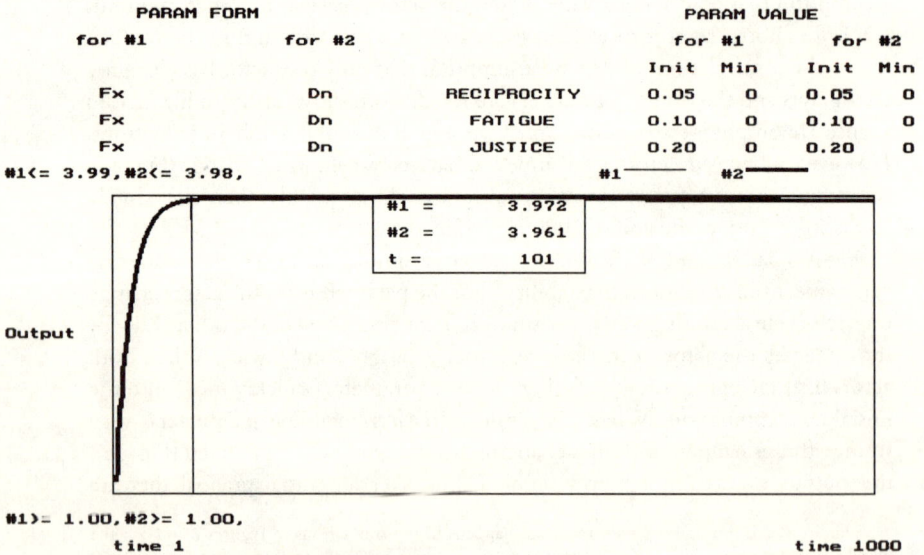

Fig. 2b. Additive model, initial parameter values leading to stability, all parameters for #1 are Fixed, for #2 Down

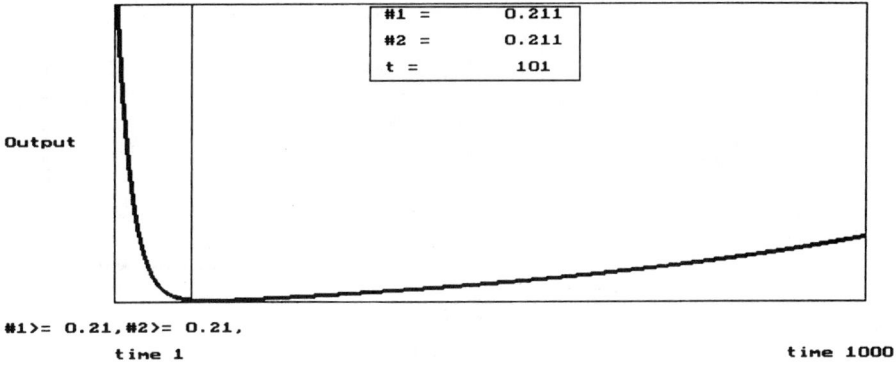

```
1000 cycles   tau = 0.010   discount = 0.950   #1,t0 = 1,  #2,t0 = 1
                             Additive

      PARAM FORM                                    PARAM VALUE
   for #1          for #2                        for #1          for #2
                                              Init   Min      Init   Min
      Dn              Dn        RECIPROCITY    0.05    0       0.05    0
      Dn              Dn        FATIGUE        0.10    0       0.10    0
      Dn              Dn        JUSTICE        0.20    0       0.20    0
#1<= 1.15,#2<= 1.16,                          #1————   #2————

                            ┌──────────────────────┐
                            │ #1 =        0.211     │
                            │ #2 =        0.211     │
                            │ t =          101      │
                            └──────────────────────┘

Output


#1>= 0.21,#2>= 0.21,
     time 1                                              time 1000
```

Fig. 2c. Additive model, initial parameter values leading to stability, all parameters for both #1 and #2 are Down

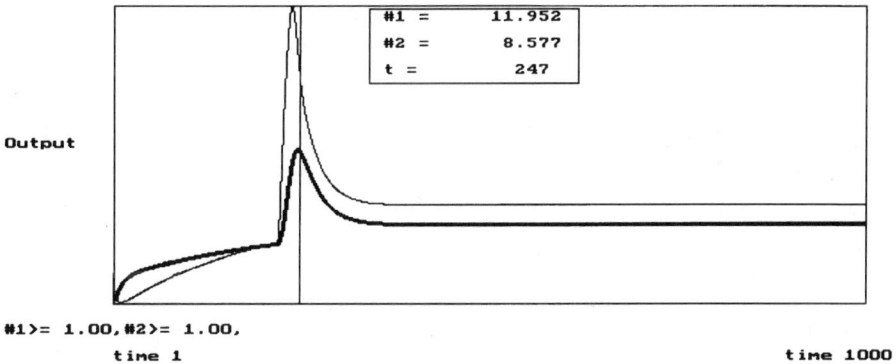

```
1000 cycles   tau = 0.010   discount = 0.950   #1,t0 = 1,  #2,t0 = 1
                             Additive

      PARAM FORM                                    PARAM VALUE
   for #1          for #2                        for #1          for #2
                                              Init   Min      Init   Min
      Up              Fx        RECIPROCITY    0.05    0       0.05    0
      Up              Fx        FATIGUE        0.10    0       0.10    0
      Up              Fx        JUSTICE        0.20    0       0.20    0
#1<=16.07,#2<= 8.78,                          #1————   #2————

                            ┌──────────────────────┐
                            │ #1 =       11.952     │
                            │ #2 =        8.577     │
                            │ t =          247      │
                            └──────────────────────┘

Output


#1>= 1.00,#2>= 1.00,
     time 1                                              time 1000
```

Fig. 3a. Additive model, initial parameter values leading to stability, all parameters for #1 are Up, for #2 Fixed

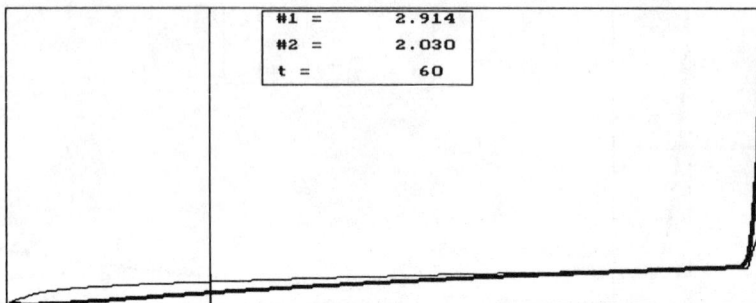

```
      220 cycles   tau = 0.010   discount = 0.950  #1,t0 = 1,  #2,t0 = 1
                              Additive
            PARAM FORM                                       PARAM VALUE
        for #1          for #2                          for #1          for #2
                                                    Init    Min     Init    Min
          Fx              Up          RECIPROCITY    0.05     0      0.05     0
          Fx              Up           FATIGUE       0.10     0      0.10     0
          Fx              Up           JUSTICE       0.20     0      0.20     0
  #1<= 7.53,#2<=25.39,                            #1━━━━    #2━━━━
                                    ┌─────────────────────────┐
                                    │ #1 =       2.914         │
                                    │ #2 =       2.030         │
                                    │ t  =          60         │
                                    └─────────────────────────┘

  Output

  #1>= 1.00,#2>= 1.00,
          time 1                                              time 220
```

Fig. 3b. Additive model, initial parameter values leading to stability, all parameters for #1 are Fixed, for #2 Up

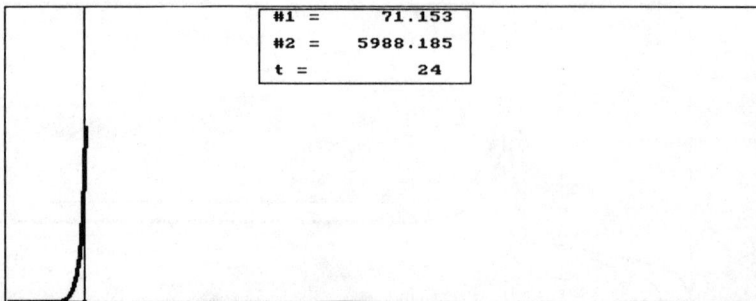

```
      220 cycles   tau = 0.010   discount = 0.950  #1,t0 = 1,  #2,t0 = 1
                              Additive
            PARAM FORM                                       PARAM VALUE
        for #1          for #2                          for #1          for #2
                                                    Init    Min     Init    Min
          Up              Up          RECIPROCITY    0.05     0      0.05     0
          Up              Up           FATIGUE       0.10     0      0.10     0
          Up              Up           JUSTICE       0.20     0      0.20     0
  #1<=10001.00,#2<=10001.00,                       #1━━━━    #2━━━━
                                    ┌─────────────────────────┐
                                    │ #1 =       71.153        │
                                    │ #2 =     5988.185        │
                                    │ t  =          24         │
                                    └─────────────────────────┘

  Output

  #1>= 0.77,#2>= 0.87,
          time 1                                              time 220
```

Fig. 3c. Additive model, initial parameter values leading to stability, all parameters for both #1 and #2 are Up followed by a very sharp increase and sharp drop-off. Furthermore, the system is differentiated, with one actor's output higher than the other's at equilibrium. On the other hand, when #1 has fixed parameters and #2's parameters increase when ahead of the other, the system is unstable (Fig. 3b). The simulation in Figure 3b was only run for 220 iterations, because it explodes so rapidly after that. It looks very much like its counterpart in Figure 3a until about iteration 200, where the outputs of the two actors cross. After that, in Figure 3b the output of the higher actor explodes rapidly; in Figure 3a it also rises rapidly but peaks and then descends to an equilibrium.

We see from these results that the assumption that inequity is a motivating force when the actor is behind rather than ahead produces more stable and equal outcomes. However, for both the assumption that equity is activated by being behind and the assumption that it is activated by being ahead, we have the counterintuitive result that stability is reached *only* when the two actors have *different* approaches. When both are assumed to react to inequality the same way, the system explodes (we have also found this in examination of simulation runs with more complex interaction models). This suggests one possible value of diversity in a conflict or interdependent interaction. Perhaps the search for a universal formula to express social comparison or equity is less useful than a search for multiple formulas.

We also have an example of one set of assumptions (inequity means being behind) in which it makes no difference which of two actors with different approaches goes first, and another (the assumption that inequity means being ahead) in which the actor who goes first makes a major difference. This suggests that for some interactions having a formal structure, requiring the taking of turns can be an important factor in determining the outcome, while in other interactions it may not. Also, in some interactions, having the initial advantage of taking the first turn may translate into long-term differences in outcome, while in others it may not. This may suggest some of the processes by which individuals or groups with initial disadvantages (for example, gender, race, prestige of family or education) get further behind in social exchanges.

An Inductive Use of the Simulation

In another application (Meeker and Leik 1994), we used the simulation to ask a set of inductive questions about the relationship between reciprocity and equity, setting the "justice" parameter equal to zero and keeping "satiation" constant. We first examined exchange without assuming an effect of equity. This seems like a very plausible "bare bones" model for dyadic social exchange: each participant reciprocates the actions of the other modified by satiation resulting from own acts. However, it does not predict a stable exchange. We then asked, in the absence of a "justice" parameter, what assumptions about reciprocity changes in response to inequity create a stable result? We also asked the theo-

retical question, what assumptions about parameter values for both actors produce equality of outcomes?

Only one out of the eight combinations investigated produced stable, non-
zero exchange. The others all either escalate indefinitely or decline to zero, with
some producing inequalities along the way. The one combination of assumptions that produces a stable, non-zero exchange is UP DN under initial values
meeting conditions for instability. In other words, in the absence of the "justice"
parameter, it is once again only when we assume that the two actors have *different*
definitions of equity that we can use those assumptions to predict a stable and
equal exchange. We can explain this intuitively by saying that when the rates of
output depart from stability, if the actors have different views of equity, the actions of one actor will pull the rate back to stability when it departs in one
direction while the actions of the other will pull it back from the other direction.
When both actors have the same reaction, their mutual reactions cause the system to keep on either escalating or declining. This observation might suggest a
theoretical application to role differentiation, or once again the usefulness of
diversity of orientations among actors in exchanges.

The fact that introducing an assumption of equity as a motivating process
produces the prediction of a stable, non-zero exchange in only one of eight
combinations of assumptions suggests that even simple processes such as reciprocity, satiation, and equity are sensitive to initial conditions, and that development of stable social exchanges based only on these processes is problematic.
A variety of additional processes could be added to try to introduce stabilizing
influences; these might include influences from outside the dyad (such as constraints on resources) or actions of the actors that are not responsive to the history
of the exchange (such as role obligations—this could be operationalized in this
simulation by making the "justice" parameter non-zero). In general, these results
support the view that normative processes such as equity or conformity to role
obligations are necessary to explain the development and maintenance of stable
social exchanges.

An Application to "Real" Data

Although the major purpose of our simulation has been to explore theoretical
issues, we have used data from early trials of a two-person game experiment to
estimate parameters for the model, and then used those estimates in a simulation
to compare with data from a later part of the same experiment (Meeker and Leik
1996). In this experiment, the subjects had displayed a tendency common in such
situations, to "lock in" to a response. That is, they tended to repeat a response
given on a previous trial. In previous analyses of this type of process, a probabilistic model, a discrete-state Markov process, had been used to model the data
(Leik and Meeker 1975: ch. 10). In our new simulation, this phenomenon can
be modeled well by assuming that "Satiation" is negative—that is, that the actors

are more likely to repeat what they just did rather than less likely—and by giving some actors high starting values for contribution and others low. This means that the assumption of randomness is applied at the beginning of the interaction, though the choices made once the interaction has begun are not random.

Summary

In this paper, we have tried to make the following three points. First, that computer simulations are emerging as an important tool in sociological theory construction, especially as addressed to issues of how social structure, networks, and decisions develop and how different levels of analysis can be combined. Second, we have discussed a number of current examples of probabilistic simulations and one deterministic model. Third, we have suggested that as this technique emerges, theorists should be aware of and should discuss explicitly a variety of issues of both method and interpretation.

Issues such as relations between individual and structural processes (or micro- and macro-levels, or "agency" and "structure"); relationships between objective and subjective processes; and issues of reciprocal causality and equilibrium in social systems are often referred to as "metatheoretical" issues. This tends to mean they are defined as issues one can talk about but not study analytically. Computer simulations allow the researcher to make assumptions about processes at different levels and examine the consequences of making different assumptions about how systems composed of different levels and reciprocal effects operate.

In addition to allowing systematic construction of more complex theoretical models, computer simulation can contribute to increasing abstraction of theories. In a way, this is inherent in the use of a computer model, because the elements of a simulation are entirely abstract. It is our impression that simulators often fail to take advantage of this possibility because of the tendency we have to label the elements of a simulation with the concepts of the theory and then assume they represent *only* those concepts. For example, both the Macy and the Heckathorn simulations mentioned above show effects of increasing the number of other actors whose actions must be "monitored" at one time point in order to take action at the next time point. For another example, in both the Carley and the Feinberg-Johnson simulations, very similar assumptions are made about the spread of "information" through a "crowd" or "society" based on processes of contagion and differential association. They also have similar end states, of either unity or polarization.

The fact that they are combining very similar assumptions to simulate very similar phenomena may be obscured by the theoretical labels they use. These theoretical labels are different because the empirical phenomena for which the simulations were developed are different. On the empirical level, formal organizations and crowds are very different entities, and it would be a mistake to apply empirical generalizations from one to the other. However, the blips on the computer screen are equally (good or poor) representations of employees of a formal organization and members of a crowd. To the extent that all formal organizations contain features that make them different from all crowds, those features have been lost in the simulation. If we believe that such abstraction is a goal of scientific theory development, this is a benefit. But we do not reap the benefit unless we recognize that the labels may be too concrete.

If, on the other hand, we believe that in this case too much has been lost by the abstraction, recognizing that the simulation represents equally well two quite different social objects leads us to suggestions about what needs to be added into the theory in order adequately to represent reality. That is, it contributes the "positive heuristic" of the research program.

This discussion leads us to several points. First, to reiterate a point made above, it is very important to distinguish between empirical data and simulation-generated data. The history of social science is littered with mistakes made through trying to apply empirical concepts from one object (for example, individual personality types) to inappropriate other objects (for example, nations). Since computer simulations are not empirical, we can usefully apply them to very different objects, but treating them as if they "really are" empirical reality can lead us to make mistakes both of inappropriate generalization from one empirical area to another, and of failing to recognize the similarity between different empirical areas at a more abstract level. Second, it is useful to attempt quite different mathematical approaches to the same empirical phenomenon. For example, although most simulations assume a probabilistic process, our exercise in integrating two different areas of theory via a simple, deterministic model shows that such a model can also produce predictions of complex patterns involving instability, differentiation, rapid reversals of direction, and so on.

Third, it is very important for reports of simulations to give enough information about the algorithms used, so other researchers can see when the processes are really the same as their own even if the conceptual labels are different. Finally, it becomes apparent that the adequate use of computer simulations in theory development requires careful attention to concept formation and definitions. Exclusive attention to the question of whether the algorithms represent the processes under study may obscure the importance of concept formation and definitions of the objects, states, outcomes, and transitions. This of course is true of theories generally, and brings us back to our starting point: simulations are a form of theory construction, increasingly emerging as an important component of theoretical research programs in sociology.

Beyond Experimental Inference:
A Decent Burial for J. S. Mill
and R. A. Fisher

$$\blacktriangleright\blacktriangledown$$
$$\blacktriangle\blacktriangleleft$$

Bernard P. Cohen

This paper addresses a fundamental problem: Using empirical evidence (if that is not a redundant expression) for theory choice. It starts out from the view that current sociological methodology places almost exclusive emphasis on assessing single studies and does not deal adequately with the problem of theory choice. In addition, it presumes that current methodological writing does not reflect the way many of us behave, a way that makes considerable sense and a way that ought to be codified.

We all learned that empirical studies cannot verify a theory, so Popper's "falsification" (1959) became the guiding principle. Falsification may work as a criterion for demarcation, as Popper proposed, but it does not work as a method for empirically evaluating theories. Most of us do not regard even reproducible falsification as sufficient grounds to abandon a theory. A bit of reflection reveals the fact that every theory is false by this criterion because no theory exactly predicts observation values. Furthermore, as Duhem (trans. 1954) pointed out early in this century, what is tested is not a theory but a complex conjunction of the theory and auxiliary assumptions, for example, an error theory. Hence it is not clear what is falsified—an assertion of the theory or one or more of the auxiliary assumptions.

Lakatos's "methodology of scientific research programs" (1970) is not a solution to empirically based theory choice either. The "irrefutable hard core" of Lakatos's theoretical research program makes many of us uncomfortable. For one reason, adopting this idea would insulate from evidence many things that we would not want to consider scientific theories.

Some of the critics of scientific sociology recognize these issues. They use Kuhn's (1962) analysis to justify an extreme relativism that argues that there are

Revised version of a presentation at the 100th Anniversary Congress of the International Institute of Sociology, Paris, France, June 23, 1993.

no rational means to use observations to choose among theories. These critics falsely conclude that all empirical criteria are in the end subjective; from this it is only a step to the view that every theory is as good as every other theory. These views represent what Crews (1987) has called "theoreticism," which he defines as "a frank recourse to unsubstantiated theory, not just as a tool of investigation, but as anti-empirical knowledge in its own right." Is there any alternative to such an extreme relativism?

Obviously, this author believes there is an alternative. However, those of us who believe that there are rational ways to use observation to evaluate theory must confront the issues; we cannot leave the arguments to either the positivists or the antipositivists. In these controversies, the empirical character of science is at stake. If there is no rational means for using evidence to assess scientific claims, then, as the relativists argue, theories are little more than personal preferences and scientific claims are no different from literary, political, or religious affirmations. Empirically based theory choice is not just an issue for the philosophers of science to resolve; those practicing scientists involved in the methodology of their research have critical contributions to make.

We need new methods, new criteria, and new strategies for the empirical evaluation of ideas. This paper is a call for a new methodology which elsewhere the author has termed the "methodology of cumulative research" (Cohen 1989: 291) to replace the methodology of experimental inference. It reflects the author's strong belief that the present models of experimental inference do not address the key issues. These models do not reflect the way we operate nor the way we should operate. They place unwarranted emphasis on the single empirical study and give insufficient weight to the theoretical and empirical context in which that study takes place.

Later sections of this paper will discuss cumulative research and cumulative research programs in some detail, but first it is necessary to clarify the term "cumulative." It is not used in a simple additive sense to mean a linear accretion of facts and findings; the antipositivist critique is correct on this point—facts and theories do not cumulate additively. Freese (1980b) offered a more congenial conception of cumulation in which cumulation involves using prior research to generate and solve new problems, problems which could not be defined or solved without the knowledge base of the prior research.

Building on this conception, the present author defined a cumulative research program, or CRP, as a series of interrelated theoretical and empirical studies, each of which is associated with an identifiable stage of development where stages are ordered according to their capacity to identify and solve sociological problems (Cohen 1989: 293).

While the focus of this paper is the CRP, there are some preliminary issues to consider. The next section will present a brief critique of the methodology of experimental inference. Following this critique, the paper will discuss some work in the philosophy of science that provides a context for the proposals it will make. The central section of the paper will describe this writer's conception of a CRP and some of the ways that researchers operate in the context of a CRP. This paper will conclude with a comparison of the methodology of CRPs with the methodology of experimental inference and a consideration of a few critical questions a methodology of CRPs must address. Throughout the analysis of a CRP, the discussion will offer some preliminary proposals for methods, criteria, and strategies to be incorporated in a methodology of cumulative research programs.

The Methodology of Experimental Inference

Many sociologists, whether they do experimental or nonexperimental research, operate with some approximation to an ideal experimental model. J. S. Mill (1872 [1934]) and R. A. Fisher (1938) have provided the basic models for using empirical evidence to choose among theories, employed even by many of us who reject the empiricist position. In brief, these models involve comparisons of experimental and control groups where alternative predictions are eliminated through experimental intervention, statistical manipulation, or randomization. Nonexperimental work employs between-group comparisons often based on nominal categories and without random assignment of individuals to comparison groups. Continuous variable comparisons are a direct extension of the basic canons. Research designs based on these models provide an opportunity to reject a theory's predictions; if the data do not contradict the theory's predictions, then the researcher concludes that the study supports or confirms the theory.

One could characterize these inference models as updated and more sophisticated versions of Mill's canons (Mill 1872, quoted in Cohen and Nagel 1934) supplemented by R. A. Fisher (1938) and the analysis of variance. This writer suggests that the basic experimental inference model underlies all empirical inference in quantitative sociological research.

Lieberson (1985) criticizes sociologists for aping the natural sciences by using an experimental model that is inapplicable to nonexperimental research. Lieberson claims that the experimental model is inappropriate for sociologists because nonexperimental or quasi-experimental research has built-in biases that violate basic assumptions of the model.

The problem, however, is not that sociological research does not fit the Fisher-type model; what Lieberson does not recognize is that model itself is flawed. It doesn't work even in areas where highly rigorous, randomized experiments are possible, even in the most rigorous experimental research. And it is not at all clear that successful natural scientists operate with this model, although it does clearly dominate psychological research.

Philosophers of science have long recognized that experiments are neither

$$A \quad B \quad C \quad \longrightarrow \quad E$$

Fig. 1. Mill's Method of Difference　　　$A \quad B \quad \sim C \quad \longrightarrow \quad \sim E$

methods of discovery nor methods of proof (Cohen and Nagel 1934). Most sociologists have had at least a passing acquaintance with the Cohen and Nagel analysis of Mill's canons, but have probably forgotten the details. It is illuminating to review their critique of Mill's Method of Difference. The method of difference is a good case for analysis because it reflects a simple experimental control group design. Figure 1 shows Mill's two circumstances alike in all respects but one—A and B stand for all respects in which they are alike; C and $\sim$C are the single respect in which they differ. E and $\sim$E stand for the presence and absence of some effect. Mill argues that this model allows the inference that C causes E.

To concretize Figure 1, consider an experiment dealing with the effects of status equality in a group on the group's level of idea generation. In the experimental treatment, "C" represents groups whose members are status equals and "E" signifies a high level of idea generation. In the "control" treatment, "$\sim$C" stands for groups whose members are not status equals, that is, groups with status hierarchies, and "$\sim$E" indicates a low level of idea generation. In both treatments, "A" and "B" symbolize factors, such as sex of members and group task, that are constant across treatments.

As we all are aware, proving that C causes E requires that all other known causes are contained in A and B, and we are never in a position to know that. Hence, the method of difference is not a method of proof. It is not a method of discovery because it depends on a priori identification of A, B, and C. In short, Mill's Method of Difference—and his other canons of experimental inference—fails as an "inductive logic."

Some experimentalists believe that R. A. Fisher solved this difficulty with Mill's canons by introducing the idea of random assignment. Random assignment equates experimental and control groups on all the unknown and unknowable causal factors. Elsewhere (Cohen 1989), this author has shown that randomization does not solve the problem; this paper can only summarize the main arguments. First, as the set of unknown factors increases, the probability that subjects randomly assigned to experimental and control groups will differ significantly on at least one of these factors approaches 1.0. Second, randomization never guaranteed the equating of treatments on any single variable except in the limit, and experiments are not done in the limit. Hence, there is always some unknown alternative causal factor operating. There are other difficulties, but suffice it to say that randomization does not turn experiments into methods of proof or methods of discovery.

While many researchers recognize that experimental models do not provide a logic of proof, experimentalists have found powerful justification for these models as tools of choice. In their analysis, Cohen and Nagel also showed that Mill's method works as a method of elimination. In the method of difference, if A and B are the same when E or E occurs, then A and B cannot be causes of E. And this is the basis on which most of us operate, as I noted earlier. We design an experiment or a quasi experiment to provide an opportunity to reject our theory, and if it is not rejected, then we provisionally accept the theory.

In the use of this model, a subtle point often is overlooked: The evaluation is relative to a small number of alternative predictions. A central principle, then, is:

> *All theory evaluation is comparative; choice, or nonrejection, is relative to a limited set of explicitly specified alternatives.*

A major obstacle to theoretical development is that many people may be aware of this principle but pay only lip service to it. Our critics, the proponents of both Theoreticism and Empiricism, are still looking for the statistical magic bullet to evaluate the nature of the world. It follows from this principle that these critics have an incorrect formulation of the problem. The implication is that we cannot evaluate the nature of the phenomenal world; we can only evaluate *analyses* of limited segments of the world.

But the problem goes deeper. There is a fundamental difficulty that this author only appreciated recently. *Developing Sociological Knowledge* (1989) promotes the strategy of eliminating alternative explanations using the Cohen-Nagel modification of Mill's Method of Difference. Although he discusses the inadequacies of single empirical studies, the writer as researcher, too, is a prisoner of conventional methodology; hence, he misses the inconsistency between advocating methods of elimination in single experiments and questioning the utility of single studies in general. Once one recognizes the inconsistency, it is terribly obvious. An experiment deals with one instantiation of a theory and its alternatives. To eliminate alternatives involves the same generalization process that cannot be justified in the absence of a valid inductive logic.

In Figure 1, what A, B, C and E stand for is not the relevant entities of the alternative theories but their operationalizations. A reproducible experiment may demonstrate that a particular operationalization of A cannot account for a particular operationalization of E under a particular operationalization of the scope of the theories. But to conclude from this that therefore Theory A is eliminated as an explanation of Phenomenon E requires an inference from the particular to the general.

Does this, then, mean that we must concede to our relativist critics that there is no rational way to use evidence to choose among rival theories? that there is no point in doing experiments? that, as far as the phenomena are concerned, one theory is as good as another? Obviously, this methodologist's answer to these questions is an emphatic No. (Otherwise, there would be no reason for this paper.) Before the author sketches an alternative approach, it is necessary to touch briefly on the broader philosophical context. The following discussion is presented not as a critical analysis of alternative views in the philosophy of science but rather to indicate some of the sources of the current proposal.

Verifiability, Falsifiability, and What Else?

Philosophy of science has dismissed verifiability as a basis for evaluating theories. Furthermore, Popper has argued that his "falsifiability" is a criterion of demarcation rather than a standard for theory choice (1959, 1982). To be scientific, a theory must be capable of being falsified, but this is not a guide to dealing with the falsifying instance. If falsifiability and verifiability do not provide standards for theory choice, can we look to the philosophy of science for guidance?

One philosopher of science, Larry Laudan, argues that we should abandon the concern for truth or falsity (1977). He writes: "The first and essential acid test for any theory is whether it provides acceptable answers to interesting questions; whether, in other words, it provides satisfactory solutions to important problems" (pp. 13–14). He does make solution of empirical problems a key element and distinguishes among solved problems, unsolved problems, and anomalies. He adds, "Of any and every theory, we must ask how many problems it has solved and how many anomalies confront it? This question, in slightly more complex form, becomes one of the primary tools for the comparative evaluation of theories" (p. 18).

"Interesting" and "important" present difficulties, and his proposed criteria are not sufficient. We can't get intersubjective definitions of basic sociological ideas, so one does not have much hope for consensual agreement on interesting questions and important problems. Laudan does, however, recognize that in early stages of development of a science, there is "usually no good reason for singling out one [problem] . . . as more important or crucial than another. Once we have one or more theories in the domain, however, we immediately have certain criteria for *increasing* the importance of certain empirical problems" (p. 33). These include: (1) some theory in the domain has solved the problem, and (2) solution of a problem that has resisted solution by other theories in the domain, that is, resolving an anomaly.

Laudan's proposals have other difficulties as well in the comparative counting and weighting of solved to unsolved problems. He formulates his appraisal measure in these words, "the overall problem-solving effectiveness of a theory is determined by assessing the number and importance of the empirical problems which the theory solves and deducting therefrom the number and importance of the anomalies and conceptual problems which the theory generates" (p. 68). One has difficulty envisioning this type of quantification.

Despite its difficulties, Laudan's analysis offers a promising direction for answering the relativist critics and preserving the empirical character of science. He writes:

> In appraising the merits of theories, it is more important to ask whether they constitute adequate solutions to significant problems than it is to ask whether they are "true," "corroborated," "well-confirmed," or otherwise justifiable within the framework of contemporary epistemology. (1977: 14)

In proposing this dramatically different criterion, he also argues that theories may not be the appropriate object of evaluation. His unit of appraisal is what he calls the "research tradition." He acknowledges the influence of Lakatos in this concept, but since he is not concerned with refutation, he has no need for an "irrefutable hard core."

Laudan preserves the empirical character of science by providing criteria for the acceptability and pursuitability (*sic*) of a research tradition. Although the present writer was not aware of Laudan's work at the time of writing *Developing Sociological Knowledge*, the concept of a CRP has many similarities to Laudan's research tradition. The two concepts are not identical, but both stem from common concerns. This is not at all surprising, since the present author, too, was influenced by Lakatos.

Cumulative Research Programs

While this writer's initial formulations predate exposure to Laudan's work, his current thinking has been influenced by two of Laudan's major books, *Progress and Its Problems* (1977) and *Science and Values* (1984). This discussion will not explicate Laudan's work further, since the purpose here is not to examine philosophical similarities and differences, but rather to raise issues for sociological methodology.

The definition of a CRP specified that each series of interrelated studies had to be tied to a particular stage of development. Since identifiable stages are a key feature of this definition, it is important to describe and provide some examples of the three key stages. The discussion of each stage will incorporate Laudan's concerns with appraisal and pursuitability.

A Stage 1 CRP represents what we might call a "pretheory" stage of development. Theoretical studies range from essays to propositional inventories; empirical investigations address demonstrating a phenomenon or establishing an empirical regularity. Many inquiries focus on defining and formulating a problem to be solved, and the solutions advanced are usually *ad hoc*. Theoretical propositions, which are called "knowledge claims" in *Developing Sociological Knowledge,* are usually unconnected and concepts are not well explicated. Empirical propositions, or observation statements, are similarly unconnected and usually imprecise. Attempts to define domains of inquiry are characteristic, whereas most researchers pay little attention to specifying the scope of their propositions.

There are a large number of examples of Stage 1 CRPs. Perhaps the best-known of these is the large literature dealing with gender differences in occupational and organizational behavior, an important segment of which is the research on gender discrimination in recruitment and rewards (for example, England, Farkas, Kilbourne, and Dou 1988). Social psychologists are very familiar with the body of conformity studies employing the Asch experimental situation (Allen 1965, 1977); this array of empirical studies is almost prototypical of a Stage 1 program.

Appraisal of a Stage 1 CRP

What constitutes successful problem solution in a Stage 1 CRP? First of all, we know that more than a single study is necessary to establish regularities and to determine what is problematic and, certainly, to evaluate solutions to the problematic. Hence, without several studies, it is undoubtedly premature to ask about acceptability of the program. What is there to accept? One or two studies provide almost nothing that can be called established knowledge or useful theory. Even after several studies that produce statistically significant findings and successfully demonstrate regularities, there is not sufficient reason for the sociological community to pay much attention to this program. Of course, if the regularities are counterintuitive or challenge conventional wisdom, then there may be a reason for others to orient their own work to support or attack the program.

Presumably a successful first-stage CRP not only finds regularities but attempts to account for them with some formulation. In other words, the program takes explaining the regularities as its problem and constructs some kind of theoretical argument as a solution to the problem. However, it is always possible to find some solution that fits the problem if there are no other constraints and all it has to do is solve the one problem that motivated the investigation. That is what we mean by calling a solution *ad hoc.* Hence, fitting a model to a known set of data can't really count as a success, regardless of R^2. Nor can deducing an observation statement from a set of premises constructed solely for that purpose be regarded as an accomplishment.

One principal objective of a Stage 1 CRP is to transform *ad hoc* solutions into heuristic mechanisms that have consequences above and beyond any single problem. Heuristic mechanisms include theories, measurement models, standardized experimental situations, and engineering interventions. These also include extensions of the domain and/or scope of the original problem solution. Successfully achieving this objective marks the transition to a Stage 2 CRP. Before we turn to Stage 2 CRPs, it is important to examine pursuitability.

Abandonment of a Stage 1 CRP

Are there empirical criteria on the basis of which a researcher can rationally decide to abandon a program? One may lose interest or be unable to obtain funding, but those are not empirical criteria. Consider three cases: (1) After several attempts, researchers accumulate only inconsistent results; (2) A set of studies produces weak but consistent results; (3) A set of studies generates strong, consistent relationships.

Case 1. Even if researchers fail to find any regularities after several studies, the arguments about the lack of an inductive logic do not allow one to conclude that the next study will also fail. However, there is a point where, being reasonable, a sociologist will conclude that pursuing something else is better for his or her soul; that point will vary from researcher to researcher. Besides, there certainly have been instances where what some will call irrational tenacity has paid off. It is doubtful that one can find empirical criteria to cover this case, but we need not worry too long about it. Continued lack of success will eventually lead to abandoning an incipient program unless it has become a pathological obsession to those who pursue it.

Case 2. Where a set of studies produces weak and inconsistent results, current methodology does not provide adequate direction for deciding whether or not to abandon a CRP. For example, the present author is currently investigating the impact of group structures on group productivity (Cohen, forthcoming). Suppose he finds weak first-order relationships between some structural property and productivity. Does he abandon the quest for structure-outcome connections? No. What he did—and what most of us do in similar circumstances—was to look at other properties and other structures; refine measures; and include additional factors in the analysis. Most researchers attempt to reduce noise in their observations and try to identify disturbance factors that may be obscuring relationships. One may try to identify outliers and remove them from the analysis. In some situations, one may restrict the scope of these relationships and exclude certain instances that may be problematic. These behaviors may not be typical, but they are certainly not unique. What the author wants to suggest, however, is that there is a certain amount of rationality to these actions, especially since in his own work he was successful in strengthening what were initially weak relationships.

It is important to emphasize that the path described is hardly one suggested by the ideal model of a randomized experiment. The fact of weak relationships is not nearly so important as the nature of the efforts to explain why they are weak. Current methodology provides little guidance to these efforts, but the nature and implications of the attempts to account for weak relationships are probably the ultimate arbiter of whether to abandon a CRP or to continue to pursue it. In general, weak empirical findings *by themselves* are not a rational basis on which to abandon a first-stage CRP.

Case 3. There are only a few comments to make about this case. While weak findings are not adequate justification for abandoning a CRP, strong consistent findings are not sufficient to require its continuation. Strong consistent findings are likely to generate questions concerning mechanisms, processes, generality, and scope limitations. Notice the qualification, *likely*; there is no guarantee that researchers will raise heuristic questions, and in the absence of anything problematic, no empirical criterion can justify continuation of a CRP. To take just one example, in the 1950's and 1960's, a large number of experiments found substantial correlations between personality tests and conformity behavior in the Asch Conformity situation, but psychologists offered no serious alternatives to a trait conception of conformity. The lack of heuristic implications for this conception led to abandoning what had held an important place in experimental social psychology.

To summarize the discussion of abandoning a Stage 1 CRP, the following offers a criterion that is empirically based, if not fully empirical.

A Stage 1 CRP should be abandoned when the empirical research no longer has heuristic implications.

Heuristic value is the ultimate test, and many of us believe that it is possible to evaluate heuristic value intersubjectively and rigorously. How to do so is a question that the methodology of CRPs must address.

Stage 2 Cumulative Research Programs

The development of a heuristic mechanism marks the initiation of Stage 2. This mechanism integrates and generalizes elements of the problem solution to create a substantive theory or a theory of measurement or, perhaps, a general research strategy. The successful problem solution has received an abstract formulation, and the implications of this formulation have received support in more than one instance. At this stage, limitations of the formulation become clearer; anomalies appear and may remain unresolved. Research also addresses modification of the scope of the formulation and extensions of its domain. As we envision a Stage 2 program, it typically—although not exclusively—involves a single well-developed theory and its related empirical research. As the CRP becomes widely known to scientists who are not working within it, it may motivate rival theories or alternative CRPs.

Examples of Stage 2 CRPs include status attainment models and the numerous empirical studies dealing with these models (for example, Sewell and Hauser

1975; Treiman and Yip 1989). One could also consider the extensive developments in network analysis to exemplify a Stage 2 program (for example, Marsden and Lin 1982).

How do researchers operate in a Stage 2 CRP? They have a theory which solves the problem that motivated it. Since the theory has untested implications, the researchers engage in investigations to test these consequences. They may do experiments or nonexperimental studies and, in their experiments, may randomly assign subjects to treatments. But are they trying to falsify their theory? Are they trying to eliminate alternative hypotheses and not eliminate their own? It is at least reasonable to argue that they are *not* trying to falsify their theory. However, they *are* trying to eliminate some alternative hypotheses. Those alternative hypotheses usually are *ad hoc* and usually concern avoiding artifacts and ruling out mundane everyday explanations. At this stage, we don't ask ourselves what other theories could explain our results, and one may suggest that it is *not* our obligation to do so. It is the researchers' obligation to conduct studies that demonstrate success for their theories.

If there are a number of studies in a Stage 2 CRP, the results are very likely to be mixed. Anyone who has done any empirical research knows that a study never turns out exactly as anticipated. Indeed, it probably would not be very interesting if it did. With a series of studies, there will be some support for the theory, some nonsupport, and some indeterminate results. Some studies may provide genuine discoveries, and others may produce serious anomalies. How does one evaluate the theory and/or the CRP in the face of this mixed collection of empirical outcomes? Neither the philosophy of science nor current methodology provides much help in answering this question. Yet this is the situation that confronts those sociologists who have made long-term intellectual commitments.

Appraisal of a Stage 2 CRP

This paper has asserted the principle that all theory evaluation is comparative. Hence, the appraisal of a Stage 2 CRP depends on what alternative theories are available. The question then becomes, how do the problem-solving successes of the Stage 2 CRP compare to the successes of other available problem-solving alternatives?

If no other theories exist, or, as is more likely, the available alternatives are *ad hoc*, then, relative to these alternatives, the theory of the Stage 2 CRP is more successful. Almost by definition, the mixed collection of empirical results must contain solutions to more than one empirical problem; the CRP's theory must explain more than one set of observations. The *ad hoc* alternatives deal only with single problems and do not have heuristic value. Despite the tendency among some sociologists to treat theoretical and *ad hoc* arguments as equivalent, the constraints on a theory that are absent in *ad hoc* problem solutions make correct predictions from the theory all the more impressive. Theory choice in this case should be neither problematic nor controversial.

Where there are rival theories or CRPs, appraisal is more complex. While it is possible to propose some guidelines for choosing among the rivals, many details need to be worked out. (Another critical task for the new methodology that this essay advocates.) Appraisal depends on the problems that are solved by one of the competitors and not solved by its rivals and in particular the anomalies in one program that are solved problems in the other. If program A solves all of program B's anomalies and A has no unsolved problems that B solves, then the evaluation is clear-cut—program A is more successful. The world, however, is not that neat; it is more likely that A will solve some of B's anomalies and unsolved problems while B does likewise for some of A's anomalies and unsolved problems. It may be possible to weight and count problems, but weighting and counting proposals have hidden traps reminiscent of attempts to quantify "explanatory power."

Note that this discussion argues not for the "truth" or "confirmation status" of theories but rather for a theory's relative success at predicting and explaining observed relationships that are not predicted or explained by its rivals. Furthermore, it does not appeal to a "generalization" of success to future problems; rather, it focuses on what each rival program has accomplished at the time of its appraisal. Appraisal, then, is relative not only to available alternative problem-solving mechanisms but also to available empirical research.

Abandonment of a Stage 2 CRP

Here again we can ask what empirical criteria would lead to a rational decision to abandon a program that has reached Stage 2. When there is no competing program and no alternative theory, it is unlikely that one would cease pursuing a program that has had sufficient success to achieve Stage 2. However, should the program stagnate, that is, should it no longer identify new problems or generate new solutions, we would then be in a situation similar to that discussed in connection with Stage 1 where criteria other than empirical outcomes—for example, loss of interest in the problems already solved—would determine the decision to abandon the program. It is important to emphasize that these other criteria would only be triggered by empirical studies that together did not increase problem-solving success.

Where there are competing programs, the above discussion of appraisal implies a principle on which to base the decision to abandon a program or a theory within a program:[1]

> *Abandon a Stage 2 program or a theory within the program only if there is an alternative that is decisively more successful in solving empirical problems.*

[1] We use the phrase "program or theory within a program" to allow the possibility that a theory might be abandoned but its related empirical research transferred to a rival program.

In theory choice, let us call the theory that is decisively more successful the "preferred theory." In a comparison, either the theory under attack or one of its alternatives could turn out to be the preferred theory. Where each of two theories deals successfully with some of the other's unsolved problems, we must allow the possibility that there are no preferred theories and no preferred programs. Where there is no clear-cut winner, there is no reason to abandon any of the rivals; competitors can exist side by side, each useful in its area of success. Sometimes rationality requires not choosing among theories or the CRPs in which they are embedded.

While it is difficult to specify "decisively more successful" except in the unlikely extreme case discussed above, it is possible to indicate the dimensions that are relevant to this choice. Although these dimensions are familiar, their comparative use is more uncommon. It is taken for granted that the rival theories can approximately predict and explain sets of observations; if the predictions of one theory generally have a higher degree of approximation, or precision, that should weigh in its favor. The degree of overlap of the domains of the rival theories is another dimension of evaluation; domains must overlap to some extent, or the theories are not competitors. It follows that decisive success within the area of overlap is weakened if each rival also has success in areas that do not overlap. A similar analysis applies to the scope of each of the rival theories. It may turn out that we would want to restrict decisive success to those rivals that have nearly total overlap in their domain and scope. Finally, evaluating decisive success in any decision to abandon a program must consider whether a CRP is progressive or degenerative in continuing to identify new empirical problems. More precise specification of these dimensions and their relative importance must await further methodological work.

A Stage 3 Cumulative Research Program

A CRP is at Stage 3 when the program contains a number of related theories using the same concepts and similar principles. The family of theories covers several distinct domains and has demonstrated success in more than one of these. The expectation states program exemplifies a Stage 3 CRP (Berger 1992); it employs ideas about state-organizing processes to explain and predict task interaction, justice processes, and, most recently, affect phenomena.

Wagner and Berger's analysis of theoretical research programs (1985) fits well with the present meaning of a Stage 3 CRP;[2] although their focus is on a retrospective analysis of programs, their concepts of proliferation and elaboration of theories are relevant to the development of criteria for appraisal and program choice. Competition is also a key process in their analysis.

The comparative assessment that the present author has stressed requires us

[2] See also Berger and Zelditch 1993.

to distinguish between competition from within a program and competition from outside the program. Competition within a program is relevant to Stage 2 evaluations of one theory against another, whereas Stage 3 appraisal demands external competition from either an alternative program or at least a theory that is not compatible with the CRP being assessed. A theory is not compatible if it deals with some problems in the CRP's domain but conceptualizes those problems in terms of different entities or processes. For example, Archibald (1976) conceptualized group member differences in interaction rates in terms of alienation from power, a conception that is not compatible with a formulation built around expectation states based on status.

Appraisal of a Stage 3 CRP

Many of the considerations presented in the discussion of appraising Stage 2 CRPs are applicable to Stage 3 as well. Given the demonstrated success of a Stage 3 CRP, the only appropriate comparative evaluation is with rival Stage 3 programs. That is, a Stage 3 program by definition is more successful than rivals that have not achieved Stage 3. In an appraisal of Stage 3 programs, a most important question is, does the program demonstrate problem-solving success in a range of different domains? Compared to rival programs, a more successful program has solved empirical problems in more different domains. Another way to address this issue is to assess how many of the theories of a CRP are more successful in their own domains than their rivals. It is a matter not of treating each theory or each domain as a unit, but of looking for clear domination of one CRP over its rivals—in other words, a set of empirical successes that decisively favors one program over another.

Anomalies are most informative to Stage 3 CRPs. Unless they open new domains, additional successful predictions add diminishing increments to the evaluation of a highly developed program; where success is commonplace, one more is not very exciting. Failure to solve an empirical problem in its domain, however, is unexpected for a Stage 3 CRP and is likely to have a dramatic impact. The inability to resolve an anomaly may weigh heavily against a program, and there is strong motivation for program adherents to find a resolution.

Abandoning a Stage 3 CRP

Since a Stage 3 program has demonstrated considerable success in a range of domains, the presumption should favor its continuation. At the same time, it cannot be totally insulated from termination, or it becomes no different from dogma. Furthermore, competitor CRPs can coexist for long periods of time, each with its own successes and anomalies, with only partially overlapping domains. Persistence of one CRP or coexistence of rivals can occur without programs having any "irrefutable hard core" that must be preserved by nonrational or irrational means; persistence can result from quite rational calculations and choices.

We are all aware that research traditions can peter out. A Stage 3 CRP can stagnate if it no longer generates new solutions to new problems. Other symptoms include the end of the expansion of the domain and scope of problem solving or even their contraction. The domain of a CRP contracts when a rival takes over part of it by virtue of its greater success there. There are circumstances when rationality dictates abandoning the program. While more analysis is required, it is appropriate to propose the following decision rule:

> *A Stage 3 CRP should be abandoned if it has no preferred theory in any of its domains, and there is an alternative CRP that overlaps some of its domains and contains at least one preferred theory in the area of overlap.*

This rule should at least cover situations where a rival is decisively more successful or a program becomes completely stagnant. Since the determination of preferred theories rests on an empirical base, this proposal preserves the empirical character of scientific sociology without invoking impossible standards and without appealing to a nonexistent logic of induction.

A Methodology for CRPs

In developing the concept of a cumulative research program and describing its stages, this paper has presented suggestions, criteria, and proposed rules for a new methodology. A reader may well ask how these proposals differ from traditional methodology. Is success at solving empirical problems any different from confirmation status, degree of corroboration, and so on? In this author's view, the following list briefly captures the main differences.

1. Successful problem solving is different from failure to refute, and it is not necessarily critical to eliminate rival explanations.

2. Problem-solving success is explicitly comparative, relative to available alternatives.

3. There is a need to evaluate against standards other than the null hypothesis.

4. A single empirical study is insufficient for either appraisal or the decision to abandon a program; hence it is necessary to attend to more than a single study.

5. There are different criteria for different stages of a CRP; successes and failures are not tallied equally—success is more important than failure for Stage 1.

6. Failure is more important than success for Stage 3.

7. This approach does not generalize "truth" in evaluating theories.

8. Appraisal requires explicit specification of domain and scope.

A methodology of cumulative research programs is itself at the beginning of Stage 1; the development of workable standards for determining successful problem solution is at the top of the agenda. We need criteria that will recognize that a "black box" prediction is not as successful as a prediction that derives from a formulation of mechanisms or processes; that will build "understanding" and measures of understanding into the evaluation; and that will take into account the stage of development of the program.

This methodology must address the design of research; efficient research designs that facilitate comparative assessment of theories or CRPs are an urgent priority. To replace the "crucial experiment," we require designs that incorporate multistudy approaches. Such designs, in turn, require the operationalization of ideas like precision, scope, and domain which play a key role in comparisons of theories or CRPs. A major challenge for this new methodology is the formulation of standards and the construction of techniques for combining the outcomes of several empirical studies. Meta-analysis, about which one can have many reservations on other grounds, at least reflects the right concerns.

These issues are formidable, and there are many others that this paper has not considered. This writer is confident, however, that with an effort comparable to that put into current sociological methodology, we will successfully create a methodology of cumulative research programs.

Testing Elementary Theory
for Universality

◥◤

Jacek Szmatka

Contemporary sociology is a diversified and divided science. Not only do we have several different substantive theoretical frameworks and perspectives (see Turner 1991; Berger and Zelditch, eds. 1993), but we also witness deep controversies over the methodological status of sociology as a science. The universality of sociological theory is not taken for granted across these different perspectives.

Many theoretical approaches programmatically exclude the possibility of universal laws and theories in sociology, that is, laws and theories that hold true in all times and all places. For example, the interactionist tradition overtly proclaims the impossibility of universal laws and theories in sociology. Similarly, humanistic sociology (Scimecca 1989) claims universal laws are impossible due to the agency of human actions. Structuration theory also argues that there can be no universal and abstract laws in sociology. First, they are impossible because social organization is changeable by social agents altering its allegedly invariant properties (Giddens 1984: 326). Second, social theory cannot be natural science–like. Instead, social theory is by its nature social criticism (Giddens 1984: 335), where there is no room for any universal laws and theories.

Historical sociology and historical social psychology argue that the social world, as opposed to the natural world, is a historical one. This is why social psychology (and sociology) should progress as a history looking for "historically situated conventions" (Gergen 1973, 1976, 1982: 203). Bernard Cohen writes that disciples of this orientation

argue that sociological principles of necessity are historically conditioned. They argue that the distinction between natural and social science rests precisely on the fact that the natural sciences can have laws that hold true in all times and all places while the social sciences can

This research has benefited from Polish Committee for Scientific Research (KBN) research grant no. PB 0870/P1/94/07 and from the Research Support Scheme of the Open Society Institute grant no. 746/94. The author thanks David Willer, John Skvoretz, and Barry Markovsky for comments on earlier drafts of this paper. I also thank Izabella Uhl for assistance in running Polish experiments.

have only historical laws, true for particular places and times. Such an argument denies the possibility of social science in any but a symbolic meaning of the term. (Cohen 1980: 77)

Thus, there is no doubt that for historical sociologists (Skocpol 1979; Moore 1966; Anderson 1974; Mann 1986; and also Tilly 1984), the issue of universality of sociological theories and laws is a nonexistent problem simply because there are no such theories. As Richard Münch writes, it is impossible to find general and universal theory on the level of historical concreteness. "This is the level on which historical study of the concrete cases with special sensitivity to the very concrete circumstances on the levels of economics, politics, solidarity structures, and legitimation is required" (Münch 1994: 198).

Similar reasoning lies behind the dismissal of the search for universal laws in sociology by members of the hermeneutic camp. They claim that general (universal) theories are visibly lacking in sociology (S. Turner 1989). As a consequence, or in addition to that,

there are no true empirical theories in social science which are non-trivial. Either it is easy to produce counterinstances to every such supposed law, i.e., they are false, or these "laws" are true but merely descriptive or true by virtue of the logical form or the meaning of the terms in which they are stated. (S. Turner 1989: 130)

Perhaps the most extreme standpoint contesting sociology's right to universal laws and theories derives from postmodernist camp. Those who represent this orientation not only oppose universal theories and laws, they oppose sociological theory in any form. Universality of laws and theories in sociology is inconceivable because such laws and theories "become so contentless as to lose whatever explanatory value they have" (Seidman 1991: 137). If universality of sociological laws and theories is impossible in any form, then the very term "theory" should also be abandoned as an inappropriate label for a sociological product. What is left, then, is a social theory as social narrative. "To be revitalized, theory must be reconnected in integral ways to ongoing national public moral and political debates and social conflicts. To reestablish that tie I have urged that sociological theory reaffirm a core concept of itself as a broad, synthetic narrative" (Seidman 1991: 144). By social narrative, Seidman understands an event-based, nation/society-based narrative.

I address this paper to those who claim not only the possibility of universal laws in sociology but their necessity, too. Fortunately, I am not alone in this quest.

There are a number of excellent examples of successful elaboration and empirical testing of such laws in sociology and social psychology. Three volumes of *Sociological Theories in Progress* (Berger, Zelditch, and Anderson 1966, 1972, 1989) contain perhaps the best examples. As Fararo says, "Berger and his colleagues tried to provide a way for physics-like interplay between *abstract theories, appropriate formalisms*, and *relevant data*" (Fararo 1984: 155. See also Webster and Foschi 1988; and Berger and Zelditch, eds. 1993).

In this paper, I will follow the view that theoretical propositions must be of universal form (Sell and Martin 1983: 346), that experimental social psychology and sociology do not necessarily create research about advanced industrial societies or about any existing society (Sell and Martin 1983: 349; see also Jasso 1988: 1–20), and that "there can be unchanging laws about sociological phenomena even though what are instances of those phenomena may change just as the value of the constant in Galileo's law changes as one tests the law in places remote from the surface of the earth" (Cohen 1980: 83).

First, I would like to offer a method by which to test a sociological theory for its universality. I will argue that cross-national as opposed to cross-cultural comparative research is an appropriate vehicle for that kind of test. Second, I will test a particular theory, elementary theory, for universality.

Universality and Three Genera of Sociological Theories

Universality of theory and universality of scientific laws are not equally sound problems in all kinds of sociological theorizing. To show where universality makes sense, and where it does not, let me introduce briefly the concept of three genera of sociological theories (see Szmatka 1994, and Szmatka and Sozański 1994, where this issue is more thoroughly elaborated). To do so, let me assume that the history and the development of sociological theories can be interpreted in terms of continuous attempts at making sociology a scientific discipline. By "scientific," I mean a discipline able to build abstract theories that have empirical import. Contrary to many other methodological standpoints in sociology, I maintain that there is one universal scientific method for all sciences. Sociology to be a scientific discipline must be able to meet these standards instead of creating its own (Willer 1967; Willer and Willer 1973; Cohen 1989).

The Grand Theory Genus

I claim that in the process of the development of sociology, three families or genera of theories in sociology can be isolated. The grand theory genus emerged along with nineteenth-century classical sociological systems. Theories of this kind suffer from the lack of explicitly stated "scope conditions" (Cohen 1980, 1989; Walker and Cohen 1985), and therefore they remain untestable. They stay in close relation to philosophy; are usually presented as abstract, general, and overarching conceptions of the social world; and are usually presented in narrative form. Since they are untestable, they do not meet the basic requirements of the scientific method.

Theories of the first genus do not belong to the past of sociology by any means. Although the whole classical tradition belongs to that category, contemporary theories of Blumer, Coser, Giddens, Goffman, Habermas, Homans, Luhman, and Parsons (to mention few) must also be classed as first-genus theories.

Their methodological underdevelopment, however, and especially their untestability make them an inappropriate platform from which to consider the issue of universality of theory.

The Social Theory Genus

These theories have their own verification procedures and are testable, but they are endowed with scope conditions which make reference to concrete people and societies rather than to abstractly defined social actors and systems. Sociology is filled with these theories. Theories of social stratification, of meritocratic justice, of social structure in comparative perspective (Słomczyński, Miller, and Kohn 1981; Słomczyński 1989), theory of social mobility (Wesołowski and Mach 1986), organizational theory of collusion (Baker and Faulkner 1993), and theory of differential social control (Matsueda 1992; Heimer and Matsueda 1994) are good examples of second-genus theories. Although their methodological sophistication, especially in terms of advanced statistical analyses, is very high, the reference to concrete people and societies makes it impossible for these theories to produce true universal laws. That means that the second genus itself cannot be universal either.

The Sociological Theory Genus

Third-genus theories like elementary theory (Willer 1992), expectation states theory (Wagner and Berger 1993), and power-dependence theory (Cook and Yamagishi 1992) accept the methodological standards of the "hard sciences." They are both abstract and empirically testable, unlike the theories of the first genus (old and new "grand theories"). The merger of these two features is possible thanks to a qualitatively new conception of theory verification (new in sociology, but well known in the "hard sciences"). According to this conception, theory relates directly not to the "real world" but to a "theoretical universe." The method of theory testing is scientific experiment as opposed to empiricist experiment (Willer 1987). In scientific types of experiments, an investigator creates an artificial social world in the laboratory which is maximally similar to a theoretical model of it. Then, he or she observes the behavior of this artificial world to tell the difference (if any) between the theoretical model and the experimental artificial situation. These unique features of the third-genus theory allow it to produce not only universal sociological laws but an empirical test for universality as well. The third-genus theory is, then, the only type of sociological theory where the test for its universality is possible.[1]

[1] The meaning of the distinction between descriptive theoretical approach and formal theoretical approach (Martin and Sell 1979; Freese 1980a; Freese and Sell 1980) is close to my distinction between first and second genus theories on the one hand and third genus theories on the other. Note also that the concept of an interactor theory (Berger, Eyre, and Zelditch 1989) is in a very close neighborhood to our concept of the theory of third genus.

The Meaning of Theory

By "theory," I understand, then, a set of interrelated, general, universal, and abstract statements which have an empirical import, supplemented by a set of scope conditions, which specify a theory's scope or domain of applicability (Cohen 1980, 1989; Walker and Cohen 1985). Since such a theory does not address any real situation, it is not culture bound. But because it is not about any real situation or any real society, it has implications for a variety of real processes and societies.

Abstraction, Generality, and Universality

Let me define three dimensions of theory and its laws. The first dimension I would like to analyze is the abstract character of theory itself and of its laws. Not all empirical sciences and not all their theories must be abstract. The subject of history, for example, is always "concrete" historical events or people. In theoretical (or nomothetical) sciences, as well as in theories of the third genus in sociology, the requirement of abstractness must be met. In brief, the notion of abstraction (that knowledge claims are abstract) "requires that knowledge claims be considered apart from application to any particular object" (Cohen 1989: 76). Statements, and whole theories as well, do not refer to any aspect of the "real world." Rather, they refer to ideal objects like "perfect gas," "rigid body," or "null connected exchange structure." The theory must then create an abstract world composed of abstract, theoretical objects that exist beyond time and place.

Generality of theory (and of theoretical statements) is referred to the scope or domain of the theory (or statement) and indirectly to its scope conditions as well. The broader the scope (or domain) of a given theory, the higher its generality. Most old and new grand theories (theories of the first genus) are very general, because their domain is the whole society. They also have no precisely stated scope conditions. Although "relaxing a scope restriction on the theory, by eliminating it entirely or by substituting a less restrictive form of the statement, increases the class of hypotheses that the theory . . . explains" and makes the theory clearly more powerful, it makes the theory also much more vulnerable to the empirical test (Cohen 1989: 298). We see that if the abstraction dimension is an absolute characteristic of the theory (the theory can or cannot be an abstract one), the generality dimension is its relative characteristic (Such 1972). As many authors claim, although the goal of science is to create theories as general as possible, to be testable the theory must be conditional. Empirical, abstract theory without scope conditions is unrealistic (Webster and Kervin 1971; Cohen 1980, 1989; Sell and Martin 1983).

Universality of the theory as a necessary condition for a theory to be a scientific one, means the truth of the theory is independent of time, space, or historical circumstance (Cohen 1989: 78). As opposed to the two previous dimensions of theory—abstraction and generality—universality surpasses "the world of theory" and refers to the relation of the theory to the "real world." The question of universality is exactly the question of the independence of the truth of the theory from time, space, historical circumstance, cultural or national context, and so on. The more universal the theory, the larger the number of different, real, time and space determined systems in which the theory has been empirically confirmed. However, to claim the theory passed the test of universality, one has only to replicate the original experiment in a different, contrasting setting.

From the three dimensions of the theory, *abstraction* is a constant value and cannot be a subject of the empirical test. *Generality* is not a subject of any empirical test, either. We can, however, attempt to extend the level of generality of a given theory by formulating a new version of it with relaxed scope constraints, as compared with the old one. That is a standard method of cumulative theory development (Wagner and Berger 1985; Berger and Zelditch 1993). Only *universality* of a given theory can be empirically tested with no further substantial consequences for its content. Universality is the only dimension of the theory the test for which can affect the methodological status of that theory.

Universality and Cross-National Research

Cultural-Based Inference and Cultural Difference Studies

The well-established tradition of cross-cultural and cross-national studies (experiments) allows only theories of the second genus to form a subject for a test. Formal, third-genus theory is usually claimed to be an inappropriate vehicle for cross-cultural comparisons. As I will show below, the disjunction between theory of the third genus and cross-cultural comparisons is particularly unfortunate, because cross-cultural comparisons are the only method for a test for universality. As a result of this disjunction:

1. In most cross-cultural and cross-national comparisons (see Marsh 1967; Hopkins and Wallerstein 1967; Przeworski and Teune 1970; Elder 1976; Nowak 1977; Tilly 1984; Ragin 1987, 1989; Kohn 1989b,c), "theories tested systematically on a cross-national basis refer to some 'natural social objects' ('family,' 'school,' 'village,' 'city'), the meaning of which is specified by the everyday experiences of the members of the studied populations and is defined in the way that these people see and define them" (Nowak 1989: 45). Meanwhile, it is a condition for a theory to refer to abstract, "theoretical" objects, as opposed to "real world" ones. Referring to natural social objects, theories of the second genus must be culture bound. Cultural differences must usually serve to operationalize theoretical variables and, through that, to be a part of such a theory. Such a theory can never be a universal one.

2. Cross-cultural and cross-national research is usually claimed to be a standard method of testing theory for its generality. Rohner, for example, says that the aim of cross-cultural research is "to test for the level of generality of a theory or proposition" (1977: 6). Apparently, his concept of the generality of theory is different from mine:

Can the theory be generalized to all humanity, or is it valid only for certain kinds of people, for example, people living in certain physical environments, in certain types of cultural systems, or populations sharing certain genetic characteristics, and so forth? (Rohner 1977: 6)

Not only generalizability of the theory is defined by Rohner differently. His notion of theory obviously does not involve an abstract, theoretical object if it refers to "certain types of cultural systems." Others (see, for example, Foschi and Hales 1979; Kohn 1989a) claim that cross-national studies extend the scope of sociological knowledge (see Kohn 1989a: 78). Extending the scope, however, is merely an equivalent of testing for or extending the generality of a theory (Kohn 1987: 714). As I explained earlier, for a theory of the third genus there is no test for "the level of generality of a theory," or at least any attempt at such a test has nothing to do with cross-cultural or cross-national comparisons.

3. Some authors, like Foschi and Hales (1979), claiming universality as a target of cross-cultural research, seem to treat that dimension of the theory not as a point of departure but as a point of arrival. That, in turn, contradicts the conception of the theory of the third genus in which I claim universality is a precondition for a theory. It also fits well with the research situation characteristic for second-genus theories.

The pattern of cross-cultural comparisons that I call *cultural difference studies* is, then, the following one. First, studies of this kind begin with the theory of the second genus that, by its nature, refers to real-world objects and processes. As such, these objects and processes must be located and defined in terms of a certain cultural or national context. Second, depending upon research goals, one may try to generalize the results of a study conducted in one cultural or national context to another, thus extending the scope of the theory. One can also try to set values for the independent variable (for example, mental states associated with culture) while the dependent variable is measured as it would be in single culture study.[2]

Culture-based inference characteristic for *cultural difference studies* is, then, as it is shown on Figure 1. Here, it is assumed that different culture produces different people, who are characterized by different mental states associated with their culture. That, in turn, produces different behavior, even under the same conditions.

---

[2] Types of *cultural difference experiments* and methodological issues related have been discussed thoroughly in Willer and Szmatka (1993).

CULTURE-BASED INFERENCE   **STRUCTURE-BASED INFERENCE**

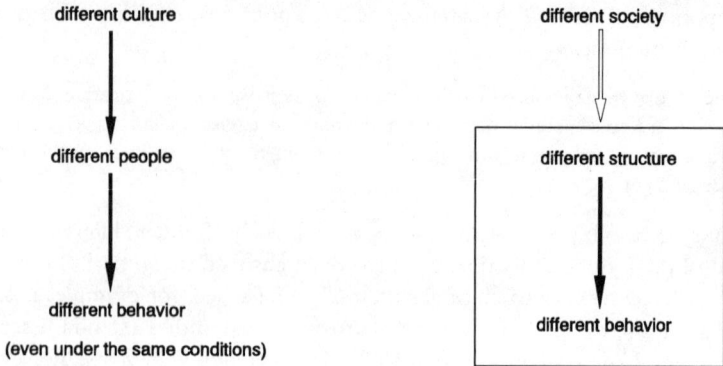

Fig. 1. Two types of inference in cross-national research

Cross-national and Cross-cultural Replication Experiments

Let me begin with the analysis of the type of inference characteristic for cross-national replication experiments, which I call structure-based inference. It is assumed that different structure produces different behavior *regardless* of the type of society or culture in which it has been implemented. Although concrete structures characteristic of concrete, real societies are considered products of a given society, for purposes of this analysis, I do not need, and must not even focus on, processes of structure formation in concrete, historical societies. Quite the contrary, what interests me is a universal, abstract process of power distribution in a social structure regardless of the social context in which such structure can be produced. At issue is not the generality of findings and the validity of interpretations derived from single-nation studies (Kohn 1989a: 77), but rather *testing theory by varying conditions that are external to the models tested and could influence results.*

In the case of cross-national replication experiments, an experimenter deals with abstract, theoretical objects. They are the subject of the empirical test only in experiments driven by theory of the third genus. Cross-national replication experiments are intended to vary conditions that are not part of theory and "can be identified by default only" (Foschi 1980: 93). Experiments of this type use test-retest reliability design and are intended to form a test for universality of the theory by showing that it can be applied, as it is assumed, independent of time and place.

The Meaning of the Test for Universality

I argue that the cross-national and cross-cultural replication experiment is the only method of testing a theory for universality. First, only formal or third-genus theory can be tested for universality, since only this theory can legitimately claim to be a universal one. Second, at issue is not how to obtain universal theory, since the theory must be such at its inception. Third, the test for universality, therefore, is not a subject of the "inductivist fallacy." That means, even one successful cross-national replication constitutes valid evidence for a theory's universality.

Cross-national replication experiments as a method of testing theory for universality are virtually unknown in sociology. Perhaps, it is because of the limited number of theories of the third genus in our discipline. The only theory (to my knowledge) intensively cross-nationally developed is expectation states theory. There are many studies and experiments conducted in countries other than the United States where this theory was first time tested, that is, in Australia (Crundall and Foddy 1981; Riches and Foddy 1988), in Canada (Foschi 1971, 1986; Foschi and Buchan 1990; Foschi and Freeman 1991; Foschi, Warriner, and Hart 1985; Maupin and Fischer 1989; Moore 1985; Pierce and Sharon 1982; Sev'er 1989; Stewart 1988; Stewart and Moore 1992; Tuzlak 1989; Tuzlak and Moore 1984), and in Israel (Cohen and Sharan 1980). Most of them, however, were not designed for cross-national replication purposes but aim at a test of further hypotheses and "standard" theory development. The only two studies that partially approach the goal of cross-national and cross-cultural replication experiments, as it is stated above, were conducted in Canada (Stewart 1988) and in Israel (Cohen and Sharan 1980).

Elementary Theory has only once been a subject of the cross-national replication test so far (Sozański 1993b). In that study, however, the power advantages were smaller than in the original experiment. Sozański attributes the difference to varying modes of negotiation across U.S. and Polish settings. The initial test by Willer and Szmatka (1993), however, provides support for the universality of Elementary Theory.

An Overview of Elementary Theory

Elementary Theory (Willer and Anderson 1981; Willer 1987; Markovsky, Willer, and Patton 1988; Willer 1992; Skvoretz and Willer 1991, 1993; Willer and Markovsky 1993; Szmatka and Willer 1993, 1995) is a theory of actors in social relationships. The central objects are individual or collective actors conditioned by structures. The two basic theoretical questions are (1) how are actions in relations conditioned by structures? and (2) how is power in the form of exploitation and domination structurally produced? (Willer and Markovsky 1993).

Actors in social relationships are motivated by two interests: an interest in gaining maximum outcomes from the exchange and an interest in avoiding the worst possible outcome at nonexchange or confrontation. Resistance Theory (Willer 1981a, 1984; Heckathorn 1983a) and Graph-theoretic Power Index (Markovsky, Willer, and Patton 1988) provide a procedure for calculating the expected rate of exchange or rate of coercive exploitation/domination as well as a method of deriving power events under a variety of conditions and structures (Willer, Markovsky, and Patton 1989: 324).

Given in Figure 2 is a schematic for the elementary theoretic research program as investigated in the United States. The model of exchange structure is a basic model for network exchange theory. It is composed of exchange relations in which two positive sanctions are paired (see Figure 3 and Willer 1987: 51–96). The main thesis is that exclusion is a structural condition of power in exchange, that is, exclusion produces the power in exchange networks. I tested for universality 3,3 weak centralized exchange structures, 4,3 and 5,3 strong centralized exchange structures, and 1-exchange profit point network. The first three are represented in Figure 2 by the box *Centralized Exchange Networks* located under *Exclusion*. The 1-exchange profit point network is represented by *1-Exchange* box located under *Exclusion*, and then under *Profit Point Networks*.

Weak Centralized Exchange Structure

This structure (in Figure 3a, a 3,3 null connected structure) has been designed so that the number of exchanges between an actor on central position is equal to the number of actors on peripheral positions in the network. In this structure, no actor is necessarily excluded. Consequently, ET predicts that exchange rates between A and B will approach equality. In the experiment, B had a counter worth ten points to A but nothing to himself, while A had several counters worth one point to both. ET predicts that on average A will give B five counters in exchange for the one counter worth ten points, for a $\frac{5}{10}$ exchange rate.

Strong Centralized Exchange Structure

These structures (in Figure 3b,c, a 4,3 and 5,3 exclusionary connected structure) have been designed so that the number of exchanges between an actor on central position is less than the number of actors on peripheral positions in the network. In these structures, ET predicts that exchange rates will come to favor the central actor who is never excluded. The peripheral actors bid against each other to avoid exclusion and offer increasingly favorable rates to the central actor.

ET predicts that in the strong centralized exchange structures, power will develop rapidly and will approach the maximum value of power exercise, namely, where A is exchanging one counter for B's counters worth ten points, for a $\frac{9}{10}$ rate in his favor.

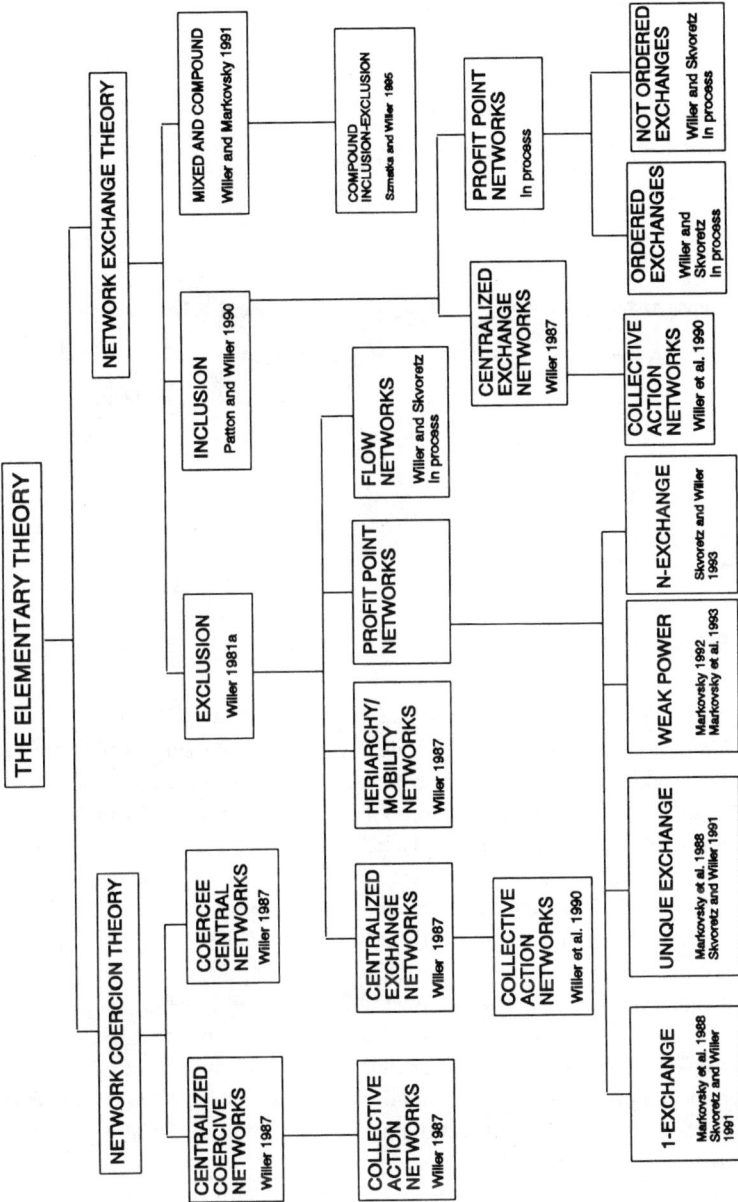

Fig. 2. A schematic for the Elementary Theoretic research program

a. Branch 3,3 weak exchange structure

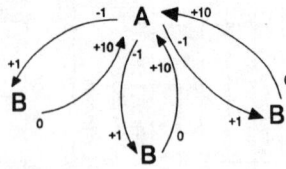

b. Branch 4,3 strong exchange structure

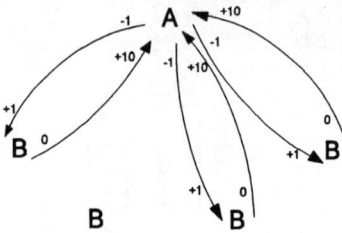

c. Branch 5,3 strong exchange structure

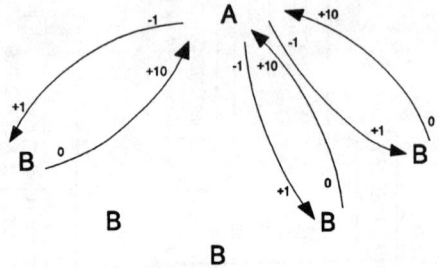

Fig. 3. Three exchange structures

1-Exchange Profit Point Network

GPI is a Graph-theoretic Power Index with associated axioms that can be applied to exclusionary networks in which all actors exchange maximally once (Markovsky, Willer, and Patton 1988; Willer 1992). Generally, GPI allows the identification of the power position in a network and measurement of its power compared with other positions. The network I tested cross-nationally is shown in Figure 5, where GPI values are indicated as superscripts.

First, GPI predicts that the network will break down between B and D positions. Having two potential partners, each at a different power level, D will prefer to exchange with the equal power E than to exchange with the higher power B. Since D will never seek to exchange with B, it is predicted that the network splits into two subnetworks: A–B–C branch and the D–E dyad.

Second, it is predicted that B is high in power and will have power only over A and C. Since in our experiments the profit point pool was 24, it is predicted that B will gain substantially better than $\frac{12}{12}$ divisions.

Third, according to the GPI index, D and E will be in equipower positions, dividing equally at $\frac{12}{12}$.

Fourth, profit made by E will be higher than that made by A and C, since E is located within the equipower dyad, whereas A and C are in low power positions (Markovsky, Willer, and Patton 1988: 226–27).

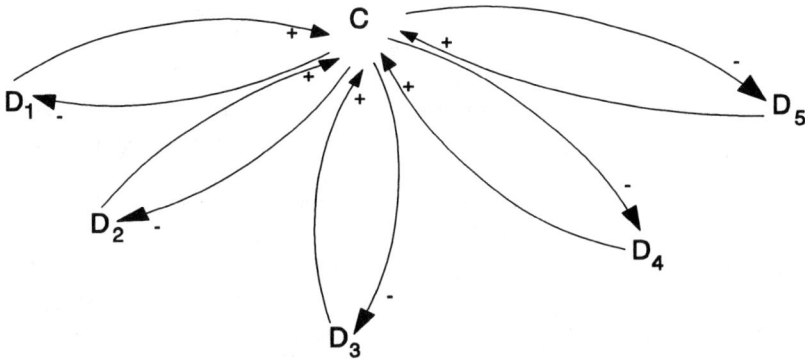

Fig. 4. A coercive structure

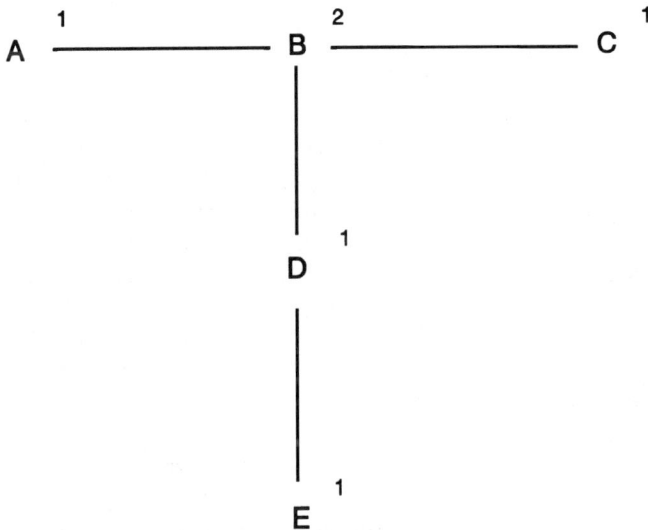

Fig. 5. A 1-exchange network with initial GPI values

Centralized Coercive Structures

As shown in Figure 2, network coercion theory is a second major branch of ET. Coercive structures are composed of coercive social relations in which a positive and negative sanction is paired (Willer 1987; see also Fig. 4). In these networks a single coercer threatens use of negative sanctions to extract positives from coercees at the periphery. Rates of coercion vary with the costs of transmission of the negative (Willer 1987: 97–123).

I tested for universality weak centralized coercive structures and two types of strong centralized coercive structures. All three are represented in Figure 2 by the box *Centralized Coercive Networks* located under *Network Coercion Theory*.

In the experiment, in weak structures each D initially is allocated ten resources while C is allocated two negative sanctions each of which costs a D ten points when received. In strong coercive structures the negative sanction is replaced by the confiscatory sanction the effect of which is to confiscate the resources of any D receiving it. In both cases, the negatives C holds cost C one to transmit to D.

In weak coercive structures the rate of coercive exploitation C_x is defined as the ratio of resources transmitted to resources initially held by the coercee. For each relation of the weak structure $C_x = .45$ is predicted. In strong 1 coercive structure, C is allocated one confiscatory sanction, and in strong 2 coercive structure, C is allocated two confiscatory sanctions. The $C_x = .9$ rates are predicted for both, though strong 1 structure is expected to move more slowly to the extreme than strong 2.

The Experiment

The Two Settings

The two settings were the United States and Poland. The U.S. research on exchange and coercion structures was completed in the mid-1970's and research on 1-exchange profit point networks in the late 1980's. All the Polish research was completed in the late 1980's. During that time, Poland was a socialist society, and the decision to replicate U.S. experiments was based on the presumption that both societies were fundamentally different, especially in terms of their social structures. I was looking, then, for a setting that was culturally different from the United States and that also had deep differences in politics, economy, and stratification. Therefore, the best setting for the replication of U.S. experiments would be a socialist (communist) society.

The socialist system reveals particularly strong systemic features and to operate smoothly must reveal a certain set of properties. These properties are syndromatic, which means that there are strong positive statistical and functional associations between them. This feature makes the system extremely sensitive to any changes of core elements and, in consequence, extremely rigid. Students of socialist societies highlight the enormous stability of the structure of this system—it has virtually the same end products regardless of the target society (Szmatka, Mach, and Mucha 1993; Kornai 1992). For my purposes it was important that in all three structural dimensions, politics, economy, and stratification, a socialist society is diametrically opposed to a capitalist one (Staniszkis 1992).

At the time of the research, the Polish political structure was characterized by:

1. Vanguard role of the Communist Party, with extensive authoritative power under conditions of a one-party political system;

2. Total domination by the Communist Party limited neither by received laws or codes nor even by the boundaries of governmental functions;
3. Control over formal organizations ("nomenklatura");
4. Control over flow of information (censorship);
5. Control over means of violence.

The Polish economic structure was characterized by:

1. Centrally planned economy where economic development was subordinated to the extension or maintenance of Communist Party control;
2. State-Party control over the means of production and state ownership of the means of production;
3. Lack of "free labor" (no labor market, full employment);
4. Incomplete and nonexclusive property rights;
5. Extensive allocation of power (through the central economic plan, state authorities decide where, when, and how major means of production are to be developed);
6. Control over the means of collective consumption;
7. Control over the means of personal consumption.

The Polish stratification system was characterized by:

1. Party bureaucracy as a new ruling class;
2. Unqualified egalitarianism and decomposition of class attributes (see Wesołowski 1979, who explains these features of Polish society);
3. Potentially dichotomous class structure–Party bureaucracy versus people's class. (For more information about characteristics of Polish society, see Mucha, Skąpska, Szmatka, and Uhl 1991; Szmatka, Mach, and Mucha 1993. Kohn and Słomczyński [1990] support the thesis of profound structural differences between Polish and U.S. societies.)

The Rationale

Taken together, 13 different networks were investigated in both settings—a total of 48 Polish and 60 U.S. experiments (see Willer and Szmatka 1993). For purposes of this analysis, however, I discuss 7 different networks replicated in both settings—a total of 30 Polish and 41 U.S. experiments. Although to replicate all studies conducted in the United States would give more impressive and convincing data, it was unnecessary from a methodological point of view. To demonstrate that structure created in the laboratory produces the same phenomena in both settings (our test for universality), it is only necessary to replicate in Poland studies from different parts of the theory's scope. This cross-national experimental replication investigates structures composed of each of the three different kinds of ties that may compose networks according to Elementary Theory—exchange, coercion, and profit point.

The Method

U.S. subjects were undergraduates at the University of Kansas. Polish subjects were graduate students at Uniwersytet Jagielloński in Kraków. In both settings the same experimental procedure was used. Before being taken to the laboratory, subjects were given instructions that explained the general nature and goals of the experiment, the rules by which negotiations were to be conducted, and the values of the resource. They had an opportunity to ask questions regarding procedures and were assured that the instructions contained no misdirection. Then they were randomly assigned to positions previously arranged for the experiment. Physical barriers were used to restrict communication between occupants of the B positions. Counters served as resources to be exchanged.

For each type of exchange structure A was allocated thirty-three counters worth one point each to A and to B. Each B was initially allocated a set of ten counters which had to be transmitted as a unit. B's resources were worth nothing to B, but were worth ten points when received by A.

For weak coercive structure C was allocated two counters each of which cost a D ten points when received. In both types of strong coercive structures, C held one counter that confiscated the resources of any D receiving it, while D initially was allocated ten counters worth ten points each. In both cases, it cost C one point to transmit a negative to D.

Experiments were organized by rounds, periods, and sessions. For each structure, three sessions were run, each with a different group of subjects. They were told that they would have an opportunity to occupy each position of the network. Thus, each session was divided into four or six periods, depending upon the number of positions. Each period was divided into four rounds for negotiation and exchange. For example, for each 3,3 weak exchange structure, there were four subjects and thus four periods with four rounds; in each 4,3 strong structure, there were five subjects and five periods with four rounds; and in each 5,3 strong exchange structure, there were six subjects and six periods with four rounds. Thus, subjects had sixteen, twenty, or twenty-four rounds in which to bargain and exchange, depending upon the size of their structure. The same procedures were applied to three types of coercive structures investigated, with one exception: in the U.S. setting, four sessions were run; in Poland, three (Willer 1987).

For the 1-exchange profit point network, twenty-four counters were placed between related positions. These were to be divided by mutual agreement. Each position was limited to one agreement per round. There were five subjects and thus five periods with four rounds (Markovsky, Willer, and Patton 1988). In the U.S. setting, five sessions were run; in Poland, three.

Scores were recorded and announced at the conclusion of a round. After the first four rounds of negotiation and exchange were completed, subjects were rotated to new positions. Subsequently, at the end of each period there were further rotations such that each participant occupied each position and bargained in each four times. This rotation provided systematic control of individual differences, although no attempt was made to control for gender. Upon completion of the experimental session, participants were paid for points earned and dismissed.

Analysis

The cross-national studies suggest the two types of tests shown in Figure 6. First, were the phenomena of the theory produced in the two settings? The answer comes from a comparison of the rates in weak structures to the rates in strong structures. In exchange networks, resources gained by peripherals in the weak 3,3 branch should be substantially higher than resources gained by peripherals in either the strong 4,3 or strong 5,3 branch. In coercive networks, the number of resources retained by peripherals in the weak branch should be substantially larger than the number retained in either strong branch. The 1-exchange profit point network should behave similarly across branch types. If the phenomena were successfully produced in both settings, these weak-strong differences should appear in each setting.

Section B tests for universality. If elementary theory is not limited by the particularities of time and place, rates of exchange and of coercion will be similar across the two settings. As indicated in Figure 6b, tests compare rates for similar structures across settings. I test whether the number of resources gained by peripherals in weak exchange branches is similar in Poland and the United States—and similarly for each of the remaining types of coercive and exchange structures. Since Polish and U.S. societies at the time of the experimental work were quite different, this is a severe test for universality. Section B gives both hypotheses and

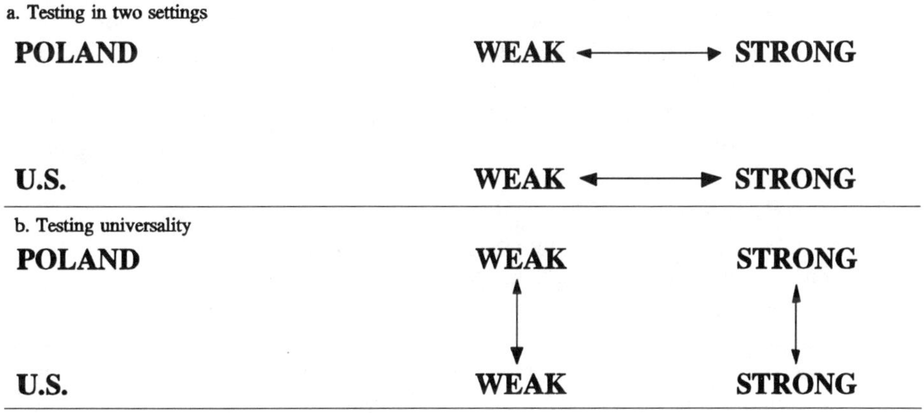

a. Testing in two settings

POLAND   **WEAK ◀——————▶ STRONG**

U.S.   **WEAK ◀——————▶ STRONG**

b. Testing universality

POLAND   **WEAK**   **STRONG**

                              ↕   ↕

U.S.   **WEAK**   **STRONG**

Fig. 6. Schematic for the cross-national tests

results of these comparisons. In addition, to evaluate the effects of structure and setting I applied a two-way analysis of variance to data from experiments in the United States and Poland.

Hypotheses and Results

Testing in Two Settings: Hypotheses

1. Elementary Theory predicts that in the weak 3,3 (null connected) branch the rate of exchange at equiresistance is $\frac{5}{10}$. Therefore, the theory predicts $P_A = 5.0$ and $P_B = 5.0$ for central and peripheral positions. For strong 4,3 and 5,3 branches it predicts that the rate approaches the $\frac{1}{10}$ extreme where $P_A = 9$ and $P_B = 1$. Null hypotheses predict no differences in rate of exchange between the weak and both types of strong branches for each setting.

2. Elementary Theory predicts that in the weak coercive branch the rate of coercive exploitation will be $C_x = .45$. At that rate $P_C = 4.5$ and $P_D = -4.5$. Since each D position begins with ten resources, this prediction means that Ds will each retain, on the average, 5.5 counters. For strong 1 and strong 2 branches it predicts that the rate of coercion will move to the $C_x = .9$ extreme. Null hypotheses predict no difference in rate of coercive exploitation between weak and both types of strong branches in both settings.

3. Elementary Theory predicts for the 1-exchange profit point network ("T-shape" network) that B exercises power over A and C gains more than one-half the pool of resources. The theory predicts that D and E divide the resource pool evenly. In both cases, the resource pool contains 24 points. Thus for both relations in the two settings the null hypotheses are that resource pools are divided equally at $\frac{12}{12}$.

Testing in the Two Settings: Results

Table 1 shows the observed mean resources received by peripheral positions. In the Polish strong 4,3 branch, B's average earnings were 2.54 and in the strong 5,3 branch, 2.36 points. Both means are significantly different from the observed mean earnings of 5.42 in the weak 3,3 branch. The first set of null hypotheses are rejected and thus ET's prediction for the Polish setting is supported. Similarly, results for the U.S. setting reject the null hypotheses and support the hypotheses drawn from NET.

Table 2 shows the mean number of resources retained by occupants of position D—the smaller the number retained the higher the rate of exploitation. In the Polish setting, the mean in strong 1 branch was 1.77 and was 1.25 in strong 2, both significantly lower than the mean of 4.61 for the weak coercive structure. In the U.S. setting, the mean rate in the strong 1 was 2.01 and in strong 2 was 1.65, both being significantly lower than the mean rate in a weak coercive branch

TABLE 1

Mean Points Received by Peripherals in Two Settings by Type of Exchange Branch

Setting	Type	Mean	t	df	p.
Poland	Weak 3,3	5.42	7.238	25	<.001
	Strong 4,3	2.54			
	Weak 3,3	5.42	9.961	28	<.001
	Strong 5,3	2.36			
U.S.	Weak 3,3	6.88	9.674	34	<.001
	Strong 4,3	3.09			
	Weak 3,3	6.88	18.715	38	<.001
	Strong 5,3	2.10			

TABLE 2

Mean Points Retained by Peripherals in Two Settings by Type of Coercive Branch

Setting	Type	Mean	t	df	p.
Poland	Weak	4.61	23.29	70	<.01
	Strong 1	1.77			
	Weak	4.61	32.44	70	<.01
	Strong 2	1.25			
U.S.	Weak	4.60	15.82	94	<.01
	Strong 1	2.01			
	Weak	4.60	20.18	94	<.01
	Strong 2	1.65			

of 4.60. Thus, all null hypotheses for the coercive networks can be rejected, supporting ET's predictions.

Table 3 lists the mean observed earnings of the B position and of the D position. As displayed, Polish B's obtained favorable divisions from A and C averaging 19.62, while in the United States, B's averaged 19.20. Both are significantly higher than the null hypothesis predictions of 12, thus supporting NET's predictions. Table 3 shows also that Polish D's mean earnings in divisions with E were

TABLE 3

Mean Points Gained in "T" Network vs. Theoretical Null of 12

Setting	Position	Mean	t	df	p.
Poland	B	19.62	19.67	14	<.001
	D	11.64	1.902	14	NS
U.S.	B	19.20	10.31	24	<.001
	D	12.17	1.622	24	NS

11.64 and that U.S. D's earned 12.17. Both are not significantly different from the predicted value of 12, thus supporting ET's predictions.

Summing up, results from Poland and the United States all support predictions from NET and NCT, the two parts of Elementary Theory. These results support the universality of ET by showing that it can produce its phenomena in the two contrasting settings. Let me now turn to the issue of universality as tested by Polish-U.S. comparisons.

Testing Universality

Eight comparisons test ET for universality. In each comparison the null hypothesis is that the mean earnings of a position in a particular network will not differ as they do between settings. The results are in Table 4.

Of the eight comparisons, the null hypothesis would be rejected in two at the .01 level and in one more at the .05 level. The remaining five t statistics are small enough that the null hypothesis of equality between settings cannot be rejected. These results directly support the universality of ET, showing that it produces significantly the same phenomena regardless of the setting of its implementation.

Finally, I applied the two-way analysis of variance—unbalanced design (General Linear Models Procedure) to data from the three exchange and three coercion structures in two settings, the United States and Poland (see Table 5). For exchange structures, I found that the main effect of structure was significant (p = .0001), the main effect of setting was not (p = .33), and the interaction between structure and setting was also not significant (p = .70). For coercion structures, I found similarly that the main effect of structure was significant (p = .0001), while effects of setting and interaction between structure and setting were not (p = .59 and .85 respectively). Finally, testing the effect of structural position versus national setting for "T-shape" structure, I found that the main effect of position was significant (p = .0001) and the effects of setting and interaction between position and setting were not.

TABLE 4

Mean Points Received by Peripherals/Positions in Three Exchange Branches,
Three Coercive Branches, and "T" Network by Setting

Network/Position	Setting	Mean	t	df	p.
Weak 3,3 Exchange Branch	Poland	5.42	4.783	26	<.01
	U.S.	6.88			
Strong 4,3 Exchange Branch	Poland	2.54	1.171	33	NS
	U.S.	3.09			
Strong 5,3 Exchange Branch	Poland	2.37	1.062	40	NS
	U.S.	2.10			
Weak Coercive Branch	Poland	4.61	.0645	82	NS
	U.S.	4.60			
Strong 1 Coercive Branch	Poland	1.77	1.425	82	NS
	U.S.	2.01			
Strong 2 Coercive Branch	Poland	1.25	2.975	82	<.01
	U.S.	1.65			
B	Poland	19.62	.5182	38	NS
	U.S.	19.20			
D	Poland	11.64	2.448	38	<.05
	U.S.	12.17			

Discussion

Cross-national and cross-cultural replication experiments are intended to test theories for universality. In this paper, I have shown that an array of derivations from Elementary Theory have survived tests in two very different settings. Whereas further tests would add confidence, the tests offered here provide a basis for theory applications without regard to the particulars of time and place. These tests directly support the universality of Elementary Theory because they show

TABLE 5

Analysis of Variance of Power Use by Type of Structure and Type of Setting

Source	df	f	p.
Exchange Structures (ES)	2, 15	34.81	.0001
Setting Polish/U.S. (P/US) for ES	1, 15	1.96	NS
Structure x Setting ES x P/US	2, 15	1.47	NS
Coercion Structures (CS)	2, 36	241.15	.0001
Setting P/US for CS	1, 36	2.73	NS
Structure x Setting CS x P/US	2, 36	.87	NS
B and D position in "T" shape structure	2, 76	237.18	.0001
Setting P/US for BD	1, 76	.01	NS
Position x Setting BD x P/US	1, 76	.94	NS

that it produces significantly the same phenomena regardless of the setting of its implementation.

In three cases, predictions had not been confirmed experimentally. The test of the weak exchange branch as shown in Table 4 did not confirm theoretical predictions. The main reason for that was an unexpectedly high rate of 6.88 received in the U.S. setting as compared to 5.42 observed in the Polish setting—the result much closer to the theoretical value. I can't offer, however, any speculations on why in the U.S. setting such salient deviation from the theoretical value occurred.

When I compared the data for strong 2 coercive branch, as shown in Table 4, the results, t = 2.975, p < .01, have not confirmed the prediction that the rates in both settings will be insignificantly different. The raw data show that the rate of coercive exploitation developed more rapidly in the Polish setting than in the U.S. setting. That made the Polish data support the theoretical value, but differ significantly from the U.S. ones.

A similar kind of effect I found analyzing data related to the mean rate of exchange of D in a "T-shape" network. When I compared D's mean rates of exchange in both settings against the theoretical value, the data, as shown in Table 3, supported the hypothesis. However, the mean rates of exchange for D compared across settings, as Table 4 shows, are significantly different, and the hypothesis that they are similar was not confirmed. The raw data show that the rate of exchange in the U.S. setting was very stable as opposed to the Polish setting. That made the *t*-test results more conservative and led to rejection of the hypothesis.

Despite these flaws, the results obtained can be legitimately interpreted as strong support for the universality of Elementary Theory. ANOVA tests provided further support for the thesis that ET is universal. Additionally, these tests show that the failure to produce the data supporting three of the eight comparisons was not due to cultural differences in both settings, as the null hypothesis would suggest. This analysis shows also clear drawbacks in the test for universality: it can be applied only to formal (third genus) theories and conducted through cross-national and cross-cultural experimental replications.

Informal Theory Testing Through
Mathematical Analysis

▶◤
◣◢

M. Hamit Fisek

At the time I started graduate school, mathematical models were seen as the wave of the future, and arguably the salvation of sociological theory, or even the salvation of sociology as a scientific discipline. Any primer of mathematical models of the time, and there were quite a few, would list a number of advantages that mathematical models offered over more mundane versions of theoretical statements. One of these advantages, the one that impressed me the most, was that mathematical models made it easier to see or derive the logical implications of a theoretical statement, making it more testable. This virtue I thought very important.

It has been about thirty years since those days, and we have a more modest view of mathematical models, but they certainly are established as a significant mode of sociological knowledge, and their virtues are accepted as I earlier stated. However, over this time period of about thirty years, I cannot think of a single instance of a sociological mathematical model where the mathematical nature of the model was used to derive the implications of the model to test it.

This of course is overstatement: Any test of a mathematical model involves a prediction of the model which technically is an implication of the model. Typically, models are used to make numerical and/or ordering predictions for a variable to be measured, and the test of the model is a comparison of the predicted and the observed values. In such cases the numerical or ordering predictions are implications of the model in the logical sense. However, the connotations of the term "implication" in everyday usage involve more than numerical or ordering predictions—an implication should be more of a general effect rather than a specific result. I use the term in this sense, when I say that sociological models are not tested through derived implications. The distinction I am trying to make may best be conveyed through example.

The author's work on this paper has been partially supported by the Turkish Academy of Sciences.

Let me present, very briefly, a sociological model, a standard test of the model, and what I see as a test by derivation of implications from the model. These "implication tests" derive general properties from a formal model and ask whether these general properties accord with commonsense understandings of the phenomena being modeled. The point I would like to make is that such tests are possible, useful, and furthermore a lot less expensive than standard tests.

A Mathematical Model

The mathematical model I would like to use for illustrative purposes is the model embedded in the 1977 formulation of the theory of status characteristics and expectation states (Berger, Fisek, Norman, and Zelditch 1977). This particular model is especially well suited for my purposes, as it is an integral part of a theory, rather than a translation of a verbal theory into mathematical terms. I will give a very brief statement of the theory, to put my current remarks in context.

The theory of status characteristics and expectation states is concerned with status behavior such as acceptance or rejection of influence in the task-oriented collective action settings. A situation in which two or more actors work on a collective valued task is represented as a graph structure. The actors, the status characteristics they possess, the possible task outcomes, and a few theoretical entities such as expectation states are the points, or nodes, of the graph. These points may be connected to each other by three relations: Two of these relations, possession and relevance, are straightforward in their usage; the third—dimensionality—is less so, but we need not dwell on it for our current purposes.

An actor's task expectations are given by the paths connecting the actors to the task outcomes. These paths can be positive or negative, and they can vary in "strength," depending on length. The strength of a path is given by a monotonically decreasing function of its length, thus the strength of a path of length l, is $f(l)$. (A lot, and all that I want to say in this paper, can be said without assuming a particular form and parameter values for this function.) The combined strength of a given set of paths is given by a "combining rule."

The parts are first organized into subsets by sign and then combined within each subset according to a form which may be expressed as below for two paths of lengths i and j:

$$f(i \cup j) = f(i) + f(j) - f(i)f(j)$$

The combined values carry the sign of the paths being combined, and the final value is obtained by algebraically summing the two combined subset values. Generalizing the above basic combination formula to more than two paths, the complete combining rule may be expressed as below.

Given that an actor p is connected to the task outcomes by m positive paths of lengths $\{l_1, l_2, \ldots l_m\}$ and n negative paths of lengths $\{l'_1, l'_2, \ldots l'_n\}$, the actors' expectations are given by the expression below.

$$e_p = \{1 - [1 - f(l_1)][1 - f(l_2)] \cdot \cdot [1 - f(l_m)]\}$$
$$- \{1 - [1 - f(l'_1)][1 - f(l'_2)] \cdot \cdot [1 - f(l'_n)]\}$$

An actor's power and prestige position (and therefore his or her rates of rejecting or accepting influence) vis-à-vis another is given by the actor's expectation advantage (the difference between their expectations) over the other.

This combining principle, sometimes called the subset combining principle, postulated by the theory of status characteristics and expectation states has generated considerable interest (and indeed some controversy), and a good deal of empirical research has been carried out to test it (Webster and Driskell 1978; Zelditch, Lauderdale, and Stublarec 1980; Hembroff, Martin, and Sell 1981; Hembroff 1982). The latest and certainly the most definitive empirical study on the combining principle of this theory is by Robert Z. Norman and his associates (Norman, Smith, and Berger 1988).

A Standard Test of the Model

Norman and his associates do an experiment to discriminate between the combining principle of the theory and two alternative hypotheses to be found in the literature. One of the alternative hypotheses is the *cancellation principle*, according to which positive and negative paths of equal length cancel each other out and the remaining paths of one sign combine according to the basic combining rule. The other alternative hypothesis is the *balancing principle*, which says that of the positive and negative paths the weaker subset is ignored and the expectations are determined solely by the stronger subset. The difference between the three alternative hypotheses is best seen by limiting our attention to situations where all the paths are of the same length l and actor p possesses more positive (m) than negative (n) paths. Then the subset combining principle says that the actor's expectations are given by the following expression.

$$e_p = [1 - f(l)]^m - [1 - f(l)]^n$$

According to the cancellation principle, the actor's expectations are given by a different expression, as shown below.

$$e_p = [1 - f(l)]^{m-n}$$

The balancing principle leads to the following expression.

$$e_p = [1 - f(l)]^m$$

Norman and his colleagues designed and carried out a five-condition experiment to test these alternative theories in the generalized experimental situation associated with the theory of status characteristics and expectation states. This experimental situation has been described many times in the literature (for example, Berger, Fisek, Norman, and Zelditch 1977), and I will not describe it again; let me just say that subjects work with a partner on a common task and their rate of rejecting influence is measured. The subjects are put through status manipulations before working on the common task so that the effects of different status situations can be assessed. Three of the five conditions of this experiment are essentially control and baseline conditions with which we need not be concerned for our current purposes. The real test is yielded by two conditions—conditions two and three in their presentation.

In condition two, the subject possesses two positive status characteristic states while the subject's partner possesses the negative states of the two status characteristics. Thus the subject is "high status" compared to his partner and is expected to have a high rate of rejecting influence. In the third condition, the subject possesses the positive states of three characteristics and the negative state of a fourth characteristic while the subject's partner possesses the negative states of the first three characteristics and the positive state of the fourth.

Now in a comparison of these two conditions, the cancellation hypothesis says that the rejection of influence rates for subjects in the two conditions will be the same. In the third condition, the negative state the subject possesses will cancel out one of the subject's three positive states, leaving the subject with just two positive states, and the partner will similarly possess two effective negative states. Therefore, the third condition is just the same as the second.

The balancing hypothesis says that the weaker subset of paths will be ignored, therefore in the third condition it is as if the actor possessed only three positive, and the partner only three negative, characteristics. Therefore the actor is even higher status than the actor in the second condition and should have a higher rate of rejecting influence.

The subset combining principle, on the other hand, says that in the third condition, the three positive states the actor possesses will first be combined. The combining function is such that the combined strength of a set of paths is less than their algebraic sum, that is, path strengths are attenuated in combination. Then the strength of the negative path will be subtracted from the combined strength of the three positive paths. The result will be less than the combined strength of two positive paths. The same argument applies to the partner, and the conclusion is that the actor should have a lower rate of rejecting influence than the actor in the second condition.

The results are that the rate of rejecting influence in the second condition is .754, and in the third condition it is .701. The difference is significant at the .005 level of significance by *t*-test. It is abundantly clear that the subset combining hypothesis is supported while the balancing and cancellation hypotheses are rejected.

It should be clear that I have no intention of being critical of this experimental test of the model—in fact, I believe it is a great piece of work which has added significantly to our understanding of these processes. What I do want to point out is that this experiment involved 317 subjects, and it must have taken about six months for a research team of four or five researchers to conduct. What it involved in financial terms I will not try to estimate.

An Informal Test of the Model

I will now try to present an informal test of this model through mathematical analysis. I have tried to work out the implications of the subset combining principle embodied in the model through mathematical analysis. I have written up elsewhere (Fisek 1993) six lemmas and four theorems which can be derived from this principle. I want to present two of the theorems here, and the first theorem I call the "No man can be a prophet in his own land" theorem.

The First Theorem

Given that an actor, p, is connected to task outcomes by a set of paths of one sign and a single path of the other sign, then as the total strength of the set of paths increases, p's expectations will approach a limit which is less in magnitude than the limiting value for expectations.

What the theorem says, and what I tried to capture in naming it, is that an actor who possesses a negative characteristic will never achieve maximum status, that is, the effect of the negative characteristic will never be entirely erased. It is equally true that the effect of a positive characteristic will not be erased either, but it is enough to present the argument in terms of a negative characteristic at this point. This is, of course, just the opposite of what the cancellation and balancing hypotheses have to say: Both say that the effect of a negative characteristic will be entirely erased if there are enough positive characteristics.

Now I would like to invoke your assessment as "lay psychologists" in Heider's (1958) sense. In other words I would like to appeal to your common sense: In assessment of social status, are people's negative characteristics ever completely erased? It seems very clear to me that the answer is negative. I remember my father saying about my mother, whom he revered, after more than forty years of marriage in an evaluation of task competence in a context which had nothing to do with gender, "After all, she is a woman."

I would say that subset combining agrees better with common sense than the cancellation and balancing in this respect.

The second theorem, which I call the "Familiarity leads to equality" theorem, is given below.

The Second Theorem

Given that an actor, p, is connected to task outcomes by paths of equal length such that n $(n > 1)$ are of one sign and d $(d > n)$ are of the other sign, and an actor, o, is connected to the task outcomes with paths which are of equal length and number as p's but of the opposite sign, then if n is sufficiently large, the power and prestige differentiation between p and o will be arbitrarily small.

The theorem says that if an individual has a number of negative characteristics, no matter how many more positive characteristics the individual may have, he or she will never have really high status. It is also true that if an individual has a number of positive characteristics, then no matter how many more negative characteristics he or she has, the individual will never have really low status.

Once again, both the cancellation and balancing hypotheses make the opposite prediction. In terms of both, an individual possessing a number of characteristics of one sign can be entirely rid of their effects merely by possessing more characteristics of the other sign.

Again I appeal to your common sense: Which is a better portrayal of the way individuals are assessed in status situations? My perception of status situations in everyday life is that people with a few negative characteristics, perhaps two or three, never acquire high status regardless of their positive characteristic, and people with a few positive characteristics similarly never acquire really low status regardless of the negative characteristic they may possess. Thus I would argue that subset combining is the clear winner of this test as well.

Concluding Remarks

Clearly the informal test of the model which I presented above cannot have the same weight as the rigorous empirical test by Norman and his associates. But when you consider that the final result of all theory testing is our faith in the truth of a theory, which after all is a subjective matter, and also take into consideration the relatively low cost of informal testing as portrayed above, it seems to me that informal testing through mathematical analysis is a procedure that should not be ignored.

Thus as well as deriving specific predictions for specific situations for purposes of empirical testing of mathematical models, we should also derive general implications of the models through analysis and evaluate these implications in commonsense terms. In fact, such research should in general precede more rigorous empirical testing, as it is certainly cheaper and may result in avoiding needless expensive, rigorous tests. After all, if scientific methodology is a refinement of common sense, we should first resort to common sense.

PART II

Status, Sentiments, and Comparison Processes

Social Structural Analysis and Status Generalization: The Contributions and Potential of Expectation States Theory

J. David Knottnerus

This paper explores the major developments in theory and research in expectation states theory (EST) and assesses what we've learned about structural analysis from this literature in the past several decades. Such an endeavor will provide a clearer idea of what work in EST contributes to our understanding of a core concept in contemporary sociology, that is, social structure.

EST has developed numerous theories that are formally presented in a precise manner and normally focus on various aspects of group processes. It is a theoretical research program with many branches, which are founded on extensive bodies of research. Dedicated to the goals of deductive theorizing and cumulating, much of the research utilizes experimental procedures to progressively develop a body of theoretical formulations which explain the processes involved in the creation of social phenomena such as social inequality and social structure.[1]

At the heart of this program is the development of metatheory, which Berger, Wagner, and Zelditch (1985, 1989, 1992; Berger and Zelditch 1993) treat as a working strategy for formulating testable, empirical theories. More precisely, the metatheoretical conception underlying work in EST is a "state organizing process" which is "a framework for the construction of theories of interpersonal processes" (Berger, Wagner, and Zelditch 1992: 107).

Metatheoretical Assumptions of Expectation States Theory

A state organizing process involves two key dimensions: the social framework and the situation of action (Berger 1992; Berger, Wagner, and Zelditch 1992; Berger and Zelditch 1993). The social framework is composed of three elements which are more enduring and inclusive than those in an action situation. "Cul-

---

[1] A theoretical research program is defined by Berger, Wagner, and Zelditch (1985: 2) as "an interrelated set of theories together with theoretical research relevant to them and applied research grounded in them."

tural elements" involve social categories, norms, beliefs, and values. "Interpersonal elements" include networks of communication, influence, and sentiments. "Formal elements" refer to institutionalized and formalized roles and positions in authority structures. The framework is an abstract concept whose elements can be found at different levels of the social order, for instance, in society as a whole or in particular subcultures.

Within the social framework is the situation of action which refers to the properties of the situation of immediate action in which social processes occur. Significant features include the focus of the interaction process, that is, the goal states toward which actors are oriented, such as solving a collective task. These properties of the situation of action also define the "scope conditions" of the theory, that is, the conditions under which the process should occur (for example, actors being collectively and task-oriented and number of actors in a situation). Under these conditions a social process will develop in which information used by actors results in "states, which are stable structures that define the relations of the actors to each other within their immediate situation" (Berger, Wagner, and Zelditch 1992: 115). Eventually, this process may end (deactivate) and/or influence the social framework (construction effects) or other interaction episodes (succession or transsituational effects).

Given this state-organizing process, more specific principles must be formulated by the theorist which describe the various dynamics of this process and its consequences. As we shall see, of the different branches of EST, status characteristics theory has been most fully developed according to this metatheoretical scheme.

For the present, what is of interest is the makeup of this conception's social framework whose elements—formal, interpersonal, cultural—play a crucial role in the development of specific theoretical explanations of a social process. These three elements, it is suggested, seem to correspond to three basic modes of structural analysis found within sociological theory and research.

Approaches to Structural Analysis in Sociology

Social structure is a core concept within sociological analysis which has been defined and discussed in numerous ways. Such diversity makes it practically impossible to deal with each specific perspective. A close reading of the literature in modern sociological theory suggests, however, that it is possible to distinguish among these various orientations and to identify three basic approaches to understanding this concept (Prendergast and Knottnerus 1994; Knottnerus and Prendergast 1994; see also Knottnerus and Prendergast 1992, for a partial discussion of this idea). They are the objectivist, transactional, and idealist conceptions of social structure. Each approach is identified by the unit of structural analysis which is used to represent the whole. Different theoretical/research traditions select one of these dimensions or features of social structure as the indispensable or primary component to represent social structure and, therefore, to analyze it. Of course, in certain cases we may find that more than one of these orientations is utilized by a particular school to understand social structure. Usually, however, one of these approaches plays a dominant role in the mode of structural analysis developed within any particular tradition.

The objectivist perspective emphasizes the autonomous and causally powerful role of social relations. The agent has little or no place in this approach, which tends to focus upon patterns of social organization and system-centered analysis in larger social orders. The deeds, decisions, and beliefs of actors are often a reflection of or strongly determined by the dynamics of these supra-individual structures which tend to operate according to their own logic and mechanisms. Several examples of this popular approach would include world systems theory, structural versions of Marxism, Peter Blau's macrostructuralism, structural sociologists such as Bruce Mayhew, the population ecology model of organizations, and structural functionalism to a large degree.

The transactional conception of social structure views social organization as a process or an activity involving two or more parties that affect or influence each other. Social structure is the accretion of recurrent transactions between individuals. Even if it is not consciously designed, social structure is depicted as a flexible arrangement which is the product of individual choice-making, usually of an instrumental nature. Here, actors create and extend networks and hierarchies in order to obtain valued resources. Social structure is depicted less from the outside than from the inside, as an arrangement of opportunities for interaction. The vulnerability and dynamic nature of social organization are emphasized, along with its tendency to disassemble when it fails to fulfill individual goals. Such an approach quite often defends methodological individualism, that is, the role of the purposive, goal-directed actor, while yet explaining to varying degrees the emergence and impact of social structures. Examples of this perspective would include social exchange theory and research, rational choice theory, and to a certain extent the resource dependency theory of organizations by Pfeffer and Salancik (1978).

The idealist view of social structure suggests that social relations and organization are mind dependent, or, put differently, culturally dependent. This approach emphasizes the normative or significative aspect of social structure. Social organization is made possible by and ultimately consists of principles of action, rules, routines, or programs that are part of an actor's stock of knowledge. These routines or codes are applied by actors to situations, depending on the cues provided in the setting. With this emphasis upon actors' cognitive maps, the idealist tradition draws our attention to structure making, that is, the cognitive operations of categorization and enactment. In this approach would be found theoretical/research traditions such as symbolic interactionism, ethnomethodology, neo-Parsonians (for example, Alexander), and significant parts of structuration theory by Anthony Giddens. A more holistic strand emphasizes the cultural systems from which expectations, typifications, or categories derive (for example, Durkheim and Mauss 1963).

To varying degrees the three elements within EST's metatheoretical social framework correspond to these three orientations for representing and analyzing social structure. The formal element, with its emphasis on institutional, formalized positions and authority structures, appears to correspond to the objectivist ⁓conception of structure with its focus on the causally efficacious and enduring patterns of social organizations and systems. The interpersonal element, which refers to networks of communication and so on, is quite similar to the transactional conception of structure, which also focuses on processes among actors (for example, influence) that result in networks and social arrangements. Finally, the cultural element with its focus on social categories and beliefs is nearly identical to the idealist view of structure with its emphasis on signification and cognitive constructs in the creation of social structure.

Given these points, the pertinent question to be addressed is where does the work conducted in EST, contributing to our understanding of social structure, fit with regard to this metatheoretical model (that is, its social framework) and the typology of approaches to structural analysis. This examination of EST will argue that much of this work falls within the idealistic and transactional orientations or, to use this program's own metatheoretical framework, within the cultural and interpersonal elements. Certainly, with its focus on group processes or micro-interaction episodes, the transactional/interpersonal orientation to structure is quite evident. However, the most significant component of analysis rests upon idealistic/cultural assumptions. This is because a close reading of EST reveals that the key explanatory concepts for describing the emergence of structure in groups have often focused upon beliefs and cognitive processes.

In this regard, EST has contributed much to the analysis of group structures over the past several decades. Furthermore, recent work has been expanding its investigations of the idealistic realm of structure and has begun to examine various aspects of the other two dimensions of social structure: the objectivist and transactional spheres. To substantiate these points, let us examine this research in greater detail.

Status Characteristics Theory

Status characteristics theory is one of the oldest and most developed branches of EST and the theory most closely associated with the metatheoretical conception of "state organizing process." This branch provides an explanation for the repeated finding that inequalities in power and prestige emerge in group interaction when an actor possesses and is differentiated by some social characteristic, such as occupational rank, sex, or ability, whether or not the characteristic is relevant to the group task (for useful discussions of the theory and related developments, see Cohen, Berger, and Zelditch 1972; Berger, Fisek, Norman, and Zelditch 1977; Berger, Rosenholtz, and Zelditch 1980; Berger and Zelditch 1985; Webster and Foschi 1988).

To explain this phenomenon, the earliest formulation of the theory (Berger, Cohen, and Zelditch 1966) utilized a number of concepts from the original and related "power and prestige" theory. This theory examined the formation of expectations in groups whose members are not differentiated in terms of characteristics such as age or race. It specified the process by which group members develop expectations for each other, based upon each member's performance in the group. As these expectations emerge in a group actors come to believe that certain members' contributions are valuable and should be accepted while others' contributions are valueless and should be ignored. Through this process the group develops a social structure in terms of activity and influence.

Building upon these ideas, status characteristics theory argues that social characteristics serve as cues from which actors form expectations concerning their own and others' task abilities. Once formed, these expectation states shape the power and prestige order of the group. Over the past several decades, Berger and others (Berger, Cohen, and Zelditch 1966, 1972; Berger, Conner, and Fisek 1974; Berger, Fisek, Norman, and Zelditch 1977; Humphreys and Berger 1981; Berger and Zelditch 1985) have constructed and tested a formal theory which explains this process.

This process involves two types of status characteristics, specific and diffuse. Specific status characteristics contain two or more states that are differentially evaluated (for example, high and low), and associated with each state is a specific expectation state or belief about how actors will perform certain tasks, such as solving mathematical or verbal problems (Humphreys and Berger 1981). A diffuse status characteristic, such as race or gender, "involves two or more states that are differentially valued; and associated with each state are distinct sets of specific expectation states, each itself evaluated; and associated with each state is a similarly evaluated general expectation state" (Berger, Wagner, and Zelditch 1992: 110). Examples of general expectations would include intelligence or overall competence. In addition to these expectations, diffuse status characteristics also contain "invidious social evaluations (in terms of differences in honor, respect, esteem, and the like)" which are associated with its states (Berger, Wagner, and Zelditch 1985: 12). The theoretical concept of a status characteristic, it should be noted, applies only to empirical situations which fit its definitions.

Furthermore, the theory deals only with situations that satisfy certain scope conditions. As Berger, Wagner, and Zelditch (1992: 110) point out, "Actors in the situation may be interactants or referents." Interactants are two actors interacting with each other at any particular point in time. The referent is an actor who is a "noninteractant . . . whose status information is used by the interacting pair" (ibid.). Finally, there has to be a valued collective task toward which the interactants are oriented (for example, all actors are motivated to solve some type of problem).

At the heart of status characteristics theory are five principles. The "salience assumption" specifies when status information will be operative in a situation: when the status characteristic is clearly defined as relevant to a task or when the characteristic discriminates among actors in a situation (for example, actors are distinguished by their ethnic background). The second principle, the "burden of proof assumption," states that a salient status characteristic will link the actor to the outcomes of the group's task, that is, any salient status characteristic will be normally applied to every new situation or task unless its inapplicability is definitively established. The third assumption, the "sequencing assumption," states that the restructuring of a situation will occur in sequence as new actors enter or depart the task setting. The fourth assumption, the "aggregation assumption," argues that actors combine all information that has become salient and relevant to the task to form overall performance expectations for themselves. All positive status characteristics are combined according to an attenuation principle to produce a value of positive performance expectations while all negative characteristics are combined to form negative performance expectations (the "principle of organized subsets"). These positive and negative subsets are then summed to generate aggregated expectations for an actor. The fifth assumption, the "basic expectation assumption," states that an actor's position in the power and prestige structure (chances to perform, communicated evaluations, distribution of performance outputs, and influence among group members) is a direct function of his or her aggregated performance expectations relative to those for the other actor.

As the theory has progressed it has evolved through distinct stages "marked by an increase in its generality, empirical range, and deductive capacities" (Berger, Wagner, and Zelditch 1992: 112). In the initial formulation of the theory, attention was restricted to the effect of a single status characteristic on interaction in a task group. Later, the theory was altered to deal with multiple and single status characteristics and specific and diffuse status characteristics (Berger and Fisek 1974). And the theory has been extended to deal with more actors and types of actors including referents and interactants (Berger, Fisek, Norman, and Zelditch 1977).

Numerous studies utilizing standardized laboratory settings have supported these theoretical formulations. For instance, the effects of diffuse status characteristics such as age (Freese 1974), military rank (Berger, Cohen, and Zelditch 1972), race (Webster and Driskell 1978), and education (Markovsky, Smith, and Berger 1984) and specific status characteristics such as verbal or mechanical ability (Freese 1974) have been confirmed, and the argument that such characteristics are accompanied by differential evaluations, which lead to differential expectations and interaction inequalities, has been demonstrated (Greenstein and Knottnerus 1980).

As the theory has been progressively reformulated certain issues have received the greatest attention. Perhaps most important, a large amount of research has examined the question of how multiple status characteristics are processed by actors especially where actors are simultaneously differentiated by contradictory status and performance information (that is, the problem of status inconsistency). Besides raising theoretical questions concerning the dynamics of social cognition and status generalization processes, this is a significant issue because it is directly relevant for efforts aimed at reducing the pernicious effects of negatively evaluated diffuse status characteristics. Presently, a significant amount of research supports the aggregate combining model, which argues that all status information that is salient is combined by actors to form performance expectations (Berger and Fisek 1974; Webster 1975; Webster and Driskell 1978; Zelditch, Lauderdale, and Stublarec 1980; Markovsky, Smith, and Berger 1984; Wagner, Ford, and Ford 1986; Balkwell et al. 1992). What this suggests is that in group interaction, structured inequalities generated by a diffuse status characteristic will be decreased due to the presence of a performance characteristic with the opposite evaluation (although not totally eliminated).

An alternative model of multicharacteristic processing known as the balancing or discounting principle does exist, which argues that expectations from a diffuse status characteristic can be blocked if a more specific status characteristic is present with a different evaluation (Freese and Cohen 1973; Freese 1974). What this suggests is that structured inequalities in a group created by a negative status cue will be completely eliminated. Besides diverging from the combining principle in its predictions for altering the structure of group interaction, this model also presents a very different theoretical conception of social cognition (Knottnerus 1988). Actually, other research has suggested that there are situations in which both combining and balancing processes occur (Hembroff 1982; Hembroff, Martin, and Sell 1981; Hembroff and Myers 1984; Martin and Sell 1980; Sell and Freese 1984). It should be appreciated, however, that a substantial amount of evidence supports the combining model (for more recent studies supporting the combining argument, see Balkwell 1991b; Berger, Norman, Balkwell, and Smith 1992; Balkwell et al. 1992).[2]

A limited amount of research has also examined how actors process information when they are differentiated by consistently high or low evaluations on both specific and diffuse status characteristics. Knottnerus and Greenstein (1981) investigated this issue and found that such a situation results in the exacerbation

---

[2] A significant body of applied research in EST exists which examines problems such as how intervention techniques can reduce inequalities among status groups (e.g., Cohen and Roper 1972; Cohen 1993).

of inequalities in group interaction. In contrast to the combining principle, however, they argue that an interactive effect may occur between status characteristics. In this situation a status validation process operates in which actors utilize specific status information to reinforce already existing status stereotypes or diffuse status characteristics. Such a finding and argument (whether one utilizes the combining principle or the validation model) has important theoretical implications concerning the perpetuation and reinforcement of status inequalities in social interaction (for a discussion of how EST's investigation of such processes are also relevant for public policy, see Knottnerus 1986).

In short, because of studies such as these, status characteristics theory provides the most comprehensive analysis within EST of the determinants of social structure in group interaction. Through a cumulative body of research and theory development examining status generalization processes, our understanding of how status structures are created, maintained, or altered has been significantly advanced. Furthermore, in addition to this research, there have been major extensions of the theory. Two deserve special mention because they are directly relevant for understanding social structure.

The first extension, which is most fully elaborated in Berger, Fisek, Norman, and Wagner (1985; for an earlier discussion, see Berger, Zelditch, Anderson, and Cohen 1972), is concerned with the processes by which reward expectations are created in status situations. The idea of "referential structures" is central to this discussion. These refer to "taken for granted" beliefs in society concerning the association between rewards (for example, positions in society, material rewards) and categories of persons (for example, gender or age), performance outcomes, or ability levels. Basically, new assumptions and concepts already developed in status characteristics theory are utilized to explain how expectations for rewards are formed and derived from such beliefs. Attention is also directed to a "reverse process" in which the distribution of differential rewards leads to task expectations consistent with the rewards. This theoretical extension is very important for structural analysis because it could increase our understanding of how different kinds of status expectations are linked to patterns of rewards received by actors in different situations. At this time, however, this extension is not at an advanced level of development because while a theory has been proposed, the need exists to empirically test it in a rigorous manner (Berger, Wagner, and Zelditch 1985: 44, 52).

The second major extension of status characteristics theory examines the transsituational outcomes of status organizing processes. The key assumption underlying this work is that the structures created in one situation can influence the status structures which emerge in subsequent situations. Such succession effects, which deal with how expectations are transferred from one situation to another or from one actor to another, are quite important because they can explain "cross-situational consistencies in the individual's behavior" (Berger 1992: 6). As

Berger (ibid.) emphasizes, the analysis of these processes enables us to "account for the existence of more stable structures on the individual and social level by starting from the interpersonal or group process level."

Markovsky, Smith, and Berger (1984) have examined this process by building upon the work of Pugh and Wahrman (1983). Pugh and Wahrman's research draws upon the theoretical discussion in Berger, Fisek, Norman, and Zelditch (1977) which argues that the expectations an actor forms for a former partner will continue to operate as long as he or she remains in the same situation. The former interactant (for example, first female) becomes a referent actor to the other (for example, a male) while he remains in the status situation interacting with a new partner (for example, second female). In their investigation of how to eliminate status-generated inequalities, Pugh and Wahrman (1983) show that this referential process does occur, that is, status expectations transfer from one status occupant to another.

Markovsky, Smith, and Berger (1984) further the analysis by examining a status intervention in a task group setting. An inconsistently evaluated specific status characteristic is introduced into a group in the effort to reduce status-based inequalities. After doing this, an actor from the first group participates in a different task situation with a new partner who has the same status rank, that is, diffuse status characteristic, as the first partner. It was found that the intervention effect transferred to the second setting involving a new group task and a new partner. At the same time, the strength of the transfer effect decreased.

In addition to these studies of the transfer-of-expectations process, several other theoretical works address these issues. Berger, Fisek, and Norman (1989) specify how the structure of one task setting is connected with that of a subsequent setting. In this formulation they discuss some of the dynamics by which expectations and behavior change or stabilize when actors interact in a series of tasks. In a different vein, Markovsky (1988b) has demonstrated how diffusion models can help us understand how expectations (that is, status interventions) generated in small groups might spread throughout a population resulting in changes at more macro levels.

In brief, these studies clearly indicate that the transferral of expectations has transsituational effects which can play a central role in the transmission and modification of status structures across social situations and different levels of the social order.

Further Developments in Expectation States Theory

In addition to status characteristics theory, several other research efforts within EST are making (or show the potential to make) significant contributions to our understanding of social structure. Most of these are more recent and are at various stages of development. I will briefly describe this work, beginning with research focused on legitimation processes (for a more detailed discussion of these developments, see Knottnerus 1994a).

Despite an extensive body of literature examining the role of legitimacy in social institutions and organizations and the strong impression that it is important for informal decision-making groups, little theoretical analysis of legitimacy in face-to-face groups exists. Recently, however, Ridgeway and Berger (1986, 1988), Ridgeway (1989), and Ridgeway, Diekema, and Johnson (1991) developed an expectation states theory of legitimation in informal task groups. In their work, "legitimacy" generally refers to actions within a group being governed by norms supported by the members of the group; more specifically, it refers to the exercise of power with the collective consent of the governed. Legitimacy enables actors to generate support for their normative-based actions and obtain compliance from other members of the group. Because it increases compliance to the status order of the group, it enhances the stability of that order. Consequently, legitimacy plays a significant role in the creation and strengthening of group structures.

The EST of legitimacy draws on analyses of legitimation processes in large-scale, formal organizations, especially the work of Zelditch and Walker (1984), who emphasize the importance of authorization (resources derived from outside the system) for generating collective support for an authority. Building upon these insights, EST outlines several processes by which members in a collective task group begin to believe that their status order is or could be supported by something outside the group (that is, authorization). For task groups, outside support for an informal hierarchy in the group comes from the larger collectivity or, more precisely, the normative cultural order in society. Support for the status order of a group develops from actors' "referential beliefs" (that is, "referential structures") about the kinds of people that normally occupy higher or lower status positions in society. These are widely shared, socially validated beliefs that describe what is thought to be the usual association between a characteristic of actors and the occupation of valued status positions in social hierarchies.

These beliefs about reality give rise to expectations that take on a normative quality and legitimate a status order within a group. When referential beliefs are activated in a group, actors use them to form expectations for the status rank of group members. These are referred to as "status expectations." Included among the three kinds of referential structures which can be activated are "categorical beliefs," which associate the occupation of status positions with status characteristics. An example would be the belief that men in U.S. society hold more highly valued positions than women. According to the theory, the more referential structures activated in the group which consistently confirm that a particular type of actor usually has higher status than another, the more differentiated are group members' expectations that this will be the case in the local group. The stronger the group members' expectations, the more likely actors are to consider as legitimate a status hierarchy that is consistent with their expectations (Ridgeway 1989; Ridgeway, Diekema, and Johnson 1991). Based upon these arguments, the theory discusses a number of issues including the differences and interconnections between this process and the process by which the power and prestige order emerges according to performance expectations, the kinds of groups that should produce different probabilities of legitimation, and the behaviors of actors within legitimated informal status orders.

Overall, the theory argues that legitimacy of a group structure is based upon norms actors have defined as socially valid. It is a cultural explanation of legitimation in which actors are viewed as socially constructing their reality, giving it a truth and moral quality grounded in objectified referential beliefs (see Berger and Luckmann 1966). An important source of this group "reality" is the sense that the status order's defining norms are derived from a collective reality that transcends the group situation. Through processes such as these, legitimacy can further strengthen the structural arrangements which emerge in informal groups.

In contrast to this theory of legitimation, a very different type of structural analysis has recently been proposed by Ridgeway (1991). In this essay she argues that simple structural conditions are sufficient but not necessary to make a nominal characteristic such as gender or ethnicity acquire independent status value. Peter Blau's (1977a,b) macrostructural theory is linked with EST to show how structural conditions influence interaction, and then the products of unique interaction processes are diffused across social space, altering status at the system level. As such, the theoretical argument encompasses both macro- and micro-dimensions of the social order.

This theoretical work shows how a nominal characteristic, which is any socially recognized feature on which people are viewed as differing in a categorical manner, can come to be associated with cultural beliefs that give it independent status and connect it to expectations for overall competence. An explanation is presented of how structural conditions can generate and perpetuate the status value of nominal characteristics. Various conditions are assumed to exist, including the unequal distribution of a resource which can be exchanged among members of a population, the collection of actors being divided into categories of a nominal characteristic, and a correlation between the nominal characteristic and the resource characteristic in which one of the categories of the nominal characteristic has a greater likelihood of being a member of the resource-rich than the other category. Blau's (1977a,b; Blau and Schwartz 1984) heterogeneity theorem is then employed to show that while actors seek to interact with resource-similar others, they will still interact with a substantial number of resource-different actors because of the distribution of potential interactants in the two categories.

Principles from EST are introduced at this point to demonstrate how interaction created by the structural conditions leads to status associations with the nominal characteristic. Research in EST suggests that performance expectations will develop in interaction which match the level of exchangeable rewards possessed by actors (Berger, Fisek, Norman, and Wagner 1985; Cook 1975). Working from this research, Ridgeway suggests that actors possessing more resources are viewed as those who are most likely to contribute to the group task and are seen by group members as more competent and worthy. Moreover, the effects of an interaction setting can transfer to other groups and shape their status structures. Essentially, it is argued that in interaction higher performance expectations will be created for resource-rich actors than for resource-poor actors. In patterns of interaction where actors differ in both resources and the nominal characteristic, higher performance expectations will become associated with the category of actor who has a greater likelihood of being rich while lower performance expectations will become associated with the other category of actors who are more often poor. These expectations will then transfer and diffuse throughout the population becoming macro-level status beliefs.

In sum, a combination of interactional and macrostructural processes are responsible for a nominal characteristic acquiring status value and impacting upon the stratification system at the societal level. Of course, research examining this formulation is needed, since this theory has not been fully tested. Nevertheless, the argument developed in this work represents a unique contribution to EST. With EST linked to a different theoretical perspective, an explanation is provided for how the interplay between distinct structural processes can produce enduring forms of social inequality.

Finally, several areas of investigation deserve mention, even though they are in their early stages of development. To varying degrees, they stress the importance of interpersonal processes for explaining the dynamics by which group structures are maintained and solidified.

Some research focuses on status cues—verbal and nonverbal information actors use to infer another's status—and their role in status generalization processes (Ridgeway, Berger, and Smith 1985; Berger, Webster, Ridgeway, and Rosenholtz 1986; Tuzlak and Moore 1984; Tuzlak 1988). Investigations of these issues have included the development of a typology of status cues (Ridgeway, Berger, and Smith 1985; Berger, Webster, Ridgeway, and Rosenholtz 1986) and limited research of issues such as the impact of status characteristics on behavioral cues—for example, eye gaze (Ridgeway, Berger, and Smith 1985). What this work suggests is that status cues may play a major role in the structuring of groups, either through their direct effects on interaction or as part of a generalization process generated by status characteristics.

Other work is examining the role of dominance behavior, legitimacy, and status in group interaction (Ridgeway 1984, 1987, 1993; Ridgeway and Diekema 1989; Ridgeway, Diekema, and Johnson 1991). Several studies show that the status structure of a task group is quite stable and resistant to dominance behaviors directed toward individual gain. Such opportunistic behaviors may actually lead to collective efforts aimed at controlling them. Moreover, external status characteristics may serve to legitimate high-status actors' use of dominance behaviors to control others, thereby preserving the collective interests and status structure of the group.

Elsewhere, limited research has begun to delineate how socio-emotional behaviors are involved in the creation, and especially the maintenance, of status orders in informal groups. Ridgeway and Johnson (1990; see also Houser and Lovaglia 1993) have made an initial effort in this regard by discussing several processes involving socio-emotional behavior which may influence the status hierarchy of informal groups. This work points to the important role emotions surely play in the emergence of group structures.

Lastly, attention has recently been directed to the possible linkages between social exchange / power processes and the development of status structures. Lovaglia (1992, 1994) has examined several hypotheses, including the idea that if actors differ in power that produces a difference in rewards, status differences will result corresponding to these power differences. Such research raises many questions concerning the ways status structures and exchange networks may impact upon each other.

Contributions to Structural Analysis

This review suggests that EST research has made significant progress with regard to broadening our understanding of the idealist dimension of social structure and to investigating more formally the objectivist and transactional dimensions of social structure. Status characteristics theory, with its focus upon the dynamics of status generalization and the crucial role of cognitive processes in shaping group behavior, grounds much of its analytical arguments in concepts that are idealist in nature. Although the investigation of interaction episodes clearly involves the study of transactional dimensions of social structure, idealist constructs play a pivotal role in these explanatory formulations. Indeed, their essential role in EST is highlighted by Berger, Wagner, and Zelditch (1989: 23), when they describe a "core set of ideas about human behavior" which have provided the "roots from which the trunk and branches" of EST have developed:

(1) Actors generate expectations for self and others on the basis of various kinds of information in the situation—cultural definitions, referential beliefs, specific personal evaluations, and so on; (2) these expectations in turn govern actors' behavior toward each other in the situation . . . and (3) this behavior reinforces the existing expectations unless the conditions of the situation change (e.g. new or contradictory information is introduced).

In this respect, EST provides us with an impressive body of theoretical formulations and research findings concerning how status generalization processes—involving, for instance, multiple status characteristics of actors—organize group interaction. In addition, investigations into succession and transfer effects demonstrate how generalization processes can be the source of similar patterns of interaction across different situations. These developments hold the potential for explaining how status generalization can structure social processes at progressively more macro levels of analysis.

Research into legitimation processes, on the other hand, directs our attention to a different aspect of the idealist dimension of social structure. This theory shows how norms that shape the status structure of a group are derived from a collective realm, that is, a cultural domain, external to the group. This expansion of our understanding of the idealist dimension of structural processes emphasizes the importance of referential beliefs which are found throughout society. It is an analytical perspective that explicitly focuses upon the role played by normative beliefs at both micro and macro levels of the social order while demonstrating how such legitimating beliefs are involved in the construction and stabilization of group structures.

The analysis of the social construction of status value integrates concepts from the idealist, objectivist, and transactional dimensions of structural analysis. Arguments from EST are combined with the objectivist macrostructural theory of Peter Blau, which deals with the dynamics of societal populations. An explanation is provided for how structural factors can influence interaction, and then these interactional processes have consequences for status structures throughout society. This impressive integration of theoretical concepts clearly shows how very different structural processes can be interrelated and have macro-level effects.

Finally, we find that in several recent areas of inquiry focusing upon, for example, dominance behavior and exchange processes, behavioral and interpersonal factors play a key role in analyzing structural dynamics, especially the stabilization of group orders. While these developments are certainly linked to formulations dealing with other dimensions of structural analysis (for example, idealist concepts in status characteristics theory), each contributes to the formal analysis of different aspects of the transactional dimension of social structure. For this reason, it appears that such work increasingly involves theoretically integrative formulations explicitly grounded in the transactional and idealist approaches to structural analysis.

Possible Future Developments

These are all positive developments which are expanding EST's capacity for analyzing social structure. Of course, this examination of EST also raises certain concerns and suggestions for future research. Though not exhaustive, several points can be addressed here.

Certainly, as noted by various researchers in EST, further theory development and research are needed in a number of areas. While this review has shown that an expanding array of structural issues is coming under scrutiny, it is also apparent that much of this research is still in its early stages. Even within the most developed area of status characteristics theory, more work on issues such as the transsituational and construction effects of generalization processes is needed.

A different suggestion for future research would involve integrating EST with other theoretical traditions focusing on structural issues at various levels of analysis, that is, from micro interactional levels to more macro levels up to and including the societal and perhaps even transsocietal level. Though quite useful, Blau's macrostructural theory is certainly not the only candidate for such integrative endeavors. In this regard, it is possible that the "new institutionalism" in organizational analysis (for example, Powell and DiMaggio 1991) and EST could be productively integrated. Notwithstanding certain differences between the two approaches (Berger, Eyre, and Zelditch 1989), part of the conceptual framework of the "new institutionalism" could be of value for broadening EST's analysis of structural processes in different settings and at different levels of analysis. This is especially the case, since both perspectives utilize idealist concepts to a great extent to analyze social structure.

The neo-institutional analysis of organizations focuses upon the "social meanings" that underlie all types of organizational phenomena. Key components of formal organizations such as authority positions and policies rest upon interpretations of reality which may take the form of legitimating rules and myths. "Idealist" elements such as these define and shape institutions. Such a perspective seems directly relevant for work examining how group norms and status structures are legitimated and how generalization processes operate in groups located within institutions. The collective beliefs of organizations could, for instance, be the source of status beliefs which determine what characteristics influence (or do not influence) status generalization processes operating in different settings and groups within this organizational subculture (for example, beliefs about occupational positions and rank, policies opposed to bias based upon certain status characteristics).

Exchange theory and EST could also be productively combined in different ways to further our understanding of how social structure develops and endures. Part of the reason for this assessment is the diversity of concepts and findings in the exchange tradition, especially in the two main approaches to structural analysis (Knottnerus 1994b): elementary relations theory (Willer and Anderson 1981; Markovsky, Willer, and Patton 1988) and power-dependence theory (Emerson 1972a; Cook 1987). One possibility is that the concept of "exclusion" in elementary relations theory could be linked with EST to explain how status value may be formed.

According to elementary relations theory, power is determined by structural conditions. The main condition involves the exclusion of actors from exchange relations with others in which excluded actors engage in bidding to avoid further exclusion. The greatest power in exchange relations accrues to those who can avoid this predicament and profit from the bidding of others. I suggest that structural exclusion could be a source of status differences. More precisely, it is possible that actors subject to the structural condition of exclusion acquire low status while nonexcluded actors acquire high status.

One way in which this causal process might operate would involve differences in power and rewards resulting from nonexclusion and exclusion generating corresponding differences in status value. According to this line of reasoning, the structural condition of exclusion creates differences in power, resources, and rewards which produce corresponding expectations for competence formed from these different reward levels. These expectations for ability then result in consistently evaluated differences in status value. The more often certain actors, or groups of actors, are the object of such structural and generalization processes, the greater the effect on status value and the more likely that status differences will persist (for research relevant to this general argument, see Berger, Fisek, Norman, and Wagner 1985; Lovaglia 1992; Ridgeway 1991). If these ideas were formally developed and tests of them were devised, we could further our understanding of how status distinctions and structures of exclusion and exchange can generate structural inequalities at various levels of the social system.

It is also possible that EST and exchange theory could be linked to describe a "reverse process" in which status value contributes to the formation of zones of exclusion and nonexclusion. The low status of a potential exchange partner could increase the likelihood that the individual will be excluded from exchange relations while the high status of an actor could decrease the probability of his or her exclusion. A causal chain which could account for this process would involve status value leading to expectations for ability or competence, which in turn shape inferences about the potential power and resources associated with an actor. The likelihood of exclusion or nonexclusion of an actor is then determined by these inferred power and resource levels. In this hypothetical process, evaluated status beliefs would serve as a cognitive or ideational mechanism contributing to the creation, or possibly even the legitimation, of spheres of exclusion and nonexclusion.

A more speculative observation concerns the possible value of linking EST with more macro perspectives dealing with inequalities in economic or material goods and power. Programs investigating issues such as the dynamics of elites and corporate concentration, the structural aspects of status attainment (for example, segmented markets, occupational labor markets), or the role of the state direct our attention to the ways resources and power are distributed within societies, organizations, and occupational groups and the ways these patterns sometimes change. Such distributional patterns could, for instance, generate and fuel status beliefs and expectations for occupational groups, economic elites and nonelites, and even corporate entities. Indeed, it is conceivable that such macro conditions of exclusion and nonexclusion could lead to the creation of status differences and patterns of exclusion at the micro interactional level through the previously described process for creating status value. At the same time, under the proper conditions these types of cognitions or status beliefs could be an important mechanism contributing to the perpetuation of economic and power structures.

This last comment brings us to our final point concerning the metatheoretical conception underlying EST. While it was earlier suggested that the three elements of the social framework in this scheme correspond to the three approaches to structural analysis, there are differences in the degree of correspondence. More precisely, the formal element and the objectivist approach to social structure are not exactly the same. By focusing upon institutionalized and formalized roles and positions of authority, the formalist element is clearly referring to normatively and cognitively prescribed positions and expectations, especially as found within formal organizational settings or subcultural traditions. This idealist interpretation of the meaning of the formal differs from that of the objectivist approach.

In objectivist perspectives, social structure refers to arrangements of channels or "containers" that constrain and facilitate decisions. Structure guides and objectively influences social behavior whether or not it is interpreted by actors or legitimated. It may include organizational along with more macro structural arrangements which actors are incapable of influencing or changing. Such a perspective significantly differs from the more idealist understanding of the social order in the formalist framework. Given this metatheoretical scheme, perhaps this is why only one study (Ridgeway 1991) has so far theoretically integrated idealist and transactional concepts with an objectivist approach to structure, such as Peter Blau's. For this reason, it is suggested that modifications in the conceptualization of the formalist element to include, or at least not explicitly rule out, more objective components of the social order could be quite useful. Thus, the metatheoretical base or working strategy of EST would better lend itself to theory construction and integrative endeavors with work in more objectivist traditions.

Conclusion

EST has been and is a very productive program which continues to grow. Because of this progress and its grounding to a large degree in the idealist tradition, it is one of the major idealist approaches in U.S. sociology examining social interaction and social structure. With its commitment to cumulation and theory development, EST focuses in a rigorous manner on a clearly defined subject matter, that is, state organizing processes, especially the formation of expectations in task group settings which guide interaction. The result of these endeavors is a formal explanation of the cognitive and behavioral dynamics generating certain types of structures, particularly status structures in informal groups.

Furthermore, EST's presuppositional commitments in terms of the three-part framework in its metatheoretical scheme would facilitate further developments characterized by more extensive analyses of the different aspects of social structure. The challenge for EST is to continue developing theories and conducting research along the directions outlined by this orienting strategy while considering how its metatheoretical conception might be adjusted to accommodate other theoretical perspectives. In the process of pursuing these goals, the opportunities for integrative endeavors with other theoretical programs will only increase. Because of developments such as these, EST is making and will most certainly continue to make a major contribution to social structural analysis in contemporary sociology.

Where Do Status Value Beliefs Come From? New Developments

◥◣

Cecilia L. Ridgeway

Even the most casual observer of human affairs cannot fail to be impressed by the powerful role that status plays in the organization of social life. From the teenager on the street to the corporate board, relations of social esteem and respect (that is, status) are a major component in the structure of power, influence, social networks, and inequality within and between social groups. Three decades of research have shown that the development of status relations among actors depends heavily on their shared cultural beliefs about the status value of the characteristics and possessions which are perceived to distinguish them (Strodtbeck, James, and Hawkins 1957; Berger, Fisek, Norman, and Zelditch 1977; Webster and Foschi 1988; Wagner and Berger 1993a). Some of the most diffusely powerful of these beliefs, such as those associated with gender, race, ethnicity, or occupation, differentially evaluate the social categories to which people belong.

But where do status value beliefs come from? How are they maintained or changed? We have surprisingly little systematic knowledge with which to answer these fundamental questions. It is unlikely that any single answer will suffice. One recent theory, status construction theory, specifies some mechanisms by which widely shared status value beliefs could develop with regard to an initially unordered (that is, nominal) distinction among people (Ridgeway 1991). A distinctive aspect of this theory is that it posits a crucial role for interactional groups, especially small groups of between two and six members, in the creation, maintenance, and change of status value beliefs. This paper reviews this theory and presents recent developments with regard to the theoretical issues it raises about the creation, acquisition, and diffusion of status value beliefs.

Before we turn to the theory, it is useful to clarify a few points about the nature of status value beliefs themselves. They can be defined as widely held

Work for this chapter was partially supported by the National Science Foundation grant SES-921071, which I gratefully acknowledge.

beliefs that attach differential social worthiness and competence to states (such as male and female) of characteristics on which people are perceived to differ (such as sex). Status value beliefs are cultural schemas that represent x_1 as somehow "better" than x_2 (Sewell 1992). Note that status value beliefs are distinct from the familiar in-group bias described by social identity theory (Tajfel 1978, 1981; Turner 1985; Abrams and Hogg 1990). As research in that tradition has shown, mere difference can cause people to evaluate their own social category more favorably than the other category. But with status value beliefs, people in both categories come to agree (or at least concede) that one category is better than the other.

As this implies, an essential quality of status value beliefs is that they are shared. They are roughly consensual across a population of actors. Consensuality "objectifies" these evaluative schemas, according them a kind of social reality (Berger and Luckmann 1966). Regardless of what I think about x_1 and x_2, if I think you believe, and you and you and you believe, that x_1 is better than x_2, then that constructs a social reality that I believe I must respond to. Consensuality is the factor that causes status value beliefs to have such a powerful impact on the organization of social life. Thus, to understand how status value beliefs are created and changed, one must explain how they gain or lose consensuality. This is a process in which interactional groups play a critical part.

Status Construction Theory

Since Max Weber, sociologists have argued that status value develops from the possession of material resources. But it has never been clear exactly how (that is, through what processes) this occurs. Status construction theory postulates one set of processes by which this could happen. The theory provides an abstract model of social processes that are sufficient, if not necessary, to create consensual status value beliefs about an initially unordered (that is, nominal) distinction among people. Since it is an abstract model, it is not intended to represent the actual historical processes by which any particular status belief arose. Rather, it presents an a priori theoretical argument about structural processes that can underpin the status value of nominal distinguishing characteristics. If the theory is sound, then if these structural conditions are present for any given status belief, they will affect the maintenance or change of that belief regardless of its exact historical origins.

I will begin by describing the theory and then turn to recent developments with regard to it. These developments include simulations of the sets of interactional processes by which, according to the theory, status value beliefs can become consensual, as well as experiments testing the belief acquisition processes posited by the theory. Each suggests some further insights into the processes by which status value beliefs develop.

Initial Structural Conditions

The theory begins with an abstract population in which three structural conditions obtain. (1) The members differ in the level of material resources they possess. (2) They also differ on an unordered, nominal characteristic, N, that has been cognitively distinguished in the culture. (3) The distribution of states of the nominal characteristic and resources is correlated such that those with one state of the characteristic (for example, Na) are more likely to be resource rich than those with another state of the characteristic (for example, Nb).

The material resource involved is assumed to be an exchangeable resource with exchange value for the entire population, making it a kind of wealth. Although the logic of the theory can accommodate diverse distributional inequalities, it is easier to present the argument if we assume, as an example, that there is a simple dichotomous division between those with more of the resource and those with less of it. Assume as well that the population is evenly divided into these resource-rich and resource-poor categories.

The theory further assumes that the nominal characteristic is an attribute on which people are easily perceived to differ but which has not yet acquired consensual status value. Although the social salience of any attribute will increase as it acquires evaluative significance in the culture, it is important to note that people can distinguish at least some individual characteristics before they acquire the type of evaluative significance that constitutes consensual status value. Research suggests that attributes of appearance that are easily observed without close inspection and that show clear differences among interactants are the strongest candidates for such salient descriptive characteristics (see Fiske and Taylor 1991: 144–45, for a review). As noted, mere recognition of difference on such an attribute can create in-group bias, but this is quite different from consensual status value (Doise et al. 1972; Tajfel 1978).

A characteristic's potential to acquire independent status value is affected by its social salience relative to other such descriptive, nonresource characteristics recognized in the population. The more distinctive it is, the more susceptible it is to acquiring status value. For this reason, the theory assumes that the nominal characteristic is not systematically correlated with nonresource characteristics more salient than itself. Again, for a simple example, assume that the nominal characteristic, N, has two categories, Na and Nb, that evenly divide the population. Finally, to complete the example, assume that the correlation between level of resources and the nominal characteristic is such that 60 percent of Nas but only 40 percent of Nbs are resource rich.

The theory then considers the impact of these structural conditions on interactional events in the population that could give rise to status value beliefs. It asks three questions. First, how will the distributions of resources and the nominal characteristic, N, affect who encounters whom in the population? Second, how will the individuals' similarities or differences in resources and N affect the development of informal status and influence in these encounters? Third, what are the implications of these two processes, taken together, for the creation and spread of status value beliefs about the nominal characteristic? The logic of the theory unfolds in the answers it offers to these questions.

Who Encounters Whom?

The theory borrows from Blau's (1977b; Blau and Schwartz 1984) structural theory of association to describe the impact of the initial structural conditions on patterns of interaction in the population. Blau argues that the likelihood of encounters among people similar or different on given characteristics is a joint function of the structural availability of similar or different others and the strength of people's preference, if any, for associating with others who are similar to them in given ways. Thus, Blau's argument incorporates people's well-established tendency for homophily in their associations (for example, Huston and Levinger 1978; McPherson and Smith-Lovin 1987) while acknowledging that tendencies to homophily vary considerably depending on the characteristic involved. But most important, Blau's theory recognizes that all such associational tendencies are constrained by the structural availability of similar others.

Skvoretz (1983) has formalized Blau's principles of association. His formulas can be used to predict the likelihood, under different assumptions, of encounters between people who are (1) similar in resources and the nominal characteristic, N; (2) different on one variable but not the other; or (3) different on both variables. The last type, called "doubly dissimilar" encounters, plays a crucial role in status construction theory.

Under most assumptions about the distribution of resources and the nominal characteristic in the population, the correlation between them, and the strength of preferences for similar others on one or both characteristics, doubly dissimilar encounters are a small minority of all encounters. For instance, with the distributions and correlation assumed above and the further assumptions that people have a 50 percent preference for resource-similar others, but no particular preference for N-similar others, doubly dissimilar encounters will compose 13 percent of all encounters (Ridgeway 1991: 373). Yet status construction theory argues that doubly dissimilar encounters are nevertheless the crucial sites where the construction of status value beliefs begins. They are able to have widespread impact, despite their relative rarity because they engender a diffusion process through which they continually pump reinforcement of the status belief into the population.

Difference and Status in Encounters

To describe the development of status and influence in encounters where actors are similar or different in resources and/or the nominal characteristic, status construction theory draws from expectation states theory (Berger, Conner, and Fisek 1974; Webster and Foschi 1988). Several expectation states studies document that the possession of superior resources or rewards in goal-oriented interaction tends to create corresponding differences in expectations for competence and performance in the situation (Cook 1975; Harrod 1980; Stewart and Moore 1992). These performance expectations, in turn, tend to become self-fulfilling, so that the resource rich develop more influence and social standing in the encounter than the resource poor (Berger, Fisek, Norman, and Wagner 1985; Miller and Turnbull 1986).

For resources to have this differentiating effect on standing in an encounter, the actors involved must differ in their resource levels, according to expectation states theory. Thus, this effect applies only to resource-different encounters in the population. When actors are similar on an attribute, either resources or the nominal characteristic, that attribute itself cannot become a basis for differential status and influence in the encounter.[1] Since the nominal characteristic is assumed to lack, as yet, a systematic, socially shared evaluation, it should not effect the initial development of hierarchies in a manner that is consistent across multiple encounters. However, once a hierarchy of influence and status develops in an encounter where people differ on the nominal characteristic, it is possible that actors could associate the characteristic after the fact with the differing levels of social standing each had in the situation. This is especially likely, since the nominal characteristic is assumed to be a fairly salient attribute perceptually, in that it is easily recognized and not highly correlated with other characteristics more easily noticed than itself.

If people did associate standing in the encounter after the fact with their corresponding differences in N, it would create for those people an implicit, fledgling assumption about the competence and social worthiness of people who differ in N that could provide the beginnings of status value beliefs. This suggests that encounters where actors differ in N could possibly provide a site where status value is initially associated with N. If this were true, then further evidence indicates that actors would transfer these fledgling beliefs to future encounters, creating a diffusion process (Markovsky, Smith, and Berger 1984). The theory turns to an account of this diffusion process and the likelihood that it would produce consensual status beliefs.

Transfer, Diffusion, and Consensus

Expectation states research suggests that when interaction modifies actors' performance expectations for people with a given social attribute, the actors

---

[1] According to expectation states theory, attributes which do not distinguish among actors can still become salient and affect expectations when they are relevant to the situational goals. However, in this case, they contribute to similar, rather than differentiating expectations for the actors involved.

transfer their modified expectations to future goal-oriented encounters with such actors (Pugh and Wahrman 1983; Markovsky, Smith, and Berger 1984). While the effect of the modifying interaction diminishes with each subsequent transfer, a modest diffusion process is nevertheless created (Markovsky 1988). This is because the actor with modified expectations acts on those expectations in subsequent encounters, treating the person with the given attribute differently. By acting on the modified expectation, the actor "altercasts" the person with the attribute and effectively teaches the modified belief to others in the encounter (Weinstein and Deutschberger 1963; Miller and Turnbull 1986). Thus, the effects of N-different encounters in creating differential expectations for actors who differ on N could potentially diffuse widely, creating more general status beliefs about N.

There are two types of N-different encounters that could produce status beliefs about N: encounters where actors are similar in resources and doubly dissimilar encounters where they differ in resource level as well as N. The effects of the structural conditions, especially the correlation between resources and N, on the distribution of different types of encounters affects the potential of the two types of N-different encounters to create consensual status value beliefs.

In encounters where people differ in N but not resources, people could indeed associate their resulting hierarchies with states of N. But in the population of such encounters, there should be just about as many instances where Na is associated with high standing in the situation as where Nb is. Consequently, the effects of the transfer and diffusion of the status associations with N developed in these encounters should be effectively to cancel each other out. As a result, the micro-level associations between status value and N formed in these encounters should, by themselves, be insufficient to result in consensual status value beliefs about states of N.

The consequences of doubly dissimilar encounters are different, however, in ways that are important for the construction of status beliefs. The effect of resources on standing in the encounter means that the resource rich, whatever their state of N, are likely to become the influential, high-status actors in doubly dissimilar situations. Although standing in the encounter initially develops from resource differences, once it does, actors may again associate it after the fact with their corresponding differences in N. Thus, these groups, too, create a potential basis for status beliefs about N. But in this case, the macro-level correlation between being resource rich and being Na means that there will be more doubly dissimilar encounters that create an association between Na and positive status value than do so for Nb. For instance, using the assumptions given as an example above, 69 percent of doubly dissimilar encounters should result in high-Na and low-Nb expectations and only 31 percent in the reverse. When these associations between states of N and competence and worthiness transfer and diffuse, the 31 percent reversals should eventually counteract a like number of high-Na—low-Nb associations. But this still leaves in force the effects of 38 percent of the associations favoring Na over Nb.

This systematic advantage for Na over Nb will not be cancelled out by the effects of other sorts of encounters, since these produce either no or equally counteracting associations between N and expectations for competence and worthiness. As a result, the micro-level associations between states of N and status value developed in doubly dissimilar encounters are likely to diffuse widely, creating macro-level consensual beliefs associating status value with N and advantaging Nas over Nbs.

For instance, at least some actors are likely to transfer what they learn about N in doubly dissimilar encounters to resource-similar, N-different encounters. Such generalization of situationally modified expectations to partially similar situations has been shown to occur, as when actors transfer expectations from one type of goal setting to similar actors in a very different goal setting (Markovsky, Smith, and Berger 1984). Standing in resource-similar, N-different encounters is usually determined by idiosyncratic behavioral differences. But when one of the actors has previously learned to associate states of N with status value, he or she is likely to treat the others accordingly, biasing the development of standing in the situation and "teaching" the status value of N to the other interactants.

This process of belief formation may not be effective in a single encounter. But over multiple encounters, the process will repeat itself and, as people circulate through different types of encounters, they may have additional experiences in doubly dissimilar encounters. Although always a minority, at any one time, there will always be a certain percentage of the population in doubly dissimilar encounters, so that these situations continually pump support for status beliefs about N into the population. Over time, the likely result will be increasingly firmly held and increasingly consensual beliefs about the status value of N. By these processes, then, status construction theory argues, interactional groups can create consensual status value beliefs about an initially nominal distinction from structural conditions in a population.

Developing and Evaluating the Theory

The theoretical argument here turns on two related sets of processes. In the first set, individuals initially acquire status value beliefs in particular types of encounters. In the second set, assumptions are made about the consequences of the diffusion of these beliefs through the population.

The initial acquisition of status beliefs actually involves a pair of interrelated processes of belief formation, both of which are rooted in group dynamics. There is the process of initially inferring status value beliefs from the circumstances of doubly dissimilar encounters through a kind of misattribution or overgeneralization of the source of actors' standing in the encounter. Then there is an altercasting process by which one in the situation who already holds the belief enacts it in an encounter by treating others in accord with it and, in so doing, "teaches" the belief to others present.

Whether or not these belief acquisition processes actually occur as the theory describes requires empirical tests. However, whether, if they do occur, they would logically lead to near consensual status value beliefs in a reasonable lapse of time is a question that can be examined through simulations. Therefore, recent work on status construction theory has proceeded in two directions. The first project develops a formal, group-based model of the diffusion of status value beliefs to examine the logical sturdiness of the theory's arguments about diffusion and the emergence of consensual beliefs. Simulations, of course, cannot tell us what empirically would occur. But they can examine the complex and sometimes unexpected implications of a theory under various assumptions to show what logically should occur if the theory is correct. The second project, which is still in process, is a set of behavioral experiments designed to test the theory's arguments about belief acquisition. The results of these projects have thus far strongly supported the theory. They have also suggested new insights into results predicted by the theory. Of particular interest is what these insights indicate about the importance of group dynamics to the acquisition and spread of status value beliefs.

Simulating the Diffusion Process

A Formal Model

Drawing on previous mathematical approaches to the diffusion of social beliefs or practices (for example, Coleman, Katz, and Menzel 1957; Coleman 1964; Daley and Kendall 1965), James Balkwell and I created a formal diffusion model that incorporated the main arguments of status construction theory (Ridgeway and Balkwell 1992, 1997). As a means of exploring the relative importance of interactional (that is, group) processes in the formation and spread of status value beliefs, the model incorporated some extratheoretical factors as well, which I will describe shortly.

Since the formal model itself is fairly complex and is presented in detail elsewhere (Ridgeway and Balkwell 1992), I will not reproduce it here. Instead, I will give a general sketch of its logical strategy and then turn to the relevant results. We followed the logic of many diffusion models in viewing the spread of status beliefs as a continuous time, birth-death process in which holders of the belief are "born" or "die" in the population (for example, Coleman 1964). But unlike most such models, we took the goal-oriented encounter, not individuals, as our unit of analysis. Thus, we viewed the "birth" or "death" of an individual's belief as a transition of the goal-oriented encounter the person is in from having X believers to having either $X + 1$ or $X - 1$ believers. Then we developed a stochastic model of the probability of these transitions in doubly dissimilar and other group types based on the theory's assumptions about the kind of belief acquisition or loss likely to occur there.[2]

We further developed the model to include two extratheoretical factors as well. First, we included in our model of transition intensities a parameter that represents the possibility that people might individually infer status value for the nominal characteristic directly from their own observation of the correlation between N and resources in the larger population regardless of their interactional context. This parameter is equivalent to the "broadcast" parameters of many diffusion models that represent a stimulus for belief acquisition that is constant across actors in the population (compare Lave and March 1975; Markovsky 1988). Putting such a parameter in the model allows us to examine explicitly the added effects of belief acquisition through the interactional processes posited by the theory.

A second extratheoretical element we incorporated into the model was a consideration of encounter size as a factor in belief acquisition. There are two reasons for examining the effects of encounters of different sizes. The first is realism. The logic of status construction theory is implicitly dyadic. Dyads are the building blocks of groups of all sizes. However, they do leave out third-party effects that can be important to behavior in interactional groups greater than the dyad. If the diffusion processes posited cannot be shown logically to persist when groups larger than dyads are considered, then this is a serious limitation on the theory. A second reason for examining encounter size goes to the heart of the theoretical logic itself. If simulations incorporating large groups show that belief acquisition is a linear function of group size, so that the largest groups produce the highest rate of belief adoption, it would challenge the theory's basic contention about the importance of face-to-face interaction in the construction of status value. Thus, incorporating the extratheoretical factors of direct structural effects and encounter size allows the model to provide a more critical examination of the theory's claims about the importance of interactional processes to the creation of consensual status value.

To incorporate the effects of group size as well as summarize across encounters of different types, we situated our stochastic birth-death model for group types in a probability distribution representing two factors. First was the likelihood of encounters of different sizes, assumed to be roughly distributed as a Poisson distribution. Second, within each encounter size, was the relative likelihood that encounters would be doubly dissimilar groups, N-different but resource-similar groups, or other groups, given varying assumptions about the distribution of resources and N in the population, the correlation between them, and the

---

[2]Because of the computational complexities of including death as well as birth processes in the model, belief loss was represented more simply than the more elaborately specified processes of belief acquisition.

strength of preferences for resource- or N-similar associations. This second factor captured Blau's theory of association, using a generalization of Skvoretz's (1983) formalization. Using this full model, we could run computer simulations to see how the expected number of believers in the population changes over time under different assumptions.

The Importance of Small Groups

Ridgeway and Balkwell (1992) describe a number of results from such simulations, but here I focus on those that demonstrate the importance of group processes in the emergence of consensus about a status value belief. We first examined the importance of interactional groups by simulating how close to consensus a population would come if all groups were of a particular size or type. That is, we examined the asymptotic expected percentages of believers under these assumptions (Table 1). If "groups" were all size 1, so that no group processes were involved at all, a maximum of about 70 percent of the population could eventually acquire the belief. On the other hand, if all groups were doubly dissimilar encounters of two or more people, between 94 percent (if all were dyads) and 99 percent (if groups were of eleven or more) would acquire the belief. So group processes are clearly crucial in the development of consensus. These results also showed, as expected, that doubly dissimilar groups were the most powerful producers of believers in comparison to other types. Finally, and most interestingly, these results indicated that, while larger groups do produce more believers than smaller ones, most of the added effects of size occur in groups of between three and six people. Thus, it is small groups that have the most powerful rate (per person) of belief induction.

We used the full model, which includes groups of all sizes and types, to examine how the diffusion process would work under different assumptions about the initial structural conditions, particularly the correlation between N and resources and the strength of homophily biases on N or resources (Ridgeway and Balkwell 1992). The results most relevant here indicated that the correlation between N and resources is the key factor in the speed of diffusion. The impact of any homophily bias on N, which moderates the diffusion rate, is clearly less powerful. The percentage of believers quickly approaches a ceiling effect with high correlations (for example, phi = .60) between N and resources.

The relevant implication of this result here is that, in order to explore further the importance of group size in producing believers, it is best to examine size effects under a relatively low correlation to avoid ceiling effects. As a result, we chose a correlation of phi = .10, which is roughly equivalent to a 53–47 percent split between rich Nas and rich Nbs. As in the initial example described earlier, we also assumed no homophily bias on N and a .5 bias on resources. We then compared the levels of consensus that would be achieved under these conditions if all encounters were of a given size (Fig. 1).

TABLE 1

*Diffusion of Status Value Beliefs in a Hypothetical Population
with No Initial Carriers*

Group Size	Same on N		Different on N	
	Same R	Diff R	Same R	Diff R
1	70.5	-	-	-
2	70.5	70.5	86.4	93.7
3	70.5	70.5	92.7	96.0
4	70.5	70.5	95.0	97.1
5	70.5	70.5	96.2	97.7
6	70.5	70.5	96.9	98.1
7	70.5	70.5	97.4	98.4
8	70.5	70.5	97.7	98.6
9	70.5	70.5	98.0	98.8
10	70.5	70.5	98.2	98.9
11	70.5	70.5	98.4	99.0
12	70.5	70.5	98.5	99.1

Note: The figures in the body of this table are the asymptotic

expected percentages of carriers. Source: Ridgeway and Balkwell

(1992).

The results showed the striking importance of small-group interaction for the production and spread of status value beliefs (Ridgeway and Balkwell 1992). Groups of 2, 3, 4, and 5 each provided significant increments over no groups (that is, size = 1) or over the next smaller group in both the rate that believers were produced and the asymptotic level of consensus achieved. There was a large leap between dyads and triads, representing the added effects of third-party observation on the acquisition of status beliefs. By group size 6, however, virtually all the incremental value of increasing size has been attained. Groups of 7 or more produce a level of consensus so close to that of 6-person groups that the lines would be difficult to distinguish on a graph.

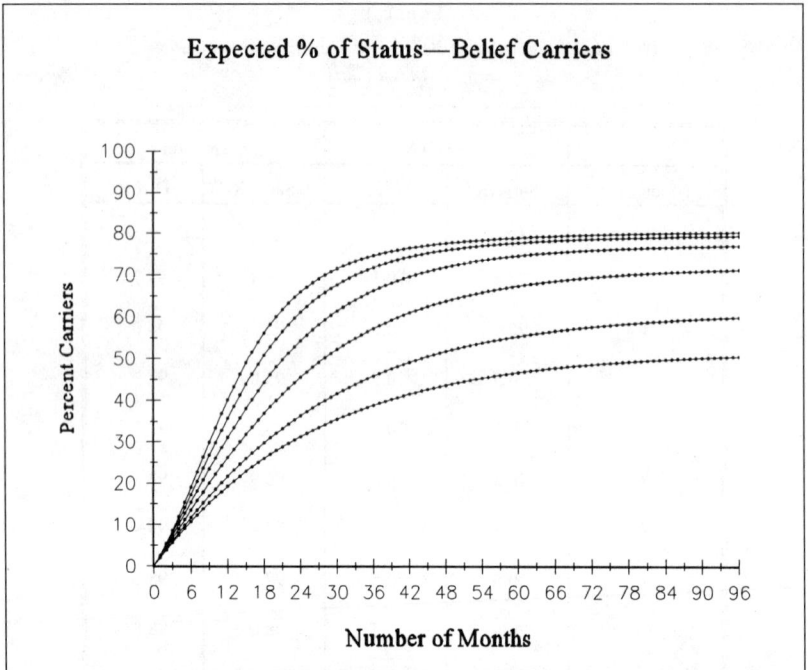

Fig. 1. Group size and the production of believers

It is clear, then, that within the logical assumptions of status construction theory (as represented in the formal model), small groups of three to six are the most powerful contexts for the creation and spread of status value beliefs. Small groups, of course, are the social context most strongly characterized by direct, face-to-face interaction. They are just the context where one would expect the interpersonal processes described by status construction theory to be most powerful.

It is important to note that this finding about the power of small groups was not an obvious or predicted effect of the theory, even though it is in strong support of it. The original theory says that it is encounters that are crucial to the development of consensual status beliefs, but says nothing about encounter size. When we added a size factor to the formal model, we could not be certain that the resulting simulations would not produce logical challenges to the importance the theory attaches to face-to-face, interpersonal contexts. That they did not, and in fact confirmed that importance, is strong support for the theory's underlying logic.

The results of the simulation project demonstrate the logical sturdiness of the theory's argument about the development of consensual status beliefs. They suggest that if the belief acquisition processes posited by the theory do occur, the process should, on logical grounds, be sufficient to create a consensual belief. Furthermore, they provided new insight into the power of small groups larger than the dyad to speed the process along. The crucial next question, then, is whether the processes of belief acquisition described by the theory are empirically plausible. The following section describes a project under way to test arguments about belief acquisition.

Forming Status Value Beliefs

The theory argues that beliefs are formed and spread through two related processes. First, there are the processes of inference and association that foster the creation of status value beliefs in doubly dissimilar encounters, even when none of the actors initially holds such beliefs. These, of course, are crucial to the theory. Then, second, there are the more familiar altercasting processes by which actors who already hold the belief "teach" it to others by enacting it in N-different encounters of any sort (that is, N-different, resource-similar or doubly dissimilar interactions). A more careful review of these processes clarifies the issues involved in testing the theory's arguments with regard to them.

Belief Acquisition Processes

In goal-oriented, doubly dissimilar encounters, the argument is that members' differences in resources create corresponding differences in performance expectations that tend to become self-fulfilling. Several studies have documented that this does occur in resource-differentiated interaction (Harrod 1980; Stewart and Moore 1992). Acting on their expectations, the resource rich take the initiative more, participate more, are evaluated more highly, and become more influential (Berger, Fisek, Norman, and Wagner 1985). As a result, the actors enact and experience an implicit structure of status inequality in the situation. How do they interpret this? They know, of course, that they differ in resources, but in this case, they also differ on N, which is assumed to be a relatively salient characteristic. The argument is that they generalize and, in that sense, misattribute their social standing in the situation to their corresponding differences in N. On the basis of such experiences, they make implicit evaluative assumptions about people who differ on N as well as those who differ in resources. Over multiple such experiences, these become increasingly stable beliefs.

The second set of belief acquisition processes occurs because, according to the theory, people who form such beliefs in doubly dissimilar encounters are likely to transfer them to encounters with people who are similar in resources but also different on N. Imagine, for instance, an Na who implicitly assumes that

Nas are more worthy and competent than Nbs in an encounter with a resource-similar Nb. The Na speaks up and acts confidently, assuming she has more to offer than the Nb. She pays little attention to the Nb's suggestions, effectively treating them as of lower value. The Nb (and any third parties in the encounter) see in the Na a display of the behaviors usually associated with high-status actors who are presumed to be competent (Ridgeway, Berger, and Smith 1985; Fisek, Berger, and Norman 1981). They also see the Nb treated as apparently less competent and status worthy.

The likely result is a self-fulfilling prophecy. The Nb and others assume the Na must really be more competent and worthy than the Nb. Such altercasting effects, where others' expectations for you affect your own expectations for yourself, are well documented (Weinstein and Deutschberger 1963; Moore 1985; Miller and Turnbull 1986). The added point here is that, according to the theory, the actors, in trying to make sense of the status hierarchy, implicitly associate differential expectations for actors with their distinguishing attributes such as N. In this way, actors "learn" status beliefs about N by being treated as though N were status valued. Again, multiple experiences may be necessary for such beliefs to fully develop and stabilize.

What these two sets of processes have in common is that actors experience an interactional status hierarchy that they come to associate with their corresponding differences in N. What they differ on is the initial source of the hierarchy, which is resources in the original doubly dissimilar situation and the altercasting behaviors of a believer in the second situation.

In both cases, certain parts of the process are well documented. Specifically, the effect of resources on status and influence has been demonstrated, as have the corresponding effects of altercasting on self-expectations. The key, then, is the association of local status differences between specific actors with the social category of actors and a given state of N. Thus, the belief acquisition process here differs from many reward or feedback learning processes because the actor is forming a positive or negative belief not just about self or another but about social categories to which they belong, people with different states of N. This is what must be demonstrated. The most important situation in which to do so is the doubly dissimilar encounter, since in this context local status differences are potentially confounded with resource differences as well as differences in N. A series of experiments with doubly dissimilar encounters is currently under way to examine the belief acquisition process.

Before we turn to them, however, it may be helpful to clarify further the relationship between the associational/inference processes described by status construction theory and cognitive-evaluative effects with regard to group categorization and stereotyping that are well established in the research literature. Particularly relevant are "illusory correlation" effects and established conditions for out-group, rather than in-group, bias.

Other Cognitive-Evaluative Processes

The processes central to belief acquisition here are distinct from the cognitive bias known as "illusory correlation," which has been shown to encourage the development of positive and negative stereotypes about social categories (Hamilton 1981; Hamilton, Stroessner, and Mackie 1993). On the other hand, there are some similarities in overall logic of the two types of processes. With illusory correlation, actors overestimate the association between membership in a statistical minority and exceptionally good or bad behaviors or traits merely because both are rare and therefore cognitively distinctive. The belief formation described by status construction theory does not require that either a state of N or a resource group be in a statistical minority. Rather, N and resources become cognitively distinctive in some *encounters* and, thus, potentially affect belief formation, because they *differentiate* the actors. In those encounters, actors experience an actual, nonillusory correlation between N, resources, and social standing which they then do overgeneralize to situations where actors don't differ on resources. Thus, these are distinct, if related, processes. Illusory correlation biases, however, could intensify the belief formation processes described here if the distribution of resources or states of N were, in fact, skewed so that some categories were in a statistical minority among the population.

The conditions under which doubly dissimilar encounters are predicted to induce evaluative consensus about N are also a bit different from the conditions which have already been shown to create such consensus. Note that established in-group bias effects work with the acquisition of status beliefs about N for actors advantaged by N. But for those disadvantaged by N, acquiring status value beliefs means overcoming in-group bias and coming to accept an out-group bias. Thus, the development of status beliefs by those disadvantaged by them is the key to consensuality. One study has shown that an evaluative consensus (that is, in-group bias by one group and out-group bias by the other) can be created when a legitimate authority assigns to one arbitrarily created group power to distribute resources for the other group as well as itself (Sachdev and Bourhis 1985). The development of evaluative consensus here, however, is more complex, since no higher authority directly assigns power or social standing in an encounter to the resource rich or to Nas. Rather, actors jointly construct power and status inequalities in the encounter from expectations they themselves form about one type of social category (resources), which they later generalize to an often associated category (N). It is clear, then, that the belief formation processes posited by status construction theory are plausible in terms of established research on cognitive-evaluative biases in group categorization and stereotyping as well as documented altercasting effects. But they are nevertheless distinctive and require independent tests.

Experiments with Doubly Dissimilar Encounters

The task, then, was to design experiments to examine whether doubly dissimilar encounters, as described by the theory, could cause participants to develop not merely in-group bias about N but consensual status evaluations of states of N. I had a special interest in understanding the relative impact of actors' social standing in a doubly dissimilar encounter on their formation of status evaluations of N, since assumptions about this process are a distinctive part of the theory.

I began the project with an exploratory pilot study that simply placed participants in a task-oriented, doubly dissimilar encounter. I brought same-sex undergraduates to the laboratory two at a time for a study supposedly of diversity and problem-solving in groups. To create a nominal distinction between them, participants were placed in individual rooms where they looked at a series of paintings by Klee and Kandinsky and recorded their preferences, supposedly as a measure of Personal Response Style. This is a version of a group categorization procedure used in many studies to create a "mere difference" between groups (for example, Tajfel, Billig, Bundy, and Flament 1971). Participants were then told that they had been assigned a pay level of $7 (or $10) and their partner $10 (or $7) and that they were an "S2" (or "Q2") in Personal Response Style while their partner was a "Q2" (or "S2"). The two participants were then brought together to complete a 10-trial cooperative decision-making task, after which they separated to fill out a post-experiment questionnaire.

Among other items, the questionnaire contained four questions designed to be unobtrusive measures of their evaluative beliefs about S2s and Q2s. These items asked which of the following people would be more likely to be chosen as foreman of a jury, to be the first speaker at a community function, to be promoted early in a major corporation, and to be in a responsible position in the university. Participants chose answers from a series of contrasts such as a westerner or an easterner, an S2 or a Q2, someone from a large family or a small family.

Note that the design of this pilot study offers only a very weak realization of the conditions of doubly dissimilar encounters that are presumed by the theory to give rise to status beliefs. There is only a single, brief round of interaction. The resource manipulation is quite weak, since it is not a stable, transsituational difference between the participants, as it is in the theory. Indeed, since it was a one-time-only difference between them in pay, participants may have been encouraged to minimize its impact on their treatment of one another out of "politeness" (Mikula 1980). Finally, the interaction between the participants was unconstrained and "noisy" from an experimental point of view. Interaction was face-to-face with no elimination of confounding differences in status characteristics such as attractiveness or ethnicity, although, of course, these were random-

TABLE 2

Mean Preferences for Own Group by Pay, Sex, and Personal Response Style (PRS)

	Male Dyads		Female Dyads	
PRS	S2	Q2	S2	Q2
High Pay ($10)	68%	79%	77%	78%
	(n=18)	(n=19)	(n=17)	(n=16)
Low Pay ($7)	61%	71%	62%	48%
	(n=16)	(n=18)	(n=19)	(n=14)
ANOVA Results						
						Pay x Sex
Effects	Pay	Sex	PRS	Pay x Sex	Pay x PRS	x PRS
F Test	8.70	0.39	0.21	2.16	3.40	0.35
P	p=.004	p=.530	p=.653	p=.141	p=.072	p=.553

ized across conditions. Probably as a result of these factors, interactional hierarchies of influence in the dyads were only weakly differentiated on average.

Yet, despite these several weaknesses, the results provided some evidence of the effects of pay differences on the beginning of a status valuation of the nominal characteristic, Personal Response Style. On the questionnaire items, strong majorities in almost all conditions rated their own response style group as more likely than the other group to be in the higher status position. This is the classic in-group bias effect (Tajfel 1978; Turner 1985). But, importantly, the strength of this in-group preference was significantly (p = .004) weaker for low-paid subjects than high-paid subjects (Table 2). Thus, even in this weak, one-time-only situation where only slight differences in social standing emerged and other confounding factors were present, an encounter with someone who differed on the nominal characteristic and was paid more was enough to begin the erosion of lower-paid actors' preference for their own nominal group. This is the essential transformation that must occur for a characteristic to acquire consensual status value.

For some of these groups, after the participants completed the questionnaire, we took them to meet another subject who also differed from them in response style but not, this time, in pay. This was exploratory, and I do not have systematic data to offer with regard to it. However, it appeared from videotapes that people who were low paid on the first round of interaction (their first doubly dissimilar encounter) often tried to assert themselves more strongly in round two. It appeared to be a kind of reactance or equity restoration response.

Such reactance was probably encouraged by the weak, one-time-only nature of the resource difference created in round one. Nevertheless, it points to a fundamental, if unsurprising, observation. There may be a basic asymmetry in the processes by which status value beliefs are acquired. People in the advantaged group may infer the beliefs directly from experiences such as those in the doubly dissimilar settings. There, their normal cognitive bias toward their in-group is given broader social meaning by its apparent association with a resource advantage and the performance expectation and influence advantages those create.

But in a classic example of self-centered biases in attribution (for example, Ross and Sicoly 1979), people in the disadvantaged group may resist attributing a devaluing experience to something stable about themselves. In this case, it is their membership in a given nominal characteristic (for example, response style) category. Consequently, it may require more exposure to interactions where the devaluation is clearly enacted for persons in the disadvantaged group to accept implicitly the status valuation of the characteristic. As a result, the way the diffusion of status beliefs may actually work is that the beliefs develop more rapidly and stably among those advantaged by it, who then act on those beliefs by repeatedly treating the disadvantaged group in terms of them. It is this direct altercasting in N-different encounters of all sorts that eventually forces the beliefs on those disadvantaged by them. The power of these encounters is reinforced by the fact that some of them are doubly dissimilar encounters where the resource advantage creates an undeniable superiority for the N-advantaged actor.

It is probably only the repeated experience of being cast in a negative light by a characteristic, so that the evaluation seems to have a social reality, that makes people actually accept a devaluing belief about a self-attribute. This is particularly the case when the belief is not just about ourselves, but about all who share the self-attribute with us. Thus, we may accept negative beliefs about such self-attributes only when interactional experiences make it seem that such beliefs have some apparent social currency. This observation brings us back to the importance of perceived consensuality in the transformation of group categorization effects into status value beliefs. It suggests that a major importance of interaction contexts and group dynamics is their power to create local experiences that appear to represent such agreed-upon reality to individual actors, even before, at a population level, such consensuality actually exists. This is the process by which interactional groups foster or undermine the social construction of consensual status value beliefs.

If there is an asymmetry in belief formation between actors who would be advantaged or disadvantaged by a status belief, what are the implications of this for the theory itself? Clearly, a slower rate of belief acquisition on the part of N-disadvantaged actors (for example, Nbs) would slow down the overall rate of diffusion. In general, the larger the proportion of the population that is N-disadvantaged, the greater the potential for slowing diffusion. But will the ultimate effect be a substantial retardation of the diffusion process and a possible drop in the overall level of consensuality achieved? This may not be too likely for a number of reasons.

If those who would benefit from a belief are more prone to adopt it, then the rates of belief formation in a given doubly dissimilar encounter could be higher for Nas than for Nbs. But this suggests that Nas, carrying a firmer status belief, will be more likely to enact such a belief in subsequent N-different encounters. Thus, in such encounters, other Nbs will receive more interactional "teaching" from Nas than Nas do from Nbs. While an Nb is unlikely to acquire the belief from one such enactment alone, it does increase Nbs' exposure and, thus, susceptibility to the belief, relative to Nas. As a result, rates of belief acquisition may begin higher with Nas but fairly quickly almost even out. As a result, the effect of the asymmetry of belief acquisition on the overall rate of diffusion and eventual consensuality may be fairly small.

At present, a series of more controlled experiments are under way to realize more fully the circumstances of doubly dissimilar encounters as described by the theory. The purpose is to test whether these circumstances are in fact sufficient to overcome people's prior tendencies to in-group bias. Are they sufficient to actually create status beliefs that are ascribed to by those they disadvantage as well as those whom they benefit? In contrast to the pilot study, these experiments strengthen or control a number of factors and combine them in several ways. To strengthen the resource manipulation, pay, and give it a less intensely local, one-time-only context, participants are given unobtrusive referential information indicating varying pay rates for other S2s and Q2s that have participated in the experiment before them. To reduce confounding differences in existing status characteristics (for example, attractiveness, ethnicity), participants interact with their partners verbally, through an audio hookup, rather than face-to-face. To ensure that a clearly differentiated local hierarchy is created during interaction, the role of partner is played by student confederates who act appropriately assertive or deferential, depending on their relative pay level.

If the theory is correct, this set of factors, in combination, should be sufficient to induce both disadvantaged and advantaged actors to infer shared status value for the nominal characteristic, response style. Other experiments will disaggregate these factors in various ways to determine their contribution to the formation of shared status beliefs. Together this set of experiments should provide evidence of whether the crucial belief acquisition processes that underlie status construction theory do indeed occur.

Final Thoughts

This paper began by asking where status value beliefs come from. Status construction theory suggests one set of answers to this question. Status value beliefs come from associations between the distribution of resources and the distribution of other distinguishing characteristics in a population, as Weber proposed. But more specifically, they come from the way these factors constrain (1) who encounters whom, (2) the local beliefs about competence and worthiness that are fostered in these encounters, and (3) the likelihood that these local beliefs will be transferred by actors to other encounters and their participants and become increasingly firmly held and broadly consensual beliefs about the status value of a distinguishing characteristic.

As this indicates, the construction of status value beliefs is a multilevel process. It is a joint product of structural conditions at the macro-level and the group dynamics of encounters at the interactional level. Not surprisingly, then, projects to develop and test status construction theory have also had to address processes at two levels, the more macro-level of diffusion processes and the micro-level of belief acquisition through group dynamics in encounters.

The results of both the simulation project addressing diffusion processes and the experiments on interactional belief formation have thus far supported the theory. They have also added significant new insights. First, they indicate that it is small groups, encounters larger than dyads but less than seven or eight, that are the most powerful producers and spreaders of status value beliefs. Second, the spread and maintenance of status value beliefs have asymmetric qualities, since they are more readily acquired and enacted by those advantaged by them rather than by those disadvantaged. Because the advantaged and disadvantaged interact with one another, they mitigate the effect of this asymmetry on the overall diffusion of the status value belief. But the asymmetry does create distinctive dynamics that suggest, for instance, that when structural conditions allow, change in a given status belief will come first from those disadvantaged by it.

In suggesting that status value beliefs are created, maintained, and changed through a multilevel process, status construction theory is consistent with what three decades of research have taught us about status relations (see Wagner and Berger 1993; Ridgeway and Walker 1995 for reviews). People construct their status relations by combining and acting on the multiple shared status beliefs evoked in the situation by their characteristics and behaviors, and by contingent events. These local status relations in turn mediate the distribution of resources, the evaluation of individuals, and access to opportunities that in turn have far-reaching effects on patterns of inequality in society. Thus, status processes are always and inherently multilevel.

The image of this multilevel process offered by status construction theory has some interesting parallels with recent theories of social structure and its relationship to cultural knowledge or schemas and action (for example, Sewell 1992; Giddens 1976, 1984). Like those "dualist" theories of social structure, status structures are described in terms of both the widely shared cultural schemas people use to organize their status relations (that is, status value beliefs) and the actual behavioral and resource inequalities that result. In this case, however, status construction theory provides a more detailed and specific account of the development of these cultural schemas for status relations. Perhaps, in the process, it can suggest some general circumstances that could foster change for other structural schemas as well.

Status construction theory suggests that people create and learn the shared cultural schemas (such as status beliefs) that they use for initially defining and organizing interaction with others from structurally constrained encounters with people who are similar or different from them in socially defined ways. People carry the cultural schemas they acquire along social networks to future encounters where they are evoked by circumstances and become the basis for action. Because networks are also structurally constrained, and homophily is common on many attributes, most others that people encounter will roughly share their cultural schemas for organizing interaction. As a result, their enactment of these schemas will not be resisted or challenged by interactional events in many encounters. Perhaps, it is because of this that widely shared cultural schemas can develop at all.

However, because people have multiple socially defined characteristics, networks are multiplex. Furthermore, there are structural constraints on homophily under most circumstances. Consequently, some people in the population, some percentage of the time, must encounter others who are different from them in multiple ways that have the potential for changing the actors' cultural schemas, including status beliefs (Ridgeway and Smith-Lovin 1994). This is the situation described for doubly dissimilar encounters in status construction theory. An insight of the theory is that these multiple difference encounters are the relatively rare but crucial sites for schema change or development.

There are at least two circumstances under which such encounters have the potential for changing actors' cultural schemas. The multiple differences among the actors may evoke inconsistent cultural schemas, forcing actors to combine or integrate these schemas in order to organize interaction. In the process, the actors create an interactional order that has the potential to modify their schemas about people with the attributes evoked in the situation (Pugh and Wahrman 1983; Markovsky, Smith, and Berger 1984). A second possibility is that the multiple differences salient in the situation may evoke cultural schemas about one characteristic which shapes interaction in such a way that encourages actors to create new or transformed schemas about another attribute for which they did not have clearly developed or shared schemas. The last is the case described by status construction theory.

A central point of the theory, however, is that the long-term potential of multiple difference encounters to affect shared cultural schemas depends once again on larger structural conditions. Actors do not abandon established cultural schemas after one disconfirming experience (Rothbart and John 1986; Ridgeway, Johnson, and Diekema 1994). Neither do new, fledgling beliefs or assumptions become firm bases for action after a single experience. The pattern of confirming, nonchallenging, and disconfirming encounters brought about by structurally constrained networks will be all-important in determining whether new or changed schemas take hold for a significant number of actors and diffuse to become consensual beliefs.

Thus, once again, it is the structurally constrained pattern of networks, working together with the dynamics of encounters, that determine the development and change of the consensual cultural schemas that people use to enact the social structures through which they live their lives. By this analysis, the answer to where status beliefs come from may be the same as that for other cultural schemas for social structures: from structured networks and interaction. In this view, then, the specific processes described by status construction theory may be part of a more general multilevel process by which a variety of social structures, in their dual nature as cultural knowledge (or schemas) and distributions of resources, are enacted, maintained, or changed.

Status, Emotion, and Structural Power

Michael J. Lovaglia

The emotional reactions of individuals play a role in the complex social relationships that determine their status and power. This conclusion coalesced from a program of theory and research that attempts to integrate *status characteristics* and *expectation states* theories with theories of power in exchange networks (Lovaglia 1992, 1994, 1995). Recent work allows specification of the role played by different emotions in the creation and maintenance of individuals' status in the hierarchy of task groups (Houser and Lovaglia 1993, 1994; Lovaglia and Houser 1994, 1996). In addition, a study now under way investigates emotional reactions of high- and low-status individuals working together in face-to-face groups. Finally, an investigation of emotional reactions associated with high and low power positions in exchange networks is being designed. The goal is to link theories of power and status using emotion. This requires demonstrating that (1) during interaction power creates distinct emotions for low- and high-power actors and (2) that these emotions act on the status hierarchy of a group in specific ways. Here I summarize completed, ongoing, and planned research in this program.

The theory has developed, and each new development has been tested by empirical research. Credit for this progress should be given to the program's rocky beginning. The original theory linked power to status through a process of attribution. But hard evidence to support it has proven elusive (Lovaglia 1992, 1995). I was about to give up when serendipity intervened to launch the program as it has so much other research. In order to find an explanation for results that repeatedly failed to support the original theory, I began to observe subjects' behavior closely during the experiments. I noticed that low-power subjects became visibly upset. This led me to search out the little literature available that dealt with the effect of emotion on social structure. With Jeff Houser's help, a theory emerged that included emotion but no longer needed attribution to explain the way that power differences relate to status in task groups. This called for a series of experiments, as we had become wary of letting theoretical development outstrip the empirical base.

The following section presents the theoretical foundations of the relationship between power and status. Next is a section that reviews some literature on emotions and social structure. Then I describe the theory and the empirical results that punctuate each stage of its development.

Conceptions of Power and Status

Both terms are fundamental to sociology and are used in a wide variety of ways. Here they are arbitrarily restricted to a narrow range of meaning that allows theoretical development in the tradition of structural social psychology (Lawler, Ridgeway, and Markovsky 1993).

Exchange Theories of Power

Power-dependence theory (Emerson 1962) locates power in the relations between actors rather than within individual actors. Power, then, is a product of social structure rather than differences in individual capacity. Power results when an actor has the ability to deprive another of a desired goal, either by imposing a cost or withholding a reward. Power in exchange networks requires enduring relations among actors (Emerson 1972). Exchange consists of a series of transactions, each beneficial to actors who complete exchanges. Alternatives are the key to power in exchange networks (Emerson 1972; Cook and Emerson 1978; Cook, Emerson, Gillmore, and Yamagishi 1983). A low-power actor who finds alternative partners for profitable exchange reduces her dependence on a more powerful actor. The theory proposes that reducing dependence increases power.

Network exchange theory focuses on exclusion, the obverse of alternatives, as the key to power (Willer 1981; Markovsky, Willer, and Patton 1988; Markovsky et al. 1993). Power is identified as the ability to exclude an actor from profitable exchange. This occurs when an actor cannot find a profitable alternative. For example, if two dealers in town sell the same model, a customer for a car is in a better bargaining position than she would be if the desired car is available from only one source. The only dealer in town can charge a higher price, knowing she has the ability to exclude a customer from exchanging money for a desired car.

Power, then, is defined as the social structural capacity to acquire contested rewards. This is in keeping with definitions of power used by both power-dependence and network exchange theories.

Power exists as a capacity but can also be *used*. Molm (1990) points out that power in the absence of power use may not affect exchange outcomes. An actor may choose not to use a power advantage, or attempts to use power may be ineffective. Samuel and Zelditch (1989: 309) define power use as "the use of rewards and/or penalties to induce or coerce compliance." Power use requires that an actor attempt to dominate another.[1] In exchange research, the amount of rewards obtained in a competitive situation commonly indicates power use and, indirectly, power itself (Emerson 1962; Cook and Emerson 1978; Cook, Emerson, Gillmore, and Yamagishi 1983; Molm 1985; Markovsky, Willer, and Patton 1988).

Status Characteristics Theory

Status refers to an individual's standing in the hierarchy of a group based on the prestige, honor, and deference accorded her by other group members. *Status characteristics* are features of individuals that influence group members' beliefs about each other.[2] Such features of individuals can have different states. One state of a status characteristic is generally considered to be more desirable, esteemed, and honored than another. For example, people in some cultures consider light skin more desirable than dark skin. Skin tone is a cue to the state of the status characteristic, race. Status characteristics can be diffuse, like race, in that different states are associated with competence in a wide variety of situations. Status characteristics may also be specific, such as the ability to play chess. Chess-playing ability is associated with competence at chess but not in as many other areas of life as is race. Both diffuse and specific status characteristics are associated with expectations for competent performance. For members working together in a task group, the theory proposes that these expectations then produce a status hierarchy in which high-status members (1) are given more opportunities to perform, (2) perform more, (3) are given higher evaluations for their performances, and (4) have more influence over group decisions. A member's influence over group decisions is a frequently used indicator of status in status characteristics research (see Berger, Fisek, Norman, and Zelditch 1977; Berger, Wagner, and Zelditch 1985; Webster and Foschi 1988 for overviews).

The theory links status characteristics to observable patterns of behavior and influence using five logically related assumptions:

1. Status characteristics become *salient* to group members if they are initially defined as relevant to the task, or if group members possess different values of the characteristic. For example, the status characteristic, gender, would be considered relevant for the task of nurturing young children because women are assumed to be trained for this task while men are not. However, the theory further assumes that gender would be salient in any task group composed of both men and women.

[1] This definition may be too restrictive. It will become apparent in the section "Distinguishing Power from Status" that actors can use power without being aware they have it.

[2] This incomplete and informal description is taken from Berger, Rozenholtz, and Zelditch (1980) and Berger, Fisek, and Norman (1989). These provide a more thorough account and a formal statement of the theory. I have included only those parts of the theory useful to my thesis. See also Driskell and Webster (this volume) for a lucid exposition.

2. Salient characteristics will be used by group members to form expectations for members' competence unless those characteristics have been specifically dissociated from the task at hand. This has been called the *burden of proof* assumption because it says that actors will use all salient characteristics to form expectations unless convinced they do not apply. For example, a judge might warn a jury to disregard a witness's race when weighing her testimony. This is an attempt to dissociate the characteristic, race, from the jury's task, which is to evaluate the evidence.

3. Groups restructure interaction when a new actor joins a group according to the salience and burden of proof assumptions.

4. Actors combine all relevant status information, though they may not be aware of the process. All positive information is combined, all negative information is combined, and then these two subsets are combined to form an *aggregated expectation* state. This combining is subject to attenuation. That is, each additional piece of positive status information adds less weight to the positive subset than did the previous piece of positive status information. The same holds for negative information.

5. A group member's position in the status hierarchy of a group relative to another is a direct function of that member's aggregated expectation advantage or disadvantage relative to that other.

The process produces exceptionally stable status hierarchies. The theory accounts for the "self-fulfilling prophecy" effect. High-status members are evaluated as more competent because they are high status. This ensures they will maintain their rank in most situations, barring strategic intervention (Cohen and Roper 1985; Cohen 1993).

Distinguishing Power from Status

Power as a structural capacity is independent of the intentions and expectations of actors. For example, consider a simple exchange network in which three actors bargain for resources, A_1—B—A_2. Dashes signify potential exchange relations. Actor B can exchange with A_1 or A_2. The two A actors cannot exchange with each other. We create power in this network by restricting actors to only one possible exchange per round of bargaining. B now has power because the A actors must bid against each other for the single profitable exchange available. It is not necessary that B knows why the A actors are offering favorable exchange rates, or even that the rates offered are favorable. When B accepts terms favorable to herself at another's expense, she has used power. The structure of the network confers power on B, and a favorable exchange rate indicates that power.

Status operates quite differently. It is conferred on a member by the expectations of the group as a whole. Group members form expectations for each other's ability that combine to produce a status hierarchy. A low-power member of an

exchange network may or may not develop high expectations for the competence of a high-power member. Thus, a high-power member may or may not
attain a high rank in the status hierarchy of the group. The theory developed
here explains how the emotional reactions of group members intervene to determine whether a power advantage becomes a status advantage as well.

Emotions and Social Structure

Emotions are a subtype of affect, a global term that comprises emotion,
mood, and sentiment. Emotions are short-term evaluative states with neurophysiological components that also may have cognitive aspects (Kemper 1978; Gordon 1981; Hegtvedt 1990; Lawler 1992). Emotions are transitory positive or
negative feelings such as anger or happiness, resentment or sympathy. When social interaction triggers emotion, we call it an emotional reaction. In contrast,
moods are affective states that last longer, usually are of lower intensity, and lack
a salient antecedent cause (Forgas 1991). Sentiments are relatively enduring, usually mildly arousing, affective states such as disliking or liking toward a person
(Shelly 1993; Driskell and Webster, this volume). These three categories of affect
relate in complicated ways. For example, it is possible to have an angry emotional
reaction toward a person you like very much, but this is less apt to happen if you
are in a good mood. This section selectively reviews research on mood, sentiment, and emotional reactions that was useful in developing a theory of emotions and social structure.

Several theorists suggest ways that affect alters group processes. Collins (1984)
argues that emotional energy upholds the social structure. Isen (1987) links positive affect to increased sociability and cooperation. Lawler proposes that positive
emotions strengthen ties to collectivities. Moore and Isen (1990) suggest that
negative emotion increases the psychological distance between persons.

Ridgeway and Johnson's (1990) theory relates socioemotional behaviors to
status in groups. The theory suggests that interaction in a task group produces
emotional reactions. These emotional reactions are expressed or suppressed, depending on the status of the group member. High-status members are freer to
express negative emotion than are low-status members. Socioemotional behaviors are thought necessary for group cohesion. This theory attempts to focus on
socioemotional behavior in part because emotions themselves are difficult to
measure. Ironically, this aspect also makes the theory difficult to test. It requires
a distinction between instrumental behavior motivated by task concerns and socioemotional behavior motivated by emotional reactions. The problem develops
because interaction in task groups provides incentives to express emotions different from those felt in order to complete that task. For example, a boss may feel
considerable satisfaction in wielding her power when giving an assistant a stern
dressing-down. Meanwhile, the subordinate's ingratiating smile may mask seeth-

ing resentment. A frown can be either instrumental or socioemotional, depending on the motivation for it. These problems suggest new and potentially fruitful avenues of research. But because motivation is as difficult to measure as emotion, it is more direct to pursue a theory of emotional reactions.

Kemper's (1984) theory links emotional reactions to social structure in ways that seem consonant with the above ideas. He sees positive emotions such as loyalty, pride, and love as *integrating*. Integrating emotions typically motivate behaviors that bind groups together. Negative emotions such as anger, fear, or envy are *differentiating*. These typically motivate behaviors that push group members away from each other. George (1990) provides some correlational empirical support. She found less prosocial behavior in groups prone to negative affectivity. Groups of salespeople whose members reported more negative affect also reported being less helpful to their customers than groups whose members reported more positive affect.

Theoretical Development and Tests

The original theory linked power to status through an attribution process (Lovaglia 1992, 1994). People have a tendency to attribute acts to persons—that is, enduring characteristics of actors—rather than to situation factors in the environment (Heider 1958). This tendency has been called *correspondence bias* (Jones 1986) and the *fundamental attribution error* (Ross 1977). Attribution to the person persists even when ample evidence is present that situational factors were responsible for a person's behavior (Jones and Goethals 1971; Ross, Lepper, and Hubbard 1975). For example, we tend to doubt the competence of a person who has lost her job, even though there is evidence of an economic recession that may have triggered the layoff. However, Gilbert, Jones, and Pelham (1987) found that information about the situational cause of a power advantage can reduce correspondent inferences. Correspondence bias suggests that high power will usually increase an actor's status rank while the status of low-power actors will decrease. Power in exchange relations increases the capability of high-power actors to acquire resources and restricts that capability in low-power actors. If people have a tendency to attribute that capability to some personal talent of the high-power actor, then they may form high expectations for that actor's abilities in general. In status characteristics theory, status rank is a direct function of such expectations.

There are other good theoretical reasons to think that a power advantage might be turned to status advantage. The *reward expectations theory* (Berger, Fisek, Norman, and Wagner 1985) relates resource levels to expectations of ability using referential structures. Referential structures are commonly held beliefs in a particular culture. In the United States, for example, it is commonly believed that competent performance is rewarded. This implies that high rewards—such as those acquired through a power advantage—will likely be seen as evidence of competent performance. Expectations of competence form. These lead to higher status for the powerful. This "reverse process" has received empirical support (Harrod 1980; Bierhoff, Buck, and Klein 1986; Stewart and Moore 1992).

Analysis of evaluation/expectation states theory provides another mechanism by which a power difference may produce a corresponding status difference. This theory (Berger, Conner, and McKeown 1974; Berger and Conner 1974; Fisek, Berger, and Norman 1991) explains how status hierarchies emerge in groups of status equals. The theory assumes that differences in performance expectations develop from differences in acceptance rates for performance outputs. (A performance output is a problem-solving attempt by a group member.) Thus, the theory predicts that when a group regularly accepts the ideas of a member, that member's status increases. An individual's role in the group is seen as an external factor that contributes to the emergence of differences in group evaluations of individual performance outputs. Moore (1985) tested the theory by placing subjects in the role of a person rejecting the performance of a partner while accepting and staying with her or his own performance. Then in the second phase of the study, subjects did in fact reject the influence of the partner more often than did subjects who had not been placed in the role. This relates to power because in many situations, a position of power affects the rate at which performance outputs are accepted. For example, in an exchange situation where a high-power position with several alternative partners seeks to exchange with a low-power position who has no alternative, an offer by the high-power position to the low-power position is more likely to be accepted than an offer by the low-power position to the high. In the theory, accepting another's offer is a reward action that signifies a positive evaluation of the performance output. When this pattern of acceptance is repeated over time, the high-power actor is effectively placed in the role of a high-status actor.

Ridgeway's (1990) resource expectations theory can also be used to connect power and status. She argues that resources, such as those accumulated by the powerful, can be used to further group goals. They represent competence to achieve goals that require these resources. This produces more general expectations that lead to higher status rank for those who have used their power to amass resources.

A Test of the Attributional Hypothesis

I devised an experimental situation that should have been capable of detecting the proposed effects of attributions (Lovaglia 1992, 1994). To manipulate power, I placed undergraduate subjects in either high- or low-power positions in an exchange network. The exchange rate was manipulated such that high-power subjects had a bargaining advantage that allowed them to acquire more money than a low-power partner. Low-power subjects made considerably less than a high-power partner. The role of the partner was played by a computer program in an experimental situation similar to that used by Cook and Emerson (1978).

Following attribution theory, I assumed subjects would attribute reward levels to the personal competence of themselves and their partner. Then in an attempt to reduce such attributions, I informed half the subjects that their position in the power structure and their reward levels were determined entirely by chance. This should have induced subjects to attribute reward differentials to the bargaining situation rather than to the competence of bargainers.

The dependent variable for the study was a subject's resistance to the influence attempts of the partner. Following the bargaining, subjects engaged in a "Contrast Sensitivity" test, a standardized experimental setting used in status characteristics research (Berger, Fisek, Norman, and Zelditch 1977). No power differences existed between subject and partner at this point in the study. Both benefited equally by getting the correct answer. Subjects engaged in twenty trials of a binary choice test where they were told their partner disagreed with their decision. They then had the opportunity to change their mind to agree with their partner or stay with their original decision. The proportion of trials in which a subject stayed with his original decision was the dependent measure of resistance to influence, $P(s)$.[3]

The study is a 2×2 factorial design. Two levels of power (high reward and low reward) crossed with two levels of attribution to the person (no situational knowledge and situational knowledge). Using analysis of variance, I predicted a main effect of power and an interaction effect of situational knowledge and power on the dependent variable, $P(s)$. Resistance to influence should decrease when high-power subjects have knowledge that their reward advantage is the result of luck. The resistance to influence of low-power subjects should increase when they have this knowledge.

Table 1(a) shows that no differences in $P(s)$ levels occurred between any of the conditions. This happened despite subjects' common reports that the high-power partner was more competent and the low-power partner was less competent than subjects at bargaining. During the study, I noticed that low-power subjects were emotionally involved during bargaining. Joseph Berger suggested to me that this might be a factor increasing their resistance to influence. The study included subjects' semantic differential ratings of their partners on seven-point scales including items such as pleasant-unpleasant, likable-unlikable, and modest-egotistical. I combined these into a scale that served as a rough indicator of a subject's negative emotional reaction to the partner. Table 1(b) shows the

---

[3] Men were used in this study primarily because more men than women were available in the subject pool at the time. No effect of gender was expected.

TABLE 1

Power, Knowledge, and Influence

(a) Behavioral Measure of Influence, P(s): Means by Condition

	Low power– no knowledge	Low power– knowledge	High power knowledge	High power– no knowledge	Total
P(s)	.54	.55	.58	.56	.56
SD	(.14)	(.17)	(.17)	(.18)	(.16)
N	13	13	13	13	52

(b) Logistic Regression Model of Influence Behavior with CHOICE to Stay or Change as Dependent Variable Controlling for Emotional Reaction, REACT

Variable	B	S.E.	*p*
POWER	.26	.07	.00
KNOW	−.07	.09	.44
REACT	1.04	.23	.00
POWER X KNOW	−.01	.06	.97
Constant	.41	.08	.00

Goodness of fit Chi Square   1038.48, df (1035), $p = .46$

results of a reanalysis of the data with emotional reactions statistically controlled using the REACT scale. Power now has a clear effect.[4] High-power actors resist influence more often than low-power actors. The REACT scale also has a significant effect. However, KNOW and the interaction term, KNOW × POWER, show no effect. Whether subjects knew the difference in rewards was due to chance made no difference in their resistance to influence. That is, attribution to situation versus attribution to person seemed to have no effect on the behavior of subjects.

The reanalysis demonstrated an interesting correlation between negative emotional reactions and resistance to influence. It further suggested that power differences may in fact produce status differences when emotional reactions are controlled. Testing these ideas requires a modest research program. To demonstrate the relationship between power and status, as well as the possible role of emotion in that relationship, requires a series of studies where emotion is experimentally rather than statistically controlled. Power differences must be shown to produce specific emotional reactions, and the effect of these emotional reactions on status processes must be determined.

[4]Following Balkwell (1991a) I used a logistic regression model to test hypotheses. This avoids problems caused by violated assumptions when using analysis of variance. For this paper I replicated all logistic regression analyses using ANOVA. In all cases, results point unequivocally to the same conclusions.

A Theory of Emotional Reactions and Social Structure

The first big problem in studying emotions is categorization. How do we specify which of the bewildering array of emotions a person will feel? Dichotomizing emotional reactions as positive or negative helps. People probably feel constellations of related emotions rather than one in particular (Polivy 1981). For example, this makes it difficult to separate fear from anger or sadness. However, it less likely that a person will feel joy and anger simultaneously.

Theoretical work on the emotional reactions produced by power differences has been deferred primarily because it seems relatively straightforward. Individuals in high-power positions probably have more positive emotional reactions during group interaction than do individuals in low-power positions. Houser and Lovaglia (1993; Lovaglia and Houser 1996) began by investigating the effects of emotional reactions on status processes.

We used Kemper's distinction between integrating and differentiating emotions to explain how typical emotional reactions of group members reinforce the status hierarchy of a task group. We assume that interactions among group members typically produce positive, integrating emotional reactions in high-status members. This follows from status characteristics theory. High-status members are given more opportunities to perform and perform more often than low-status members. High-status members receive higher evaluations for their performances, and they have greater influence over group decisions than do low-status members. Thus, high-status members will likely feel happier and more satisfied than low-status members. This motivates them to engage in integrating behaviors that bind the group together. We say that high status is *compatible* with positive, integrating emotions. However, low-status members who receive little opportunity to perform, seldom perform, receive low evaluations for their performances, and have little influence on group decisions will typically feel more anger, disappointment, and resentment than will high-status members. Thus, they would be motivated to engage in differentiating behaviors that increase the distance between group members. We say that low status is *compatible* with negative, differentiating emotions. Empirical work by Kemper (1991) and Smith and Kluegel (1982) supports the idea that status rank promotes such compatible emotional responses.

Houser and Lovaglia (1993) proposed that compatible emotions decrease status differences in task groups. When high-status members feel positive emotions, they should respond with attempts to bind low-status members to the group. These responses likely include giving low-status members more opportunities to perform, giving those performances higher evaluations, and giving low-status members more influence over group decisions than they otherwise would. Status characteristics theory proposes that these behaviors determine the status hierarchy. Thus, responses to compatible emotions by high-status members increase the status of low-status members. When low-status members feel negative emotions, they likely respond by distancing themselves from high-status members. Responses may include refusing to give high-status members opportunities to perform, negatively evaluating those performances, and resisting their influence. Thus, compatible emotions of low-status members decrease the status of high-status members. The overall result would be a less stratified group. Status rank would remain unchanged, but the gap between high- and low-status members would be reduced.

Research on sentiments and moods is consistent with these ideas. Shelly (1993) induced sentiments in experimental subjects (mild liking or disliking). Group members who were liked participated more than members who were disliked. In addition, research on the effects of moods in social interaction identifies a wide range of mood-congruent social judgments (Bower 1991; Forgas and Bower 1987, 1988; Mackie and Worth 1991; Schwarz, Bless, and Bohner 1991). For example, Baron (1987) placed interviewers in either a positive or a negative mood by giving them positive or negative feedback on a task they performed. Interviewers in a negative mood evaluated job applicants more negatively than did interviewers in a positive mood. This suggests that mood alters expectations for competence.

The proposition that compatible emotional reactions decrease status differences in task groups rests on three assumptions connecting emotional reactions to three assumptions of status characteristics theory. (See the section "Conceptions of Power and Status," above.) (Assumption 1) Salience: Emotional reactions are salient if they occur during or immediately preceding group interaction. (Assumption 2) Burden of proof: Emotional reactions are relevant unless they have been specifically dissociated from the task. (Assumption 4) Aggregation: Relevant emotional reactions combine with other status information to form aggregated performance expectations according to the attenuation principle of status characteristics theory. When a group member's emotions are compatible with status, their effect on performance expectations for a partner is opposite to the relative status held by the partner. For example, negative emotion is compatible with low status; it has the effect of decreasing a low-status member's performance expectations for a high-status partner. When emotions are incompatible with status, their effect on performance expectations is in the same direction as the status held by the partner. For example, positive emotion is incompatible with low status; it has the effect of increasing the performance expectations of a low-status member for a high-status partner. Once the effects of emotional reactions have been included in aggregated performance expectations, the fifth assumption of status characteristics follows: Status rank is a direct function of aggregated performance expectations.

The combined effect of compatible emotional responses of high-status and low-status members decreases differences in status among group members. How-

ever, in a task situation, the self-fulfilling nature of the status characteristics process continues to stratify the group. The effects of the compatible emotions
process and the status characteristics process oppose each other. This is what
produces stable status hierarchies noted for their remarkable resistance to change.

Testing Emotional Effects on Status Processes

Several testable hypotheses are apparent from the theory. The first hypothesis
predicts that subjects who experience negative emotion will have higher resistance to influence, P(s), than will subjects who experience positive emotion
(Lovaglia and Houser 1996). Testing this hypothesis requires that we induce
positive or negative emotion in groups of subjects and then measure their resistance to influence. Resistance of the positive emotion group should be lower
than that of the negative emotion group. A second hypothesis predicts that effects of emotional reactions will combine with effects of status characteristics to
determine P(s). Both hypotheses were tested in a single experiment using a 2 ×
2 factorial design. Two levels of emotion (positive and negative) were crossed
with two levels of status characteristics (high and low). Then P(s) was measured
as before and results among the four conditions were compared. In addition, two
baseline conditions calibrated the effectiveness of the status manipulation.

Subjects were 159 freshman women. Data from 9 subjects (6 percent) were
discarded for subjects who failed to meet the requirements of the study, according to the conservative guidelines in Moore (1985). This left data from 150 subjects to be analyzed, 25 in each condition.

Emotion was manipulated using a reciprocal gift exchange setting that proved
effective. Subjects were asked to choose from among five gifts to give to their
(fictitious) partner. They were told the cost of the gift sent would be deducted
from their pay at the end of the study. They expected that their partner would
reciprocate. To induce positive emotion, the partner reciprocated a flower in an
attractive vase. To induce negative emotion, subjects received no gift from their
partner. Status characteristics were manipulated by giving subjects personal information about their partner's age and education. Freshman women possessed
low status characteristics when their partner was presented as a graduate student,
a 26-year-old woman doing biomedical research. Subjects possessed high status
characteristics when their partner was presented as a 16-year-old high school girl.

Table 2(a) and (b) shows the results of this experiment. The first hypothesis
predicted a main effect of emotional reaction. Resistance to influence in negative
emotion conditions should be higher than in positive emotion conditions. This
was supported (B = −.21, p < .01). If emotional reactions combine with status
characteristics information as predicted by status characteristics theory, there
should also be a main effect of status characteristics on P(s). This was not the case
(B = .09, p = .16). Lovaglia and Houser (1996) concluded that emotions do
have effects on status processes in the predicted direction. However, the experi-

TABLE 2

Status, Emotion, and Influence

(a) Behavioral Measure of Influence, P(s): Means by Condition

	Low status characteristics		High status characteristics	
	Positive emotion	Negative emotion	Positive emotion	Negative emotion
P(s)	.50	.62	.54	.65
SD	(.14)	(.19)	(.20)	(.17)
N	25	25	25	25

(b) Logistic Regression Model of Influence Behavior with CHOICE to Stay or Change as Dependent Variable

Variable	B	S.E.	p
EMOTION	−.21	.06	<.00
STATCHAR	.09	.06	.16
EMOTION X STATCHAR	.08	.18	.65
Constant	.30	.06	<.00

Goodness of fit Chi Square   1999.99, df (1996), $p < .01$

ment left doubt as to whether emotional reactions combine with other status information or eliminate other status information.

The question of whether effects of status characteristics can be eliminated in some situations is an important one (Freese and Cohen 1973). However, there is another, perhaps more plausible, explanation for the lack of a status characteristics effect. The manipulation of status characteristics may have been weak. This would produce the differences found in the predicted direction that were too small to reach statistical significance. Lovaglia and Houser (1996) designed a second experiment in which the effect of status characteristics would be larger. If this produced main effects for both emotions and status characteristics, then we could conclude that the lack of significance was in fact due to a weak manipulation in the previous experiment. This would support the hypothesis that effects of emotions combine with effects of status characteristics.

The previous study was replicated, with the following changes. To manipulate status characteristics, we used the same partners as in the previous experiment, but with two additions. First, we included high school grade point average in the personal information given to subjects. Low-status subjects had a high-status partner with an A grade average. High-status subjects had a low-status partner with a D+ average. We also included five trials of a "Spatial Judgment" task similar to "Contrast Sensitivity." Low-status subjects were told they did poorly on this task. High-status subjects were told their performance was supe-

TABLE 3

Status, Emotion, and Influence: Replication

(a) Behavioral Measure of Influence, P(s): Means by Condition for Strengthened Status Characteristics Manipulation

	Low status characteristics		High status characteristics	
	Positive emotion	Negative emotion	Positive emotion	Negative emotion
P(s)	.23	.49	.59	.70
SD	(.17)	(.10)	(.16)	(.10)
N	10	10	10	10

(b) Logistic Regression Model of Influence Behavior with CHOICE to Stay or Change as Dependent Variable for Strengthened Status Characteristics Manipulation

Variable	B	S.E.	p
EMOTION	−.24	.06	.02
STATCHAR	.78	.06	<.01
EMOTION X STATCHAR	.68	.18	.02
Constant	−.18	.06	.11

Goodness of fit Chi Square   800.00, df (796), p = .45

rior. Subjects were 42 freshman women. Data from 2 subjects were excluded for failing to meet the conditions of the study. This left data from 40 subjects to be analyzed, 10 in each of four conditions.

Table 3(a) and (b) shows that with a strengthened status characteristics manipulation, status characteristics and emotion have independent effects on subjects' resistance to influence, P(s). The effect of status characteristics is very strong (B = .78, p < .01). The effect of emotion is also strong (B = −.24, p = .02). Lovaglia and Houser (1996) concluded that these results support the assumption that effects of emotion combine with effects of other status information according to the aggregation assumption of status characteristics theory. However, the significant effect of the interaction term suggests that the exact way in which emotions combine with status information may require a closer look.

Inducing Emotion without Exchanging Gifts

Inducing emotion through gift exchange is a complex process by experimental standards (Lovaglia and Houser 1996). The objection was raised that some unknown aspect of the exchange situation other than emotion may have caused the results in the previous two experiments. One way to answer this objection is a partial replication that induces emotion in subjects in some other way—that is, without gift exchange. This presented a problem for the original theory. Houser and Lovaglia (1993) proposed that emotional reactions must be directed at a group member to alter behavior in task groups. Negative emotion in general might not be effective. However, just as the effects of status characteristics generalize to other settings and other actors, so might negative emotion from some other source generalize to group members. Theoretically, generalization weakens the effect of status characteristics. Thus, we can expect differences in behavior between subjects feeling general positive or negative emotion to be less dramatic than in the gift exchange setting. There, subjects were angry at their partner who failed to reciprocate, or happy with their partner who gave them a flower. Nonetheless, it might still be possible to find an effect of emotion not directed at a group member.

One reliable way to induce positive emotion is to give subjects an unexpected gift without requiring reciprocation (Isen, Clark, and Schwartz 1976; Isen and Simmonds 1978; Worth and Mackie 1987; Moore and Isen 1990). Lovaglia and Houser (1996) changed the design of the previous study so that the research assistant gave subjects the flower at the beginning of the study. It was presented in appreciation for their help with the research.

Inducing negative emotion is a more difficult problem. Lovaglia and Houser (1996) used the manipulation described by Wiggins and Heise (1988).[5] Subjects were asked to fill in an "Administrative Questionnaire" before the study began, using a bubble-in test blank, the type used for most multiple choice tests. The research assistant handed subjects the test blank and a pen to fill it out. Subjects usually asked, "Shouldn't I use pencil?" The research assistant responded, "Just fill it out," and then left the room. After subjects completed the questionnaire in pen, a confederate entered the room in the role of an officious administrative assistant. The confederate said, "Oh bother! Don't you students know you are supposed to fill these out in PENCIL?" Chastizing subjects for following instructions reliably produced negative emotional reactions.

All subjects possessed low-status characteristics for this replication because we were only interested in whether a different emotion manipulation would have effects similar to gift exchange. Subjects were 43 freshman women. Data from 3 were discarded (6 percent) for failing to meet the conditions of the experiment. This left 20 subjects in a positive emotion condition and 20 in a negative emotion condition. As before, resistance to influence, P(s), was the dependent measure.

A simple *t*-test is sufficient to test the hypothesis that subjects in the negative emotion condition will have higher P(s) than subjects in the positive emotion condition. Mean P(s) for negative emotion subjects was .41, SD = .18. Mean P(s) for positive emotion subjects was .30, SD = .15. The mean for the negative emotion condition is significantly higher than the mean for the positive emotion condition, t(38) 2.08, p = .02, one tailed.[6] This supports the hypothesis. Lovaglia

[5] I would like to thank Lynn Smith-Lovin for suggesting this very effective experimental design.
[6] This analysis was replicated using the nonparametric, Mann Whitney U test. Results pointed unequivocally to the same conclusion.

and Houser (1996) conclude that emotion—and not some other aspect of an exchange relation—produced changes in resistance to influence in this series of experiments.

Comparing these means with the low-status conditions of Table 3(a), notice that negative emotion subjects were less resistant to influence than they were in the previous experiment. Also notice that positive emotion subjects were more resistant to influence than in the previous experiment. Because of this, the difference between positive and negative emotion conditions is not as large as it was in the previous experiment. This supports the idea that generalization weakens the effect of emotion on status processes just as it weakens the effect of status characteristics. Overall evidence to this point suggests that emotion acts very much like status characteristics do in organizing behavior in task groups.

Emotion and Status in Face-to-Face Groups

Another proposal from the theory has been investigated (Lucas, Wynn, and Vogt 1995). The theory proposes that during the course of interaction on a task, high-status group members will feel more positive emotion while low-status group members will feel more negative emotion. This proposition follows from the idea that high-status members are getting more opportunities to perform and are getting high evaluations for their performances. This preferential treatment seems likely to produce positive emotions. On the other hand, low-status members, whose input is ignored or given poor evaluations by the group, would likely feel negative emotion. Nonetheless, the point requires experimental test. It can be argued that more responsibility is given to high-status members and this can weigh heavily on them. The burdens of leadership can cause stress and a negative mood. For example, it is common to hear the high rates of suicide and depression among doctors attributed to the responsibilities of their high-status profession.

Lucas, Wynn, and Vogt (1995) tested the hypothesis that during group interaction on a task, a high-status leader would feel more positive emotion during group interaction than would other, lower-status group members. This test required a quite different experimental setting than had previously been used. Laboratory experiments are used to manipulate status characteristics because subjects cannot be randomly assigned a gender or race or level of education in face-to-face task groups. The use of confederates and bogus information makes possible the random assignment to a high- or low-status condition. But the isolation of laboratory experiments severely restricts group interaction. To test the hypothesis that high-status members will feel more positive emotion in the course of normal group interaction requires a face-to-face group where members can interact freely.

Lucas, Wynn, and Vogt (1995) used 254 subjects from eight discussion sections of an introductory sociology class and one section of an introductory social psychology class at the University of Iowa. Subjects were randomly assigned to groups of four to six members. Each group was given a "Meaning Insight" test. This test requires subjects to match words from arcane languages to a common English word. They were told that research has found this ability (in fact, fictitious) to be related to a talent for facilitating group interaction, and that those who do well on the test are potentially good leaders. One person in each group was randomly assigned a score of 14 or more out of 20, a superior score. Other group members were randomly assigned scores between 4 and 10, below average to average. The person who scored above 14 was appointed leader of the group because of her or his leadership potential. Thus, one group member was randomly raised to the status of leader, and expectations for competence were formed by her or his performance on the "Meaning Insight" test.

Group members then interacted for about twenty minutes on a task. They made decisions about planning and expenditures for an "annual company banquet for a medium-sized electronics firm in Silicone Valley, California." They were given information about budgetary and political constraints involved in their decisions. They were told that consensus was important, that there was one correct way to plan this event, and that their group would be evaluated on how close their decisions came to the correct ones. They were also told that their scores would be boosted by 10 percent if they achieved consensus on their decisions. The leader's role was no different from that of other group members except that she or he was supposed to "facilitate consensus." If consensus was not reached in a few minutes on a particular decision, the leader was to go with the majority decision.

Emotion was measured with a self-report post-test questionnaire. Subjects were asked to rate on a ten-point scale how they felt during group interaction. Anchors for scale items included Extremely happy–Extremely unhappy, Extremely angry–Not angry at all, and so on, for the emotions Anxious, Frustrated, Guilty, Dissatisfied, Disappointed, and Resentful. The items were combined for analysis into a positive emotion scale. The scale ranged from 0, very negative emotion, to 10, very positive emotion.

Table 4 gives the results of a regression analysis with POSEMOT, the positive emotion scale, as dependent variable. Note the regression coefficient for DLEADER, the dummy variable for leadership position (Leader = 1, Other group member = 0) is positive and significant, p = .01. Lucas, Wynn, and Vogt conclude that the hypothesis is supported. Subjects randomly assigned to a high-status leadership position did report more positive emotion during interaction on a task than did group members assigned to a lower-status position.

The regression coefficient for the dummy variable, DFEMALE (0 = male, 1 = female) is also positive and significant (p < .01). This finding suggests that women subjects reported more positive emotions during group interaction than did men. This is interesting because female is considered the low state of the

TABLE 4

Regression Coefficients Testing the Effect of Leadership Position on Positive Emotion

(N = 252)

Variable	B	S.E.	p
DLEADER	.57	.22	.01
AGE	.03	.07	.62
DFEMALE	.78	.19	$<.01$
YEAR IN SCHOOL	−.23	.13	.07
Constant	7.26	1.15	$<.00$

R^2 .109

status characteristic gender in most task situations. Yet women report more positive emotional reactions than do men. How can this finding be explained in light of the finding that high status leads to more positive emotional reactions? There are several possible explanations. Recall Ridgeway and Johnson's (1990) theory. Women may be constrained from expressing negative emotion. Much has been written about how women in this society are socialized not to express negative emotions. It is also possible that the gender of the leader has an effect. Men may react negatively to working in a group led by a woman, but women do not. These findings demonstrate how important random assignment is to theoretical tests. Sex is a diffuse status characteristic. Had Lucas, Wynn, and Vogt (1995) used gender as an independent variable, they might well have reached the erroneous conclusion that low status produces positive emotion during interaction in task groups. Just the opposite, however, this study provides strong evidence in support of the theory: having high status in a group results in more positive emotion than does having low status.

Conclusion: Work Planned and in Progress

This program of research has made progress in determining the relationship between power and status. Emotions play a role in this relationship. Results of several studies suggest that negative emotional reactions decrease performance expectations individuals have for other group members. Positive emotional reactions increase such performance expectations. If, as the theory proposes, being in a low-power position in an exchange relationship produces negative emotion while being in a high-power position produces positive emotion, the theoretical connection between power and status will be made.

The emotions and status project has taken on something of a life of its own. Houser and Lovaglia (1994) are developing Houser's ideas on emotion and group solidarity. This comes from Kemper's conception of positive emotions as integrating and negative emotions as differentiating. Do positive emotions act to increase group solidarity? An experiment is being designed that allows a direct answer to this question. We will first manipulate emotion in subjects who then participate in a group task. We will interrupt the task and find out how much money it would take to pry members from the group they are currently in. The money required to pry members from a group is a good indicator of group solidarity.

More work is planned using face-to-face groups. Groups similar to the ones described above will interact in a mock-jury task. This should generate more involvement, commitment, and negative emotion in group members than the previous "corporation committee" task did. It will also be possible to use synopses of real cases with known outcomes. This will allow a test of the effectiveness of group work.

Finally, we return to the question that started the program. What is the relationship between power and status? We have gone some way toward demonstrating that power differences do in fact create status differences in group interaction. This can occur through any or all of several proposed mechanisms: (1) In reward expectations theory (Berger, Fisek, Norman, and Wagner 1985), rewards that result from power use symbolize competence and increase status. (2) In evaluation/expectation states theory (Berger, Conner, and McKeown 1974), powerful actors engage in high-status role behavior that increases expectations for their ability, thus increasing their status. (3) Ridgeway's (1990) resource expectations theory suggests that because resources can be used to accomplish some group goals, general expectations of competence and higher status accrue to members whose power allows them to control resources. More research is needed to sort out how these various processes contribute to the relationship between power and status.

Emotions can intervene to impede the process that converts power to status. Lovaglia and Houser (1996) demonstrate that negative emotion increases resistance to influence and that positive emotion reduces it. This has known effects on the creation and maintenance of status orders in groups. When group members' performance expectations for an actor increase, this increases the influence that actor has, and that actor's status in the group increases as well. Left to demonstrate is the theoretical prediction that being in a low-power position induces negative emotion while being in a high-power position induces positive emotion.

In designing an experiment to investigate the emotions produced by power differences in exchange networks, I came upon an interesting idea now called the "Honest Car Dealer" problem. Some bargaining situations produce stronger emotions than others. And it occurred to me that this could be detrimental to the ethics of businesspeople. Suppose there are two car dealers. One tries to be as honest and fair as possible. Immediately after a short haggle, she offers all customers the lowest price she can afford to take for the car. After haggling, the second car dealer says he has offered the best price, but he is not being honest.

He always keeps a cushion of five hundred dollars between what he says is his best price and the amount he is willing to accept. The research question is, which car dealer makes more money and which has happier customers? The dishonest car dealer will probably make more money, not just because he may get a better price for a car, but because he may make more sales. In addition, and this is surprising, I believe his customers will be happier.

The reason that a dishonest car dealer may have happier customers stems from the process of bargaining. What is the likely response to a car dealer who offers you her last, best price? It seems that most customers would counter with an offer a few hundred dollars lower. If the car dealer has been honest, she must stubbornly refuse this offer. She cannot afford to accept it. She appears obstinate and unhelpful. Many customers likely leave frustrated. When those customers get to dealer number two, the bargaining process repeats itself. (Seldom do customers get the chance to bargain with two dealers over exactly the same car.) But when the dealer makes his final offer and the customer comes back a few hundred dollars lower, the dishonest dealer reluctantly accepts. The customer feels she got a great deal, and the dealer makes a sale and a profit. Meanwhile, the honest car dealer goes slowly out of business.

These ideas can be tested using a computerized exchange partner. Subjects will bargain in either high- or low-power positions. That is, they will have a structural advantage or disadvantage that allows them to make either more or less than their partners. In addition, the computerized partner will either honestly inform her partner of the best offer she is willing to make, or she will claim she has made her best offer when she will really accept somewhat less. Subject and partner will bargain over twenty rounds for a total of perhaps twenty dollars in potential profit. Then we can measure emotions in a post-test as before. Will we find that low-power bargainers report more negative emotion? It seems likely, but anything can happen in a laboratory. Will more exchanges be made by the dishonest computer partner? Will subjects who exchange with the dishonest computer partner be happier? I will let you know.

Status and Sentiment in Task Groups

◥◣

James E. Driskell and Murray Webster, Jr.

Several decades of theory building and empirical research have developed a well-elaborated understanding of ways in which status characteristics affect interpersonal behavior. As a result of this sustained program of research, (1) we possess rigorous definitions of diffuse and specific status characteristics; (2) we know scope and interaction conditions that lead to status generalization, and details of how the process occurs; (3) it is possible to predict precisely the effects of any combination of status characteristics for certain situations; and (4) several successful interventions have been designed to control aspects of status generalization in natural settings.[1]

This body of knowledge has come about through abstractly formulating questions, testing and extending theoretical propositions, modifying propositions in light of evidence, and incorporating them into the logical structure of theories of status characteristics and social behavior. In this paper, we report results of first investigations to extend the propositions of status characteristics theory in a new direction; namely, to integrate a second social process, *sentiment*, or liking/disliking, with effects of status generalization. Our investigations include theoretical extension and empirical evidence.

Sentiment processes, like status processes, are very common in face-to-face behavior. Liking and disliking emerge in virtually every case of ongoing interaction, including some that are very brief. Sometimes the sentiment is weak, sometimes powerful; and it may change, strengthen, or attenuate as interaction continues. As status generalization may lead to enduring relations of power, prestige, and authority in groups, sentiment processes can lead to favoritism, friendship cliques, feuds, lifelong friendships, and enduring enmity. However, unlike status generalization, the actual processes of sentiment formation and develop-

[1] For summaries of this research program, please see Webster and Foschi (1988), and Berger and Zelditch (1993). Research directly related to the work presented here is reported in Berger, Wagner, and Zelditch (1985); Berger, Fisek, Norman, and Zelditch (1977); Driskell (1982); Driskell and Mullen (1988); Webster and Sobieszek (1974); and Webster and Driskell (1978, 1983).

ment are understood only anecdotally, and few investigators have gone beyond statements such as those above when they describe it. In this paper, we offer some leads for developing greater understanding of the processes of sentiment development.

The starting point of our investigation is a *similarity of behavioral outcome*. One of the most sensitive and reliable measures of status generalization in many situations has been *acceptance or rejection of influence in case of disagreement*. Indeed, this measure has become the standard dependent variable in laboratory experiments designed to test extensions of theories of status generalization (see Berger, Fisek, Norman, and Zelditch 1977; Webster and Foschi 1988; Wagner and Berger 1993). Across a wide variety of empirical situations and with a range of subject populations (including male and female high school and college students, military personnel, civilian adults, and individuals from many different ethnic backgrounds), the influence measure has been robust. People in relatively low status positions defer to people in relatively high status positions more often than vice versa.

That same effect sometimes occurs as the result of sentiment. Some studies suggest that people defer more to those they like than to those they dislike. Moreover, this effect occurs under (at least) the same scope conditions as status generalization. Status generalization occurs under scope conditions of task orientation and collective orientation of actors. That is, we reject influence from those we dislike or accept influence from those we like when we are both task oriented and collectively oriented—and, no doubt, under other conditions as well. Similarity of effect is the starting point for our efforts to develop theoretical understanding of how sentiment functions in interpersonal behavior. We expect that sentiment processes can occur under the status generalization scope conditions of task and collective orientation.

We begin with the theory of status characteristics and expectation states, describe some similarities between outcomes of that process and outcomes of sentiment, and ask how to conceptualize the combined effects of sentiment and status. A primary question is whether to conceive sentiment and status as distinct theoretical processes, or whether sentiment effects have important similarities to status effects. We describe a preliminary experiment designed to differentiate predictions from two variant approaches, and follow that with abstract generalizations on sentiment and status. Next we describe and analyze an experimental test of our ideas on how sentiment and status function to affect behavior in face-to-face interaction. We conclude with a review of what is known as the result of this work and with suggestions for further theoretical and empirical research.

Theoretical Development

Chart 1 shows a version of a theory of status generalization, based upon one or more status characteristics.

CHART 1

The Theory of Status Characteristics and Social Interaction

Given:

Actors p (person) and $o_1 - o_n$ (others); a task T with outcome states T+ (success) and T− (failure); and a specific ability C* that is relevant to T, such that C*+ is linked to T+ and C*− is linked to T−:

Definition 1: C is a *specific status characteristic* iff:

(a) there are at least two states of C, C+ and C− that are differentially evaluated; and

(b) with every state of C there are associated specific performance expectations.

Definition 2: D is a *diffuse status characteristic* iff:

(a) there are at least two states of D, D+ and D− that are differentially evaluated;

(b) with every state of D there are associated specific performance expectations; and

(c) with every state of D there are associated general performance expectations without limit as to scope.

Assumption 1 (Salience):

All D or C characteristics that are already considered by the actor p to be linked to outcome states of T become salient in the situation, and all D or C characteristics that discriminate between actors also will become salient.

Assumption 2 (Burden of Proof):

If any D or C characteristic is salient, then (1) for each D, the associated general expectation state Γ will also become salient and will become relevant to a similarly evaluated state of C*; and (2) for each C, the relevant task outcome state τ will become salient, and τ will become relevant to a similarly evaluated state of abstract task ability Y, and Y will become relevant to the similarly evaluated outcome state of T.

Assumption 3 (Sequencing):

A structure of status characteristics and expectation states will become fully connected through the salience and burden of proof processes as described. If actors leave or enter the situation after it has been completed, new connections will appear according to the same processes, and all parts of the structure previously completed will remain in subsequent interaction.

Assumption 4 (Aggregation):

If an actor p is connected to outcome states T+ and T− in a completed structure, then p's aggregated expectations e_p may be represented by:

$$e_{p+} = [1 - (1 - f(i)) \ldots (1 - f(n))];$$
$$e_{p-} = -[1 - (1 - f(i)) \ldots (1 - f(n))]; \text{ and}$$
$$e_p = e_{p+} + e_{p-}.$$

Assumption 5 (Behavior):

Once p has formed aggregated expectation states for self and other, p's power and prestige position relative to o will be a direct function of p's expectation advantage over o $(e_p - e_o)$ in this situation.

Adapted from Webster and Foschi 1988.

Status generalization processes occur under two general scope conditions, task orientation and collective orientation. Task orientation means that individuals are *primarily motivated by the prospect of solving some problem(s)*, rather than primarily oriented to benefits of the interaction process itself. People in a committee or a classroom usually are task oriented; people at a social gathering, usually less so. Collective orientation means that individuals view their task as a *team task*, one in which it is legitimate and necessary to consider each individual's suggestions. The outcome, thus, is success or failure for the group, not for certain individuals in the group. Members of a basketball team or a jury are collectively oriented; individuals competing at a computer game are not.

In status generalization, the first assumption of the theory says that, given the scope conditions of task orientation and collective orientation, individuals may *activate* status characteristics; that is, status characteristics may become important facts about individuals' identities in their immediate interaction. Activated status characteristics then function to affect performance expectation states, through a *burden of proof* process (assumption 2). That is, without clear, convincing evidence that the status characteristics are *not* relevant, actors behave *as if* they were relevant. They form specific performance expectations consistent with the societal evaluations of their status characteristics: high expectations for individuals displaying highly evaluated status characteristics, and low expectations for individuals displaying disfavored characteristics.

The third assumption says that if individuals enter or leave the interaction situation, status effects are preserved, and they cumulate. Every interaction is affected not only by the status information immediately present but also by status characteristics of individuals who were present earlier and who have departed (as long as the focal actor p remains in the situation). This feature of the theory has been important in developing interventions. It predicts, for instance, that a man who has had contact with a highly competent woman will later display effects of the earlier interaction (for example, higher expectations for women's performance) when he meets a second woman.[2]

The fourth assumption describes how activated status information is combined in reaching aggregate expectations for each actor. In most cases, all activated status information will function in a burden of proof process. Thus, the resulting performance expectation states reflect all activated status characteristics; none is eliminated, and none becomes a "master status," so important that everything else is ignored. Assumption 4 incorporates an "attenuation effect" and an "inconsistency effect." The attenuation effect is that when one or more status characteristics have become salient and all possess the same valence (positive or negative), adding one more consistently valued status element has less incremental effect than it would by itself.[3] The inconsistency effect is that when a new

---

[2] For data on this issue, please see Pugh and Wahrman (1983).

[3] The attenuation and inconsistency effects are comparable to the economic principle of diminishing marginal utility and to the psychological principle of reward satiation.

Observable Initial Conditions:	Unobservable Theoretical Construct:	Observable Behavioral Outcome:

| Distribution of Status Elements | → | Performance Expectation States | → | Power and Prestige Behaviors (e.g., influence rejection) |

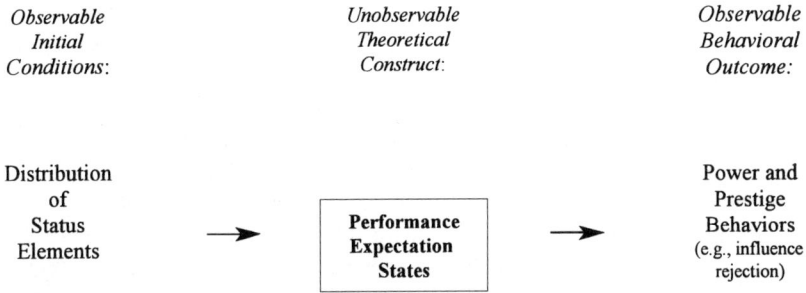

Fig. 1. The process of status generalization

status element appears having a different valence from already salient statuses, the new element has greater effect than it would by itself. (Please see Webster and Foschi 1988: 11–12 for more detailed exposition of the attenuation effect and the inconsistency effect.)

Finally, assumption 5 translates performance expectation states into behavior. It claims that all components of the group's power and prestige structure—such as giving each other chances to perform, the likelihoods that each individual will try to solve the group's task, evaluations of performances and ability, choices for leadership positions, and acceptance or rejection of influence in case of disagreement—will be direct functions of differences in the level of performance expectations associated with each group member. The higher the expectations associated with a given individual relative to expectations associated with another interactant, the more likely it is that other (o) will defer to him or her (to p) when disagreements arise, and the less likely it is that p will accept influence from o.

Thus, the theory posits a process having the form diagrammed in Figure 1. Activated status information (which is observable) creates performance expectation states (a theoretical construct), which in turn determine power and prestige behaviors (also observable).

For instance, in a society such as ours where *gender* is a status characteristic for most people, jurors may notice that some of them are women and some are men, thus activating a status difference based on the gender characteristic. Jurors form performance expectation states consistent with society's evaluation of the status characteristics—they treat the women *as if* they were less capable of reaching a good verdict than the men. That is, the burden of proof process produces specific performance expectation states for the group's task. As a result, *both the women and the men* treat the women as if they knew less about deliberating. When disagreements arise, the women are more likely to back down than the men are.[4]

---

[4]Notice that status generalization processes in this case are largely independent of actual ability of the jurors. That is, the gender characteristic alone will predispose actors to form higher expectations for the men. A complete picture of expectation patterns in the group would require knowing

Status generalization usually occurs below the level of consciousness. Thus, we do not believe, for instance, that women on a jury think to themselves, "I am a woman and he is a man; therefore I expect he will know more about how to do this than I do." Rather, they are likely *to behave as if* they went through such a cognitive process. The fact that status generalization usually is not conscious has at least two important implications for most situations. First, people possessing the (socially evaluated) lower state of some characteristic are just as likely to show behavioral effects as those possessing a status advantage. While many women, for instance, would deny gender as a basis for forming ideas about individuals' abilities if that question were brought to their conscious attention, still they will often defer to men in situations where only gender is available as a differentiating principle. Second, people possessing the (socially determined) higher state of the characteristic likewise need not consciously seize interaction advantages on that basis. Men may well deny letting gender differences determine their behavior in mixed sex groups, and that denial will be sincere. The theory of status generalization predicts the behavioral effect of status differences. It does not (without some additional assumptions) predict cognitive or judgmental effects.[5]

Because sentiments may have an impact on influence, we ask first whether sentiments can be seen most usefully as additional types of status information, or whether they must be conceptualized separately, though having in common with status that behavioral outcome. In other words, the first issue in constructing a theory of sentiments is whether to see them as producing status generalization (perhaps under differing conditions), or as operating according to different principles that lead to some of the same behavioral outcomes.

To ask the question somewhat differently, does sentiment affect the chain of events in Figure 1 at the beginning (where status information becomes activated), or at the end (where performance expectations are translated into behavior)? From the point of view of theory construction, the task would be simpler if sentiment functioned as a type of status characteristic. In that case, the definition of status elements would be generalized to incorporate this new type of status information. The task would be to determine conditions under which sentiment did and did not function as status information, and possible limits on the behavioral consequences of that type of status generalization.

On the other hand, if sentiments act at the end of the chain, if they affect

---

in addition how actors evaluate performance attempts by each other. However, we would not expect the status and expectation advantages and disadvantages conferred by gender to disappear. Rather, they will be combined with effects of performance evaluations in forming aggregate expectations for actors.

[5] Of course it would constitute a serious misunderstanding of the theory of status generalization to infer that it justifies inequality based upon gender or any other status difference. Whether inequality is justified in a particular situation is a separate question. In fact, this theory provides the basis for some effective interventions to overcome undesirable effects of status generalization (see, for instance, E. G. Cohen 1993; and Entwisle and Webster 1974). Understanding why certain behavioral advantages and disadvantages get created is the first step to changing things, where that is desirable.

behavior independently of status generalization, the theoretical task is more complex. In that case, although sentiment affects some of the same behaviors as status generalization, sentiment works through a different theoretical process. That is, a separate theory is needed to predict such effects as rejecting influence based upon sentiment. Then the need would be to develop an adequate conceptualization of the independent variables such as liking and disliking, to develop a catalog of behaviors affected by sentiment, and to specify the processes by which sentiment comes to affect behavior. The former route is simpler and is obviously therefore more appealing.

However, we need more information before beginning theoretical development in either avenue. Most helpful would be empirical results indicating whether it is indeed possible to conceive of sentiment as a type of status information, or whether the process involved is quite different from status generalization.

Study 1

Imagine a situation with two actors, p and o, differentiated by a single status characteristic, either diffuse or specific. For this example, p has low status and o has high. From that fact, p is disposed to accept influence from o (or at least p is *more likely to* accept influence from o, rather than vice versa).

Next add sentiment; suppose in addition that p dislikes o. Sentiment dampens, or reduces, p's propensity to accept influence. By comparison to the simple status-only situation, sentiment reduces the behavioral evidence of status organizing. The question is whether the status organizing process has actually been affected, or whether its effect in this situation has been masked by a second process, sentiment. To evaluate these possibilities, we use a function developed by Berger, Fisek, Norman, and Zelditch (1977) for the widely used expectation states experimental situation.

In a two-person group where individuals make repeated two-stage choices (each individual makes an "initial choice," sees the partner's supposed initial choice, reconsiders the question, then makes a private "final decision") on a series of binary problems, and where controlled disagreements are introduced on most of the initial choices, it is possible to measure expectation states by the *probability that an individual will reject influence*, or P(s), estimated from the proportion of decisions on which the individual makes the same final decision as his or her initial choice. That is, given that two individuals are working on a collective task where they exchange initial choices before making final choices, and given that they disagree on initial choices, each individual's level of performance expectations may be estimated from his or her P(s).

P(s) is estimated as follows:

$$P(s) = m + q(e_p - e_o).$$

e_p and e_o are, respectively, the performance expectations associated with individuals p and o, so $(e_p - e_o)$ represents p's "expectation advantage" (which in some cases may be negative). m is a population parameter absorbing all influences that make individuals more or less likely to accept influence (such as past experiences, or training that emphasizes sticking to one's own ideas or trying to see the other person's point of view). q is a situational parameter, incorporating all properties of the situation making expectations more or less effective in determining behavior (such as level of task orientation). This gives the key to experimental design.

If sentiment is a status characteristic, it affects the $(e_p - e_o)$ expectation advantage. If, on the other hand, sentiment intervenes between expectations and behavior, then it affects q. An experiment manipulating other factors in q, such as importance of the decision, could, we feel, help identify where sentiment enters the equation.

In the 1960's, Camilleri and Berger (1967; Camilleri et al. 1972) conducted an experiment in which *level of responsibility* for the group's decision varied from none through full. Responsibility was varied by defining the team's scoring system. In different conditions, one individual had *full* responsibility while the other had *none*; or both individuals had *equal* responsibility. The Camilleri-Berger experiment also included a status manipulation. However, because here we are concerned with the effect of responsibility, we look only at a condition where S's had equal status. Where actors had equal status (low for both self and other) for no responsibility, P(s) = .73; for equal responsibility, P(s) = .66; and for high responsibility, P(s) = .52. Those differences suggest that manipulating responsibility can produce visible effects upon behavior in a standard experimental situation.

In our preliminary experiments, we first induced low status, then added the negative sentiment *disliking*. The effect of low status will be to increase acceptance of influence—that is, to lower P(s)—while the effect of disliking will be to decrease influence acceptance, or to raise P(s). Finally, for two conditions, we induced *responsibility*, using the manipulation Camilleri and Berger developed. Subjects in this study were 92 volunteer college student women between ages 18 and 22, assigned randomly to the four conditions of the experiment.

We expected that, while the effect of added dislike would be to increase P(s), the increase would be greater for low responsibility conditions than for high responsibility. The idea was that, although disliking predisposes an individual to reject influence, she or he will be less likely to do that if the consequences of an error are severe (high responsibility) than if they are low. Thus, the experiment depended upon detecting a "difference of differences" across conditions.

Results of this first experiment were equivocal. Sentiment (dislike) raised P(s), and it raised P(s) somewhat more when responsibility was equal than when it was high. That seems to support a view that two distinct processes are involved. On the other hand, the differences were not statistically significant. The reason they were not may be high variance in one cell (low status, disliking, full responsibility). However, since we had no independent evidence for that interpretation, we decided to treat the results of experiment 1 as preliminary and to devise a second experiment which we hoped would clarify these issues.

Overall, we concluded that results were more consistent with the idea that sentiment must be conceived distinctly from status,[6] and we pursued that conclusion further with a second set of experiments.

Study 2

Study 2 addresses the same general theoretical question as Study 1: What impact do status and liking have on group behavior? However, Study 2 was designed to allow the following specific questions to be examined. First, we wanted to observe effects of status alone on performance expectations and influence. As noted earlier, differences in external status produce differential performance expectations, which determine observable power and prestige behaviors such as influence. Thus, higher status relative to one's partner should lead to higher performance expectations for self versus other and greater influence; whereas lower relative status leads to lower performance expectations and less influence. Second, we wanted to observe the effects of external status on sentiment relations in the group. Evidence suggests that, at least in some cases, we are more attracted to those of higher status (Hurwitz, Zander, and Hymovitch 1960; Suls and Miller 1978). Thus, Study 2 was designed also to examine the effect of high and low status on liking or disliking for one's partner.

Third, we wanted to observe the impact of manipulating positive and negative sentiment or liking on performance expectations and on influence behavior. More specifically, we wanted to examine the impact of liking and disliking when that is the sole differentiating information available to interactants. The first comparison of interest is the effect of positive or negative sentiment on liking for one's partner. We expect positive sentiment (operationalized here as attitude similarity) to produce liking for one's partner, and negative sentiment to induce disliking. However, a question of more direct theoretical interest is the effect of sentiment relations on status. For example, when group members know only that they like or dislike their partner, is that information sufficient to produce differentials in power and prestige? There is experimental evidence (see Back

---

[6] While the three manipulations (status, sentiment, and responsibility) all had their anticipated effects, one condition of the experiment (low status, dislike, full responsibility) produced variance too high to yield clear support for either case. The pattern of results, however, was more consistent with case 2 (separate process) than with case 1 (sentiment as status). In retrospect, we believe it was a mistake to create *dis*liking rather than liking. We did that based on an intuitive belief that it would be easier to create dislike quickly in a laboratory. However, the stress induced by all three of these independent variables at once may have caused some participants to "escape" from the situation psychologically, thus creating variance and blurring our results. Complete data and other analyses of this experiment are available from the authors.

| Distribution of Status Elements | → | **Performance Expectation States** | → | Power and Prestige Behaviors |

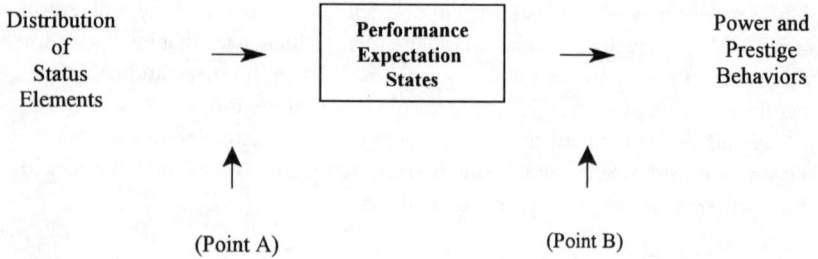

(Point A)   (Point B)

Fig. 2. Actions of sentiment as a status characteristic (Point A) or as a separate process (Point B)

1951; Berkowitz 1957) that individuals tend to be influenced more by those they like. Therefore, one comparison of interest in this study is the effect of liking and disliking, when that is the sole differentiating information, on status relations in the group.

Fourth, we wanted to examine how the effects of status and sentiment combine. For example, if p is of lower status relative to o, does the fact that p also dislikes o affect the extent to which p accepts or rejects influence from that person? Therefore, we created experimental conditions in which subjects possessed a status disadvantage relative to their partners, but also either liked or disliked them.

Finally, we took a different approach to examine the question of whether sentiment intervenes to determine performance expectations (at point A in the status→performance expectations→behavior sequence; see Fig. 2), or whether sentiment may determine some of the same behaviors as does status, but independently of the process through which performance expectations are developed (in this case, sentiment may impact behavior at point B). To evaluate these alternatives in this study, we assessed the impact of status and sentiment on both the behavioral measure of rejection of influence and on questionnaire items assessing subjects' expectations for self and other. This questionnaire measure has been used successfully in prior studies (Driskell and Mullen 1988, 1990) as a subjective measure of performance expectations.

Study 2 also differed somewhat from Study 1 in concrete features. Study 2 was conducted in a research laboratory at a navy base, with military personnel as subjects. The general experimental paradigm was similar to that of Study 1. Differences in design and procedure are described in the following.

Subjects

Subjects in this study were 115 male technical school students between the ages of 17 and 25 who volunteered to take part in a study of group performance. They were randomly assigned to one of six experimental conditions.

CHART 2

Conditions of Study 2

Condition	Status Relations (Self, Other)	Sentiments
1	$(+-)$	—
2	$(-+)$	—
3	—	$(+)$
4	—	$(-)$
5	$(-+)$	$(+)$
6	$(-+)$	$(-)$

Status relations: $(+-)$ is "high-self, low-other," meaning p has a positive status advantage; $(-+)$ is "low-self, high-other," meaning p has a status disadvantage.

Sentiments: $(+)$ means p likes o; $(-)$ means p dislikes o.

Design

The design of this study is shown in Chart 2. The study contained six conditions. In conditions 1 and 2, status was manipulated into relatively high $(+ -)$ or low $(- +)$ states. In conditions 3 and 4, sentiment was manipulated by reporting attitude similarity $(+)$ or dissimilarity $(-)$. Similarity and dissimilarity of attitudes have been shown by Byrne (1961) and others to produce, respectively, liking and disliking. In condition 5, subjects were placed in a low-status position $(- +)$ relative to their partners and were told their attitudes were similar to their partner's to induce liking for the partner. In condition 6, subjects were again placed in a relatively low-status position $(- +)$, but in this case they were told their attitudes were dissimilar and would probably lead to dislike for their partner.

Procedure

Subjects were seated in individual laboratory rooms and instructed that they would be working as two-person teams over closed-circuit laboratory equipment. In conditions 1 and 2, they were differentiated by a single status cue, military rank. Subjects all were ranks E-2 and E-3, called "Seaman."[7] In condition 1, subjects were introduced to their partner (actually a stimulus person on videotape), a "Recruit Webster," identified as grade E-1. Since the subjects themselves were of higher rank, this constitutes a relatively high-status manipulation for subjects in condition 1. In condition 2, subjects were introduced to their partner, a commissioned officer, "Lieutenant Webster." Since subjects in this case were of lower rank, this constitutes a relatively low-status manipulation

[7] Seamen in the navy are comparable to privates in the army and the air force. Grades E-4 through E-7 are noncommissioned officers, comparable to corporals and sergeants. Grade E-1 is entry level, boot camp, usually called "seaman recruit" or just "recruit." There is considerable status differentiation between E-1 and E-2 or E-3.

for them.[8] Following the status manipulation, subjects in conditions 1 and 2 began work on the data collection task.

In conditions 3 and 4, liking/disliking was manipulated. After being seated in laboratory rooms, subjects were asked to complete the "Team Cohesiveness Index" (TCI), a questionnaire purported to measure the extent of team members' compatibility. On this questionnaire were a number of items addressing likes, dislikes, opinions, and values. For example, one subscale of the TCI asked subjects to choose the characteristics that he would describe as the worst traits and the best traits to have in a team partner. Other items asked subjects to indicate the extent to which a series of statements (for example, "I enjoy working with people") described themselves. After the index was scored, the experimenter explained team scores. In condition 3, each subject was told that he and his team partner scored very similarly on index scales of consideration, flexibility, and team orientation, and that this indicated team members would like each other and get along very well. In condition 4, subjects were told that their scores were quite discrepant, indicating that the subjects would not like each other, and that they as team members were likely to get along very poorly.

In conditions 5 and 6, subjects received both status and sentiment manipulations. In condition 5, subjects met their partner, "Lieutenant Webster," placing the subjects in a relatively low-status position. Both individuals were then administered the TCI, and were scored as very similar to their partners on the compatibility scales. In condition 6, subjects received the same status manipulation, but in this case the TCI scores revealed strong incompatibility.

Following the status and/or sentiment manipulations, subjects worked on the data collection task, which required them to make initial and final choices on a series of ambiguous binary choice slides. The task consists of a series of slides, each containing two black and white checkerboards, one above the other.[9] Subjects made initial choices on each slide to determine whether the top or bottom checkerboard contained the greater area of white (in fact, the slides are ambiguous). Following each initial choice, subjects could see their partner's initial choice, and then they would make a final decision. There were 23 trials, 20 of them experimentally created disagreements.

On each disagreement trial, subjects could accept influence from the partner

---

[8] Recruits (E-1) are housed separately from seamen (E-2 and E-3), and of course officers also live separately. Thus, there is little occasion for interaction across the three status levels of this study. In conditions 3 and 4, where status is not manipulated, it would be reasonable for subjects to infer that their partners were of equal status to themselves. Post-session interviewing established that no subjects inferred that their partners differed from themselves on status in these conditions. Note that the theory claims (assumption 1) that status characteristics that do not differentiate actors will not become salient nor function in the burden of proof process. Thus in Chart 2 we show status for conditions 3 and 4 as absent. Theoretically, it makes no difference whether status is absent or equated in these conditions (see Webster 1977).

[9] The task is obviously unrelated to military rank; there is no reason to presume that officers will be better able to judge the slides than recruits will. According to assumption 2, burden of proof will produce status generalization for cases where the link to status is unknown, as it is here.

by taking the partner's choice as their own final choice, or reject influence by keeping their own choice. The measure P(s), the proportion of stay responses, was recorded as the primary behavioral dependent variable.

A second dependent measure assessed sentiment relations (positive or negative affect toward the partner). Immediately following the data collection task, subjects completed a postexperimental questionnaire. The sentiment questionnaire included seven items designed to assess sentiment relations in the group. The following items were presented on a seven-point scale:

1. If you were to return to take part in a face-to-face discussion group, would you prefer the same partner or a new partner?
2. How satisfied are you with this team?
3. Based on your impressions at this point, how much do you think you would like your partner?
4. Do you think that your partner had attitudes concerning the team's goals and performance similar to yours?
5. How well do you believe that your partner would get along in most teams?
6. How desirable would you rate your partner as a teammate?
7. Do you think that you would like to socialize with your partner in today's group?

A third dependent measure was a questionnaire measure of performance expectations. The purpose of this questionnaire was to obtain a direct measure of the unobservable construct "expectation states" by treating them as accessible to retrieval using appropriate questions. Berger, Wagner, and Zelditch (1985) caution against relying too heavily on self-reports of expectations, noting that we have no satisfactory theoretical explanation of how individuals verbalize expectations. However, Driskell and Mullen (1988) show that questions such as Who has the most ability? tap information that must be available to interactants to solve a group task. In a statistical integration of studies using both self-reported expectations and behavior, Driskell and Mullen (1988, 1990) found a strong and significant relationship between questionnaire measures of expectations and behavior. Performance expectations were assessed in the postexperimental questionnaire to provide a subjective measure of task competence. Questionnaire measures of performance expectations also proved workable in other studies (Webster and Driskell 1983; Webster and Hysom, forthcoming). We consider behavioral measures as preferable when they may be used, and all conclusions from performance expectations in this study are consistent with behavioral data. Questionnaires provide supplementary information.

Two items were included in this miniscale:

1. How capable do you think you are compared with your partner at most tasks?
2. Compared to you, how well do you expect the other group members to do in situations in general?

Results of Study 2

Effects of Status and Similarity on Performance Expectations

Analysis of the items assessing perceptions of task competence reveal an alpha reliability $= .813$, and so we combined these two items into a composite questionnaire measure of performance expectations. Table 1 presents the mean performance expectation scores and standard deviations by condition and the results of the primary comparisons of interest.

Data show the expected effect of status on performance expectations. Results indicate that high-status subjects in condition 1 developed significantly higher performance expectations (4.40) than did low-status subjects in condition 2 (3.53), $F(1, 37) = 6.71$, $p < .01$.

Comparison of conditions 3 and 4 indicates no significant effect of liking (similarity) on perceptions of task competence, $F(1, 40) = 0.31$, $p > .10$. Thus liking or disliking one's partner, when that is the only discriminating information available, is not sufficient to develop differentiated performance expectations. This outcome is inconsistent with an idea that sentiment is a type of status characteristic.

Analyses reveal no significant difference between condition 5 (low status + liking) and condition 6 (low status + disliking), $F(1, 32) = 0.61$, $p > .10$. Thus, in this case, where status information discriminated interactants (in both conditions 5 and 6, subjects perceived themselves to be interacting with a higher-status partner), the addition of information on similarity and dissimilarity still had no

TABLE 1

Mean Performance Expectation Scores and Standard Deviations by Condition

Condition	Performance expectations[a]	Comparison
1. High Status	4.40 (1.35)	1 vs. 2; $F(1, 37) = 6.71$, $p < .01$
2. Low Status	3.53 (0.59)	
3. Liking	4.07 (0.78)	3 vs. 4; $F(1, 40) = .31$, $p > .10$
4. Disliking	4.21 (0.87)	
5. Low Status + Liking	3.74 (1.39)	5 vs. 6; $F(1, 32) = .61$, $p > .10$
6. Low Status + Disliking	4.06 (0.98)	

[a] Higher numbers indicate more positive expectations for self versus other. Thus the relatively high status actor in condition 1 has higher expectations for self than the relatively low status actor in condition 2.
2 vs. 5; $F(1, 34) = .36$, $p > .1$
2 vs. 6; $F(1, 34) = 4.0$, $p > .05$

impact on performance expectations. We may examine this phenomenon more closely by comparing condition 2 (low status) with conditions 5 (low status + liking) and 6 (low status + disliking). Taking condition 2 as a baseline, we found no significant modification of performance expectations from adding liking in condition 5, $F(1, 34) = .36$, $p > .1$, or from adding disliking in condition 6, $F(1, 34) = 4.0$, $p > .05$.

Effects of Status and Similarity on Sentiment

Analysis of the seven-item sentiment scale reveals an alpha reliability of .854. Therefore, we combined these items into a composite measure of sentiment relations. Table 2 presents mean sentiment scores and standard deviations by condition and results of the primary comparisons of interest.

Comparison of conditions 1 and 2 indicates that we do indeed tend to like those of higher status. High-status partners were perceived as considerably more likable than low-status partners, $F(1, 37) = 15.05$, $p < .001$. The sentiment effect here is striking, especially in view of the minimal, highly controlled interaction permitted between subjects.

There was also a significant difference in sentiment relations between conditions 3 and 4, $F(1, 40) = 9.30$, $p < .01$. Subjects who received the similarity manipulation in condition 3 reported more positive affect toward their partner than subjects who received the disliking manipulation in condition 4. This finding confirms satisfactory manipulation of sentiment by the method used.

Finally, comparison of conditions 5 and 6 reveals that low-status subjects re-

TABLE 2

Mean Sentiment Scores and Standard Deviations by Condition

Condition	Sentiment[a]	Comparison
1. High Status	3.68 (0.93)	1 vs. 2; $F(1, 37) = 15.05$, $p < .001$
2. Low Status	2.61 (0.78)	
3. Liking	3.14 (0.64)	3 vs. 4; $F(1, 40) = 9.30$, $p < .01$
4. Disliking	3.78 (0.72)	
5. Low Status + Liking	2.29 (0.89)	5 vs. 6; $F(1, 32) = 34.69$, $p < .001$
6. Low Status + Disliking	4.10 (0.90)	

[a] Higher numbers indicate greater negative affect (less liking). Thus the relatively high status actor in condition 1 has less liking for his partner than the relatively low status actor in condition 2.

2 vs. 5; $F(1, 34) = 1.28$, $p > .10$

2 vs. 6; $F(1, 34) = 28.41$, $p < .001$

ported more positive affect for the higher-status, similar partner than for the higher-status, dissimilar partner, $F(1, 32) = 34.69$, $p < .001$. Using condition 2 (low status) as a baseline, we see that the effect of adding dissimilarity in condition 6 is to produce greater negative sentiment $F(1, 34) = 28.41$, $p < .001$. Comparing conditions 2 and 5, we see that the effect of adding similarity is to increase positive affect somewhat, although this difference is not statistically significant, $F(1, 34) = 1.28$, $p > .10$. Thus, adding inconsistent sentiment information (that is, dislike of a high-status partner) seems to have a greater impact than adding consistent sentiment information (like of a high-status partner). This is consistent with the attenuation and inconsistency effects incorporated in assumption 4 of the theory.

Effects of Status and Similarity on Behavior

Table 3 presents mean P(s) scores and variances about the mean number of self-resolutions by condition. The comparison of P(s) data for conditions 1 and 2 shows that, as expected, the high-status subjects in condition 1 are less likely to accept influence from their partner (.708) than are the low-status subjects in condition 2. P(s) for condition 1 = .708, and for condition 2, .553; $F(1, 37) = 8.07$, $p < .01$.

The analysis reveals no significant difference in P(s) between conditions 3 and 4; $F(1, 40) = 0.15$, $p > .10$. Thus, liking/disliking has no effect on influence when it is the only information differentiating group members. This behavioral result is consistent with the result on the questionnaire measure of expectations above.

TABLE 3

Mean P(s) Scores and Variances About the Mean Number of Self-Resolutions by Condition

Condition	P(s)	Comparison
1. High Status	.708 (9.50)	1 vs. 2; $F(1, 37) = 8.07$, $p < .01$
2. Low Status	.553 (13.72)	
3. Liking	.631 (12.95)	3 vs. 4; $F(1, 40) = .15$, $p > .10$
4. Disliking	.610 (12.96)	
5. Low Status + Liking	.491 (21.65)	5 vs. 6; $F(1, 32) = 7.67$, $p < .01$
6. Low Status + Disliking	.676 (8.76)	

2 vs. 5; $F(1, 34) = .77$, $p > .10$
2 vs. 6; $F(1, 34) = 4.84$, $p < .05$

By examining conditions 5 and 6, we can observe the combined effects of status and sentiment on behavior. First, results reveal a significant difference in P(s) between condition 5 (.491) and condition 6 (.676); $F(1, 32) = 7.67$, $p < .01$. We may examine this more closely by comparing condition 2 (low status) with condition 5 (low status + liking) and condition 6 (low status + disliking). Using condition 2 as a baseline, we see that the effect of adding liking in condition 5 is to reduce P(s) somewhat from .553 to .491, although this difference is not statistically significant; $F(1, 34) = .77$, $p > .10$. The effect of adding disliking in condition 6 is to increase P(s) from .553 to .676; in this case, a significant increase, $F(1, 34) = 4.84$, $p < .05$. Again, we note that *inconsistent* sentiment information (for example, finding that one dislikes a higher-status partner) seems to have a greater impact on behavior than consistent sentiment information (for example, finding that one likes a higher-status partner). As noted above, this is consistent with the attenuation effect and the inconsistency principle incorporated in assumption 4.

Study 2 Discussion

Status structures (who influences whom) and sentiment structure (who likes whom) are primary features of most small groups. This research is an initial attempt to integrate these social processes by examining several independent and combined effects of status and sentiment in groups. Overall results of Study 2 illuminate the question of how status and sentiment affect group interaction.

First, external status was a significant predictor of both performance expectations as measured by questionnaires and of actual influence as measured by P(s) data. Subjects considered higher-status group members to be more competent at "most tasks" and at "situations in general," and deferred to them more often during decision making.

In a new finding, status also predicted sentiment relations: subjects viewed higher-status group members as more likable. Thus, we have experimental demonstration of the idea that high status conveys an additional advantage, predisposing people to find a high-status individual likable, with a corresponding disadvantage for low status. People who have just met a person of high status in the military (for example, a flag officer) or in civilian life (for example, the President) frequently report, "I was surprised at how warm, likable, and nice he was," sometimes despite the famous person's reputation for being "difficult." This effect may help us to understand such puzzling reports. In brief, experimental results indicate that we defer to and are more influenced by those of higher status, *and*, at least sometimes, we like them, too.

Attitude similarity was a significant predictor of liking for one's partner and also for attraction to the group. Those with similar partners liked them more and reported higher satisfaction with the team. However, the data revealed that when sentiment (liking/disliking) is the sole characteristic differentiating group members, it had no significant impact on performance expectations or behavior. Recall that status characteristics of individuals determine status structures of groups through a three-stage process:

external status $\rightarrow$ expectations $\rightarrow$ behavior.

Conditions 3 and 4 demonstrate that liking alone does not provide sufficient information to induce differentiation in either expectations or behavior. The probable reason for this is that a status structure is a normatively supported cooperative process, whereby some group members give deference in exchange for what they expect will be superior task contributions of others. For instance, if we are deliberating a task in a corporate boardroom, we may defer to someone having a senior position in the organization in exchange for that person's expected superior contributions to solving the task at hand.

Thus, expectations for performance capacity are a primary basis for confirming status. Whereas external status characteristics may be directly related to performance expectations (that is, external characteristics such as occupational position, military rank, and so on, imply task capability), sentiment or liking seems to imply no such performance connotations. Knowing that one shares similar attitudes with one's partner, or that one likes one's partner, if that is the only discriminating information available, is not sufficient to produce status differentiation. Knowing only that I like person A does not cause me to see person A as more competent. Knowing that I share attitudes with Person A causes me to develop more positive sentiment, as conditions 3 and 4 demonstrate; however, it does not affect status in this study.

How, then, do we account for studies, such as that by Berkowitz (1957), that have shown an effect of liking on influence? The possibility exists that information on sentiment may combine with information on status to determine influence. That is, if individuals are differentiated by status, knowing also that the other person is likable or dislikable may affect status relations. Based on these experimental results, we believe that when this effect occurs it is due to lowered responsibility for the decision, or lowered task orientation (concern with getting the right answer), or both.

Recall that we considered two mechanisms through which the effect of sentiment might occur. First, we posited that it might function as an additional status characteristic. That process may be illustrated by the statement "My partner is higher rank, but I dislike him, so he must not be that competent." Results of these experiments indicate this did not occur.

The second mechanism, sentiment intervening to make less salient the performance expectations that have formed on the basis of external status, is what appears to have occurred in this experiment. This process is illustrated by the statement "My partner is higher rank, so he must be competent. However, I dislike him. Therefore, although I think he is competent, I'm not going to defer to him as often." In this second case, sentiment makes less salient the expectations that have formed on the basis of status. For example, working with a higher-status person results in formation of positive performance expectations for that person. If sentiment also figures in the situation, it will affect influence as an additional process. If we like that person, we may defer more often than we would, based solely on the performance expectations formed. Conversely, if we dislike that person, we may defer less. In both cases, what happens is that expectations continue to affect behavior, as assumption 5 predicts, but there is an additional process activated in the situation. Behavior, then, is determined not solely by expectations, but by a combination of expectations and sentiment.

Evidence from conditions 5 and 6 of this study supports this alternative. Adding liking or disliking had no effect on performance expectations—the high-status disliked partner was perceived to be just as competent as the high-status liked partner. However, subjects rejected influence from the high-status disliked partner more often than from the high-status liked partner. Sentiment does not impact performance expectations, but, under certain conditions, sentiment may impact decision-making behavior. This suggests that sentiment operates on the status structure primarily by affecting the salience of performance expectations that have been formed for group members.

In fact, it seems that this is the type of condition under which earlier studies found an effect of liking on influence. In the Berkowitz (1957) study, subjects met face to face before performing the group task. We would expect subjects upon meeting to use available cues, such as dress, language, and nonverbal behavior, to form initial task expectations. In that liking was then manipulated, this study is similar to our conditions 5 and 6, in which status *and* sentiment were manipulated. Results of the Berkowitz study also were similar—liking had an effect on the perceived merit of others' opinions. We conclude that if this study had been similar to our conditions 2 and 3, in which liking was the only information present, liking would have had little or no effect on task expectations or on actual influence.

There are, of course, limitations to conclusions that can be drawn from this analysis. First, Study 2 was designed to examine the independent effects of status (when that is the only differentiating information) and the independent effects of similarity (when that is the only differentiating information) on status and liking processes. To examine how status and sentiment information combine, we contrasted a low status + liking condition to a low status + disliking condition. Whether the obtained results would hold under high status + liking and high status + disliking conditions should be determined by further research.

Second, a possible alternative explanation of the results of Study 2 is that status affects behavior, which then determines performance expectations. That is, the postexperimental questionnaire measure of performance expectations may reflect subjects' attempts to develop an explanation consistent with their prior behavior. Munroe and Shelly (1994) have recently shown that under certain conditions in discussion groups, any of several structural advantages can organize status structures consistently with the initial structures. Two factors argue against that interpretation for this experiment. First, in a meta-analytic evaluation, Driskell and Mullen (1988, 1990) found strong support for the status-expectations-behavior relationship as specified by the theory. Results of the meta-analysis provided no support for a status-behavior-expectations pattern of effects. Furthermore, in the present study, conditions 5 and 6 instantiate a situation in which there is differentiation in behavior, with higher P(s) in condition 6 than in condition 5, but not in expectations as measured by questionnaire. If we were to assume that performance expectations were simply cognitive attempts to reconstruct recent behavior, we would expect that in every case, expectations would be consistent with behavior. The results of conditions 5 and 6 do not support such a conclusion. Therefore, although there may well be situations in which sentiment affects types of behavior that then influence performance expectations, there is no empirical evidence to support this position from our experiments.

Discussion and Conclusions

We began with the question of how to conceptualize sentiment relations in face-to-face task-oriented groups. Two possibilities appeared likely. The first and simpler is to see sentiment as an additional status characteristic, perhaps operating under somewhat different conditions; the second is to see it as a separate process having some of the same behavioral effects. Rather than attempting an analytic solution, we devised situations in which the two approaches would produce different empirical consequences.

Results of the first experiment better supported the "separate process" concept, but not unambiguously. Thus, we conducted a second experiment having both high- and low-status conditions, and liking and disliking sentiment conditions, and this time sentiment appears clearly as a separate process from status generalization.

We were fortunate to be able to conduct the two experiments in diverse settings (a university campus for the first one, a military base for the second) with widely different subject populations. About all the people in the two experiments had in common was age: all were between 17 and 25 years old. They differed (at least) on gender, educational level, socioeconomic status, maturity, and family background. Women university undergraduates were the first group; navy recruits, the second. Behavioral data were similar for the two experiments, supporting the idea that the status and sentiment processes are general.

Theoretically, experimental results show the status and sentiment processes are distinct, and the tasks for theory construction appear to be the following.

First, the concept "sentiment" needs further development. We operationalized it as liking and disliking produced by attitude similarity and dissimilarity. It appears important now to develop a clearer conceptualization of sentiment, perhaps along the lines of the explicit definitions of diffuse and specific status characteristics. Such definition might include delineation of classes of sentiment situations, perhaps suggesting some types not now recognized as sentiments. It also might include ideas for kinds of situations in which sentiments appear, or kinds of situations that produce different sentiment relations.

After further explication of the concept of sentiments, their theoretical functioning needs attention. Status generalization has been seen as a "state-organizing process" (see, for instance, Wagner and Berger 1993a: 56–58). That is, under certain conditions status elements become activated; they come to affect interaction in well-understood ways; and under other conditions status de-activates or no longer functions to affect behavior. Sentiment structures may function in similar ways. Viewing sentiment as a state-organizing process may offer the advantage of sensitizing theorists to ways in which status generalization and sentiment processes operate similarly. Whatever the approach, the goal is to incorporate sentiments in explicit testable propositions.

These experimental results add to the literature on status effects, for as we saw in conditions 1 and 2 (as well as the more complex conditions 5 and 6), status effects appear both in the questionnaire measure of expectations and in the P(s) measure of behavior. Given the history of this research program, these results are not surprising; however they augment the evidentary basis for status generalization theories.

The experiments also produced several new results involving sentiment. First, status and sentiment combine to affect influence behavior but as two separate processes operating to produce similar effects. Second, at least in this situation, sentiment effects are weaker than status effects. Status generalization theories treat all characteristics as if they had equal degrees of effect, a simplifying assumption that may not be justified in specific cases. Whether sentiment effects are as great as status effects may require theoretical attention, or it may be advisable to pursue a similar simplifying approach and not ask that question at this time. Certainly for this specific case, it is easy to imagine some reasons why status might be a stronger determinant of behavior than are sentiments. First, the population: for military recruits, status characteristics may be especially salient, particularly for those new to the military, as our subjects were. Second, sentiment relations may take longer to become salient, or for their effects to become apparent, than do status relations. It may simply take longer to decide we like or dislike someone than to be impressed with his or her high or low status. As theoretical development of sentiment relations proceeds, it may become necessary to consider what determines degree of effect.

A most intriguing finding here is that status affects sentiment, but not vice versa. That is, there is a tendency to like high-status people and to dislike low-status people, but the causation does not run in reverse. Are there only some conditions under which the status-produces-liking effect appears? What are some consequences of this effect in natural settings, such as where authority or leadership are important? Further research should address these questions.

We close by noting that the study of sentiment relations has only begun. Besides our program, at least two other research programs are investigating related issues. Robert Shelly (see, for instance, Shelly 1988, 1993) is studying the ways sentiment and other structures interact in discussion groups. Michael Lovaglia and his associates (see, for instance, Houser and Lovaglia 1994) have developed a somewhat different experimental design from ours for investigating how status and sentiment interact. While these programs investigate differing aspects of sentiment relations, in many respects they are complementary, and together they hold out a prospect of growing knowledge about these important phenomena.

Status, Affect, and Multiple Standards for Competence

⧎

Martha Foschi

Many everyday contexts, both formal and informal, involve the performance of a valued task and the assessment of the outcome. For example, employees in bureaucratic organizations are formally evaluated for their performances on a routine basis, and so are students in educational institutions. Performance evaluation is no less central to informal groups where the goal is to complete a task, as when a group of volunteers meets to plan a fund-raising event. The performances in question may be individual, or they may be the result of a collective endeavor. In either case, the evaluation of units of performance is used to arrive at generalized appraisals of competence at the task at hand (and sometimes even at other tasks). Assessors as well as performers engage in this process. Depending on the context, these appraisals can have wide-reaching implications at various levels, from individual to macro-structural. Examples of the variables thus affected are self-confidence, work-related stress, reward allocation, and organizational stability.

How *do* evaluations of units of performance result in overall judgments of competence? This paper addresses some aspects of that question. Although evidence of ability to perform a given task is a necessary condition for the inference of competence, there are many situations in which biases nevertheless affect that inference. There are many such biases—here I begin by examining the role that those grounded on status of performer have in that inference. The focus of my interest is on the conditions under which *different standards*, stricter for lower-status than for higher-status persons, are used to judge the same performance. This phenomenon is perhaps best exemplified in the case of gender,[1] as it is not

The ideas presented in this paper were developed as part of the work supported by research grant #482-88-0015 from the Social Sciences and Humanities Research Council of Canada (Strategic Grants Division, Women and Work Theme). This support is gratefully acknowledged. I also thank Andrea Bull and Marie Lembesis for their helpful comments on an earlier version.

[1] As generally agreed in the social psychological literature, I use the term "sex" to refer to biological differences between men and women, and "gender" to the associations individuals, as mem-

uncommon to observe that such double standards are applied when men and women produce performances at the same level.

This paper begins with the presentation of background material, followed by a theory on status and multiple standards for competence. The theory asserts that the application of a stricter standard to the performance of a lower-status actor constitutes a subtle mechanism through which the status quo is maintained. Here I propose several extensions involving status-related factors and review the evidence for the theory's key propositions. Finally, I introduce a theoretical extension that incorporates affect sentiments among participants in the evaluation setting, and propose conditions under which those sentiments also activate different standards for competence.

Theoretical Background: Expectation States Theory

Basic Notions

Expectation states theory is an extensive research program on how inequalities of interaction emerge and prevail in task groups (Berger, Cohen, and Zelditch 1972; Berger, Fisek, Norman, and Zelditch 1977; Berger, Rosenholtz, and Zelditch 1980; Berger, Wagner, and Zelditch 1985; Webster and Foschi 1988; Wagner and Berger 1993a). The focus is on the effects that a group member's relative status has on level of assigned competence, and on the consequences this assignment carries for group interaction. The work also includes intervention research aimed at creating equitable patterns of interaction (see, for example, Cohen 1982). Expectation states theory constitutes the most comprehensive account to date of status effects on competence assignment. Furthermore, empirical results provide strong support for its predictions. The work presented in this paper extends and refines aspects of the theory.

Two key concepts are "status characteristic" and "expectation state." A status characteristic is any valued attribute implying task competence. Such characteristics are defined as consisting of at least two states (for example, either a high or a low level of mechanical ability; either limited or extensive formal education), one evaluated more positively than the other. These attributes are conceptualized as varying from specific to diffuse, depending on their perceived applicability. A specific characteristic has well-defined expectations associated with it while a diffuse characteristic carries, in addition, general (that is, broadly defined) performance expectations. In many societies, gender, ethnicity, socioeconomic class, organizational rank, and physical attractiveness have the latter

---

bers of a given society, make with these differences. Thus, beliefs about the relative competence of men and women are social products and therefore a gender issue, whereas what activates these beliefs is usually nothing more than the perception of the performer as either male or female. When the evidence available involves only such perceptions, or when the only intention is to identify participants in a study as either men or women, I use the term "sex."

implications for a substantial number of individuals. Thus, women, for example, are not only expected to be inferior to men in various specific skills, but are also assumed to have inferior competence in general.

An expectation state is an anticipation of the quality of group members' future task performances. Expectation states are based on status characteristics and thus reflect assignments of task competence. These assignments are viewed as relative to two or more actors rather than absolute (for example, "I am better than my partner at this task" instead of "I have a high degree of this ability"). Expectation states link status characteristics to observable behaviors by directly affecting several features of group interaction: the distribution of the offer and acceptance of performance opportunities, the types of evaluations received (either positive or negative), and the rates of influence exerted among group members. This set of interrelated behaviors is known as "the power and prestige order of the group." Such an order is both the result of each person's relative status and a factor contributing to its maintenance.

Status in a group may be acquired in one of two ways: *directly* or *indirectly*. To begin with, let us consider a situation involving only the first process. In such a case, participants have no basis for forming differential expectations about each other at the onset of their interaction. Initially, then, they behave as status equals. The theory predicts that a status order will nonetheless eventually develop, and that this order will be the *direct* result of the evaluation of the performances that the group members produce as they try to solve their task. Such evaluations may be made either by the group members themselves or by an external source (that is, a person with evaluative experience or with the objective means to assess performances, such as an answer key to a test). For example, if the group is engaged in a fund-raising drive, as ideas related to meeting that goal are proposed and either adopted or discarded during the discussions, those participants with the better ideas will emerge as the higher-status members of the group.

A status order may also develop through an *indirect* connection. In this case, a status characteristic that is perceived to be related to the group's goal is "imported" into the interaction. For simplicity, let us assume that no other bases for expectations exist. The characteristic will then be used to classify both the potential and actual contributions of the participants as having either much or little value in the solution of the group's task. Thus, depending on whether the characteristic differentiates or equates group members, it will organize interaction by either providing an instant status hierarchy or defining the participants as status equals.

These direct and indirect processes of status assignment correspond to the two major branches of expectation states theory. The first is known as "evaluations and expectations theory"; the second, as "status characteristics theory."

Status Characteristics and Biased Evaluations

Let us consider some of the main ideas of the latter theory in more detail, focusing on the effects of status on evaluations. The status characteristic in question, be it specific or diffuse, results in biased evaluations whereby higher-status actors' contributions to the group task are assessed as more valuable than those of lower-status participants. This occurs under the following conditions: (1) group members value the ability required for task performance and are motivated to do the task well, (2) they are convinced that status is a useful cue to competence, (3) they have no other cues in this regard, and (4) they must evaluate each other's performances but have no objective criteria with which to do this. It would actually be surprising if, under such conditions, biased evaluations did not occur when status and the task at hand are known to be associated—a situation referred to as "explicit relevance." Thus, bias in evaluations is predicted if, for example, the task involves assessing the logic of arguments and the participants classify themselves into philosophy and nonphilosophy majors. The bias would also show itself if, for instance, all group members were philosophy majors and this fact were salient to them; then every person would feel as highly qualified as the next.

An important proposition of the theory, however, states that biased evaluations occur even when status and task are *not* deemed to be associated, *provided* the characteristic differentiates the participants, and status and task have not been explicitly dissociated. In other words, relevance between the two develops as long as the possibility of such a link is left open and the characteristic provides discriminating information. This situation, referred to as "implicit relevance" or "status generalization," involves a burden of proof argument: those who are considered to be of lower status will be seen as making inferior contributions unless they demonstrate otherwise.

Biased evaluations are important because of their critical role in a circular reasoning: under the circumstances described above, they are not only the result of status effects but also an agent that helps to maintain them, particularly when actors are initially differentiated in status. Notice that the other elements of the power and prestige order of the group also conspire in this same direction.

Two Bases for Performance Expectations

What happens, however, when participants who *differ* regarding a status characteristic produce performances of *equal* quality (that is, either equally good or equally poor)? The most theoretically interesting case is the one involving two very different grounds for inferring status. Let us then assume that the evaluation of these performances has been made through the use of objective criteria (that is, the operation of biased evaluations has been blocked) and that the status characteristic is diffuse in nature. In expectation states theory terms, this is a situation where both direct and indirect bases for status are available. It is this issue that is at the core of the present paper. Would the diffuse status characteristic still have an effect? Expectation states theory proposes that it does.

The answer is presented in a graph-theoretic model that formalizes a major part of the theory (Berger, Fisek, Norman, and Zelditch 1977); the situation described above is one of its special cases. According to the model, an actor is said to "possess" a given state of a characteristic (for example, to have or not have artistic talent, to be male or female). Furthermore, an actor is said to be linked through "paths of relevance" to the other components of the situation, such as states of additional characteristics, general performance expectations, and outcomes (both anticipated and actual) for the task at hand. Let us examine how an actor may be connected to such outcomes. First, this may occur through paths of different lengths. For example, as discussed earlier, an actor may be linked to success in one of two ways: directly, through actual performance, or indirectly, through a burden of proof process. The former represents a shorter path of relevance than the latter. Second, an actor may be consistently connected to the same outcome through alternate paths (as the previous example illustrates), or there may be some paths connecting the actor to success, whereas others link the person to failure. The shorter the paths and the larger the number of consistent paths, the stronger the resulting expectations (for either success or failure). Thus, a woman performing a masculine task well, although connected to success through a direct path, is still indirectly linked to failure on account of gender-based expectations. Conversely, a man performing well at the same task does not have this liability, and therefore stronger expectations for his success are in place. Experimental tests provide clear support for these predictions. For reviews of studies and empirical assessments of the graph-theoretic model, see Fox and Moore 1979; Balkwell 1991b; Fisek, Norman, and Nelson-Kilger 1992; for examples of experiments, see Pugh and Wahrman 1983; Wagner, Ford, and Ford 1986.

Notice that the above situation is also of central interest in the literature on social category membership and the attribution of success and failure. In fact, the concept of "social category" has much in common with that of "diffuse status characteristic." Work from this tradition also indicates that social category has an impact in spite of equal performances, resulting in asymmetrical attributions. Thus, for example, success by men tends to be attributed to ability, whereas the same success by women tends to be assigned to nonability factors such as good luck or additional effort. For reviews of studies, see Sohn 1982; Hansen and O'Leary 1985; Whitley, McHugh, and Frieze 1986; Foschi and Takagi 1991. For the most part, however, the support found in these reviews has been moderate rather than strong, a result that may be due mainly to variation in the quality of the studies.

Expectation states theory and attribution theory thus differ in their conceptual tools and in the level of empirical support received. Since they nevertheless overlap in their substantive interests, it should be worthwhile to try to integrate the two. Moreover, in my opinion both approaches have overlooked one important factor, namely, the *standards* through which the performances are assessed. In Foschi (1989) I have proposed a formulation incorporating this variable. The proposal both elaborates and extends aspects of expectation states theory while including elements of attribution work. Another way of viewing the proposal is to consider it a reformulation of the attribution ideas on social category and outcome that incorporates them into the framework of expectation states research (Foschi and Takagi 1991). The core idea is that, under certain conditions, different standards are used to appraise the same performance when actors differ in status. This is discussed next.

Status Characteristics, Performances, and Standards

Standards and the Inference of Competence

As used in this paper, the term "standard" refers to performance requirements for the inference of ability and lack of ability. In other words, standards are viewed as norms rather than descriptions, and as such play a major role in how performance evaluations are processed. For example, depending on the standards used, the same level of success may be interpreted as either conclusive or inconclusive evidence of competence. Performance scores provide an apt illustration: a score of 70 percent is usually sufficient indication of ability if the standard is at least 60 percent, whereas the same score becomes an unconvincing performance if the standard is at least 80 percent. The same holds for the interpretation of failure. Since a large number of everyday task situations involve inferences of competence as well as incompetence, it is important that both types of standards be included in the discussion.

The concept of "standards" has a long-established tradition in the social sciences. Although couched in other terms and defined somewhat differently from the use adopted here, it has appeared in connection with the study of a variety of processes. "Standards" as used in this paper can be traced to the writings of William James (1981 [1890]: 296) and his definition of "self-esteem" as the ratio of successes to pretensions. A recent example of work on standards is Frey and Ruble's (1990) examination of the idea that people choose different evaluation criteria (be they intrinsic to the task or socially derived) in order to maintain a sense of competence and self-esteem.

The concepts of "level of aspiration" and "goal setting" are similar to that of "standards" as defined here, and have also received considerable attention (for reviews, see Locke, Shaw, Saari, and Latham 1981; Lee, Locke, and Latham 1989). This literature, however, as well as most of the more recent work dealing directly with standards (e.g., Higgins, Strauman, and Klein 1986), does not have the same focus as the present paper (Frey and Ruble 1990 is one of the few exceptions). The most important difference is that this other work is concerned with the level of performance that a person who values success will strive for, or would prefer to achieve, rather than with requirements for ability inference. Accordingly, this literature deals mostly with the effects of performance goals on actual outcome; subsequent affective reactions are a particular focus (Hoffman 1986). Furthermore, this related work has not examined standards for *lack* of ability.

The literature on social comparison, stemming from Festinger's (1954) work, also has some relevance to the present discussion. This literature is concerned with those contexts where the ability level of comparison others is used as a standard. However, the focus is again different. My interest is in standards for performance defined in relation to the task itself, whereas social comparison research concentrates on situations where such a standard is lacking and, instead, one measures one's showing against the performances of others (or vice versa) (see, for example, Suls and Miller 1977; Felson 1993).

Clearly relevant to this paper is the theoretical and empirical work on standards carried out within the expectation states tradition. Foschi and Foddy (1988) propose a conceptualization of "standards for ability" and "standards for lack of ability" that is particularly well suited to the study of multiple standards. Consistent with expectation states theory, a task situation involving a person p (or "self") and a partner o (or "other") is assumed; propositions are formulated from the point of view of the person occupying the role of self.[2] Both individuals are task oriented and motivated to form correct expectations about each other. Several tasks are involved, each consisting of a series of equally difficult trials, and each requiring either a single ability or a number of related abilities. The proposal concerns the standards used by p to infer that a person (self or other) either does or does not have the ability in question. The standards may be imposed by a third party, or they may be generated by p.

Foschi and Foddy (1988) propose that, under such conditions, standards be defined in terms of five dimensions: (1) the degree of difficulty of the trials in one of the tasks requiring the ability, (2) the proportion of correct responses in that series of trials, (3) the number of times the series has to be repeated, (4) the number of additional tasks requiring the ability, and (5) the number of additional tasks requiring *related* abilities. Each of these dimensions is conceptualized as having two values, one more demanding than the other. These values, in turn, are used to construct "standards for ability" differing in *strictness*. For example, a standard for ability of at least 80 percent correct responses requires more evi-

[2]If the group consists of more than two persons, expectation states theory views it as a network of dyadic interactions in which each person takes turns at being the focal actor p and interacts with every member of the group one at a time. In addition to interactants, the theory identifies others playing important roles in the task setting, such as referents, audiences, and sources of evaluation (Berger, Wagner, and Zelditch 1985: 15).

dence and is therefore stricter than a standard of at least 65 percent. A similar definition is proposed for "standards for lack of ability." Accordingly, a standard that defines "lack of ability" as 35 percent or fewer correct responses is more lenient than one that sets the figure at 55 percent.

Such standards are, in turn, used to define various "expectation states" differing in strength, depending on whether or not p and o meet the requirements applied to their respective performances. For example, if p's performances meet the standard for ability and o's performances meet the standard for lack of ability, p is said to form "strong" (that is, definite or conclusive) higher expectations for self than for other. If p performs better than o but neither person meets the imposed standard, p will still form expectations of superior competence relative to the partner, but these will be "weak" (that is, less definite). Intermediate degrees of strength result if one standard (either for ability or for lack of ability) is met by one person but not the other. Two experiments (Foschi, Warriner, and Hart 1985; Foschi and Freeman 1991) designed to test some of these ideas provide direct evidence of the effect of standards imposed by an external source on strength of expectations. For a review of other work on standards and expectations, see Foschi 1992.[3]

A Theory on Status and Multiple Standards for Competence

Let us now go back to the task situation of central interest in this paper and specify its conditions in more detail. Suppose, then, that there are two performers, a man and a woman, working individually toward the solution of a valued task. Only one ability is required for success and both persons are task oriented and motivated to form accurate expectations about self and partner. The two treat gender as a diffuse status characteristic, and because of the sex difference between self and other, gender is a salient factor in the situation.[4] At the initial stages of interaction, sex of performer is the only cue they have about their respective levels of task ability. Following this, both persons receive evaluations for

---

[3] Note that the use of standards for the assessment of competence is basically a comparison whereby individuals judge their level of a certain attribute in relation to a set level of that attribute. Other examples involving similar comparisons are inferences about well-being, relative deprivation, beauty, or just treatment. Thus, fairness of the reward one receives is determined by a comparison with a "reward standard" (Lawler, Ridgeway, and Markovsky 1993). A similar idea is incorporated in Berger, Fisek, Norman, and Wagner's (1985) discussion of "referential structures," based on either status characteristics or on outcomes, that act as standards for the allocation of rewards. For an important formulation subsuming these various types of comparisons under a general theory of comparison processes, see Jasso 1993a.

[4] The different states of the status characteristic provide a clear condition for its salience. Such characteristics, however, may also become salient or "activated" under other circumstances. The following have been identified: (1) actors are equated with respect to the characteristic, but there is an explicit relevance link between it and the task at hand (Berger, Fisek, Norman, and Zelditch 1977: 64–74), and (2) actors make comparisons between themselves and non-interacting others (e.g., sources of evaluations) (Ridgeway 1982, 1988; Foschi and Freeman 1991; Foschi, Sigerson, and Lembesis 1995). In this paper, I consider only situations where the status characteristic is activated through a difference between the performers.

their own and the partner's performances. These assessments are made by an external source considered by the two actors to be objective. Furthermore, the evaluations indicate that the two have been either *equally successful* or *equally unsuccessful*. The question is: what level of competence do they assign to each other?

In Foschi (1989) I have proposed an account of the effects that sex of performer has even under such conditions of equal performances. A key element of the proposal is the assumption that there are *no previously set and agreed-upon standards* available to the actors to infer either ability or lack of ability from the performances. My theory is formulated to apply to the standards activated by any status characteristic, be it specific or diffuse; however, since in this paper I focus on the latter, I use gender for the illustration. Notice also that although most of the discussion that follows is about double standards, the ideas are easily extended to multiple standards if the characteristic in question has more than two states (as, for example, in the case of three levels of socioeconomic class).

The nature of the linkage between status and perceived ability to do the task at hand is a central variable in this formulation. For example, in p's view, task ability and sex of performer may be (1) explicitly dissociated, (2) explicitly associated, or (3) neither (1) nor (2). Since it is safe to assume that sex of performer would not have an effect in the first case, only the remaining two situations are of interest here.

Let us start by considering that there is an established linkage between sex and task that defines the latter as *masculine*, and that the two persons have been *equally successful*. Foschi (1989) proposes that, despite their equal performances, different expectations are formed for the two persons because they are held to different standards. More specifically, sex of performer activates different ability requirements, and these are stricter for the woman than for the man. Thus, once a performance occurs, the man is more likely to meet the more lenient standard applied to him than the woman is to meet the stricter standard employed to evaluate her. As a result, his performance will be seen as sufficient evidence of ability while hers will be attributed to nonability factors such as additional effort or good luck. This, in turn, will lead to expectations for future success that will differ in strength: strong for the man, weak for the woman.[5]

The proposal also extends to contexts in which p forms expectations about two or more performers (o_1, o_2, etc.) without being a performer himself or herself. This person is motivated, first of all, to arrive at correct estimates of the performers' ability, and he or she may or may not have formal authority over them (Foschi 1989; Foschi, Lai, and Sigerson 1994). Again, performance evalua-

---

[5] It is important to note that it is not assumed that p goes through the steps specified in the theory in a conscious way—he or she may or may not. In particular, p is not necessarily seen as setting standards in an explicit manner or as calculating probabilities. Similarly, no such purposeful connotations are attached to the terms "mechanism," "exclusion rule," "to activate," or "to process." Rather, the theory is only a model to be used to predict p's behavior, not an account of this person's thoughts. To this end, it is convenient to think of p *as if* this person performed the operations specified in the theory.

MARTHA FOSCHI

o_1 —— $D(+)$ —— $C(+)$ —— $\begin{bmatrix} T(+) \\ SA(1), \ \overline{SA}(1) \end{bmatrix}$

p

o_2 —— $D(-)$ —— $C(-)$ —— $\begin{bmatrix} T(-) \\ SA(s), \ \overline{SA}(s) \end{bmatrix}$

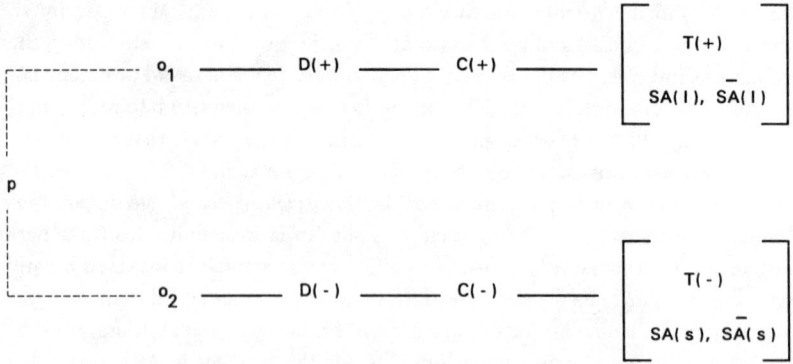

Fig. 1. Effects of status at t_1: Predicted outcomes and activated standards

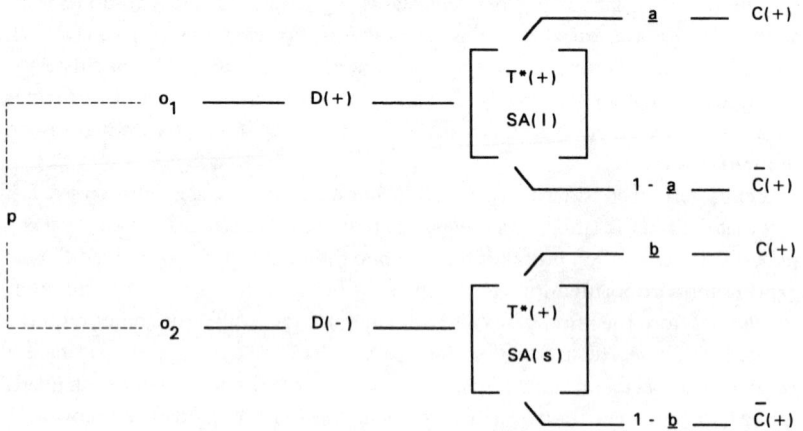

o_1 —— $D(+)$ —— $\begin{bmatrix} T^*(+) \\ SA(1) \end{bmatrix}$ $\begin{cases} \underline{a} \ — \ C(+) \\ 1 - \underline{a} \ — \ \overline{C}(+) \end{cases}$

p

o_2 —— $D(-)$ —— $\begin{bmatrix} T^*(+) \\ SA(s) \end{bmatrix}$ $\begin{cases} \underline{b} \ — \ C(+) \\ 1 - \underline{b} \ — \ \overline{C}(+) \end{cases}$

Fig. 2. Effects of status at t_2: Inference of levels of competence. Prediction: $a > b$

tions are made by an outside source assumed to be objective. Such contexts are of special interest in this paper because of their similarities to the evaluation settings commonly found in the workplace and educational institutions. To facilitate comparison with the last section of this paper, next I illustrate the effects of status on standards in the p, o_1 and o_2 context. (For representation of these effects in the p and o context, see Foschi 1989.)

Adapting ideas from Berger, Fisek, Norman, and Zelditch (1977), I represent the situation in terms of two graphs, one at t_1 (before the performances have taken place), the other at t_2 (after the performances have occurred). These graphs are shown in Figures 1 and 2, respectively. The broken lines indicate that the situation is described from p's point of view. Solid lines represent either a "possession" or a "relevance" relation; when I assign probabilities to these relations, the values are shown on the solid lines themselves. Brackets indicate that the enclosed elements are activated as a set. Note that I distinguish between a *predicted* task outcome T and an *actual* outcome T*.

In Figure 1, o_1 and o_2 are connected to opposite states (one positive and one negative) of a diffuse status characteristic D. C is the specific characteristic required to do the task. Since D and C are explicitly associated, p's activation of the corresponding opposite states of C follows. In other words, p makes a preliminary judgment of task ability. In turn, expected task outcomes T are also assigned to the performers in line with their status difference, and either strict (s) or lenient (l) standards for ability (SA) and lack of ability ($\overline{SA}$) are activated.

Figure 2 represents the situation after the two actors have performed the task at equally successful levels T*(+). Now p makes a subsequent assignment of levels of C. Because both actors have done well, of the two standards activated for each performer at t_1, only those for ability are used now. C(+) represents possession of ability, whereas $\overline{C}(+)$ represents its complementary state. (Note that $\overline{C}(+)$ is not equivalent to C(−). $\overline{C}(+)$ includes assigning C(−) *as well as* attributing T*(+) to nonability factors such as good luck or effort, *and* suspending judgment.) The application of different standards results in different probabilities, *a* and *b*, that competence will be inferred in the two persons. The probabilities of inferring $\overline{C}(+)$ in o_1 and o_2 are indicated by $1 - a$ and $1 - b$, respectively. The prediction is that *a* will be larger than *b*.[6]

The formulation makes the opposite predictions for the case of a *feminine* task. In that situation, it is the man who would be treated with a stricter standard. However, if the task is *neutral* (that is, neither explicitly associated nor explicitly dissociated from sex of performer), a status generalization process would define the task as one at which men are better than women. This, in turn, would again activate a stricter standard for the latter group. Since the association between gender and task is less direct, it is expected that the double standard will not be as pronounced as in the case of a masculine task. (Note that these arguments assume that the masculine, feminine, and neutral tasks are equally valued.)

A double standard is also predicted for the case of *equally unsuccessful* performances: in this case, unless the task is seen as feminine, lack of competence is inferred in women with *less* evidence of failure—that is, a stricter standard—

---

[6] There are also some conditions under which the lower-status person is ostensibly treated with a *more lenient* standard than the higher-status counterpart, and is told that the performance is sufficient demonstration of ability when in fact it is not. Such statements are rarely the result of a genuine assessment error but are, rather, made for other purposes; for instance, to avoid conveying a poor evaluation, or to meet quotas set to redress inequalities. For this reason, such patronizing standards fall outside the scope of this paper. They are nevertheless worth investigating, since depriving the lower-status person of a truthful appraisal is yet another practice through which the status quo can be maintained. There are also corresponding patronizing standards for lack of ability. Moreover, different standards for different classes of actors (be the standards stricter or more lenient for the lower-status person) are often applied in areas other than competence, such as beauty and morality. For a discussion of various types of multiple standards, see Foschi 1992.

than it takes to make the same inference about men (see Foschi 1989 for the graphic representation). In other words, provided that the task is either masculine or neutral, the use of different standards for men and women results in parallel processes whereby the former's failure and the latter's success are minimized.

The formulation also extends to other situations, such as those involving more than one status characteristic (specific, diffuse, or both) in either consistent or inconsistent combinations (Foschi 1989). In Foschi (1992), I discuss the role of level and number of performances in the activation of multiple standards. In all cases—albeit to different degrees, depending on these factors—the prediction is that the status characteristics of the performers will result in the activation of standards varying in strictness. Also, as discussed earlier, the degree of relevance between the characteristic(s) and the task is a key variable affecting the extent to which this occurs. Once a performance has taken place and is processed through one of these standards, expectations of differing strengths will result. Double (and multiple) standards are thus another component of the power and prestige order of the group contributing to the self-maintenance of the status quo.

Two useful features of this theory derive from the expectation states approach. The first is the *situational* character of the account: the same person p is expected to behave differently, depending on variations in the context, such as those involving the status characteristic(s) of self and partner and the sex linkage of the task. For example, if a man considers that gender is a cue to competence and that the task to be completed is masculine, he will tend to form higher expectations for self than for a female other. The same man, however, will form expectations of equal competence if the partner for the same task is another man. This relative character is captured in the notion of an expectation *state*, that is, an assignment of competence that responds to changes in the key elements of the context. The second feature, closely related to the first, is the *conditional* nature of the propositions. Thus, the above example also serves to illustrate that the theory does not apply to every man. Rather, it is only about those who view gender as a source of information about the quality of performances, that is, to those who are sexist by that definition. Because of the inclusion of such a scope condition, the theory is sensitive to cultural, historical, and individual differences. The scope condition itself also makes it possible, as the next step, to discuss levels of such sexism and to formulate propositions about their effects. For example, one would expect that the higher this level, the wider the gap between the standards for male and female performers. Notice also that women as well as men may meet this scope condition—whether they do or not is an empirical matter. If both sexes are equal in this respect, both male and female actors will treat women with a stricter standard than they will treat men. Other scope conditions of the formulation specify the perceived sex linkage of the task at hand, and stipulate that actors should assign a high value to performing it well.

Foschi's (1989) model on multiple standards for competence elaborates and extends aspects of expectation states theory. The new elements are the incorporation of standards as a factor in the formation of expectations, and the linkage between status differences and the activation of multiple standards. An alternative account of these processes has been proposed by Foddy and Smithson (1989). Their model is also based on expectation states theory, but includes the innovation of using fuzzy sets instead of graphs and paths of relevance. Although we propose different accounts for the use of multiple standards, the two models treat them as a mechanism contributing to the preservation of the status quo, and both make compatible predictions.

Finally, the work by Biernat and associates (Biernat, Manis, and Nelson 1991; Biernat and Manis 1994), proposing a model of stereotype-based shifts in judgment standards, should also be mentioned here. Their focus is on situations that are the reverse of the one discussed in this paper, and thus the work adds to the scope of the present discussion. These authors examine conditions under which members of different social groups show *differences* in an attribute (for example, a man who is 2 m tall and a woman who measures 1.80 m) but are nevertheless judged to be *equal* in that respect (in this case, tall) because of the application of different standards (namely, "tall for a man" and "tall for a woman"). Their model includes predictions about the relative impact of objective and subjective judgments on this process.

These three models propose a relationship between stereotypes and standards. Moreover, they share the theoretical advantage of their abstract treatment of the variable which activates multiple standards (that is, that variable is seen either as a status characteristic or as a social group). Together, the models represent a comprehensive effort to understand the operation of multiple standards. I now turn to a review of the evidence on this practice.

Empirical Evidence on Status and Multiple Standards for Competence

The expression "double standards" as used in this paper is of course not a new one—it is often employed in everyday language. ("Multiple standards" does not occur in that context as often, but its meaning would usually be readily understood.) A number of references to the practice of using different standards of competence for different categories of people may also be found in the social sciences literature. Although often insightful, these references nevertheless consist, for the most part, of descriptions of the practice rather than reports of research on it. Often the status characteristic in question is gender (see Foschi 1992 for a review of this work).

The topic has not received the research attention it deserves. Direct as well as indirect research evidence comes from a limited number of studies. I define "direct evidence" as that resulting from work specifically designed to test hypotheses about either double or multiple standards; "indirect evidence" comes from research that, although not employing those terms, nevertheless investigates this practice.

Four studies providing indirect research evidence are of special relevance here. All are based on expectation states theory and investigate situations in which men's and women's competence on various experimental tasks and corresponding influence over group members are being assessed. In all cases, performance requirements differ by gender. In Pugh and Wahrman (1983) and Wagner, Ford, and Ford (1986), results show that women were required "to prove themselves" more than men. In the first of these two studies, women had to demonstrate a higher level of performance than men before the two sexes achieved parity regarding influence; in the second study, a woman's superiority over her male partner did not result in the same high degree of influence as a man's comparable superiority over his female partner. The other two pieces in this group are Ridgeway (1982) and Carli (1990). In Ridgeway (1982), women had to show group orientation in order to be influential, whereas this was not required of men. Carli (1990) reports a comparable result: women who spoke tentatively had more influence over men than women who spoke assertively; male speakers, on the other hand, were equally influential regardless of their language style. In terms of the definition of "standards" used here, findings from these two studies show women having to demonstrate qualities that are not required of men. It is worth noting that only in Wagner, Ford, and Ford (1986) was the task explicitly described as masculine.

As for work providing direct research evidence, Yogev and Shapira (1987) examine credentials for employment—a variable closely related to perceived competence. The authors propose the existence of a double standard of "credentialism" for members of two ethnic groups in Israel, and the data support their claim: in actual employment practices, educational requirements were differentiated by level and type of education acquired which, in turn, were associated with different ethnic groups. To my knowledge, apart from this study, all the other direct evidence originates in work designed to test the three models described earlier. These studies may be summarized as follows.

Let us begin with the work by Biernat and associates. Biernat, Manis, and Nelson (1991) report results from three studies on gender stereotypes and standards. Subjects judged male and female target persons with respect to gender-related attributes (height, weight, and income), using either a subjective or an objective scale. Results show, as predicted, that targets differing in an attribute (for example, a man taller than a woman) were nevertheless judged to be equal if the scale was couched in subjective terms. In other words, such a scale enabled subjects to use gender-based double standards for tallness. Also as predicted, this did not occur when judgments were made on an objective scale. The issue is further explored in Biernat and Manis (1994), an article more closely related than the earlier one to the topic of social category membership and standards for competence. Four studies are reported, investigating academic competence and verbal ability in relation to gender, and verbal and athletic abilities in relation to race. In all cases, the predictions about subjective and objective judgments were supported.

The next four pieces have the closest relevance to this paper, as they test hypotheses derived from the two expectation states models. Foddy and Graham (1987) investigated subjects' standards for their own ability and lack of ability in same-sex and opposite-sex dyads. Participants first performed a "pattern recognition" task, described to them as being either masculine, feminine, or of no known sex linkage. Next they received prearranged scores indicating either one person's definite superiority or definite inferiority relative to the other. The results regarding standards for ability imposed on self in the opposite-sex conditions are particularly interesting. As expected, the authors found that when the task was described as masculine, women set a stricter standard for themselves than did men. This effect was larger when the female subject had performed worse than her male partner than when she had outperformed him. A double standard was also found when the task was defined as neutral, but here the effect was stronger when self had received higher scores than the partner. Also as predicted by the authors, no double standard was evident when the task was presented as feminine.

Two experiments reported in Foschi (1996) investigated a situation similar to that studied by Foddy and Graham (1987); nonetheless, there are several important differences. The central interest in the first of these studies was in standards for ability applied to *either* self or partner, and the "pattern recognition" task was defined as one on which men usually do better than women. (Most subjects of both sexes, however, considered it to be gender-neutral.) Subjects participated in opposite-sex dyads and were assigned at random to either control or experimental conditions. After performing the task individually, those in the latter conditions were informed that both self and partner had scored at an ordinary level. However, in half of these conditions self's scores were marginally better than the partner's while in the other half it was the partner who was marginally better. Subjects then set standards for ability for the performer with the higher scores. As expected, results show that, regardless of whether the person occupied the role of self or other, the female better performer was treated with a stricter standard than her male counterpart. The effect, however, was stronger when the standard was set for the partner rather than for self. The second experiment investigated level of accountability for one's assessments, and the effects of this variable on the use of double standards. As expected, the practice emerged clearly when accountability was low, but diminished when accountability was raised.

A study by Foschi, Lai, and Sigerson (1994) tests hypotheses about the use of double standards in the self-and-two-others context, and includes both sex of performer and sex of assessor as variables. The design involves the examination of files of applicants for engineering jobs, and recreates several features of a hiring decision. Subjects were male and female undergraduates who believed they were members of a university-wide committee making recommendations on the selection of applicants. The critical choice to be made by each subject was between a male and a female applicant with average but slightly different academic records. In one experimental condition the man held the better record; in the other the situation was reversed. Results from male subjects indicate that when the male candidate was the better performer, he was chosen more often, and considered more competent and more suitable for the job, than when the female candidate was in that position. Female subjects, on the other hand, did not exhibit such a double standard. This corresponds with the authors' hypothesis that men and women would differ in the extent to which they treated sex as a cue to competence.

In sum, the four studies show consistent support for the key propositions I presented earlier in this paper. Using gender as the status characteristic, they demonstrate the effects of sex of assessor, sex of performer, sex linkage of task, and accountability on the use of double standards. They also provide evidence that the practice occurs regardless of whether the level of advantage of one performer over the other is minimal or substantial, or the standard for ability is set for self or the partner.

Affect States and Multiple Standards

Up to this point I have discussed multiple standards for competence as they are activated by status characteristics. Is it, however, possible for other types of attributes to have a similar effect? Two such attributes have been described within the context of expectation states theory: personality characteristics (such as "gregarious," "introvert," or "empathic") and moral characteristics (such as "honest," "responsible," or "devious"). Both imply broadly defined attributions of what is perceived to be a person's true nature or character, but the latter also include judgments of what is right and what is wrong. As with status characteristics, personality and moral characteristics have differentially evaluated states, and these evaluations are affected by cultural, historical, and individual differences. For example, what is a moral characteristic in culture A may not have that connotation in culture B, or it may have the connotation to a different extent. Driskell (1982) examines conditions under which personality attributes function as status characteristics, and Webster (1982) discusses how moral characteristics may have similar consequences. It is therefore likely that each of these attributes can also activate multiple standards for competence.

Other, more recent developments in expectation states theory have involved extensions of the research to include socioemotional behavior and in particular *affect processes* (see, for example, Berger 1988; Johnston 1988; Ridgeway and Johnson 1990; Shelly 1993). These concern the degree of liking generated among participants in a task group. In such a setting, although the formation of performance expectation states is still the crucial process taking place, it is by no means the only one—the development of affect states often occurs concurrently. In fact, these are rarely avoidable. This point has also been noted in work from other research traditions (see, for example, Kemper 1991; Esses, Haddock, and Zanna 1993). Thus, one may acknowledge superior competence in a partner but at the same time dislike him or her simply because one is being inferiorized by the comparison. Alternatively, one may dislike a lower-status partner who is performing as well as oneself because the partner poses a threat to one's status. Furthermore, being liked by a higher-status person can in itself be a source of higher status. Affect states can also result from the assignment of personality or moral characteristics. For instance, one may feel sympathy for the "shy" group member and like that person more than the "outspoken" others. Similarly, it is common to like the person defined as "moral" more than his or her less virtuous counterparts. Finally, affect states may also result from more transient feelings, such as being annoyed or pleased by a group member's specific action (for example, a word or a gesture). As can be seen, there are many potential bases for an affect state; these in turn would impinge on its intensity.

As described in the previous section, multiple standards are an exclusion rule: they decrease the chances of a lower-status person being assigned competence and increase his or her chances of being considered incompetent, thereby contributing to the maintenance of the status quo. What activates multiple standards is the status difference. Thus, preliminary judgments about levels of competence are made on the basis of this difference; subsequently, more evidence of competence (or less evidence of incompetence) is required (or tolerated) from the lower-status person. Such multiple standards, however, may also be applied for other reasons.

Let us consider a situation involving affect states. These may develop either between p and o or in the p, o_1, and o_2 setting. An affect state then describes either the feelings of like or dislike (or even indifference) between two performers p and o, or the feelings that p (an assessor but not a performer) has toward performers o_1 and o_2. Here, I develop an example for the latter case. Several elements remain the same as in the status-activated multiple standards illustrated in Figures 1 and 2. Thus, the situation is seen from p's point of view; the fact that this person is not a performer is indicated by the broken lines. Again, p is motivated to form correct performance expectations about o_1 and o_2, and there are no previously set and agreed-upon standards from which to infer levels of competence. For simplicity, I assume that o_1 and o_2 are now equated with respect to a status characteristic; in this case they are both D(+). However, one of the performers is liked by p (L(+)) while the other is disliked (L(−)). As indicated above, the reasons for these feelings may vary; nevertheless, these reasons are not treated as a factor in this discussion.

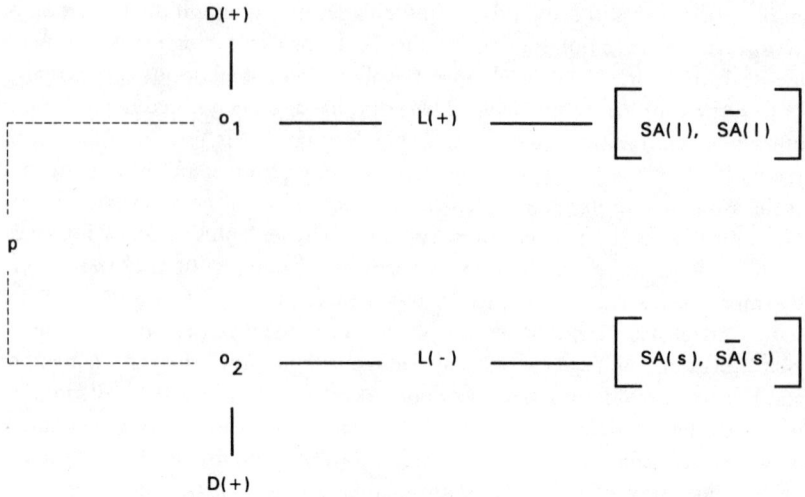

Fig. 3. Effects of affect at t_1: Activated standards

From p's point of view, then, nothing differentiates the two actors except the levels of affect toward them. I propose that under these conditions, different standards for competence are activated by the opposite affect states, so that standards for ability as well as lack of ability are more lenient for the liked person than for the disliked one. This is shown in Figure 3. Once again, the motivation is exclusion, but now this is done on the basis of differences in affect.

This proposal is consistent with and expands upon the ideas presented in Shelly (1993). He argues that affect states have consequences for the power and prestige order of a group: well-liked actors receive more chances to perform, are awarded more positive evaluations, and are more influential than those who are less liked. Since standards are another element contributing to the maintenance of that order, it is reasonable to assume that affect states would also have a similar effect on them. (See also Schwarz 1990 for an interesting discussion of how mood can affect evaluative judgments.)

Notice that since actors in Figure 3 are equated with respect to a status characteristic at t_1, the characteristic is presumed not to be activated.[7] Accordingly, its states do not lead to performance expectations and standards (as the differen-

[7] In the future, the model could be elaborated by proposing that states of the status characteristic are activated even though they equate the performers. This could occur if, for example, there is a strong relevance link between the characteristic and the task at hand. Suppose again that both performers are D(+). In that case, both would be connected to T(+) in Figure 1 and to lenient standards for ability and lack of ability in Figures 1 and 3. In Figures 3 and 4, the effects of affect would be moderated by those of status.

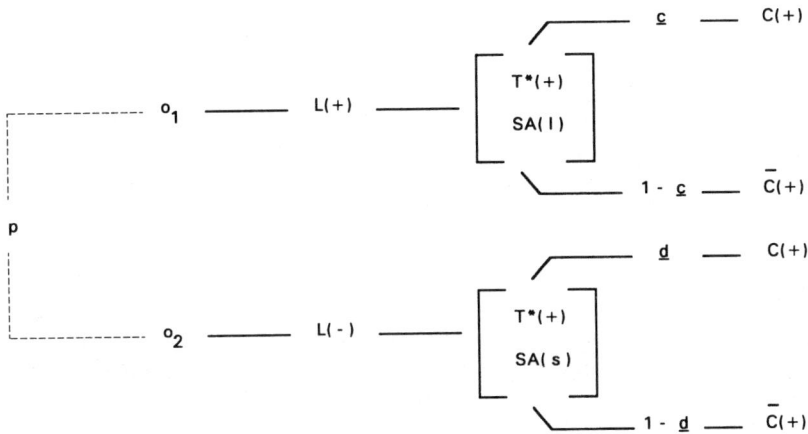

Fig. 4. Effects of affect at t_2: Inference of levels of competence. Prediction: $c > d$

tiated states of D do in Figure 1). Furthermore, affect states do *not* result in the expectation that o_1 will perform well or that o_2 will perform poorly.

Figure 4 illustrates the situation at t_2, after both actors have completed their performances. Again, I assume that the evaluations have been objective and that the two persons have been *equally successful*. The status characteristic is not included in this figure, as its states have not been activated. On the other hand, since the performance has been successful, the different standards for ability, activated at t_1, are now being used (whereas the standards for lack of ability are not). This results in a lower probability of the disliked person being assigned competence. Thus the prediction is that c will be larger than d. I propose a comparable situation for the case of two *equally unsuccessful* performers. Then it will take *less* evidence of failure to infer lack of competence in the disliked actor than it will take to arrive at the same conclusion regarding the liked person.

The next task is to develop hypotheses assessing the relative strengths of the variables considered in the four figures presented in this paper, namely, type of standard (lenient or strict) and type of process activating it (status or affect). It is important to remember that, as discussed earlier, one cannot assume that affect processes will be nonexistent in Figures 1 and 2, or that status processes will be totally suppressed in Figures 3 and 4. With that in mind, I submit that the activated standards are more pronounced when status-based than when resulting from affect, since they are reinforced by a prediction about quality of performance (levels of T) in the former case but not in the latter (cf. Figs. 1 and 3).[8]

---

[8] It is also likely that the activation of multiple standards by status is supported by a legitimacy process. In the situation examined in this paper, at the beginning of the interaction p associates status and expected performance in a consistent manner. When confronted with an inconsistency between

220   MARTHA FOSCHI

This argument is consistent with Shelly's (1993) predictions and results. In an experiment comparing the effects of sentiments and task ability, he found that the former did organize interaction in task groups, but that they did so more weakly than task ability. My predictions are thus that $a > c$ and that $d > b$. The resulting overall prediction is that both type of standard and type of activating process will have an effect, and that these two variables will interact: $a > c > d > b$.

Tests of the status characteristics and multiple standards formulation have shown clear support for its predictions. Its extension to affect process now awaits empirical testing. Once this is done, the next step would be to empirically assess the relative strength of status and affect in activating multiple standards. For a thorough understanding of these effects, it will be important to operationalize these two variables in a wide variety of ways. Thus, it would be useful not only to include different instances of status characteristics (with different levels of relevance to the task at hand) but also to vary the reasons underlying the affect states. Further, for both status and affect, it would be worthwhile to investigate situations resulting in multiple as well as double standards.

Summary and Conclusions

This paper addresses an issue of central interest in task groups, namely, how the evaluation of units of performance generalizes into appraisals of an individual's level of task competence. I discuss the role of performance standards as filters through which such evaluations are processed. I propose that, under certain conditions, status characteristics activate the use of multiple standards for competence. The core idea in this proposal is that, even if two actors perform at the same level, those who are perceived to be of lower status are treated with stricter standards than their higher-status counterparts. As a result, the former have diminished chances of being assigned ability when they are successful, and increased chances of being deemed incompetent when they fail.

My formulation elaborates and extends aspects of expectation states theory and, as such, has theoretical and empirical advantages derived from its association with this larger framework. A review of the evidence specifically obtained to test double standards hypotheses is also presented; although work on this topic is new and thus necessarily limited in quantity, it shows clear support for the formulation.

---

these two items, he or she activates different standards in line with each performer's status. The standards define what is sufficient evidence, and the model assumes that caution motivates p to require more evidence of ability of the lower-status person (and more evidence of lack of ability of the higher-status person). However, p may consider not only that it is prudent to use a double standard but also that it is the proper (that is, right) action to take. For a discussion of legitimacy and formation of expectations, see Ridgeway and Berger 1986.

Finally, I also present an extension of the status characteristics and multiple standards theory to include affect states. These states, or feelings of like and dislike toward performers, are proposed as another factor triggering the use of multiple standards. As in the case of status and standards, the interest is in situations where actors produce performances of equal worth. Now, however, it is the difference in affect that is predicted to activate standards of varying strictness and to result in inequalities of interaction. By incorporating both status and affect processes, the proposal now encompasses the two key aspects of interaction in task groups. This paper thus offers a ground plan for generating cumulative knowledge on an important exclusion practice.

Operation of Status in the Middle Grades: Recent Complications

Elizabeth G. Cohen and Rachel A. Lotan

Middle school classrooms in the United States have complex social structures. Students, typically of ages 11, 12, and 13, come from a wider social and ethnic range of backgrounds than is the case for elementary schools. There are few adult work situations that are so consistently and strongly evaluative, directly encouraging social comparisons between actors. As students move from elementary to middle schools, there is less emphasis on effort and more stress on purely meritocratic criteria. Through recitation and grading practices, evaluations of students by teachers tend to be frequent and public; they create a publicly agreed-upon rank order of academic status on how good each student is in that subject.

Boys and girls come out of the sex-segregated world of the elementary school and begin to be intensely interested in each other. Issues of attractiveness and popularity with same- and opposite-sex classmates lead to a constant process of peer evaluation in which students are ranked as to peer status. Criteria for this social ranking may include dress, athletic prowess, physical attractiveness, and elements of personal style.

Peer and academic status characteristics have a *local* character that distinguishes them from diffuse status characteristics. As is true of diffuse status characteristics, there are general expectations for competence attached to high and low states of the characteristics. However, as is not the case with diffuse status characteristics, the beliefs underlying these expectations for competence do not lie in the general culture. Rather, the definitions of high and low states of these characteristics and their accompanying expectations stem from local school culture concerning what it means to be "smart" in school and what it means to be popular and socially desirable. This set of beliefs can and does vary from school to school and from class to class.

Hypotheses and Exploratory Questions

In previous work on the elementary school classroom, we have shown that peer and academic status predicts rates of task-related talk in cooperative classroom groups (Cohen 1984; Cohen, Lotan, and Catanzarite 1988). The practical importance of these status effects on interaction lies in the relationship of interaction to learning when groups are engaged in collective tasks that are ill-structured problems (Cohen 1994). Under these conditions, those who talk and work together more frequently gain more in learning outcomes than those who participate less (Cohen 1984).

In this paper, we present an analysis of middle school data in which we investigate whether or not the relationships will hold in the middle school as they did in the elementary school data. Specifically, we test the following hypotheses:

> When working in groups on open-ended tasks, students who are seen as good in the subject matter and those who are popular will be more active than those who are not popular or seen as good in the subject matter.

> Those students who have higher rates of participation within groups will show greater learning gains than those students who are less active.

When strong local status characteristics are affecting interaction, the relationship of diffuse status characteristics to interaction is much less clear. One such characteristic is gender. Although Leal (1985) found no evidence of the effects of gender on interaction in cooperative classroom groups at the elementary school level, there is ample evidence that gender operates as a status characteristic by the time students reach puberty (Lockheed, Harris, and Nemceff 1983). Reasoning from the general social importance of race/ethnicity and gender, from their effects in controlled laboratory situations, or from the correlation of academic performance with race/ethnicity, one might assume that there will be strong direct effects in mixed-gender, interracial classroom settings. However, there are reasons to expect a weaker or more indirect relationship. The local characteristics are far more relevant to classroom activities and thus would have a more direct path of relevance. Moreover, deriving hypotheses is complicated by the earlier research showing that as students move toward middle school, peer status may have no direct relationship to diffuse status characteristics or to academic status (Wilson 1979). In other words, students who are popular may or may not be seen as good students and are often members of racial and ethnic minority groups. Thus, we have a mixed status characteristic situation with varying paths of relevance. Because of this complexity, we treat the effects of diffuse status characteristics on interaction in groups as an exploratory issue.

The way in which academic and peer status characteristics relate to each other is a separate feature of local social structure that varies between classrooms. Below the sixth grade, we have always found these dimensions to be positively related, that is, those who are high in academic status are often highly chosen as friends (Cohen, Lotan, and Catanzarite 1988). Wilson's (1979) study of sixth graders was the first to show that these dimensions may be negatively related or unrelated. With older students, peer status is a source of prestige that may be independent of academic success.

Theoretically, when students who are high on only one status characteristic work together with students who are high on another status characteristic, the result will be equal-status behavior. This occurs because people combine status information from different sources to form one aggregated expectation for the competence of self and others in the group. When peer and academic status are not positively related, there will be many more groups which combine students who have inconsistent states on these low-status characteristics. There should be fewer groups combining students who have consistently high states on peer and academic status with students who are low on both peer and academic status. When this is the case, the overall impact of status on interaction should be less severe than when peer status and academic status are positively related. In this middle school study, we explore the impact of variation in this structural feature of the classroom on the severity of observed status problems.

The Setting and the Sample

This is an observational study of status and interaction in nineteen social studies classrooms. All the classrooms were in middle schools that were in the process of eliminating academic tracks (in some countries, referred to as "streams"). The schools were all located in the San Francisco Bay area, California, USA. They were selected for study on the basis of their racially and ethnically mixed populations.

All teachers and students in classrooms in the study used complex instruction—an approach developed for heterogeneous classrooms by the staff of Stanford University's Program for Complex Instruction. The approach consists of instructional strategies and special group tasks requiring multiple intellectual abilities. The teachers had all participated in two weeks of staff development during the preceding summer and were receiving systematic feedback throughout the school year from the Stanford staff developers. Feedback was based on observations made during the implementation of complex instruction in their classrooms.

In many of the seventh grade classes, social studies were integrated with language arts in what is called a "core" approach. This means that there was a two- and in some cases even a three-hour time block allocated to instruction, permitting ample time for an orientation to the lesson, time to complete a variety of tasks in small groups, and time to come back together for presentations from each of the groups and a wrap-up by the teacher.

During groupwork, each group of three to five students had a different task to complete; each task reflected the central idea of the curriculum unit. In the multiple ability curricula specifically developed for complex instruction, tasks also involved many different intellectual skills and abilities. For example, one curriculum unit is called "How Do Historians Know?" Each group had an activity card requiring students to discuss and analyze open-ended questions. Following the discussion, groups put on a role play, created a model of a Crusader castle, wrote an advertising campaign for Pope Urban's Crusade, and created a mural depicting the defense of Jerusalem by the Muslims. In addition to the group product, each individual was supposed to write his or her own report based on specific discussion questions given to the group. Teachers were instructed to rotate groups between tasks, so that for a given unit, students experienced the central idea in various formats. The goal of this design was the understanding of the sources of historical knowledge through examination of physical ruins, ancient text, artwork, and music.

In order to ensure that the group proceeded smoothly and efficiently, each student played a specific role. For example, one student was the facilitator, whose job it was to see that group members got the help they needed. Another was a materials manager, a third was a reporter, and a fourth might be a harmonizer or a recorder. These roles rotated over time.

Students in each class received special preparation for cooperation in groups. Not only did they learn to ask each other questions and to help each other, but they were given specific training in articulating their ideas and in giving reasons for their positions.

When students are poorly prepared for cooperation and when tasks are weakly engineered for interdependence, one may see certain students doing all the work while others look on or engage in social interaction. Under these conditions, it is difficult to conclude that inequalities in participation are solely a function of expectations based on status. We are bringing out these particular features of the classrooms so that it will be clear that any status problems we observed were not a function of weak preparation for cooperation or inadequate attention to group and individual accountability.

Nor were inequalities in participation between high- and low-status students a function of uninteresting and unsuitable tasks. Students were engaged in their work, for the most part, and analysis of results of a content-referenced test showed that complex instruction classrooms gained significantly more from the pre- to the post-test on items requiring higher-order thinking than a set of comparison classrooms that did not utilize complex instruction (Cohen and Lotan 1995, forthcoming).

Research Design and Procedures

The research design called for a comparison of the rate of task-related inter-action of a subset of high- and low-status students (referred to as target students) within the same classroom. In order to estimate a stable rate of interaction for these students, it was necessary to observe them on multiple occasions as they worked on different group tasks and with different members of their class.

According to expectation states theory, the rate of task-related talk is an in-dicator of the operation of status generalization. High-status individuals will talk more about the task than low-status individuals. The basic data on task-related talk for the test of the hypotheses and for the exploratory questions came from classroom observations of high- and low-status students while they were engaged in collective tasks. Groups were composed heterogeneously by the teacher with respect to academic achievement. We took measures of the behavior of the target students in any group in which we found them, reasoning that the highest-status students in the class would be found in groups where some others were of lower status. Likewise, we assumed that the lowest-status students in the class would be working in groups where most other members were of higher status.

Because of the field setting of the study, we used a multivariate analysis to control other variables that have been shown to affect the rate of task-related interaction in complex instruction. Multivariate analysis was also necessary to test the effects of diffuse status characteristics while taking into account the impact of local status characteristics. In addition, in order to test the hypothesis concerning the impact of interaction on learning outcomes, it was necessary to control pre-test scores while estimating the impact of interaction on the post-test scores.

Measurement of Status Generalization

In order to assess the status order prior to the beginning of complex instruc-tion, we administered a sociometric test in each classroom in the fall. With each sociometric criterion, we gave students a list of classmates and asked them to circle as many people as fit the criterion. For example, to measure academic status, we asked students: "In your opinion, which students are the best at the subject in this class?" To measure peer status, we asked: "If your class had a popu-larity contest and you could vote for as many students as you wanted, who would you vote for?" We tallied the number of choices received by each student on these two criteria. The distribution of choices for each criterion was divided into quintiles. Each student received a score of 1 to 5, depending upon the quintile in which lay the number of choices he or she received. Because people combine the status information they receive (Humphreys and Berger 1981), we combined the scores on academic and peer status into a single index called the

"Costatus Score." Students who received a score of 2 received very few or often no choices on either criterion. Students who received scores of 9 or 10 received, relative to their classrooms, many choices on both criteria.

In order to gauge the observable status problems in the groups, we selected a set of target students in each of the nineteen classrooms. After calculating the costatus scores for all students, we selected five high-status and five low-status target students from each classroom. We classified all students who had a score of 2, 3, or 4 as "low status" and all students who had a score of 8, 9, or 10 as "high status." If there were not five students available with high and low scores defined in this way, we selected students from the closest middle category in order to complete the sample.

We collected at least six observations for each of 145 target students: 58 low status, 71 high status, and the remaining 16 middle status. Some students moved in the middle of the year; others were frequently absent and therefore we were unable to complete the full set of observations required for the entire sample.

Using the target student observation instrument (see Appendix), the observers recorded the frequency of task-related talk, of talking like a facilitator, and of selected nonverbal behaviors such as behaving like a facilitator (pointing or directing others how to behave), and working together. The observation instrument was divided into six 30-second intervals, so that if a person were talking about the task continuously during the observation, he or she would be scored six times. If a person shifted from task-related talk to talking like a facilitator and back to task-related talk within a 30-second interval, he or she could receive more than one score for task-related talk per time interval. An instance of talk or behavior in any of the categories was scored by a single check as long as it was not interrupted by another student talking or by a change of category. Interobserver agreement on the target student instrument was 94.69 percent.

To calculate an average rate of talking or behaving across observations for each target student, we divided the total frequency of these speeches and behaviors by the number of observations for each student. The average rate of peer task-related talk was 7.33 utterances per three minutes (S.D. = 3.53) (see Table 1). An analysis of variance of individual observations was conducted to test for the effects of the individual student on observations for task-related talk made on separate occasions. After finding that there was more variability between observations made on different individuals than between observations made on the same individuals (F = 10.2; p = .001), we averaged the rate of peer task-talk across all observations made of each target student.

In order to examine the effects of structural variation at the classroom level on the incidence of status problems, we used the same basic data on task-related talk but aggregated it to the classroom level. We estimated the relationship between costatus and observed rate of interaction for the classroom as a whole by

TABLE 1

Rate of Peer Task-Related Talk by Status, Gender and Ethnicity for Individual Target Students

	N	Mean	S.D.	Range
Status				
Low	58	6.48	3.66	0.60–17.0
High	71	7.84	3.13	1.67–16.4
Gender				
Boys	75	7.22	3.54	0.60–16.4
Girls	70	7.44	3.53	1.60–20.0
Race/Ethnicity				
White/Asian	89	7.70	3.52	1.67–20.0
Other	56	6.69	3.49	0.60–16.4
All Target Students	145	7.33	3.53	0.60–20.0

creating an index of status problems to measure the extent to which status was affecting interaction in the small groups. We calculated a correlation coefficient (Pearson r) between the costatus scores of all target students and their observed average rate of interaction during group work for each classroom. In some classrooms the correlation between status and talk was not different from zero, indicating no observable status problems. In other classrooms there was a significant positive relationship, indicating that the higher the status of the student, the more active he or she was within the small groups.

Measurement of Achievement

Students took a pre-test in the fall and a post-test in the spring. We created items for this test from the specific content material covered in the units we developed for the complex instruction classes. The content was based on the curricular frameworks developed for the seventh and eighth grades by the state of California and what was in the state-adopted textbooks. We did this so that the same test could be administered to classrooms that did not experience complex instruction.

The test was made up of factual items and of items requiring the students to draw analogies between what they had learned and some other situation. The following is an example of the kind of analogy we employed: The way the Muslims felt after the Crusaders captured Jerusalem was like the way you would feel after: (a) winning a lottery; (b) not getting invited to a party; (c) catching a cold; (d) having your home robbed of all its valuables. The items using analogies required higher-order thinking. Our experience at the elementary level had demonstrated that work on demanding open-ended tasks leads to gains in higher-order thinking (Cohen and DeAvila 1983; Cohen 1990).

Because our curriculum has a particular focus on higher-order thinking, we selected out the items requiring students to form analogies in order to test the effects of interaction on learning. For each student in the analysis, there was a pre-test and a post-test score based on the percentage of the items on which he or she had the correct answer. Since the classes did not cover all the units represented in the test content, we used for each class only those items representing content covered in that particular class.

Status, Interaction, and Achievement

To test the two hypotheses concerning status, interaction, and achievement, we examined the impact of status on interaction and the effect of interaction on learning. Peer status and academic status are the two status characteristics making up the costatus score. Table 1 presents the observed rates of task-related peer talk for low- and high-status students. The rate of participation for high-status students was significantly higher than that of low-status students (t = -2.42; p $<$ .05), although the average difference between the two groups was only .36. The rate of participation in peer task-related talk was markedly higher for both low- and high-status students (6.48 and 7.84 per three minutes, respectively) in the middle school than in the elementary school. The standard deviation of these statistics was also much higher. For example, the range of talk by low-status students ran from 0.6 per three minutes to 17 times per three minutes (which was slightly higher than the most talkative high-status student), yielding a standard deviation of 3.66 for low-status students.

Table 2 presents a regression of task-related talk on the costatus variable.

TABLE 2

Regression of Task-Related Talk on Status Characteristics, Controlling on Implementation

(N = 145)

Predictor	B	Beta[a]	t	p(1 tail)
Constant	-2.908	.000 (2.039)	-1.427	.079
% Talk/Work	0.186	.335 (.043)	4.139	.000
Costatus	.276	.213 (.101)	2.742	.004
Gender	-0.165	$-.023$ (.546)	-0.301	.382
Race/Ethnicity	0.759	.105 (.564)	1.344	.096

[a]Standard Error in Parenthesis
Dependent Variable = Task-Related Talk with Peers
R^2 = .425

TABLE 3

Regression of Post-test Scores on Higher Order Thinking on Pre-Test Score,
Peer Task-Talk, and Reading Scores

(N = 102)

Predictor	B	Beta[a]	t	p(1 tail)
Constant	.150	.000 (.059)	2.54	.007
Pre-Test Higher-Order Thinking	.429	.401 (.093)	4.62	.000
Peer Task-Talk	.009	.161 (.005)	1.91	.03
Reading Score	.002	.271 (.001)	3.07	.002

[a]Standard Error in Parenthesis
Dependent Variable = % Correct on Higher Order Thinking Items on Post-test
$R^2 = .579$

There was a highly significant effect of status on the rate of task-related talk; higher-status students talked more than lower-status students (Beta = .213; p = .004). In this regression, we controlled several other variables with potential effects on the rate of talk. The most important control is the general rate of interaction in the classroom as measured by the percentage of students talking and working together. This statistic was taken from the Whole Class Instrument; observers counted the number of students engaged in various activities on multiple occasions when the small groups were in operation. The average proportion talking and working together across multiple observations of a given classroom is a critical measure of the extent to which the teacher was able to foster peer interaction in the groups; if the teacher had difficulty in delegating authority, then both low- and high-status students talked less. This general rate of interaction and interdependence for each classroom had a major effect on the rate of participation of all students (Beta = .335; p = .000). The diffuse status characteristics in this regression did not have a significant impact, and this will be discussed in more detail in the next section on the interrelationship of costatus and diffuse status characteristics.

In order to test the effects of interaction on achievement, we used multiple regression. Table 3 shows the results of regression of the post-test score on higher-order thinking on the pre-test score, on the students' rate of task-related talk, and on the students' sixth-grade standardized reading score. Peer task-talk had a significant positive effect on the post-test score, holding the pre-test score constant. This means that the amount of interaction we observed was a predictor of gains on the items requiring higher-order thinking. Early reading score was also a predictor of how well the students did on the post-test.

Status scores do not appear in this regression because they did not have a direct effect on learning gains. As in the analysis of elementary school data (Cohen 1984), status had an indirect effect on learning gains. Those with higher status talked more and therefore learned more.

The effect of the early reading score on learning gains may reflect the strong demands for reading skills made by the test as well as the curriculum. One cannot tell whether those with reading difficulties experienced problems gaining access to the task or whether their difficulty lay with showing what they did know on an instrument that required more reading skill than they possessed. Nonetheless, regardless of one's early reading score, those who interacted more showed better gains on these items requiring higher-order thinking. In a separate analysis not reported here, we carried out a similar examination of the factual items on the test. Interaction was not a significant predictor of gains on factual items.

Gender, Race, and Ethnicity

The first diffuse status characteristic we examined was gender. Table 1 presents the means and standard deviations for task-related talk among peers for boys and girls while Table 4 presents rates according to gender *within* the low- and high-status groups. The results indicate that there are no overall differences by gender. According to Table 4, boys are somewhat more active than girls in both status groups, but the differences are not statistically significant.

Still another possible status characteristic we should examine is that of race and ethnicity. In more controlled laboratory settings, there is considerable evidence that African-American or Mexican-American students will be less active and influential on a collective task than white or Anglo students (Cohen 1982). In ordinary classroom settings, belonging to these two groups is often associated with lower academic status. Thus, it is not always easy to detect the operation of race and ethnicity as a status characteristic independent of academic status. In these data, we classified whites and Asians as high on the race/ethnicity sta-

TABLE 4

Rates of Peer Task-Related Talk by Gender and Ethnicity, Controlling for Costatus

	Costatus low			Costatus high		
	N	Mean	S.D.	N	Mean	S.D.
Gender						
Boys	35	6.68	3.65	32	7.98	3.41
Girls	23	6.17	3.72	39	7.72	2.91
Race/Ethnicity						
White/Asian	35	6.74	3.24	43	8.29	3.25
Other[a]	22	5.90	4.28	28	7.14	2.85

[a]Other = African-American, Hispanic, "other"

TABLE 5

Regression of Task-Related Talk on Gender and Ethnicity: Low-Status Students

(N = 57)

Predictor	B	Beta[a]	t	p(1 tail)
Constant	−4.463	.000	−1.670	.055
Facil. Talk Behavior	4.134	.585 (.682)	6.064	.000
% Talk/Work	.227	.394 (.058)	3.879	.000
Gender	−2.074	−.278 (.765)	−2.711	.005
Race/Ethnicity	1.511	.203 (.743)	2.032	.024

[a]Standard Error in Parenthesis
Dependent Variable = Task-Related Talk with Peers
R^2 = .721

tus characteristic and African-Americans, Mexican-Americans, Central Americans, and "other" as low on this status characteristic. Racial and ethnic classifications are based on the teacher's categorization and are only a rough guide to observable racial and ethnic differences. Table 1 presents the average rates of task-related talk among peers for the two broad racial/ethnic categories. White/Asian students have a significantly higher rate of task-related talk among peers than African-American and Latino students ($t = -1.68$; $p < .05$). Table 4 presents rates separately for low- and high-status students. When the sample is broken down in this way, the difference between whites and Asians and other racial/ethnic groups is in the same direction as that for the whole sample, but in neither case are the mean differences statistically significant.

In order to determine whether these different status characteristics had an independent effect on the rate of participation, we used regression techniques. Table 2 shows the results of regressing the rate of task-related talk with peers on the costatus score, gender, and race/ethnicity. For the sample as a whole, neither gender nor race/ethnicity has a statistically significant effect on task-related talk.

Tables 5 and 6 test the effects of gender and ethnicity in separate regressions for low- and high-status students. In these regressions, we use an additional control variable: the rate at which the target student talks and behaves like a facilitator. This kind of talk was scored separately from task-related talk. In earlier research on elementary schools, there was a suggestion in the data that when a low-status student plays the role of the facilitator, it has a boosting effect on that individual's rate of task-related talk (Cohen and Lotan 1995). Playing the role of a facilitator has considerable potential for changing competence expectations for a low status student. This role allows students to tell each other what to do in a legitimate manner that will not be resented by others.

The results in Table 5 demonstrate that for low-status students, both gender and race/ethnicity were significant predictors of interaction. Among the low-status students, boys were more active than girls, and whites or Asians were more active than African-Americans, Latinos, or those classified as "other." In addition, playing the role of a facilitator had a strong and significant positive effect on the rate of task-related talk. The effect was far stronger than any we observed for the elementary students.

When the same analysis was conducted for high-status students (Table 6), neither gender nor race/ethnicity had a significant effect on rate of interaction. Only the variables measuring quality of implementation (%Talk/Work) and playing the role of a facilitator had a significant positive effect on rate of task-related talk.

This finding means that there is an interaction effect between costatus and the two status characteristics of gender and race/ethnicity. If the student were high on academic or peer status, then these two status characteristics did not matter. If, however, the student were low on peer or academic status, then being male or being white/Asian predicted higher rates of interaction than being female or African-American / Latino. According to this analysis, the student who suffered the most from effects of status problems was the minority female who was neither particularly popular nor seen as a good student.

TABLE 6

Regression of Task-Related Talk on Gender and Ethnicity: High-Status Students

(N = 71)

Predictor	B	Beta[a]	t	p(1 tail)
Constant	−.252	.000 (3.021)	−.083	.467
Facil. Talk Behavior	1.369	.241 (.645)	2.121	.019
% Talk/Work	.161	.294 (.071)	2.263	.014
Gender	.156	.025 (.731)	.213	.416
Race/Ethnicity	.179	.028 (.798)	.225	.412

[a]Standard Error in Parenthesis
Dependent Variable = Task-Related Talk with Peers
$R^2 = .411$

TABLE 7

Classroom Variables

(N = 19)

	Mean	S.D.	Range
Index of Status Problems	0.34	0.35	−.23−+.79
Index of Congruence	0.04	0.242	−.26−+.60
% Low–Status Students	26.97	8.53	14.3−48.3

Status Problems at the Classroom Level

Table 7 presents the mean value of the index of status problems as well as the range. Classrooms in this study showed considerable variability in the extent to which status and interaction were correlated. Index values ranged from −.23 to +.79. There were three classrooms with a negative index value below −.10. In these classrooms, there was a tendency for low-status students to be more active on the task than high-status students. In contrast, there were nine classrooms with an index value of +.50 or higher, indicating a statistically significant association between being higher status and talking more.

Index of Status Congruence

It will be recalled that the costatus score is composed of two status characteristics: peer status and academic status. The degree to which the two status dimensions were congruent or incongruent was an important classroom characteristic for understanding the occurrence of status problems. Incongruent classrooms are classrooms where peer status and academic status are *unrelated* or *negatively related* to each other. Congruent classrooms are those where peer status and academic status are positively related.

Table 7 shows the descriptive statistics for the index of congruence. On average, the correlation between the two dimensions in these classrooms was 0.04. Thus, on average, these were incongruent classrooms. The index value, however, ranged from −.26 to +.60.

Predicting Status Problems at the Classroom Level

In order to evaluate the effects of structural factors on the index of status problems, we carried out a regression analysis on all nineteen classrooms (see Table 8). The effects of congruence in the classroom were not clear in the regression analysis until we entered the percentage of low-status students in the classroom as a control variable. The power of status congruence in predicting status problems was not observable in a simple correlation matrix where status congruence was unrelated to the index of status problems (see Appendix,

Table C). This occurred because status congruence was correlated with the percentage of low-status students. Congruence operates to *increase* status problems while the percentage of low-status students operates to *decrease* status problems. These contrary effects were masked by simple correlations.

Table 7 shows that there was a wide range in the proportion of low-status students in these classrooms. The statistic ranges from only 14.3 percent in one classroom to 48.3 percent in another. There is a large standard deviation of this statistic: S.D. = 8.53.

Another variable of interest in this regression is the presence or absence in the classroom of "mainstreaming," in which students who are classified as disabled with respect to the ordinary school program are combined with more typical students. There has been, in the past few years, a strong trend toward ending the segregation of such students in special education classes by bringing them into the regular classrooms, often accompanied by a special education teacher who teams with the regular classroom teacher. Students, however, often exhibit marked prejudice toward special education students, calling them "retards" and "dummies." This kind of behavior suggests the operation of still another status characteristic, in which special education students are seen as generally incompetent intellectually, although in reality they may only suffer from a very specific type of learning disability. There were two mainstreamed classes among the nineteen in the study. They were both taught by our most experienced and skilled teachers who had a thorough understanding of status problems and how to treat them. Nonetheless, both these classrooms exhibited severe status problems.

Table 8 presents the results of regressing the index of status problems on main-

TABLE 8

Regression of Status Problems on Status Congruence, Mainstreaming and Percentage of Low-Status Students: Classroom Level

(N = 19)

Predictor	B	Beta[a]	t	p(1 tail)
Constant	.213	.000 (.334)	.636	.267
Mainstream	.670	.597 (.237)	2.829	.007
% Low-Status	−.024	−.577 (.011)	−2.259	.010
Status Congruence	.726	.495 (.382)	1.899	.039

[a]Standard Error in Parenthesis
Dependent Variable = Index of Status Problems
R^2 = .410

streaming, the proportion of low-status students, and the index of status congruence. All three variables showed statistically significant and independent effects on the occurrence of status problems. The index of status congruence was a statistically significant predictor of status problems. Looking at this result another way, we found that the incongruent classrooms, as we predicted, had less severe status problems. Mainstream classrooms had more severe status problems, holding status congruence and the proportion of low-status students constant. And finally, those classrooms with a higher proportion of low-status students had less severe status problems.

Discussion

The favorable effects of status incongruence suggest that something may be reducing the severity of status problems that is quite independent of what the teacher is doing. When students create an alternative status characteristic that is unrelated to the official school value on academics, it is almost as if they are creating a natural status treatment. They are creating a situation in which they are not dependent on the school as the only way to gain status with one's peers. This situation need not create problems from a teacher's perspective unless peer status and academic status are negatively related to each other. This latter case can be a challenging teaching situation. If a student gains in academic status, it may be at the cost of personal popularity. This may well be the common situation of which teachers complain: there is peer pressure to avoid looking like a good student.

Status congruence in the classroom was associated with the occurrence of a higher proportion of low-status students. Since the same persons in a status congruent classroom rank highly on peer status and academic status, there are many other students receiving relatively few choices on either criterion. In contrast, when there is a status incongruent classroom, there are many students who receive a costatus score in the medium range, that is, they are high on one dimension and low or average on the other dimension. The concentration of students in the medium range of choices received means that there are not so many students receiving few choices on both status dimensions.

The effect of the percentage of low-status students may be partly an artifact of our measurement procedures. In classrooms where there are many low-status students and status is concentrated in a relatively few "sociometric stars," a number of groups we might observe should lack very high-status students and should contain all relatively low-status students. Since status problems are only activated in mixed-status groups, low-status students will not necessarily be inactive in such homogeneous groups. It should be recalled that we observed selected low-status students in any group in which they were working. We did not ascertain whether groups met the theoretical requirement of "a mixed-status group" for the status problems to appear. For classrooms where there are many low-status students, therefore, we should not expect to see such severe status problems as in classrooms where we are more likely to find low-status students in interaction with students who have a higher status.

Status Treatments

Teachers learned how to carry out two types of status treatments: the Multiple Ability Treatment and Assigning Competence to Low-Status Students. In the Multiple Ability Treatment, teachers discussed all the different kinds of intellectual abilities required by the cooperative learning tasks. They then created a mixed set of competence expectations for each student by saying, "No one will be good at all these abilities. Everyone will be good at some of these abilities."

To carry out the other treatment, teachers were advised to observe low-status students very carefully while they were at work in their groups on tasks requiring multiple abilities. If they saw one of these students exhibiting competence in an intellectual ability such as observing, reasoning logically, or solving a spatial problem, they were to publicly and specifically evaluate that student's competence in a particular ability. They were also advised to point out the relevance of this particular ability to the task, indicating that this student could be an important resource to his or her group.

The teachers in this study exhibited such variability between the different classrooms they taught that the observed rate of assigning competence did not meet our basic criterion of less variability between observations taken on the same teacher than between observations taken on different teachers. Thus, we were unable to analyze the effects of this treatment separately.

When we examined the teachers' rate of using both kinds of status treatments combined, we found that their rates of using treatments varied significantly according to the nature of the classroom. Those classrooms where we observed more severe status problems, such as the congruent classrooms, were the classrooms where the teachers were observed more frequently trying to treat status problems. In those incongruent classrooms where the status problems were less severe, the same teachers used status treatments less frequently. This suggested to us that it was not so easy to pick out low-status students and to observe status problems in the incongruent classrooms.

Because we did not know what the status problems in each classroom were *prior to the teachers' attempt to treat those problems*, there was no way to disentangle initial differences in the severity of the problem and the effect of differences in the rate of treatment. Statistical analysis showed no effects of the teachers' rate of using status treatments. This may have occurred because the teachers working in the classrooms with more severe status problems may have brought those classrooms up to the point where they looked indistinguishable from those classrooms where the natural status treatment of incongruent status orders was taking place.

Theoretical Implications of Our Findings

Some of these results are clearly explained by expectation states theory, and some are not. Although race/ethnicity and gender seem at first glance to be the most general and powerful status characteristics, academic status and peer status more consistently account for differences in interaction between high- and low-status students. The superior power of status characteristics that have a direct path of relevance to the task and situation is not surprising in terms of the theory. Clearly, academic status and peer status are much more relevant than diffuse status characteristics to the collective tasks assigned in the classroom setting. Although peer status does not logically seem to have a direct path of relevance to a collective task for young adolescents in a classroom, we believe that peer status is uppermost in the minds of these students, even as they work on academic tasks.

The interaction effect between the diffuse status characteristics and the local status characteristics is puzzling. If it is true that these local status characteristics have greater relevance, it should be true unconditionally. If this were the case, we shouldn't see the effects of the diffuse status characteristics for low-status students. Somehow, if a minority student is high in popularity or is seen as a very good student, ethnicity is irrelevant. If this minority student is neither of those things, then he or she is more silent than a nonminority student of the same academic and peer status. The same can be said of low-status girls in comparison to equally low-status boys.

In the minds of many educators with whom we have worked, the very term "low status" is another name for minority student. However, there were just as many minority students who were "high" on the costatus variable as were "low" on this variable. The same was the case for girls: they were evenly distributed over the high- and low-status groups divided according to a combination of peer and academic status. Thus, at least in middle school classrooms where there is a good representation of both genders and minority groups, it is a mistake to assume that the classroom will faithfully reflect the status order of the outside society.

We have called the effect of status incongruence at the classroom level on reducing the severity of status problems observed in groups a "natural treatment." The development of a status order among the peers that is independent of the academic status order seemed to have a moderating effect on status problems in the classroom. This natural treatment for status problems might be explained as a combining effect. As students who are in inconsistent states on the two status characteristics work with each other, the combining or averaging of expectation states might be expected to produce an equal status outcome. However, this cannot fully explain equal status behavior in status incongruent classrooms in this set of data because we chose those students with the lowest and highest status on the two characteristics combined. This would mean that, on average, we would be observing low-status students in interaction with others who had higher status, very likely with students who had "medium" costatus scores. Rosenholtz (1985) demonstrated strong status effects in groups made up of students of average and low perceived reading ability as well as in groups made up of students of high and average perceived reading ability. Thus, we should still expect to observe status generalization operating with the target students we chose in status incongruent classrooms.

The most interesting theoretical issues raised by this research have to do with the emergence of *local* status characteristics and the effects of local context on the operation of status generalization. How do structural features such as the relationship of two important local status characteristics come to affect expectations for competence? Somehow the independence of the status dimensions at the classroom level had an effect on the occurrence of status generalization at the group level. With the exception of the seminal work on the referent actor (Berger, Fisek, Norman, and Zelditch 1977), the various developments of expectation states theory have not yet solved this problem of moving between levels of the group and the immediate context of that group. But this is a critical problem for those of us who use the theory as a basis for intervention in specific organizational settings.

Appendix

TABLE A

Intercorrelation of Task-Related Talk, Implementation, Facilitator Talk and Behavior, and Status Characteristics Individual Level of Analysis

(N = 145)

	Task-Related Talk	% Talk/ Work	Costatus	Gender	Race/ Ethnicity
Task-Related Talk	1.00				
% Talk/Work	.362***	1.00			
Costatus	.210	.042	1.00		
Gender	−.030	.038	.122	1.00	
Race/Ethnicity	.139	.156	−.074	.086	1.00

***p < .001

TABLE B

Intercorrelation of Task-Related Talk, Implementation, Facilitator Talk and Behavior, Gender, and Race/Ethnicity

	Task-Related Talk	Facil. Talk/ Behavior	% Talk/ Work	Gender	Race/ Ethnicity
	Low Status Students (N = 58)				
Task-Related Talk	1.00				
Facil. Talk/Behavior	.585***	1.00			
% Talk/Work	.330	.052	1.00		
Gender	−.069	.077	.274*	1.00	
Race/Ethnicity	.113	.026	−.136	.184	1.00
	High Status Students (N = 71)				
Task-Related Talk	1.00				
Facil. Talk/Behavior	.282*	1.00			
% Talk/Work	.330**	.047	1.00		
Gender	−.042	.021	−.245*	1.00	
Race/Ethnicity	.182	.113	.427**	.022	1.00

*p < .05   **p < .01   ***p < .001

TABLE C

Intercorrelations of Index Status Problems and Other Classroom Level Variables

(N = 12)

	Index of Status Problems	Mainstream	% Low Status	Status Congruence
Index of Status Problems	1.00			
Mainstream	.441	1.00		
% Low Status	−.235	.082	1.00	
Status Congruence	.023	−.218	.592**	1.00

**p < .01

TABLE D

Intercorrelations of Post-Test Scores on Higher Order Thinking and Pre-Test Scores, Task-Related Talk, and Early Reading Score: Individual Level Analysis

(N = 102)

	Post-Test Score	Pre-Test Score	Task-Related Talk	Reading Score
Post-Test Score	1.00			
Pre-Test Score	.476***	1.00		
Task-Related Talk	.190	−.041	1.00	
Reading Score	.420***	.303**	.086	1.00

***p < .001   **p < .01

Derivation of Predictions in Comparison Theory: Foundations of the Macromodel Approach

Guillermina Jasso

Theory-based scientific work may be regarded as consisting of three partially overlapping phases: (1) construction of postulates; (2) derivation of predictions; and (3) testing of predictions. The first two phases are considered theoretical work proper—that is, they are the main task of theoretical analysis—while in the third phase the fruits of theoretical work are submitted to rigorous empirical test. When working with a fledgling general theory, a theory already possessed of that minimum of postulates capable of generating testable predictions, it is the second phase that commands the most time and attention. An important focus is on the development of tools for deriving predictions from the postulates, and thus a large segment of what is called the methods of theoretical analysis consists of methods for theoretical derivation.[1]

This paper describes one method for deriving predictions, a method called the macromodel approach because it begins with the *distribution* of a theoretically based quantity and the parameters, subdistribution structure, and other features of that distribution. There are two main goals in the macro approach. The first is to obtain distribution-independent results; the second is to obtain results for a wide variety of distributional forms that can be considered as approximations to real-world distributions of the theoretically based quantities.

The macromodel method has proved useful in deriving predictions from the postulates of comparison theory, and the description of the method in this paper

---

This work was partially supported by the National Science Foundation under Grant No. SBR-9321019.

[1] At least since Merton (1945) it has been recognized in sociology that theoretical work requires much more than speculation (though speculation is so important a part of theoretical work that the physicist Fermi set aside an hour a day for pure speculation) and that progress in theoretical development requires a systematic array of methods for constructing postulates and for deriving implications. Important contributions to this task have been made by Berger and his associates (Berger, Zelditch, and Anderson 1972; Berger and Zelditch 1993), Blau (1960, 1977b), Coleman (1964, 1973, 1986a, 1990), Fararo (1973, 1989), and a host of younger sociologists.

will be stated in terms of comparison theory. However, the method is general, and can be used to derive predictions from the postulates of diverse theories. Conversely, it should be emphasized that there are many methods for deriving predictions, and the macromodel approach is only one of them; indeed, as of this date the majority of the predictions derived in comparison theory have been derived using another approach, called the micromodel approach. The micromodel approach is less technically demanding, and there is a suspicion that increased familiarity with the macromodel approach will trigger a burst of new derivations, possibly landing in new fields of phenomena. The same may occur in other theories.

The paper is organized as follows. The first section provides an overview of the macromodel approach. The second section presents procedures for choosing modeling distributions and finding their basic associated functions. The third section describes techniques for obtaining the distribution of a function of the initial variables and for obtaining the new distribution's main parameters and subdistribution structure. The fifth section considers examples of predictions derived by using the macromodel approach. A short note concludes the paper.

Overview of the Macromodel Approach for Deriving Predictions

The macromodel approach begins with a "something" specified for individuals—say, a behavior, an action, a sentiment, a judgment. This something is postulated by the theory to vary with certain factors. The objective of the macromodel approach is to show how the distribution of the something—and the parameters of the distribution as well as the subdistribution structure—depends on the distributions of the factors which produce the outcome.

In comparison theory, the something is the experience of a Z, the outcome of a comparison process. The class of Zs is large, and includes such outcomes as happiness, satisfaction, well-being, self-esteem, and the sense of justice. What all the Zs have in common is that they are thought to arise from the comparison of an actual holding of a good (or a bad) to a holding regarded as just or desirable or expected, termed the comparison holding.

This starting idea (to use Merton's apt phrase) of comparison theory—that humans compare their attributes and material possessions to those of others and/ or to some level desired or thought just for themselves and thereby experience happiness, self-esteem, well-being, relative deprivation, and the sense of justice—is of ancient origin, and appears in diverse literatures; early examples include Aristotle, Seneca, and Genesis. Social scientific treatments begin with Marx (1849), James (1891), and Durkheim (1893, 1897), and continue in such twentieth-century scientists as Stouffer et al. (1949), Merton and Rossi (1950), and Festinger (1954), to name only the earliest. The outcomes of comparison processes are thought to influence a wide range of behaviors at both the individual and social levels.

The starting postulate of comparison theory states that Z depends in a specified mathematical way on the actual holding A and the comparison holding C:[2]

$$Z = \begin{cases} \ln\left(\dfrac{A}{C}\right), & \text{for a good} \\[3ex] -\ln\left(\dfrac{A}{C}\right), & \text{for a bad} \end{cases} \tag{1}$$

The Z function thus requires that the actual holding and the comparison holding be positive numbers. The outcome Z can assume any value on the real-number line. Importantly, it assumes the value zero when the actual holding equals the comparison holding; and it assumes negative (positive) values when the actual holding is less than (greater than) the comparison holding. Besides unboundedness and the naturalistic mapping onto the real line, other useful properties of the Z function are symmetry, additivity, and the signs of the second derivatives. By symmetry, a ratio of the actual reward to the just reward and its reciprocal yield Zs of identical absolute magnitude; for example, the magnitudes of happiness and unhappiness are equal when one earns twice or half one's desired earnings. By additivity, it is possible to examine separately the effects of the actual reward and the effects of the just reward. The signs of the second derivatives ensure that, in the case of goods, deficiency is felt more keenly than comparable excess. Among other things, these properties make it possible to predict an important phenomenon empirically documented by Tversky and Kahneman (Kahneman and Tversky 1979; Tversky and Kahneman 1986)—that the response to gains is concave and the response to losses is convex.

The Z function is a general function that can be applied in many contexts. For example, the outcome Z may be experienced about one's own situation (a reflexive Z) or about another's situation (a nonreflexive Z). Put differently, the rewardee may or may not be the observer himself or herself. In the case of nonreflexive Zs, distinction is made, via subscripts, between the observer and the rewardee. Moreover, the observer and the rewardee need not be individual persons but may also be corporate persons.

For ease of exposition, we will restrict attention to the case of goods; hence,

---

[2]Description of the development of the comparison function will be found in Jasso (1978, 1980, and 1990). Note that this paper focuses on the *experience* of the outcome Z. In empirical work, distinction is made between the experience and the expression of Z, and the formulas include a multiplicative constant, known as the Signature Constant, which transforms the experienced Z into an expressed Z.

all formulas will be expressed for goods. Note, however, that extension to the case of bads is straightforward, given that all that has to be changed is the sign of the logarithm.

An important special case of the class of Zs is the justice evaluation, denoted J. The corresponding formula is written:

$$J = \ln\left(\frac{actual\ reward}{just\ reward}\right). \tag{2}$$

In fact, the current formalization of comparison theory originated with a theory of distributive justice (Jasso 1980), and the comparison function can be traced to the justice evaluation function proposed by Jasso (1978), which in turn built on the insights and analyses of Homans (1961) and Berger, Zelditch, Anderson, and Cohen (1972).[3]

Like all Zs, the justice evaluation can be reflexive or nonreflexive; that is, a person may experience the sense of justice about his or her own or about another's situation. The rewardee may be an individual or a corporate person; for example, studies of distributive justice have judged the fairness of the earnings of married couples, and studies of retributive justice have judged the fairness of the punishments meted out to corporations. The observer, too, need not be an individual person, as in cases of wage boards and juries.

The formulas shown in expressions (1) and (2) can be used directly to develop the macromodel approach for deriving predictions. However, in order to build a more general set of macromodel procedures, we will introduce two further postulates of comparison theory. These are the measurement rule and the identity representation of the comparison holding.[4]

Expressions (1) and (2) make plain that if the good (or bad) under scrutiny is cardinally measurable, the formulas are immediately usable. For example, the reader can substitute into equation (2) the values of earnings—actual earnings and just earnings—for any rewardee and obtain a J. A problem arises, however, when the subject of the comparison is not cardinally measurable, as, for example, for goods such as beauty, intelligence, bravery, athletic skill, and so on. The measurement rule states that ordinal holdings are to be measured as relative ranks within a comparison group. Specifically, the levels of the actual reward and the just reward are represented by $i/(N+1)$, where i denotes the rank–order statistic (arranged in ascending order) and N denotes the size of the group or population. The relative ranks thus lie on the unit interval. Two important properties of this measurement procedure are symmetry with respect to the endpoints and symmetry with respect to the midpoint. The relative ranks of the bottom and top

---

[3] For a detailed account of development of the theory of distributive justice and its generalization to comparison theory, see Jasso (1993b).

[4] The measurement rule and the identity representation of the comparison holding were proposed in Jasso (1980) and Jasso (1986), respectively.

person are equidistant from zero and one, respectively. For example, the relative ranks of the bottom and top persons in a group of size 12 are 0.0769 and 0.9231. In groups of even size, the two middle persons have relative ranks equidistant from 0.5; for example, in a group of size 12, the sixth and seventh persons from the bottom have relative ranks of 0.4615 and 0.5385. In groups of odd size, the middle person has a relative rank equal to 0.5.

The identity representation of the comparison holding is designed to cope with theoretical ignorance of the comparison holding in the eyes of particular observers. That is, the just reward is often far more difficult to ascertain than the actual reward. The identity representation states that the comparison holding is expressed as the product of the arithmetic mean of the distribution of the good (or bad) and a parameter ϕ, which captures everything unknown to the theorist about a particular individual's comparison holding: $C = \phi\mu$. For example, consider two persons who are in the same group, where the mean earnings amount is \$25,000. Person A considers his or her own just earnings to be \$20,000, and person B's just earnings amount is \$30,000. These facts are not known to the theorist, who represents the two persons' comparison holdings by $\phi \times 25$, where person A's value of ϕ equals 0.8 and person B's value of ϕ equals 1.2.[5] In the case of ordinal holdings, the arithmetic mean of the relative ranks is always $\frac{1}{2}$; hence, the comparison holding is represented by $2/\phi$.

Combining the three postulates—logarithmic specification, measurement rule, and identity representation—yields the following formula, written for the case of a good:

$$
Z = \begin{cases} \ln \dfrac{x}{\phi\mu}, & \phi > 0, \quad \text{cardinal holding} \\[2ex] \ln \dfrac{2i}{\phi(N+1)}, & 0 < \phi < 2, \quad \text{ordinal holding.} \end{cases} \tag{3}
$$

As shown, the formula for Z in the case of cardinal holdings includes the term x, which represents the actual holding, and the terms μ and ϕ, which represent, respectively, the arithmetic mean of X in the collectivity and the idiosyncrasy parameter. In this paper we will be using two kinds of arithmetic means, the arithmetic mean of the cardinal good X and the arithmetic mean of the outcome Z. To avoid confusion, we adopt the convention of always denoting the arithmetic mean of the cardinal good X by μ and that of the outcome Z by $E(Z)$.

In the macromodel approach, we will be using mathematically specified continuous distributions, and hence it is useful to introduce an equivalent restate-

---

[5] The identity representation has an additional feature. In the case of cardinal holdings, the mean can be expressed by its two constituent factors, the total amount of the good, denoted S, and the population size N. This feature proves extremely useful in the micromodel approach for deriving predictions, but does not come into play in the macromodel approach developed in this paper.

ment of the formula for Z in the case of ordinal holdings. The observed relative rank $i/(N+1)$ is an approximation of the quantity α, which can be interpreted as the theoretical relative rank. The quantity α can also be interpreted as the probability associated with a variate, and below we will make use of this fact.

First, however, we restate the basic comparison formula, replacing the observed relative rank $i/(N+1)$ by the theoretical relative rank α:

$$Z = \begin{cases} \ln \dfrac{x}{\phi\mu}, & \phi > 0, \quad \text{cardinal holding} \\[3mm] \ln \dfrac{2\alpha}{\phi}, & 0 < \phi < 2, \quad \text{ordinal holding.} \end{cases} \tag{4}$$

The objective is to establish the properties and subdistribution structure of the Z variate. There are two sets of procedures we can now follow. First, we can separate out the ϕ-component and establish the properties of the holding-component of Z. Second, we can eschew ϕ the identity representation and directly model both the actual holding and the comparison holding. In this paper, we develop the first set of procedures, leaving the second for a future paper. Denoting the holding-component of Z by Z^h, we rewrite the basic comparison function formula:

$$Z^h = \begin{cases} \ln \dfrac{x}{\mu}, & \text{cardinal holding} \\[3mm] \ln(2\alpha), & \text{ordinal holding.} \end{cases} \tag{5}$$

We now review two basic functions associated with probability distributions and their relations. The probability that the variate X assumes a value less than or equal to x, regarded as a function of x, is the cumulative distribution function (cdf), usually denoted $F_X(x)$. The inverse of this function, called the quantile function (qf) or inverse distribution function (idf) and variously denoted $G(\alpha)$ or $Q(\alpha)$ or $F^{-1}(\alpha)$, expresses the value of the variate as a function of the probability α. That is:

$$F(x) = \alpha \quad \text{and} \quad Q(\alpha) = x. \tag{6}$$

Important relations include:

$$F[Q(\alpha)] = \alpha, \quad \text{for } F \text{ continuous} \tag{7}$$
$$Q[F(x)] = x, \quad \text{for } F \text{ continuous and strictly increasing.}$$

(See Johnson and Kotz 1969, 1970a; Eubank 1988; Evans, Hastings, and Peacock 1993.)

It is obvious from expression (5) that the formula for Z^h in the case of ordinal holdings is itself the quantile function of the associated Z^h distribution. That is, we recognize the qf form in the fact that the variate is expressed as a function of the probability. Of course, we could have derived the qf in a totally different way, for example, by first obtaining the probability density function (pdf) of Z, using change-of-variable procedures on the given Z function and the distribution of relative ranks, which is a unit rectangular (as done in Jasso 1980).

However, we cannot proceed any further with the formula for cardinal holdings without first selecting a set of modeling distributions for them.

Selecting and Preparing the Modeling Distributions for Cardinal Holdings

Selecting the Modeling Distributions

We need probability distributions that can serve as useful models for the distribution of cardinal holdings. Because comparison theory is general and aims to encompass diverse kinds of goods (and bads) and to yield predictions for diverse times and places, it is important that the set of modeling distributions include many possible forms. Note that there is a lively area of research whose objective is to provide faithful models of the current income distribution. Results of that work will provide modeling distributions for comparison theory. But the set of modeling distributions used in comparison theory cannot be restricted to models of the current income distribution. We must have modeling distributions for many cardinal goods (and bads), including children's allowances, land and stock of animals, and prison sentences.

The first requirement is almost obvious, yet it is useful to state it. The required modeling distributions must be defined on a positive support. That is, the variate must be one that assumes only positive numbers. This requirement immediately rules out many distributions which are defined on the entire real line, for example, the normal, the Cauchy, and the logistic.

A useful way to categorize positive variates is by the activity at their lower and upper bounds. At the lower bound, we examine whether the variate approaches zero from the right. In ordinary language, we are interested in whether or not there is a minimum holding. Technically, however, it is the infimum that is of interest and not the minimum. The minimum of a set is its smallest element, if it has one; the infimum is the largest lower bound. Thus, a continuous positive variate which approaches zero from the right has a zero infimum but no minimum. Of course, if the variate has a minimum, that minimum is also the infimum. Accordingly, we will distinguish between variates with a zero infimum and variates with a nonzero infimum.

At the upper bound, we examine whether the variate has a supremum. In ordinary language, we are interested in whether or not there is a maximum holding. As with the lower bound, however, it is the supremum which is of interest and not the maximum. The maximum of a set is its largest element, if it has one; the supremum is the smallest upper bound. Thus, we are interested in distinguishing between variates with a supremum and variates without any upper bounds. Accordingly, we will distinguish between variates with and without a supremum. (See Binmore 1980: 67–70.)

TABLE 1

Prototypical Distributions of Material Goods

Infimum > 0	Supremum	
	Yes	No
Yes	Quadratic	Exponential Pareto
No	Power-function	Lognormal

NOTES: In both the power-function and the quadratic variates, the supremum is also the maximum. The lognormal and the power-function have an infimum at zero; the power-function of $c>1$ also has a minimum at zero.

Treating each dimension as a dichotomy, this approach leads to four combinations of interest: (1) a variate with nonzero infimum and a supremum; (2) a variate with nonzero infimum and no supremum; (3) a variate with zero infimum and a supremum; and (4) a variate with zero infimum and no supremum. To illustrate, the wealth distribution of a primitive society in good times may be modeled by the first type and in bad times (such as famine) by the third type; the wealth distributions of advanced societies near the end of a war may be modeled by the second type among the winners and by the fourth type among the losers.[6] Table 1 provides example(s) of each of the four combinations of properties. As shown, the Pareto variate, as well as the exponential variate, exemplify the combination of nonzero infimum and no supremum. The lognormal exemplifies the combination of zero infimum and no supremum. The power-function variate has a supremum but no infimum. Finally, the quadratic, a symmetric variate, has both an infimum and a supremum.

Work to date on comparison theory has utilized the five distributions in Table 1. It is important, however, to have a larger set of modeling distributions. To that end, current work is systematically adding new variates. These include the Weibull, beta, chi-squared, F, Gamma, log-Laplace, log-logistic, log-t, and log-Cauchy. Except for the beta, these variates are characterized by a zero infimum and no supremum. Note, however, that some of these variates can be

[6] Note that these idealized types of wealth distributions play a prominent part in ethical discussions of the just distribution of wealth; for example, while Plato (*Laws*, Book V) prescribed both a minimum and a maximum income (the maximum set at five times the minimum allotment), Rawls (1971) prescribes only a minimum income. Note also that the philosophical propositions use the terms "minimum" and "maximum" in their ordinary-language sense, not in the mathematical sense in which the minimum and maximum are special cases of the infimum and the supremum, respectively.

shifted rightward to produce versions with nonzero infimum and no supremum. Description of candidates for modeling distributions is found in the standard sources (Johnson and Kotz 1970a,b; Hastings and Peacock 1974; Stuart and Ord 1987; articles in the *Encyclopedia of Statistical Sciences*, such as Kotz, Johnson, and Read 1985; and so on).

Preparing the Modeling Distributions for Theoretical Analysis

To date, it has been found useful to employ two-parameter distributions as the modeling distributions in comparison theory, defining the two parameters as the arithmetic mean and a general inequality parameter. Fixing the two parameters at the mean and inequality is useful in comparison theory for two main reasons: First, the formulas for Z include μ, and, as we shall see, the mean cancels out of the formulas for the distribution of Z^h. Second, it will be useful to assess the dependence of properties of the Z distribution on inequality in the holding's distribution.

In general, there are three basic parameters, a location, scale, and shape parameter. For convenience, we adopt the uniform notation proposed by Hastings and Peacock (1974) and continued in Evans, Hastings, and Peacock (1993), using the lower-case italicized English letters a, b, and c to denote the location, scale, and shape parameters, respectively. The location parameter is a point in the variate's domain, and the scale and shape parameters govern the scale of measurement and the shape, respectively. Variates differ in the number and kind of basic parameters. Thus, our first task is to adapt the selected variates so that the versions to be used have two parameters and those two parameters are the arithmetic mean and the general inequality parameter. Because a can be any location parameter, our final formulas for the variates will be expressed in terms of the more specific μ rather than in terms of the generic a. We shall use c to denote the general inequality parameter, even though in some cases the inequality parameter may be based on a scale rather than a shape parameter.

Upon selecting a variate as a modeling distribution, it is useful to derive expressions for the major associated functions. The most fundamental associated function is, of course, the cumulative distribution function (cdf). Other critically useful functions are the probability density function (pdf), the quantile function (qf), the moment-generating function (mgf), and the characteristic function. In special cases, it will also be useful to have at hand expressions for the survival function and its inverse, as well as for the hazard function. Accordingly, the goal is to find the formulas for all these functions, written in terms of the two parameters μ and c.

As a last step, the investigator will check the operation of the inequality parameter c, making sure that it is indeed operating as a general inequality parameter. Two useful checks are: (1) to verify that two or three well-known measures of inequality are monotonic functions of c; and (2) to verify that as c ap-

TABLE 2

Quantile Function in Six Variate Families

Variate Family	Quantile Function $Q(\alpha)$	
Exponential	$\mu\left[\dfrac{1}{c} + \dfrac{c-1}{c}\left(\ln\dfrac{1}{1-\alpha}\right)\right]$	$c > 1$
Lognormal	$\mu\exp\left[cQ_N(\alpha) - \dfrac{c^2}{2}\right]$	$c > 0$
Pareto	$\dfrac{\mu(c-1)}{c(1-\alpha)^{1/c}}$	$c > 1$
Power-Function	$\dfrac{\mu(c+1)\alpha^{1/c}}{c}$	$c > 0$
Quadratic	$\mu\left\{1 + c\sin\left[\dfrac{\arcsin(2\alpha-1)}{3}\right]\right\}$	$0 < c < 2$
Rectangular (Power: $c=1$)	α	---

NOTES: The term $Q_N(\alpha)$ denotes the quantile function of the unit normal variate. Inequality is a decreasing function of c in the Pareto and the power-function variates and an increasing function of c in the exponential, lognormal, and quadratic variates.

proaches its low–inequality limit, the distribution becomes degenerate, that is, collapses onto a single point, the point of equality. Of course, the direction of the relation between inequality and c may differ across variates. For example, in the Pareto and power-function variates, inequality is a decreasing function of c; in the exponential, lognormal, and quadratic variates, inequality is an increasing function of c.

Table 2 presents the formulas for the pdf and qf of five variates which may be used to model the distribution of cardinal holdings, all specified as two-parameter distributions (a location parameter fixed at the arithmetic mean and a general inequality parameter) and ready for use in comparison theory or in any other theory whose quantities of interest include material resources. The table also shows the quantile function for the rectangular distribution which approximates the distribution of ordinal holdings. The following section illustrates the procedures used to obtain the expressions.

Illustration: The Pareto Variate

The Pareto variate is widely known in social science, and thus it serves as an ideal variate for illustrating the procedures described in this paper. In this section, we illustrate the tasks described in the preceding section, that is, the tasks associated with preparing the Pareto for use in theoretical analysis.

The Pareto—more precisely, the Pareto distribution of the first kind—is characterized by a nonzero infimum and no supremum; that is, it ranges from a minimum value to infinity. It is usually presented as a two-parameter distribution, the two parameters being a location parameter equal to the minimum value and a shape parameter known as Pareto's constant. Consulting two standard sources, Johnson and Kotz (1970a: 233–49) and Evans, Hastings, and Peacock (1993: 119–22), we find two expressions for the cumulative distribution function which are identical except for notation. While Johnson and Kotz (1970a: 234) denote the location parameter (minimum value) by k and the shape parameter by a, Evans and associates (1993: 119) denote these by a and c, respectively. Following their notation, the formula is:

$$F(x) = 1 - \left(\frac{a}{x}\right)^c, \quad a > 0, \; c > 0; \; x \geq a. \tag{8}$$

Our first objective is to reparametrize so that the location parameter is fixed at the arithmetic mean rather than the minimum value. Accordingly, it is necessary to find the arithmetic mean and express it in terms of the minimum value. If the source did not provide the arithmetic mean, we would find it using the procedures to be described below. However, most presentations of the Pareto include the expression for the arithmetic mean. That formula, as shown in Evans, Hastings, and Peacock (1993), is:

$$\mu = \frac{ca}{c - 1}, \quad c > 1, \tag{9}$$

where the restriction indicates that the arithmetic mean in the Pareto is defined only for values of c greater than one. By algebraic manipulation, we express the minimum as a function of the arithmetic mean:

$$a = \frac{\mu(c - 1)}{c}. \tag{10}$$

Substituting this expression for the minimum a in equation (8) and incorporating the new restriction on c, we obtain the final formula for the Pareto's cumulative distribution function:

$$F(x) = 1 - \left[\frac{\mu(c-1)}{cx}\right]^c, \quad c > 1; \; x \geq \frac{\mu(c-1)}{c}. \tag{11}$$

The next step is to obtain the final formulas for the other associated functions. In general, there are two ways to do this, by adapting existing formulas (for example, replacing a by μ, as in the cdf above), and by deriving the formulas from that for the cdf. It is useful to perform both sets of procedures, as a check on the results. Below we illustrate the second procedure, obtaining the formulas for the probability density function and for the quantile function.

In continuous variates, the probability density function is the first differential of the cumulative distribution function. Accordingly, the task is to differentiate the cdf with respect to x. We find:

$$f(x) = F'(x) = \left[\frac{\mu(c-1)}{c}\right]^c cx^{-c-1}, \quad c > 1; \; x \geq \frac{\mu(c-1)}{c}. \tag{12}$$

Because the quantile function is the inverse of the cumulative distribution function, we can use simple algebra to find it, isolating x on one side and obtaining:

$$Q(\alpha) = \frac{\mu(c-1)}{c(1-\alpha)^{1/c}}, \quad c > 1. \tag{13}$$

Finally, we are ready to check the operation of the inequality parameter c. We perform two procedures. The first is to verify that two well-known measures of inequality are monotonic functions of c. For the two measures, we choose the Gini index of concentration, denoted GIC, and the measure Δ proposed by Atkinson (1970, 1975), defined as one minus the ratio of the geometric mean to the arithmetic mean. The formulas for these two measures in the Pareto may be available in published sources, or they may be derived by well-known methods. In this case, one or both formulas (or key components, such as the geometric mean) may be found in Johnson and Kotz (1970a), Cowell (1977), Dagum (1988), and Jasso (1982).

The formula for Atkinson's inequality in the Pareto is:

$$\Delta = 1 - \frac{(c-1)\exp(1/c)}{c}. \tag{14}$$

The first derivative is:

$$-\frac{\exp(1/c)}{c^3}, \tag{15}$$

which is always negative (given that c must be positive). Thus, as c increases, Atkinson's inequality declines. Further, the limits of Atkinson's inequality are exactly the desired limits:

$$\lim_{c \to 1^+} \Delta = 1 \quad \text{and} \quad \lim_{c \to \infty} \Delta = 0. \tag{16}$$

The formula for Gini's index of concentration is:

$$\frac{1}{2c - 1}.$$

(17)

The first derivative is:

$$-\frac{2}{(2c - 1)^2},$$

(18)

which again is always negative. The limits are exactly the same as for Atkinson's inequality. Thus, c governs these measures of inequality, inequality declining as c increases.[7]

We turn now to a second check on the operation of the general inequality parameter. Intuitively, the limiting distribution of the variate, as the general inequality parameter approaches its low-inequality limit, should be degenerate. That is, the distribution should collapse onto a single point, the point of equality. A simple procedure utilizes the quantile function, which expresses the variate's value corresponding to magnitudes of α. Accordingly, if the presumed inequality parameter is indeed operating as an inequality parameter, then the limit of the quantile function, as the inequality parameter approaches its low-inequality limit, should equal the arithmetic mean. Formally, and denoting the low-inequality limit by q:

$$\lim_{c \to q} Q(\alpha; \mu, c) = \mu.$$

(19)

In the Pareto, it is straightforward to show that the limit of the quantile function, as c goes to infinity, is equal to the arithmetic mean:

$$\lim_{c \to \infty} \frac{\mu(c - 1)}{c(1 - \alpha)^{1/c}} = \mu.$$

(20)

The proof utilizes three limits and the theorem that the limit of a product(quotient) equals the product(quotient) of the limits (provided, in the case of a quotient, that the divisor does not equal zero). The three limits are as follows:

$$\lim_{c \to \infty} \mu = \mu$$

(21)

$$\lim_{c \to \infty} \frac{c - 1}{c} = 1$$

$$\lim_{c \to \infty} (1 - \alpha)^{1/c} = 1.$$

Thus, as the inequality parameter approaches infinity, its low–inequality "end," the distribution collapses onto the point of equality.

[7] In fact, it is known that all measures of relative inequality are monotonic functions of the Pareto's shape constant. Note, however, that the coefficient of variation is defined only for values of c greater than two.

Deriving the Z^h Distribution and Its Parameters and Subdistribution Structure

The Z^h Distribution

With the modeling distributions for cardinal holdings in hand, we are ready to derive the distribution of the holding-component of Z, namely, Z^h. The objective is to find the distribution of Z^h, given the function that connects the holding x to Z^h and given the holding's distribution. There are many procedures for achieving this objective. The best known is the change-of-variable procedure, which uses the probability density function of the input variable (the holding x, in this case) and yields the probability density function of the outcome variable (Z^h, in this case). That procedure is described in Hoel (1971); description of its use in comparison theory is found in Jasso (1980), and will not be repeated here. A second useful procedure is based on the quantile function, and we shall describe it in this paper.

Recall that the quantile function expresses the value of the variate as a function of the probability α. That is, x is expressed as a function of α. Transformation of x by an increasing function will then produce the quantile function of the new variable. Formally, we begin with

$$x = Q(\alpha). \tag{22}$$

Applying the transformation, an increasing function h, yields:

$$h(x) = h[Q(\alpha)]. \tag{23}$$

The resulting expression is the quantile function of the new variate.

Applying this procedure to the case of comparison theory, we begin with the quantile function for the holding x, and then apply the transformation:

$$\ln\left(\frac{x}{\mu}\right) = \ln\left(\frac{Q(\alpha)}{\mu}\right). \tag{24}$$

Of course, from equation (5),

$$\ln\left(\frac{x}{\mu}\right) = Z^h. \tag{25}$$

Hence, we restate in the language of quantile functions:

$$Q_{Z^h}(\alpha) = \ln\left(\frac{Q_X(\alpha)}{\mu}\right). \tag{26}$$

Equation (26) is the master equation that is used to obtain the distribution of Z^h in comparison theory.

To illustrate with the Pareto variate, we begin with the Pareto's quantile function, given in equation (13), and repeated here with the subscript P for Pareto:

$$Q_P(\alpha) = \frac{\mu(c-1)}{c(1-\alpha)^{1/c}}, \quad c > 1. \tag{27}$$

Accordingly, the quantile function of the holding-component of the Z distribution is:

$$Q_{Z^h}(\alpha) = \ln\left(\frac{c-1}{c(1-\alpha)^{1/c}}\right), \quad c > 1. \tag{28}$$

As noted earlier, the mean μ vanishes, so that the distribution of Z^h depends only on the inequality parameter in the distribution of the underlying good (or bad).

The cumulative distribution function is readily obtained by algebraic manipulation:

$$F(z) = 1 - \left[\left(\frac{c-1}{c}\right)^c \exp(-cz)\right], \quad z \geq \ln\left(\frac{c-1}{c}\right). \tag{29}$$

The probability density function is obtained in turn by differentiating the cumulative distribution function:

$$f(z) = c\left(\frac{c-1}{c}\right)^c \exp(-cz), \quad z \geq \ln\left(\frac{c-1}{c}\right). \tag{30}$$

The Z^h variate arising from the Pareto is recognized as belonging to the positive exponential family. While the formulas can be restated in terms of the basic parameters of the positive exponential (as in Jasso 1980), we retain their parametrization in terms of the holding's inequality parameter because it emphasizes the dependence of Z^h on a single parameter of the holding's distribution and because in the development of the parameters and subdistribution structure, it will be useful to examine the dependence on the inequality in the holding's distribution.

Table 3 presents the quantile functions associated with the holding-component of the Z distribution which arises when the collectivity values one ordinal holding or one cardinal holding whose distribution is modeled by one of the five variates in Tables 1 and 2. As noted, the formulas for the Z^h variates arising from cardinal goods are expressed in terms of the inequality in the holding's distribution.

Parameters of the Z^h Distribution

Two parameters are of major interest. These are the arithmetic mean and the Gini's mean difference (GMD). These quantities are so important in comparison theory that each has been given special meaning and made the focus of a postulate. The arithmetic mean is regarded as summarizing the social welfare in the collectivity; and it is thought that social cohesion varies as the negative of

TABLE 3

Quantile Function of the Z^h Distribution Arising from Six Variate Families

Good's Distribution	Quantile Function $Q_{Z^h}(\alpha)$	
Exponential	$\ln\left\lvert \dfrac{1}{c} + \dfrac{c-1}{c}\left(\ln\dfrac{1}{1-\alpha}\right)\right\rvert$	$c>1$
Lognormal	$c Q_N(\alpha) - \dfrac{c^2}{2}$	$c>0$
Pareto	$\ln\left\lvert \dfrac{(c-1)}{c(1-\alpha)^{1/c}}\right\rvert$	$c>1$
Power-Function	$\ln\left\lvert \dfrac{(c+1)\alpha^{1/c}}{c}\right\rvert$	$c>0$
Quadratic	$\ln\left\{1 + c\sin\left[\dfrac{\arcsin(2\alpha-1)}{3}\right]\right\}$	$0<c<2$
Rectangular (Power: $c=1$)	$\ln(2\alpha)$	---

NOTES: $Z^h = \ln(x/\mu)$. The term $Q_N(\alpha)$ denotes the quantile function of the unit normal variate. Inequality is a decreasing function of c in the Pareto and the power-function variates and an increasing function of c in the exponential, lognormal, and quadratic variates.

the GMD. Accordingly, finding the formulas for these parameters is an important task.

The Arithmetic Mean of the Z^h Distribution

It is evident that in comparison theory one routinely works with both the arithmetic mean of the holding's distribution and the arithmetic mean of the Z^h distribution. Thus, as noted above, to avoid any ambiguity, we adopt the convention of using the symbol μ exclusively to denote the arithmetic mean of the holding's distribution. For the arithmetic mean of the Z^h distribution, we shall use, again exclusively, the symbol $E(Z^h)$, which makes use of the expected-value operator.

As usual, there are several procedures that one can use to find $E(Z^h)$. The most widely used is based on the probability density function, and we write:

$$E(Z^h) = \int_{-\infty}^{\infty} z^h f(z^h)\, dz^h. \tag{31}$$

A second procedure is based on the quantile function; in this case, we write:

$$E(Z^h) = \int_0^1 Q_{Z^h}(\alpha)\, d\alpha. \tag{32}$$

It is useful to have several procedures at hand, for it may happen that one or another of a variate's associated functions is more or less demanding mathematically. For example, it may be quite easy to find the arithmetic mean with formula (32) but quite difficult with formula (31), or vice versa.

We now illustrate with the Pareto. Using the qf-based formula, we write:

$$E(Z^h) = \int_0^1 \ln\left(\frac{c-1}{c(1-\alpha)^{1/c}}\right) d\alpha. \tag{33}$$

This is an improper integral, given that the integrand is discontinuous at the endpoint 1, and we shall have to test for convergence by evaluating the limit. The antiderivative is:

$$\alpha\left[\ln\left(\frac{c-1}{c}\right) + \frac{1}{c}\right] + \frac{1-\alpha}{c}\ln(1-\alpha). \tag{34}$$

Evaluating the antiderivative at α equals zero yields zero. Examining the limit at α equals one shows that the limit exists, so that the definite integral in (33) exists and yields the expression for the expected value:

$$E(Z^h) = \ln\left(\frac{c-1}{c}\right) + \frac{1}{c}. \tag{35}$$

The pdf-based procedure begins with statement of the integral:

$$E(Z^h) = \int_{\ln(c-1)/c}^{\infty} \left[c\left(\frac{c-1}{c}\right)^c z \exp(-cz)\right] dz. \tag{36}$$

The antiderivative is:

$$-\frac{\left(\frac{c-1}{c}\right)^c [\exp(-cz)](cz+1)}{c}. \tag{37}$$

The integral is improper because one of its limits is infinity. Evaluating the antiderivative at $\ln(c-1)/c$ and taking the limit at infinity yields the same expression given in equation (35), namely, the formula for $E(Z^h)$.

It has been previously established that the arithmetic mean of the Z^h distribution is a decreasing function of inequality (Jasso 1980). This relationship is easy to verify by differentiating the mean with respect to the general inequality parameter c.

The Gini's Mean Difference of the Z^h Distribution

For the Gini's mean difference, too, there are several formulas that one can use. One is based on the quantile function and is written:

$$GMD = 2\mu - 4 \int_0^1 \int_0^\alpha Q(\alpha)\, d\alpha. \tag{38}$$

Applied to the Z^h distribution, we write:

$$GMD(Z^h) = 2E(Z^h) - 4 \int_0^1 \int_0^\alpha Q_{Z^h}(\alpha)\, d\alpha. \tag{39}$$

To illustrate use of this formula, we again turn to Pareto-distributed goods. We already know the antiderivative for the inner integral (it was given in expression (34)), and we already know that it evaluates to zero at the zero endpoint. Thus, the definite integral is equal to the expression evaluated at α. The required outer integral is thus:

$$\int_0^1 \left\{ \alpha \left[\ln\left(\frac{c-1}{c}\right) + \frac{1}{c} \right] + \frac{1-\alpha}{c} \ln(1-\alpha) \right\} d\alpha. \tag{40}$$

As usual, there are several ways to proceed. One way is to make use of the theorem that the integral of a sum equals the sum of the integrals and separate the integral into two component integrals:

$$\int_0^1 \alpha \left[\ln\left(\frac{c-1}{c}\right) + \frac{1}{c} \right] d\alpha + \int_0^1 \frac{1-\alpha}{c} \ln(1-\alpha)\, d\alpha. \tag{41}$$

The lefthand integral is easy to evaluate, quickly yielding the antiderivative,

$$\int \alpha \left[\ln\left(\frac{c-1}{c}\right) + \frac{1}{c} \right] d\alpha = \left[\ln\left(\frac{c-1}{c}\right) + \frac{1}{c} \right]\left[\frac{\alpha^2}{2}\right], \tag{42}$$

and the definite integral,

$$\int_0^1 \alpha \left[\ln\left(\frac{c-1}{c}\right) + \frac{1}{c} \right] d\alpha = \frac{1}{2}\left[\ln\left(\frac{c-1}{c}\right) + \frac{1}{c} \right]. \tag{43}$$

The righthand integral is obviously improper, with a discontinuity at α equals one. Integrating by parts, we find the antiderivative:

$$\int \frac{1-\alpha}{c} \ln(1-\alpha)\, d\alpha = \frac{1}{c}\left[\frac{\alpha^2 - 2\alpha}{4} - \frac{(1-\alpha)^2}{2} \ln(1-\alpha) \right]. \tag{44}$$

At α equals zero, the antiderivative equals zero. Taking the limit as α approaches one, we find that the limit exists and equals $-1/4c$. Thus, we have

$$\int_0^1 \frac{1-\alpha}{c} \ln(1-\alpha)\, d\alpha = -\frac{1}{4c}. \tag{45}$$

Combining all the component results, we find the expression for the Gini's mean difference of the holding-component of Z when the collectivity values one Pareto-distributed good:

$$GMD(Z^h) = 2\left[\ln\left(\frac{c-1}{c}\right) + \frac{1}{c}\right] - 4\left\{\frac{1}{2}\left[\ln\left(\frac{c-1}{c}\right) + \frac{1}{c}\right] - \frac{1}{4c}\right\} \quad (46)$$

$$= \frac{1}{c}.$$

Subdistribution Structure in the Z^h Distribution

The Z outcome describes a sentiment or a judgment such as happiness, well-being, self-esteem, or the sense of distributive justice. Thus, the distribution of Z in the collectivity will include positive and negative values, representing, for example, happiness and unhappiness or overreward and underreward. An intuitively appealing subdistribution structure arises by dividing the population at $Z = 0$—forming the underrewarded and overrewarded subdistributions.

More generally, in derivation of predictions, there are two kinds of subdistribution structures that are of interest. The first is the structure formed by separating segments bounded by particular values of Z; the underrewarded and overrewarded subdistributions constitute a special case of this kind of subdistribution structure. The second kind of subdistribution structure arises when the collectivity is divided according to proportions, for example, the bottom half and the top half, or the bottom fourth and the top three-fourths.

These two kinds of substantively meaningful subdistribution structure correspond to censored and truncated subdistributions. In censoring, the distribution is divided at a percentage point α; in truncation, the distribution is divided at a value of the variate.[8]

Analysis of subdistribution structure in comparison theory focuses on finding three quantities: (1) endpoint quantities—in censoring problems, the values of the variable corresponding to the given censoring point(s), while in truncation problems, the probability levels α corresponding to the given truncation point(s); (2) the arithmetic means in the subdistributions; and (3) the Gini's mean difference in each subdistribution. In this section we describe methods for obtaining the endpoint quantities and the subdistribution arithmetic means, leaving development of the Gini's mean difference of each subdistribution to future work.

[8] Our distinction between censoring and truncation follows the usage in Moses (1968: 196–201) and in Johnson and Kotz (1969: 27). We use the term "censoring" to refer to selection of the units in a subdistribution by their ranks or percentiles in the parent distribution; for example, the bottom one-fourth of the population is a right-censored subdistribution. In contrast, we use the term "truncation" to refer to selection of the units in a subdistribution by values of the variable; for example, the group with incomes greater than the mean is a left-truncated subdistribution.

Truncated Subdistribution Structure

Finding the proportion in each subdistribution of a truncated structure. In comparison theory, the most common kind of truncation involves, as noted above, separating the positive-Z subdistribution from the negative-Z subdistribution. The first task is to find the proportion in each subdistribution, that is, the proportion underrewarded and the proportion overrewarded. To do this, it is only necessary to evaluate the cumulative distribution function at the point zero, that is, $F_Z(0)$. In the special case of the holding-component of Z, it is evident that

$$F_{Z^h}(0) = F_X(\mu), \qquad (47)$$

where, as before, X denotes the distribution of the good.

To illustrate with the Pareto, the cumulative distribution function of the Z^h distribution is:

$$F_{Z^h}(z) = 1 - \left[\left(\frac{c-1}{c}\right)^c \exp(-cz)\right], \quad z \geq \ln\left(\frac{c-1}{c}\right). \qquad (48)$$

Evaluated at the point zero, the cdf solves to:

$$F_{Z^h}(0) = 1 - \left(\frac{c-1}{c}\right)^c. \qquad (49)$$

The cumulative distribution function of the underlying Pareto variate is:

$$F(x) = 1 - \left[\frac{\mu(c-1)}{cx}\right]^c, \quad c > 1; \; x \geq \frac{\mu(c-1)}{c}. \qquad (50)$$

Evaluated at the arithmetic mean, the cdf solves to the same expression given in (50).

Thus, the proportion underrewarded is given by the expression in (49). A natural question is how the proportion underrewarded varies with the inequality in the distribution of the valued good. Differentiating (49) with respect to c yields

$$\frac{d}{dc}\left[1 - \left(\frac{c-1}{c}\right)^c\right] = -\left(\frac{c-1}{c}\right)^c\left[\ln\left(\frac{c-1}{c}\right) + \frac{1}{c-1}\right], \qquad (51)$$

which, given that c exceeds one, is negative. Thus, as inequality decreases (that is, as c increases), the proportion underrewarded decreases and its complement, the proportion overrewarded, increases.

Other kinds of truncation also arise in comparison theory. For example, there is a conjecture that individuals whose Z scores lie in the interval between -1 and $+1$ constitute the mainstream, while individuals with scores less than -1 represent a particularly disadvantaged group and those with scores greater than $+1$ a particularly advantaged group. In this case, in order to find the proportions in each of the three groups, it is necessary to evaluate the cdf at -1 and at $+1$. The proportion disadvantaged is equal to $F(-1)$; the proportion advantaged is equal to $[1 - F(1)]$; and the proportion in the mainstream is equal to $[F(1) - F(-1)]$.

When attention focuses on the holding-component of the Z distribution, it is of interest that the values of the variate that correspond to Z scores of -1 and $+1$ are μ/e and μe, respectively, or approximately 37 percent of the mean and 2.72 times the mean.

It may happen that a particular distribution does not extend to the left of -1 and/or to the right of $+1$. The Pareto variate provides a good illustration. Recall that the Pareto has a nonzero infimum, so that the left bound of the variate equals $\mu[(c - 1)/c]$ and the left bound of Z^h equals $\ln c - 1/c$. The Z^h distribution extends to the left of -1 only if $c < e/(e - 1) \approx 1.582$. Thus, some collectivities will not have a group of downtrodden, though others will.

Finding the arithmetic mean of each subdistribution in a truncated structure. As before, the arithmetic means can be found in a number of ways, of which we highlight two, the pdf-based procedure and the qf-based procedure. The pdf-based formula for the mean of a truncated subdistribution is written:

$$\frac{1}{F(b) - F(a)} \int_a^b xf(x)dx, \tag{52}$$

where a and b denote the values of the variate at the endpoints of the subdistribution. The qf-based formula for the mean of a truncated subdistribution is written:

$$\frac{1}{F(b) - F(a)} \int_{F(a)}^{F(b)} Q(\alpha)\ d\alpha. \tag{53}$$

When the required mean is for a subdistribution that is either the leftmost or the rightmost, the endpoints are adjusted accordingly. For example, the mean of the truncated subdistribution containing the bottom group bounded above by the value b is written, using the qf-based formula:

$$\frac{1}{F(b)} \int_0^{F(b)} Q(\alpha)\ d\alpha. \tag{54}$$

Similarly, the mean of the truncated subdistribution containing the top group bounded below by the value a is written:

$$\frac{1}{1 - F(a)} \int_{F(a)}^1 Q(\alpha)\ d\alpha. \tag{55}$$

To illustrate with the Pareto, the formula for the mean of a leftmost truncated subdistribution is written:

$$\frac{1}{F(b)} \int_0^{F(b)} \ln\left(\frac{c - 1}{c(1 - \alpha)^{1/c}}\right) d\alpha. \tag{56}$$

If truncation is at zero—for example, to find the mean of the underrewarded group—the formula reduces to:

$$\frac{1}{F(0)} \int_0^{F(0)} \ln\left(\frac{c-1}{c(1-\alpha)^{1/c}}\right) d\alpha, \tag{57}$$

which, substituting for $F(0)$, becomes:

$$\frac{1}{1 - \left(\frac{c-1}{c}\right)^c} \int_0^{1-[(c-1)/c]^c} \ln\left(\frac{c-1}{c(1-\alpha)^{1/c}}\right) d\alpha. \tag{58}$$

From work discussed above, we know the antiderivative of the integral in (58)—expression (34)—and we know that, evaluated at zero, the antiderivative equals zero. Evaluating the antiderivative at the upper limit of integration, we obtain

$$\text{Underrewarded Mean} = \frac{\ln\left(\frac{c-1}{c}\right)}{1 - \left(\frac{c-1}{c}\right)^c} + \frac{1}{c}. \tag{59}$$

Similarly, to obtain the mean of the overrewarded segment, we evaluate:

$$\text{Overrewarded Mean} = \left(\frac{c}{c-1}\right)^c \int_{1-[(c-1)/d]^c}^1 \left[\ln\left(\frac{c-1}{c(1-\alpha)^{1/c}}\right)\right] d\alpha. \tag{60}$$

The definite integral is improper, given that the integrand is discontinuous at α equals one. Again, from our earlier work, we know the antiderivative—expression (34)—and we know that its limit, as α approaches one, exists and is equal to the expression in (35). Using the expression at the upper limit and substituting the value at the lower limit in the antiderivative, we find the formula for the overrewarded mean:

$$\text{Overrewarded Mean} = \frac{1}{c}. \tag{61}$$

It is good practice to check the means using the weighted-mean formula:

$$E(Z^h) = \left(\begin{array}{c}\text{Proportion} \\ \text{Underrewarded}\end{array} \times \begin{array}{c}\text{Underrewarded} \\ \text{Mean}\end{array}\right)$$
$$+ \left(\begin{array}{c}\text{Proportion} \\ \text{Overrewarded}\end{array} \times \begin{array}{c}\text{Overrewarded} \\ \text{Mean}\end{array}\right) \tag{62}$$

The check is completed, and the formulas are seen to be correct.

The procedures described in this section are easily generalized to the case of several truncated subdistributions and the means of the truncated subdistributions readily obtained. Moreover, if interest centers on a further function of Z, the means of the function are readily obtained. For example, in the case where interest centers on the three subdistributions described above, formed by setting -1 and $+1$ as the inner endpoints, the three means are easily obtained, as are means of functions of Z.

Censored Subdistribution Structure

Finding the values at the endpoints of each subdistribution in a censored structure. Suppose now that the problem of interest begins with given proportions of the collectivity, for example, the bottom 30 percent and the top 70 percent or the bottom half and the top half. The first task is to find the values of Z at the endpoints of the subdistributions. One may want to know, for example, whether a particular subdistribution includes both positive and negative Z scores. In this case, the quantile function provides the natural way to proceed. The value of Z corresponding to a particular percentage point α is $Q_{Z^h}(\alpha)$. The endpoints for any subgroup are found by evaluating the qf at the percentage endpoints.

We now illustrate, again using the Pareto variate to model the distribution of a valued cardinal good. The qf of the Z^h distribution is given by:

$$Q_{Z^h}(\alpha) = \ln\left(\frac{c-1}{c(1-\alpha)^{1/c}}\right), \quad c > 1. \tag{63}$$

Accordingly, the right endpoint of the leftmost subdistribution is found by evaluating the quantile function in (63) at the proportion in the subdistribution. For example, suppose that $c = 2$ and the leftmost group contains 25 percent of the population; then

$$Q_{Z^h}(\alpha) = \ln\left(\frac{1}{2(1-.25)^{1/2}}\right) \approx -0.549. \tag{64}$$

That is, the bottom quarter of the collectivity have Z scores less than -0.549. Similarly, the bottom half of the collectivity have Z scores less than -0.347.

Finding the arithmetic mean of each subdistribution in a censored structure. To obtain the means of the censored subdistributions, we again have several procedures available, and we highlight two. The pdf-based formula for the mean of a censored subdistribution is written:

$$\frac{1}{\alpha_2 - \alpha_1} \int_{Q(\alpha_1)}^{Q(\alpha_2)} xf(x)\ dx, \tag{65}$$

where α_1 and α_2 denote the probability values at the endpoints of the subdistribution. The qf-based formula for the mean of a censored subdistribution is written:

$$\frac{1}{\alpha_2 - \alpha_1} \int_{\alpha_1}^{\alpha_2} Q(\alpha)\ d\alpha. \tag{66}$$

If the substantive context refers to a structure of two groups, then there is only one censoring point, denoted α^*, and the two means may be defined as follows:

$$\text{Lower Mean} = \frac{1}{\alpha^*} \int_0^{\alpha^*} Q(\alpha)\, d\alpha, \qquad (67)$$

and

$$\text{Upper Mean} = \frac{1}{1 - \alpha^*} \int_{1-\alpha^*}^1 Q(\alpha)\, d\alpha. \qquad (68)$$

Again, the means obey the weighted-mean relation:

$$E(Z^h) = (LM)(\alpha^*) + (UM)(1 - \alpha^*), \qquad (69)$$

where LM and UM denote the Lower Mean and Upper Mean, respectively.

We now illustrate, using the Pareto variate to model the good's distribution.

To find the Lower Mean, we evaluate the definite integral in (67), for the case of the Pareto:

$$\text{Lower Mean} = \frac{1}{\alpha^*} \int_0^{\alpha^*} \ln\left(\frac{(c - 1)}{c(1 - \alpha)^{1/c}}\right) d\alpha. \qquad (70)$$

By now this integral is very familiar to us, and thus we quickly evaluate it:

$$\text{Lower Mean} = \ln\frac{c - 1}{c} + \frac{1}{c} + \frac{(1 - \alpha^*)\ln(1 - \alpha^*)}{c\alpha^*}. \qquad (71)$$

Similarly, to find the Upper Mean, we evaluate

$$\text{Upper Mean} = \frac{1}{1 - \alpha^*} \int_{1-\alpha^*}^1 \ln\left(\frac{(c - 1)}{c(1 - \alpha)^{1/c}}\right) d\alpha, \qquad (72)$$

which we quickly find:

$$\text{Upper Mean} = \ln\frac{c - 1}{c} + \frac{1}{c} - \frac{1}{c}\ln(1 - \alpha^*). \qquad (73)$$

Notice that both the expression for the Lower Mean and that for the Upper Mean contain the formula for the overall mean $E(Z^h)$; that is, the first two terms are equal to the overall mean in (35). The Lower Mean is equal to the overall mean minus a quantity (in the expression above, plus a negative quantity), and the Upper Mean is equal to the overall mean plus a quantity (in the expression above, minus a negative quantity). In fact, the weighted-mean check can be performed visually. It is obvious that the third term in (71), weighted by α^*, and the third term in (73), weighted by $(1 - \alpha^*)$, sum to zero; and it is obvious that the overall mean, weighted by α^*, and the overall mean, weighted by $(1 - \alpha^*)$, sum to the overall mean.

Our development has built on the distinction between truncated and censored subdistribution structures. But it is useful to make explicit the fact that often both kinds of procedures are combined in the analysis of a single problem. For example, suppose that one is interested in the truncated structure formed by the underrewarded and overrewarded subgroups. A simple way to find the means of the underrewarded and overrewarded subdistributions is to first use truncation-based procedures to find the proportion underrewarded and overrewarded and next use censoring-based procedures to find the means in the groups defined by the proportions they contain. That is, first evaluate the cumulative distribution function of Z^h at the point zero, as we did for the Pareto-based distribution in equation (49), and next substitute that value for the value of the censoring point α^* in the formulas for the Lower Mean and Upper Mean. To illustrate, the proportion underrewarded in Z^h arising from the Pareto is, as given in equation (49):

$$F_{Z^h}(0) = \alpha^* = 1 - \left(\frac{c-1}{c}\right)^c. \tag{74}$$

Replacing α^* in (73) by this quantity yields

Overrewarded Mean =

$$\ln\frac{c-1}{c} + \frac{1}{c} - \frac{1}{c}\ln\left\{1 - \left[1 - \left(\frac{c-1}{c}\right)^c\right]\right\}, \tag{75}$$

which quickly yields the value reported in (61):

$$\text{Overrewarded Mean} = \frac{1}{c}. \tag{76}$$

Examples of Theoretical Derivation Using the Macromodel Approach

In the macromodel approach to derivation of predictions from the postulates of comparison theory, the starting point is the instantaneous Z distribution and one or more of its parameters. In this section we provide several examples.

The Effect of Inequality on the Collectivity's Mean Well-Being

It is widely thought that wealth inequality has a pernicious effect on society. Two early examples of this view appear in Plato and in the Old Testament. Plato, who has Socrates say in the *Gorgias* that "justice is equality," also argues, in the *Laws* (Book V), that the ratio of the maximum to the minimum wealth should not be allowed to exceed five. And the writer of Leviticus (25) prescribes the establishment of a jubilee year every fiftieth year, when inequalities are erased and the ancestral allotments are restored.[9]

A key feature of comparison theory is that it enables rigorous derivation of

[9] For discussion of the idea that equality is a "good" and inequality a "bad," see Kristol (1968) and Oppenheim (1968).

the proposition that, in collectivities which value material resources, mean well-being is a decreasing function of inequality in the distribution of the valued good. This proposition can be derived in two ways. First, it is straightforward to derive the distribution-independent prediction that the mean well-being is a decreasing function of inequality in the distribution of the valued good, where inequality is measured by Atkinson's (1970, 1975) measure, defined as one minus the ratio of the geometric mean to the arithmetic mean. Second, it is easily shown that, when the valued cardinal good is modeled by two-parameter variates such as the ones described in this paper, the mean well-being is a monotonic function of the general inequality parameter c, with mean well-being declining as inequality increases.

To illustrate with the Pareto variate, recall the formula for $E(Z^h)$, given in equation (35). It is easily seen that the first derivative with respect to the inequality parameter c,

$$\frac{d}{dc} \ln\left(\frac{c-1}{c}\right) + \frac{1}{c} = \frac{1}{c^2(c-1)}, \tag{77}$$

is always positive, given that c must be greater than one. Given that inequality is a decreasing function of c, it follows that mean well-being is a decreasing function of inequality.

This link between inequality and mean well-being has far-reaching implications, for it provides precise meaning, based on universal principles, to the idea that inequality is a "bad." This result is also the first in a long line of results linking inequality to a variety of undesirable consequences—for example, in the section below entitled "Conflict Severity," it is shown that conflict between the warring subgroups of a collectivity (in which the people value wealth) is always exacerbated by wealth inequality. But note that the predictions stretch to remedies for the undesirable consequences—for example, in the cloister predictions in the next section, it is shown that the salutary effect of the cloister is heightened, the greater the inequality in the distributions of valued cardinal goods.

Public Benefit of the Cloister

In an analysis of the benefit to the society at large (called the public benefit) of monastic and mendicant institutions (collectively referred to as the cloister), Jasso (1991) modeled the public benefit of the cloister as the signed difference between the mean well-being of the entire population at the precloister period and the mean well-being of the noncloistered population during the cloister period. The model notices and highlights one important feature of the classic monastic and mendicant institutions—that the members assume the lowest places in the distributions of the goods valued by the society. In the classic monastic institution, the monks give up personal freedom and the perquisites of birth, taking the lowest places in the distributions of many valued ordinal goods;

in the classic mendicant institution, not only do the friars take a vow of poverty, but the institution itself takes on corporate poverty, so that the friars are unambiguously the poorest members of society.[10]

Accordingly, the population during the cloistered period may be regarded as having a censored subdistribution structure, the censoring point equal to the proportion who are cloistered. Thus,

$$B = (Upper\ Mean)_2 - E(Z)_1, \qquad (78)$$

where B denotes the public benefit of the cloister and the subscripts 1 and 2 denote the precloister period and the cloister period, respectively.

In the monastic institution, the valued good is ordinal, and hence the Z distribution is the negative exponential. In the mendicant institution, the valued good is cardinal, and hence its distribution must be modeled, a task for which we may use the modeling distributions discussed earlier. It is then straightforward to find formulas for the public benefit B for a variety of possible situations. For example, in the case of the Z^h distribution arising from a Pareto variate, we form the benefit term by subtracting the upper mean (expression (73)) from the overall mean (expression (35)), obtaining:

$$B = \left[\ln \frac{c-1}{c} + \frac{1}{c} - \frac{1}{c} \ln(1 - \alpha^*) \right] - \left[\ln \frac{c-1}{c} + \frac{1}{c} \right] \qquad (79)$$

$$= \frac{1}{c} \ln(1 - \alpha^*).$$

As shown, the public benefit of the cloister is a function of two quantities, the proportion cloistered, given by α^*, and the amount of inequality in the distribution of the valued good, given by the general inequality parameter c. In the case of ordinal goods, the formulas for the upper mean and for the overall mean contain only the factor α^*, so that the public benefit of the cloister in such cases is a function only of the proportion cloistered. It is then natural to ask two questions: First, how does the public benefit of the cloister vary with the proportion cloistered? Second, in societies that value cardinal goods, how does the public benefit of the cloister vary with inequality in the distributions of the cardinal goods?

To answer those questions, it is only necessary to take the corresponding derivatives. Differentiation of B with respect to the proportion cloistered (partial differentiation, in the case of cardinal goods) shows that the public benefit of the cloister is always an increasing function of the proportion cloistered. In the case of cardinal goods and mendicant institutions, partial differentiation of B with respect to the general inequality parameter c indicates that the greater the

---

[10] See Jasso (1991) for discussion of the use of the classic monastic and mendicant institutions as Weberian ideal types and for discussion of the extent to which particular orders and houses lived up to the ideal.

inequality in the distribution of valued cardinal goods—such as wealth—the greater the benefit conferred by the cloister on society at large.

A further question concerns differences across distributional regimes in the level of the public benefit of the cloister and in the effects of the proportion cloistered and of inequality. Jasso (1991) examines graphs of B across distributional regimes. These graphs suggest that the public benefit of the cloister tends to be small in societies where there is a safety net (the nonzero infimum variates) and large in societies where there is extreme poverty (the zero infimum variates). Another procedure for assessing the impact of the distributional form of the wealth distribution is to investigate the dependence of B, not on the within-variate inequality parameter, but rather on a conventional and well-understood measure of inequality, such as the Gini coefficient.

Comparison of the ordinal-good and cardinal-good cases also makes it possible to develop a new interpretation of the rise of the mendicant institutions in the thirteenth century and of the vision of the inventors of this new type of religious order, Saint Francis of Assisi (1181–1226) and Saint Dominic (1170–1221). In brief, when the societal valued goods shifted from quality goods—such as birth—to quantity goods—such as wealth—the monastic institution no longer conferred a public benefit on society, because the houses could be wealthy, even if individual monks made a vow of poverty. The invention of the mendicant institution, characterized by corporate poverty as well as individual poverty, ensured that the friars would be at the lowest places in the hierarchies of the new valued goods—chiefly, wealth—and hence that the cloister would again provide a public benefit.

Conflict Severity

In an analysis of conflict between the subgroups of a population, Jasso (1993a) set up a model in which the valued good in a collectivity is perfectly correlated with a grouping variable such as race, ethnicity, or sex. Thus, the wealthiest (or most skilled, etc.) person in the disadvantaged subgroup is poorer (or less skilled, etc.) than the poorest (or least skilled, etc.) person in the advantaged subgroup. This condition is termed "cleavage" and sets the stage for conflict between the subgroups. Clearly, the cleavage condition can be precisely mathematized by means of censored subdistributions, with the censoring point α^* representing the proportion in the disadvantaged subgroup.

Reasoning that the well-being of each subgroup can be represented by the average Z in the subgroup, Jasso (1993a) represents conflict severity, denoted S, by the signed difference between the mean well-being in the advantaged subgroup and that in the disadvantaged subgroup. Formally:

$$S = Upper\ Mean\ -\ Lower\ Mean. \qquad (80)$$

It is thus straightforward to obtain the formulas for conflict severity S in many distributional regimes.

As in the cloister example, it is evident that S depends on the censoring point α^* and on the general inequality parameter c. Accordingly, it is natural to pose the two questions: First, how does conflict severity vary with the proportion in the disadvantaged subgroup? Second, in collectivities which value cardinal goods, how does conflict severity vary with the amount of inequality in the distributions of the valued cardinal goods?

(Partial) differentiation of S with respect to α^* and the inequality parameter c provides the answers. First, the direction of the effect of the proportion disadvantaged on conflict severity S differs across distributional regime. For example, in societies which value an ordinal good, conflict severity declines as the relative size of the disadvantaged subgroup increases; in societies which value a cardinal good and the cardinal good is Pareto distributed, conflict severity increases as the relative size of the disadvantaged subgroup increases; and in societies which value a cardinal good and the cardinal good is lognormally distributed, conflict severity is a nonmonotonic symmetric function of the relative size of the disadvantaged subgroup, decreasing to its lowest point when the disadvantaged and advantaged subgroups each contain half the population and subsequently increasing. Second, in collectivities which value cardinal goods, the within-variate partial derivative shows that conflict severity is always an increasing function of inequality in the distribution of the valued cardinal good.

It was noted earlier that a major objective is to obtain distribution-independent results. The conflict work provides another example. As the summary just provided indicates, the analysis using modeling distributions showed that conflict severity is a monotonic function of the relative size of the disadvantaged group in all the variates examined except in the single variate whose Z distribution is symmetric. In this case, where the valued good is lognormal and the resulting distribution of well-being is normal, the graph of the conflict severity function is symmetric with respect to its vertical axis, which is the line $\alpha = 0.5$. This result immediately raised the possibility that all symmetric Z distributions would similarly have symmetric conflict severity functions. Consideration of the properties of symmetric variates led us to conclude that such indeed is the case. Whenever the Z distribution is symmetric, the conflict severity function, too, is symmetric (about the line $\alpha = 0.5$). As noted above, work is underway to model the distributions of cardinal goods by the log-Laplace, the log-logistic, the log-t, and the log-Cauchy variates. In all those cases, the Z distribution is symmetric; and hence we know already that the conflict severity function will be symmetric.

Concluding Note

This paper described the foundations of the macromodel approach to theoretical derivation. Although the development was in terms of comparison theory, the macromodel approach is applicable to all cases in which a theoretical quantity of interest is defined in the individual and hence has a distribution in the collectivity. We described procedures for selecting and preparing modeling distributions, for finding expressions for the principal parameters, and for working with subdistribution structures arising from either censoring or truncation.

The procedures described in this paper constitute the basic building-blocks of the macromodel approach. Elaboration of these procedures is in three main directions. First, the set of modeling distributions is being expanded; it is important that all quantities discussed in this paper be obtained for the resulting new Z^h distributions. Second, procedures are being developed to model the full Z distributions, obtained by modeling both the actual holding term and the comparison holding term; these procedures highlight two dimensions of interest— whether A and C are identical or different; and whether A and C are independently distributed, perfectly positively associated, or perfectly negatively associated—giving rise to six polar cases, or ideal types. An important part of this work is to find expressions for all the associated functions and subdistribution formulas discussed in this paper. Third, a new set of procedures is being developed to systematically derive distribution-independent results.

To illustrate the ongoing work, here are two kinds of results that have been obtained, the first referring to specific variates, the second to distribution-independent results.

Results for specific variates. First, it can be shown that if A and C are independently and identically distributed (iid) Paretos or power-functions, then Z is Laplace. Second, it can similarly be shown that if A and C are identical Paretos or power-functions and perfectly negatively associated, then Z is logistic. Third, it can be shown that if A and C are different Paretos or power-functions, and perfectly negatively rank-correlated, then Z is an exponential, and is positively or negatively skewed depending on whether A or C has the greater inequality.

Distribution-independent results. First, if A and C are iid, then Z is symmetric about zero. Second, if A and C are identical and perfectly positively associated, then Z is degenerate at zero. Note that the first result enables immediate extension of one of the conflict severity predictions to a more general case: If the actual holding and the comparison holding are independently and identically distributed, then conflict between the high-Z and low-Z subgroups—whether these are defined via censoring or truncation—will decline the more nearly equal in size are the two subgroups, reaching its nadir when the two subgroups are of equal size.

Future work will provide systematic description of these further procedures which build on the procedures described in this paper. Meanwhile, use of the macromodel approach to theoretical derivation may yield many new predictions, not only in comparison theory, but also in a wide range of other theories.

PART III

Structure, Social Networks, and Rational Choice

Structural Formulations and Elementary Theory

◥◣

David Willer and Jacek Szmatka

This paper examines structural formulations used in elementary theory, offers new applications for those formulations to solve three neglected problems stemming from the use of the concept "structure," and points to new directions. Elementary Theory models actors in relationships, contains a structural conception of social life, and studies networks of sanction flows as they are mapped onto populations. Paraphrasing Mayhew (1980: 338), we identify that network, the interactions which proceed through it, and the consequences which follow from it as its subject matter.

This paper does not trace the development of the theory. In fact, Elementary Theory has been intensively developed in a direct line for almost twenty years. By a "direct line of development," we mean that concepts and procedures which were early formulations, such as the theory's modeling procedure and its resistance equations, are still being used *in their original forms* and are now being applied over a much broader range of structures than originally envisioned. During the same time period, new procedures, such as the Graph-Theoretic Power Index, have been developed to solve problems which could not be addressed with older formulations alone. We make no attempt here to begin with basic concepts and work through to the theory's current scope; nor is such needed, for it is available elsewhere (Willer 1981a,b; Willer and Markovsky 1993; Szmatka and Willer 1993). The paper also will not recount recent developments in theory concerned with weak power and testing for universality, for both are also available elsewhere (Markovsky 1992; Markovsky et al. 1993; Skvoretz and Willer

The authors acknowledge grants from the National Science Foundation, Polish National Science Foundation, KBN (PB 0870/P1/94/07), and Research Support Scheme of the Open Society Institute (Grant no. 746/94) supporting research mentioned in this paper and thank John Skvoretz, Michael Lovaglia, Barry Markovsky, Patricia Willer, and the Iowa Workshop on Theoretic Analysis for helpful comments and suggestions.

1993; Willer and Szmatka 1993). Instead, we focus on problems in the theory of structure as seen from the perspective of Elementary Theory.

Concepts of Structure in Sociology

To place Elementary Theory's structural formulations, we begin with a brief review of structural perspectives in sociology. Our first comments concern the level at which structures are located, a macro-micro issue. Then we turn to differing views concerning the composition of social structures.

In the analysis of structure, some sociologists focus on large-scale objects. Lenski, for example, takes a macrosocial perspective defining structure as the pattern underlying the history of human societies. His evolutionary conception sees a configuration of far-reaching, directional trends determined by evolutionary processes (Lenski 1975). Parsons's view of structure is also macrosocial, but his interest focuses on relations between subsystems and larger systems (Parsons 1975). Regarding Parsons, Blau notes, "A theoretical scheme on such a high level of abstraction makes people disappear from view and with them not only the motives and behavior of individuals but also the structures of social relations and the differentiated collectivities in society" (Blau 1975: 4–5). Other examples of the macro approach include Marx (1973 [1857]); Skocpol (1979); and Tilly (1973). (For more examples, see Kontopoulos 1993.)

Other sociologists focus on the structure of small-scale objects as in Homans' analysis of elementary social behavior (Homans 1950, 1974, 1975). According to Homans, social structures are merely enduring and persistent aspects of social behavior (1975: 53). (Also see Homans 1950.) From Homans' point of view, structures are produced at the individual level and can, in principle, be explained by individual-level laws alone. While James Coleman's approach is quite different from Homans', his focus is also on the micro level where individual behavior is governed by rational choice (Coleman 1975, 1986a, 1990).

A third approach is concerned with structure at both the micro and the macro level (Merton 1968, 1975). (See also Lipset 1975.) Here, structure is found in both small-scale and large-scale social objects and in the linking of the two levels. Many studies take this multilevel view (for example, Blalock and Wilken 1979; Collins 1981; Burt 1982; Markovsky 1987). Recently, Kontopoulos revived the idea of "meso" structures (for example, organizations) located between small- and large-scale social objects (Kontopoulos 1993).

Elementary Theory distinguishes social structures qualitatively, not quantitatively in terms of size. For example, social structures composed of coercive relations are fundamentally different from social structures composed of exchange relations. Furthermore, social structures which have "exclusive" connections are fundamentally different from ones with "inclusive" connections. Early Elementary Theory work focused on two different kinds of structures, normative versus power. In the field, normative structures are relatively small; power structures are relatively large. But variations in size alone do not necessarily result in qualitative changes. It is quite possible to model a social structure containing one hundred people, the processes and outcomes of which are identical to one which is structurally similar but contains only ten people.

Differing sociological perspectives take widely different views of the composition of structures. Some see structures as composed of observable events. For others, structures are hidden patterns. For still others, structures are sets of parameters. Following Simmel, Elementary Theory models structures as compositions of simpler parts (Willer 1984).

Homans sees structures as observable patterns of interactions characterized by persistence and stability (Homans 1975). For example, a relatively persistent complex of roles and positions in a formal or informal organization is a social structure. A social institution such as marriage which is associated with persistent patterns of interactions is structural.

Alternatively, for structuralists (see Bottomore and Nisbet 1978), "structure" is not directly observable. Thus, structuralists seek the "inner," "hidden," or "deep" structure (ibid.: 593) which is associated with or determines observable human events. According to Boudon (1971), "structure" is that which is more fundamental and also somehow more hidden than other more superficial or observable characteristics. According to Bottomore and Nisbet, "The essential step in the constitution and development of any science is the theoretical construction of the object of scientific inquiry by the formation of concepts which refer to 'hidden' realities" (1978: 593). (See also Lévi-Strauss 1952, 1963; Althusser and Balibar 1970; Rossi 1981.)

A third view sees "structure" as a multidimensional space of differentiated social positions of individuals in a collectivity (Coser 1975; Lenski 1975; Blau 1960, 1975, 1977a,b). Here "structure" is not specific component parts but the properties of the entity which is composed of those parts.

Finally, in the tradition of Simmel, structure can be seen as a configuration of interconnected relations between elements (Simmel 1964 [1917], 1978). Network connection or, as Simmel might say, the "geometry of an arrangement" is the crucial factor which conditions the behavior of elements such as social actors. For Simmel, structure is the *form* of social phenomena, the parameters of space within which the actors' behaviors are generated (Simmel 1964 [1917]). (See also Magala 1980.) At issue is how structure determines interaction between actors (Nowak 1975). It is Simmel's tradition of theorizing structure which is found in Elementary Theory.

Because Elementary Theory builds models of social structures, its viewpoint is fundamentally different from both Homans and the structuralists. Like Homans, we see structures as real complexes of events, but, unlike Homans, we see as the first step toward explaining those events the building of theoretical models corresponding to them. Contrary to Homans, we use some formulations in these models, such as "type of connection," that cannot be reduced to individual-level laws. Like the structuralists, we recognize that, from the point of view of everyday interaction, the configuration of social structures is largely if not wholly hidden. Contrary to the structuralists, we assert that structural configurations are precisely knowable, not directly and by observation alone, but indirectly, by interaction between modeling and observation.

The Concept of Structure in Elementary Theory: Three Neglected Issues

Elementary Theory is a theory of (1) actors in (2) positions in (3) relationships in (4) structures. Social structure is defined here as a set of social positions with valued resources connected by social relationships. These positions are occupied by actors whose interests, values, and beliefs spring from the relationships, positions, and resources (Willer 1992b; Willer and Szmatka 1993: 39). These four levels result in *three general structural problematics*.

The first problematic arises from the interrelation of actions in relations, a condition we call "the joint action problem." *Predicting how actors resolve their joint action problems is tantamount to predicting actors' acts.* This problem was first recognized by Hobbes and is the Hobbesian problem of order (Hobbes 1968 [1651]: 104). Expectation states theory offers one well-developed theoretic solving joint action problems which leads to the study of influence. Rational actor principles adopted by Elementary Theory lead to the study of power.

The second problematic results from connecting relations in structures. While social relations generate actors' interests, the ways that relations are connected in social structures determines how and to what extent these interests are realized. For example, high- and low-power positions are inferred from properties of relation and connection, none of which can be reduced to attributes of discrete individuals. We claim that *structures affect action because network connections and configurations condition the joint action problem.* The solution to the second problematic predicts the effect of structure, through relations, on activity.

Elsewhere, in a critique of Homans, we called the second condition "the structural residue problem" (Willer and Patton 1987: 202). According to Homans, structures are simply patterns of events emanating from the properties of the people composing them. Therefore, structures can be analyzed into their component parts—individuals and their properties—leaving no residue whatsoever. This is Homans' reductionist position. As is evident from this and other of our papers, however, research produced by Elementary Theory offers proof after proof that Homans' view is false.

For instance, "strong" and "weak" exchange structures may be identical except for the configuration of relationships connecting positions. Because that configuration is not a quality of the people in the network, when the network is analyzed into its component parts, the configuration is the *structural residue*. Configurations have important effects. The processes and outcomes of strong and weak power structures are distinct even when the two differ only by configuration. It follows that only configuration, a structural residue, can explain this difference. Therefore, Homans' reductionist position is false.

The third problem considered concerns the efficacy of different kinds of structures. Here we investigate the efficacy of coercion relative to exchange. At its inception, exchange theory maintained that coercion, which it defined as punishment, fails as an effective social relation. Because Elementary Theory is not an exchange theory, but is a theory of social relations, we reject that parochial claim. At issue is whether there are effective coercive power structures and, if so, how effective they are. We show that there are such structures and evaluate their effectiveness relative to exchange by applying a cross-relational measure.

The comparison of coercion with exchange raises important ethical issues which are too frequently trivialized. It would be comforting to believe that the brutalities of coercive power—for example, in slavery—have been displaced by the less objectionable qualities of exchange power—for example, in capitalism—because people will not long tolerate subjection through coercion. As Weber (1963 [1919]) and Fogel and Engerman (1974) have shown, however, the fall of slavery structures has nothing to do with a triumph of the human spirit over coercion. As Weber explained, slavery in Rome persisted until the fall of the empire in the West. Fogel and Engerman explain that U.S. slavery was profitable to the end. Only military defeat of the Confederacy led to slavery's downfall.

To believe that coercive power was confined to some previous time and that only "ethically clean" exchange power is found today is naive. Insofar as modern societies are concerned, exchange and coercive power are intermixed (Foucault 1979). As Gilham (1981) and Willer (1985, 1992b) have shown, modern exchange structures could not exist without coercive power at their base. Outside the laboratory, there is no "reward-based" power which is not underpinned by negatives.

Nevertheless, exchange and coercive power are analytically separable, and, in the laboratory, the two can each be studied in their theoretically pure forms. Our analysis draws on experimental studies to (1) locate the conditions of power which are particular to coercive and not exchange *relationships*, (2) determine the conditions of power which are general for coercive and exchange *structures*, and (3) compare the efficacy of the two.

The Joint Action Problem

Social structure in Elementary Theory has multiple levels (Markovsky 1987; Markovsky, Willer, and Patton 1988; Lawler, Ridgeway, and Markovsky 1993). Actors and positions form two levels; social relationships which are paired sanc-

a. A positive sanction

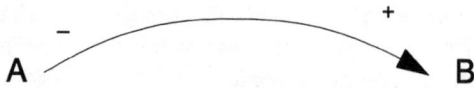

b. A negative sanction

Fig. 1. Two bisigned arcs

tions (see Fig. 2) form the third level; and the fourth level is given when rela-tionships are connected into social structures (see Figs. 3–4). The first three levels, which give the structure *within* social relationships, are the focus of this section. Our discussion will indicate why theories of social structure, which do not analyze the structure within relationships (see Burt 1982), miss an important step in the prediction of action.

Since it is now well known that Elementary Theory uses bisigned arcs to connect nodes, as in Figure 1 (Willer and Anderson 1981; Willer 1987; Willer, Markovsky, and Patton 1989), only two examples are displayed. Briefly, arcs are either positive sanctions or negative sanctions, depending upon the sign adjacent to the *receiving* node. Thus Figure 1(a) is a positive sanction and 1(b) is a negative sanction, even though, for both, there is a negative sign adjacent to the transmit-ter of the act. A negative sign of transmission represents the cost of (or effort associated with) the act.

Here, nodes are actors in positions. Actors are endowed with preferences, beliefs, and the ability to make decisions to transmit sanctions which affect own and/or others' preference states. Numerical values can be added to signs indicat-ing the amount of preference change per unit flow, as shown in Figure 2. Unless otherwise specified, preferences are determined by sanction values and the size of flows which are possible for the structure. *In other words, actors' preference systems (their values) are read directly from the model of the structure.* Similarly, changes in actors' preference states are found by noting sanction transmissions and recep-tions. For example, when C transmits its negative sanction, C's preference state is reduced by one and D's is reduced by ten. In both figures and elsewhere, only transmitting actors decide whether a sanction will be sent.

Similarly, unless otherwise specified, actors' beliefs reflect the modeled struc-ture. This specification has a number of consequences. Obviously, an actor's beliefs which reflect the modeled structure are both complete and accurate. For example, any actor having alternatives, knows it has alternatives. Less obviously, actors can infer other actors' values and their beliefs as well. These "default" specifications were chosen because they result in the simplest models and because they are optimal for applying rational actor principles. Although default specifications do not restrict the range of further models which can be constructed under other specifications, all those models will necessarily be more complex (Willer 1984, 1992a). For example, when one actor's beliefs do not accurately reflect the modeled structure, another structure which represents those beliefs needs to be constructed, doubling the theorist's task.

Conceptualizing actors in this way uncovers the joint action problem, an important issue for theory which is central to Elementary Theory's understanding of social action. By "joint action," we mean that, in all social relationships, the outcomes which are *valued* by each actor are determined *jointly by the acts of both*. For example, examination of the relationships in Figure 2 shows that A's valued outcomes in exchanging are determined partly by the sanctions A decides to transmit to B and partly by the sanctions B decides to transmit to A. The same is true for B's outcomes. For the coercive relation, outcomes are again jointly determined: C's outcomes are determined by both C's and D's transmissions, and so are D's. Since actors directly control only their own acts and not the acts of others, it follows that both actors have an interest in *relating* their own to the other's acts. In other words, social action is not an issue of pursuing goals. Instead, actors seek to manage relationships by relating their own acts to related acts of others.

While relating acts is a problem faced by actors, it is also a problem for theory. Modeling actors' solutions allows the theorist to infer outcomes including ex-

a. Exchange

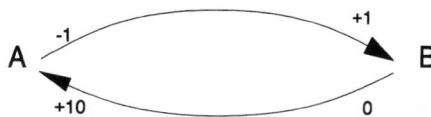

b. Coercion

Fig. 2. Two social relations

change rates and rates of coercion. Also inferred are interaction processes which lead to those outcomes. In our models, actors seek to solve the joint action problem through communications which link sanction flows such as offers, orders, and threats.

The joint action problem defines a choice situation that differs greatly from the "parametric" choice situations that dominate neoclassical economics and its offspring, rational choice theory. There, payoffs are contingent on one actor's choices alone (Elster 1986: 7). Here, actors' payoffs occur only after actors agree upon the number or amount of sanctions to be sent by each. In fact, joint action problems are open to a variety of solutions, each with distinct implications for action. We consider three, beginning with justice and expectation states, then turning to Elementary Theory's solution.

We begin with Aristotle's conception of distributive justice, a solution limited to exchange relationships. Let A and B be the "merit" of the two actors A and B, respectively, in Figure 2, and the total value distributed be $\alpha + \beta$ which is the net payoff of the two sanction flows. Let α be A's net benefit and β be B's. For Aristotle the distribution is just if $A/B = \alpha/\beta$. This is a structural theory of exchange, and according to Aristotle, the payoff to each actor is determined by (1) the type of political structure in which the exchange occurs and by (2) the actors' positions within that structure. For all actors in a democracy $A = B$ and value in all exchanges is divided equally. For an aristocracy, when A is an aristocrat and B is not, $A > B$. Therefore $\alpha > \beta$: A gains the larger proportion of value and B the smaller. Since exchanges with those of lower status favor aristocrats, wealth differences upon which the aristocracy is founded are maintained (Aristotle 1976 [330 B.C.: 178 ff.]).

It is not clear whether Aristotle's theory was intended to be normative, explanatory, or both. If explanatory, it is also not clear whether rates of exchange are governed directly by justice evaluations, or by some social mechanism outside the exchange relations which enforces justice norms. In the case of equal exchange, exchange occurs when the labor of the two actors is equal, apparently a precursor of Marx's labor theory of value (Marx 1967 [1867]). Why should rates of exchange be proportional to amounts of labor? The reason is no clearer in Aristotle than in Marx (Cutler, Hindess, Hirst, and Hussain 1977). In Jasso's recent theory of distributive justice (1980, 1989), the normative versus explanatory issue is resolved. Still, as currently formulated, that theory does not predict rates of exchange and cannot be used to solve the joint action problem (Jasso: personal communication).

Expectation states theory (hereafter EST) offers a second basis for solving joint action problems (compare Berger, Zelditch, and Anderson 1966; Berger, Conner, and Fisek 1974; Berger, Wagner, and Zelditch 1992). Perhaps the simplest application of EST to the Figure 2(a) exchange relation attributes to the actors A and B one status characteristic each which is salient to the joint action problem. That is to say, the two actors have a collective task—to determine how much each should transmit to the other—and each has a status relevant to that task. Let A and B agree that A is higher on the status characteristic. Thus, both will have higher performance expectations for A than B; A will influence B, not the reverse; and A gains a preferred outcome.

Though this application may be outside the range of phenomena for which EST was initially intended, we believe that it is formally within its scope. EST is scope limited to collective tasks, but joint action problems certainly are collective, and there is a task. Let the task be solution of the joint action problem, and the outcomes, which are exchange rates, be valued as successes or failures (Berger, Zelditch, and Anderson 1966: 34). Subject to these provisos, EST solves joint action in exchange. When it does, however, actors do not believe that an exchange rate is selected because it balances interests or favors one actor over the other. Instead, a rate is selected because it is the best solution for the relation.

The application of EST to exchange may explain why, in face-to-face experiments, offers of high-status subjects may be passively accepted by low-status subjects even when resulting rates strongly favor those with high status. When generalized status characteristics are investigated in EST experiments, normally the power and prestige order of the society outside the laboratory is an initial condition. Those with high status influence those with low status. By extension, in exchange, high-status subjects can gain favored rates from low-status subjects. While we are satisfied that there have been status effects in some of our experiments, whether they are a reproducible remains to be seen.

Elementary Theory and the Joint Action Problem

We now turn to the Elementary Theory (hereafter ET) solution to the joint action problem, a solution which applies to both exchange and coercive relationships. The first principle of ET is that

> *All social actors act to maximize their expected preference state alteration* (Willer 1981a: 28).

This principle asserts that actors select actions which they believe will realize their greatest gain. Actors acting in accordance with that principle will be attracted to positions like A and B of Figure 2 by the possibility of gain through exchange. But no actor will transmit sanctions to another unless she or he believes that that transmission will be reciprocated. This belief is a necessary condition for exchange, because any actor transmitting and not receiving only loses, does not gain, and violates principle 1 (Willer 1992b). Grounding that belief are offers which, if accepted, become contracts relating the two flows. A second necessary condition for exchange is the opportunity for *both* actors to gain from the exchange. Both actors can gain when at least one sanction is differentially valued. In Figure 2, the flow from B to A is differentially valued: there is no loss to B, and a gain of ten to A.

Actors will also be attracted to the C position in the coercive relation by the possibility of gain, but repelled from the D position, where all inputs and outputs are negative. It follows from principle 1 that a necessary condition for action in the coercive relationship is that the actor in the D position, the coercee, cannot escape. It also follows from principle 1 that, unlike exchange, coercion has only one of the two sanctions flowing. C gains by receiving positives from D, but principle 1 asserts that D will transmit them only if the loss from their transmission is smaller than the loss which would occur if C's negative was received. That sanction flows are mutually exclusive is the second necessary condition of coercion.

Note that communications in coercion have the same effect as communications in exchange: In both cases communications link actions of the two actors. In the case of coercion, however, communications are not offers but threats which link the coercee's positive transmissions to the coercer's inaction or the coercee's inaction to the coercer's transmission of the negative sanction. When the two sanction flows are exclusive only because a threat is communicated, the threat is a necessary condition of the relation.

Principle 1 also allows us to infer the range of rates possible for each relation. Let Pi be i's preference state alteration consequent to transmitting and receiving sanctions. Rational actors will not exchange unless at least a minimal gain is possible. Thus, for the flow of the two sanctions both $P_A > 0$ and $P_B > 0$. A "rate of exchange" is the ratio of either actor's benefit to total benefit. Here, we express the ratio from A's point of view such that $Ex = P_A/(P_A + P_B)$. Let Ex be undefined when exchange does not occur. When A's sanctions are lumpy, the range of feasible rates is $1/10 \leq Ex \leq 9/10$. Outside the range, one or the other does not benefit: when $Ex = 0/10$, A does not gain, and when $Ex = 10/10$, B does not gain. Within Ex's range, A can benefit more only if B benefits less and conversely. In the terms of neoclassical microeconomics, all rates in that range are on the contract curve (Rubinstein 1982).

We now define Cx, the rate of coercion and infer its range similarly. Let P_D be the loss to D when transmitting sanctions to C and P_{Dc} be D's loss when receiving C's negative sanction. Then the rate of coercion is defined as $Cx = P_D/P_{Dc}$ which is the ratio of D's loss through transmissions to C to D's potential loss from C's transmission. Let Cx be undefined when C transmits its negative. As in exchange, principle 1 allows the range of feasible rates to be inferred. When D's sanctions are lumpy, $0 \leq Cx \leq 9/10$ and within that range C can benefit more only if D loses more. Note that the $Cx = 0$ rate is feasible because transmission of the negative sanction is costly; but $Cx = 10/10$ is not, because D prefers reception of the negative to sending ten to C. Neoclassical microeconomics does not draw contract curves for coercive relations.

Actors who agree upon a rate of exchange or of coercion link their actions.

From the point of view of the actors, that agreement solves the joint action problem. From the point of view of the theorist, the agreed-upon rate predicts the outcome of the relationship. Actors who act only upon principle 1, however, cannot solve the joint action problem in either relationship.

Principle 1 leads actors to maximize, but in social relationships actors cannot both maximize. Consider the case of exchange. When both attempt to maximize, A selects Ex = 1/10 and B selects Ex = 9/10. The two rates are not the same, joint action is not solved, and exchange cannot occur. The relationship is in "*confrontation*," and since no sanctions flow $P_A = 0$ and $P_B = 0$. Yet both actors prefer any of the feasible exchange rates to confrontation.

It follows that both actors prefer to employ any decision procedure which allows them to agree upon any feasible exchange rate to being limited to decisions based on simple maximization. Exactly the same holds for the coercive relationship. "Resistance theory" is such a procedure. We see actors negotiating and reaching agreements at "equi-resistance" in exchange and coercive relations. We first consider the exchange and coercion as isolated dyads and then in a variety of structural conditions.

Resistance, Rates, and Power

When joint maximization does not solve the joint action problem, ET asserts that actors do not fall into confrontation by default. Instead, a second interest is triggered, the interest in avoiding confrontation. Then that interest and the interest in maximization are combined in resistance. Let $P_i\text{max} - P_i$ be the size of the interest in maximizing and $P_i - P_i\text{con}$ the size of the interest in avoiding confrontation. Then, resistance divides the first interest by the second, such that

$$R_i = \frac{P_i\text{max} - P_i}{P_i - P_i\text{con}}$$

Principle 2 of ET asserts that

actors agree at equi-resistance.

For exchange $P_A + P_B = 10$ and setting $R_A = R_B$, resistance predicts $P_A = 5$ and $P_B = 5$ at Ex = 5/10. For the coercive relationship, $P_C = -P_D$ and setting $R_C = R_D$ predicts that $P_C = 4.5$ and $P_D = -4.5$ at Cx = 4.5/10. (Note that when a coercive relation is at confrontation the negative sanction is transmitted. Thus, for calculating these rates of coercion, $P_{Ccon} = -1$ and $P_{Dcon} = -10$.)

Exchange theories express rates such as those calculated above in terms of power, but do so in different ways (Willer 1992a). For example, in power-dependence theory, i is said to exercise power over j when i is advantaged relative to j (Stolte and Emerson 1977). As Heckathorn points out, however, comparing the size of payoffs directly is not a satisfactory measure of relative advantage (Heckathorn 1983a,b). A better measure of relative power will not directly compare actors' utilities and will have an appropriate point of zero power. Ideally, a designation of relative power advantage will have a zero point that is (1) unaffected by linear utility transformations and (2) independent from units of measurement. Furthermore, it will consistently express relative advantage across types of relationships.

In ET, relative power is defined in the following way. For exchange we define relative gain of any actor as the ratio of preference state alteration to maximal preference state alteration initial to the relationship. Thus when $Pi/P_{imax} = Pj/P_{jmax}$ relative advantage of i and j is equal and power is zero. It can be shown that zero power occurs at equi-resistance when $P_{icon} = P_{jcon}$. Then the equi-resistance point, $Ex = 5/10$, which is the predicted rate of the exchange relationship, is equipower.

Assessing the presence of power in coercion is straightforward. All coercive relations are power relations, and power is always in the hands of the coercer. In coercive relations, coercees never gain. If the threat succeeds, coercees always lose and coercers are always advantaged. Therefore, power is never equal, but a power event is present only when the coercer's threat succeeds. Then the coercer is exercising power over the coercee. When the threat fails, power is absent because there has been no power event.

Thus far, our analysis shows that resistance solves joint action problems in isolated relations. We now turn to structures and how "structural residues" affect the way actors solve joint action problems.

"Structural Residue" and the Joint Action Problem

In many sciences, connecting parts into structures produces properties not found in the parts. For example, properties of molecules such as water cannot be inferred from the properties of hydrogen and oxygen, and the properties of DNA cannot be inferred from its base pairings. Since new observational properties occur, it is a problem for theory to conceptualize them. In chemistry, biochemistry, and a variety of other sciences, new properties are produced in theory by formulations for linkages connecting the elements and for resulting shapes (Watson 1969). These formulations are used to build from parts to wholes and to analyze from wholes to parts. Then the behavior of the whole is seen to be a consequence of its shape, the qualities of its parts, and their connections. In ET, we use types of connection and network shape to predict structural power.

These issues in conceptualizing structure are not new in sociology; they were recognized from its inception. According to Durkheim, the "social" consists, not in its elements which are people, "but in the entity formed by the union of these elements" (1982 [1901]: 39). To capture these ideas of structure, a formal theory would, according to Simmel, make use of "isolation and recomposition," "Geometric abstraction," and "spacial forms" (1964 [1917]: 21). Weber attempted to reflect social structure in the structure of his theory. Its element was social action.

Social relationships were formed by the union of two or more social actions, and combining social relationships produced social orders (1968 [1918]: 31 ff.). Much earlier, Marx emphasized the movement in theory from the complexities of the concrete, by analysis, to simple formulations and, by synthesis, back to the concrete (1973 [1857]: 100 ff.). We now turn to ET's formulations for social structure.

The Types of Network Connection

For ET, social structures are connected social relationships. In the following sections we introduce ET's five types of connection and trace their effects from the structural level through relationships to acts. Resistance is applied to predict rates. We begin with triads in which one actor is connected to two others and then move to connections with larger numbers of relations. Complex networks in which more than one type of connection occurs are beyond the scope of this paper.

Triads

In triads only three of the five types of connection are possible. They are:

1. Exclusion: A benefits when exchanging with B or C but not with both.
2. Inclusion: A benefits only when exchanging with both B and C.
3. Null: A benefits when exchanging with B or C or both. (Willer 1992a)

It is the triad of Figure 3 (left), a "2-branch" which will be discussed here. In the 2-branch, the A-B relationship of Figure 2 is connected at A to A-C, the latter being a second relationship identical to the first.

When two relationships are exclusively connected, the behavior of all three actors is very different from behavior that would occur in either relationship if not connected to the other. As seen earlier, resistance asserts that actors in unconnected exchange relations will bargain to compromise. In the 2-branch,

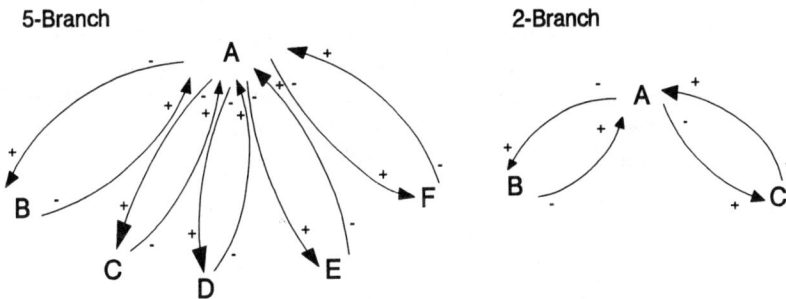

Fig. 3. Exchange networks

resistance asserts that offers move successively toward the extreme. This is an iterative process in which A considers an offer in the A–B relation only if it is better than the last offer in the A–C relation and an offer in A–C only if better than the last in A–B.

Resistance traces the movement of rates toward the extreme favoring A as follows. Because offers on one side set the maximum payoff for the actor on the other, P_{Bmax} and P_{Cmax} decline such that $P_{Bmax} - P_B = 0$ and $P_{Cmax} - P_C = 0$ for offers successively more favorable to A. The end point of the process is reached when $P_A = P_{Amax}$ where resistance of all actors is zero and A's payoff and power exercise are maximal (Willer 1984, 1987). The exclusively connected 2-branch dissolves the joint action problem. A is necessarily in confrontation in one of the relations, and, since that confrontation is costless, A exercises power in the other. Therefore, interaction processes of triadic 2-branch are fundamentally different from the dyad.

Like exclusion, inclusive connection introduces conditions and dynamics not found in isolated relationships. When inclusively connected in the 2-branch, the joint action poses a greater problem for A because A's cost of confrontation in either relationship transfers to the other. For example, when A completes its first exchange with B, $P_{Acon} = P_{Ab}$: the better the settlement gained with B, the greater the jeopardy faced by A when exchanging with C. As a result, A's resistance is lowered, and power is at the periphery. Inclusion's effect is in the opposite direction from exclusion, but its size is substantially smaller.

Inclusion's effect in each relation is determined by the timing of exchanges. When exchanges are sequential, the peripheral exchanging first gains the same rate as in the dyad, but the second peripheral gains the better rate. When the two peripherals recognize the advantage of exchanging second, both will hold out. As a result, time pressures generate effectively simultaneous exchanges in which both peripherals are favored (Patton and Willer 1990). In the next section, we offer a resistance solution which predicts exchange rates for simultaneous exchanges in inclusively connected branches of any size.

Null connection does not alter the joint action problem in either of the connected relations from dyadic conditions. Unlike exclusion, when the connection is null, exchanging in one relation does not dissolve the jointness of A's action in the other. Unlike inclusion, when the connection is null, exchanging in one relation does not heighten A's costs in the other. Therefore, in each of the null connected exchange relations, actors will bargain to compromise exactly as they would in an isolated dyad and power is equal throughout.

Generalizing to N-Branches

An N-branch is a network in which one node is connected to N other nodes which are not connected to each other. The triads above were 2-branches. We now generalize types of connection to N-branches by defining three types of networks: Ni, Mi, and Qi. Ni is i's potential network, the largest network which i can reach for exchanging. Mi is i's maximum possible network: it is the largest network in which i can exchange and benefit in each relation. Qi is i's minimum necessary network, the smallest network in which i must complete all exchanges to benefit from any one. When $N > 2$, five types can be defined. They are:

—i is exclusively connected if $Ni > Mi \geq Qi = 1$.
—i is inclusively connected if $Ni = Mi = Qi > 1$.
—i is null connected if $Ni = Mi > Qi = 1$.
—i is inclusively-exclusively connected if $Ni > Mi \geq Qi > 1$.
—i is inclusively-null connected if $Ni = Mi > Qi > 1$. (Willer 1992a)

For the first three types, the effects of connection in N-branches are qualitatively similar to those of the 2-branch traced above. As in 2-branches, in larger branches null has no effect on the processes and outcomes of relations. In the case of inclusive and exclusive, however, there are quantitative issues which deserve mention and which will be discussed before we turn to the other two connection types.

A straightforward extension of the iterative analysis of the 2-branch asserts that, in any exclusively connected branch, the rate of exchange will move toward the one most favorable to the central actor. Resistance asserts that all exclusive branches will reach the same extreme, but not that they will reach that extreme in the same time interval. Brennan (1981) found that the slope of the line of power development over time is $Ni/Mi - 1$. Consider the implications of Brennan for two cases: for the first $Ni = 100$ and $Mi = 99$ and for the second $Ni = 100$ and $Mi = 50$. For both, i is exclusively connected, and the end point of the iteration process is the same: the extreme rate most favorable to i. But power will develop 99 times slower when $Mi = 99$ than when $Mi = 50$. In fact, the rate of change in the first branch is so slow that the theoretic extreme exchange rate might not be reached even in the highly controlled conditions of the laboratory.

In inclusively connected branches, N, M, and Q are equal and the exchange rate varies with size. Here we consider only the theoretically simplest case in which all peripherals exchange simultaneously. In the inclusive 2-branch when exchanges are simultaneous, $P_{Acon} = -P_A$. Thus, relative to the dyad, the denominator of the resistance factor is increased from Pi to $2Pi$. More generally, since i is at jeopardy in all Q relations but the one where negotiations are current, i's loss at confrontation is $Pi(Qi - 1)$ and i's resistance factor is

$$\frac{P_i\max - P_i}{P_i - (-P_i[Q - 1])},$$

which simplifies to

$$\frac{P_i\max - P_i}{QP_i}.$$

Therefore, as Q increases, the settlement in all relationships approaches the rate of exchange most favorable to peripherals. For example, when $Q_A = 10$, $P_A = 2.70$ while $P_B = 7.30$, $P_C = 7.30$ and similarly for the remaining eight peripherals. Results reported by Patton and Willer (1990) fit well the above formulation.

Compound Connection

When $Ni > 2$, two further types of connections are possible. When $Ni > Mi \geq Qi > 1$, the connection compounds exclusion and inclusion. When $Ni = Mi > Qi > 1$, null and inclusion are compounded. Of the two we limit this discussion to the compound inclusion-exclusion type. For that type, it is straightforward to combine factors from exclusion and inclusion in the resistance equations. Placing Q in the denominator of the central actor of the branch lowers that actor's resistance. But that effect is not decisive, for the effect of exclusion on the resistance of peripherals is greater. As a result of exclusion, the resistance of the peripherals will go to zero for rates of exchange successively more favorable to the central. Therefore, in any compound inclusive-exclusive branch, power will develop toward the maximum. In other words, exclusion overwhelms inclusion, and power is centralized in the branch exactly as it is when the connection is purely exclusive (Szmatka and Willer 1995).

Coercion versus Punishment—Structural versus Psychological Factors Producing Behavioral Differences

During development of Exchange Theory in the 1960's and 1970's, prominent theorists claimed that only positives and never negatives were effective resources in social relationships. But this claim was based on a confusion. Exchange theorists used terms casually borrowed from operant psychology. More specifically, negative reinforcement was conflated with punishment, and as a result, all negatives were referred to as punishments—an error that persists today.

We now show how the effect of this error was to rule out coercion as a subject worthy of study and to focus attention on exchange alone. According to Homans (1974: 26),

The use of punishment is an inefficient means of getting another person to change his behavior. . . . Punishment makes rewarding *any* action that allows him to avoid or escape punishment and not just the one we have in mind.

And according to Blau (1964: 224),

Punishment is not a very effective method of influencing behavior. . . . Later experiments by Skinner and Estes essentially confirmed the conclusion that punishment is a poor reinforcer.

To find the error here, we need to examine the meanings given to negative reinforcement and to punishment by operant psychology. In operant terms, an event that increases the frequency (or probability) of a behavior is a "reinforcer." There are two types of reinforcers, positive and negative. A *reinforcement* is positive when its reception by an organism *increases* the frequency of an act. A *reinforcement* is negative when stopping its reception by an organism *increases* the frequency of an act. Punishments have the opposite effect. *Punishments* always *decrease* the frequency of an act and, at the extreme, will extinguish it.

Both theorists were wrong. Blau was mistaken in asserting that punishment is a "poor reinforcer," because punishment is *not* a reinforcer. Homans was also wrong. Punishment does not change one behavior into another. On the contrary, punishment only reduces the frequency of an act or extinguishes it. At issue is more than technical inaccuracy: both quoted statements imply that negatives are always ineffective. For operant psychology, however, the effectiveness of both negative reinforcement and punishment is as well established as the effectiveness of positive reinforcement (Don Bushell: personal communication to the first author).

In this section, we intend to show that negatives, as they occur in the social relation of coercion, are not ineffective. We recognize that coercive systems of exploitation are held to be reprehensible, and we share that judgment. Coercion is reprehensible, but it is not ineffective. In fact, exactly the opposite is the case. Coercive systems such as slavery earned their negative evaluations precisely because they were effective means of subjection and exploitation.

Slavery, a power structure based on coercive relations between master and slave, existed over very long periods of time in Roman antiquity, in the U.S. South, and elsewhere. Later we will discuss Weber's analysis of why slavery was effective in antiquity. For the United States, Fogel and Engerman (1974: 4–5) claim that slavery was quite profitable: "Slavery was not a system irrationally kept in existence by plantation owners who failed to perceive or were indifferent to their best economic interests. . . . The slave system was not economically moribund. . . . Slave owners were not becoming pessimistic about the future of their system. . . . Slave agriculture was not inefficient compared with free agriculture." In light of the long history of slave systems and the proofs of effectiveness offered throughout Fogel and Engerman's work, it is surprising that the idea that coercion is ineffective is given credibility today. Nevertheless, a new claim has surfaced, and this one is backed by experimental evidence. According to Molm (1993: 1–2), "Contrary to the classical exchange theorists (e.g., Blau 1964; Homans 1974), who argued that punishment is an ineffective and unreliable way of controlling behavior because of the *consequences* of its use, I argue that coercive power is ineffective primarily because of the *failure* to use it." She asserts that coercive power is limited because it is risky to the coercer (ibid.: 2). "Actors fear the retaliation that punishment might bring" (ibid.: 13). Certainly

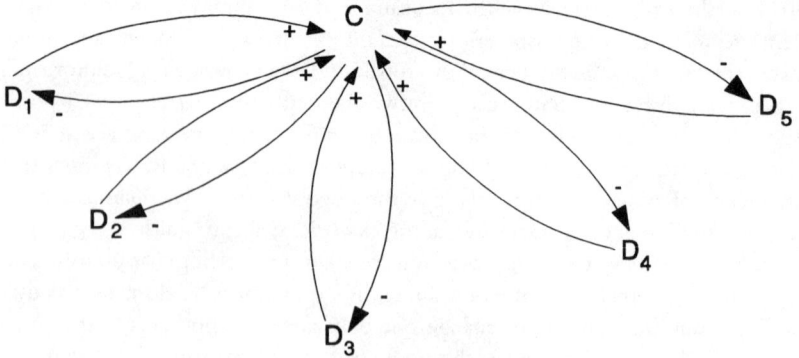

Fig. 4. Coercive 5-branch

U.S. slave masters feared retribution. Yet slavery did not dissolve as a consequence of that fear. On the contrary, slavery was profitable until put out of business by the Civil War.

As shown earlier in this paper, coercion has two necessary conditions: (1) the flow of positives from the coercer and negatives from the coercee must be mutually exclusive, and (2) the escape of the coercee must be blocked. It is doubtful that Molm's experimental study satisfied either condition. In that study, subjects were not allowed to communicate. Since threats could not be communicated, positive and negative flows could not be made mutually exclusive. Because no subject could transmit positives in order to avoid negatives, the first condition was not satisfied. Subjects could not entirely escape. But all were linked to two relations, and those subject to negatives in one exchanged in the other. Thus subjects experiencing periodic losses from negatives could attempt to maximize gain by increasingly focusing their activity on the exchange relation. In Molm's design, coercion should have failed and it did.

Prior to Molm's study, the effectiveness of coercive power was demonstrated and the determinants of different rates of coercive exploitation were investigated by Willer (1987). Given in Figure 4 is the coercive structure investigated, which is composed of five of the Figure 2 coercive relations connected at C. Since all relations are coercive, resistance predicts that C will exercise power over the Ds. The Figure 4 structure resembles null connected exchange structures in that the connection at C has no effect on any of the relations. In other words, the power exercise is due to the conditions of each relationship only, and the C will have *exactly* the same amount of power over each D in Figure 5 as C has over D in the disconnected coercive relation of Figure 2. Thus, the rate of coercive exploitation predicted for each of the relations of Figure 5 is $Cx = 4.5/10$ which is exactly the same rate as that predicted for the coercive relation of Figure 2.

Willer reported a mean observed rate of exploitation of $Cx = .538$ which is higher than predicted by resistance. Negatives were shown to be effective in these experiments because threat of their transmission extracted substantial numbers of positives. In fact, coercers extracted slightly more than half the valued resources initially held by coercees. But higher rates of coercive exploitation are possible. Here the amount of power exercised was due to qualities of each coercive relationship alone. But there are structural conditions that can increase exploitation.

There is historical evidence that coercive structures can have structural power *in addition to* the relational power of their parts. According to Marx, the master has an interest in the preservation of the slave only as long as she or he is not replaceable or, at least, not cheaply replaceable. When slave trading is practiced, however, the aim becomes to extract "the uttermost toil of the slave; for, when his place can at once be supplied from foreign preserves, the duration of his life becomes a matter of less moment than its productiveness while it lasts" (1967 [1867]: 266). Marx compared the U.S. South, where slave importation was illegal and profits were lower, to Jamaica, where slave importation was legal and profits were higher. Both cases were contemporary for Marx. By contrast, Weber's focus was on Roman antiquity: "The ancient slave estate devours human beings as the modern blast-furnace devours coal. The slave market . . . is the indispensable presupposition of the slave barracks producing for the market. The buyer looked for cheap ware" (1963 [1919]: 346).

The power condition in coercive structures first noted by Marx and Weber is an analogue of exclusion in exchange structures. For example, in a branch with exclusion, the central actor has one or more *free confrontations*. These confrontations generate competition among peripherals, producing rates of exchange maximally favoring the central actor. In coercion, confrontation is the transmission of the negative. To transmit a negative is never free, but may be nearly so. For example, when slaves are replaceable, sending a negative is cheap, but it is expensive when they are not. In history, there is no coercive analogue of the completely costless confrontations in exchange. Nevertheless, resistance analysis infers that coercive exploitation should increase as the cost of slave replacement declines, an inference which fits Marx's and Weber's observations.

In the laboratory, however, exact analogues of exclusion in exchange can be generated for coercive structures by making the sending of negatives costless. In the Figure 4 structure, this has been done in two ways: (1) by requiring C to send two negatives, or (2) by allowing C two negatives which confiscate D's resources. In either case, resistance predicts $Cx = .9$ and that rate was approximated in both. For the first and second, $Cx = .850$ and $Cx = .841$ respectively (Willer 1987). In both types, the pattern of competition among low-power actors typical of exclusion in exchange was observed. Thus, like exchange branches with exclusion, power increased over time to the maximum, which was the $Cx = .9$ predicted rate.

A general measure of effectiveness in exploitation allows the power exercised in exchange and coercion to be compared. For this comparison we take effectiveness to be *gain* received by the high-power actor in value of sanctions received from those low in power *minus the cost* in sanction transmissions expended to receive that gain. Efficiency of exploitation increases as gains increase and costs decline. For the second coercive structure mentioned above, high-power Cs extracted, on the average, 8.41 resources in each of *four* relations—a total 33.64 points—expending only a single negative with a transmission cost of one. Thus, gain minus costs was 32.64 points or 8.16 per relation. The maximal power exercise reported by Willer (1987) in any exchange structure occurred when high-power As gained resources worth ten from each of three peripheral Bs at a mean cost of 2.20 per relation. Gain minus cost in exchange was 7.80 points per relation. Thus, effectiveness of power exercise in coercion is slightly higher than in exchange. We do not claim, however, that power exercise in coercion is always more effective than in exchange. Nor is that claim necessary. Our aim is only to show that coercion is not ineffective. To demonstrate that, it is enough to show that the effectiveness of power exercise in coercion and exchange is of a similar magnitude.

Conclusion

Structural wholes are distinct from and not reducible to parts. This claim is at least as old as the field of sociology itself. Elementary Theory is capable of explaining why wholes are not reducible because formulations for wholes are embedded in the structure of the theory itself. Elementary Theory predicts behavior by modeling the ways that actors solve their joint action problems in relations and how the solutions of those problems are changed when relationships are connected into structures. We have shown how Elementary Theory employs the principles of rationality and resistance to solve joint action problems in relations and structures. Initial conditions of relations and structures at t_0 predict activity at t_1.

Power structures persist over time such that, starting from a structure at t_0, the power exercised at t_1 that results from the structure, produces the same or a similar structure at t_2. Only the first part of this process is now covered by Elementary Theory. Yet for any power structure to persist, its power exercise must generate the resources needed for its reproduction. An older view of power considered resources to be the basis of the reproduction of structure (Bierstedt 1950; Lukes 1974). There are may directions for Elementary Theory in the future. One of the most important of these is to develop an integrated view of the complete power process so that the reproduction of power structures over time can be predicted and explained.

Power and Dependence in Exchange Networks: A Comment on Structural Measures of Power

▶▼
▲◀

Karen S. Cook, Toshio Yamagishi, and Shawn Donnelly

The explicit treatment of social structure as the primary dependent variable in exchange theory is associated with Emerson's (1972b) chapter on exchange relations and exchange networks. In this piece he attempts to develop concepts and formal propositions linking exchange principles to the emergence of various forms of social structure and to structural change. A primary aim of this theoretical effort was to extend exchange theory and Emerson's (1962) original power-dependence formulation beyond its fundamentally dyadic focus. Emerson set about this task by developing formal propositions that applied to networks of exchange relations (or sets of connected exchange relations) and to corporate groups viewed as bounded entities that typically engage in collective action through some mechanism of agency (for example, a principal or set of principals selected to represent the group). Subsequent work has focused more on the application of exchange concepts to networks of exchange relations rather than on the processes of group formation (for example, coalition formation) and collective action (exceptions include Gillmore 1987; Cook and Gillmore 1984; Yamagishi and Cook 1993). In this paper, we will comment primarily on current work in the network branch of the theory, specifically focusing on the development of structural measures of power.

Power and Dependence: From Dyads to Networks

An exchange relation is conceived by Emerson (1972a,b) as a series of temporally interspersed opportunities for exchange, initiations, and transactions. Thus, the focus is on the relation as the unit of analysis and not independent transactions (as is typical in micro-economic theory; see Molm 1993). "The exchange relation focuses attention upon the relatively enduring interaction between specified actors A and B, with behavior variable both in kind and magnitude over the lifetime of the relation. By contrast, market economics focuses upon the transaction as a unit, with actors interchangeable" (Emerson 1972b: 60). Exchange theory within sociology thus has developed primarily to focus on the emergence, maintenance, and termination of relatively enduring social relations and the social structures they generate over time. It is not surprising, as a result, that the theory has developed as a major approach to the analysis of social structure and structural change (see Cook 1992). Exchange theory takes as theoretically problematic the very social institutions that micro-economists assume exist as the context for transactions. This theme is clear even in the initial work of Homans (1974 [1961]) and Blau (1964).

The dependence of one actor upon another is taken as the key determinant of power in exchange theory. Dependence varies directly with the value of the domain (or set of reinforcers or resources) to the actors involved in the exchange relation and varies inversely with the number of alternative sources of this domain of value (Emerson 1972b: 59). In subsequent theoretical development the latter condition was changed to the "availability of alternative sources" of the domain(s) of value (see Cook and Emerson 1978: 723), since it is really the availability of alternatives and not strictly the number of alternatives that is critical in determining levels of dependence. (Cook and Emerson 1978: 723 note that availability is determined jointly by access to alternative sources of Y, the resource of value, and by the comparison levels based on a history of exchange with each source.)

Power is linked to dependence in the well-known theorem: In any exchange relation A:B, Pab = Dba or the power of A over B is equal to the dependence of B upon A for resources of value. An imbalance in the dependencies of two actors upon each other results in a power advantage for the actor who is the less dependent upon the relation. A's power advantage in the A:B exchange relation is represented as Pab − Pba. When a power imbalance exists in an exchange relation, the theory states that actor A's use of power will increase across continuing transactions as a function of power advantage (Emerson 1972b: 66). These fundamental concepts and propositions formed the basis for subsequent developments in the theory to apply to networks of connected exchange relations.

Power and Dependence: Early Network Formulations

In our earliest attempts to extend exchange theory to deal explicitly with networks, we proposed several different measures of power at the network level which we thought had the potential to be quite general, incorporating what Emerson referred to as both positive and negative connections, or what Yamagishi (1992) calls exchange relations involving complementary and substitutable goods or services. Our first attempt drew upon graph-theoretic representations of exchange networks in order to evaluate the significance of various network relations in determining the power of each position in the network. This formulation was developed primarily to apply to negatively connected exchange networks in which the exchange relations were between actors with alternatives that provided access to substitutable goods or services (for example, a network in which one actor has access to two potential sources of the same resource).

The idea behind our first attempt to develop a network-level measure of the relationship between dependence and power was based on a fairly simple concept: how "vulnerable" is the network-level flow of resources (and profit) to the existence of specific connections within the network? Put more simply, are the occupants of some positions in the network more critical than others in terms of the network-level flow of resources? The general focus was upon developing a conception of the dependence of the network on a particular position in the network (as an analogy to determining the level of dependence of an actor on his or her exchange partner). The extent of network-wide dependence on a position (or set of positions) would be a measure of the power of that position within the network in terms of resource distribution or flow.

As an initial approach we conceived of exchange and the flow of resources in a network as critical and measured power in terms of the "reduction in maximum flow" (or RMF) of the profits to be obtained in the network when a particular position was removed from the network. Thus, we calculated what we called a "residual" or the remaining amount of potential network profit to be obtained, given the omission of a specific point (or set of equivalent points). Residual graphs represented the remaining networks, providing a picture of the nature of a network's "vulnerability" (in terms of effects on maximum resource flow or distribution) to the presence or absence of a particular network position (see Cook, Emerson, Gillmore, and Yamagishi 1983 for further explication). This conception of vulnerability in a negatively connected network located points of minimum dependence in the network, which is equivalent to locating points of maximum network-wide power under Emerson's assumption that dependence is the determinant of power.

As various authors and critics (for example, Willer 1986) suggested subsequently, this approach was flawed for several reasons. First, it was not as general as we had hoped—it failed to locate power differentials in some networks. Second, it was not sensitive to more subtle power shifts. A major reason for this shortcoming was that it was a dichotomous measure; it represented only the presence or absence of a network link along which resources might flow or be distributed. It was not equipped to deal with a proportional reduction in the flow of resources at a particular point as a continuous measure (for example, reduced to half or a third of the potential value of the profit relation between two points representing an exchange event or relation).

One effort to alter the measure to take into account this particular difficulty was the creation of a revised measure which we referred to as CRMF (that is, the cost of exercising power). This measure was based more on the concept of line vulnerability than point vulnerability. A network is viewed as "vulnerable" at a line if removal of that line (or, in this case, exchange relation) reduces resource flow throughout the network (see Cook, Gillmore, and Yamagishi 1986: 446–47 for details). A combined measure of network-wide dependence (or Dni) was developed based on both the notion of point vulnerability (RMFi) and line vulnerability (CRMFi). However, as noted below, this approach, while improved, did not yield a fully general measure of network-wide power. Subsequently, we developed formal algorithms for calculating network power differentials. Others pursued alternative graph-theoretic approaches (for example, Markovsky, Willer, and Patton 1988).

Structural Measures of Power in Exchange Networks: Alternative Approaches

Markovsky, Willer, Patton, and Skvoretz in the tradition of elementary theory (see Willer and Anderson 1981) have developed several approaches to the measurement of power differences in networks of exchange relations. Their major contribution is referred to as the graph-theoretic power index, or GPI. According to Skvoretz and Willer (1993: 805): "GPI sums 'nonintersecting' paths from a node by adding odd length paths, which are advantageous, and subtracting even length paths, which are disadvantageous." Such a measure takes into account the existence of alternative exchange relations (as alternative paths), since advantage is conferred by the existence of alternatives. Disadvantage refers to the effect of competing alternatives or actors who have difficulty gaining access to alternatives because of the limits established by the nature of the exchange connections, especially in paths of even length. The original GPI measure (see Markovsky, Willer, and Patton 1988) generated ordinal predictions regarding the earnings differentials among network positions ordered by the magnitude of their GPI scores. For any two actors in an exchange relation, if GPIi > GPIj, then actor i should receive a larger share of the proceeds from exchange than actor j in the i–j exchange relation.

Departing from graph-theoretic approaches, Friedkin (1993) has developed an expected value model of social power which he has tested in simulations. This formal model is quite broad, applying to any power structure defined as a pattern of opportunities for relational events among actors. The events could be exchange, influence, attraction, or anything that can be classified as "relational." The model developed by Friedkin specifies a sample space for each power structure (or network). Such a space is "unrestricted" if it contains all possible R-networks or all the different ways in which the actors in the network can be uniquely connected. Probabilities can then be assigned to each possible R-network in several different ways. For instance, if they are analytically assigned, then probability of a particular R-network is given by the product of the probabilities for the activation of the links that compose the network. Further calculations determine the expected values of a power structure's outcomes (for example, density, point centralities, and so on). This approach has promise because it represents a general method of linking network structure to network outcomes and takes advantage of recent developments in network measures. In addition, it is linked to a formal model of social influence processes or power; thus, its scope extends beyond exchange relations.

Structural Measures of Power in Exchange Networks: Power-Dependence Formulation

Power-Dependence Principles: Further Refinements

In a recent effort to extend power-dependence principles to apply to negatively connected exchange networks, Cook and Yamagishi (1992) abandoned their earlier vulnerability approach and subsequently developed a set of more formal procedures for determining the relative power of the positions in an exchange network. This step allowed them to formalize earlier conceptions of the determinants of network-wide power. Let us briefly describe this effort.

According to Emerson (1972a,b), the power of A over B is an inverse function of B's dependence on A for resources of value, as noted above. This fairly simple proposition has been quite powerful in predicting the distribution of power in dyadic exchanges and in networks of exchange relations (for example, Cook and Emerson 1978; Cook, Emerson, Gillmore, and Yamagishi 1983). Another central proposition in power-dependence theory, as developed over time by Emerson, Cook, and their associates, is the notion that the dependence of one actor, B, on another actor, A, is a positive function of the total value of the resources actor B acquires from A compared to the total value of the resources B can acquire from the best alternative exchange partner (Cook and Yamagishi 1992). In the terminology developed earlier by Thibaut and Kelley (1959), the dependence of actor B on A is a positive function of the difference between CL and CLalt (that is, the comparison levels of the outcomes obtained in the A-B exchange relation, CL, and an alternative exchange relation, CLalt).

Based on these two primary propositions defining the sources of dependence, and thus power, and two additional auxiliary assumptions of the theory, Cook and Yamagishi (1992) developed an algorithm for predicting the distribution of power in negatively connected exchange networks composed of two or more connected exchange relations. The auxiliary assumptions refer to exchange ratios at equi-dependence (Cook and Yamagishi 1992) and the predicted "equilibrium" which emerges in structures in which exchange rates tend to stabilize at equi-dependence. First, auxiliary assumption (A1) proposes that as exchanges proceed over time, the exchange ratio shifts toward the point at which both partners to the exchange depend on each other to the same degree. This assumption is referred to as the equi-dependence principle by Cook and Yama-gishi (1992). According to a second auxiliary assumption (A2), as "equilibrium" at equi-dependence is reached, the relative exchange ratios reflect the structur-ally determined power of the two actors in the network. As Cook and Yamagishi (1992) argue, when this equi-dependence ratio is reached, neither actor has the "ability" (in a strictly structural sense) to alter the exchange ratio in his or her favor. Of course, this equilibrium does not necessarily refer to an equal division of profit, but to that point at which neither actor in the exchange can gain further comparative advantage based on network position.

These fairly simple theoretical principles allowed Cook and Yamagishi (1992) to develop a more formal set of procedures for deriving predictions concerning the distribution of power in negatively connected exchange networks. The initial algorithm developed by Yamagishi is based on the following reasoning: (1) Exchange ratios in all exchange relations shift toward equi-dependence throughout the network of connected exchange relations. If we let D_{ij} represent the dependence of actor i on another actor j, and if R_{ij} is used to represent the profit actor i acquires from an exchange with actor j, then relative structural power is reflected in the R_{ij} matrix when D_{ij} is equal to D_{ji} for all dyadic ex-change relations i-j in the network (where i-j represents possible partner pairings as determined by the network structure). If the network, for example, includes three actors connected by exchange relations, a, b, and c, then dependencies are calculated for each pair a-b, a-c, and b-c. (2) The dependence of any actor i on another actor j (D_{ij}) is defined as the difference between R_{ij} (the profit i gets in exchange with j) and A_{ij}, where A_{ij} is the profit i acquires from the best alter-native exchange partner, k. That is, $D_{ij} = R_{ij} - A_{ij}$ (where $A_{ij} = $ max, for all j not equal to k). A more detailed description of this algorithm and its applica-tions is included in Cook and Yamagishi (1992).

The results of an experiment reported in Cook, Donnelly, and Yamagishi (1992) provided the first results in support of the predictions derived from these refined power-dependence principles for several particular exchange networks. The predictions presented in that paper were derived from the application of the algorithm described briefly above. This algorithm is used to find exchange ratios which produce equi-dependence throughout a network. The dependence of actor i on actor j, using this algorithm, is defined as the difference between the profit i earns from j, R_{ij}, and the profit i earns in his or her best alternative exchange relation (A_{ij}). This operationalization of dependence (fundamentally based on the original conception of Thibaut and Kelley 1959, and reflected in the early work of Cook and Emerson 1978) and the associated algorithm pro-vides an adequate approximation of the actual dependency relations in many network structures. However, this definition and the algorithm based on it are just a first approximation. The primary weakness of this algorithm is that it does not take into account accessibility of the alternatives, that is, how easy or difficult it is to get access to the best alternative exchange partner. Two actors i and j may each have alternatives but may differ markedly in the likelihood of obtaining their respective "best" alternatives when they decide not to deal with each other. A refined definition of dependence can be introduced to deal with this additional factor. We offer a provisional definition and a revised algorithm based on this revised definition of dependence in order to stimulate additional theoretical and empirical work on this topic.

The refined definition of dependence uses the same basic concepts and the formula developed in Cook and Yamagishi (1992):

$$D_{ij} = R_{ij} - A_{ij} \qquad (1)$$

However, it alters the nature of the determination of the best alternative, A_{ij}. In the original algorithm developed by Yamagishi, A_{ij} was defined as the maximum of R_{ik}. That is,

$$A_{ij} = \max\{R_{ik}\}, \text{ for } k \text{ not equal to } j \qquad (2)$$

In the refined algorithm, the best alternative is replaced by the notion of expected profit. That is, the alternative A_{ij} in the new algorithm is defined as the amount of profit i can obtain when i decides not to exchange with j. Expected profit used in the revised algorithm is calculated in the following way: (1) Identify the alternative partner, m, who gives i the best profit. That is, $R_{im} > R_{ik}$ for all k not equal to i or j. (2) Determine the "availability" (denoted as V) of m as a potential exchange partner for actor i, according to the following formula:

$$V_{mi} = R_{mi} / \text{sum}\{R_{mk}\}. \qquad (3)$$

That is, the availability of alternative actor m to i is determined by the relative "attractiveness" of i's offer, or the amount of profit m can obtain from i standardized by the total amount of profit m can obtain from all of his or her exchange relations. The greater the availability of m (based on expected profit), the more strongly m will prefer to engage in exchange with i rather than with his/her other partners. (3) (It is assumed that the more strongly m prefers to engage in exchange with the focal actor m is more easily available for i as exchange partner.) Use this availability value as an approximation of the probability that i can successfully trade with m when he or she makes an offer to m. Then the expected profit for i in the i-m exchange relation is the product of R_{im} and V_{mi}. (4) Using V_{mi} as an approximation of the probability that i's offer to m is successfully accepted, $(1 - V_{mi})$ represents the probability that i fails to exchange with m. When this happens, i turns to the second best alternative, m'. The expected profit i obtains from m' is, similarly, $R_{im'} \times V_{m'i}$. Thus, the expected profit for i if she or he first turns to m and then (when m does not accept his or her offer) to m' is given by: $R_{im} \times V_{mi} + (1 - V_{mi}) \times R_{im'} * V_{m'i}$. (5) The expected profit for i outside the i-j relation is thus obtained by summing the expected profit and repeating the same calculation with all of i's alternative ex-

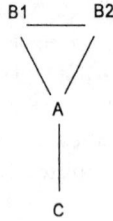

B1 _____ B2

\ /

A

|

|

Fig. 1. Stem   C

Fig. 2. Diagonal Square   A1 _____ B2

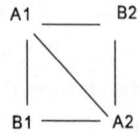

B1 ——— A2

change partners. This refined conception of an alternative, taking into account the likelihood that alternatives are accessible (and interested in exchange with the focal actor), is still an approximation, but may be more fruitful as a general approach to determining dependency in networks than our prior attempt because it incorporates a more subtle comparison of alternatives than did the first algorithm (Cook and Yamagishi 1992).

We can use this revised algorithm to make refined predictions concerning the distribution of power in the stem network (see Figure 1). These results are also reported in Cook, Donnelly, and Yamagishi (1992). (Additional results for this network using our original algorithm are reported in Skvoretz and Willer 1993.) The A-C exchange ratio (in a relation with a 24-point profit overlap) is predicted to be 16–8, using the revised algorithm. According to calculations using the original algorithm, the predicted exchange ratio between A and C in the stem network is 18–6. The prediction based on the revised algorithm (17.04–6.96) actually better approximates the observed exchange ratio of 16.74–7.26 for the A-C exchange relation in this network as reported by Cook, Donnelly, and Yamagishi (1992). However, because these predicted differences using the two algorithms are often quite small, we conducted another experiment using a different network structure, referred to as the "diagonal square" (see Figure 2), for testing the refined algorithm.[1]

According to the original algorithm (Cook and Yamagishi 1992), all four points in the diagonal square network are predicted to have the same power. However, using the refined algorithm, A is predicted to have a slight power advantage over B, and the A-B exchange ratio (assuming a profit overlap of 24) is predicted to be 13.58–10.42 for this network. (In this case, a 12–12 split of

[1] Details of the algorithm and the predictions of the distribution of power for all possible 5-actor network structures and the corresponding simulation results are available in Japanese (Takahashi and Yamagishi 1993).

the profit would represent "equal" exchange.) Thus, it appears that for some networks the refined algorithm is able to make subtle power distinctions undetected, using a less sophisticated measure of dependency. Below we report briefly the empirical results for the diagonal square network diagrammed in Figure 2, using the Cook, Emerson, and associates' experimental setting (see numerous publications for full descriptions of this experimental setting, for example, Cook and Emerson 1978; Cook, Emerson, Gillmore, and Yamagishi 1983; Yamagishi, Gillmore, and Cook 1988).

Forty undergraduates, recruited from introductory sociology classes at a large state university, participated in the experiment. Ten same-sex groups (four male and six female groups) were run in the study. No manipulated factor was involved in the experiment. All procedures were exact replications of the earlier studies conducted in this series and reported in Cook, Donnelly, and Yamagishi (1992). The study involved simple negotiations with each exchange partner over resources that could be exchanged for mutual profit (that is, negotiations over a 24-point profit overlap or range of mutual benefit). Subjects had information only about their own exchange opportunities and potential profits but were not given information on each transaction about what their partner's profit would be. In other words, the subjects were unable to make equity comparisons concerning the amount of profit each party to the exchange received when they reached an agreement over the terms of trade.

Groups were used as the unit of analysis due to the nature of the interdependency of the subjects' behavior within each group. The reported A-B exchange ratio is the average of the four A-B exchanges, A1-B1, A1-B2, A2-B1, and A2-B2. The 42 trial periods were aggregated into two blocks of 21 trials each. The analysis focuses on the second block of trials, since the predicted power differential is expected to emerge over time in the experiment. The results are quite consistent with the predicted exchange ratio. The average profit A earned during the last half of the experiment (that is, during the last 21 transactions) was 13.65 (S.D. = 2.42), which was quite close to the prediction of 13.58 (for actor A in exchanges with B). The observed A-B exchange ratio provided actor A with a significantly larger amount of profit than B (t = 2.05, df = 9, p < .05, one-tailed). This result provides some supporting evidence for the utility of the revised algorithm in making predictions concerning network power differentials, in networks in which there are more subtle power differences. In this case the existence of subtle power differences can be attributed to what Cook and Yamagishi (1992) have referred to as "latent" relations. Latent relations represent exchange opportunities that may be used infrequently but, as viable alternatives, have a significant effect upon the distribution of power in the network (see Cook and Yamagishi 1992 for more details on this distinction). Examples of latent relations include the existence of an available but infrequently called friend or former partner, or the presence of an alternative supplier who might be occupied primarily with other customers, but who could become a reliable resource if approached in the right manner. Such relations are important determinants of power, but have not been treated sufficiently in the literature on exchange networks.

Conclusion

At present, there are a variety of methods being developed for generating structural measures of power in exchange networks. These include GPI and its revisions by Markovsky, Willer, Skvoretz, and their collaborators, game theoretic measures being developed by Bienenstock and Bonancich (1992), network expectancy measures being developed by Friedkin (1993), and, more recently, math-modeling by Yamaguchi (1996). It is not yet a simple matter to decide which of these approaches will yield the most general results. Friedkin's recent work is the only approach that extends beyond exchange theory, treating a power structure as determined by a network of relational events, one subcategory of which involves exchanges between actors. The other approaches are all primarily attempts to formalize measures of the distribution of power in exchange networks specifically and derive from efforts to build a more comprehensive theory of exchange relations. Few of these approaches have been directly compared, using the same experimental setting. Thus, additional empirical work will be needed to investigate the scope and specific range of applicability of the various alternative methods for detecting power differences in exchange networks. In the past, two factors have hampered progress. The first is the existence of fairly major differences in the experimental paradigms (and thus the exact conditions under which prior data have been obtained), making comparisons of methods difficult. The second is that only recently have there been concerted attempts to analyze the underlying theoretical differences between the various approaches to the study of exchange networks and processes (for example, Molm 1993). However, the explosion of interest in this topic in sociology promises resolutions to these issues in the near future.

Toward a Formal Theory of Equilibrium in Network Exchange Systems

■

Tadeusz Sozański

Structural Approach in Network Exchange Theory

This paper deals with the issue of formal modeling in Network Exchange Theory (NET). NET is not one comprehensive general theory. It is more of a *theoretical perspective* with a fairly clear identity defined by the type of problems it addresses. As a theoretical perspective, it encompasses a range of *specific theories*. Some of them are complementary, as they are to account for phenomena occurring in different systems or situations; others compete with each other by offering incompatible predictions for same or overlapping scope conditions.

What NET currently is can be seen from the special issue of *Social Networks* (1992: no. 3–4). In comparison with earlier exchange theorizing, the network approach is much less concerned with a single dyad. The focus is on structural analysis of exchange *systems*. Structural approach is based here on a more specific meaning of "structure." In most classic "structural" theories, structure is more of a spell than a scientific term. Technically, "structure" has been identified with a "network," or a configuration of relations (ties, connections). These terms still remain vague unless they are translated into the formal language of mathematical graph theory.

Before we consider the issue of formalization, we must say that the meaning given to the term "structure" in the context of a structural theory of social interaction seems to be richer than an arrangement of constituent elements in a

The first part of this paper (two initial sections) was presented at the 31st Congress of the International Institute of Sociology, Paris, June 1993. The second part reports on the results of further research supported by grant PB 0870/P1/94/07 from the Polish National Committee for Science Research. A summary of mathematical theory offered here appeared first in print in volume 3 of the Proceedings of the International Conference on Social Networks, London, July 1995. Some results were also presented earlier at the 13th World Congress of Sociology, Bielefeld, Germany, July 1994. Send correspondence to: Tadeusz Sozański, Jagiellonian University, Institute of Sociology, 52 Grodzka, 31-044 Kraków; email: ussozans@cyf-kr.edu.pl.

social whole. What do we mean when we say that "interaction" is "structured"? First, "structure" can be conceived of as a relatively stable, distinct, somehow regular, "non-isotropic" pattern of actions occurring within a relatively closed set of social actors. Then the interaction process is assumed to run in conditions which do not basically restrict the freedom of "emitting" and "receiving" actions among the members of the social whole. However, freedom need not result in chaos, or the lack of any regularity of joint actions. Whenever a pattern of interacting has been observed, one must solve the problem of why an initial "entropy" of social actions has evolved into a relatively stable arrangement or network of social relationships. This kind of network approach encompasses, in particular, classic sociometry and more recent studies aimed at discovering structural biases such as, for instance, the predominance of triads of a special structural form within a small social group (Davis and Leinhardt 1972).

Second, one can qualify the interaction process as "structured" if it is subject to structural constraints. Then a network structure is interpreted as a set of interaction opportunities which delimit the range of possible dyadic interactions—that is to say, they enable certain interaction opportunities and disable others. This need not mean that structure determines interaction. Actually, structure alone is never able to set or maintain the social system in motion. The network defining for any actor his potential partners does not by itself determine how the interaction will run, that is, which available channels will actually be used. Thus, to account for observed patterns of network-constrained interaction, one has to resort both to extranetwork structural conditions and to nonstructural or actor-dependent determinants that give direction to actors' conduct within structurally imposed limits.

Generally, in sociology the term "structure" can be referred to any "constraint on variety" of events within a social system (Ashby 1950: chap. 7; see also Buckley 1967: 94, 128). The factors which are out of the actors' control and restrain the range of their possible actions are both "hard" logical and physical necessities and "soft" (vulnerable to violation) social norms or rules. To build a specific structural theory of socially constrained interaction, one must assume that the rules of the social system are effectively enforced. At the same time one should not embrace structural determinism by taking the existence of these rules and actors' conformity as the only source of theoretically explicable regularity. Let us add that the distinction between structural and nonstructural determinants of social actions, for all its theoretical importance, is relative rather than absolute. To extend the structural approach to modeling actors, one has to replace a real actor by an ideal decision-maker whose activities are subject to internal structural constraint. Such an actor is assumed to use certain rules of strategy choice and in the extreme is functionally equivalent to an automaton. The "movement away from complex actors and simple structures toward simple actors and complex structures" (Willer 1992a: 187–88) is a promising path of theory development, but it should be balanced by parallel modeling of an actor as a decision maker who is not only driven by certain general "principles" (such as "maximization of expected payoff state") but who is able to translate these principles into dynamic programmable strategies generating his behaviors in an interaction setting.

An explicit interpretation of "structure" as a restraint on the freedom of interaction appeared first in experimental investigations of the effectiveness of problem-solving groups (Bavelas 1950; see also Flament 1963: chap. 2 for a graph-theoretic analysis) where the circulation of messages was limited by the experimenter to a "communication network," or a fixed set of channels. Currently, such an understanding of structure has become characteristic of most network exchange theories and tends to pervade some other network approaches. One of the basic differences between exchange perspective and these approaches lies in a more special view of the nature of interaction (see Cook and Whitmeyer 1992 for a comparison of network analysis with the exchange perspective).

Exchange even if conceived as broadly as possible is but one of many elementary forms of social interaction. The idea of a general Network Interaction Theory has begun to materialize with the appearance of the Elementary Theory (Willer and Anderson 1981; Willer 1981a,b; Willer 1987; Willer and Markovsky 1993), which has offered a more comprehensive framework for studying interaction than the exchange paradigm. The Elementary Theory (ET) is an elaborate intellectual construction of which a hard-science methodological creed is an important part. Substantively, a system of terms and conceptual distinctions is developed and a number of research problems are stated. Last but not least, ET contains some specific interaction theories such as the Resistance Theory (Heckathorn 1980; Willer 1981b). Recently, ET has been qualified as a "scientific research program of the dynamics of social structure" (Szmatka and Willer 1993). It is not our intention here to analyze ET as a whole or to assess its ambitions to become *the* theory of social relations with the largest scope possible. Let us only remark in this connection that ET is focused on the question of how "actions in relations are conditioned by structures" (Willer and Markovsky 1993: 323), that is, what regular patterns of interaction will be observed in a social system operating under the given network and extranetwork structural constraints.

One can argue that there are even more fundamental problems that social theory should pose and solve, namely, how structures constraining social actions come into being, how they are maintained in existence and operation, and why they occasionally break up or change shape (cf. Cohen 1968: chap. 2). The problem of order and the problem of structural change or "morphogenesis" have so far been the favorite topic of grand theorizing. It is an open question whether such issues will always remain intractable for abstract, experimentally testable theories ("theories of the third generation"; see Szmatka and Sozański 1994). Today's network exchange theories take as given the system's structure and, on assuming that structural constraints do not change over time, attempt to predict the course of the interaction process or at least its results, such as the final allocation of resources among the actors. The decision to consider a system's structure as fixed has stemmed in part from discovering how easily the experimenter can create in the laboratory a miniature social system with arbitrarily imposed network constraints. Originally, the network structure was viewed by Richard Emerson (1972a,b) as a set of "exchange relations" basically determined by the allocation of resources differentially valued by group members. The experimental procedure that he and his associates invented (Stolte and Emerson 1977; Cook and Emerson 1978) prompted them to change the conceptual image of structure; in their experiments the network structure began to function as a fixed precondition of interaction rather than a set of actually observed exchange relations.

If structural conditions of interaction are kept constant over a time interval and an exchange system is protected from the impact of external factors, it is natural to expect that the interaction process will run regularly and will lead to a distribution of resources which remains stable even if it is not equally beneficial for all actors, reflecting power differentials among them. The concept of "equilibrium" has always played an essential role in economic theory; it can also be found in the works that marked the beginning of contemporary social exchange theory (Homans 1958, 1961; Thibaut and Kelley 1959; Emerson 1962; Blau 1964). However, when we look back on the past thirty years which have lapsed since the publication of Emerson's seminal paper (1962), we notice few if any attempts to define a network-wide equilibrium for exchange systems larger than a dyad. Until very recently, this has apparently been too difficult a task for all network exchange theories, including the Elementary Theory and the Power-Dependence Theory (PDT) originated by Emerson and developed by his associates (Emerson 1962, 1972; Stolte and Emerson 1977; Cook and Emerson 1978; Cook, Emerson, Gillmore, and Yamagishi 1983).

Outside NET, the situation looks better, since there already exists an elaborate mathematical theory of system-wide equilibrium. Unlike other exchange theories beginning from the dyad, the theory proposed by James Coleman (1972, 1990) deals from the outset with a system of n actors who have differential *control* over and *interest* in m *events*. For such a system, the theory predicts the distribution of control at equilibrium. Coleman's theory in its original formulation makes little reference to network constraints on interaction: it is assumed that each actor has "free access" to all other actors. It has been shown, however, that network restrictions can be incorporated into Coleman's model of an exchange system (see Marsden 1983; Braun 1994). Thus, one can expect that various approaches within NET will gradually come close to each other.

Theoretical unification of NET requires full formalization of the concept of an exchange system. What is needed is both a formal model of the system's structure and a proper representation of the system's dynamics, including the negotiation process in which transactions are initiated and concluded (cf. Skvoretz and Fararo 1992: 338–39). The first part of this paper takes up the issue of formalization, which the author dealt with in his paper published in Polish (1993a).

The second part is devoted to the recent version of PDT proposed by Cook and Yamagishi (1992). Drawing on Emerson's (1962, 1972b) definition of "balance" for a dyad A—B ($D_{AB} = D_{BA}$ where D_{AB} measures the dependence of actor A on actor B), they managed to operationalize the notion of inter-actor dependence in the context of the network; next they stated the network-wide equidependence principle as the postulate that *all* dyads within the system simultaneously approach the state of balance. The equidependence principle was finally proposed as a new core of PDT in the hope that it would yield more adequate predictions for empirical networks than the authors' earlier approach (Cook, Emerson, Gillmore, and Yamagishi 1983; Cook, Gillmore, and Yamagishi 1986), which did not stand up to the criticism launched by Willer (1986) nor to a confrontation on both theoretical and empirical grounds with Graph Power Index Theory of Markovsky, Willer, and Patton (1988). The latter theory, which appeared within the framework of ET, is directly comparable with Cook and Yamagishi's Equidependence Theory, since both deal with the class of network exchange systems called "profit pool networks."

Leaving aside the empirical problem of which of the two theories finds stronger support in experimental data, we confine the discussion to the mathematical content and form of both theories. We think that Equidependence Theory is a noteworthy attempt to build a new full-fledged equilibrium theory of exchange under the assumption of network-constrained interaction. One can expect that the Elementary Theory will also be able to elaborate its own system-wide equilibrium perspective. Its foundations have already been laid in Resistance Theory (see Lovaglia, Skvoretz, Willer, and Markovsky 1995 for recent developments).

A thorough examination of Cook and Yamagishi's approach reveals that it consists of four components of unequal weight. The first and most important component is the general principle of "equal dependence throughout the network," which is combined with an operational definition of inter-actor dependence. The latter in turn is based on a particular definition of alternative profit in a given relation, or expected reward from possible exchange outside this relation. This definition can be seen as a new interpretation of the old concept of "comparison level" (Thibaut and Kelley 1959; Emerson 1972a). The fourth, last, and most controversial component of Cook and Yamagishi's formulation is their method of "solving the network" or an algorithm for determining the equidependence profit allocation.

Formal Modeling of Network Exchange Systems

In an earlier paper (1993a), we suggested that an exchange system should be modeled as a multistructured mathematical object (see Sozański 1986, 1992 for an explication of the notion of structure in mathematics). A general *two-resource network exchange system* was defined as a complex construct characterized by a set of nonspecific axioms or postulates that bind together the structures within the system. One can also regard these axioms as structural scope conditions of one or more specific exchange theories which can be stated and tested for the given class of systems. Such theories can contain further postulates as additional scope conditions, concerning, for instance, the motivation directing actors' behavior. These conditions are basically controlled by the experimenter but often need to be verified, if, say, it is not certain that the actors are actually willing to pursue their theoretical interests induced by the instructions. Finally, a particular exchange theory should offer testable predictions deducible from its specific axioms, which may entail, in particular, a formula for the rate of exchange at equilibrium.

Along with several general postulates, our formal model contains as nonspecific axioms a list of more restrictive technical conditions which complete the description of the system so that its synthesis in a computer-aided laboratory is possible. Our aim was to remove any indeterminacy from the procedure for generating experimental data by ensuring maximum control over the conditions in which all elementary system-relevant actions (choices of behavior options) and events (transactions) are to be observed. As a result we get a fully standardized record of the negotiations at an experimental session (see Skvoretz and Willer 1991 for a description of the experimental procedure used in ET investigations of profit pool networks).

We will not repeat in this paper all the details given in our earlier paper (1993a). What we are going to do now is to outline a range of theoretical options which one has to consider in constructing the model of a class of network exchange systems.

Let us start with listing elementary units of analysis dealt with in the investigations of exchange systems. These basic units are *actors*, *positions*, *resources*, *behaviors*, and exchanges, or, more generally, *transactions* (cf. the ET glossary in Morris 1981). Although all these elements are important, in a structural system-oriented exchange theory, *position* is the most fundamental primitive term, and positions are referred to as the "system's constituent components." The structural approach means that it is the positions, not actors, that are primarily assigned control over resources, action options, and transaction opportunities (access to other positions). However, actors must be included in the description of an exchange system, since without being manned the system would remain "dead."

The definition of a network exchange system can be given by specifying interrelated structures that together define the system's identity, or total structure, and model both the static and dynamic facet of the system.

The first of these structures is an *assignment of actors to positions*. Then, all exchange systems can be divided into two classes: those with a fixed actor-position assignment and those admitting of the movement of a fixed set of actors across positions during the system's lifetime, or the time of its functioning. This distinction is crucial for the decision on what is to be considered a sample of the system's behavior. A single interaction process is a sequence of behaviors that is obtained by filling positions with actors (more precisely, the actors must be endowed with a proper motivation to act; then they will start negotiations and conclude transactions so that relevant data will be produced). To test the effect of structure against the operation of individual and group-dependent determinants of actors' behavior, one needs a number of such behavior sequences, called runs, trials, or *rounds* in the experimental procedure. They are generated by having the same system work with varying actor casts. Usually the method of *rotation* is used, that is, a fixed group of actors move across all positions during the experimental session divided into *periods*, with fixed assignments of actors to positions. This method, for all its virtues and convenience, may sometimes appear inadequate, since the systematic character of rotation suggests an alternative and even more natural interpretation of the data from one group as one sample of the dynamics of a system with interposition mobility.

The term "exchange network" is often used in NET as a synonym for "exchange system." Here, we refer the term "network" solely to the transaction opportunity structure. It is given as the set of pairs of positions between which bilateral transactions are permitted (the nature, physical or social, of the restrictions on the access between positions is a matter of empirical interpretation of the model). Then a basic choice to be made is whether the opportunity structure should be introduced into the model of an exchange system as its constant component or is allowed to vary during the system's functioning (due to an external manipulation and/or postulated actors' ability to establish and remove network linkages). The first step toward a dynamic conception of the network structure has already been made (Leik 1992); for now, however, the static approach is the rule.

A constant *transaction opportunity structure* will be defined here as a connected graph whose points are identified with positions. The literature in mathematical graph theory (GT) varies in the ways of defining its basic terms. For applications in the social sciences, the best source remains Harary, Norman, and Cartwright's (1965) book. For the convenience of the reader and to prevent possible misunderstandings, we include below the elementary definitions of several fundamental terms of GT.

A *digraph* (short for "directed graph") is a collection of *n* points (or *nodes*) and *m* lines (or *arcs*) together with a mapping which assigns to any line an ordered pair of points called the *first and second point* of a line. A digraph can be drawn on a plane by means of arrows going out of the first to the second point of a line: an arc from point P to Q is drawn as $P \to Q$. In early sociometric research, a *geometrical representation* of a digraph has often been confused with the digraph itself.

Yet the same digraph admits of many geometrically dissimilar images, and their properties should not be identified with the (often "invisible") structural or invariant properties of the digraph. Actually, digraphs form a *category* of abstract *mathematical objects* that are distinguished "up to isomorphism."

Let us assume that for any ordered pair of points (P, Q), there is at most one line having these points as its first and second point. Then, each line can be identified with the ordered pair of its end points, and the digraph is formally given as $(\mathbf{P},\mathbf{L})$ where $\mathbf{P}$ is the *set of points* and $\mathbf{L}$ is the *set of lines*; then, $\mathbf{L}$ is a *binary relation* on a finite set $\mathbf{P}$. If this relation is *symmetric* (PLQ implies QLP), the digraph $(\mathbf{P},\mathbf{L})$ is said to be *undirected*. Then (P,Q) and (Q,P) are either both in $\mathbf{L}$ or both not in $\mathbf{L}$. The pair of inversely oriented lines is often called an edge; it is drawn as a curve without arrows. Following Harary (1969), we use the term *graph* for undirected digraphs.

Two digraphs $(\mathbf{P},\mathbf{L})$ and $(\mathbf{P}',\mathbf{L}')$ are *isomorphic* if there exists a one-to-one correspondence ϕ between their point sets (a $1-1$ mapping of $\mathbf{P}$ onto $\mathbf{P}'$) such that PLQ if and only if $\phi(P)\mathbf{L}'\phi(Q)$ for any P,Q in $\mathbf{P}$. An isomorphism of a digraph $(\mathbf{P},\mathbf{L})$ with itself is called its *automorphism*.

Let $\mathbf{D}$ denote the set of all digraphs with the same point set $\mathbf{P}$. It is not difficult to see that isomorphism is an *equivalence relation* on $\mathbf{D}$, that is, this relation is *reflexive, symmetric*, and *transitive*. The set of all digraphs from $\mathbf{D}$ which are isomorphic with a given digraph in $\mathbf{D}$ is called the *equivalence class of the digraph*. The set of equivalence classes is a *partition* of $\mathbf{D}$: its elements will be called *structural forms of digraphs* (see Sozański 1986, 1992).

Let f be any function assigning numerical values to the digraphs from $\mathbf{D}$. If f assumes the same value for isomorphic digraphs, then f is called a *global structural parameter* or an *invariant* of a digraph. The number of lines in a digraph is the simplest example. In particular, if 0 and 1 are the only values assumed by f, f can be called a *structural property* of a digraph. We define in turn a *local structural parameter* of a point as a numerical function defined on the set of points of a digraph which takes the same value for any two *structurally indistinguishable* points. Structural sameness of two points P and Q means by definition that Q is the image of P through an automorphism α of the digraph. The condition $Q = \alpha(P)$ for some automorphism α defines an equivalence relation on the set of points; the respective equivalence classes are called *orbits of the automorphism group acting on* $\mathbf{P}$ (see Sozański 1992 for a presentation of the mathematical theory of group action on a set and related combinatorial issues). Orbits have been proposed as a formalization of the sociological notion of position (Everett 1985; Sozański 1986). Here, we speak of *structural classes of positions*, as the term "position" has already been used to denote nodes of an exchange network.

The simplest local structural parameters are the outdegree and indegree of a point. The *outdegree* (*indegree*) of P is defined as the number of lines with P as their common first (second) point. The outdegree and indegree of a point P are equal for graphs, and the common value of these parameters, or the number of *edges incident to P*, is called the *degree* of P. Various point centrality measures (Freeman 1979; Bonacich 1987) are also examples of local structural parameters. Borgatti and Everett (1992) have postulated explicitly that all measures of positional power be defined as invariants of automorphisms.

A point Q is said to be *adjacent* to point P if PLQ, or (P,Q) is a line of a digraph $(\mathbf{P,L})$. If P and Q are interpreted as positions in an exchange system, we will also say that position Q is *accessible* to P, or Q is a *potential transaction partner* of P.

Let us label the points with numbers $1,...,n$, that is, let $\mathbf{P} = \{P_1,...,P_n\}$. Then one can represent the digraph $(\mathbf{P,L})$ by its *adjacency matrix*, which is defined as a zero-one square matrix G such that $G_{ij} = 1$ if point P_j is adjacent to point P_i; otherwise $G_{ij} = 0$. Henceforth we shall not distinguish a digraph from its adjacency matrix (points will be identified with numbers $1,...,n$). Then ϕ is the isomorphism of digraphs G and G' if and only if $G_{ij} = G'_{\phi(i)\phi(j)}$.

Graph theory provides tools for modeling not only transaction opportunities but other structures, such as, for instance, the interest of an actor in the resources controlled by another actor (details are given in our 1993a paper). Then, for each particular relation, a different set of structural properties may be required. Thus, transaction opportunity structure will be modeled by a digraph with three properties: (1) the absence of *loops*, or lines of the form (P,P), that is, no transaction with oneself is ever possible; (2) the symmetry of the accessibility relation; (3) connectedness; intuitively, this property means that an exchange system is a whole made up of elements linked together directly or indirectly.

Two distinct *lines* in a digraph are said to be *connected at point* Q if Q is common to the two lines. That is, one of three cases takes place: (1) Q is the common beginning of the two lines (graphically, $P \leftarrow Q \rightarrow P'$); (2) Q is the common end of the two lines $(P \rightarrow Q \leftarrow P')$; (3) Q is the end of the first line and the beginning of the second line $(P \rightarrow Q \rightarrow P')$. A *semipath of length k from point P to point Q is* a sequence of k lines such that: (1) P is one of the end points of the first line and Q is one of the end points of the last line of the sequence; (2) any two lines immediately following each other in the sequence are connected; (3) all the points at which the lines in the sequence are connected are distinct except, possibly, P and Q. If any two neighboring lines in the sequence are connected according to the pattern (3), then a semipath is called a *path.*

If for any ordered pair (P,P') of distinct points of a digraph, there exists a path (semipath) from P to P', the digraph is said to be *strongly (weakly) connected* (see Harary, Norman, and Cartwright 1965: chap. 3 for details). For graphs, or undirected digraphs, strong and weak connectedness are equivalent, and one term *connectedness* is used (for graphs a path is also defined as a sequence of edges rather than lines). For any two points P and P' in a connected graph, the *distance* between P and P' is defined as the length of the shortest path from P to P'.

A closed path (a path from P to P for some point P) is called a *cycle*. Connected graphs having no loops and cycles of length 3 or more are called *trees*. All trees have the same number of edges equal to $n - 1$ and are minimal connected graphs with n points (the graph obtained by removing any edge from a tree is no longer connected). So far, almost all research in NET has assumed that the transaction opportunity structure has the form of a tree. The tree structure imposes maximum restrictions on transaction opportunities while still maintaining unity of the system. The *complete graph* G_n, having $n(n - 1)/2$ edges, is located on the opposite pole: all possible channels are open, and at least $n - 1$ edges must be removed to make the network disconnected. Between these two extremes lie all other types of opportunity structure, including connected bipartite graphs, which have thus far been given little attention in NET, despite their theoretical importance as a model of bilateral markets such as the labor market. A graph is called *bipartite* if its point set is the union of two disjoint non-empty subsets such that every edge joins the points from different subsets. In particular, in the *complete bipartite graph* G_{kl} (where $k \leq l$ and $k + l = n$), every point in a subset of k elements is linked with every point in the other subset of l elements (hence the number of edges in G_{kl} is kl). If $k < l$ these two subsets of the point set coincide with two distinct structural classes of points; if $k = l$ all points form one structural class. The only complete bipartite graph which is a tree has the form $G_{1(n-1)}$, that is, one position, say, P_1, is tied to $n - 1$ remaining positions $P_2,...,P_n$. If $n \geq 3$ this unique position is called *central* while the other positions are called *peripheral*. Indeed, P_1 has all attributes of centrality discussed by Freeman (1979): easiest access to other positions (the degree of P_1 is $n - 1$; all P_i for $i = 2,...,n$ are directly accessible to P_1), maximum closeness to other positions (measured by the sum of distances from a given point to other points), and indispensability for maintaining the communication between other positions (P_1 falls on every path from P_i to P_j for $i,j = 2,...,n$).

For small values of n it is not difficult to list all structural forms of connected graphs with n points, and draw on the plane the graphs representing them. Specifically, the total number of structural forms of connected graphs with the number of points ranging from 2 through 6 equals 142 (see Harary 1969: Appendix 1).

Let us proceed to discuss further structures in a network exchange system. Its dynamics amounts to two intertwined processes: the circulation of resources across positions, and the interaction process in which periods of negotiations are followed by transactions. As a consequence, one needs to distinguish within the system two interrelated structures: *resource-control structure* and *social action structure*. Their interdependence is expressed in two statements. First, any change in the allocation of resources among the positions can come about only as a result of a transaction; any transaction must in turn be preceded by an appropriate sequence of actors' behaviors. This condition leaves outside the scope of NET the class of social systems in which resource flows are brought about by an external factor, as has been the case with a socialist economy controlled by the state. Second, the range of admissible actions open to each actor at a given time should depend on the current distribution of resources among the positions. This may mean, in particular, that the actors are not permitted to offer what they do not actually possess or to address their offers to those who have nothing to trade off.

Any specific model of the resource-control structure must take into account the nature of the resources which are available in the system (divisibility, durability, and so on) and the type of control attributed to positions (for example, unlimited alienability). For instance, ET assumes that control over resources in exchange systems is governed by "private property rules" (see Willer 1987: 81–88). These rules are not stated explicitly in the formal model itself.

To give an example of how control over the resources can be formalized, assume that there are m types of divisible resources and the total amount of each type of resource is constant throughout the system's lifetime. Let $c_k > 0$ denote the total number of resource units of type k available in the system. The formalization of the resource-control structure can be given in terms of the *space of states* **X** whose elements, called *resource allocations*, are all $n \times m$ matrices X such that $X_{ik} \geq 0$ and

$$\sum_{i=1}^{n} X_{ik} = c_k \quad \text{for all } k;$$

X_{ik} denotes the amount of kth resource currently controlled by the occupant of ith position. The *transition* from state X to state X' can be described by the formula $X' = X + F$ where $F = X' - X$ is a matrix called a *resource flow*. A matrix F is a resource flow if and only if

$$\sum_{i=1}^{n} F_{ik} = 0 \quad \text{and} \quad F_k^+ = \sum_{i: F_{ik} > 0} F_{ik} \leq c_k \quad \text{for all } k$$

(F_k^+ is the *total flow of kth resource*). If F is a flow then $-F$ is also a flow. The sum of these two flows, which are said to be *inverse* to each other, is the *zero flow*; it does not change the current resource allocation. The set of flows is not, however, an additive group, since in general the sum $F + F'$ of two flows need not be a flow; if it is, then $F + F'$ is called the *composition* of F and F'. A flow F is *feasible in a state X* if $X' = X + F$ is in **X**.

F is a *dyadic flow* between positions i and j if $F_{hk} = 0$ for all k and all h other than i and j. One can prove that any flow is the composition of a finite number of dyadic flows. Let us call a flow F *unilateral* if for any position i either $F_{ik} \geq 0$ for all k or $F_{ik} \leq 0$ for all k. Then we can define an *exchange between positions i and j* as any dyadic flow between i and j which is not unilateral. When only two types of resources are transferred between two positions, an exchange between P_i and P_j will be written as $P_i(x_k / x_l) P_j$, which means that x_k units of kth resource flow from P_i to P_j and at the same time x_l units of lth resource flow from P_j to P_i. The ratio x_k/x_l is called the *rate of exchange* of kth resource for lth resource.

The social action structure has thus far remained somewhat in the background, considered as part of the experimental technique rather than an integral component of the theoretical definition of a network exchange system. ET assumes that theory-relevant characteristics of the interaction process are determined by the network and "actor conditions" (see Markovsky, Willer, and Patton 1988: 223). The regularity of the course of negotiations may also result from a certain organization of collective behavior instituted by means of a set of explicit rules or spontaneously arrived at by the group upon previous experience of its members. Any exchange theory that attempts to predict as accurately as possible the results of negotiations should not leave out of consideration a possible effect of the *negotiation protocol* on exchange rates agreed upon by the actors. Thus, the level to which the competition among peripheral actors negotiating with the central actor in a centralized exchange system (Willer 1987: chap. 3) brings down the exchange rate may vary under various negotiation protocols (see Sozański 1993b for a more extensive analysis of this issue).

The fact that most of theoretical work has yet to be done as regards modeling the interaction process is not a surprise, once we note that NET, no longer tied to the psychological operant theory, could equally little benefit from the "action approach" in sociology (see Cohen 1973: chap. 4). What was wrong with the traditional action perspective was its preoccupation with the "unit act" (Parsons's term) or at best interaction in a dyad. A single action was viewed as a pill containing in itself the whole society. In our view, NET should build on a quite opposite approach, one much less concerned with the nature of a single action. What counts in a formal theory of action is the possibility of *concatenating* elementary acts into somehow organized sequences (*strings*). A formalization of social action structures has become possible by resorting to mathematical theory of formal languages (Nowakowska 1973; see also Skvoretz and Fararo 1989 and the papers quoted there). The structure of the stream of actions can be defined as a *grammar* of the *action language*. We will not explain here what in formal linguistics is meant by a grammar—in particular, a "generative grammar." Suffice it to say that a grammar determines a class of *syntactically admissible strings* of elements from a set of elementary symbols; this set is called an *alphabet*. Regardless of how a grammar is specifically defined, it should provide an effective (programmable) means of ascertaining whether a given string is or is not admissible.

The construction of a formal language for modeling the interaction process in a network exchange system must start from the choice of an action alphabet whose elements are interpreted as action options available to the actors occupying positions in the system. What types of actions are legal in a given system is a matter of defining the system's normative constraints. For instance, coalition offers may be permitted or not. Similarly, property rights define legal ways of using resources by the actors. In the laboratory system, all these rules are laid down and enforced by the experimenter. The use of a computer network has made this task easier and has allowed the elimination of both illegal and irrelevant behaviors. What an actor is permitted to do at any moment is to pick an option from the current menu given by the program managing the experimental session.

The action options that have been used in NET experiments are offers and responses to offers: acceptances or rejections (Skvoretz, Willer, and Fararo 1993). A *parametric directed offer* is a proposal to conclude an exchange at a given rate with a given partner. The tradition of interpreting the interaction process within a group as a series of two-party negotiations (run in public, however, and thus interdependent) accounts for the common practice of using only directed offers in experimental systems. We would like to suggest a different construction of the action language to allow an actor to send his offers to the "market," that is, to all whom it may concern, as well as to address proposals to particular partners.

Let **A** be the set of *action options*. For any a in **A** and any position P the expression $P:a$ will denote the *action* of the occupant of P which consists in selecting option a. Let us assume that **A** contains only two types of options: *partner choices* and *offers*; these terms will be used to denote also the respective actions. The choice of the occupant of position P_j as the current negotiation partner, made by the occupant of P_i, will be written as $P_i:j$. Two *complementary partner choices* are those of the form $P_i:j$ and $P_j:i$.

In order to define offers, one must specify the nature of admissible transactions. If the resource-control structure is introduced in such a way as we did, transactions can be identified with exchanges, or special resource flows. Then, an offer is defined as a vector $z = (z_1,...,z_m)$. The sign of its kth coordinate tells us if an actor who makes the offer is willing to receive ($+$) or would like to give up ($-$) a given number ($|z_k|$) of units of kth resource. This definition implies that $P_i:z$, or an offer made by the occupant of P_i, is not addressed to any particular partner but to all who can respond with a complementary offer. Two *offers* $P_i:z$ and $P_j:z'$ made by the occupants of two distinct positions P_i and P_j are said to be complementary to each other if $z' = -z$.

For the sake of parsimony, we shall not enlarge the repertoire of elementary actions by adding a variety of reactions to the offers. Accepting an offer will be treated as equivalent to making a complementary offer. Rejecting an offer will in turn be considered as one of the meanings of making a *zero-offer* ($z_k = 0$ for all k). We permit also other interpretations of zero-offers such as temporal withdrawal from negotiations, canceling a previous offer and partner choice, or just waiting for actions of others. Strictly speaking, an actor's intention expressed in his particular action should not be confused with the meaning given to an action by the negotiation protocol. Thus, the meaning of the zero-offer is partially established by the following condition which restricts the freedom of breaking negotiations and loosely corresponds to the maxim *Audiatur et altera pars*: *After its last partner choice $P_i : j$ the occupant of P_i must not make a zero-offer until the occupant P_j makes a non-zero offer.* This condition (Axiom 9 in our 1993a paper) shows how the rules of continuing interaction endow the action language with a syntactical structure.

Let us suppose that an actor occupying position P_i is given an opportunity to act at time t. Then, the range of action options available to him at t is assumed to be completely determined both by the current system state X (allocation of resources among positions) and by the sequence of actions (of P_i and other positions) that have occurred in a round since the beginning of the bargaining cycle up to time t. Let us call a *bargaining cycle* the sequence of actions between two consecutive transactions. We assume that the dynamics of the system is governed by the following principle (Axiom 3 in 1993a):

> *An exchange between P_i and P_j comes about at time t if and only if last non-zero offers and last partner choices made by P_i and P_j are complementary.*

Accordingly, an exchange is an event that happens automatically as soon as the interaction process reaches the point in which $P_i : z$ and $P_j : -z$ are valid offers of the occupants of P_i and P_j, $P_i : j$, and $P_j : i$ are their valid partner choices (all four actions may appear in any order). An offer/partner choice made by P_i at time t remains *valid* until P_i makes its next offer/partner choice at some $t' > t$; in addition, we assume that a zero-offer invalidates both the last offer and last partner choice. A *directed offer* valid at t is defined as a pair consisting of a non-zero offer and a partner choice both valid at t.

The opportunity structure constrains the interaction in the sense that the occupant of P_i is allowed to choose P_j if and only if P_j is accessible to P_i (Axiom 2 in 1993a; Axiom 1 is the assumption of connectedness of the opportunity graph). The resource-control structure imposes the ban on making unreliable offers. An offer $P_i : z$ is *reliable* with respect to the current resource allocation X if $X_{ik} + z_k \geq 0$, that is, the number of units of kth resource that P_i is willing to give up must not exceed the amount of kth resource currently possessed by P_i. A non-zero offer $P_i : z$ is *realistic* if there exists a position P_j accessible to P_i such that the offer $P_j : -z$ is reliable. Again, we assume that unrealistic offers are forbidden.

The freedom of making offers can be limited even further by assuming that certain offers are *socially approved* while others are illegal, which implies that certain feasible transactions (those allowed by the network and the distribution of resources) will be excluded. This third constraining structure will be termed *social control over resource flows*. In our earlier paper (1993a), we assumed that social control operates in an invariable manner throughout each bargaining cycle. This assumption is part of a more general condition (Axiom 4 in 1993a) which requires that the terms of negotiations stay fixed between any two consecutive transactions. Then, in particular, control over resources remains unchanged during each bargaining cycle so that exchanges are the only resource flows which can happen during the system's lifetime.

In the case of exchange systems with two types of resources, social control over resource flows can be introduced by defining for any bargaining cycle an upper and/or lower limits for currently proposed exchange rates. As for any other normative structure, the source of the restrictions must remain unspecified in the formal model. Exchange systems may essentially differ with respect to what is the range of socially approved rates and how it may vary during the system's functioning. There are systems in which resources are allowed to be exchanged at any rate; if in addition any two positions which have an interest in a resource flow are accessible to each other, then such systems can be termed *free markets* (Sozański 1993a). In other systems, the exchange rate may be subject to social control, say, in such a way that only "equitable" exchanges are permitted. In still other systems, social control can produce a sort of status hierarchy (Willer 1987: chap. 6).

In the case of a centralized system with a mobile hierarchy, the terms of consecutive exchanges change in such a way that a peripheral actor who contrives to make a deal with the central actor before others do will achieve a better rate of exchange. This generates competition among peripheral actors, which in turn gives the occupant of the central position the power over the peripherals. In the paper (1993b) reporting our replication of Willer's experiment, we claimed that the degree to which the central actor benefits from the competition among his partners may depend on how the stream of actions is organized in time. As a consequence, in order to define a negotiation protocol, it is not sufficient to specify the set of elementary actions and to define grammatical rules of continuing interaction. One also needs to specify who may enter into the negotiations and when. The competition among actors (produced by "exclusion," as claimed by ET) consists not only in the actors' making competitive offers but also in their struggle for a chance to come up with any offer before others do. If all peripheral actors are guaranteed the right to make their offers in a bargaining cycle and hear the offers made by their rivals, they can discover that collective resistance to the central actor is their common interest and act accordingly, even if they are not permitted by the system rules to propose to one another that they coordinate action.

Any negotiation protocol resembles a score, since it must tie together the synchronic and diachronic dimension of the collective action of many players. In particular, any public stepwise procedure organizes interaction into a sequence of coactions in consecutive time intervals, or bars. An actor can make at each stage only one offer or partner choice without knowing the actions of others at this stage. The ordering of these actions within a given time interval is unimportant; hence they are said to form a coaction. The assumed public character of negotiations means that all actions that happened at a given stage become known to all actors before the next stage begins. The above paradigm admits of many protocols specifying which actors, with what types of actions, at which stages, and in what order are supposed to enter into the negotiations. For instance, the protocol used in our replication (1993b) of Willer's experiment assumed that at every stage only one actor could act. The negotiations were organized as a series of biddings, each followed by the central actor's choice of a peripheral partner. A bidding was defined as a sequence of offers made by distinct actors. The ordering of positions within a bidding was randomly determined by the computer program managing the experimental session. Using this procedure, we were able to find out, among other things, that the central actor gains greater power when his offer made in the first bargaining cycle precedes the offers of his partners (1993b: 261).

The discussion of the dynamics of an exchange system should not leave out of consideration the global time span of the system's functioning. To see how the system works in time, one must generate a sample of its behavior. This not only means that people have to occupy positions and act in accordance with the rules. The experimenter must also choose a time interval or intervals in which the system's behavior will be observed, taking into account how the system's lifetime is defined in theory. Without going into details, let us distinguish three ideal types of systems.

1. Systems that function in a theoretically infinite time span, possibly with periodical renewal of resources.
2. Systems with the probability of "death" (a system's breakdown) assigned to any moment; in particular, the systems that stop working at the moment set in advance, regardless of the events that may have taken place before a system's lifetime elapsed.
3. Systems for which the *end condition* is defined in terms of an event or a sequence of events that whenever it occurs (no matter how much time is needed for these events to happen) brings the system's action to an end (for instance, the system stops working after a preset number of transactions).

The ET deals with systems of type 3. The end condition is introduced by means of an *exchange regime* (Markovsky, Willer, and Patton 1988; Friedkin 1992), which permits each position to conclude at most one transaction with each partner and imposes a limit on the number of transactions with distinct partners. A round comes to an end when all transaction opportunities are exhausted for all positions. In experiments this condition is combined with a time limit (usually two to five minutes). If multiple transactions with the same partner are not allowed and the order in which transaction occur is ignored, then an end condition can be specified by defining a family of subgraphs ("potential networks," in ET terminology) of the transaction opportunity graph G. The lines of each subgraph represent transactions that may occur in a single round. The only requirement imposed on the *class of transaction subgraphs* $\mathbf{T}$ is that for any position i there must be at least one subgraph in $\mathbf{T}$ in which the degree of i is greater than 0, that is, the rules do not exclude any position from the game. The minimum and maximum values of the degree of i over all subgraphs in $\mathbf{T}$ and the degree of i in G are used to define the *type of connection of the network at point i* (see Willer 1992a: 205–8 for a new, more precise explication of this concept). One can also define the *type of interdependence of two positions i and j* in terms of a set-theoretic relationship between the set $\mathbf{T}_i$ of transaction subgraphs in which point i has a non-zero degree and the similar set $\mathbf{T}_j$ corresponding to j. If the two sets do not intersect, then positions i and j are said to be *negatively interdependent*; if $\mathbf{T}_i = \mathbf{T}_j$, i and j are said to be *positively interdependent*. If $\mathbf{T}_i \subset \mathbf{T}_j$ and $\mathbf{T}_i \neq \mathbf{T}_j$, i is *unilaterally dependent* on j. Unilateral dependence of j on i is the fourth type of relationship possible. In the last, fifth type the sets $\mathbf{T}_i$ and $\mathbf{T}_j$ overlap, but neither of them is contained in the other.

The definition of a network exchange system must contain also a *start condition* which points out a class of initial resource allocations under which negotiations can begin. It is natural to assume that the actors will not start negotiations unless they have an interest in exchanging resources. It is generally agreed that any exchange model must somehow reflect the fact that the resources which the actors transmit are evaluated by them. A sociological or economic theory of exchange cannot analyze resource flows solely in terms of the quantities of resource units circulating within the system. However, how to build the valuation structure into the exchange model has always been and still is a controversial issue, despite the efforts by Emerson (1972a, 1987) to clarify the meaning of the concept of value. The debate is focused on two general questions. The first is how the evaluations of resources by the actors are related to their behaviors and how the process of resource circulation is driven by the actors' interests. What is at issue here is whether the valuation of resources should be introduced into the model as an independent characteristic of the actors (say, as the collection of actors' fixed utility functions) or should the actors' evaluations be derived from the exchange process itself, which in turn might lead to defining the value of a given resource in terms of the ratio at which this resource is actually exchanged for another resource.

The second major question concerns the validity of interpersonal utility comparisons. It is debatable whether the values assigned by the two actors to a resource allocation can be meaningfully compared with each other, especially by means of the formula (Cook and Emerson 1978: 723) in which the profits (utility increments) of the two parties from a possible transaction are equated with each other in order to find an "equitable" exchange ratio. Without going into the dispute between Heckathorn (1983a,b) and Emerson, Cook, Gillmore, and Yamagishi (1983) over this issue (we think that Heckathorn's position rejecting inter-actor utility comparisons is more convincing), let us go ahead with the formalization of the valuation structure. Let us begin by noticing that NET has not yet developed its own formal language for modeling the valuation of resources. That is why one must make use of the tools of classic microeconomy and the theory of games and decisions. Both Elementary Theory and Power-Dependence Theory actually deal with "utilities," even though the term is hardly ever used explicitly.

Let us assume that $u_i(X)$, the *utility for an actor i of a resource allocation X*, depends solely on $X_{i1},...,X_{im}$ where X_{ij} is the amount of resource j ($j = 1,...,m$) currently in possession of actor i and u_i is actor's i's *utility function*. Then $u_i(X)$ can be written as $u_i(X_{i1},...,X_{im})$ and identified with the *value for i of one's own resources*. In microeconomy, certain mathematical properties are required from an individual's utility function (see Kemeny and Snell 1962: Appendix B for an elementary introduction), but the formula for u_i may be left unspecified on the level of general theoretical formulation. On the other hand, a more concrete definition of u_i may enrich the formal theory, even if its scope will be limited. For instance, the recent version (1990) of Coleman's interest-control exchange theory is based on the Cobb-Douglas utility function, which, under the notation used in this paper, can be written as $u_i(X_{i1},...,X_{im}) = X_{i1}^{a_{i1}},....,X_{im}^{a_{im}}$ where a_{ij} is a measure of the "interest" of actor i in resource j.

Another simple formula is grounded on two assumptions. The first says that an actor's satisfaction from having a single resource is directly proportional to the quantity of this resource possessed by the actor (that is, the effect of satiation is ignored). The second assumption defines the overall level of satisfaction from a "commodity bundle" as the sum of utilities of all resources. The assumptions of proportionality and additivity lead to the following formula for the utility function of actor i:

$$u_i(X_{i1},...,X_{im}) = \sum_{j=1}^{m} u_{ij}X_{ij},$$

where u_{ij} is the *unit value* of resource j for actor i. Then the *profit of actor i from the resource flow* $F = X - X'$, defined as $u_i(X) - u_i(X')$, can be computed as the sum $\Sigma u_{ij}F_{ij}$ over $j = 1,...,m$. For the case of two resources, the latter formula is equivalent to Cook and Emerson's (1978: 723) profit calculation formula as well as to Willer's (1981b: 111) "first law," or the formula for "preference state alteration."

We restrict our discussion to the simplest system in which there are only two actors and two resources. Let us assume that the total amount of each resource remains constant throughout the system's lifetime. For simplicity, let these two constants be equal to 1 so that X_{ij} can be interpreted as the fraction of the total amount of good j controlled by actor i. Then, the space of possible resource allocations can be identified with the square on the plane with vertices $(0,0)$, $(0,1)$, $(1,0)$, $(1,1)$. Any point (x_1,x_2) of the *unit square* represents the resource allocation such that x_1 and x_2 describe the possession of resources 1 and 2 by actor 1; the possession of the two resources by actor 2 is given by the numbers $1 - x_1$ and $1 - x_2$.

A resource allocation (y_1,y_2) is said to be *jointly at least as good as* (x_1,x_2) if $u_1(x_1,x_2) \geq u_1(y_1,y_2)$ and $u_2(1 - x_1, 1 - x_2) \geq u_2(1 - y_1, 1 - y_2)$, and *jointly better than* (x_1,x_2) if at least one of these inequalities is sharp. The allocation (x_1,x_2) is called *jointly best* if there is no allocation (y_1,y_2) jointly better than (x_1,x_2). The postulate that the final resource allocation should be jointly best and at least as good for both parties as the initial allocation does not suffice as the basis of a theory of bilateral exchange capable of determining uniquely the final allocation of resources for any given initial resource allocation. More than a hundred years ago (1881), Edgeworth demonstrated that under certain regularity conditions imposed on the utility functions, all jointly best outcomes form a curve which was called the *contract curve*. This "indeterminacy" had been a serious challenge to exchange theorists until early 1950s, when John Nash proposed his solution to the bargaining problem. Although Nash was interested first of all in solving cooperative games (1953), his general model of bargaining (1950) admits of several applications which include the exchange of goods in conditions of "bilateral monopoly."

The *bargaining problem* was formally defined (see Luce and Raiffa 1958: chap. 6; Myerson 1991: chap. 8) as a pair made up of a subset S of the plane, and of a point $a = (a_1,a_2)$. The elements of S represent all possible bargains. The two coordinates of any point $s = (s_1,s_2)$ in S are the levels of satisfaction of the two parties from a given contract. It is assumed that the set S satisfies some regularity condition: S should be *convex* (for any two points in S, the segment of the straight line joining them is contained in S), *bounded* (S is contained in circle of a sufficiently large radius), and *closed* (the limit of any convergent sequence of points of S lies in S). The point a may lie inside or outside S. In the first case a is usually interpreted as the *status quo outcome*, or the initial level of satisfaction of the bargainers. If a is not in S, it can be regarded as the *confrontation outcome* with which the two parties end up if they fail to agree on a point from S. The definition of the bargaining problem contains also the assumption that there is at least one point $s = (s_1,s_2)$ in S such that $s \geq a$, that is, $s_1 \geq a_1$ and $s_2 \geq a_2$. Thus, it is always possible to avoid confrontation or move from the status quo to a state in which both parties are better off.

The *solution* of a bargaining problem is conceived of as a unique point s^* in S determined for (a,S) with the use of a rule applicable to the whole class of bargaining problems, that is, $s^* = F(a,S)$ where F denotes a given rule. The next step must be to define the properties required of any "reasonable" rule and to prove the existence and uniqueness of a rule with these properties. Nash himself proposed four axioms and demonstrated that there is only one rule satisfying his postulates. Specifically, his rule defines the solution of (a,S) as the unique point at which the product $(s_1 - a_1)(s_2 - a_2)$ attains the maximum value on the set of all s in S such that $s \geq a$.

The first axiom requires that the solution be both jointly at least as good as a ($s^* \geq a$) and *jointly undominated*. The latter property, called also *Pareto optimality*, means that there is no s in S different from s^* such that $s \geq s^*$. The subset of S made up of all Pareto optimal points which are at least as good as a is called the *negotiation set*.

Let (a',S') be the image of (a,S) through the transformation $s'_1 = \alpha_1 s_1 + \beta_1$, $s'_2 = \alpha_2 s_2 + \beta_2$ with $\alpha_1 \alpha_2 > 0$, that is, the actors change arbitrarily their satisfaction scales as permitted by interval measurement of utility. The second axiom assumes that the solutions of (a',S') and (a,S) should be functionally related with each other via the same transformation. Similarly, if (a,S) is transformed onto (a',S') by having the actors interchange positions ($s'_1 = s_2$, $s'_2 = s_1$), the third axiom requires that the solution of (a',S') be obtained in the same way from the solution of (a,S).

The fourth axiom has the following statement: if the solution of (a,S) lies in the subset S' of S, then it must coincide with the solution of the bargaining problem (a,S') with a smaller set of possible outcomes. Formally, for any two bargaining problems (a,S) and (a,S'), if $S' \subset S$ and $F(a,S) \in S'$ then $F(a,S') = F(a,S)$. The last axiom seems at first glance reasonable and obvious. It is no longer so if we assume that the parties seek only a compromise solution of their conflict of interests. The solution reached under a restricted set S' of available outcomes need not be identical with that arrived at in conditions when there are more options from which to choose, even if the "global" point of compromise happens to fall into S'. Nash's axiom is justified if we require that the bargainers find first a bilaterally acceptable *complete* ordering of all outcomes in S (which is an extension of the *partial* order defined on S by the condition $t \geq s$ if and only if $t_1 \geq s_1$ and $t_2 \geq s_2$) to choose next the best outcome accordingly.

This and other objections to Nash's axiom gave rise to the search for an alternative rule for solving the bargaining problem. Kalai and Smorodinsky (1975) retained Nash's axiomatic approach but replaced his fourth axiom with the *monotonicity axiom*. To state the latter axiom, we need further definitions. Let us define the *conditional best hope* of actor 1 as the maximum satisfaction that actor 1 can attain if actor 2's satisfaction is at least t_2. The conditional best hope of actor 2 is defined similarly. Formally,

$$b_1(t_2,S) = \max\{s_1 : (s_1,s_2) \in S \text{ for some } s_2 \geq t_2\}$$
$$b_2(t_1,S) = \max\{s_2 : (s_1,s_2) \in S \text{ for some } s_1 \geq t_1\}.$$

The *best hopes* $b_1(S)$ and $b_2(S)$ of actors 1 and 2 are defined as $b_1(a_2,S)$ and $b_2(a_1,S)$, respectively. The best hope of actor 1 is simply the maximum satisfaction actor 1 can attain from any bargain in S jointly no worse than the baseline level a.

Let (a,S) and (a,S') be two bargaining problems such that $b_1(S) = b_1(S')$ and $b_2(t_1,S) \leq b_2(t_1,S')$ for any t_1 ranging from a_1 to $b_1(S)$. This assumption means that if one party in each of the two situations proposes an agreement which ensures it the minimum satisfaction t_1, then the other party can gain more in the second situation than in the first one. The monotonicity axiom requires that the relatively better bargaining position of actor 2 in (a,S') be reflected in the solution, that is, $F(a,S)_2 \leq F(a,S')_2$.

Kalai and Smorodinsky demonstrated that the axiomatics obtained by appending the monotonicity axiom to the first three axioms introduced by Nash is also satisfied by exactly one rule. Their solution, which is different from that of Nash, is defined for (a,S) as the unique point at which the negotiation set intersects the segment of the straight line joining the points $a = (a_1,a_2)$ and $b = (b_1,b_2)$ where $b_1 = b_1(S)$, $b_2 = b_2(S)$ for a fixed S.

Let us assume that $b_1 > a_1$ and $b_2 > a_2$ (if $b_1 = a_1$ or $b_2 = a_2$ the negotiation set reduces to the single point). Heckathorn (1980) observed that the equation of the straight line going through a and b can then be written in the form:

$$\frac{b_1 - s_1}{b_1 - a_1} = \frac{b_2 - s_2}{b_2 - a_2}.$$

For any $s \geq a$ in S, the left- and right-hand sides of this equation were termed by Heckathorn the *resistances* of actors 1 and 2, respectively, to a possible bargain s. The resistance of each party is defined as the ratio of two utility differences, which implies that its value will not change after any appropriate transformation of the utility scale.

The concept of resistance became one of the key ideas of ET. Willer (1981b) modified the definition of resistance by replacing $b_i - a_i$ in the denominator with $s_i - a_i$. As a consequence, the variable defined by him can assume infinitely great values while under Heckathorn's definition it is always a number between 0 and 1. It is not difficult to verify that Willer's equation of equal resistance is equivalent to Heckathorn's equation given above.

The abstract mathematical model of bargaining can be applied to bilateral exchange to derive the solution of the indeterminacy problem. The concrete formulas are obtained if the actors' utility functions are assumed to have the following linear form:

$$u_1(x_1,x_2) = u_{11}x_1 + u_{12}x_2,$$
$$u_2(1 - x_1, 1 - x_2) = u_{21}(1 - x_1) + u_{22}(1 - x_2).$$

Under these formulas, the unit square is transformed onto the convex hull of the set of 4 points: $U(0,0) = (0, u_{21} + u_{22})$, $U(0,1) = (u_{12}, u_{21})$, $U(1,0) = (u_{11}, u_{22})$, $U(1,1) = (u_{11} + u_{12}, 0)$, or images of the vertices of unit square $(0,0)$, $(0,1)$, $(1,0)$, $(1,1)$. Recall that the *convex hull* of a set is the minimal convex set containing the

given set. The convex hull, which is to play the role of the set S in Nash's definition of the bargaining problem, is the quadrangle with vertices $U(0,0)$, $U(0,1)$,
$U(1,0)$, $U(1,1)$ unless no 3 out of these 4 points lie on a straight line. Since the
actors in an exchange relation do not suffer any loss if they fail to agree on a
bilateral resource flow, the point a in the bargaining problem (a,S) will be an
element of S so that it will mean the level of satisfaction from the initial resource
allocation.

We will put off for another paper the derivation the Kalai–Smorodinsky solution of the bargaining problem just defined. Let us say only that this solution
will give us the predicted rate of exchange of good 1 to good 2.

To conclude, the knowledge of the actors' utility functions is needed to make
specific predictions of resource flows in a dyadic system. However, there are
some reasons why NET has preferred to avoid elaborating on a model of resource valuation, especially in the case of exchange systems with many actors.
The interpretation of the situation of bilateral exchange as a bargaining problem
leads to the conclusion that a transaction may be conceived of as the choice of
an option from a negotiation set (the contract curve in the "Edgeworth box,"
or the northeast border of the utility quadrangle). Then the actors' utility functions seem to be less important than the "mixed-motive" structure of the conflict
of interests (cf. Heckathorn 1983a) of the actors whose common interest is to
move from the status quo to the negotiation set on which their preferences are
opposite to each other. In fact, to start negotiations, an actor does not need to
know the other party's utility function. Even if the players have such a knowledge, they can disregard it. If the actors are informed about the others' values
and they are willing to make interpersonal utility comparisons, it is natural to
aim at a theory that would use equity expectations to predict resource flows in
the system. The idea of equitable exchange seems to be a good starting point if
one aims at an equilibrium theory in a network exchange system. However, if
the actors are not guided by a norm of fair division, but all of them want to score
as many "profit points" as possible, then mutually acceptable transactions are also
possible, and the search for an equilibrium theory is natural as well. Basically, the
term "profit point" may be referred to any formal parameter that is used to
represent the unidimensional negotiation set contained in the two-dimensional
set of all feasible bargains. However, both in theory and in experiments, profit
points are often given an intrinsic value common to the actors. Then the comparisons of relative benefits and equity hypotheses become meaningful again.

A Mathematical Theory of Equal Dependence in Profit Pool Networks

A *profit pool network* is a connected graph G whose edges have been assigned
positive numbers. The number assigned to the edge ij, called the *profit pool* in $i—j$
relation, is interpreted as the number of points that the actors occupying two
connected positions i and j can split between each other in a single transaction.

It is convenient to represent a profit pool network by a square matrix $C = (C_{ij})$, $i,j = 1,...,n$ (n is the number of points of G), with numerical entries satisfying the following condition.

$$C_{ij} \geq 0, \quad C_{ii} = 0, \quad C_{ij} = C_{ji} \quad \text{for all } i,j$$

The case $C_{ij} = 0$ will be identified with the absence of a tie between positions i and j. Then the adjacency matrix of the transaction opportunity graph G is determined uniquely by the matrix C: $G_{ij} = 1$ if $C_{ij} > 0$; $G_{ij} = 0$ if $C_{ij} = 0$. It is assumed, as part of the definition of a profit pool network C, that the graph G obtained from C is connected.

Let us define a *homogenous profit pool network with constant pool size c* by the condition:

$$C_{ij} = c \text{ if } C_{ij} > 0;$$

The next step to develop a formal *structural* theory must be to define an appropriate notion of isomorphism for the class of objects under study. Let ϕ be a permutation of the set $\{1,...,n\}$ and let k be a real number greater than 0.

The n-point profit pool networks C and C' are said to be *isomorphic* through (ϕ,k) if

$$C'_{\phi(i)\phi(j)} = kC_{ij}.$$

Then ϕ is an isomorphism of the graphs G and G' corresponding to C and C'. The constant $k > 0$ in the above definition means that the profit pool size is scaled arbitrarily (under the type of measurement known as ratio scale). Since all homogenous networks with the same underlying graph G are isomorphic with each other the constant c can be set to 1 (in experiments c has usually been set to 24 points).

Let (ϕ, k) denote an automorphism of C. By applying the formula $C'_{\phi(i)\phi(j)} = kc_{ij}$ to ij (such that $C_{ij} > 0$) sufficiently many times until $\phi^p(i)\phi^p(j) = ij$ for some power p of ϕ we arrive at the formula $C_{ij} = k^p C_{ij}$ which may be true only for $k = 1$. As a consequence, the automorphisms of any network C can be identified with the automorphisms of the associated graph G.

The matrix C specifies the constraints imposed on the functioning of a *dynamical system* which is obtained when the positions are manned with actors who can negotiate pool splits with their neighbors on the transaction opportunity graph.

The current state of negotiations will be formally described by a *profit demand* matrix $R = (R_{ij})$ with all entries satisfying the condition

$$0 \leq R_{ij} \leq C_{ij}.$$

The ij entry is interpreted as the offer, addressed by actor i to actor j, to divide the pool assigned to ij so that actor i will receive R_{ij} profit points and j will get the rest of the pool, that is, $C_{ij} - R_{ij}$.

Two profit demands R_{ij} and R_{ji} are said to be *complementary* to each other if

$R_{ij} + R_{ji} = C_{ij}$. If this is the case for all ij, R will be called a *self-complementary profit demand matrix*. If $R_{ij} + R_{ji} \neq C_{ij}$, then two cases $R_{ij} + R_{ji} < C_{ij}$ and $R_{ij} + R_{ji} > C_{ij}$ will be called *weak complementarity* and *conflict of demands*, respectively.

The set of all profit demand matrices, noted **R**, will be the *space of states* of our dynamical system. The *demand adjustment transformation* U of **R** into **R** given by the formula

$$U(R)_{ij} = \tfrac{1}{2}(C_{ij} + R_{ij} - R_{ji})$$

makes the actors change their demands in such a way that they will both demand either more points or less points than they originally claimed. Specifically, new profit demands are obtained from the old ones by adding or subtracting half the length of the interval between them. In both cases, the result is always a self-complementary profit demand matrix.

The negotiation process can be modeled as a sequence of two-step cycles. At the first step, all actors make offers to their neighbors, and at the next step, they modify their demands by means of the demand adjustment transformation U. The matrix $U(R)$ becomes in turn the starting point for making new, possibly conflicting demands, and so forth, until a state of equilibrium is reached.

For homogenous networks, another approach to modeling the negotiation process is possible. It is based on the assumption that the same offer is sent to all "whom it may concern." Then the initial matrix R must satisfy the condition that $R_{ij} = r_i$ for all j adjacent to i, where r_i is the profit demand addressed by i to all of its potential partners. Next the transformation U is applied to R to obtain R': $R'_{ij} = \tfrac{1}{2}(c + r_i - r_j)$ for any i,j such that $G_{ij} = 1$. R' should be replaced in turn by R'' similar to R in that the new demand made by i is also addressed to the "market" (r_i'' can be defined, for instance, as the maximum R'_{ik} over all k adjacent to i).

This path of developing a theory of negotiation process will not be pursued here. We will examine the general case where the actors are permitted to address different offers to different potential partners. Then it is reasonable to assume that the next offer made by actor i to actor j will depend on the set of current offers received by i from other partners than j. The idea of defining for any current profit demand matrix R an *alternative profit matrix* $A(R)$ functionally related to R admits of various operationalizations. In general, $A(R)_{ij}$ should be defined as the number of points the actor i expects to gain from a transaction with a potential partner other than j. In other words, what we need is a formalization of Thibaut and Kelley's (1959) concept of "comparison level." In particular, $A(R)_{ij}$ can be defined as the weighted sum $\Sigma w_{ik;j} R_{ik}$ over all k linked with i except j. One can also consider the formula in which R_{ik} is replaced by $C_{ik} - R_{ki}$, which means that actor i takes into account the number of points he can get by accepting his partner's demand rather than the number of points he hopes to receive if he persuades his partner to accept his own demand. The weight $w_{ik;j}$ is the probability with which actor i anticipates a transaction with actor k other than j. Cook, Donnelly, and Yamagishi (1997) derive these probabilities from the current R-matrix. One can also define $w_{ik;j}$ as dependent solely on the fixed transaction opportunity graph G. For example, if i has m potential partners except j ($m = d_i - 1$, where d_i is the degree of point i on G), then $w_{ik;j}$ can be set to $1/m$. This amounts to the assumption that i's partner choices are directed by i with the same probability to all its neighbors different from j. Such a simple model is probably most appropriate in the case where each actor's knowledge of the transaction opportunity structure is limited to one's own immediate neighbors on G (actor i does not know whether potential partner k has other potential partners than i).

For the case where full information on interposition connections is available to all actors, one can propose a more complicated but possibly more realistic formula which takes into account that the probability of i's transaction with an alternative partner k may depend not only on the probability that i will choose k but also on the probability that k will reciprocate i's choice. Let p_{ik} denote the probability that i will choose k. In the general formulation we require only that $p_{ik} = 0$ if i is not linked with k, and that the sum of p_{ik} over all k be equal to 1. Let us assume in turn that all actors' choices are *stochastically independent* of one another. Then the probability that i's choice of k is reciprocated by k is $p_{ik}p_{ki}$. To calculate the anticipated profit of i outside the i—j relation, one can take as $w_{ik;j}$ the conditional probability that i's choice of k is reciprocated by k, given that i excludes j as a potential transaction partner, symbolically, $w_{ik;j} = p_{ik}p_{ki}/(1 - p_{ij})$.

The assumption of *isotropy* of actors' choices allows us to derive p_{ik} from the transaction opportunity graph, namely, $p_{ik} = 1/d_i$. Then $w_{ik;j} = ((d_i - 1)d_k)^{-1}$. Note that these weights need not add up to 1 and the complement to 1 is the conditional probability that no choice made by i from among all alternatives to j will be reciprocated. By assigning 0 to such an event, we get a well-defined expected value for i's anticipated profit outside i—j.

To conclude, there is a range of plausible ways of defining the "comparison level." We will not discuss them in this paper. Instead, we shall examine in more detail the consequences of the original formula for $A(R)$ proposed by Cook and Yamagishi (1992: 249). Their definition of $A(R)_{ij}$ is based on the assumption that actor i will compare the current offer made to j with the best of all offers he directs to partners other than j. Following this suggestion, let us define the *best alternative profit matrix* by the formula:

$$A(R)_{ij} = \min\{C_{ij}, \max\{R_{ik}: k \neq j\}\}.$$

According to this formula, $A(R)_{ij} = 0$ if i and j have no transaction opportunity ($C_{ij} = 0$) or j is the only potential partner of i. Otherwise, $A(R)_{ij}$ is the best result that i expects to get having excluded j as a possible transaction partner. In addition, since we have assumed that the "comparison level" will be used by i only in negotiations with j, its value should not exceed the maximum number of points available in i—j relation. That is why $A(R)_{ij}$ is defined as the minimum of the pool size in i—j relation and of the maximum number of points that actor i would like to gain in other relations (the same modification should be applied to other definitions of $A(R)$).

Although the definitions given by Cook and Yamagishi (1992: 248–49) and their principle of equidependence are suitable for mathematical elaboration, the algorithm for determining the final R-matrix they offer does not fit their formulation as a whole, since in some cases it yields a result that does not satisfy the two conditions they tend to assume for any R-matrix: self-complementarity and equidependence.

The *self-complementarity condition*, which has already been stated, can be written as the following system of equations

$$R_{ij} + R_{ji} = C_{ij} \quad \text{for all } i,j.$$

The *equidependence condition* has the form of another system of equations

$$D(R)_{ij} = D(R)_{ji} \quad \text{for all } i,j,$$

where $D(R)_{ij}$, or the *dependence of actor i on actor j with respect to R*, is defined by the formula

$$D(R)_{ij} = R_{ij} - A(R)_{ij}.$$

We will also use matrix notation for its compactness. Let M^t stand for the *transpose* of an $n \times n$ matrix M. Then the two conditions and the definition of dependence can be written as the following matrix equations:

$$R + R^t = C$$
$$D(R) = D(R)^t$$
$$D(R) = R - A(R)$$

The matrix $C - R^t$ will be called the *complement* of R. While the ij entry of R shows how many points actor i currently wants to gain from a transaction with actor j, the ij entry of the complement of R (equal to $C_{ij} - R_{ji}$) shows how many points actor i will gain if he accepts actor j's demand. R is self-complementary if and only if the complement of R is equal to R.

The definition of the dependence matrix implies that the equidependence equation can be written in the form:

$$R - A(R) = R^t - A(R)^t$$

Note also that all these definitions and derivations make no reference to the particular form of $A(R)$.

We will say that R is *balanced* if it satisfies the self-complementarity and equidependence conditions. It is not difficult to show that R is balanced if and only if

$$R_{ij} = \tfrac{1}{2}(C_{ij} + A(R)_{ij} - A(R)_{ji}) \quad \text{for all } i,j,$$

which can be written in the matrix form as

$$R = \tfrac{1}{2}(C + A(R) - A(R)^t).$$

Let us define the transformation T_A of **R** into **R** by the formula:

$$T_A(R) = \tfrac{1}{2}(C + A(R) - A(R)')$$

Clearly, R is balanced if and only if $T_A(R) = R$. In other words, any balanced R is a *fixed point* of T_A. Note that $T_A(R) = U(A(R))$, that is, T_A is the *composition* of two transformations of **R** into **R**. The demand adjustment transformation U, which restores self-complementarity, can be defined now by the matrix formula:

$$U(R) = \tfrac{1}{2}(C + R - R')$$

We have already suggested that the negotiation process can be described mathematically as a sequence of two-step cycles of the form $R \to A(R) \to U(A(R))$. What is obtained now is the stop condition for this process. It will end as soon as a balanced R is attained. The process of approaching the equilibrium can be viewed as the sequence

$$R_o \to T_A(R_o) \to T^2_A(R_o) \to \cdots \to T^m_A(R_o) \to \cdots,$$

where R_o stands for an initial matrix which is assumed to be self-complementary. For instance, one can take as R_o the *equitable profit split matrix* $\tfrac{1}{2}C$.

It is interesting to know for which matrices the sequence $T^m_A(R_o)$ converges to a matrix R^* (we will explain the meaning of "convergence" later in this section). Then $T_A(R^*) = R^*$ and R^* is balanced. Another important question is whether R^* depends on the choice R_o. In other words, one can ask whether the final result of the negotiation process is independent of initial offers made by the actors. However, the most fundamental problem is whether the equilibrium exists at all. We shall prove the following:

EXISTENCE THEOREM. *If A is a continuous function which assigns to any R in **R** a matrix $A(R)$ in **R**, then there exists a balanced matrix R^* in **R**.*

Readers who are familiar with mathematical tools that are used to prove such theorems as Nash's theorem on the existence of equilibrium in a normal form game with mixed strategies (see Luce and Raiffa 1958: Appendix 2) will not be surprised by the method that will be used to prove our existence theorem. Indeed, the proof is straightforward as soon as we notice that the assumptions of the Brouwer fixed point theorem (see Kemeny and Snell 1962: Appendix A for an elementary introduction to the topic) hold for the set **R** and the transformation T_A. Indeed, **R** is a convex, closed, and bounded subset of the space of $n \times n$ matrices, and T_A is a continuous mapping of **R** into **R**. These assumptions imply that the equation $T_A(R) = R$ must have at least one solution.

The *convexity* of **R** means that for any two matrices R and R' in **R** and any two non-negative numbers λ and λ' such that $\lambda + \lambda' = 1$ the matrix $\lambda R + \lambda' R'$ is also in **R**. This property has to do with the *algebraic structure* of the space of real-valued $n \times n$ matrices: matrices are treated as *vectors*, which can be added and multiplied by a real number.

The space of matrices can be endowed also with a metric structure to give a precise meaning to the notion of convergence of an infinite sequence of matrices. In general, a *metric structure* is introduced in a set X by assigning to any two points x and x' of X a non-negative number $d(x,x')$ called the *distance* between x and x'. The distance function is assumed to satisfy three axioms: (1) $d(x,x') = 0$ if and only if $x = x'$; (2) $d(x,x') = d(x',x)$; (3) $d(x,x') \leq d(x,x') + d(x',x'')$.

A subset Z of X is *bounded* if there is a number $\delta > 0$ such that the distance between any two points of Z does not exceed δ. The *neighborhood* of a point x with the *radius* of $\epsilon > 0$ is defined as the set of points whose distance from x is less than ϵ. An infinite sequence x_i, $i = 1,2,\cdots$ is *convergent* to the *limit* x if in any neighborhood of x with an arbitrarily small radius lie almost all elements of the sequence ("almost all" means "except for at most a finite number of the initial elements of the sequence"). A subset Z of X is *closed* if the limit of any convergent sequence of points of Z is also in Z. A mapping F of X into X is *continuous* if for any sequence x_i which is convergent to an x, the sequence $F(x_i)$ is convergent to $F(x)$. A sufficient (but not necessary) condition of continuity of F is the *Lipschitz condition*, which is stated as follows: there exists an $\mu > 0$ such that $d(F(x), F(x')) \leq \mu d(x,x')$ for any two distinct points x and x' of X. In particular, F is called *contracting* if $\mu < 1$, and *non-expansive* if $\mu = 1$.

A metric structure in the set of $n \times n$ real-valued matrices is obtained, for instance, by defining the distance between R and R' as the square root of the sum of $(R_{ij} - R'_{ij})^2$ for $i,j = 1,\cdots, n$. This distance is called *Euclidean*. Another specific definition of distance is given by the formula

$$\rho(R,R') = \max\{|R_{ij} - R'_{ij}| : i,j = 1,\cdots,n\}.$$

These two definitions of distance are *topologically equivalent*—that is, any sequence R_i which is convergent to R under one metric is also convergent to R under the other metric; the converse also holds.

We will use the non-Euclidean distance in order to prove that then the transformation U of $\mathbf{R}$ into $\mathbf{R}$ is non-expansive, that is, $\rho(U(R), U(R')) \leq \rho(R,R')$. This results from the following series of inequalities: $\rho(U(R), U(R')) = \max|\frac{1}{2}(C + R - R')_{ij} - \frac{1}{2}(C + R' - R'')_{ij}| = \frac{1}{2}\max|(R - R')_{ij} + (R'' - R')_{ij}| \leq \frac{1}{2}\max(|(R - R')_{ij}| + |(R'' - R')_{ij}|) \leq \frac{1}{2}\max(|(R - R')_{ij}| + \frac{1}{2}\max|(R'' - R')_{ij}| = \frac{1}{2}\rho(R,R') + \frac{1}{2}\rho(R',R'') = \rho(R,R')$.

We will show in turn that if $A(R)$ is defined as the best alternative profit matrix, then the transformation A is also non-expansive. The proof is based on the following two inequalities, which can be demonstrated by examining cases: $|\min\{a_1,b\} - \min\{a_2,b\}| \leq |a_1 - a_2|$ and $|\max\{a_1,a_2\} - \max\{a'_1,a'_2\}| \leq \max\{|a_1 - a'_1|, |a_2 - a'_2|\}$. By applying these inequalities we get: $\rho(A(R),A(R')) = \max|\min\{C_{ij}, \max\{R_{ik}:k \neq j\}\} - \min\{C_{ij}, \max\{R'_{ik}:k \neq j\}| \leq |\max\{R_{ik}:k \neq j\} - \max\{R'_{ik}:k \neq j\}| \leq \max\{|R_{ij} - R'_{ik}|:k \neq j\} \leq \rho(R,R')$. If U and A are nonexpansive, then so is their composition:

$\rho(T_A(R), T_A(R')) \leq \rho(R, R')$. If T_A were a contracting transformation, we could apply the Banach fixed point theorem, which would ensure uniqueness of a fixed point and allow us to compute it as the limit of the sequence of *iterations* $T^m{}_A(R)$ for $m \to \infty$. We examined the behavior of this sequence by means of a computer program. Convergence to a balanced matrix is a rule, and the limit does not depend on R provided that the fixed point equation $T_A(R) = R$ has a unique solution.

Unfortunately, the uniqueness theorem is not true. Consider, for example, a 5-point homogenous profit pool network in which points 1 and 2 are tied to points 3, 4, and 5 and no other connections are present (the transaction opportunity structure has the form of a bipartite graph). Then, any profit demand matrix R in which $R_{ij} = x$ *for* $i = 1,2; j = 3,4,5; R_{ij} = c - x$ for $i = 3,4,5; j = 1,2$ is balanced with any x such that $0 \leq x \leq c$ (c is the constant pool size). Note that this R-matrix satisfies the *condition of invariance*

$$R_{\alpha(i)\alpha(j)} = R_{ij} \quad \textit{for all } i, j \textit{ and any automorphism } \alpha \textit{ of } C.$$

The condition of invariance requires that the negotiation behavior of an actor solely depend on his location on the network. Thus, any two actors whose positions on the network are structurally indistinguishable should make identical demands.

The existence theorem can be strengthened by showing that for any profit pool network, there exists a balanced matrix R which is invariant under any automorphism of the network C. To prove this, one can resort again to the Brouwer fixed point theorem, having replaced **R** by the set of all invariant R-matrices. This set is never empty because it contains at least the equitable profit demand matrix $\frac{1}{2}C$. If $A(R)$ is left unspecified, one must also assume that A preserves invariance (for any automorphism α of the network if $R_{\alpha(i)\alpha(j)} = R_{ij}$ for all i,j, then $A(R)_{\alpha(i)\alpha(j)} = A(R)_{ij}$ for all i,j). For the best alternative profit matrix, this property results from the definition.

Having imposed the invariance condition on admissible solutions of the fixed point equation, we set ourselves the task of solving it for all 142 homogenous networks with 2 to 6 points. We had to use paper and pencil to analyze almost every case separately, since we did not manage to devise a general algorithm for determining for any network the set of solutions of the equation $T_A(R) = R$. The results of computations can be summarized as follows. For 98 out of 142 networks, there is only one invariant solution (in 43 cases, it is $\frac{1}{2}C$). For 40 networks, the set of invariant solutions is infinite; more exactly, the solutions can be described as linearly dependent on one parameter. For the remaining 4 networks, the solution set is the union of two one-parameter sets intersecting in one point.

We also examined the class of homogenous networks with 2 to 9 positions in which the transaction opportunity structure has the form of a tree. The results

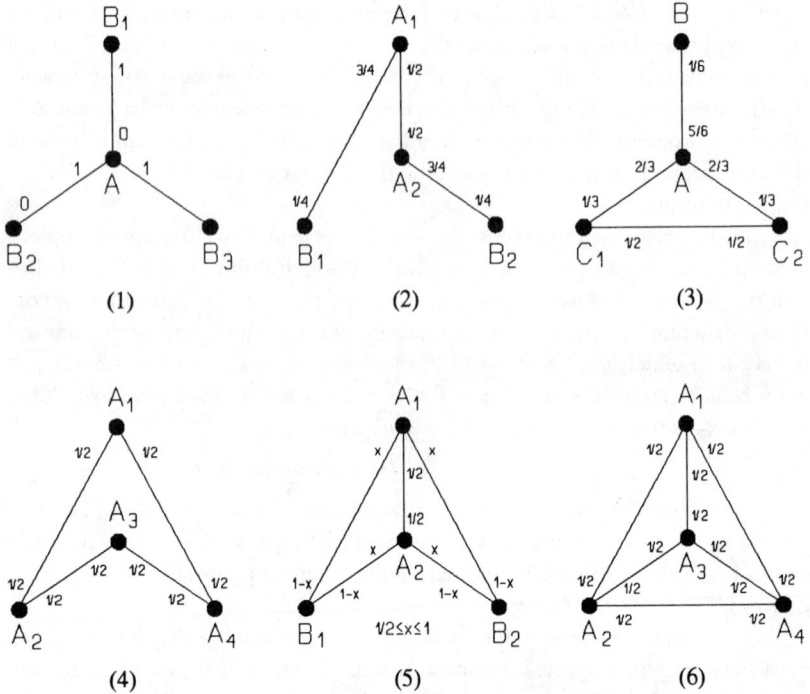

Fig. 1. Balanced solutions for 4-point homogenous networks

justify the *conjecture that any homogenous network over a tree admits of exactly one invariant balanced profit demand matrix.*

For any homogenous network C over the n-point complete graph the only invariant balanced matrix is the equitable profit split matrix $\frac{1}{2}C$. For $n = 2$ the complete graph A_1—A_2 is the only connected graph. For $n = 3$ there are two connected graphs: the complete 3-point graph whose points can be labeled A_1, A_2, A_3 and the 3-point tree B_1—A—B_2 (points in one structural class are labeled with the same letter). In the latter case, the only balanced R-matrix is farthest from the equitable split: A will demand the entire pool for himself while B_1 and B_2 must accept no profit points. The solutions for 6 structurally distinct 4-point homogenous networks are given in Figure 1 (the pool size is set to 1).

Let us show how to find an invariant balanced R-matrix by direct solving the equidependence and self-complementarity equations. We use as an example the 4-point homogenous network (3) in Figure 1, called the stem, which has been given most of the attention in NET literature.

The condition of invariance implies that we are left with three unknowns $x=R_{AB}$, $y=R_{AC_1}=R_{AC_2}$ and $z=R_{C_1C_2}=R_{C_2C_1}$ (the transposition of C_1 and C_2 is the only automorphism of network (3) besides the identity transformation). Then, by self-complementarity, $R_{BA}=1-x$, $R_{C_1A}=R_{C_2A}=1-z$. Since $R_{C_2C_1}=z$, we have $z=1-z$ and $z=\frac{1}{2}$. The values of unknowns x and y will be found from equidependence equations for $D_{AB}=D_{BA}$ and $D_{AC_1}=D_{C_1A}$, which can be written as $x-y=1-x$ and $y-\max\{x,y\}=1-y-\frac{1}{2}$. The first equation implies that $x-y\geq0$, $x\geq y$ and $\max\{x,y\}=x$, which allows us to rewrite the second equation as $y-x=\frac{1}{2}-y$. Thus, we arrive at two linear equations $2x-y=1$ and $2y-x=\frac{1}{2}$ whose only solution is $x=5/6$, $y=2/3$. In terms of a 24-point pool, the solution is $x=20$, $y=16$, $z=12$.

The final R-matrix obtained by Cook and Yamagishi by means of their algorithm (1992: 252–53) has $R_{AB}=18$, $R_{BA}=6$, $R_{C_1C_2}=R_{C_2C_1}=12$, $R_{AC_1}=R_{AC_2}=12$, $R_{C_1A}=R_{C_2A}=6$. The profit demands in A—C_i relation are not complementary here but only weakly complementary to each other ($12+6<24$). In fact, their algorithm differs from our iterative method (based on hypothetical convergence of the sequence $T^m(R)$) in that they use the formula $R'_{ij}=\frac{1}{2}(C_{ij}+A(R)_{ij}-A(R)_{ji})$ for the transition from $A(R)$ to R' only if $A(R)_{ij}+A(R)_{ji}\leq C_{ij}$. In the case of conflicting alternative profit demands ($A(R)_{ij}+A(R)_{ji}>C_{ij}$), they put $R'_{ij}=C_{ij}-A(R)_{ji}$, that is, the complement transformation is used instead of the demand adjustment transformation. Cook and Yamagishi define the stop condition for their procedure as $R'=R$. Then, regardless of how R'_{ij} is computed for a particular i—j relation, the equidependence equation $D(R)_{ij}=D(R)_{ji}$ holds for all i,j. It is not required, however, that the self-complementarity equation $R_{ij}+R_{ji}=C_{ij}$ be satisfied throughout the network. According to Cook and Yamagishi's theory, the relations i—j for which this is the case are those in which exchanges are most likely to occur. In particular, for the stem network the transactions should take place in A—B and C_1—C_2 relations. Since our theory defines the state of balance as the combination of two conditions, equidependence and self-complementarity, another condition must be used to distinguish between complementary demands which are likely to result in a transaction and those which are not.

Axiom 3 of Markovsky, Willer, and Patton's (1988) theory states that "i and j can exchange only if each seeks exchange with the other." "Exchange-seek relation," which appears also in Axiom 2, is a primitive term of their formal theory. The authors provide us also with an empirical interpretation of the notion of exchange-seek: "'i seeks exchange with j' means that i makes competitive offers to j" (1988: 225). Our formal theory will be more parsimonious. Instead of introducing exchange-seek relation as a primitive term, we will define it as a function of the current system state. Our immediate aim is to show that the approach founded on Emerson's equidependence principle can be developed into a mathematical theory which is rich and elegant enough to rival with Markovsky and associates' theory at least on formal grounds.

We will start by defining for any position i of a profit pool network two variables related to a current system state R: the *aspiration level* $p_i(R)$ and the *satisfaction level* $q_i(R)$ of actor i.

$$p_i(R) = \max\{R_{ik}:k\}, \quad q_i(R) = \max\{C_{ik} - R_{ki}:k\}$$

The aspiration level of i is the maximum number of profit points actor i would like to receive at the current state of negotiations; i's satisfaction level is the number of points that actor i can get by accepting the best of all offers currently made to him by his partners.

The aspiration level was first introduced by Cook and Yamagishi (1992: 253) under the name of the "power" of a position. We will use the term *power* only in the case of a self-complementary matrix R. Self-complementarity implies that $q_i(R) = p_i(R)$ while for any R we have $q_i(R)=p_i(C - R')$.

If R is an invariant profit demand matrix, then $p_i(R)$ and $q_i(R)$ are local structural parameters of a position in the transaction opportunity graph G. That is, if $R_{\alpha(i)\alpha(j)} = R_{ij}$ for any i,j and any automorphism α of G, then $p_{\alpha(i)}(R) = p_i(R)$ and $q_{\alpha(i)}(R) = q_i(R)$ for any automorphism α.

For any matrix R in **R**, we will define in turn a binary relation $S = S(R)$ on the set of positions by the following conditions:

$$iS(R)j \quad \text{if and only if } C_{ij} > 0 \text{ and } R_{ij} = p_i(R).$$

Using the matrix representation of $S(R)$, we will write also $S(R)_{ij} = 1$ if $iS(R)j$ and $S(R)_{ij} = 0$ otherwise. If $iS(R)j$, we say that actor i *seeks exchange with* actor j at the current state R. To simplify the notation, we will write S^* instead $S(R^*)$ if R^* is balanced; $A(R^*)$, $D(R^*)$, $p_i(R^*)$ and $q_i(R^*)$ will be noted similarly.

The set of positions with the exchange-seek relation is a subdigraph of the transaction opportunity graph G. If R is invariant, then any automorphism α of G is also an automorphism of this subdigraph: $S(R)_{\alpha(i)\alpha(j)} = S(R)_{ij}$ for any i,j.

We are going to derive several theorems characterizing power and exchange-seek relation in the state of balance. Unlike the above definitions which do not make reference to $A(R)$ *all of the theorems that follow assume that $A(R)$ is defined as the best alternative profit matrix. We will also assume henceforth that the profit pool network C is homogenous.* Recall that then $A(R)_{ij} = 0$ if $C_{ij} = 0$ and $A(R)_{ij} = \max\{R_{ik}:k \neq j\}$ if $C_{ij} > 0$.

THEOREM I. $R^*_{ij} - R^*_{ji} = p^*_i - p^*_j$ *for any i, j such that $C_{ij} > 0$.*

To prove Theorem 1, let us notice first that in a homogenous network $p_i(R)$ is equal to the maximum of R_{ij} and $A(R)_{ij}$, which is true for any $j \neq i$ such that $C_{ij} > 0$. The formula $R^*_{ij} - R^*_{ji} = p^*_i - p^*_j$ can be written equivalently as $R^*_{ij} - p^*_i = R^*_{ji} - p^*_j$, or $R^*_{ij} - \max\{R^*_{ij},A^*_{ij}\} = R^*_{ji} - \max\{R^*_{ji},A^*_{ji}\}$. The latter equation is a consequence of the equidependence equation $R^*_{ij} - A^*_{ij} = R^*_{ji} - A^*_{ji}$ which implies in particular that $R^*_{ij} - A^*_{ij} \geq 0$ if and only if $R^*_{ji} - A^*_{ji} \geq 0$. Indeed, the two sides of the equation to be demonstrated are either both equal to 0 (case $R^*_{ij} - A^*_{ij} \geq 0$) or (case $R^*_{ij} - A^*_{ij} < 0$) they coincide with the two sides of the equidependence equation.

Theorem 2 says that at equilibrium the exchange-seek relation is symmetric: if actor i seeks exchange with actor j, then j also seeks exchange with i.

THEOREM 2. $S^*_{ij} = S^*_{ji}$ *for any* i,j.

The proof of Theorem 2 is straightforward. Suppose that $S^*_{ij} = 1$, that is, $C_{ij} > 0$ and $R^*_{ij} = p^*_i$, or $R^*_{ij} - p^*_i = 0$. Then, by Theorem 1, $R^*_{ji} - p^*_j = 0$ and $R^*_{ji} = p^*_j$, which together with $C_{ji} = C_{ij} > 0$ means that $S^*_{ji} = 1$.
The next theorem is another simple consequence of Theorem 1.

THEOREM 3. *If* $C_{ij} > 0$, *then* $R^*_{ij} \geq R^*_{ji}$ *if and only if* $p^*_i \geq p^*_j$; $R^*_{ij} = R^*_{ji}$ *if and only if* $p^*_i = p^*_j$; $R^*_{ij} > R^*_{ji}$ *if and only if* $p^*_i > p^*_j$.

Note that the proofs of Theorems 1–3 do not make use of the self-complementarity condition. These theorems will therefore remain true if R^* satisfies solely the equidependence condition. We will need the self-complementarity condition $R^*_{ij} + R^*_{ji} = c$ to derive in turn a simple formula for the profit demand directed at balance by actor i to actor j. This result will be stated as Theorem 4.

THEOREM 4. $R^*_{ij} = \frac{1}{2}(c + p^*_i - p^*_j)$ *for any* i,j *such that* $C_{ij} > 0$.

Thus, R^*_{ij} is linearly related to the power differential between i and j. Our formula, obtained as a consequence of Theorem 1, resembles the formula derived by Lovaglia, Skvoretz, Willer, and Markovsky (1995) from the equiresistance equation. The resistance of actor i to the demand of actor j at a given system state R can be computed using either Heckathorn's or Willer's formula, provided that to any i there have been assigned certain numbers $m_i(R)$ and $M_i(R)$ interpreted, respectively, as the minimum and maximum profit currently anticipated by actor i. If these two numbers for any i satisfy the condition $M_i(R) = m_i(R) + a$ with some constant a (Lovaglia and associates define m_i as $l_i \frac{1}{2}c$ and M_i as $m_i + \frac{1}{2}c$ where l_i is the network-dependent likelihood that i will be included in a transaction), then the solution of the equiresistance equation is given by the formula $R_{ij} = \frac{1}{2}(c + m_i(R) - m_j(R))$.
Our next theorem gives a characterization of the exchange-seek relation.

THEOREM 5. $S^*_{ij} = 1$ *if and only if* $G_{ij} = 1$ *and* $p^*_i + p^*_j = c$.

The necessary and sufficient condition given in Theorem 5 remains valid for any self-complementary R such that the relation $S(R)$ is symmetric. To prove such an extension of Theorem 5, we must first notice that for any self-complementary R we have $p_i(R) + p_j(R) \geq C_{ij}$. Suppose now that $p_i(R) + p_j(R) = C_{ij}$ for two connected points i and j ($G_{ij} = 1$). Clearly, $S(R)_{ij} = 1$; if this were not the case, then $p_i(R) > R_{ij}$, which, together with $p_j(R) \geq R_{ji}$, would imply that $p_i(R) +$

$p_j(R) > R_{ij} + R_{ji} = C_{ij}$. Suppose in turn that $S(R)_{ij} = 1$, or $p_i(R) = R_{ij}$. By symmetry of $S(R)$ we have $S(R)_{ji} = 1$, or $p_j(R) = R_{ji}$. Hence $p_i(R) + p_j(R) = R_{ij} + R_{ji} = C_{ij}$.

The ordering of values of $p_i(R)$ defines an antisymmetric transitive relation on the set of positions: a position i is said to be *more powerful* than position j at R if $p_i(R) > p_j(R)$. According to Theorem 3, the equilibrium power ordering of two positions determines relative profit of each party from a possible transaction as postulated by Axiom 4 of Markovsky, Willer, and Patton's (1988) theory.

The power hierarchy can be further simplified to obtain three groups of positions. The *upper*, *middle*, and *lower power group* are defined, respectively, by the conditions: $p_i(R) > \frac{1}{2}c$, $p_i(R) = \frac{1}{2}c$, $p_i(R) < \frac{1}{2}c$. Theorem 5 implies that at balance the members of the upper group will seek exchange only with the members of the lower group, and conversely, while the middle group will look for transaction partners only among themselves. The lower group may not have any transaction opportunity among themselves or with the middle group. Indeed, if $p_i(R) < \frac{1}{2}c$ and $p_j(R) \leq \frac{1}{2}c$, then $G_{ij} = 0$. Otherwise the inequality $p_i(R) + p_j(R) \geq c$ would imply that $p_i(R) \geq c - p_j(R) \geq c - \frac{1}{2}c = \frac{1}{2}c$.

Before we provide further characterization of the exchange-seek relation, we will show that the equilibrium power of a position is functionally related to the powers of adjacent positions as required of "centrality measures" by Bonacich (1987).

THEOREM 6. $p^*_i = c - \min\{p^*_j : G_{ij} = 1\}$.

Theorem 4 allows us to replace R^*_{ij} by $\frac{1}{2}(c + p^*_i - p^*_j)$ in the formula $p^*_i = \max\{R^*_{ij} : G_{ij} = 1\}$. To complete the proof of Theorem 6, it is sufficient to observe that $\max\{\frac{1}{2}(c + p^*_i - p^*_j) : G_{ij} = 1\} = \frac{1}{2}(c + p^*_i) - \frac{1}{2}\min\{p^*_j : G_{ij} = 1\}$.

It follows from Theorem 6 that any two positions which have equally powerful neighbors are also equally powerful. We will first define the *equipower relation* corresponding to R by the condition $p_i(R) = p_j(R)$. Let us call the *power partition* the partition of the set of positions into *power classes*, or the equivalence classes generated by the equipower relation. If $p_i(R)$ is a local structural parameter of i (this is the case if and only if R is invariant), we will speak of a *structural power partition* (cf. Borgatti and Everett 1992: 291–98). Then any power class is the union of some structural classes (recall that two positions are in the same structural class if one is the image of the other through an automorphism of G). In general, we will say that a *partition* of a set X into classes $A_1,\cdots,A_r$ (non-empty pairwise disjoint subsets of X whose union is X) *is finer than* a partition of X into classes $B_1,\cdots,B_s$ if any A_l is contained in a B_j. Then any class in the coarser partition is the union of some classes from the finer partition.

Let E be an arbitrary equivalence relation on the set of points of a graph G. We say that i and j are *neighbor-equivalent with respect to E*, symbolically, $iN(E)j$, if for any point k adjacent to point i $(G_{ik} = 1)$ there is a point k' adjacent to point j $(G_{jk'} = 1)$ such that kEk', and conversely, for any neighbor h of j one can find a neighbor h' of i such that hEh'. If $iN(E)j$ implies iEj for any two positions i and j, the relation E is called *ecological equivalence*. Then the partition into equivalence classes generated by $N(E)$ is finer than the partition generated by E. The notion of ecological equivalence is given here after Borgatti and Everett (1992: 299), whose original formulation has been slightly rephrased. Borgatti and Everett also noticed that the condition of ecological equivalence need not be satisfied by the equipower relation obtained by equating values of the power measure, which was invented by Markovsky, Willer, and Patton (1988: 224; Willer 1992: 201) and called the "graph-theoretic power index." The equipower relation defined by the equation $p^*_i = p^*_j$ is ecological, which is a simple consequence of Theorem 6.

GPI or *graph power index* is defined as a specific structural parameter of a point in the transaction opportunity graph. In order to compute the value p_i of this parameter for a point i, one must find first for any $k = 1, \cdots, n - 1$ the *maximum number m_{ik} of pairwise point-disjoint paths of length k from point i* (two paths from i are *point-disjoint* if i is the only point that the lines of the two paths have in common). Note that m_{i1} is equal to the degree d_i of point i. Note also that $m_{ik} = 0$ if k is greater than the length of the longest path from i. The definition of p_i, called Axiom 1 by Markovsky, Willer, and Patton, is as follows:

$$p_i = \sum_{k=1}^{n-1} (-1)^{(k-1)} m_{ik}.$$

The formula defining p_i can be rewritten as $(m_{i1} - m_{i2}) + (m_{i3} - m_{i4}) + \ldots$ or alternatively as $m_{i1} - (m_{i2} - m_{i3}) - (m_{i4} - m_{i5}) - \ldots$. These formulas and the inequalities $m_{i1} \geq m_{i2} \geq \ldots m_{i(n-1)}$ which follow from the definition of m_{ik} imply that $0 \leq p_i \leq d_i$. Since d_i does not exceed $n - 1$, the latter number is also the maximum value of the GPI in an n-point graph. If G is a tree then the value $n - 1$ is achieved at point 1 i if and only if $G_{1i} = 1$ for any $i \neq 1$ and $G_{ij} = 0$ for any $i,j \neq 1$, that is, position 1 is central in $G = G_{1(n-1)}$.

We computed the GPI for all connected n-point graphs with $n \leq 6$ and all trees with $n \leq 9$ using our own Quick BASIC program (available upon request). For any connected graph G with $n = 3,4,5$ the values p_i for $i = 1, \cdots, n$ are displayed in Tables 1–3 along with the values of $p^*_i = p_i(R^*)$ calculated for all invariant balanced matrices over G. Let us call the latter parameter the *equidependence power index*.

The unique connected graph with two points A_1 and A_2 can be drawn as a line.

$$A_1 \; \bullet\!-\!\bullet \; A_2$$

The GPI assumes the same value 1 for A_1 and A_2 while p^* is equal to $\tfrac{1}{2}c$ where c is the constant pool size. The unique collection of values of p^* is also obtained for all homogenous profit pool networks over 3-point connected graphs. In Table 1, the two structural forms of such graphs are represented by two non-

TABLE 1

3-Point Connected Graphs

(1)

	A	B_1	B_2
A	0	1	1
B_1	1	0	0
B_2	1	0	0

	A	B_i
GPI	2	0
p^*	1	0

(2)

	A_1	A_2	A_3
A_1	0	1	1
A_2	1	0	1
A_3	1	1	0

	A_i
GPI	1
p^*	$\frac{1}{2}$

isomorphic graphs. For each graph, there is given its adjacency matrix and geometrical representation. The positions are labeled so as to reflect the partition of the point set into structural classes. In all tables the constant pool size is c has been given value 1.

For many connected graphs, there exists exactly one invariant balanced R^* so that a unique collection of values p^*_i can be compared with the respective GPI values. For the maximally centralized tree $G_{1(n-1)}$ with $n \geq 3$, the two power orderings perfectly agree with each other: $p^*_1 = c$, $p_1 = n - 1$, and $p_j = 0$, $p^*_j = 0$ for any $j \neq 1$.

In general, the comparison of the two power measures can be based on two criteria. The first criterion describes the relationship between the two power orderings by pointing to the presence of particular types of pairs of points. The two *orderings are identical* if all (unordered) pairs are concordant; a *pair* $\{i,j\}$ of distinct points is called *concordant* if $p_i > p_j$ and $p^*_i > p^*_j$ or $p_i < p_j$ and $p^*_i < p^*_j$ or $p_i = p_j$ and $p^*_i = p^*_j$. The *pair* $\{i,j\}$ is called *discordant* if $p_i > p_j$ and $p^*_i < p^*_j$ or $p_i < p_j$ and $p^*_i > p^*_j$. We will say that the two *orderings are discordant* if there is at least one discordant pair. Two orderings which are neither identical nor discordant will be called *tied* with each other. Then, apart from concordant pairs, there must be at least one *tied pair* in which $p_i = p_j$ and $p^*_i \neq p^*_j$ or $p_i \neq p_j$ and $p^*_i = p^*_j$.

The second criterion refers to the power partitions generated by the two measures. Then, four cases can be distinguished: (1) The two power partitions coincide; (2) the equidependence partition is finer than and different from the GPI partition; (3) the GPI partition is finer than and different from the equidependence partition; (4) neither of the two partitions is finer than the other.

By combining the two criteria, we arrive at the classification scheme with 8 classes.

1. The two power orderings are identical, and as a consequence, the two power partitions coincide. Then $p^*_i \leq p^*_j$ if and only if $p_i \leq p_j$ for any i,j.

2. The two orderings are tied, and the GPI partition is finer than the equidependence partition. Then, for any $i \neq j$, if $p^*_i < p^*_j$ then $p_i < p_j$, but the reverse may not always be true, since there are at least two distinct points a,b such that $p_a < p_b$ and $p^*_a = p^*_b$.

3. The two orderings are tied, and the GPI partition is coarser than the equidependence partition. Then $p_i < p_j$ implies that $p^*_i < p^*_j$ for all $i \neq j$, but we have also $p^*_c < p^*_d$, $p_c = p_d$ for some $c \neq d$.

4. The two orderings are tied, and the two partitions are not comparable. The two types of ties ($p_a < p_b$, $p^*_a = p^*_b$ and $p^*_c < p^*_d$, $p_c = p_d$), which occur separately in classes 2 and 3, are now both present.

In the remaining four classes, the two power measures disagree more seriously than in their ability to discriminate between levels of power. The discordance of two power orderings means that there exist two distinct points i and j placed by the two power measures in opposite order: for one measure position i is more powerful than j, for the other measure i is less powerful than j.

5. The two power orderings are discordant, and the two power partitions coincide.

6. The two power orderings are discordant, and the GPI partition is finer than the equidependence partition.

7. The two power orderings are discordant, and the GPI partition is coarser than the equidependence partition.

8. The two power orderings are discordant, and the two partitions are not comparable.

Let us illustrate the above classification scheme with some examples. Five out of six connected 4-point graphs (see Fig. 1 and Table 2) admit of a unique invariant balanced solution. Among these five graphs, only classes 1 and 3 are represented: graphs 1, 4, 6 fall into class 1; and graphs 2, 3 into class 3.

Graph 2 is an example of an n-point tree made up of a unique path of length $n - 1$. The allocation of power to positions in such a tree depends solely on n. If n is odd, then GPI and our equidependence power measure induce the same power ordering and the same partition of positions into two power classes. The low-power positions ($p_i = 0$, $p^*_i = 0$) alternate with high-power positions ($p_i = 2$, $p^*_i = c$) along the path beginning from its end points, which are low power. If n is even, then the value of GPI is 1 for all i, which implies that all positions form one power class. By contrast, the equidependence measure assigns different power levels to all structural classes of positions. The lowest value $(1/n)c$ is assigned to the ends of the path.

Similar data are given in Table 3, in which are listed all structural forms of connected graphs with 5 points. The data for all 112 non-isomorphic 6-point connected graphs is omitted here (the author will send the data upon request).

If $n \geq 4$, then the equidependence power index is not determined uniquely

TABLE 2
4-Point Connected Graphs

(1)

	A	B_1	B_2	B_3
A	0	1	1	1
B_1	1	0	0	0
B_2	1	0	0	0
B_3	1	0	0	0

	A	B_i
GPI	3	0
p^*	1	0

(2)

	A_1	A_2	B_1	B_2
A_1	0	1	1	0
A_2	1	0	0	1
B_1	1	0	0	0
B_2	0	1	0	0

	A_i	B_i
GPI	1	1
p^*	$\frac{3}{4}$	$\frac{1}{4}$

(3)

	A	B	C_1	C_2
A	0	1	1	1
B	1	0	0	0
C_1	1	0	0	1
C_2	1	0	1	0

	A	B	C_i
GPI	2	1	2
p^*	$\frac{5}{6}$	$\frac{1}{6}$	$\frac{1}{2}$

(4)

	A_1	A_2	A_3	A_4
A_1	0	1	0	1
A_2	1	0	1	0
A_3	0	1	0	1
A_4	1	0	1	0

	A_i
GPI	2
p^*	$\frac{1}{2}$

(5)

	A_1	A_2	B_1	B_2
A_1	0	1	1	1
A_2	1	0	1	1
B_1	1	1	0	0
B_2	1	1	0	0

	A_i	B_i
GPI	3	2
p^*	x	$1-x$

$$\tfrac{1}{2} \leq x \leq 1$$

(6)

	A_1	A_2	A_3	A_4
A_1	0	1	1	1
A_2	1	0	1	1
A_3	1	1	0	1
A_4	1	1	1	0

	A_i
GPI	3
p^*	$\frac{1}{2}$

TABLE 3

5-Point Connected Graphs

(1)

	A	B₁	B₂	B₃	B₄
A	0	1	1	1	1
B₁	1	0	0	0	0
B₂	1	0	0	0	0
B₃	1	0	0	0	0
B₄	1	0	0	0	0

	A	Bᵢ
GPI	4	0
p*	1	0

(2)

	A₁	A₂	B₁	B₂	C
A₁	0	0	1	0	1
A₂	0	0	0	1	1
B₁	1	0	0	0	0
B₂	0	1	0	0	0
C	1	1	0	0	0

	A₁	B₁	C
GPI	2	0	0
p*	1	0	0

(3)

	A	B₁	B₂	C	D
A	0	1	1	1	0
B₁	1	0	0	0	0
B₂	1	0	0	0	0
C	1	0	0	0	1
D	0	0	0	1	0

	A	B₁	C	D
GPI	2	1	1	1
p*	1	0	$\frac{2}{3}$	$\frac{1}{3}$

(4)

	A₁	A₂	B₁	B₂	C
A₁	0	1	1	0	1
A₂	1	0	0	1	1
B₁	1	0	0	0	0
B₂	0	1	0	0	0
C	1	1	0	0	0

	A₁	B₁	C
GPI	3	0	1
p*	1	0	0

(5)

	A	B	C₁	C₂	D
A	0	1	1	1	0
B	1	0	0	0	0
C₁	1	0	0	0	1
C₂	1	0	0	0	1
D	0	0	1	1	0

	A	B	C₁	D
GPI	3	0	0	2
p*	1	0	0	1

(6)

	A	B	C	D₁	D₂
A	0	1	0	1	1
B	1	0	1	0	0
C	0	1	0	0	0
D₁	1	0	0	0	1
D₂	1	0	0	1	0

	A	B	C	D₁
GPI	1	2	0	1
p*	$\frac{1}{2}$	$\frac{5}{6}$	$\frac{1}{6}$	$\frac{1}{2}$

TABLE 3 (cont.)

5-Point Connected Graphs

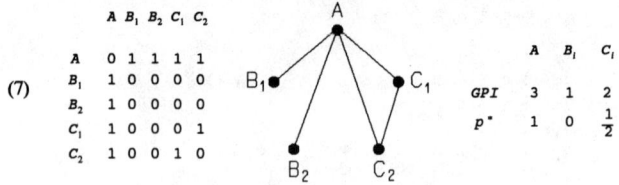

(7)

	A	B_1	B_2	C_1	C_2
A	0	1	1	1	1
B_1	1	0	0	0	0
B_2	1	0	0	0	0
C_1	1	0	0	0	1
C_2	1	0	0	1	0

	A	B_1	C_1
GPI	3	1	2
p^*	1	0	$\frac{1}{2}$

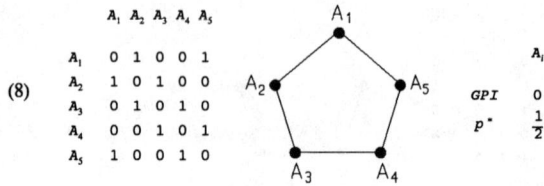

(8)

	A_1	A_2	A_3	A_4	A_5
A_1	0	1	0	0	1
A_2	1	0	1	0	0
A_3	0	1	0	1	0
A_4	0	0	1	0	1
A_5	1	0	0	1	0

	A_1
GPI	0
p^*	$\frac{1}{2}$

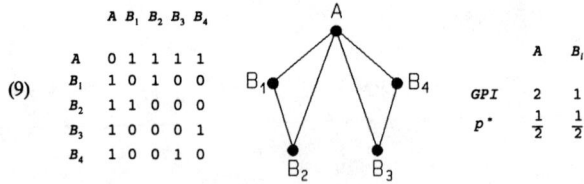

(9)

	A	B_1	B_2	B_3	B_4
A	0	1	1	1	1
B_1	1	0	1	0	0
B_2	1	1	0	0	0
B_3	1	0	0	0	1
B_4	1	0	0	1	0

	A	B_1
GPI	2	1
p^*	$\frac{1}{2}$	$\frac{1}{2}$

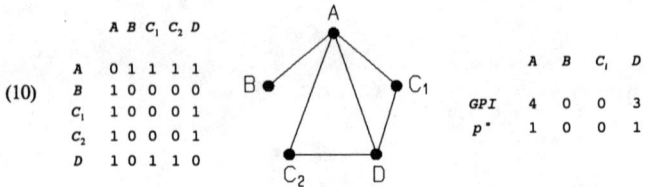

(10)

	A	B	C_1	C_2	D
A	0	1	1	1	1
B	1	0	0	0	0
C_1	1	0	0	0	1
C_2	1	0	0	0	1
D	1	0	1	1	0

	A	B	C_1	D
GPI	4	0	0	3
p^*	1	0	0	1

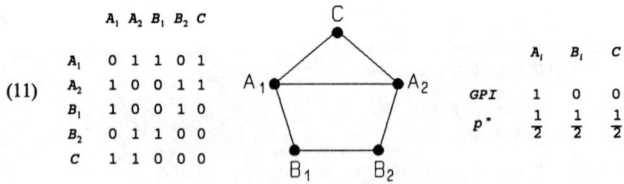

(11)

	A_1	A_2	B_1	B_2	C
A_1	0	1	1	0	1
A_2	1	0	0	1	1
B_1	1	0	0	1	0
B_2	0	1	1	0	0
C	1	1	0	0	0

	A_1	B_1	C
GPI	1	0	0
p^*	$\frac{1}{2}$	$\frac{1}{2}$	$\frac{1}{2}$

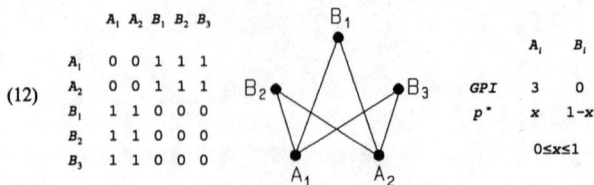

(12)

	A_1	A_2	B_1	B_2	B_3
A_1	0	0	1	1	1
A_2	0	0	1	1	1
B_1	1	1	0	0	0
B_2	1	1	0	0	0
B_3	1	1	0	0	0

	A_1	B_1
GPI	3	0
p^*	x	$1-x$

$0 \le x \le 1$

TABLE 3 (cont.)

5-Point Connected Graphs

(13)

	A	B	C_1	C_2	D
A	0	1	1	1	0
B	1	0	0	0	0
C_1	1	0	0	1	1
C_2	1	0	1	0	1
D	0	0	1	1	0

	A	B	C_i	D
GPI	3	0	1	1
p^*	$\frac{5}{6}$	$\frac{1}{6}$	$\frac{1}{2}$	$\frac{1}{2}$

(14)

	A	B_1	B_2	C_1	C_2
A	0	1	1	1	1
B_1	1	0	0	1	0
B_2	1	0	0	0	1
C_1	1	1	0	0	1
C_2	1	0	1	1	0

	A	B_i	C_i
GPI	2	0	1
p^*	$\frac{1}{2}$	$\frac{1}{2}$	$\frac{1}{2}$

(15)

	A_1	A_2	B_1	B_2	B_3
A_1	0	1	1	1	1
A_2	1	0	1	1	1
B_1	1	1	0	0	0
B_2	1	1	0	0	0
B_3	1	1	0	0	0

	A_i	B_i
GPI	4	0
p^*	x	$1-x$

$$\frac{1}{2} \le x \le 1$$

(16)

	A	B	C_1	C_2	C_3
A	0	1	1	1	1
B	1	0	0	0	0
C_1	1	0	0	1	1
C_2	1	0	1	0	1
C_3	1	0	1	1	0

	A	B	C_i
GPI	4	0	1
p^*	$\frac{5}{6}$	$\frac{1}{6}$	$\frac{1}{2}$

(17)

	A_1	A_2	B_1	B_2	C
A_1	0	0	1	1	1
A_2	0	0	1	1	1
B_1	1	1	0	1	0
B_2	1	1	1	0	0
C	1	1	0	0	0

	A_i	B_i	C
GPI	1	1	0
p^*	x	$1-x$	$1-x$

$$0 \le x \le \frac{1}{2}$$

(18)

	A_1	A_2	B_1	B_2	C
A_1	0	1	1	1	1
A_2	1	0	1	1	1
B_1	1	1	0	1	0
B_2	1	1	1	0	0
C	1	1	0	0	0

	A_i	B_i	C
GPI	2	1	0
p^*	$\frac{1}{2}$	$\frac{1}{2}$	$\frac{1}{2}$

TABLE 3 (cont.)

5-Point Connected Graphs

(19)

	A	B_1	B_2	B_3	B_4
A	0	1	1	1	1
B_1	1	0	1	0	1
B_2	1	1	0	1	0
B_3	1	0	1	0	1
B_4	1	1	0	1	0

	A	B_1
GPI	2	1
p^*	$\frac{1}{2}$	$\frac{1}{2}$

(20)

	A_1	A_2	A_3	B_1	B_2
A_1	0	1	1	1	1
A_2	1	0	1	1	1
A_3	1	1	0	1	1
B_1	1	1	1	0	0
B_2	1	1	1	0	0

	A_1	B_1
GPI	2	1
p^*	x	$1-x$

$$\tfrac{1}{2} \le x \le 1$$

(21)

	A_1	A_2	A_3	A_4	A_5
A_1	0	1	1	1	1
A_2	1	0	1	1	1
A_3	1	1	0	1	1
A_4	1	1	1	0	1
A_5	1	1	1	1	0

	A_1
GPI	2
p^*	$\frac{1}{2}$

for some graphs. In most cases, the family of p^* is dependent on a single variable x running over an interval. In four cases, two one-parameter families of solutions exhaust the set of all p^*. Multiple solutions can be represented by the values obtained in the limit when the iteration process starts from the fifty-fifty split of the pool in each relation.

We examined the two power orderings and the two power partitions for all graphs in two sets, having, respectively, 98 and 94 elements: (1) connected n-point graphs, with $n = 2,...,6$, for which the respective homogenous profit pool network admits of a unique balanced invariant solution R^*; (2) all n-point trees with $n = 2,...,9$. The results of the inspection are displayed below.

No. of graphs			No. of graphs		
Type	Set I	Set II	Type	Set I	Set II
1	30	18	5	0	2
2	40	21	6	0	0
3	13	18	7	4	4
4	2	25	8	9	6

The two power measures yield opposite predictions of order in a pair of positions only in 13 percent of the graphs in each of Sets I and II. If two power orderings are compared only over the edges of G, then the number of instances of incompatibility is further reduced. The number of cases of type 5–8 drops from 13 to 10 in Set I and from 12 to 5 in Set II. The largest reduction takes place for trees of type 2: in 17 out of 21 trees with a tie of the form $p_i < p_j$, $p^*_i = p^*_j$, the tied points are not connected on G.

The definition of GPI is, in fact, an independent replaceable module within Markovsky and associates' theory. The values of GPI are needed merely to find out which positions are more powerful than the others. The dynamics of the network is depicted in axioms in which no reference is made to the particular formula for p_i. If we ignore the two specific definitions of a power parameter, we can compare the two formal theories on purely logical grounds, regardless of the degree of compatibility of the two parameters. Axiom 2 of Markovsky and associates' theory postulates that the exchange-seek relation should depend solely on the relative power of two positions. We will show that our exchange-seek relation $S(R)$ has similar properties if R is balanced. Then all positions sought by a position as exchange partners are equally powerful and so are all positions who seek exchange with a given position.

THEOREM 7. *If* $S^*_{ij} = 1$ *and* $S^*_{ik} = 1$, *then* $p^*_j = p^*_k$; *if* $S^*_{ij} = 1$ *and* $S^*_{hj} = 1$, *then* $p^*_i = p^*_h$. *If* $S^*_{ij} = 1$, $S^*_{ik} = 0$ *and* $G_{ik} = 1$, *then* $p^*_k > p^*_j$.

If $S^*_{ij} = 1$ and $S^*_{ik} = 1$, then, by Theorem 5, $p^*_i + p^*_j = c$ and $p^*_i + p^*_k = c$. Hence $p^*_i + p^*_j = p^*_i + p^*_k$, which implies that $p^*_j = p^*_k$. The second part of Theorem 7 characterizes those neighbors of a given position which are not sought as exchange partners by it. Let us suppose that $S^*_{ij} = 1$, $S^*_{ik} = 0$, and $G_{ik} = 1$. Then $p^*_i + p^*_j = c$ and $p^*_i + p^*_k \geq c$. Hence $p^*_i + p^*_k \geq p^*_i + p^*_j$, which implies that $p^*_k \geq p^*_j$. If $p^*_k = p^*_j$, then $p^*_i + p^*_k = c$, and $S^*_{ik} = 1$ (Theorem 5) contrary to the assumption. Therefore, $p^*_k > p^*_j$.

Theorem 7 will be used to derive another necessary and sufficient condition of exchange-seek relation. This condition is somewhat stronger than that given by Markovsky, Willer, and Patton in Axiom 2 (1988: 225, 233).

THEOREM 8. $S^*_{ij} = 1$ *if and only if* $G_{ij} = 1$ *and* $p^*_j = \min\{p^*_k: G_{ik} = 1\}$.

Thus, the theory based on the equidependence principle states that at balance every actor will prefer a transaction with the weakest potential partner, including the case where an actor is more powerful than all his neighbors. The Markovsky and associates' axiom predicts that i will seek exchange with all k such that $p_i > p_k$ and $G_{ik} = 1$.

To prove the necessity of the condition given in Theorem 8, suppose that $S^*_{ij} = 1$. We must show that $p^*_j \leq p^*_k$ for any k connected to i. If $S^*_{ik} = 1$ then $p^*_j = p^*_k$, by Theorem 7; if $S^*_{ik} = 0$, then $p^*_j > p^*_k$, again by Theorem 7.

The proof of sufficiency starts from the observation that *for any point i there always exists a point h such that* $S(R)_{ih} = 1$ (it is a simple consequence of connectedness of G and of the definition of $S(R)$; it is added as a supplementary condition in Markovsky and associates' theory; see 1988: 223). Thus, $S*_{ih} = 1$ for some h. The assumption $p*_j = \min\{p*_k : G_{ik} = 1\}$ implies that $p*_h \leq p*_j$. Suppose now that $S*_{ij} = 0$. If this were the case, then by Theorem 7 we would have $p*_h > p*_j$, which is a contradiction.

The main difference between GPI and the equidependence power parameter is that GPI values may be equal for two positions i and j such that j is the only potential partner of i but j has also potential partners other than i. We will show that in such circumstances our measure always attributes less power to that of the two positions which does not have an alternative neighbor. First, let us generalize the notion of a peripheral position which has so far been referred only to the points tied to the center in the star-shaped tree (graph 1 in Fig. 1). A position in the transaction opportunity graph will be called *peripheral* if it has exactly one potential transaction partner. In graph theory, a point i such that $d_i = 1$ is often called a *hanging point*.

The presence of a peripheral position in the transaction opportunity graph works for the uniqueness of $R*$. The inspection of all 142 n-point connected graphs with $n = 2,...,6$ yields the following data: 56 (85 percent) out of 66 graphs with a hanging point admit of unique invariant balanced $R*$, and only 42 (55 percent) out of 76 graphs without a hanging point.

If i is a hanging point which is connected to point j, then, by definition, $A(R)_{ij} = 0$, $p_i(R) = R_{ij}$, and $S(R)_{ij} = 1$. The equidependence equation takes the following form: $R_{ij} = R_{ji} - A(R)_{ji}$. For any R which satisfies this equation we have: $p_i(R) = R_{ji} - A(R)_{ji} \leq p_j(R) - A(R)_{ji} \leq p_j(R)$. Thus, in the state of equal dependence the aspiration level of a peripheral position is lower than or equal to the aspiration level of its unique neighbor. To prove this we did not use the self-complementarity condition nor the assumption of network homogeneity. In a homogenous network, in the state of balance, a peripheral position i always has less power than its unique neighbor j, except for the case where j is also peripheral, which is possible only for $n = 2$.

THEOREM 9. *If* $G_{ij} = 1$, $d_i = 1$, *and* $d_j > 1$, *then* $p*_i < p*_j$.

We have already shown that $p*_i \leq p*_j$. To complete the proof of Theorem 9, let us suppose that $p*_i = p*_j$ and demonstrate that this leads to a contradiction. Since j is the only point adjacent to i, we have $S*_{ij} = 1$. Hence, $S*_{ji} = 1$ (Theorem 2) and $R*_{ji} = p*_j$. The equidependence equation for ij, rewritten as $p*_i = p*_j - A*_{ji}$, implies that $A*_{ji} = 0$. Therefore, $R*_{jk} = 0$ for all $k \neq i$. Since $d_j > 1$, there exists at least one $k \neq i$ such that $G_{jk} = 1$. $R*_{jk} = 0$ and self-complementarity of $R*$ imply that $R*_{kj} = C_{ij}$. Then $p*_k \geq C_{ij} = c$, and $p*_k = c$, which is a consequence of the definition of p^*_k and the assumption of homogeneity. We have further $R^*_{kj} = p^*_k$ and $S^*_{kj} = 1$. $S^*_{ij} = 1$ and $S^*_{kj} = 1$ imply in turn that $p^*_i = p^*_k$ (Theorem 7). We conclude that $p^*_i = c$. This and the equation $p^*_i + p^*_i = c$ (obtained from $S^*_{ij} = 1$ and Theorem 5) imply that $p^*_j = 0$, which contradicts $p^*_i = p^*_j$.

If i is the only peripheral position connected to j, then the values of p^*_i and p^*_j may depend on the properties of the whole network as is the case with a chain-shaped tree. If more than one peripheral position is connected to j, then each of them has lowest possible power level 0 and j has highest possible power level c. Independent of the whole network, its subnetwork, made up of point j and all peripheral points adjacent to it, has the same power distribution as the star-shaped tree, in which power is produced by centrality.

THEOREM 10. *If $d_i = 1$, $d_h = 1$, $i \neq h$, and $G_{ij} = 1$, $G_{hj} = 1$ for some j, then $p^*_i = 0$ and $p^*_h = 0$.*

$S^*_{ij} = 1$ and $S^*_{hj} = 1$ imply that $S^*_{ji} = 1$ and $S^*_{jh} = 1$ (Theorem 2). Thus, $R^*_{ij} = p^*_i$, $R^*_{ji} = p^*_j$, $R^*_{jh} = p^*_j$. Since $h \neq i$, $A^*_{ji} = p^*_j$. Then the equidependence equation for ij takes the following form: $p^*_i - 0 = p^*_j - p^*_j$, or $p^*_i = 0$. We have also $p^*_h = 0$, since $p^*_i = p^*_h$ (Theorem 7).

According to Theorems 9 and 10, any peripheral actor i is weaker than his only potential partner j, and i's power is reduced to 0 if i has to compete with another peripheral actor h for the access to j. The *competition* between two positions i and h will be defined by the condition: $i \neq h$ and $G_{ij} = 1$ and $G_{hj} = 1$ for some j (i and h have at least one common potential partner). We will need the relation of competition to state Theorem 11, which describes the situation in which an actor seeks exchange with all his neighbors.

THEOREM 11. *The following conditions are equivalent: (1) $S^*_{ij} = 1$ for all j such that $G_{ij} = 1$; (2) $p^*_i \leq p^*_h$ for any h competing with i; (3) $p^*_k = p^*_l$ for any k, l such that $G_{ik} = 1$ and $G_{il} = 1$.*

In other words, an actor who seeks exchange with all his potential partners may not be stronger than each of his competitors, which in turn is equivalent to having all neighbors of equal power. We shall demonstrate Theorem 11 by verifying three implications (1) → (2), (2) → (3), (3) → (1).

(1) → (2). Let i and h satisfy the relation of competition. Then the set $\{k: G_{ik} = 1, G_{hk} = 1\}$ may not be empty. This set is a subset of the set $\{k: G_{hk} = 1\}$, which results in the inequality $\min\{p^*_k: G_{ik} = 1, G_{hk} = 1\} \geq \min\{p^*_k: G_{jk} = 1\}$. For any k in the smaller set, we have $p^*_k = c - p^*_i$ (Theorem 5) so that the minimum of p^*_k on this set must be equal to $c - p^*_i$. The minimum on the second set equals $c - p^*_j$ by Theorem 6. Thus, $c - p^*_i \geq c - p^*_j$ and $p^*_i \leq c - p^*_j$.

(2) → (3). Let $\min\{p^*_k: G_{ik} = 1\} = p^*_m$ for some m adjacent to i. We will

show that $p*_k = p*_m$ for any k such that $G_{ik} = 1$. Let h be a point such that $S*_{kh} = 1$. Therefore, $p*_k + p*_h = c$ (Theorem 5) and, similarly, $S*_{im} = 1$ (which results from Theorem 8) implies that $p*_i + p*_m = c$. Thus, $p*_k + p*_h = p*_i + p*_m$, or $p*_h - p*_i = p*_m - p*_k$. If $h = i$, then $p*_m = p*_k$. If $h \neq i$, then $p*_h \geq p*_i$ by (2); hence also $p*_m \geq p*_k$. Since $p*_m \leq p*_k$ by the definition of $p*_m$, again we have $p*_m = p*_k$.

(3) → (1). This implication is a straightforward consequence of Theorem 8.

It follows from Theorem 11 that all actors who are at the bottom of the power ranking seek exchange with all their potential partners who form the top power class. Indeed, if i is in the lowest power class, that is, $p*_i \leq p*_j$ for all j, then condition (2) is satisfied, and so are the two equivalent conditions. This fact will be used in the proof of Theorem 12, which says that in a tree the set of positions with the lowest power contains at least one peripheral position.

THEOREM 12. *If G is a tree, then* $\min\{p*_i : i\} = \min\{p*_i : d_i = 1\}$.

Clearly, $\min\{p*_i : i\} \leq \min\{p*_i : d_i = 1\}$. To complete the proof we must find a point j such that $p*_j = \min\{p*_i : i\}$ and $d_j = 1$. Let j be a point at which the global minimum is attained. We infer from Theorem 11 that all neighbors of j are in the same power class, which in turn implies (Theorem 1) that $R*_{jk} = R*_{jl}$ for any k and l adjacent to j. If $d_j > 1$, then there exist at least two distinct points k and l such that $G_{jk} = 1$ and $G_{jl} = 1$. Hence, $R*_{jk} - A*_{jk} = 0$. The other side of the equidependence equation for jk is also 0, so that $R*_{kj} = A*_{kj}$. $S*_{jk} = 1$ entails $S*_{kj} = 1$, or $R*_{kj} = p*_k$. Having found that $A*_{kj} = p*_k$, let us replace $A*_{kj}$ by $R*_{kj'}$ for some $j' \neq j$ such that $G_{kj'} = 1$. By Theorem 4, $R*_{kj'} = \frac{1}{2}(c + p*_k - p*_{j'})$. The equation $p*_k = \frac{1}{2}(c + p*_k - p*_{j'})$ can be rewritten as $p*_k + p*_{j'} = c$. Hence $S*_{kj'} = 1$ (Theorem 5), which together with $S*_{kj} = 1$ implies that $p*_j = p*_{j'}$ (Theorem 7). If $d_{j'} = 1$ the proof is completed. If j' is not a peripheral position we would consider the equidependence equation for $j'k'$ where k' is a point adjacent to j' and distinct from k. We would find in such a way a point j'' such that $p*_j = p*_{j'} = p*_{j''}$. The process of extending the path $j—k—j'—k'$ on which weak and strong positions alternate must stop at a peripheral position, since otherwise the construction would never end, which is impossible in a finite graph, or one would return to a point already included in the path, which may not be the case either, because a tree cannot contain a cycle.

Concluding Remarks

The task we set ourselves in this paper was to develop a formal theory of equilibrium in a network exchange system. A thorough examination of the consequences of the principle of equal dependence revealed the theoretical potential hidden in the approach initiated by Emerson. We managed to formalize his key ideas and prove several nontrivial theorems characterizing relative power of a position for a special class of systems called profit pool networks. In particular, our theory agrees with the view that a peripheral position having exactly one potential partner must be relatively weaker than a position that can communicate with more than one partner. If at least two peripheral positions have to compete with each other for access to their common neighbor, their power reaches the lowest possible level 0, regardless of the number of competitors. The graph power index behaves in a basically similar manner. The power parameter defined by Cook and Yamagishi (1992) and theoretically elaborated in our paper is intimately linked with our theory, which to a lesser degree can be said of the Markovsky and associates' power coefficient and GPI theory. The latter parameter has an advantage over ours in some respects. For profit pool networks in which transaction opportunities are defined by the bipartite graph G_{kl} with $k < l$, the equidependence theory fails to generate a unique equilibrium power distribution (except for $k = 1$, or the case of unilateral monopoly), whereas GPI assigns more power to the positions having more potential partners, which agrees with the intuitive expectation of power imbalance in such a system. Therefore a comparison between the two competing approaches must be restricted to other connected graphs of which the trees, for their simple structure, have so far been the favorite object of theoretical and experimental investigations.

We have already pointed out that structural properties of transaction opportunity graphs are not the only variables that must be taken into account if one aims at predicting the dynamics of exchange systems. Any specific network exchange theory must include in its scope conditions some assumptions on the workings of social interaction within an exchange system. Cook and Yamagishi (1992) maintain that the equidependence approach should be applied basically in conditions of a continuous exchange process which need not have predetermined time limits or be organized as a series of rounds. We tend to agree with this view; however, we do not exclude the possibility of applying our variety of equidependence theory to network exchange systems with different modes of operation, including the exchange networks investigated in the Elementary Theory. We are aware that much has yet to be done to transform the mathematical theory into a formalized empirical theory which, in particular, would be endowed with experimental procedures of generating relevant data. The most delicate theoretical issue, which has essential implications for planning experimental tests, is how to combine static analysis of positional power with the dynamic model of the negotiation process in order to arrive at a theory that would be able to predict the observed distribution of payoffs and frequency of transactions across the channels of the network (cf. Skvoretz and Fararo 1992). We think that none of the existing theories has yet offered a fully satisfactory solution of the problem.

Those who use ET as a theoretical basis for specific hypotheses and experimental tests claim that profit differentials are produced by the right of "exclusion" granted to some positions and denied to other positions. The possibility of excluding potential partners from the exchange process is a combined effect of the location of a position on the network and of a special "exchange regime" which defines the maximum number of transaction in a "round." With this constraint the probability of concluding a transaction in a round becomes the crucial variable which determines an actor's bargaining position and actual profit from the interaction with other actors. Let us notice in this connection that regardless of how this probability is computed, its value for a peripheral actor is never greater than its value for his unique neighbor. If all transaction subgraphs are assumed to be equally likely (cf. Friedkin 1992: 218), then the probability of being included in a transaction can be defined for a position as the ratio of the number of transaction subgraphs in which this position has a non-zero degree to the number of all transaction subgraphs.

For example, the one-exchange regime applied to graph 3 in Figure 1 generates 6 transaction subgraphs with the following sets of edges $\{\emptyset\}$, $\{AB\}$, $\{AC_1\}$, $\{AC_2\}$, $\{C_1C_2\}$, $\{AB, C_1, C_2\}$. Then the probabilities of concluding a transaction are equal to 4/6, 3/6, 2/6 for A, C_i, and B, respectively. If only maximal transaction subgraphs ($\{AC_1\}$, $\{AC_2\}$, $\{AB, C_1,C_2\}$) are considered as possible outcomes of the exchange process, then the respective probabilities for A, C_i, and B are 1, 2/3, 1/3. The transaction sets possible under the one-exchange regime can also be obtained from all combinations of partner choices. For example, the empty set of transactions is obtained if no partner choice has been reciprocated, which occurs in 2 out of 12 combinations (the 2 cases are: $A \rightarrow C_1$, $B \rightarrow A$, $C_1 \rightarrow C_2$, $C_2 \rightarrow A$ and $A \rightarrow C_2$, $B \rightarrow A$, $C_1 \rightarrow A$, $C_2 \rightarrow C_1$). If all combinations of partner choices are equally likely, then $P\{\emptyset\} = 2/12$, $P\{AB\} = 3/12$, $P\{AC_1\} = P\{AC_2\} = 2/12$, $P\{C_1C_2\} = 2/12$, $P\{AB, C_1C_2\} = 1/12$. Hence the probabilities of being included in a transaction are 8/12, 5/12, 4/12 for A, C_i, and B.

Markovsky et al. (1993: 203) offer still another method of calculating these probabilities that yields the values 1, 0.8, and 0.6, which lead to the same ordering of positions as the probabilities computed with other methods as well as the values of equidependence power measure. The authors regard their new model as a supplement to the GPI theory and restrict its use to the graphs for which the graph power index fails to detect differences between positions with respect to "weak power." The new version of the GPI theory has appeared able to predict more exactly uneven distribution of payoffs observed in experiments; however, it certainly needs further refinement and unification. Possibly, in the foreseeable future one can expect further developments in stochastic modeling of negotiation and transaction processes in network exchange systems. Graph-theoretic parameters will probably be replaced by new coefficients defined in the context of more sophisticated dynamical models.

Strategy in Exchange Networks: Exploitation versus Accommodation

Phillip Bonacich and Elisa Jayne Bienenstock

Cook, Emerson, Yamagishi, and Gillmore, in their article "The Distribution of Power in Exchange Networks: Theory and Experimental Results" (1983), used experimental and simulation results to support a theory about which positions have power in networks of exchange. This work spurred much research on the topic (for example, Markovsky, Willer, and Patton 1988; Markovsky et al. 1993; Skvoretz and Willer 1993; Borgatti and Everett 1992; Friedkin 1992; Bienenstock and Bonacich 1992).

Networks like those in Figure 1 have been studied extensively by social psychologists interested in power within exchange networks. The experimental situation is usually presented to subjects in a highly abridged manner that abstracts the essentials of the bargaining situation. Pairs of subjects that arrive at an agreement on how to split a fixed number of points are allowed to earn those points. The points are converted to money at the end of the experiment. There are restrictions on who can trade with whom (these restrictions define the network) and on how many agreements each individual can conclude (this creates the necessity for including some and excluding others).

Initially, Cook, Emerson, Gillmore, and Yamagishi (1983) ran their experiment on one network. To minimize cost while testing the accuracy of their algorithm for other networks, they used a simulation program (SIMNET). According to them (1983: 295), "The simulated actors were programmed to act 'rationally', that is to attempt to maximize their profits through the exchange process." Cook, Emerson, Gillmore, and Yamagishi (ibid.: 296) defined a rational actor as one who (1) accepts the better of any two offers; (2) raises its demand the next time if its offer has been accepted; (3) lowers its demand when an offer goes unaccepted.

To test that the simulation results were realistic, Cook and associates ran the simulation using the same network structure that they ran experimentally. When they found that the results of the simulation were "the same as" the results of the experiment, they used the simulation program to test the accuracy of pre-dictions of power in other structures. The presumption was that if the results for the simulations in that one network reflected reality, they could extend that to other networks. Two underlying assumptions were made: first, that similar re-sults would suggest that the strategy programmed into the simulated actors was a reasonable model for the behavior of actual subjects; second, that all subjects have the same strategies even when presented with different structural environments. We will be testing these assumptions.

It has been recognized that the results of computer simulations are sensitive to the strategies that are programmed into the simulations (Markovsky et al. 1993). The purpose of this paper is to explore some structural features that may make what is "rational" vary from network to network. While in some structures the behavior prescribed by Cook, Emerson, Gillmore, and Yamagishi (1983) may be rational, in other structures other strategies may be better at optimizing rewards. We also suggest parallels between some exchange networks and "social dilemmas."

In *The Evolution of Cooperation* (1984), Axelrod used simulation to compare the effectiveness of different strategies in accumulating resources. Initially he ran a tournament pitting strategies against one another in an iterated Prisoners' Dilemma in order to determine which strategy would accumulate the most points for itself overall. Later, Axelrod changed the environment in which the "players" had to compete and determined that some strategies did better in some structures while others did better in other structures. Our work suggests that this may be true for exchange games as well. Structural features may make what is rational vary with the overall network structure and with position in a network.

It is not our purpose to criticize the assumptions made by Cook and associates in their simulations. Indeed, their very plausibility and utility make them a good baseline model within which to explore how rationality can vary with position and network.

Excludability

The literature on power in exchange networks shows that positions differ in the advantage they may have to accumulate resources. Excludability plays a key role in theories of network power (Markovsky et al. 1993; Skvoretz and Willer 1993; Friedkin 1992). We posit that the strategies for those that can assure themselves inclusion in an exchange may be different from those that cannot. A "rational" strategy for someone who can guarantee himself or herself access may be different from that of someone who may risk being excluded.

The key structural feature determining what is "rational" is, we suggest, the degree to which a position can be excluded from a network. To be more precise, we follow Friedkin's (1992) terminology and say that an exchange network is

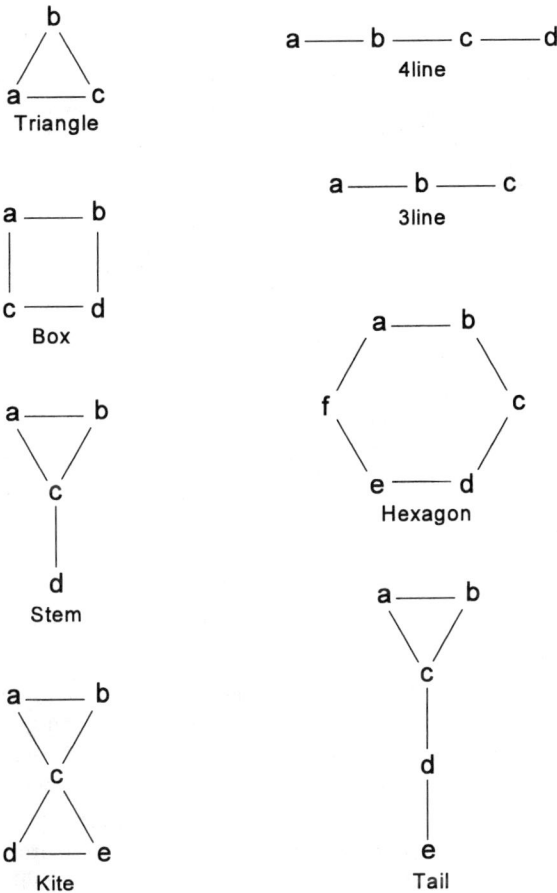

Fig. 1. Eight networks

maximally complete when no further exchanges between connected pairs can occur. For example, in the 4-line network of Figure 1, once *b* trades with *c*, no further trades are possible. Therefore, two maximally complete trading patterns are possible: *b* with *c*; and *a* with *b* and *c* with *d*. A position is *nonexcludable* if it is contained in all the maximally complete trading patterns. For example, positions *b* and *c* (but not *a* and *d*) are contained in all such patterns for the 4-line network.[1] For each network in Figure 1, Table 1 shows the maximally complete trading patterns and the nonexcludable positions.

[1] Markovsky et al. (1993) base their measure of inclusion on a baseline probability model of random offers and exchanges. Nonexcludability corresponds to the case when the measure for a position equals 1.00.

TABLE 1

Complete Trading Patterns for Eight Networks

Network	Complete Trading Patterns	Non-excludable Positions
Triangle	a-b/b-c/a-c	none
Box	a-b,c-d/a-c,b-d	a,b,c,d
Stem	a-b,c-d/a-c/b-c	c
Kite	a-b,d-e/a-c,d-e/b-c,d-e/ a-b,c-d/a-b,c-e	none
4line	a-b,c-d/b-c	b, c
3line	a-b/b-c	b
Hexagon	a-b,c-d,e-f/a-f,b-c,d-e/ a-f,c-d/a-b,e-d/b-c,e-f	none
Tail	a-b,c-d/a-b,d-e/ a-c,d-e/b-c/d-e	d

We use the assumptions of Cook, Emerson, Gillmore, and Yamagishi as a baseline model for our simulation. We run a series of exchanges in order to determine what the resource distribution would be if all players adopted the Cook and associates' strategy. Then we alter the baseline strategy for some players under certain conditions. This allows us to compare the advantages of different strategies for positions within different structural environments. Specifically we compared positions that were excludable from those that were not.

Simulations

Our simulations were designed to be similar to experiments that we and others had run on exchange networks. Players were given strategies patterned after the one used by Cook and associates with a few modifications concerning play within a game. In our computer simulation, each set of simulated players played twenty games in which the object was to divide 24 points. Each player adjusted its strategy between games, depending on the outcome of the last game. A player who had been included in an exchange lowered its initial offers to others by one point at the beginning of the next game. A player excluded from a deal raised his or her initial offers to others by two points. The initial offers to others in the first game were random variables with a rectangular distribution between nine and fifteen points inclusive.

Each game was conducted in rounds in which players had opportunities to make offers, accept offers, and confirm offers. At the start of each game in the *offer round*, each position made identical offers to all the positions to which it was connected. In the *acceptance round*, each position accepted the best offer it received, unless the best offer was less favorable to itself than an offer it had made to another. In the *confirmation round*, each position confirmed the best acceptance, unless it was less favorable than an offer by another that it had accepted. Confirmed offers became deals. If two positions confirmed the other's acceptance, the difference between the deals was averaged. No offers of 0 or 24 points were permitted. Each simulation involved twenty games. Thirty independent simulations were run in each condition.

Types of Strategies and When to Use Them

We want to distinguish between two types of strategies: *accommodative* versus *exploitative*. Accommodative strategies maximize the probability of inclusion in an exchange. Exploitative strategies maximize the gains within a completed exchange. Accommodative strategies seem to be beneficial to those positions that risk exclusion from a transaction. Exploitative strategies, on the other hand, benefit those who are sure to be included and for whom the only issue is how much they will gain in their transactions.

The following variations of the basic strategy were examined. In each simulation, one position was selected to have a more accommodative or more exploitative strategy than the other positions.

1. The selected position simply accepts the best offer received and confirms the best offer of its own that had been accepted, regardless of its own offers and acceptances. A position following this strategy is less finicky. It accepts and confirms more offers, and the additional accepted and confirmed offers are all of lower value. Such a strategy is accommodative. It should increase the probability of being included in an exchange at the cost of reward within exchanges.

2. Instead of reducing offers to others in the game after it has been included in an exchange, the selected position offers to others what his partner had earned in the last game. This results in higher offers to others, an increased probability of inclusion, but lower rewards per exchange. It is, therefore, an accommodative strategy.

3. *Only* the selected position lowers its offers to others when it has been included in an exchange, and other positions offer to others what their partners had earned in previous exchanges. If other positions don't reduce their offers to others after they have been included, then the selected position is following a relatively exploitative strategy. Making lower offers will reduce the probability of inclusion but will increase the rewards per transaction.

We expect that excludable positions will be better off with accommodative strategies and that nonexcludable positions will be better off with exploitative strategies. We examined this in a fairly crude way. We varied the strategy of one position while leaving all others constant. Using the networks in Figure 1, we selected excludable and nonexcludable positions. With respect to each comparison, we report whether the different strategy used by the altered position increased or decreased the probability of inclusion, the mean gain per exchange (a measure of *power*), and the mean total gain.[2]

Results

We present our results in three tables and discuss each table in turn. The tables show any significant increases or decreases in (1) probability of inclusion, (2) mean gain per exchange, and (3) mean total gain under strategy variations. An upward arrow means a statistically significant increase for the selected position. A downward arrow means a statistically significant decrease. A horizontal line means that the inclusion rate could not increase because the position is nonexcludable. The top rows of each table above the double line give results for excludable positions; the bottom rows, for nonexcludable positions.

Tables 2, 3, and 4 show that excludable and nonexcludable positions should adopt different strategies. Accommodative strategies may benefit excludable positions but never benefit nonexcludable positions. Conversely, excludable positions do not benefit by being exploitative, while nonexcludable positions do. Consider the first strategy: Selected Position is More Accommodative by Accepting and Confirming More Readily. According to Table 2, this strategy increases inclusion rates and decreases power. The exceptions in the first two columns were in the expected direction but not statistically significant. The effect of this accommodative strategy was negative for all nonexcludable positions. For the excludable positions, the net effect depended on whether the positive effects of greater inclusion outweighed the negative effects of reduced returns per exchange. If we had used different values for the adjustments of offers after inclusion and exclusion, we might have obtained a different pattern in the third column for excludable positions. The robust findings are that the effects of this accommodative strategy are uniformly bad for nonexcludable positions and that the effects are both positive and negative for excludable positions.

Table 3 shows the effects of the second strategy: Selected Position is More Accommodative by Not Lowering Offers to Others After It Has Been Included. The effect of this strategy change is almost identical to that of the first strategy. This more accommodative strategy increases inclusion where possible and de-

[2] If all positions in a network were structurally identical and the number of possible complete trades did not vary (the Triangle and the Box), the selected position was compared with other positions in the same network. Otherwise, the comparison was between two separate sets of simulations, those in which the selected position used a distinctive strategy and those in which it did not. All results are based on thirty independent simulations, so the degrees of freedom for the t-tests were 29 (if the comparison was between positions in one network) or 58 (if the comparison was between positions in two networks).

TABLE 2

Selected Position Accepts and Confirms More Readily

Type of position	Network and Position	Inclusion Probability	Power in Exchange	Total Reward
Excludable	Triangle - a	↑		↑
	Tail - c	↑		↑
	Kite - c	↑		↑
	4line - a		↓	
	3line - a	↑	↓	↓
	Hexagon - a		↓	↓
Non-excludable	Tail - d	-----	↓	↓
	Box - a	-----	↓	↓
	Stem - c	-----	↓	↓
	4line - b	-----	↓	↓
	3line - b	-----	↓	↓

TABLE 3

Selected Position Does Not Lower Offers to Others if Included in an Exchange

	Network and Position	Inclusion Probability	Power in Exchange	Total Reward
Excludable	Triangle - a	↑	↓	↑
	Tail - c	↑	↓	↑
	Kite - c	↑	↓	↑
	4line - a		↓	↓
	3line - a	↑	↓	↑
	Hexagon - a	↑	↓	↓
Non-excludable	Tail - d	-----	↓	↓
	Box - a	-----	↓	↓
	Stem - c	-----	↓	↓
	4line - b	-----	↓	↓
	3line - b	-----	↓	↓

TABLE 4

Selected Position Lowers Offers to Others if Included in an Exchange

	Network and Position	Inclusion Probability	Power in Exchange	Total Reward
Excludable	Triangle - a	↓		↓
	Tail - c	↓		↓
	Kite - c	↓		↓
	4line - a	↓	↑	
	3line - a	↓	↑	
	Hexagon - a		↑	↑
Non-excludable	Tail - d	-----	↑	↑
	Box - a	-----	↑	↑
	Stem - c	-----	↑	↑
	4line - b	-----	↑	↑
	3line - b	-----	↑	↑

creases power. Among the nonexcludable positions, the net effect is uniformly negative. Among the excludable positions, the net effect depends on the relative magnitude of the two opposite effects, greater inclusion but less power within exchanges.

Table 4 shows the effects of the third strategy: Selected Position is More Exploitative by Lowering Offers to Others After It Has Been Included. This exploitative strategy is uniformly good for the nonexcludable positions because it increases their power without reducing their probabilities of being included. The effects among the excludable positions are mixed because exploitative strategies also reduced the rate at which they are included.

The results are consistent across all three of our variations in strategy. Exploitative strategies are only to the advantage of nonexcludable positions, whereas accommodative strategies benefit only excludable positions. Unlike Axelrod, who found that the most successful strategies were "nice" rather then "nasty," we find that for some positions (those that can assure themselves of inclusion) nasty strategies may be beneficial while for others (excludable positions) nice strategies may prove more "rational."

Social Dilemmas Within Exchange Networks

There is an interesting discrepancy between our simulations and experimental data we have collected. In the Hexagon network, there are five possible maxi-

TABLE 5

Complete and Group-Rational Trading Patterns

Network	Complete Trading Patterns	Group-rational Trading patterns
Triangle	a-b/b-c/a-c	a-b/b-c/a-c
Box	a-b,c-d/a-c,b-d	a-b,c-d/a-c,b-d
Stem	a-b,c-d/a-c/b-c	a-b,c-d
Kite	a-b,d-e/a-c,d-e/b-c,d-e/ a-b,c-d/a-b,c-e	a-b,d-e/a-c,d-e/b-c,d-e/ a-b,c-d/a-b,c-e
4line	a-b,c-d/b-c	a-b,c-d
3line	a-b/b-c	a-b/b-c
Hexagon	a-b,c-d,e-f/a-f,b-c,d-e/ a-f,c-d/a-b,e-d/b-c,e-f	a-b,c-d,e-f/a-f,b-c,d-e
Tail	a-b,c-d/a-b,d-e/ a-c,d-e/b-c/d-e	a-b,c-d/a-b,d-e/ a-c,d-e/b-c/d-e

mally complete trading patterns (Table 1). Two of them involve three trades and three involve two trades. In the simulations, 73 percent of the games resulted in just two trades; in our experiment, 69 percent of the games resulted in three trades. This led us to speculate about what might have produced this difference (the experimental data have not yet been completely analyzed).

Borrowing from game theory, we define a *group rational* exchange pattern for an exchange network as one that produces the maximum number of points for that network. Group rational patterns are all maximally complete, but not all maximally complete patterns are group rational. For example, in the Stem network, a trade between positions *a* and *c* precludes any additional trades, but two trades are possible in this network if *a* and *b* and *c* and *d* exchange. Table 5 shows the group rational and the maximally complete trading patterns for the eight networks in Figure 1.

For three of these networks, the Stem, the 4-line, and the Hexagon, there are complete patterns that are not group rational. In these networks, there is the risk that self-interested behavior may lead to a "blind alley" in which the group as a whole is worse off. Moreover, in the Hexagon network, where all positions are equivalent structurally, the "blind alley" may in the long run be worse for *all* positions. With two trades the average gain per position per game is 8 points (48 divided by 6), but with three trades the average gain is 12 points per position per game. If all positions share equally in exclusion in the long run, this situation resembles a social dilemma. A social dilemma is a situation in which if all act in accord with their own independent self-interests, all are worse off.

In the social dilemma literature, the very simple tit-for-tat strategy has been shown to be remarkably successful (Axelrod 1984). The tit-for-tat strategy is to cooperate on the first move of a repeated Prisoners' Dilemma game and to duplicate one's opponent's last cooperative or noncooperative move on succeeding moves. In exchange games, a tit-for-tat-like strategy would take the form of making initial offers only to those with whom one has successfully completed a trade in the last round.

To examine the effects of this change, we altered our simulation. In the standard version of the simulation, positions make offers to all those to whom they are connected. In the revised version, if positions had been included in the previous game, they made an initial offer in the next game only to the position with whom they had just exchanged.

The results of this change in the Hexagon network were striking. The percentage of games with three exchanges increased from 27 percent to 98 percent. Consequently, the average earnings per game increased from 9.09 to 11.81. The reason for this change is that the pattern of three exchanges in a game becomes an "absorbing state" in a Markov chain; once entered, it is not left because all new offers are made in a symmetric pattern.

Conclusions

Using computer simulation, we have found some evidence that rational behavior varies with position in the exchange network. We distinguished between accommodative and exploitative strategies. Accommodative strategies emphasize increasing the probability of being included in an exchange. Exploitative strategies place greater emphasis on the rewards earned per exchange. Using the crude division between excludable and nonexcludable positions and the simple baseline strategy suggested by Cook and her co-workers, we found that nonexcludable positions did better using exploitative strategies and that excludable positions tended to do better using accommodative strategies.

We also found that some networks resemble social dilemmas. Through premature agreements, participants could find themselves in a situation in which all would be better off with a different pattern of agreements. This would not occur if all trades could be decided by an agreement involving all participants, but social dilemmas (and exchange networks) do not allow this degree of cooperation. Much attention has been focused on how social dilemmas can be resolved without binding agreements or a centralized authority (see, for example, Taylor 1987). As demonstrated by Axelrod, the tit-for-tat strategy is quite successful in repeated Prisoners' Dilemma games. An essential feature of tit-for-tat is that it rewards cooperative behavior in others by cooperating only with others who have cooperated. In exchange networks, an analogue to tit-for-tat (make offers only to those with whom you have successfully traded) seems to work also, although the mechanism that produces success is different. In Axelrod's experiments, tit-for-tat succeeded because it avoided exploitation by less cooperative strategies. In exchange networks, the tit-for-tat-like strategy works because it reduces the range of initial offers and makes symmetry of offers more likely.

The actual strategy employed by subjects in network exchange experiments is unknown. Our work suggests that subjects' strategies vary, depending on network structure and position in the network. Further research is necessary if we are to discover the heuristics used by subjects to determine their actual strategy. Even if it is assumed that subjects behave "rationally," we are far from being able to describe the behavior elicited under different constraints.

Synthesizing Theories of Deviance and Control: With Steps Toward a Dynamic Sociocultural Network Model

Thomas J. Fararo and John Skvoretz

In recent years, sociologists of deviance and social control have called for the integration of this field's numerous theories (Messner, Krohn, and Liska 1989). At the same time, general sociological theorists have stressed the importance of micro-macro linkage for effective explanations of macro phenomena (Alexander, Giesen, Münch, and Smelser 1987). Among the latter, those who advocate a rational choice starting point have emphasized its instrumental role in such micro-macro theorizing (Coleman 1990). The objective of this paper is to contribute to the integration of theories of deviance and social control via a micro-macro formulation that includes (but does not exclusively rest upon) a rational choice formulation at the micro level. The fundamental mechanism that leads from the micro to the macro level is what we term a dynamic sociocultural network with parallelism. Rates of deviance are macro-level outcomes of this micro-macro process.

We proceed in stages set out in a sequence of sections of the paper. First, we show how a large number of theories of deviance and control can be embedded in the framework of a dynamic sociocultural network model. Then the local situation of an actor in the network is analyzed, using the Meadian conception of self in relation to particular and generalized others. This analysis is articulated to concepts and methods of formal balance theory as it is applied to interpersonal sentiment bonds. A key idea is that the actor's action occurs in a sociomoral situation. Next we turn to the theoretical specification of a model that articulates choices based on utility with choices based on sociomoral considerations. The conception of a dynamic network with parallelism then implies that rational actors in sociomoral situations will be making choices that collectively both produce a certain frequency of deviance in a certain time period and also change the situation of action of all other actors in a recursive generative process (Fararo 1989). We conclude with a summary of the elements of the model, emphasizing its role as an initial step in a sociological process of synthesizing theories of deviance and social control in a dynamic sociomoral network framework that incorporates a micro-macro logic and an element both of rational choice and emotional balance in interpersonal relations.

Deviance and Control Theories: A Dynamic Sociocultural Network Model

Our immediate aim is to work toward an integrated theoretical model in which prior theories are interpreted as specifying types of mechanisms or important classes of parameters of the model. There are a variety of theories of deviance and social control, which can be sorted out in terms of biological, psychological, and sociological types. The biological element is especially relevant in the explanation of age and probably also of sex differences in rates of certain types of crimes. But the emphasis here will be on the sociological type, although one element highlighted in psychological explanations will be taken into account: the "impulsiveness" element in behavior (Wilson and Herrnstein 1985; Gottfredson and Hirschi 1990).

Overview of the Model

We introduce various elements of the formal approach as we discuss a series of theories of deviance and social control. This presentation motivates the various steps taken toward a synthesis within a dynamic network framework. Before we begin this constructive process, however, we give a brief overview of the model.

A network is a collection of entities called nodes, together with one or more types of ties or connections between pairs of nodes. Our fundamental type of node is the individual actor. Such actors are connected to each other by socioemotional bonds, which can change signs in the course of the processes under analysis. The sign of a bond is positive or negative, representing the emotional valence of the tie. Bonds also may be broken, represented by zero valence.

When we deal with the potential act of deviance, we use a related representation based on the point of view of the potentially deviant actor in a situation that contains others to whom that actor is connected in the network. Using the self-other ideas of Mead (1934), we represent actor-to-actor ties as relations from the actor to *particular* others and also introduce relations to *generalized* others. The primary instance of the latter is the community that defines the moral orientations from which the actor may decide to deviate. The key alternative relations to the community are alienation, which is a sense of nonbelonging, and integration, a feeling of belonging. This actor-situation analysis is carried out by using directed graphs and Heider's (1946, 1958) theory of balance as developed by Cartwright and Harary (1956). The basic idea, in our context, is dynamic: actors are motivated to reduce imbalance in patterns of signed relations that include positive and negative attitudes and moral sentiments toward potential acts. Such choices change the situation of other actors from their own point of view.

Thus, the network is dynamic in several respects. First, each actor's valuation of a particular act generates an orientation of the actor vis-à-vis the action that can be dichotomized into either of two states: oriented favorably to the law (C for conform) or oriented to rejection or defiance of the law (D for deviance). Valuations, or states, change over time as the actor nodes—the persons—respond to a mix of directed influences from others. Second, the actor's orientation to a moral community, integration versus alienation, is a problematic aspect of the whole process. It, too, can change over time in response to various influences. Third, ties of actors to others may change over time as associates are added or dropped or the strength of a tie increases or declines.

At any given time, this set of parallel processes occurs for various actors, and the whole dynamic network both generates a rate of deviance during a period of time and also recreates or changes the "sociomoral situations" of its component actors in such a way as to prepare the way for the maintenance or change of rates of deviance.[1]

Deviance Theories in a Dynamic Network Framework

In what follows, nine specific sociological theories that are frequently cited in the literature of deviance and social control will be incorporated into the framework sketched in our overview.[2] The aim is twofold: To briefly state each theory and to begin the synthesis of them in terms of the idea of a dynamic sociocultural network with parallelism.

Differential association theory (Sutherland 1924) began as an explanation of ju-

[1] For an explication of the conceptual importance of parallelism in recent science, see the papers in Metropolis and Rota (1993). Parallelism relates closely to the concept of a dynamic network process. There are several formal ways to represent such a network. One type of model is a cellular automaton: a system of N nodes (persons), each in either of two states and, on average, linked to K others. In each of a succession of discrete times, each node makes a transition of state. Such a transition depends upon the states of the nodes to which it is connected, together with its own current state. See Rietman (1989) or Kauffmann (1993) for examples. Another type of model was formulated by Coleman (1964) employing a continuous-time stochastic process model. Each actor, as above, is in either of two states (say, C for conforming and D for deviant orientation). The network state is the number (say, M) of actors in state D at time t. Then in a small time interval, there is a transition density to state M + 1 and a similar density for state M − 1, except at the boundaries of M = 0 and M = N. This density is derived by assuming that each actor to whom an actor is tied exerts an influence in the direction of that actor's own momentary disposition state. In equilibrium, there is a stationary distribution: with probability P(M) exactly M of the persons in the network are engaged in the D state. See Fararo (1973: ch. 13) for a detailed setup and analysis of the model in a social network framework. In Coleman's work, the network is treated implicitly and taken as a fixed and complete structure, that is, each person can influence every other.

[2] Stark (1994: ch. 7) provides a lucid survey of many of these theories as well as a discussion of empirical evidence relating to the assessment of them.

venile delinquency in terms of why the individual boy (as it usually was) would take up this mode of behavior in a given social environment. The theory says that the probability of becoming a delinquent depends upon the composition of the boy's contacts, namely, the strength of ties to (significant) others and the direction of orientation of the latter, favorable or not, to conduct in defiance of laws. Sutherland's theory was subsequently restated in terms of *social learning theory*, using the language of reinforcement (Akers 1973). This theory employs an actor-situation frame of reference: it explains the behavior of an actor, given the behavioral dispositions of other persons who form the social situation of the actor. These theories clearly fit nicely into the framework of a dynamic socio-cultural network. They provide mechanisms by which the change in states of nodes from conformist to deviant occurs.

Another sociological theory of deviance, *subcultural theory*, stresses that an act is only an instance of deviance in terms of certain norms or laws, the latter produced through political processes and hence dependent upon relative power. Alternative or oppositional norms may exist, so that deviance with respect to one norm implies conformity with respect to another. In the context of a dynamic sociocultural network, these bodies of norms form the moral communities to which actors are oriented and which in turn have orientations toward acts. Actors in the sociocultural network may generate their own norms, and these may be oppositional to the norms of the moral community. It follows, then, that an act by a member of the group may be deviant with respect to the moral community but compliant with respect to the group. This is a very important aspect of gang member behavior, for instance. However, we do not need to regard this formation as a new moral community. Rather, we prefer to reserve the term for a more institutionalized conception of a moral order, a legitimated moral order in Stinchcombe's (1968) sense of legitimation.

The subcultural theory is not intended to apply to every type of deviance. For instance, spouse beating seems outside its scope. It is especially useful in showing how compliance with emergent group norms is a source of deviance from the norms of the wider moral community. It has not tried to explain deviance from the group's own emergent norms. This is one of the reasons why criminologists are interested in integrating such a theory with other theories of deviance.

Another very well known theory of deviance was first proposed by Merton (1938) as a reworking of Durkheim's writings on anomie. The theory is now called *strain theory*. It begins with what is here called the moral community. By definition, there is a given consensus on certain values in this community, and there are also certain approved means for attainment of such values, the institutionalized means. From any actor's point of view, the moral community is a given. The actor's problem is one of adaptation to it. In principle, the actor can accept or reject the values and the corresponding institutionalized means or norms. An actor who accepts both is said to be a conformist. An actor who accepts the values but rejects the means is called an innovator. And so forth. The innovator in American society, for instance, is instantiated in the behavior of gang members who behave in a highly entrepreneurial manner to make money (Jankowski 1991) and thus exemplify the American way of life. The only problem is that they deal in stolen goods, illicit drugs, and the like: they do not try to make money by the approved means.

Merton thought that differential rates of deviance (especially "innovation," or, in other words, much crime) would exist by class location because these locations implied differential access to legitimate means. The theory says that an actor who values a certain goal (adapting by accepting the values of the moral community) and experiences frustrations or strains in attaining these goals by approved means will be in a situation in which there are stronger pressures to deviate, compared with actors with readier access to legitimate means to those same goals. Although this theory has been subject to revisions (Cloward and Ohlin 1960), many criminologists regard it with considerable skepticism. Its role in the integrated model presented here is more abstract than that intended by most of these critics. We consider the dynamic sociocultural network to have an emergent stratification aspect. In this case, Merton's theory applies to goals endorsed by the group's own subcultural values and to actors with differential access to attainment of these goals—all within the context of that group.

One reason for skepticism about strain theory is *labeling theory*'s emphasis on societal reactions to initial acts of deviance. Consider two gangs, one drawn from a middle-class milieu, the other from a lower-class milieu (Chambliss 1973). Behaviors by members of the former gang that are similar to behaviors of the members of the latter gang to an outside observer, both in violation of laws or customary norms, are treated differently by social control agents—police, judges, teachers, and so forth. Some such acts give rise to processing by such agents, thus giving birth to "delinquents" or "bad boys." Such a label can then enhance the likelihood of further deviance. For instance, the label could be accepted or internalized and thus lead to behaviors that attempt to maintain that self-definition. Another reason for "secondary" deviance is the objective obstacles to conforming behavior to attain cultural goals that are faced by those so labeled in public, for example, "ex-con," "dope user," and so forth.

Thus, labeling theory leads us to consider other insights from social psychology; in particular, from symbolic interaction and from experimental social psychology. A key idea of symbolic interactionism is the analysis of action in terms of self-other processes of definition and assessment. We fit this element into the theoretical model by representing the moral community as a generalized other for any actor and as a node in the dynamic network. Experimental social psychology involves a heritage of studies that also focus on the reaction to deviance, but now in controlled face-to-face interaction in small groups. The basic idea relevant to our problem is that a deviant act tends to draw out behavior from others in the group, such as negative remarks or gestures, that can be interpreted as conscious or unconscious attempts to bring the behavior back into line with group norms. A basic finding is that the more cohesive the group, the lower the frequency or rate of deviance in equilibrium. If the reactions fail with regard to a particular person, the tendency is to behave in a fashion that amounts to rejection of the person as a group member.[3]

Reactions to deviance are also central to *shaming theory* (Braithwaite 1989). From the present point of view, the theory focuses on a path potentially different from that traced out by labeling theory, given that deviance occurs. Labeling theory looks at forces that make additional deviance more likely, via stigmatization and alienation. Shaming theory stresses the alternative mechanism, sometimes used in real groups, in which the act is condemned but the actor is led to express shame and then to be *reintegrated* into the group. For instance, in a cohesive family, a child's undesirable act may be sanctioned, the child being led to feel ashamed; but not only is the child not banished from the group, but she is reintegrated—"all is forgiven." Entire societies might favor this type of mechanism, as in the case of Japan (Braithwaite 1989).

Our discussion of Merton's strain theory cited it as an interpretation of Durkheim's theory. Today, however, this theory (Durkheim 1951) survives in its own right in its original form. The deviance rate is taken as a group property. This property varies over groups, for the same type of deviance. To explain this variation, Durkheim proposes another social fact, the group's level of social and moral integration. Then Durkheim's *anomie principle* is that the deviance rate varies inversely with integration. In this form, we see that the theory matches the first of the two basic findings of experimental social psychology mentioned just above: the more cohesive the group, the lower the deviance rate.

In constructing an integrated theoretical model, we want to implement a micro-macro linkage. Through this linkage, we aim to derive Durkheim's anomie principle as a macro-level comparative statics result based on the model of the dynamic sociocultural network with parallelism. Each group will be such a network. The social integration aspect will be specified through the ties connecting actors: the greater the density of positive strong ties in the network, the greater the social integration. The cultural integration aspect will be specified through the commonness of their moral evaluations of types of acts. Note that Durkheim's principle applies to the group's own morality, not to the wider moral community. But when there is a tension between the two, our model will be able to draw out implications for the consequent equilibrated deviance rate.

---

[3] The original studies by Festinger, Schachter, and others are reprinted in Cartwright and Zander (1960).

Thus, by employing a model object—a dynamic sociocultural network with parallelism—that "concretizes" the relational and attitudinal meanings of the concept of integration, we can simultaneously deal with social learning, subculture, labeling, strain, and social integration.

We saw above that experimental social psychology has produced important findings dealing with informal social control processes activated in face-to-face interaction in small groups. Another theory has been advanced in the context of criminology and the explanation of crime rates in modern communities. This is *deterrence theory* (Gibbs 1975). The basic idea is straightforward: the more rapid, the more certain, and the more severe the punishment for a crime, the lower the rate at which such crime will occur. We interpret this theory in terms of a rational choice model of the decision between deviation and conformity. The three elements of deterrence (rapidity, certainty, and severity) can be taken in their subjective form, that is, from the standpoint of the chooser's knowledge state. Actual lags in the administration of justice will be more or less accurately reflected in tacit or explicit criminal calculations. So a subjective likelihood of being caught and punished—the certainty variable of deterrence theory—is a natural element in a rational choice model taking the form of subjective expected utility. Similarly, the severity element of deterrence theory will be reflected in the anticipated loss if a criminal act is detected, subtracting from any prospective gain. The rapidity element also can be represented, as we shall see below, by using a delay term in the rational choice model. The basic idea, then, is that a rational choice model enables us to include the elements of deterrence in the choice situation, and then the micro-macro element of the model will generate the effect on the crime rate of variations in these elements as a typical comparative statics consequence of the process model.

Many of the theories discussed above were criticized in the original formulation of *control theory* (Hirschi 1969). This theory was inaugurated by inverting the answer to the question of what needs explanation by the theory of deviance and social control. Earlier theory had presupposed that the "natural" course of socialization would produce actors oriented to conformity, so that deviance was treated as something to be accounted for. For instance, in strain theory, the "normal" actor adapts to the moral community and the stratification system by accepting the cultural goal and taking up its pursuit by legitimate means.

Control theory is a rational choice theory. The relevant decision is to deviate or to conform. But such a decision situation would not even arise unless the lure of some reward or gain from deviance presented itself. Hence, it is clear why deviance should occur. So why does it not occur more frequently? Of course, the answer is in terms of costs. The theory treats such costs in terms of a "stake in conformity." This stake normally rises with age, thereby providing one mechanism for the explanation of why certain crime rates decrease with age. It includes, for instance, social bonds and statuses that might be jeopardized, as well as internalization of social norms. It is apparent that control theory and deterrence theory fit together in their emphasis on aspects of the rational choice between deviation and conformity. While control theory may have aimed to overthrow the other theories, we shall see that there is no inconsistency in treating all the theories as specifying aspects of the general model of a dynamic sociocultural network with parallelism in which each actor, in each time unit, may be making a rational decision between deviance and conformity. In short, we have a dynamic sociocultural network of rational actors.

The General Model

The fundamental form of our model is a dynamic social-cultural network with parallelism. The network consists of persons with ties to each other, the social aspect of the network, and nodes representing moral communities and evaluated acts, the cultural aspect of the network. The dynamic aspect of the network is change of state of nodes in relation to their decisions to deviate or conform at any time and in relation to their evaluation of acts and their ties to others. Such changes of state depend upon the states of other nodes in the network. The model has a basic framework assumption that the dynamics of the process occur as actors react to two streams of randomly generated events. The first stream consists of opportunities to deviate allocated to a randomly selected actor. The second stream consists of opportunities, also allocated to a randomly selected actor, to change the state of various ties in his or her network. Network axioms describe the process by which actors select ties whose sentiment or attitude state they then change. The operating principle is to change the state of that link which would maximize local balance. Choice axioms describe the relevant utilitarian and sociomoral considerations that affect an actor's choice to conform or deviate if given the opportunity. Among the choice axioms, the articulation axiom is of special interest because it describes how utilitarian and social-moral considerations are combined. The axioms are listed in Table 1.

Sociomoral Situations and Balance

The network axioms use a qualitative form of balance theory (Heider 1946, 1958). Points in a directed graph represent concrete actors, the moral community or generalized other, and types of actions. Signed and directed lines represent sentiments and attitudes. Axiom N1 specifies that actors are connected to one another by positive, negative, or neutral sentiments; and N2 stipulates that each actor has some attitude (positive, negative, or neutral) toward the action types represented. Both sentiment states and attitude states are potentially time-variant, and thus the state of the system at time t is defined by the matrix of

TABLE 1

Model Axioms

Network Axioms	N1.	For each pair of actors, there exists a type of tie called *sentiment*, with a time-dependent state of positive, negative, or absent.
	N2.	Each actor has a relation toward an act-type X, called an *attitude*, with a time-dependent state of approval (+), disapproval (-), or indifference (0).
	N3.	The attitude of the moral community toward X is negative and time-invariant. Hence a positive attitude toward X is deviant.
	N4.	At randomly generated time points, individuals may change states of attitude and/or sentiment to reduce local imbalance (or increase local balance) with the change selected being the one that maximizes the increase in local balance.
Choice Axioms	C1.	Each actor has some amount of resource x.
	C2.	At randomly generated time points, individuals may be given opportunities to deviate (enact X) in which the lure or *temptation* is an amount g of resource.
	C3.	The subject meaning of the intrinsic gain g is relative to the amount of resource x possessed by the actor; that is, the subjective utility of a gain g in resource x if the actor's current holdings of x are g^* is: $$\frac{g}{g^*}$$
	C4.	In any occasion in which there is an opportunity to deviate, there is a chance p that the act will be detected, followed by a loss sg^* in resources x, where s is some fraction related to the severity of punishment.
	C5.	The subjective utility of the loss sg^* is relative to g^* and equal to: $$\frac{sg^*}{g^*} = s$$
	C6.	There is a delay D in the time it takes to obtain intrinsic gain g and a delay D+d in the time it takes before the intrinsic loss sg^* occurs. The effect of delays on subjective utility depends on an *impulsiveness* parameter I as follows: $$gain:\quad \frac{g}{g^*} \rightarrow \frac{g}{g^*(1+Di)} \qquad loss:\quad s \rightarrow \frac{s}{1+(D+d)i}$$ and the utility of deviance u(dev) = gain - p × loss.
	C7.	Each opportunity to deviate has associated with it two balance terms: b_1 is the local balance that would occur from the enactment of X and its implication of a positive evaluation of X; and b_2 is the local balance that would occur from the failure to enact X and its implication of a negative evaluation of X.
	C8.	In each opportunity to deviate, there is a time-invariant probability r that a rational-instrumental choice process is activated, with (1-r) the probability a sociomoral choice process is activated such that: (a) under the first process deviance occurs if u(dev)>0 (b) under the second process deviance occurs if $b_1 > b_2$

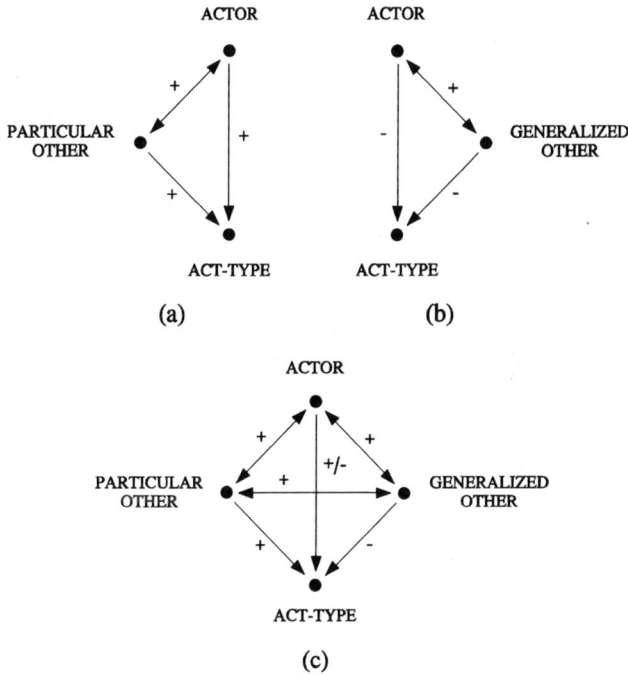

Fig. 1. Sociomoral situation of potential deviant

sentiment states and the vector of attitudes at time t. Axiom N3 makes claims about the relation between action types and the point representing the moral community. In particular, it stipulates that the moral community's attitude toward X, an action type, does not change with time and, to simplify, that the attitude is negative. This means that the act is regarded by the moral community as deviant and morally reprehensible. For example, in contemporary American society, drug use would be a type of act with a negative directed line from the moral community to it.

Figure 1 illustrates a simple case. Figure 1(a) shows a *social triad* consisting of two concrete actors and the act-type. Figure 1(b) shows a *moral triad* consisting of one of these actors, the moral community (an abstract actor), and the act-type. The two triads present an especially interesting case for analysis. Namely, the moral community disapproves of the act while the actors approve of it. We take actor A's attitude toward the act-type as problematic for analysis. We say that an actor is *balanced* in a triad if the product of the signs of the three lines is positive (Cartwright and Harary 1956). Considered individually, both triads in Figure 1(a) and (b) are balanced. If we put the two together, as in Figure 1(c), we represent the overall *sociomoral situation* of the actor. But now no matter what attitude actor A adopts, overall balance cannot be produced.

In more complex cases, particular others may disagree in their attitudes toward the act-type or the generalized other. Each particular other appears in the social graph, along with the ties among them as well as to the actor; hence, we have what network analysts call an ego-network: the actor's ties and all ties among those tied to the actor. Then each of these particular others has a directed signed line to the act-type. To simplify the analysis, suppose we consider a case in which the ego-network splits into two: one subset is uniformly positive toward the act-type and negative toward the generalized other, and the other subset has the opposite attitudes. Moreover, the two subsets are connected by mutual negative lines, indicating interpersonal hostility. For instance, one subset might be a gang to which the actor belongs, and the other represents family members. Then we can represent each of the two divisions by a single node in a graph of the social situation. Figure 2 provides an example.

Figure 2(a) shows the actor with a positive tie to both gang and family "representatives," the two particular others. It also shows their opposing attitudes toward the act-type and their mutually negative sentiment toward each other. The actor's own attitude toward the act-type cannot but produce some imbalance, since a negative cycle is implied on the left when a sign is chosen (as shown) that balances the cycle on the right. Concretely, the actor is in a state of tension with the gang when his or her attitude conforms to family feelings about the type of act. The moral situation is shown in Figure 2(b) as the same as in Figure 1(b). Figure 2(c) displays the overall sociomoral situation as a configuration that includes both the particular others and the generalized other. Depending upon the degree to which cycles in this configuration are negative, the actor is more or less imbalanced.

We view the state of the sociomoral configuration as dynamically variable over time as the actor attempts to *reduce imbalance.* An actor evaluates sentiments to others and attitudes toward action types with respect to how changes would affect local balance, that is, balance in triads involving the actor. Axiom N4 assumes that, if given the chance, an actor will make that change which produces the greatest increase in local balance. But note that changes occurring in a configuration centered on a particular person will, through the normal processes of communication, result in changes of state of other configurations that contain this particular individual. These changes of state may, in turn, evoke balancing operations by other actors. In this way, we obtain parallelism in the changes of state of sentiments and attitudes.

Choice Axioms

The choice axioms recognize that the choice between conformity and deviance involves both utilitarian assessments of costs and benefits and sociomoral

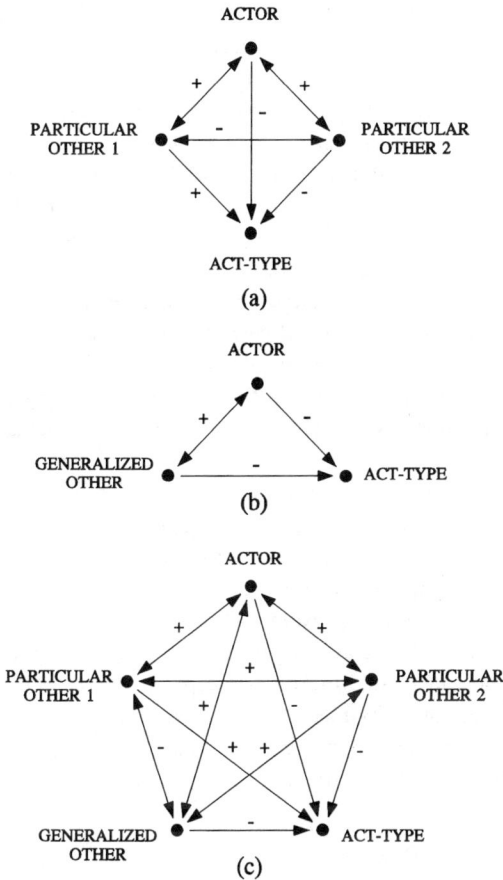

Fig. 2. Complex sociomoral situation of a potential deviant

considerations. Axioms C1 through C6 explicate the choice in utilitarian terms as a rational calculation of benefits and costs. Axiom C7 explicates the choice in sociomoral terms, and Axiom C8, the articulation axiom, indicates how these two domains are combined. We begin the explication with the utilitarian axioms.

The utilitarian perspective uses the idea from control theory that deviance arises only because, relative to the status quo of conformity, there is the possibility to gain some positive quantity G. However, from the actor's viewpoint, there is a chance p that the deviant act will be detected and lead to a loss L. Without loss of generality we can assume that conformity has expected utility zero while deviance has expected utility denoted u(dev) and given by:

$$u(dev) = (1 - p)G + p(G - L) = G - pL \qquad (1)$$

In a technical and subjective sense, the term pL is the expected loss. Thus, the actor will deviate if and only if the gain exceeds the expected loss.

Even before we introduce complications, we can show how this formula relates to some of the theories of deviance and social control. Assume that the rate of deviance in the group directly reflects the extent to which actors have greater expected utility for deviance than for conformity. First, note that any condition that makes L larger makes deviance less likely. Thus, (1) a stake in conformity will make L larger and hence will tend to reduce the rate of deviance, as asserted by control theory. (2) If there are formal punishments, then their severity affects the magnitude of L. Hence, increasing the severity of punishment makes deviance less likely (holding constant the rapidity and certainty p), as asserted by deterrence theory. (3) Increasing social integration or cohesion yields greater subjective loss in detection of a normative violation by members of the group and therefore makes deviance less likely, as stated by Durkheim and experimental social psychologists.

Second, any condition that makes p larger makes deviance less likely. Thus, (4) since p represents the certainty of punishment, in the language of deterrence theory, the greater the certainty of punishment, the lower the deviance rate (holding constant the severity and rapidity of punishment). (5) Any condition that increases the monitoring capacity of the group will make detection more likely and will correspondingly be reflected as an increase in the subjective likelihood of being detected. Hence, increasing monitoring capacity decreases the rate of deviance in a group, as discussed by Hechter (1987). Each of key terms in this equation can be expressed in terms of quantities that relate to effects postulated in existing theories.[4] We will begin with G, the gain anticipated by committing the deviant act.

Gain and Losses from Deviance

The intrinsic gain from the deviant act has two aspects. On one hand, it is some increment in a resource. We let g denote this intrinsic gain from the deviant act, measured from the current resource stock, denoted g^*. On the other hand, the gain in the sense of its subjective significance for the actor is the increment in utility that g entails, given the current resource stock. We denote this utility increment by $u(g \mid g^*)$, and then we can assert that:

$$G = u(g \mid g^*) \tag{2}$$

Strain theory suggests how the utility function should be specified. The important point for strain theory is that in certain types of sociocultural systems, a

---

[4]Neither these theories nor our theoretical integration efforts are addressed to the admitted difficulties of measurement with regard to such specifications. Some of the terms are subjective and are not really intended to be measured while others are objective and measurable (for example, balance, as indicated below).

common goal is held out for all actors independently of their legitimate opportunities to attain the goal. Thus, if we partition the actors by stratum, it follows that we should obtain differential deviance due to differential "strain." Since this strain is put as "pressures to nonconformity," it appears to some theorists as inconsistent with control theory which stresses the lure of, or gain from, deviance. However, our formulation enables consistency to be achieved by expressing the subjective significance of the intrinsic gain in terms of the utility of the resources acquired, and incorporating the common assumption that the utility of a given gain g depends upon one's total resources of the same generic kind, denoted g^*.

A typical utility function is monotone increasing in g. In fact, let us suppose the function is the natural logarithm, so that we can approximate the utility of a gain g when the resource basis is g^* by the derivative of the function evaluated at the point g^* multiplied by g.[5] That is, we obtain the equation in Axiom C3:

$$u(g \mid g^*) = \frac{g}{g^*} \tag{3}$$

This utility function directly embodies the insight of strain theory: if g^* is increasing by class location, then the utility of a gain of size g is a decreasing function of class location. Thus, for a given intrinsic gain g and net of other factors, G is greater, the lower one's class location. For instance, for a person living in poverty, the opportunity to gain \$100 has a utility that is quite different from that of a wealthy person.[6]

Detection occurs as hypothesized in Axiom C4 with probability p, but the loss depends on the stake that the actor has in the community. In particular, actors with higher levels of valued resources have more to lose through the punishment process. The amount of loss depends on the severity of the sanctions. Very severe sanctions imply nearly total loss while mild sanctions only lead to modest losses. Axiom C4 makes intrinsic loss a multiplicative function of g^*, the actor's current stock of valued resources, where the multiplier, denoted s and varying between 0 and 1, represents the severity of the formal sanctions. Therefore, sg^* is the intrinsic loss and its subjective significance is given by the size of the utility decrement it entails, given the current resource stock. Therefore, we can rewrite the equation for L as:

---

[5] The amount of the resource is represented by the x-axis in a graph of the utility function. Then at point g^* of the x-axis, the marginal utility is the derivative of the natural logarithm function at the point, namely, $1/g^*$. Hence, when the gain g is measured as an increment from amount g^* it corresponds to a utility increment of approximately g/g^*. Thus, all actors can be assumed to operate with the same general function, but the gain g is measured from different points, corresponding to different stocks of the resource reflecting different class locations.

[6] It should be mentioned that in interpreting strain theory in this way, we imply an interpersonal comparison of utility. An earlier opinion that this is to be avoided as empirically meaningless seems to be giving way to one that favors it, at least under certain conditions (Coleman 1990; Harsanyi 1990). If one insists on the avoidance, a different interpretation would be that the same actor is treated from the standpoint of how different possible states of resources of that actor correspond to distinct subjective meanings for a given intrinsic gain measured from these varying resource stocks.

$$L = u(sg^* \mid g^*) = \frac{sg^*}{g^*} = s \qquad (4)$$

Thus, in line with control theory, we have elements of the "stake in conformity" that imply more or less loss if detected in an act of deviance.

The last impact on deviance we introduce deals with the psychological element of impulsiveness. We draw upon Wilson and Herrnstein (1985) but modify their discussion and place it in a utility framework. Assume that intrinsic gain g operates through the logarithmic specification given above. Generally, there is some time lag between the act and the access to the valued resources. We propose a function that expresses the utility of a gain g delayed D units of time in terms of (a) the utility of g received immediately, (b) the length of the delay D, and (c) an "impulsiveness" factor i as follows (function is adapted from Mazur 1994):

$$u(g \mid g^*, D) = \frac{u(g \mid g^*)}{1 + Di} = \frac{g}{g^*(1 + Di)} \qquad (5)$$

Actors differ in the degree to which they "give in" to the immediacy of a gain. This is represented by the "impulsiveness" parameter i, such that $0 \leq i$. It is employed as a multiplier of the delay term D to yield Di. So in formula (5) if either the delay is zero or impulsiveness is zero, we recover formula (3) as a special case.

Figure 3 graphs utility as a function of delay, setting $g/g^* = .1, .2,$ and $.3$ and setting $i = .05$ and $.25$. When i is relatively large (.25), only gains that are nearly immediate have any appreciable value. When i is relatively small (.05), then the utility of a gain decays much more slowly with delay until its receipt. So the more impulsive the actor, the more the delay D to attain a gain g has the effect of *reducing* the attractiveness of that gain. As D decreases, the gain becomes more immediate, and thus its utility increases. A larger value of i inhibits utility increases until D is very close to 0. Figure 3 illustrates why this parameter is called impulsiveness. Imagine that the curves corresponding to $g/g^* = .2$ are moved to the right until their highest point falls on the $g/g^* = .3$ curves. When $i = .25$, the intersection corresponds to a delay of 2 time units, say, 2 days, while when $i = 0.05$, it corresponds to a delay of 10 days. The more impulsive person is indifferent to an immediate payoff of 20 percent of her current resource stock and waiting two days to get a 30 percent payoff; the less impulsive person is indifferent to an immediate 20 percent payoff and waiting ten days for a 30 percent payoff. The more impulsive person would prefer an immediate 20 percent payoff to waiting three days for a 30 percent return; the less impulsive person would prefer waiting up to ten days for a 30 percent payoff to receiving an immediate 20 percent payoff.

Axiom C6 also takes into account the reverse side of the "impulsiveness" element, namely, the deterrent effect of rapidity of sanction. The argument is

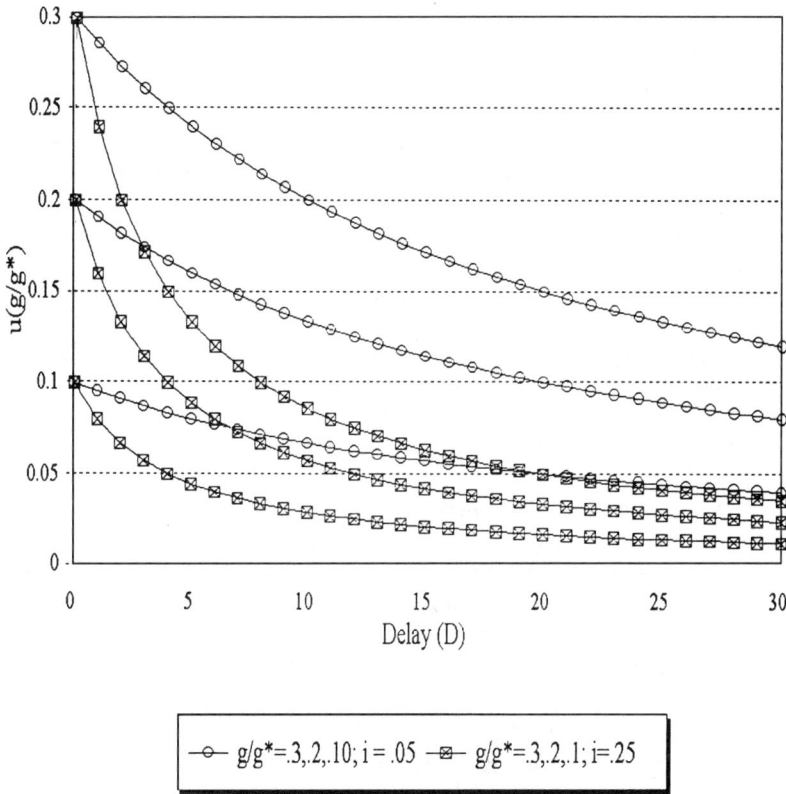

Fig. 3. Utility of g/g* as a function of delay

analogous to that for the operation of impulsiveness in relation to gain-delays. We introduce a punishment-delay parameter P and treat it as analogous to D in the earlier argument. Following the argument for utility of a gain g delayed D units of time, we express the utility of the loss sg* delayed by P time units as:

$$u(sg^* \mid g^*, P) = \frac{u(sg^* \mid g^*)}{1 + Pi} = \frac{sg^*}{g^*(1 + Pi)} = \frac{s}{1 + Pi} \qquad (6)$$

The rapidity of punishment corresponds to lower values of the P parameter, so that the greater the rapidity (the lower the value of P), the greater the subjective loss and hence (others things equal) the lower the expected utility of deviance, capturing the inhibition effect on crime intended by deterrence theory. For a person with high self-control and discipline, where $i = 0$, the punishment delay is irrelevant: it is as if the rapidity of punishment were at its maximum (where $P = 0$), no matter what the objective delays in the criminal justice pro–

cess. For a person with greater impulsiveness, on the other hand, the value of P carries its full weight: greater rapidity will reduce the attractiveness of the deviant act.

Finally, Axiom C6 makes the sensible assumption that $P = D + d$, for some d. In fact, we can safely assume that d is non-negative because formal punishment is usually quite time-delayed relative to the delay to receipt of the gain for deviance. Finally, to further coordinate with Wilson and Herrnstein, we define a loss/gain ratio:

$$m = \frac{sg^*}{g} \quad \text{or} \quad s = \frac{mg}{g^*} \tag{7}$$

and making the appropriate substitutions in formula (1), we obtain the basic rational choice formula for the utility of deviance:

$$u(dev) = \frac{g}{g^*(1 + Di)} - p\left(\frac{mg}{g^*(1 + (D + d)i)}\right) \tag{8}$$

Before we analyze the consequences of this formula, we finish exposition of the choice axioms with Axioms C7 and C8.

Axiom C7 uses the balance idea discussed earlier to describe the social-moral structure of the choice between conformity and deviance. This aspect involves psychological tensions for the actor with respect to the patterning of attitudes in the ego-network, quite apart from the number of others with one or another orientation toward the act. There are methods available for computation of a degree of balance in a directed signed graph (Norman and Roberts 1972). As-suming this as a background element and not trying to explicate it here, this means that for any given state of the sociomoral situation of the actor, there is a computable degree of balance.[7] If the actor should deviate, that would introduce some change of balance of the ego-network. On the other hand, so might the conformity choice. Let b_1 be the change in balance that would be produced by a deviant act: negative if reduced, positive if increased. Similarly, let b_2 be the change in balance that would be produced by a conforming act. The difference $b = b_1 - b_2$ is the net change in balance. If $b > 0$, then either deviance produces more balance than conformity (if the latter increases balance at all) or it produces

---

[7] A presentation of an algorithm which is the foundation for a C++ program that calculates the degree of local balance is reported in Hummon and Fararo (1995a). The same paper discusses a dynamic network simulation study in progress, in which the state of the network and the deviance/conformity states of actors co-evolve. The model generates various types of outcomes in terms of network structure and deviance. For instance, the network can evolve to a state of balance of actor relations to each other, to a type of act, and to the moral community for whom that type of act is deviant. One special case of this balanced outcome involves the formal equivalent of a gang with an isolated actor who maintains allegiance to the moral community by regarding the act as bad and refraining from it. By intent, the general theoretical model being set out in this paper is broader in possible interpretations, while the simulation study focuses attention on one family of cases within its scope.

less imbalance than conformity (if both increase imbalance). In either case, the deviant act is preferred under the general rule that actors seek balance in their sociomoral situations. These considerations build into the choice model aspects stressed in differential association (social learning) theory and control theory. Concrete interpersonal ties and their patterning in terms of attitudes toward the moral norms of the community are behind the abstract parameter b, because of the conception of a sociocultural network in which the actor is embedded.

The final axiom C8 describes how the utilitarian calculus of benefits and costs articulates with the social-moral calculus of balance. In particular, it assumes a parameter r, constant over time and over actors, gives the probability that the actor views the conformity-deviance choice in purely utilitarian terms with its complement, $1 - r$, the probability that the choice is viewed in purely sociomoral terms. We stress that this is a simple, baseline assumption that may be made more complex in various interesting ways. For instance, we could explore the consequences of r's dependence on the actor's degree of integration with the social and moral community.

This completes our axiom set. With respect to the occurrence of deviance, the axioms have the following implication. Let $Z_1 = 1$ if u(dev) > 0 and = 0 otherwise and let $Z_2 = 1$ if b > 0 and = 0 otherwise. Then

$$Pr(dev) = rZ_1 + (1 - r)Z_2 \qquad (9)$$

That is, deviance is sure to occur if the utility of the deviant act is positive and performance of the act increases local balance over nonperformance. Conformity is sure to occur if the utility is negative and conformity increases local balance more than nonconformity. In the other cases, where utility is positive but conformity increases balance more or utility is negative but deviance increases balance more, deviance occurs with probability r or $(1 - r)$, depending on which aspect of the situation is attended to.

Analysis of the Rational Choice Formula

Earlier, we showed how the basic gain-loss formula already has implications that correspond to fundamental ideas in various theories of deviance and social control. What we have just tried to do is to articulate more specifically how various theoretical ideas are represented in terms of parameters of the utility function that specify the gain and loss terms in detail. At the same time, we have articulated this rational choice aspect of our theoretical synthesis to the sociomoral situation of the actor. We now return to the rational choice formula to draw out some further points of interest.

Formula (8) can be analyzed for various interesting trade-offs. An important question is the effect of impulsiveness, under varying conditions (values of other parameters) considering the claim (especially by Wilson and Herrnstein 1985) of its considerable importance in the production of violent crime. Wilson and

Herrnstein (1985: Appendix) analyze their behavioral formula for a crossover point, that is, a point at which their model predicts a switch from the conformity to deviance or vice versa. In the rational choice formulation culminating in formula (8), a similar analysis is possible. The crossover point corresponds to the point at which u(dev) switches into or out of positive values. In terms of the element of delay to the intrinsic gain, the analysis leads to the discovery of a critical value of D such that below this value, "crime becomes irresistible (like the chocolate cake at the end of dinner), and at all longer delays, noncrime predominates" (Wilson and Herrnstein 1985: 532).

Given formula (8), we can derive results that capture the logic of their argument as a special case of our own analysis. We obtain an explicit formula for the critical value of D which is very similar to a formula derived by Wilson and Herrnstein (1985: Appendix):[8]

$$D^* = \frac{d}{pm - 1} - \frac{1}{i} \tag{10}$$

This is our critical value: if $D < D^*$, then u(dev) > 0 and, hence, deviance occurs. Another way to interpret the threshold is in terms of the concept of immediacy, as follows. Let $I = 1/D$. Since $D < D^*$ yields deviance, it follows that $I > I^* = 1/D^*$ also yields deviance. That is, if the immediacy of the reward exceeds some threshold value, the actor will deviate. By writing (10) in terms of I, we find that

$$I^* = \frac{(pm - 1)i}{id - (pm - 1)} \tag{11}$$

Then (via partial differentiation), we find that as impulsiveness i increases, the threshold I^* falls and it is "easier" for immediacy values to scale this invisible barrier to produce deviance. That is, as impulsiveness increases, deviance becomes more likely.

Returning to formula (10), we can assert that an actor with impulsiveness i and stake g^* will find attractive a deviant act with intrinsic gain g (that is subject to detection with probability p and to sanctions of severity s after delay $D + d$ if detected) if and only if D, the delay to receipt of the intrinsic gain g, is less than the threshold value D^*. If the actual delay is greater than D^*, the net expected utility from the deviant act is negative, and thus the act is no longer attractive. Therefore, any changes in parameters that increase the value of the threshold,

---

[8] We refer to their formula (4). They consider the possibility that an act of deviance may be unsuccessful. Our model, however, is somewhat simplified, inasmuch as we assume that the act (at least in the actor's mind) leads to the gain G with probability 1. Also, our operationalization of delay's effects results in a "normalization" of their term R_e to 1. Our p corresponds to their p_n, and our d to their delta term. There is one conceptual difference in the interpretation of the two formulas. The Wilson-Herrnstein derivation assumes that delay D applies to the total composition of gain G and delay $D + d$ to the total composition of loss L. For simplicity, we have partitioned G and L in such a way that social or self-administered rewards or costs are not governed by the delay parameters.

increase the range of acts that persons will find attractive. Thus from formula (10) (when D* is positive), the likelihood of deviance is enhanced by:

—greater delay (d) in the administration of sanctions
—smaller probability (p) of detection
—less severe sanction (a smaller value of s decreases m)
—lower stake in the system (a smaller value of g*)
—greater intrinsic gain (g) from deviance.

Two points about this list should be noted. First, these propositions are not in any sense surprising. Although we want nonobvious consequences from a deductive apparatus, this does not mean that we do not also want to obtain well-known and obvious results as well. One test of adequacy of a theoretical formulation is that it be comprehensive enough to include already known, and so unsurprising, propositions. But, second, lurking in the complexity of formula (10) are some relationships that are by no means obvious, as we now discuss.

Since formula (10) relates four independent quantities (or six, if we count m as composed of the independent quantities s, g, and g*), many related equations express the conditions under which the expected utility of the intrinsic gain from deviance is greater than the expected loss. Figure 4 illustrates one possibility. It graphs u(dev) for fixed values of p, m, d as functions of D and i. For a given delay, as impulsiveness increases, the utility of deviance changes sign from negative to positive. For certain low levels of impulsiveness, no delay is sufficiently short to make deviance attractive. At higher levels of impulsiveness, the effect of shorter delays on the utility of deviance is particularly dramatic. The curve created by the intersection of the 0-plane with the u(dev) surface and projected on the delay-impulsiveness plane creates what Wilson and Herrnstein call a "frontier," a line that divides parameter combinations that make the deviant act attractive from those that make it unattractive. Since these analyses only supplement what we have already done, we leave them for a later exposition.

One final point to note is an apparent paradox with respect to impulsiveness in formula (10), wherein greater impulsiveness raises the D* threshold. That is, with respect to a particular deviant act, more impulsive persons may have positive net utility even if rewards are delayed by twenty days, though less impulsive persons do not. Therefore, it seems as if the more impulsive are better able to defer gratification than the less impulsive—an apparent paradox. However, the result occurs because the more impulsive actors discount more heavily the d factor, involving the application of sanctions if detected. Heavier discounting of future rewards and sanctions leads to lower expected utility overall, given a fixed delay to rewards from deviance, but an even greater depreciation of sanctions in light of the additional delay to their application. This magnifies the difference between gain and loss, tipping the balance in favor of deviance earlier. That is, the gain from distant crimes is more attractive to—has higher utility for—less

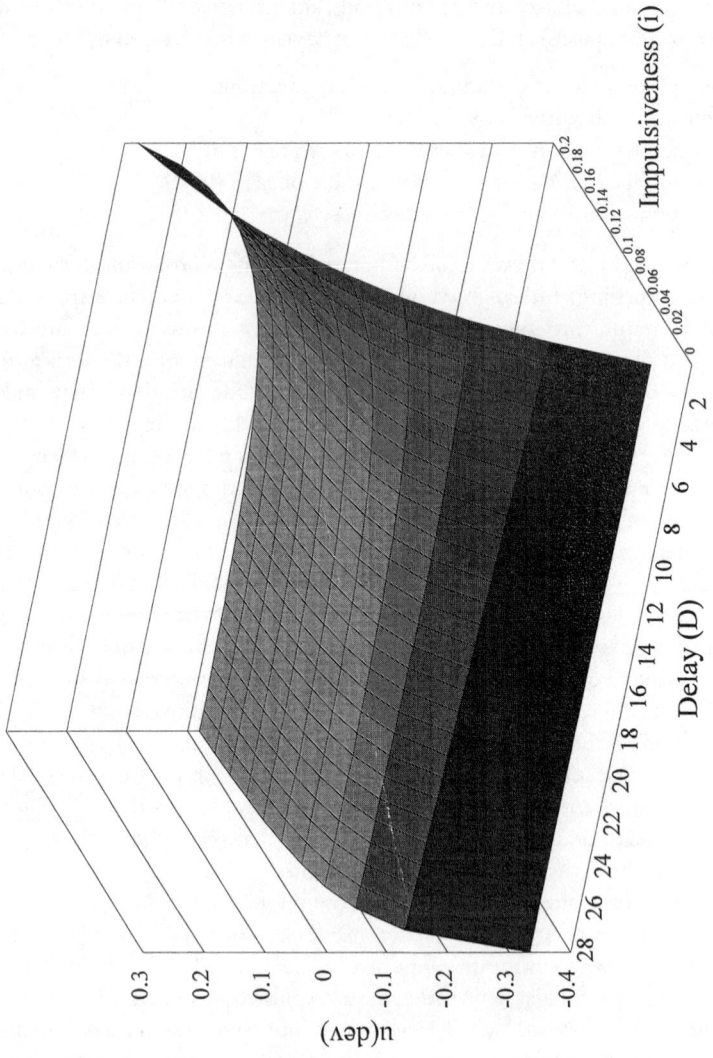

Fig. 4. Utility of deviance by delay and impulsiveness (m = 1.33, p = 1.00, d = 6)

impulsive persons. But such persons also perceive potential losses to be greater, in fact, so great that they outweigh the gain. More impulsive persons, on the other hand, discount more severely potential losses and to the extent that they no longer outweigh the perceived gain.

Rational Choice and Network Dynamics

Formula (9) captures how the probability of deviance depends on utilitarian and sociomoral considerations. But these considerations can change over time in response to individual social psychological processes and population-level competitive processes. We examine the social psychological processes first by exploring the effects of two common societal reactions to deviance, labeling and shaming.

We view labeling and shaming as changing the state of the sociocultural situation of the actor. Shaming and labeling alter the configurations for which the degree of balance is computed. In a fully dynamic sociocultural network with parallelism, as envisioned earlier, this step follows upon the actual selection of a deviant act and thereby alters the parameters of the utility function for the next episode of choice. For the present, we merely note that the sociomoral configurations of Figures 1 and 2 would be amplified with another type of point: the type-of-actor label introduced in the sanctioning phase of reaction to deviance. Figure 5(a) provides an example, focusing only on the moral triad, to isolate the core phenomenon.

A temporal sequence is involved. The initial state involves an act of deviance

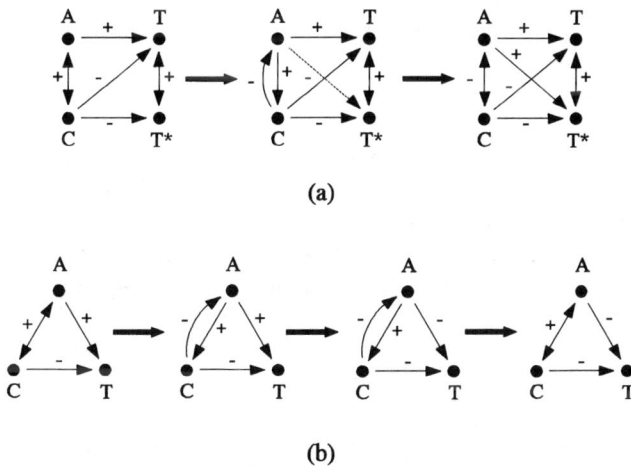

(a)

(b)

Fig. 5. Affective dynamics of labeling and shaming (A = actor; C = community [generalized other]; T = act-type; T* = label) by the actor: this is represented by a positive link to that type of act (T) morally disapproved by the moral community (C with its negative link to T). Initially, the actor is integrated into the moral community (positive link). This initial state of the moral triad is imbalanced and hence is subject to change. In the next phase, the community invokes a label (a type of actor T* of that disapproved type of act) and assigns it to the actor, shown by dashed lines to mean that the actor does not initially accept or internalize the label. At the same time, the community spurns the individual, shown by a negative line to the actor, who, as yet, is still tied positively to the community. But this situation remains imbalanced for the actor, who, in the final phase, balances the moral situation by introjecting the label positively and rejecting the community. In this final phase, balance holds. This is the route of labeling and alienation, following deviance.

The shaming mechanism avoids this labeling process, as shown in Figure 5(b). We start with an act of deviance that imbalances the triad. The community then gives a shaming response to the act, shown as a negative line to the actor, but there is no corresponding attribution of permanent negativity assigned to the actor. This provides the opening for the actor to express remorse, symbolically disavowing the type of act disapproved by the community (shown in the third step of this sequence). The triad is still imbalanced, but the community responds to the symbolic disavowal evoked by shaming through reintegration, that is, directing a positive tie back to the actor. Hence, in the final step, balance obtains. In this type of balance, we have reintegration of the actor into the moral community rather than the alienation generated by the labeling process. Of course, in a completely general process model, other paths would need to be considered beyond these two paths stressed by these two theories, shaming theory and labeling theory.

While individual-level processes may alter balance inputs to the probability of deviance, population-level precesses may alter utilitarian inputs, particularly as they influence the intrinsic gain from the deviant act. Following the ideas of Vila and Cohen (1993), we observe that at the population level, the gain to a single actor of a deviant act may often depend on the number of others in the population also executing the deviant strategy. Vila and Cohen simplify matters by assuming that actors either engage in productive behavior or play an expropriative strategy "stealing" some fraction of what the others produce. Actors meet in N-person groups, strategies are selected, and if k actors select the productive strategy (conformity), then each earns $1 - \gamma$ while the $N-k$ exploiters earn $c\gamma k/(N - k)$, where c is a depreciation constant that applies to all ill-gotten gains. It is obvious from this expression that the resource gain to each deviant depends on the number of actors that deviate. If they all choose deviance, the gain drops to 0. Gain is maximized when only one actor selects the deviant strategy. The pattern is known as negative frequency dependence.

Vila and Cohen then use ideas from evolutionary game theory to model how the proportion using the deviant strategy changes over time. The idea is that the deviant strategy reproduces at a higher rate than the productive strategy, so long as its average payoff exceeds the average payoff of the productive strategy. From our point of view, the important implications pertain to the factor g in the expression for gain—in particular, that this factor varies over time for the very same act as a consequence of the total proportion of the population selecting that act at a given point in time.

Summary of the Model

This initial work on a synthesis of theories of deviance and social control has been formulated in terms of a dynamic sociocultural network such that:

1. Each node is an actor with a utility function given by formula (8), based on the theoretical elaboration of the fundamental gain-loss formulation in expression (1).

2. Each actor is positively tied to a subset of other such actors. These ties may be created or abandoned, depending upon the efforts made by the actor to reduce imbalance.

3. Each actor is connected to the moral community, which functions as a generalized other whose attitudes toward various types of acts give these acts moral meaning.

4. Each actor may be integrated with the generalized other in a positive mutual bond or alienated with a negative mutual relation or in some transient state of imbalance with respect to it.

5. Each act taken by the actor has intrinsic significance in terms of gains and losses, but also symbolic significance in terms of what it indicates to others about the actor's attitude toward the act.

6. Each actor who is integrated into the moral community will have internalized its definition of the relevant act as morally approved or disapproved or, perhaps, morally neutral.

7. Each actor's attitude toward an act is subject to change due to pressures and tensions arising from the overall sociomoral situation of the actor in terms of the sociocultural network (that is, the particular others and their configuration of sentiments and attitudes forming the relevant ego-network) and the moral community (that is, the generalized other and its attitude toward a type of act).

8. Each actor's current attitude toward an act in the given sociomoral situation yields a degree of balance that would be shifted differentially by an act of deviance and by an act of conformity. Increases in imbalance are avoided and increases in balance sought out.

9. Sociological theories, which specify aspects of this situation but usually relate them directly to the macro-level rate of deviance without specification of the sociocultural network dynamics and its parallelism, are readily coordinated to the model: differential association and social learning; subcultural theory; strain theory; labeling theory; an experimental social psychological theory; sham-

ing theory; anomie theory; deterrence theory; and control theory. Although this list does not exhaust all the theories, it comes close to doing so.

10. Psychological theories, which stress the importance of impulsiveness in relation to delays in reward or punishment, are represented as elements in the utility function from which we obtain a threshold point analysis that corresponds closely to that given in the relevant previous literature.

11. Intrinsic gains from deviance are negative frequency dependent. Therefore, the payoff to acts of deviance that have a strong utilitarian component should be very sensitive to the number of actors engaged in the deviant activity. This factor should not affect deviant acts that have a strong social component in their payoff functions.

These eleven statements will serve to summarize our model at this stage of its development. Although in its present form the model is not completely specified mathematically, it is now ready for further work to convert it into a definite formal structure that can be studied by analytical and simulation techniques. Of great importance will be the effort to show how variations in parameters associated with various theories constitute change in conditions that produce corresponding changes in equilibrated rates of deviance under those conditions. The signs of such comparative statics results should reflect theoretical ideas about how rates of deviance depend upon prevailing structural and cultural conditions. In addition, the form of the representation of the important balance aspect of the model can be coordinated to affect control theory (Heise 1979; Smith-Lovin and Heise 1988). This theory directly incorporates some of the symbolic interactionist types of considerations introduced above, for example, the moral evaluation of types of acts.

Finally, in fully implementing the dynamic aspect of the model, we will address further questions that invoke other theoretical considerations. For instance, the act of deviance is often collaborative among members of a small group of particular others to whom an actor is tied, making the nonconforming option especially hazardous in terms of the evaluation of the actor by the others. Also, when a deviant act occurs, there is some actual outcome and not just the anticipations of rational choice. Success, in the sense of not being negatively sanctioned, will have an effect on the actor's subjective probability of being detected and sanctioned on the next occasion. In this way, not only changes in the complex of sentiments and attitudes in the sociomoral situation but concrete outcomes of deviant acts may "feed back" to alter the parameters of an actor's utility function. Thus, the next steps in model building promise to carry the current work into still further connections with other theories at the same time as the formal structure of the model is specified and its generative consequences studied through simulation.

Affective Attachments to Nested Groups: The Role of Rational Choice Processes

▚

Edward J. Lawler

This paper puts forth an emotional/affective explanation for action in the collective or group interest. The explanation is based on the *choice process theory of affective attachments to groups* (Lawler 1992)—a theory that focuses on individual-to-group ties in a nested-group context where a subgroup is encompassed within a larger group. According to this theory, choice processes that give actors a sense of control arouse positive emotions, and these lead to affective group attachments. A broader implication is that freedom, choice, and self-determination promote action on behalf of the collective interest through an emotional/affective process. The choice process, furthermore, has an important impact on the allocation of affective attachments to the subgroup and the larger group, independent of the consequences of the actual choices made. In this paper, I show how the *choice process theory of affective attachments* supplements in some respects, and modifies in other respects, a rational choice approach to collectively oriented behavior in groups.

Affective attachments are important to understanding rational choice phenomena because they promote preference shifts from the individual or self-interest to the group or collective interest. In rational choice terms, there are at least three broad ways to characterize such a preference shift. First, affective attachments lead actors to include the group welfare along with their own individual welfare as components of their utility function (Becker 1976; Harsanyi 1982). In this account, group benefit or group welfare becomes a part of and contributes to individual profit maximization. Second, affective attachments make the group welfare a distinct and separate utility function for actors (Margolis 1982). This presents them with decisions about how to allocate time, effort, or other resources to the group utility function (G-utility) versus the self-utility

The author thanks Mouraine Baker, Michael Hechter, Michael Large, and Jeongkoo Yoon for helpful comments on a earlier draft.

function (S-utility). In this account, the group's welfare is important in its own right, not just because it contributes to individual benefit (see Margolis 1982). Thus, maximizing profit does not necessarily entail maximizing individual welfare (S-utility); it can involve maximizing group welfare, individual welfare, or both. Third, affective attachments may change metapreferences, or the choice among "sets" of options, without necessarily determining the choice or preference within a given set (Sen 1973). Sen (1973, 1977) suggests that different option sets reflect different goals or values; as a result, a preference for a given option involves a choice of metapreference (for example, goal, value) as well as a choice among options within this metapreference. From this approach, the interests of a larger group, local subgroup, and individual member involve distinct metapreferences. Affective attachments should shift the choice of metapreference to the group (local or larger). "Group welfare" involves one or more distinct utility functions, but for Sen, individual maximization remains the underlying motivation.

I adopt the general approach of Margolis and Sen, focusing on their similarities. Affective attachments presuppose that the group is a distinct social object for actors, a "reality" toward which they direct emotion and action. Affective attachments give the group and its corresponding utility function (G-utility) or value in its own right, that is, something from which individuals derive intrinsic satisfaction. In Margolis's (1982) terms, the choice of metapreference is a choice of G-utility or S-utility, and the propensity toward G-utility is based on the intrinsic value of group membership. The stronger the affective attachments to groups, the greater the intrinsic value of group membership as such, and the more individuals' profit maximization will be constrained, framed, or directed toward the group interest. In this manner, group memberships which initially have an instrumental foundation become more "expressive" and "taken for granted," and actors are willing to nurture the collective welfare by, for example, contributing to public goods (Lawler and Yoon 1996).

The ties between an individual and a group, like those between individuals, can take three basic forms: utilitarian, affective, or normative (Kanter 1968, 1972). Individuals can be attached to social entities because those groups are means to particular ends, because they are valued in their own right, or because they have rules and norms that direct or guide the actors' behavior (Parsons 1951; Kanter 1968, 1972). The first is instrumental; the second is emotional/ expressive; and the third tends to contain both instrumental features (that is, group sanctions) and expressive features (internalized beliefs). These forms of attachment, of course, are interrelated. I consider in particular the connection between the instrumental and emotional/affective bases of attachment and theorize how expressiveness emerges from an instrumental foundation (see also Lawler 1992; Lawler and Yoon 1993, 1996).

Understanding the emotional aspects of person-to-group ties, apart from person-to-person ties, is fundamental to the problem of social order, as Parsons and others have suggested (Kanter 1968, 1972; Tajfel and Turner 1985; Markovsky and Lawler 1994). Once the group is "objectified" or becomes "real" to actors, people are prepared to act toward the group as a distinct entity and therefore distinguish relations to specific others in the group from relations to the "group itself" (Berger and Luckmann 1966; Tajfel and Turner 1985). This has important implications for how moral orders are created and sustained.

Background

Instrumental and expressive forms of attachment have often been pitted against one another, yet it seems fairly clear that expressive attachments often develop from instrumentally based group memberships, and expressive relations often become instrumental for actors over time. To assert that social relations are inherently either instrumental or expressive or to presume that one particular relationship obtains between the instrumental and the expressive is to ignore the fact that the instrumental and the expressive are likely to be interrelated in a variety of ways across different contexts. Of particular relevance here, the processes of making rational calculations and choices should have emotional consequences for actors, and these consequences may bear on how they perceive the group and their own connection to it. Rational choice theorists have given little consideration to the intrinsic value of choice, autonomy, or freedom, although some have acknowledged their importance and the potential that they might alter rational choice explanations (see Sen and Williams 1982; Harsanyi 1982). It is well known, for example, that perceived choice, freedom, or self-determination arouses positive emotion under certain conditions (for example, White 1959; Deci 1975, 1980; Westcott 1988). Attention to the emotions generated by rational choice processes has the potential to refashion and improve rational choice explanations of social solidarity (Hechter 1987) if we can specify how and when emotion produced by rational choice processes has an impact on affective attachments to the group.

The role of group attachments in producing preference or metapreference shifts is complicated by the fact that in most social contexts, people act and interact in "nested groups," that is, in a local subgroup subsumed within a larger group. Examples are a state within a nation, a division within a corporation, a department within a university, or an ethnic community in a larger city. When people make choices in the context of nested groups, the "group welfare" can mean the subgroup or the larger group, and clearly this choice—implicitly a choice of metapreference—has a bearing on the locus of social solidarity. My *choice process theory of affective attachments* addresses this problem. The theory formulates general principles for explaining when and how choice processes lead actors to develop stronger affective attachments to subgroups versus the more encompassing group.

Emotion and Rational Choice

The broader theoretical issue being addressed is the emotional side of rational choice processes. Just as psychologists have transcended the sharp dichotomy between cognition and emotion and have come to see these as interrelated in a variety of interesting and complex ways, theorists of rational choice and emotion can benefit from more systematic understanding of how rational and emotional processes are intertwined. Choice behavior is a good context for doing this. The recent work of Robert Frank (1988) on "passions" as commitment devices or signals and of Bruno Frey (1992a) incorporating intrinsic motivation into neo-classical economic principles offer interesting and important pathways for development, as do Hochschild's (1983) ideas on the tactical management of emotional expressions in work settings, and Clark's (1990) analysis of emotions as strategies for making status claims. A recent special issue of *Rationality and Society* on emotion suggests a shift in thinking about the relevance of emotion among sociological rational choice theorists.

An ecumenical spirit, however, should not overlook the fact that rational and emotional approaches to human behavior adopt disparate and somewhat incompatible metatheoretical assumptions. Rational choice theorists begin with the reasonable premise that social structures entail constraints on choice options and generate incentives (preferences) for adopting certain choices over others (Elster 1986). In rational choice theory, one imagines relatively "free" actors who make choices among the options available, based on the incentives associated with those options. Social institutions are regularized mappings of options and incentives that account for congruent behavior of large numbers of actors in the same group, organization, or society and for the "taken for grantedness" of much behavior. Given the emphasis on choice and its consequences, sociological rational choice theorists accord somewhat less attention to the process of means-ends deliberation by which choices are made and virtually no attention to the emotional aspects of this process (see, for example, Hechter, Opp, and Whippler 1990).

Sociological theories of emotion—although revealing less metatheoretical unity or consensus than rational choice theories—also begin with a reasonable premise, namely, that the "social" in social action presupposes a nonrational—emotional or normative—foundation for behavior (Berger and Luckmann 1966; Scheff 1990; Collins 1981). Social solidarity is in part a priori and constitutive of the social world. From such theories, one imagines actors who have a common bond to one another and who are constrained to do what is normatively sanctioned by their group; therefore, choice and choice processes play a minimal role. The choices people actually have are trivial, compared to the importance of those already structured into social institutions.

Yet people do make choices all the time; they at least act like some of these are important; and emotions such as fear, happiness, elation, and depression are clearly induced by people's choices (for example, Festinger 1959). Moreover, recent work on emotion emphasizes that the expression of emotion, while constrained by the social context, is a matter of some choice (Hochschild 1983; Frank 1988; Clark 1990). Emotions such as anger, shame, and happiness are complements of strategic choices, helping to present the desired impression or image, to convey commitment to a line of action, or to even solve the "mutual assurance problem" in mixed-motive settings (see Frank 1988, 1990). As Hochschild (1983) argues, emotions are managed by actors as much as they are dictated by the social context.

It is also reasonable to suppose that choice *processes*, not just the *actual* choices, arouse feelings and emotions that people perceive as caused by groups in the social context and that form the basis for their attachments to these groups (Lawler 1992). Outcomes are important but so is process, and my theory focuses solely on the latter. In the following sections, I synthesize the main ideas of *the choice process theory of affective attachments* and illustrate its implications for rational choice explanations of various phenemona, including the role of intrinsic motivation in persons' response to price and regulatory incentive mechanisms (Frey 1992a,b), the differences between primary and secondary labor markets (Akerlof 1982, 1984), and the impact of person-to-collective dependencies on social solidarity (Hechter 1987).

The Choice Process Theory of Affective Attachments

The broadest prediction is that *people become more emotionally attached to those groups that give them a generalized sense of control* (Lawler 1992). "Sense of control" does not necessarily mean "real control," only its perception; and it is grounded in what groups do *for* or *to* us, that is, how they enable or constrain our action. My argument is that the generalized sense of control has an impact on actors' attachments above and beyond the positive benefits actually produced by this control. A key point of the theory is that affective attachments mediate the impact of instrumental conditions on the development of commitment, solidarity, and the like.

Obviously, groups are likely to vary in the degree that they provide persons the capacity, objectively or subjectively, to have an impact on the world around them. Everyday commonsense conceptions of control tend to be embedded in myths about the primary sources and forms of "human agency" in a given group, organization, or society. Most groups, organizations, or societies contain myths about how the collective "empowers" individual members, and the everyday interaction of members can reaffirm or weaken the force of such myths. Inferences about control are therefore group-mediated, that is, they are social definitions developed and sustained in and by groups and organizations.

The scope conditions of the theory entail a choice situation in which individual actors in a nested-group context (for example, a work group in an organization) face some sort of "problem" and uncertainty about how to deal with the problem. They have a set of options to choose among and some degree of discretion (from none to much) to reshape the option set. The problem faced and the associated uncertainty constitute what is defined as a "choice situation"; the process of identifying, evaluating, and shaping options is the "choice process"; and the result is an actual choice (Lawler 1992). While group members interact with each other and therefore influence each other's interpretation of the choice process, this interpersonal influence process is treated by the theory as a given. This is not a very limiting condition, because theory and research on group formation indicate that even in the absence of interaction, people may perceive themselves as a member of a group and act differently toward in-group and out-group members (for example, Tajfel and Turner 1985; Rabbie and Horowitz 1988; Kramer 1993). Some research supports the distinct and separate effects of person-to-group, as opposed to interpersonal, ties (see also Hogg and Abrams 1990; Markovsky and Lawler 1994).

The key question addressed by the theory is: When and how do choice processes have an impact on actors' affective attachment to subgroups versus more encompassing groups? The theory holds that choice processes increase or decrease actors' *generalized* sense of control by producing more or less perceived choice, and this cognition then arouses positive or negative emotions. The social-structural context shapes these cognitions and emotions.

Social-Structural Context

Social structures have both constraining and enabling features (Elster 1986; Giddens 1984). The constraint is embedded in the "set of feasible options" among which actors are able to choose (Elster 1986); "enabling" is found in the opportunities provided by the choice. In other words, a social structure not only limits choice, it also frees actors to choose among a set of feasible options. My theory assumes a socially defined option set that is partly exogenous (dictated by social structure) and partly endogenous (shaped by means-ends deliberation). To the degree that actors construct the options or the options provide them a wide range of opportunities for action, they sense high control (Lawler 1992). The control may not be realized in the consequences or effects of a particular choice, but as a generalized capacity, it remains there to be used in the future.

Emotion is defined as a short-term positive or negative feeling that involves neurophysiological, neuromuscular, and often cognitive components (Kemper 1978). Emotion is a transitory feeling; affect, an enduring feeling or sentiment attached to an object (Kemper 1978; Gordon 1981). The objects of concern are subgroups and groups. Emotions are relatively diffuse feelings, and groups are a possible target for such feelings. The theory contends that in choice situations, cognitive appraisals of choice and freedom arouse diffuse emotion that then produces further cognitive work.[1] This additional cognitive work involves an attribution process that forms, strengthens, or weakens affective group attachments (Lawler 1992).

The attribution process concerns the inferences actors make from the choice process, rather than from the consequences of the actual choice (Lawler 1992). I argue that actors develop a commonsense understanding of the social (external) sources of their choice opportunities and their generalized capacity for control, regardless of whether they attribute choice consequences to internal or external conditions (Weiner, Russell, and Lerman 1979). These socially constructed understandings determine the responsibility that actors attribute to nested groups for the positive (or negative) feelings generated by the choice process. Thus, even in the case of an internal attribution for a behavior or actual choice (that is, an attribution to the person), I argue that actors have some understanding or interpretation about where the choice of behavioral options comes from; this can be viewed as a "second order" attribution process.

To have long-lasting effects, choice situations and, hence, choice processes need to recur so that actors repeatedly experience the sense of control or lack of it, and so their episodic attributions about control crystallize. Social structures establish such conditions by reproducing the same sort of choice situation for actors over time. If choice situations repeatedly give actors a broad range of options or substantial discretion to shape them, then choice processes should repeatedly generate a sense of control and related positive feelings. Choice processes, through such cognitions and emotions, essentially make people more aware of the constraints and opportunities embedded in social structures and also make them more likely to attribute these to relevant subgroups and groups.

Overall, people sense more control when social structures allow them to decide how to manipulate their world and thereby generate a product (see Kohn and Słomczyński 1990 for cross-national empirical support). To go further and say that a choice process arouses emotion is similar to saying that a production process (not just the product itself) engenders an emotional response because, regardless of how satisfying or dissatisfying the particular product, the process

---

[1] Actually, the uncertainties of the choice situation itself are likely to produce baseline emotions in the form of fear, anxiety, and interest (Izard 1977). Such emotions should focus people's attention on the choice problem and produce cognitive appraisal, while subsequent choice processes add another layer of cognitive appraisal that fosters other emotions such as feeling good, happy, or relieved, which, in turn, generate more cognitive appraisal. My emphasis is how individuals' cognition about the choice process (about the means-ends deliberation) impacts emotions felt by actors and how these emotions are then interpreted by the actors.

reflects actors' generalized capacity to produce better results in the future. This idea is compatible with Deci's work on intrinsic motivation and with White's analysis of "effectance motivation" (Deci 1975; White 1959). It is also compatible with Marx's (1964) notions about when the labor process alienates people from the products of their labor, and with the role of efficacy in Giddens's (1984) structuration theory. Choices that affirm a person's self-determination or freedom make him or her feel good and are likely to have intrinsic value (Westcott 1988). The question, then, is whether and when these bear on person-to-group ties.

Choice Process and Affective Attachments

Three basic ideas capture the main propositions of the theory. The first idea is that *positive emotion generated by choice processes strengthens affective ties to groups credited with making choice opportunities available; negative emotion weakens ties to those blamed for constraining choice* (Lawler 1992). I argue that actors singly or jointly attempt to understand the source or causes of these feelings, because they want to be able to reproduce good feelings and avoid bad ones; this attribution process leads to a shared understanding of the responsibility (credit/blame) relevant groups and subgroups have for such emotions. For example, an ethnic community that creates more opportunities (choices) for housing or employment for new immigrants should generate stronger affective attachments, if the new immigrant attributes responsibility for these choices to the ethnic community more than to the larger nation (Lawler 1992).

The attributions of a set of individuals "aggregate" in part because the second-order attribution—understanding the social bases or causes for choice opportunities or constraints—produces a sense of shared experience and of membership in a larger collective entity. The group or subgroup becomes more salient and also a more distinct utility function, in Margolis's (1982) terms, as people come to believe that something they experience individually (an emotion) is due in part to something they share with others—group membership. The mutual awareness of a shared emotion should be stronger where the task is a joint one involving several people, because they have an opportunity to communicate their feelings to one another, but even individual tasks can generate a sense of some larger collective under "minimal group" conditions (for example, Tajfel and Turner 1985). Sharing the emotion should further enhance the impact of a sense of control on affective attachments and, in turn, the degree that affective attachments promote behavior in the group's welfare (see Collins 1981).

To summarize, the link between social structure, the choice process, and affective attachments to groups can be portrayed as follows. Social structures generate a balance of constraints and opportunities for actors engaged in means-ends deliberation; and the choice process fosters emotions that call for a commonsense explanation or understanding by actors. The commonsense understanding is likely to make group memberships more salient and lead actors to attribute to the group some degree of responsibility for the choice opportunity (or constraint) and therefore the generalized control (or lack thereof) sensed by individuals. The greater the perceived responsibility of the group for choice, the stronger the affective group attachments.

The second basic idea of the theory is that *positive emotion produced from choice processes strengthens affective attachments to a subgroup more than to the larger group it is nested in; whereas negative emotion weakens attachments to the larger group more than to the subgroup* (Lawler 1992). The theory distinguishes two rules by which actors can distribute responsibility for a generalized sense of control and related emotion—proximal and distal. The former allocates responsibility to the smaller, immediate group; the latter, to the larger, more encompassing group. The theory predicts a proximal rule for positive emotion and a distal rule for negative emotion. Thus, actors tend to give more credit to the local group or subgroup for choice and freedom (opportunity), and more blame to the larger group for little choice and freedom (constraints).

Subgroups are likely to receive more credit for choice and less blame for constraint because of an "interaction advantage." Subgroups are closer and more immediate, especially if these promote face-to-face interaction with friends, co-workers, or others with similar social backgrounds. Proximate groups or subgroups are fertile contexts for mutual sharing of emotional responses to choice processes and also for the development of common understandings about the sources and degree of individual control that, all things being equal, favor the local group or subgroup.

One important implication is that more decentralized systems should produce a greater difference in affective attachment to the subgroup vis-à-vis the larger group. In fact, the more decoupled the subgroup from the larger group, the greater the difference in affective attachment (Lawler 1992). This helps to explain why immigrants often become more attached to ethnic communities than the host nation, why academics often are more committed to their departments than their universities, why workers often are more committed to their union local than to the national organization, and why gang members are more committed to their gang than to the local community. In each of these examples, a subgroup is perceived as a prime source of opportunities, and the larger group as a prime source of constraint. In fact, within a highly decentralized organization or society, policies of the larger organization that empower members should generally strengthen affective attachments to subgroups more than to the larger groups or organizations because of the "interaction advantage" afforded the local subgroups.

The third basic idea of the theory is that *given recurrent choice situations, repeated affirmations of control or freedom increase the likelihood of actors adopting options that are in the group's welfare*. The theory conceptualizes actors as choosing among three metapreferences (Sen 1973, 1977): the subgroup's welfare, the larger group's welfare, and the individual's welfare. The choice process involves selecting a metapreference as well as an option within it, and the main prediction is that stronger affective attachments shift metapreferences from the individual to a group and, in particular, to that group providing actors the greatest sense of control—real or imagined.

I argue further that a choice process which repeatedly affirms actors' sense of group-mediated control and freedom is likely to become symbolic or emblematic of the relevant group's empowering force. The choice process then is a ritual expression of the group, and the process is used even when it is unnecessary, that is, when the outcome of the choice is obvious and is known in advance. Once a choice process becomes symbolic of the group itself, an orientation toward that group's welfare should be a taken-for-granted reality whenever the choice process is enacted or activated. In this way, choosing the group-welfare metapreference becomes a ritual, and means-ends deliberation is confined to the options subsumed by this metapreference.

The idea of "ritual behavior" is a fruitful way to understand the result of affective attachments producing a change in metapreference. Rituals are repetitive behaviors or interaction patterns that are expressive, symbolic, or emblematic of common group memberships (Wuthnow 1987; Collins 1981, 1989). People undertake ritual behavior singly or jointly simply because they are members of the group and because such behavior is part of the group's taken-for-granted reality. My theory indicates that social structures produce repetitive choice processes that repeatedly produce positive emotion; and under such conditions, the choice process may become symbolic of the group by virtue of the fact that it is likely to produce a common focus for actors, mutual awareness of the common focus, and public displays of positive feeling (see Collins 1981, 1989 on the theory of interaction ritual chains). A "revealed" group-welfare metapreference, therefore, can be construed as ritual behavior. Such ritual frames choice without eliminating it, because considerable choice still can occur within a given metapreference.

To conclude, the *choice process theory of affective attachments* indicates one way that freedom and constraint exist side by side and, in combination, produce and reproduce stronger affective attachments than otherwise would occur. Perceptions of choice or freedom stem from the range of options within a given taken-for-granted metapreference; constraint, in the lack of choice over the metapreference (Lawler 1992). If the choice process becomes symbolic or expressive of the group as such, adopting the subgroup metapreference becomes an everyday ritual (Collins 1981). This means less free riding, less costly systems of monitoring, and more voluntary compliance with group norms, all of which remain contingent on the continued provision of choice within the ritualized metapreference.[2]

Illustrations and Implications

The theory has implications for many issues of relevance to rational choice theory, and I illustrate several here. First, rational choices that induce perceptions of control and self-determination should take on intrinsic value and impact person-to-group ties. As an illustration, I use recent articles by Frey (1992a,b) on how changes in intrinsic motivation toward certain choices alters the impact of pricing and regulation mechanisms on economic behavior. The second implication concerns the difference between primary and secondary sectors of an economy or labor market. The common notion that employees in primary compared to secondary labor markets develop greater organizational commitments could be due partly to the range of choices and resulting sense of control fostered in primary sectors. This also can illuminate the similarities and differences between Hechter's (1987) theory of group solidarity and the choice process theory of affective attachments. The third implication is that instrumentally motivated exchanges by the same actors over time may yield a more expressive relation, maintained as an end in itself. Each illustration suggests a way that the theory of affective attachments complements and builds on rational choice ideas.

Choice and Intrinsic Motivation

Sen's (1973, 1977) view that the value of autonomy, self-determination, and freedom is an important omission in rational choice theory is echoed in recent work by Frey (1992a,b). Frey (1992a) criticizes "standard economics" for ignoring the fact that external instruments, such as pricing and regulation, can affect intrinsic motivation to engage in a line of economic behavior. Intrinsic motivation is motivation to do something for its own sake, meaning the act or choice has value in and of itself. Economic structures that strengthen intrinsic motivation for a given behavior will produce more of that behavior than otherwise, and economic structures that undermine intrinsic motivation will produce less of the behavior than economic models predict. Frey's (1992a) focus is two ba-

---

[2]Departures from the theoretical predictions are likely when affective attachments become so strong that the choice of metapreference and the choice within are one and the same thing. This may be the case in highly collectivistic cultures and in some cults where the experience of control is socially defined in collective rather than individual terms, and the choice is about how the group can control the external environment impinging on individuals. However, a similar result is likely to be produced by institutionalized patterns of behavior that become so routine and ritualized that actors no longer have to deal with the problems (for example, uncertainty) that gave rise to them in the first place. My theory focuses on less extreme circumstances where affective attachments are not already so strong.

sic dimensions of economic structure, pricing and regulation. Following Deci
(1975, 1980), he argues that these economic dimensions affect the intrinsic motivation for resulting economic behavior to the extent that they bear on actors'
sense of self-determination. Autonomy or the sense of self-determination is a
key determinant of instrinsic motivation.[3]

One of Frey's key predictions is that direct regulation of economic behavior
using punishments reduces actors' perceived self-determination more than price
incentives and therefore does more damage to the intrinsic motivation for the
"desired" behavior. A second major prediction is that price incentives damage
intrinsic motivation if these make actors feel the choice is clear-cut, meaning
that it is obvious and warrants little means-ends deliberation. That choices must
seem "real" to actors is an important notion reflected in key propositions of the
choice process theory (see Lawler 1992). If little means-ends deliberation is
necessary, actors will infer less control, freedom, or self-determination from a
choice.

My theory can take the ideas of Frey (1992a) a step further by suggesting that
pricing and regulation also should modify affective attachments to the relevant
group, organization, or society. Pricing and forms of regulation that create a
greater sense of choice, control, and self-determination ostensibly should produce
more affective attachments to those groups or subgroups perceived as responsible
for the choice opportunities. In other words, the conditions that Frey views as
producing more intrinsic motivation are also conditions that tend to foster
stronger affective attachments to the subgroup or larger group that constitutes the
context for economic choices. Affective attachments to a relevant subgroup (for
example, city, state, province, nation) will be enhanced more than the attachments
to the larger society as long as the proximal rule operates.[4] If pricing and regulation
repeatedly create choice situations and processes that actors interpret as evidence
of their self-determination, then these should not only come to have intrinsic
value but also become symbolic of the relevant group.

Applied to Frey's propositions, the choice process theory predicts that regulation will not harm intrinsic motivation if it is directed at the choice of the
group's metapreference rather than at the choice among options falling within
or framed by this metapreference—assuming, of course, that there is a sufficient
range of options within the metapreference. In addition, strong price incentives
designed to induce the group's metapreference (that is, behavior in the collective interest) should not have a negative impact on the intrinsic motivation for
choices within that metapreference, so long as the options within give actors a

[3] Frey (1992a,b) also includes positive self-evaluations as a second determinant of intrinsic motivation. Economic behavior that enhances both the perception of self-determination and positive self-
evaluations will have the greatest intrinsic value.

[4] While the theory predicts that, all things being equal, a proximal rule for positive emotion will
occur, distal rules emerge when collective rituals, symbols, and the like make the larger collective
more salient and more empowering than the local subgroup (see Lawler 1992 for more discussion).

sense of control and self-determination. This illustrates one way that, in combination, constraint directed at the choice of metapreference, and freedom directed at the choice among options within the desired metapreference, can generate, maintain, or strengthen affective attachments to groups.

Primary and Secondary Labor Markets

Akerlof's (1982, 1984) idea of gift exchange specifies that primary labor sectors provide workers more wages than necessary and, in the process, purchase more loyalty from them. This loyalty is based solely on instrumental conditions—the fact that wages are higher in the primary sector. There are no wage incentives for an actor to move to a firm in the secondary sector. Thus, firms in primary sectors are "compensatory groups," in Hechter's (1987) terms, because they attain solidarity by making workers more highly dependent on the organization, that is, by providing payoffs that are greater than alternatives.

From the standpoint of my choice process theory of affective attachments, however, primary labor markets may produce greater employee commitment to a firm, partly because of the emotional effects of having a wider range of options in organizations within the primary sector. Beyond wage and salary differences, primary sectors tend to provide workers more opportunities for advancement (internal labor markets), more autonomy on the job, and more control over their career paths. Greater "generalized" control over work and career should repeatedly arouse positive feelings on the job that are attributed to the relevant organization or firm. This is a plausible interpretation of the fact that firms in a primary sector produce more worker commitment than firms in a secondary sector (see also Lincoln and Kalleberg 1985).

An important part of my argument is that the choice to stay in a firm or move elsewhere has different implications than the choice among options about how to accomplish tasks within a given firm. The choice to stay or not reflects the dependence of the actor on the organization, whereas the choice about how to do a job or shape one's career reflects the degree of self-determination within a given organization. The choice process theory suggests that the emotional/affective consequences of choice internal to the firm can counteract the effects of little choice about whether to stay in the firm. This, once again, shows how constraint and freedom operate side by side. The high levels of solidarity in Japanese organizations, for example, should be based not just on the lack of choice to leave—that is, the dependence on the work organization—but also on the way in which the organizations generate a sense of group-mediated control over work through institutional mechanisms like quality circles.

Hechter's Theory of Group Solidarity

The constrast of choices to stay in the group with choices provided within the group bears on the relationship of my theory to Hechter's (1987) theory of group solidarity. In Hechter's theory, group solidarity is based on the dependence of actors on the organization or the lack of a viable choice to exit; whereas, in my theory, affective attachments are based on the degree of perceived choice and sense of control provided by the organization the actors are dependent on. These theories are complementary in most respects, particularly if one views the internal choice as an additional source of dependence on the organization. Combining the two theories, we find that group solidarity should be greatest and have a more emotional foundation when actors are *both* highly dependent on an organization for instrumental goods and the organization internally provides greater opportunity for choice.

Yet there are noteworthy differences. When high dependence is combined with high internal choice, my theory predicts more solidarity than Hechter's theory and also suggests that less developed mechanisms of monitoring are necessary. Monitoring is analogous to regulation in Frey's analysis; it reduces actors' sense of control. In "obligatory groups"—where members confront "collective obligations" affirmed and monitored by the group (Hechter 1987)—my theory indicates that these obligations will be met without monitoring, if the relevant choices have intrinsic value. This is most likely where the "collective obligations" exercise minimal constraint over choices among the options that all meet collective obligations in some way.

Choice processes with intrinsic value could conceivably be treated as "immanent goods" by Hechter's theory, that is, goods that are jointly produced for use rather than exchange. However, this seems to stretch the meaning of "immanent goods" in Hechter's theory (see Hechter 1987: 42–43), and it would remove from my theory the expressive, symbolic aspect of action on behalf of the group welfare. If intrinsic value is a type of emergent or immanent good, emotional processes are again subject to an instrumental interpretation, and the emotional is subsumed under the instrumental. Whether to take this approach or not is a question of metatheoretical directive or theoretical strategy. The divergent assumptions of rational and emotional perspectives on behavior, noted earlier, suggest different answers, and my theory is aligned more with emotional than rational approaches in this respect.

Commitment Formation in Exchange Networks

Emerson (1981) defined an "exchange relation" as a series of repeated exchanges among the same actors over time. Exchange relations are formed and maintained solely because of instrumental conditions—actors expect and receive more benefit from these relations than what is available elsewhere. However, exchange relations also tend to foster trust or interpersonal liking, and these perceptions or affective states form the basis for some sort of commitment among the actors (Cook and Emerson 1978; Emerson 1981; Cook and Emerson 1984; Tallman, Gray, and Leik 1991). The standard social exchange explanation ties commitment to the individual rewards from interacting with familiar and/or likable others.

Homans (1961), in his classic work, proposed that the mere frequency of exchange is sufficient to produce sentiment relations, that is, ones with a significant emotional component. He argued that the frequency of exchange should have this effect in particular where (1) actors have alternative others from whom they can receive individual rewards and (2) they expect lower benefits or rewards from these alternative others. Structural conditions such as these should produce repetitive exchange and "exchange relations," as defined by Emerson (1981), and establish the foundation for emotional/affective commitments.

Recent work by Lawler and associates (Lawler and Yoon 1993, 1994, 1996; Lawler, Yoon, Baker, and Large 1995) has taken up Homans' theme and argued essentially that exchange relations, though initially instrumental, become emotional or expressive ends in themselves if structural conditions produce repetitive exchange by the same actors. They examined the impact of equal power on repetitive negotiations of a dyad within an exchange network. The results of their experiments indicate that more equal power and greater mutual dependence produced more frequent exchange between the same two actors and, in turn, more commitment behavior in the form of token gift giving and a greater tendency to stay in the relation despite a profitable alternative relation, and more willingness to contribute to a new joint venture. Instrumental conditions account for the frequent exchange; but emotional/affective processes account for the link between frequent exchange and commitment behavior. Equal power produced more commitment behavior than unequal power *indirectly* via the positive emotion produced by repetitive exchange. Thus, rational choices to exchange with another had emotional effects that altered actors' exchange relation and made them willing to stay despite profitable alternatives and to do "extra things." The fact that emotional processes mediate these effects lends credence to the notion that an expressive relation is being formed from an instrumental base.

The theorizing of Lawler and Yoon (1996) argues that when positive emotion is produced in the context of accomplishing a joint task with another, of which exchange is one example, actors attribute their positive feelings to their relation or group. The *choice process theory of affective attachments* fleshes this out. A dyadic relation in a larger network can be construed as a nested subgroup, and thus, if exchange enhances actors' sense of control over uncertainty in the context, they will feel positive emotion and tend to view it as being caused by the relation (subgroup) rather than the larger group or network. Attributions for the emotion may be partly to the other person, forming the basis for interpersonal liking, or partly to self, but my point is that the relationship itself will be accorded some of the responsibility for the positive emotion; this generates "relational cohesion," that is, "the perception of the relation as a distinct, unifying object" (Lawler and

Yoon 1996: 94). The emotions then can be reproduced by reproducing the relationship. An important implication is that if structural power conditions produce different frequencies of exchange across dyads in a network, those dyads
that exchange more frequently should endogenously generate greater cohesion
and stronger affective commitments to their relation and, as a result, be less responsive to changes in the larger network (Lawler and Yoon 1993, 1996).

Conclusions

To conclude, my argument is that instrumentally based choice in the context
of ongoing groups produces expressive or emotional attachments to something
larger—relations, groups, organizations, or societies—that subsumes the individuals. This occurs to the extent that (1) choice processes give actors a sense of
control, (2) the sense of control makes them feel good or elated, and (3) those
feelings are attributed to particular relations or groups. The emotion essentially
makes group members more aware of their collective experience and common
membership, more inclined to treat relevant groups as distinct social objects of
attachment, and more willing to affirm and symbolize these attachments through
action on behalf of one or more group's welfare.

The *choice process theory of affective attachments* shows when and how affective
attachments to groups strengthen (or weaken) group attachments and produce
preference shifts toward the group or collective interest. One implication for
rational choice theory is that actors will make inferences about their own control
from rational choice *processes*, aside from the results of their choices, and these
will produce feelings about the groups that structure and frame their choice
opportunities. These emotional processes can be construed as a by-product of
rational choice, with inadvertent effects on how people perceive and evaluate
their tie to multiple, nested groups in which their action takes place. The "con-
sequentialism" of rational choice theory diverts attention from these potentially
important emotional by-products of perceptions of autonomy, freedom, and
self-determination (Sen and Williams 1982).

There are several ways for the *choice process theory of affective attachments* to be
developed further. One is to deal with the question of whether and when the
theory applies to circumstances where affective attachments have become so
strong that there is really no choice left—either between or within metapreferences. The sense of control may remain important even in this context, but
individual control is no longer "group-mediated"; it is "group encapsulated"
because actors don't make any distinction between their individual control and
that of the group or collectivity. Some principles of the theory should still
apply—for example, "group-encapsulated" control should have the same consequences for individual emotion and for affective attachments to the empowering group. However, the duality of freedom and constraint at the heart of the
theory is no longer relevant in these contexts.

A second direction for development is to take account of the fact that a sense of control is likely to be associated with positive self-evaluations. Frey (1992a,b) treats positive self-evaluations as a second condition for economic behavior to be intrinsically motivated. If groups that foster a sense of control are also a source of positive self-evaluations, only a modest theoretical step is necessary to propose that such groups also constitute and shape persons' most salient and central identities (Stryker 1980). The theory could incorporate symbolic interactionist ideas about the impact of self-efficacy on self-esteem (Gecas 1986) and the role of identity salience in forming and maintaining identity commitments (Stryker 1980). Groups that produce the greatest sense of control and the strongest affective attachments are also likely to be the source of highly valued identities for actors.

Endorsement as Nonlegitimate Domination: An Application of Experimental Research to Historical Settings

Richard Bell

This paper applies the notion of endorsement as developed in the experimental research of Walker, Thomas, and Zelditch (1986) to Weber's historical comparative sociology of the city. I theoretically ground Weber's construct "nonlegitimate domination" more completely than is found in the original formulation by introducing Walker and associates' "endorsement principle." Their principle broadens the concept of legitimacy to include phenomena that do not entail an affirmative commitment to a given regime.

Legitimacy as Positive Belief

Until Dornbusch and Scott (1975), sociologists held that legitimacy referred to a consensus on substantive values (Lukes 1978: 634). Parsons (1968 [1937]: 659) elaborated this point with a distinction between "disinterested" and "interested" motives for obedience. Parsons asserts that legitimacy as a disinterested motivation refers to a "valuation of a thing for its own sake or as a direct expression or embodiment of an ultimate value" (ibid.: 660). This disinterested acceptance constitutes "normative constraint." Parsons's second category of motivation refers to the idea that a legitimate order is perceived to have objective validity, that is, constraining situations within which actors carry out their projects. "Thus a communist who personally does not believe in free speech may invoke the right to free speech in court to keep himself out of jail and thus further his own cause. Such a right is part of the legitimate order of present society, which he uses as a means to his own ends" (ibid.: 659).

In this formulation, a fully developed legitimate order has two motivational components. A legitimate order is viewed both as a structural element of the situation of action and as an expression of inherent values. Parsons clearly assigns greater priority to the latter component. "While interest may be a very important reason for conforming to an order, it has nothing to do with ascribing legitimacy—or illegitimacy—to it. Here only the disinterested motive elements have a place" (Parsons 1968 [1937]: 659).

This very positive and normative construction of legitimacy finds ample expression in Easton's (1965) discussion of legitimation processes as inputs for any sustained political order. Weil (1989: 683–84) states that Easton's distinction between diffuse system support and specific evaluation is probably "the most influential typology of political support in the Western democracies. . . . Most other typologies in the literature tap the same dimension." According to Easton, legitimacy operates on two levels. The first level reflects degrees of satisfaction with specific governing institutions and their policies or "outputs." The second level reflects a general satisfaction with the entire political system of which specific institutions form the various subsystems. Diffuse system support coupled with specific evaluations of state outputs constitutes political support or legitimacy (Easton 1965: 195–201).

According to Easton (1965: 273), real legitimizing support derives from those diffuse or generalized sentiments of rightness and ultimate value that must inform a compliant citizenry. As a consequence, the entire governing system is undergirded by emotionally charged beliefs which permit the possibility of delayed gratification in the face of frustration due to periodic defeat. In Parsonian terms, legitimacy rests on motives of disinterestedness. Weil (1989: 686) succinctly captures this view: legitimation is "a positive evaluation of the way the political realm is structured and political actors interact, even if one is not happy about outcomes. That is, citizens feel that the rules of the game and the conduct of the players are fair, even if their side does not win." Every long-term political order is presumed to enjoin the capacity for delayed gratification or the political order would not be long-term. This capacity is, in turn, made possible with the inculcation of positive beliefs (Easton 1965: 273).

This is what is meant by diffuse or "unconditioned" attachment to "political objects" (interestingly, the terms "diffuse" and "unconditioned" are used almost interchangeably). Unconditioned attachment not only permits toleration in the face of system failure to deliver outputs but also permits members to accept or at least tolerate outputs which damage their interests. Without this reservoir of good will, regimes would be unable to weather "the many storms when outputs cannot be balanced against inputs of demands" (Easton 1965: 273).

These representative statements reveal a central tendency and, I would argue, a central weakness in the conventional social science view of legitimacy, namely, the inclination to overlegitimize the dominant compliance structures of societies. The emphasis on values and beliefs as the basis of legitimacy implicates the members of the subject population in the compliance structures at the deepest levels of their allegiance. The argument is that such structures could not have persisted otherwise.

A more fruitful conceptualization of legitimation would be one that does not inadvertently ratify any given social order that happens to be stable by resting more or less exclusively on some claim of normative integration. Such a strategy can be found in the work of Dornbusch and Scott (1975), which I now consider.

The Dornbusch-Scott Theory of Legitimacy and the Problem of Endorsement

Legitimacy as Validity in Weber

Dornbusch and Scott's discussion employs Weber's notion of legitimacy. Weber (1968 [1918]: 53) distinguishes between domination and legitimacy where domination refers to "the probability that a command with a given specific content will be obeyed by a given group of persons." Elsewhere, Weber (ibid.: 948) states: "As far as sociology is concerned, power of command does not exist unless the authority which is claimed by somebody is actually heeded to a socially relevant degree." Legitimation, on the other hand, is tied directly to the concept of "validity," where validity refers to an orientation toward an order or command that entails a mixture of self-interest and disinterestedness. Weber (ibid.: 31) cites as an example the conduct of a civil servant. When the civil servant appears at the appropriate time in the appropriate office, he does so not merely at the behest of his self-interest but in conformance with a set of "maxims" that are regarded as being, in some fashion, obligatory. Weber does point out that his civil servant understands that disobedience would be "disadvantageous" to him as well as "abhorrent to his sense of duty." Walker, Rogers, Thomas, and Zelditch (1991: 6) summarize the Weberian concept of validity in the following manner: "The extent to which an actor knows that action will be defined, interpreted, and guided by an objective order is referred to as *validity*."

Weber (1968, [1918]: 212–14) suggests that, regardless of the historical forms legitimacy may assume, that is, traditional, charismatic, or rational-legal, they all possess the common characteristic of being perceived as imperative in nature. That is, any given command is regarded as valid "without reference to the actor's own attitude toward the value of the content of the command as such." Also, legitimacy "confirms the position of persons claiming authority and, secondly, it helps to determine the choice of the means of its exercise."

The Dimensions of Legitimacy

Dornbusch and Scott (1975: 38) stress the distinction between "validity" and "propriety." Validity is the acknowledgment of the objective nature of the normative order and an agreement that it presently operates as a standard of judgment in which sanctions are applied to those who violate that order. Propriety refers to the actual perceptions of goodness and fairness with respect to the rules (ibid.: 39–40). This distinction echoes Parsons's types of motivation orientation:

Parsons's "interested" motivations correspond to validity, and his "disinterested" motivations correspond to propriety.

Zelditch and Walker (1984: 5–6) express the distinction between validity and propriety as parallel to that between "is" and "ought." "If p knows that, whatever his/her own views, the structure will work in a certain way and that this will be supported by the conduct of other agents of authority, then the structure is valid. If p does not personally believe that that is the way it should be, then it is not proper." Weber's civil servant may feel that conformance to a valid structure regardless of the propriety of outcomes is exemplary, yet such a feeling state is not required for validity.

Weber placed primary emphasis on validity, though conventional sociology, as exemplified in the work of Parsons and Easton, emphasized propriety as the best legitimation. Interested motivations and validity, although they receive honorable mention, are not given central recognition in the conventional account. Rather, this account constitutes an extensive formulation and reformulation of legitimation as propriety.

Dornbusch and Scott (1975: 41) introduce a further distinction between authorized and endorsed power. "We will say that A's power over B is *authorized* to the extent that beliefs held by groups superior to A legitimate A's power over B; and we will say that beliefs held by B's colleagues who are also subject to A's power legitimate A's control over B. These two dimensions are conceptually independent in that authorized power may or may not be endorsed and endorsed power may or may not be authorized."

They (1975: 42) point out that the "second set of distinctions refers to the source of norms supporting the power relation." Authorizing norms or collegial norms must be present to transform power relationships into authority relationships, "persons either superior or subordinate to the power-wielder must initiate and enforce norms regulating the exercise of power if we are to speak of authority." This conception is in line with the received view which defines authority as "legitimate power" (ibid.: 38).

In the study of formal and complex organizations, sociologists tend to define power as legitimate if norms held by subordinate groups endorse the power-wielder's exercise of power (Dornbusch and Scott 1975: 44–45). This, the authors contend, is one-sided because it ignores the very important problem of authorized power. "Our view of legitimate power suggests that the norms operate in two directions: to constrain and support the behavior of those who are subject to the power; and to constrain and support the exercise of power by the power-wielder. Little attention has been directed to the latter, although we believe that it is the more significant consequence of the operation of authority norms."[1]

[1] A related point is made by Eckstein and Gurr (1975: 227), who write, "To medieval men liberty meant not so much the absence of directives as freedom from the arbitrary will of the rulers. The

As we shall see with respect to medieval cities, commands may be issued by individuals who are unauthorized by any superordinate group. The nature of the commands may, at the same time, be perceived to be lacking in propriety as well in an imperative objectivity. Yet the commands themselves enjoy a type of endorsement. From a Weberian perspective, which defines legitimation in terms of validity, such a system of domination would be nonlegitimate.

Elaborations on the Dornbusch-Scott Theory

Zelditch and Walker (1984) extend the Dornbusch-Scott theory beyond its original application to include polities that are other than trilevel and monocratic. They also incorporate experimental research on compliance and "pressures to change an authority structure" into a modified Dornbusch-Scott framework.

Interestingly, their review of the experimental literature concludes that, among other things,

validity is both necessary and sufficient to produce most of the effects usually attributed to legitimacy. A closer study of the collective legitimation of authority further qualifies and narrows the significance of individual-level propriety. It proves to be neither necessary nor, often, sufficient to produce many of the effects usually attributed to legitimacy. This leads us to conclude that legitimacy is a fundamentally collective process and seldom a question of private individual consent. (Zelditch and Walker 1984: 3–4)

Elsewhere, the authors (ibid.: 9) state that "the fundamental assumption of any theory of authority, that the propriety of a (valid) authority structure increases voluntary, unreflective compliance, has never been conclusively demonstrated." By contrast: "The legitimacy of acts has consistently had a clear effect on propriety, which in turn has had a consistent effect on compliance" (ibid.: 11). Furthermore, in one experiment it was found that the subjects "made judgments about the value of centralized networks that were consistent with their past (compliant or noncompliant) behavior rather than making their behavior consistent with prior judgment" (ibid.: 13).

The conventional account of legitimacy reduces to a version of individual-level propriety in that the social actor complies on the basis of whether the authority claim is congruent with the positive, moral beliefs of the social actor. As Zelditch and Walker point out, most theories of legitimacy agree with such an account. This does not mean, however, that accounts based ultimately on propriety are irrelevant. Zelditch and Walker (1984: 13) summarize the situation in the following manner: "In the present limited state of our knowledge, the conclusion to draw from the investigations reviewed so far is that total compliance

---

notion had less to do with the absence of constraints on subordinates than with the presence of constraints on superordinates. 'Tyranny' is the quintessence of illegitimacy as arbitrary authority."

is correlated with authority: impropriety significantly weakens this correlation; but propriety does not suffice to explain all of the effects attributed to it by most theories of legitimacy."

The authors depart from this theoretic tradition to that of Weber by shifting focus from legitimacy as propriety to legitimacy as validity. Specifically, Thomas, Walker, and Zelditch (1986) investigate the direct effect of validity on action, that is, the effect of "everyday use of rules within the given institutional contexts" on pressures for change. An institution is conceptualized as a set of rule-governed actions in which the rules are more than regulatory but actually constitutive of meaning. "Thus, a collective moral order does not presuppose 'consensus' or uniformity of individual belief; it does presuppose that there is a known institutionalized order within the collective. . . . Action is not legitimated by being grounded in disembodied abstract societal values or in the presupposed intentions of socialized members. Rather, it is grounded in specific situated rules" (Thomas, Walker, Zelditch 1986: 380).

Their research requires that the influence of validity be specified as distinct from that of propriety. They construct an experimental communication network and a corresponding reward structure that produces results which are manifestly inequitable. Subjects could mobilize others to make outcomes more equitable. In the baseline condition, the employment of these procedures is not designated as obstructing the experiment. In the "legitimation situation," such mobilizing action is presented as violating the core purpose of the experiment, by violating the actual constitutive rule of action that makes up the communication network.

They find that there is a structural bias inherent in validity itself. Mobilizing action is significantly reduced even though the reward structure and the allocation of rewards are clearly improper by any fundamental standard of fairness. "Even though maintaining the communication structure perpetuates inequality and even though it works against the material interest of the S's, they do not attempt to change the structure nearly as much when the structure is legitimated and change is delegitimated" (Thomas, Walker, and Zelditch 1986: 389).

Subsequent research (Walker, Rogers, and Zelditch 1988) suggests that validity does not necessarily or always operate in spite of propriety in instances of structured inequality. Validity can and does reinforce propriety by ratifying an inequitable outcome. Validity, however, remains the principal factor operating directly on propriety. Later research (Walker, Rogers, Thomas, and Zelditch 1991: 15–19) shows how validity reduces the likelihood of inequitable task arrangements being perceived as inequitable and reduces the "rate of protest against it" by "delegitimizing" particular forms of protest. Also, "validity seems to reinforce propriety and to provide a buffer against the effects of factors which might normally lead to a decline in the level of propriety."

Rules that are perceived as binding, that is, having validity, are not only regulatory but constitutive of meaning (Thomas, Walker, and Zelditch 1986: 380), and as such they can be activated without the direct, forceful intervention of elites (Walker, Rogers, Thomas, and Zelditch 1991: 5). Validity, as social control, also relieves elites of the need to continuously exact compliance in routine settings.

This conception of legitimacy as validity applies to situations of relative stability where rules are highly articulated. Does this conception apply to situations of comparative flux in which there is no stable allocation of rewards? I argue that the theory does apply but in terms of endorsement rather than validity.

The Principle of Endorsement

Walker, Thomas, and Zelditch (1986: 622) point to endorsement as expressive of the "collective aspect" of legitimacy in which the peers of the focal actor provide the source of legitimation. They conduct an experiment to determine if endorsement is a stabilizing influence on compliance systems, although it is not the only source of legitimacy. Their experiment selected a system of positions as the object of legitimacy (as opposed to actors, actions, or rules) and induced the false perception among the subjects that the system was endorsed by their peers. The control group was provided with no such information. "Our principal hypothesis suggests that endorsement of a system of positions will counteract pressure to change the system. . . . We argue that endorsement will inhibit attempts to alter the task structure by reducing the proportion of subjects who make such attempts or by causing them to delay taking action" (Walker, Thomas, and Zelditch 1986: 632). The results were, in a sense, counterintuitive, but they were also in the postulated direction: "The ratios indicate that for subjects in the endorsed condition there is less change observed than expected and conversely more change than was expected in the unendorsed condition" (ibid.: 633).

The authors suggest that endorsement is time dependent. Given a badly imbalanced task structure coupled with a correspondingly biased distribution of rewards, the pressure to refrain from initiating mobilizing action to alter the task structure in an equitable direction increases with each successive trial. "After completing a few trials, the subject may begin to attribute endorsement, that is, support of the task structure to co-workers. Hence, given the endorsement principle, the longer persons work under the task conditions the more reluctant they should be to change the task structure" (Walker, Thomas, and Zelditch 1986: 632).

The actor may refrain from any "change-initiating or noncompliant actions" because persistent compliance among co-workers leads the actor to assume that innovation will be met with disapproval, "and as a consequence the number of change-responses is reduced because actors find it inexpedient to make them."

Alternatively, however, "increased endorsement may simply reduce the expected probability of success for any change strategy which relies on collective action, hence making any attempt to induce change appear futile" (Walker, Thomas, and Zelditch 1986: 633).

The Weberian concept of validity as a dimension of legitimacy is most applicable to comparatively stable domination systems because the rules involved require a persistent degree of articulation. Endorsement, however, as a dimension of legitimation does not seem to carry this limitation. As a consequence, the Dornbusch-Scott framework is potentially applicable to conditions of relative instability.

For this reason and because we have been dealing with an elaboration of a fundamentally Weberian concept of legitimacy, we consider Weber's own discussion of legitimacy and destabilization. We examine Weber's historical/comparative account of the premodern city. As Roth (1968) points out, here Weber presents his own theory of revolution "in the guise of usurpation and non-legitimate domination." In the course of Weber's discussion, special problems concerning legitimacy emerge, including the issue of endorsement as a mode of legitimation of domination in revolutionary circumstances.

City-Revolts and Legitimation as Endorsement in Weber's Urban Sociology

The growth of urban culture in the medieval Occident eventuated in a legitimacy crisis for the feudal order. The validity of this system of superordination with its array of privileges and fixed statuses was not sustainable within the confines of the urban setting (Chirot 1985: 185–86). For reasons of sheer spatial ecology, among other things, the trappings of power so suitable for domination in the countryside with its physical distances came under corrosive inspection within the crowded confines of the medieval city's walls (Weber 1968 [1918]: 1307).

The reemergence of cities during the High Middle Ages served to dissolve manorial ties (Abu-Lughod 1991: 40–41). Persistent social contradictions were embedded in the very structure of the urban constitution. Authoritative resolution could only occur by stepping outside the legitimating context of manorial feudalism because that very context had become a source of intolerable conflict.

Consequently, the resulting mode of domination lacked validity, and the emerging officialdom received little or no authorizing ratification or jurisdictional restraint from a set of established superordinates, which could be found only within manorial patrimony or in the Church hierarchy. Both were consistently hostile to the interests of medieval towns (Chirot 1985: 183). Because Weber regarded validity as the core characteristic of legitimacy, he termed this urban administrative officialdom as "nonlegitimate domination" (Weber 1968: 1302). Yet these cities carried out the functions deemed essential for municipal life, such as levying taxes and conducting war.

I contend that though urban administration lacked validity and lacked authorization from superordinates outside this "state within the state" (Weber 1968: 1303, 1318), it did not lack endorsement. Endorsement functioned for the new urban administration much like validity (Walker, Thomas, and Zelditch 1986: 632–33). I also argue, in the case of the medieval city, much of the endorsement was of the negative type—that is, disapproval of peers was assumed to follow innovation, and thus actors found change responses inexpedient.

Endorsement and the Problem of Validity in the Medieval City

The city, for Weber, is a political and administrative locality. "The very fact that in these observations we had to employ categories such as 'urban economic policy,' 'urban territory,' and 'urban authority' indicates that the concept of the 'city' can and must also be analyzed in terms of a series of categories other than the purely economic ones hitherto discussed, namely, in terms of political categories" (Weber 1968: 1220).[2]

According to Weber (1968: 1227), the historical cities of the Occident possessed either partial or full "autocephaly," that is, their own judicial and administrative agencies. These agencies were founded upon two sets of urban associations: burghers in one association, and guilds and crafts in the other (ibid.: 1227). These combined to form an "associational structure," which constituted an arrangement of mutual endorsement. Weber (ibid.: 1229) characterized this arrangement as "cross-fraternal." These "urban fraternal associations" in turn composed the "city communes." Elsewhere, Weber (ibid.: 1248) described the medieval city of the Occident as a "sworn confraternity."

Thus Weber viewed the historical cities of the West as small states, having most of the authoritative characteristics of the state. Weber (1968: 1221) describes the historical city as a "special kind of a *fortress* and a *garrison*." Of particular interest, however, is Weber's (ibid.: 1250) assertion that these medieval cities were nonlegitimate; an actual working system of domination was in place, but it had no validity.

Weber takes issue with those city theorists who embrace a largely "juridical" approach toward the development of the city as a system of political and economic governance. The corporations of the burghers and their authorized officials had "legitimate" origins in privileges granted by manorial powers. However, these privileges were either real or fictitious, and when they were real they were granted only occasionally. Weber (1968: 1250) states that "it is true

---

[2] As Walton (1986: 227) points out, Weber's political view of the city is more realistic than the naturalistic or ecological view which dominated urban sociology in the United States. "Cities do not simply well up on the land. They are created by groups with political and economic goals."

that to some extent the actual process corresponded to this formal pattern. But quite often, and especially in the most important cases, the real origin is to be found in what is from a formal legal point of view a revolutionary usurpation of rights."

There were four dimensions to this revolutionary usurpation, which rendered the urban communes nonlegitimate within the feudal context:

1. Urban real estate became alienable, that is, unencumbered with feudal obligations, while peasant land was always restricted in "multiple ways" by rights reserved to the village or the patrician manor or both (Weber 1968: 1237).

2. The possibility existed for serfs to purchase their freedom through the exploitation by feudal lords of serfs in the city as sources of annuities. The Occidental city became the situs in which the serf gained ascent from bondage to freedom by means of economic acquisition (Palen 1987: 43). "This entailed a considerable stimulus for intense economic effort" (Weber 1968: 1238).

3. Once a serf became prosperous, it was not uncommon for the feudal lord to requisition him for house and stable service, often for the purpose of extracting a ransom. "The urban citizenry therefore usurped the right to dissolve the bonds of seigneurial domination; this was the great—in fact, the revolutionary— innovation which differentiated the medieval Occidental cities from all others" (Weber 1968: 1239).

4. Many of the burgher associations were usurpative from their very inception. Weber (1968: 1250) distinguishes two modes by which the burgher associations were formed. One was "spontaneous," and the other was "derived." The former was clearly a revolutionary usurpation "in defiance of the 'legitimate' powers." Weber cites the "bigger and older cities" of Genoa and Cologne as examples. A derived association possessed a quasi-legal cast in which a grant of autonomy was "issued by the city founder or his successor."

In the case of the revolutionary or spontaneous associations, legitimating fabrications were subsequently generated, thus leading astray the more legalistically oriented city theorists. "In the documentary sources of urban history, which by their nature overemphasize the continuity of legitimacy, such usurpatory confraternizations are as a rule not mentioned at all. . . . As a result, the frequency of the 'derived' origin is almost certainly overrepresented in the sources" (Weber 1968: 1250).

In actuality the typical sequence of events ran roughly as follows: first, the founder of the city was the manorial city lord. The forerunner of the city fortress was the seigneurial castle. Within the fortress resided the lord, his family, his servants, and his warriors. The burghers resided just outside the fortress walls and owed specific military duties to the military lord of the city (Weber 1968: 1251). Second, the burghers formed associations of mutual protection. The city lord was the obvious opponent of these associations and persistently raised issues of legitimacy. One issue of particular concern was whether the membership had sworn an oath of obedience to the lord. "It was, after all, in such things that usurpatory innovations would find their formal expression" (ibid.).

Third, the stratum of burghers which acted as the "driving power behind such acts of usurpation" was "from the point of view of legitimacy" nothing more than "a private club of wealthy citizens." This "guild of the rich" successfully assumed the right to grant citizenship. This right "was legally quite independent from membership in this club. . . . The majority of the larger French cities obtained their urban constitutions in a similar way through acts of sworn confraternization of the burghers" (Weber 1968: 1251).

Fourth, the revolutionary usurpations and legal innovations of these guilds were largely a response to the "peculiar anarchy" which prevailed prior to their assumption of power. The city became a situs for numerous overlapping and conflicting authority claims; all of them were "standing side by side" (Weber 1968: 1251). Apart from the confraternities or the private clubs, these included episcopal powers, political offices based on chartered privileges, and, of course, the city lord. The lord was also quite often the local bishop and, by virtue of his office, combined the "secular and religious instruments of power." The city lord, as the very embodiment of manorial legitimacy, "stood the best chance of imposing effective rulership" among all the competing powers.

Nonetheless, the confraternities were successful in their opposition to the city lord because they were able to accomplish two crucial objectives: the monopolization of the economic opportunities offered by the city (only members of the sworn associations were permitted to engage in commerce in the city) and the transformation of the confraternities into a military organization "for the purpose of expanding the political and economic power sphere of the commune against the outside." This resulted, particularly in the case of Italy, in wars of the city-communes against each other. Within the cities, the sworn associations became the chief means by which internal disputes were settled peaceably, thus displacing a core function of the manorial system (Weber 1968: 1253, 1262).

This, in outline, is Weber's depiction of the medieval Occidental city and the early development of the medieval urban constitution. Of special relevance to the problem of legitimation is the portrayal of an entire economic, political, judicial, and administrative arrangement possessing, at best, a quasi-legal authority as a kind of adornment. It is ironic that Weber's account challenges the view that a successful legitimacy claim requires an already established validating referent. This view is expressed by Griswold (1983: 677–78) in the following manner: "In order for a system of meaning to have the leverage to legitimate action, it must be, or appear to be, external to the system of action. . . . Cultural texts appear in many institutional settings (the Magna Charta, the Constitution) which are primordial, attended by myth, and whose socially celebrated origins are not regarded as simply emanating from interest. Such texts become the sources and criteria of legitimacy."

This doubtless captures the motives underlying the efforts on the part of those city theorists who have emphasized continuity and the presumed derivative nature of urban constitutions. However, those efforts did not materialize until well after the fact of the city-communes themselves. These communes functioned as fully developed administrative and military units long before they received their validating rationale.

In the case of medieval cities, it was endorsement that served as the source of textual validity. The medieval city in Europe was an autonomous judicial entity. It was not a transient political system, yet it possessed no legitimating referent beyond the relationships which obtained among the participating actors. The legitimating element for the sworn confraternaties was the confraternaties themselves. The legitimacy in question was initially derived from the mutual endorsement which constituted the burgher associations of the city-communes.

This legitimacy was largely expediential. It was contingent on the economic prosperity of a collection of freemen in a politically inhospitable world and on the physical survival offered by the associations. It was only after medieval towns had become a force to be reckoned with, as well as a source of financial support for the emerging monarchies in their unending disputes with the local nobility, that their position became formally regularized as a part of the western European political structure called the *Standestaat*, or "state of estates" (Chirot 1985: 185).

It should be noted that cities presented problems of legitimacy and control even to the monarchies. Tilly (1990: 55) has observed that "kings generally sought to limit the independent armed force at the disposition of townsmen, for the very good reason that townsmen were quite likely to use force in their own interest, including resistance to royal demands."

Weber characterized the political system of the premodern city as nonlegitimate domination. It could more accurately be characterized as nonvalidated domination, in the sense of being predicated more or less exclusively on the principle of endorsement. This particular mode of legitimation was suited to the fundamentally revolutionary nature of the political organization in question.

At first the noble and patrician families who initially made up the rich guilds and founded the burgher associations in the interest of protecting their own landed properties "would administer an oath to all inhabitants qualified by ownership; those who did not agree to take it were forced into exile" (Weber 1968: 1253). However, this did not continue. Toward the end of the eleventh century, annually elected "consuls" appeared. These consuls were to be elected by the burghers. In practice, they "were merely certified by acclamation. . . . The consuls, salaried and entitled to take fees, completed the revolutionary usurpation by seizing all or the major part of judicial powers and the supreme command in wartime; they administered all affairs of the commune" (ibid.). They razed the imperial, episcopal, and seigneurial castles within the city, and they established the principle that no castles could be built within a specified area around the city and that neither the emperor nor the city lord had the right to be quartered within the city walls. These objectives were attained by the consuls through force, extortion, or purchase (ibid.: 1253–54).

These urban revolutions clearly had a rationalizing impact on the sphere of law. Trial procedures were created which eliminated "irrational" means of evidence gathering. The duel as a legal test was barred, for example. The practice of bringing burghers before nonurban courts was prohibited, and "special rational law" to be codified by the consuls and applied by the courts was instituted. "Formally, the new urban law signified the extinction of the old personality principle of the law. Substantively, it meant the destruction of the feudal associations and of patrimonialism, but not yet in favor of the principle of general compulsory membership for all inhabiting a given territory" (Weber 1968: 1254).

The urban associations, consisting as they did of a set of utilitarian alliances unhampered by the normative constraints of externally validating criteria, could thus more readily serve as a vehicle for abrupt rationalization. In French cities, the urban communes originated in revolutionary usurpations through an alliance of burghers, merchants, and urban rentiers who often united with guilds of artisans in order to seize political power. This was the typical pattern in northern Europe. In the south, these same groups would form alliances with resident knights, also for the purpose of seizing power (Weber 1968: 1256).

There are two important aspects to the problem of endorsement that apply to this historical setting. The first aspect, which was discussed above, refers to the *source* of legitimation. The second aspect, which relates to the experimental research dealing with endorsement as a stabilizing influence, refers to the condition in which officials exercise authoritative command while lacking propriety. It is to this that we now turn.

Endorsement and the Problem of "Official Tyranny"
in the Premodern City

The urban tyrannies of the traditional Occident were the product of civil strife. This strife was due to structural contradictions in the urban constitution. On one hand, there was the dissolution of clan-based and sib-based status closures, and on the other, there was the creation of a new status association of financially prominent and leisured "notables" or honoratiores (Weber 1968: 290, 1267). This latter group constituted the urban landholding class or the urban patriciate, which asserted itself after the first revolutionary period in which the communes were established.

These urbanized and self-consciously gentrified families forming the new patriciate were able to effectively monopolize the council seats and exclude from administration the middle class, whose self-esteem was expanding with its growing wealth and education (Weber 1968: 1281, 1292). This prepared the way for the second wave of city-revolts, the "craft revolutions." These revolts, according to Weber (ibid.: 1282), constituted a genuine bourgeois seizure of power. General bourgeois participation in municipal administration was more or less equated with craft rule. Also, craft rule coincided with the "peak" of the city's external power and political independence.

Italian cities best illustrate the manner in which the rule of the urban patriciate was broken (Weber 1968: 1301). A central role was played by the *popolo*, a type of craft guild composed of both craft workers and entrepreneurs. "In the struggle against the knightly families the entrepreneurs initially played the leading role; they instigated and financed the sworn confraternity of the 'crafts' whereas the artisan guilds provided the necessary manpower for battle" (ibid.).

The Italian *popolo* was directly and simultaneously an economic and a political entity. "It was a separate political community within the urban commune with its own finances, and its own military organization. In the truest sense of the word, it was a 'state within the state'—the first deliberately nonlegitimate and revolutionary association" (Weber 1968: 1302). More than anywhere else this occurred in Italy, where the knightly families, as the embodiments of feudalism, settled in the cities for commercial reasons. The association of the *popolo*, which directly confronted these knightly families, stood outside the legitimating framework, not only of manorialism, but of the initial urban constitution as well.

One key distinction between the burgher confraternities associated with the first wave of city-revolts and the political communities, such as the *popolo*, associated with the second wave is the degree of self-consciousness on the part of the latter with respect to their nonlegitimate status. There was a strong interest on the part of the original urban confraternities in promoting a mythological city history in order to make usurpation appear as a grant from some manorial city founder. These confraternities were in origin and in practice nonlegitimate except through the process of peer endorsement by which policies and leaders were ratified. Endorsement functioned in place of validity and did so effectively.

However, the authority of command exercised by the communal leadership was not thought to actually reside in its failure to possess an external source of validity or in its failure to possess the sanction of authorizing superiors. This ceased to be the case after the second wave of urban revolts, which dismantled or attempted to dismantle the "patrician city." The *very lack* of validity and authorization was employed as a means of reinforcing the legitimating endorsement of the "state within the state," thus adding to its revolutionary character.

The association of the *popolo* established an annually elected office, *capitano del popolo*, which was invested with extraordinary powers. Most of these powers were avowedly usurpative. This official was paid a salary and provided with both a militia and a personal staff. He resided in a special "house of the people" with a tower that was the "fortress of the people" (Weber 1968: 1303).

The financial administration was carried out by representatives of the craft guilds. They were elected for short terms and claimed "the right to protect the *popoloni* in the courts, to contest decisions of the authorities of the commune [the older gentrified confraternity, which attempted to rule alongside the *popolo*], to address proposals to them, and often [had] a direct role in legislation" (Weber 1968: 1303). The *popolo* subsequently developed into a full-blown system of domination complete with its own statutes and its own tax structure.

The compliance exacted by this system was derived in no small part by the ever-present threat of banishment. Communal finances benefited directly from the administration of properties formerly owned by banished citizens. Little or no pretense was made with respect to propriety in terms of any given criterion of fairness. The *popoloni* granted to themselves special privileges of trial procedures, particularly with regard to rules of evidence. "The official judicial system with an official spying network, abetment of anonymous accusations, an accelerated inquisitorial procedure for magnates, and much simplified methods of proof (by 'notoriety') was the democratic counterpart to the Venetian trial before the Council of Ten" (Weber 1968: 1304). The penalties against the nobility were often of a redistributionist character—confiscations, penalties levied on the accused's entire family, prohibitions against the patricians on the purchase of real estate, and so forth (ibid.).

The first wave of urban revolutions in the eleventh century had a rationalizing effect in the field of law. By the time we reach the era of the *popolo*, this cannot be said. The legal innovations are directed exclusively along expropriative lines. Once more, it should be noted that Weber nowhere suggests that the *capitano del popolo* was in the least charismatic in the sense of possessing a discipleship. In other words, the second wave of city-revolts did not seem to have either of the two mutually exclusive dimensions Weber assigned to revolutions in general. They were neither rationalizing, nor were they charismatic. Rather, they constituted revolutionary seizures of power which derived their legitimacy almost solely from endorsement, certainly not from authorization, propriety, or validity.

There were several key groups that functioned in an atmosphere of practically continuous tension and "collision." First in importance, perhaps, were the associations of the *popolo grasso*, or "fat people." These made up the seven upper guilds and as such constituted the wealthy bourgeoisie. After a series of insurrections, the fourteen lower guilds were able to gain a formal share in the power of municipal government. The artisan strata obtained a share of government only after revolt in the late fourteenth century. Occasionally, the petty burghers sought to exclude not only the nobility but the wealthy bourgeoisie from the municipal councils.

In general, the nobility managed to occupy offices in the *popolo*. However, their admittance to the association was contingent upon a pledge of obedience and a renunciation of the knightly way of life. This was, at best, only partially effective. The lower guilds nonetheless enjoyed the support of the urban patriciate in their periodic assaults on upper guild rule. The patriciate also played a role in the subsequent establishment of city-state tyrannies. This role was directly analogous to that performed by the patriciate of the ancient city-states (Hammond 1971: 145–46).

As early as the thirteenth century, the nobility and the propertyless strata were able to form coalitions against the burghers. Weber (1968: 1306) notes, however, that "generally, the influence of the lower strata was contingent upon periods of political stalemate when noble families of equal strength competed for power. Only then could they gain an influence on the 'composition' at least of municipal officialdom."

It is evident that the various member groups involved in the formation of the "state within the state" lacked any stable set of shared political or economic interests. For example, in describing the situation confronting the wealthy families, Weber (1968: 1307) writes: "The nobility everywhere lived in continuous apprehension . . . and everywhere the divisions within the ranks of the nobility gave the *popolo* the opportunity to enroll the military power of one part of the knighthood in its own service."

Given the shifting nature of support for the popular associations, support based upon status aggrandizement or status retention or some combination of both, the question emerges as to what sort of structure is being endorsed. The answer can be found in the term "urban truce." Taken collectively, throughout the High Middle Ages the periods of truce between and among contending factions imposed by city bosses such as the *capitano del popolo* amounted to a system of social order.

The class privileges which dominated the social structure of the countryside became in the crowded cities a continuous and daily affront (Weber 1968: 1307). No status group could attempt to gain hegemony on the basis of its traditional claims without generating an intolerable and self-defeating level of civil strife. The only effective form of rulership could be one that stood outside the entire nexus of group entanglements and clashing status claims which passed for the urban social constitution.

The type of rulership that effectively addressed these "collisions" of interests was unavoidably usurpative or nonlegitimate in the sense of being nonvalid. The absence of propriety as defined by the feudal hierarchical system of obligations and the lack of a validating warrant did not provide a stumbling block to endorsement but, on the contrary, served to facilitate it. In the case of medieval communes, the opportunity to seek redress led to a species of collective self-help justice which received a quasi-legal character in the form of banishment and confiscation. This in turn served to reinforce the rule of the city bosses, a rule instituted by means of extraordinary violence in towns such as Florence (Painter 1965: 233).

During periods of urban truce, the association enjoyed a legitimacy predicated not upon validity but, rather, upon the general apprehension shared by each member group that the command structure of the association was fully endorsed by all the member groups. This was perceived to be the case either because of or in spite of that structure's usurpative, expropriative, and tyrannical character. Any thought of challenging the authority of the association would likely be informed by the sobering prospect of either nonsupport or outright hostility on the part of fellow confederates.

This constitutes a type of endorsement based upon a cautionary expedience discussed above. The first proposition enunciated by Walker, Thomas, and Zelditch (1986: 636) that one of the primary effects of endorsement is to prevent the "erosion" of "an existing belief in propriety" would not apply here for the obvious reason that no such belief was in place to begin with. The alternative proposition stated by the authors (ibid.: 633) has direct applicability: "Increased endorsement may simply reduce the expected probability of success for any change strategy which relies on collective action; hence making any attempt to induce change appear futile." This seems to characterize the uneasy constellation of interests that formed the nonvalidated domination of the medieval city despotisms.

Conclusion

Conventional sociology adopts an extremely positive and normative view of legitimacy. Parsons insists that for a social order to possess legitimacy, it must be perceived as embodying fundamental values, and Easton argues that any stable political order must be predicated upon unconditional attachment and a reservoir of good will. I argue that this emphasis upon values has the effect of ratifying stable political orders by implicating the beliefs of the subject population in the very persistence of stable regimes. For this reason, a sociological analysis of legitimacy so conceived could itself serve as a legitimating rationale. It is therefore desirable to seek out an alternative to the conventional account of legitimacy.

Dornbusch and Scott provide this alternative. They see legitimacy as involving four dimensions: *validity*, which is the acknowledgment of the objective nature of the normative order and which plays a subsidiary role in the Parsonian account of legitimacy; *propriety*, which refers to the actual perception of goodness and fairness with respect to the rules and which serves as the chief preoccupation of the conventional account; *authorization*, where a superordinate's authority is legitimated by his or her superior; and *endorsement*, in which the peers of the focal actor provide the source of legitimation.

Weber held that validity is the core characteristic of legitimation, regardless of any given historical variation in which that characteristic is expressed, be it traditional, charismatic, legal-rational, or some combination. Consequently, in his consideration of the medieval city and the revolts and the power arrangements that sprang from them, Weber was obliged to label these states as nonlegitimate domination because they clearly possessed no validating rationale. However, from the Dornbusch-Scott framework, the revolutionary communes of medieval cities (as Weber presents them) were actually based on another dimension of legitimacy, namely, endorsement. Endorsement, rather than validity, stabilized the regimes.

Thomas, Walker, and Zelditch (1986: 380) have found, on the basis of their experimental research, that propriety is neither necessary nor sufficient to produce the effects associated with legitimacy. They also found that endorsement inhibits change-initiating action. Furthermore, if enough time elapses, subjects may attribute endorsement of the task structure to their co-participants and for this reason are reluctant to withdraw support from a manifestly unfair distribution of rewards. This inhibition is based on expedience, that is, on the expectation of a negative collective response on the part of the co-participants.

One may question whether the legitimacy found in organizations or even society-wide legitimacy is really based on diffuse support or propriety rather than this type of expediential endorsement. A related question is whether any regime has been clearly sustained by this mode of legitimation. Ironically, we find an affirmative answer in Weber's discussion of the city as a state entity. Weber presents us with a detailed account of a nonvalid species of political rule sustained by a type of endorsement that is often all but indistinguishable from sheer calculation of interests.

Consequently, the findings of Walker, Thomas, and Zelditch concerning the endorsement principle are suggestive in developing an interpretation of Weber's one explicit theory of revolution, which is found in his account of the premodern Occidental city. The endorsement in question took the form of the sworn confraternities that instigated the first wave of city-revolts. These revolts were directed against the city lords of the manorial system. The medieval city in Europe became an autonomous judicial entity. It was not a transient political system, yet it possessed no legitimating referent beyond the relationships which obtained among the participating actors. The sworn confraternities were self-legitimating and therefore nonvalid in the Weberian sense. The actual legitimacy was initially derived from the mutual endorsement constituted by the burgher associations of the city-communes.

The second wave of city-revolts was directed against the urban gentry, who came to monopolize control over the municipal administration. The gentry were replaced by city bosses, who ruled largely through a combination of star chamber proceedings and the administration of violence in the form of self-help justice. The "official tyranny" of the city bosses drew strength from two sources,

the fact that it stood outside the internal contradictions which afflicted the medieval city-state system, and the perception on the part of each of the major
factions that all the other factions had an interest in endorsing the bosses.

Thus, the stability of the structure of nonlegitimate domination cannot rest
on validity if validity is viewed as essential to legitimation. Rather, Weber's own
theory of revolution as contained in his sociology of the city, combined with
contemporary experimental research, suggests that the stability of such structures
may derive from the endorsement principle.

References Cited

References Cited

Abrams, Dominic, and Michael A. Hogg. 1990. *Social Identity Theory*. New York: Springer-Verlag.

Abu-Lughod, Janet L. 1991. *Changing Cities: Urban Sociology*. New York: HarperCollins.

Adams, J. Stacy. 1965. "Inequity in Social Exchange." In L. Berkowitz, ed., *Advances in Experimental Social Psychology*, vol. 2, pp. 267–99. New York: Academic Press.

Akerlof, G. A. 1982. "Labor Contracts as Partial Gift Exchange." *Quarterly Journal of Economics* 90:543–49.

———. 1984. "Gift Exchange and Efficiency-Wage Theory: Four Views." *American Economic Review* 74:79–83.

Akers, Ronald L. 1973. *Deviant Behavior: A Social Learning Approach*. Belmont, Calif.: Wadsworth.

Alexander, Jeffrey, and Paul Colomy. 1990. "Neofunctionalism Today: Reconstructing a Theoretical Tradition." In George Ritzer, ed., *Frontiers of Social Theory: The New Syntheses*, pp. 33–67. New York: Columbia University Press.

Alexander, Jeffrey C., Bernhard Giesen, Richard Münch, and Neil J. Smelser. 1987. *The Micro-macro Link*. Berkeley: University of California Press.

Allen, V. L. 1965. "Situational Factors in Conformity." In L. Berkowitz, ed., *Advances in Experimental Social Psychology*, vol. 2, pp. 133–75. New York: Academic Press.

———. 1977. "Social Support for Nonconformity." In L. Berkowitz, ed., *Advances in Experimental Social Psychology*, vol. 8, pp. 1–43. New York: Academic Press.

Althusser, Louis, and Etinne Balibar. 1970. *Reading Capital*. London: New Left Review Books.

Anderson, N. H. 1976. "Equity Judgments as Information Integration." *Journal of Personality and Social Psychology* 33:291–99.

Anderson, Perry. 1974. *Passages from Antiquity to Feudalism*. London: New Left Books.

Archibald, W. Peter. 1976. "Face-to-Face: The Alienating Effects of Class, Status and Power Divisions." *American Sociological Review* 41:819–37.

Aristotle. 1976 [330 B.C.]. *Ethics*. London: Penguin Books.

Ashby, W. Ross. 1950. *An Introduction to Cybernetics*. London: Chapman and Hall.

Atkinson, Anthony B. 1970. "On the Measurement of Inequality." *Journal of Economic Theory* 2:244–63.

———. 1975. *The Economics of Inequality*. London: Oxford University Press.

Axelrod, Robert. 1984. *The Evolution of Cooperation*. New York: Basic Books.

Back, K. W. 1951. "Influence Through Social Communication." *Journal of Abnormal and Social Psychology* 46:9–23.

Baker, Wayne E., and Robert R. Faulkner. 1993. "The Social Organization of Conspiracy." *American Sociological Review* 58:837–60.

Bales, Robert F. 1951. "The Equilibrium Problem in Small Groups." In A. P. Hare, E. F. Borgatta, and R. F. Bales, eds., *Small Groups: Studies in Social Interaction*, pp. 444–76. New York: Knopf.

————. 1953. "The Equilibrium Problem in Small Groups." In T. Parsons, R. F. Bales, and E. A. Shils, eds., *Working Papers in the Theory of Action*, pp. 111–65. Glencoe, Ill.: Free Press.

Bales, R. F., F. L. Strodtbeck, T. M. Mills, and M. E. Rosenborough. 1951. "Channels of Communication in Small Groups." *American Sociological Review* 16:461–68.

Balkwell, James. 1991a. "From Expectations to Behavior: A General Translation Function." *American Sociological Review* 56:355–69.

————. 1991b. "Status Characteristics and Social Interaction: An Assessment of Theoretical Variants." In E. J. Lawler, B. Markovsky, C. L. Ridgeway, and H. A. Walker, eds., *Advances in Group Processes*, vol. 8, pp. 135–76. Greenwich, Conn.: JAI Press.

Balkwell, James W., Joseph Berger, Murray Webster, Jr., Max Nelson-Kilger, and Jacqueline Cashen. 1992. "Processing Status Information: Some Tests of Competing Theoretical Arguments." In Edward J. Lawler, Barry Markovsky, Cecilia Ridgeway, and Henry A. Walker, eds., *Advances in Group Processes*, vol. 9, pp. 1–20. Greenwich, Conn.: JAI Press.

Baron, R. A. 1987. "Interviewer's Moods and Reactions to Job Applicants: The Influence of Affective States on Applied Social Judgments." *Journal of Applied Social Psychology* 17:911–26.

Bavelas, Alex. 1950. "Communication Patterns in Task-Oriented Groups." *Journal of the Acoustical Society of America* 22:725–30.

Becker, G. S. 1976. *The Economic Approach to Human Behavior*. Chicago: University of Chicago Press.

Berger, Joseph. 1958. "Relations Between Performance, Reward, and Action Opportunities in Small Groups." Ph.D. diss., Harvard University.

————. 1974. "Expectation States Theory: A Theoretical Research Program." In Joseph Berger, Thomas L. Conner, and M. Hamit Fisek, eds., *Expectation States Theory: A Theoretical Research Program*, pp. 3–22. Cambridge, Mass.: Winthrop. Reprinted Lanham, Md.: University Press of America, 1982.

————. 1988. "Directions in Expectation States Research." In M. Webster, Jr., and M. Foschi, eds., *Status Generalization: New Theory and Research*, pp. 450–74 and 522–28. Stanford, Calif.: Stanford University Press.

————. 1992. "Expectations, Theory, and Group Processes." *Social Psychology Quarterly* 55:3–11.

Berger J., and T. L. Conner. 1974. "Performance Expectations and Behavior in Small Groups: A Revised Formulation." In Joseph Berger, Thomas L. Conner, and M. Hamit Fisek, eds., *Expectation States Theory: A Theoretical Research Program*, pp. 85–109. Cambridge, Mass.: Winthrop. Reprinted Lanham, Md.: University of America Press, 1982.

Berger, Joseph, and M. Hamit Fisek. 1974. "A Generalization of the Theory of Status Characteristics and Expectation States." In Joseph Berger, Thomas L. Conner, and M. Hamit Fisek, eds., *Expectation States Theory: A Theoretical Research Program*, pp. 163–205. Cambridge, Mass.: Winthrop. Reprinted Lanham, Md.: University Press of America, 1982.

————. 1985. "Theory, Tests, and Applications." Unpublished manuscript, Stanford University.

Berger, Joseph, and Morris Zelditch, Jr. 1993. "Orienting Strategies and Theory Growth." In Joseph Berger and Morris Zelditch, Jr., eds., *Theoretical Research Programs: Studies in the Growth of Theory*, pp. 3–19 and 453–54. Stanford, Calif.: Stanford University Press.

Berger, Joseph, and Morris Zelditch, Jr., eds. 1985. *Status, Rewards, and Influence: How Expectations Organize Behavior*. San Francisco: Jossey-Bass.

———. 1993. *Theoretical Research Programs: Studies in the Growth of Theory*. Stanford, Calif.: Stanford University Press.

Berger, Joseph, Bernard P. Cohen, and Morris Zelditch, Jr. 1966. "Status Characteristics and Expectation States." In Joseph Berger, Morris Zelditch, Jr., and Bo Anderson, eds., *Sociological Theories in Progress*, vol. 1, pp. 29–46. Boston: Houghton Mifflin.

———. 1972. "Status Characteristics and Social Interaction." *American Sociological Review* 37:241–55.

Berger, Joseph, Thomas L. Conner, and M. Hamit Fisek. 1974. *Expectation States Theory: A Theoretical Research Program*. Cambridge, Mass.: Winthrop. Reprinted Lanham, Md.: University Press of America, 1982.

Berger, J., T. L. Conner, and W. L. McKeown. 1974. "Evaluations and the Formation and Maintenance of Performance Expectations." In Joseph Berger, Thomas L. Conner and M. Hamit Fisek, eds., *Expectation States Theory: A Theoretical Research Program*, pp. 27–51. Cambridge, Mass.: Winthrop. Reprinted Lanham, Md.: University Press of America, 1982.

Berger, Joseph, Dana Eyre, and Morris Zelditch, Jr. 1989. "Theoretical Structures and the Micro/Macro Problem." In Joseph Berger, Morris Zelditch, Jr,. and Bo Anderson, eds., *Sociological Theories in Progress: New Formulations*, pp. 11–34. Newbury Park, Calif.: Sage.

Berger, Joseph, M. Hamit Fisek, and Robert Z. Norman. 1989. "The Evolution of Status Expectations: A Theoretical Extension." In Joseph Berger, Morris Zelditch, Jr., and Bo Anderson, eds., *Sociological Theories in Progress: New Formulations*, pp. 100–130. Newbury Park, Calif.: Sage.

Berger, Joseph, Susan J. Rosenholtz, and Morris Zelditch, Jr. 1980. "Status Organizing Processes." *Annual Review of Sociology* 6:479–508.

Berger, Joseph, David G. Wagner, and Morris Zelditch, Jr. 1985. "Introduction: Expectation States Theory: Review and Assessment." In Joseph Berger and Morris Zelditch, Jr., eds., *Status, Rewards, and Influence: How Expectations Organize Behavior*, pp. 1–72. San Francisco: Jossey-Bass.

———. 1989. "Theory Growth, Social Processes, and Metatheory." In Jonathan H. Turner, ed., *Theory Building in Sociology: Assessing Theoretical Cumulation*, pp. 19–42. Newbury Park, Calif.: Sage.

———. 1992. "A Working Strategy for Constructing Theories: State Organizing Processes." In George Ritzer, ed., *Metatheorizing: Volume 6, Key Issues in Sociological Theory*, pp. 107–23. Newbury Park, Calif.: Sage.

Berger, Joseph, Morris Zelditch, Jr., and Bo Anderson. 1972. "Introduction." In Joseph Berger, Morris Zelditch, Jr., and Bo Anderson, eds., *Sociological Theories in Progress*, vol. 2, pp. ix–xxii. Boston: Houghton Mifflin.

Berger, Joseph, Morris Zelditch, Jr., and Bo Anderson, eds. 1966. *Sociological Theories in Progress*. Vol. 1. Boston: Houghton Mifflin.

———. 1972. *Sociological Theories in Progress*. Vol. 2. Boston: Houghton Mifflin.

———. 1989. *Sociological Theories in Progress: New Formulations*. Newbury Park, Calif.: Sage.

Berger, Joseph, M. Hamit Fisek, Robert Z. Norman, and David G. Wagner. 1985. "Formation of Reward Expectations in Status Situations." In Joseph Berger and Morris

Zelditch, Jr., eds., *Status, Rewards, and Influence: How Expectations Organize Behavior*, pp. 215–61. San Francisco: Jossey-Bass.

Berger, Joseph, M. Hamit Fisek, Robert Z. Norman, and Morris Zelditch, Jr. 1977. *Status Characteristics and Social Interaction: An Expectation-States Approach.* New York: Elsevier Scientific.

Berger, Joseph, Robert Z. Norman, James Balkwell, and Roy F. Smith. 1992. "Status Inconsistency in Task Situations: A Test of Four Status Processing Principles." *American Sociological Review* 57:843–55.

Berger, Joseph, Murray Webster, Jr., Cecilia L. Ridgeway, and Susan J. Rosenholtz. 1986. "Status Cues, Expectations, and Behavior." In Edward J. Lawler, ed., *Advances in Group Processes*, vol. 3, pp. 1–22. Greenwich, Conn.: JAI Press.

Berger, Joseph, Morris Zelditch, Jr., Bo Anderson, and Bernard P. Cohen. 1972. "Structural Aspects of Distributive Justice: A Status Value Formulation." In Joseph Berger, Morris Zelditch, Jr., and Bo Anderson, eds., *Sociological Theories in Progress*, vol. 2, pp. 119–46. Boston: Houghton Mifflin.

Berger, Peter L., and Thomas Luckmann. 1966. *The Social Construction of Reality*. Garden City, N.Y.: Doubleday.

Berkowitz, L. 1957. "Liking for the Group and the Perceived Merit of the Group's Behavior." *Journal of Abnormal and Social Psychology* 54:353–57.

Bienenstock, Elisa Jayne, and Phillip Bonacich. 1992. "The Core as a Solution to Exclusionary Networks." *Social Networks* 14:231–43.

———. 1993. "Game Theory Models for Social Exchange Networks: Experimental Results." *Sociological Perspectives* 36:117–36.

Bierhoff, H. W., E. Buck, and R. Klein. 1986. "Social Context and Perceived Justice." In Hans Werner Bierhoff, Ronald L. Cohen, and Jerald Greenberg, eds., *Justice in Social Relations*, pp. 165–85. New York: Plenum Press.

Biernat, M., and M. Manis. 1994. "Shifting Standards and Stereotype-Based Judgments." *Journal of Personality and Social Psychology* 66:5–20.

Biernat, M., M. Manis, and T. E. Nelson. 1991. "Stereotypes and Standards of Judgment." *Journal of Personality and Social Psychology* 60:485–99.

Bierstedt, Robert. 1950. "An Analysis of Social Power." *American Sociological Review* 15:161–84.

Binmore, K. G. 1980. *The Foundations of Analysis: A Straightforward Introduction. Book 1: Logic, Sets and Numbers.* Cambridge, Eng.: Cambridge University Press.

Blalock, Huber M., and Paul H. Wilken. 1979. *Intergroup Processes.* New York: Free Press.

Blau, Peter M. 1960. "Structural Effects." *American Sociological Review* 25:178–93.

———. 1964. *Exchange and Power in Social Life.* New York: Wiley and Sons.

———. 1975. "Introduction: Parallels and Contrasts in Structural Inquiries." In Peter M. Blau, ed., *Approaches to the Study of Social Structure*, pp. 1–20. New York: Free Press.

———. 1977a. "A Macrosociological Theory of Social Structure." *American Journal of Sociology* 83:25–54.

———. 1977b. *Inequality and Heterogeneity: A Primitive Theory of Social Structure.* New York: Free Press.

Blau, Peter M., and Joseph E. Schwartz. 1984. *Crosscutting Social Circles: Testing a Macrostructural Theory of Intergroup Relations.* Orlando, Fla.: Academic Press.

Blumer, Herbert. 1969. "The Methodological Position of Symbolic Interactionism." Chapter 1 in Herbert Blumer, ed., *Symbolic Interactionism.* Englewood Cliffs, N.J.: Prentice-Hall.

Bonacich, Phillip. 1987. "Power and Centrality: A Family of Measures." *American Journal of Sociology* 92:1170–82.

Borgatti, Stephen P., and Martin G. Everett. 1992. "Graph Colorings and Power in Experimental Exchange Networks." *Social Networks* 14:287–308.

Bottomore, Tom, and Robert Nisbet. 1978. "Structuralism." In Tom Bottomore and Robert Nisbet, eds., *A History of Sociological Analysis*, pp. 557–98. New York: Basic Books.

Boudon, Raymond. 1971. *The Uses of Structuralism*. London: Heinemann.

Bower, G. H. 1991. "Mood Congruity of Social Judgments." In J. P. Forgas, ed., *Emotion and Social Judgments*, pp. 165–85. Oxford: Pergamon.

Boyce, William E., and Richard C. Diprima. 1986. *Elementary Differential Equations and Boundary Value Problems*. 4th ed. New York: Wiley.

Boyd, Lawrence H., Jr., and G. R. Iverson. 1979. *Contextual Analysis*. Belmont, Calif.: Wadsworth.

Braithwaite, John. 1989. *Crime, Shame and Reintegration*. New York: Cambridge University Press.

Braun, Norman. 1994. "Restricted Access in Exchange Systems." *Journal of Mathematical Sociology* 19:129–48.

Brennan, John S. 1981. "Some Experimental Structures." In David Willer and Bo Anderson, eds., *Networks, Exchange and Coercion*, pp. 189–206. New York: Elsevier-Greenwood.

Buckley, Walter. 1967. *Sociology and Modern Systems Theory*. Englewood Cliffs, N.J.: Prentice-Hall.

Burt, Ronald. 1982. *Toward a Structural Theory of Action: Network Models of Social Structure, Perception and Action*. New York: Academic Press.

———. 1993. *Structural Holes: The Social Structure of Competition*. Cambridge, Mass.: Harvard University Press.

Byrne, D. 1961. "Interpersonal Attraction and Attitude Similarity." *Journal of Abnormal and Social Psychology* 62:713–15.

Camilleri, S. F., and J. Berger. 1967. "Decision-Making and Social Influence: A Model and an Experimental Test." *Sociometry* 30:367–78.

Camilleri, S. F., J. Berger, and T. L. Conner. 1972. "A Formal Theory of Decision-Making." In Joseph Berger, Morris Zelditch, Jr., and Bo Anderson, eds., *Sociological Theories in Progress*, vol. 2, pp. 21–37. Boston: Houghton Mifflin.

Campbell, Donald T. 1974. "Evolutionary Epistemology." In Paul Arthur Schilpp, ed., *The Philosophy of Karl Popper*, book I, pp. 413–63. La Salle, Ill.: Open Court Press.

Carley, Kathleen. 1986. "An Approach for Relating Social Structure to Cognitive Structure." *Journal of Mathematical Sociology* 12:137–89.

———. 1990. "Group Stability: A Socio-Cognitive Approach." In E. J. Lawler, B. Markovsky, C. Ridgeway, and H. Walker, eds., *Advances in Group Processes*, vol. 7, pp. 1–44. Greenwich, Conn.: JAI Press.

———. 1991. "A Theory of Group Stability." *American Sociological Review* 56:331–54.

Carli, L. 1990. "Gender, Language, and Influence." *Journal of Personality and Social Psychology* 59:941–51.

Cartwright, Dorwin, and Frank Harary. 1956. "Structural Balance: A Generalization of Heider's Theory." *Psychological Review* 63:277–93.

Cartwright, Dorwin, and Alvin Zander, eds. 1960. *Group Dynamics: Research and Theory*. 2d ed. Evanston, Ill.: Row, Peterson.

Caudill, Maureen, and Charles Butler. 1990. *Naturally Intelligent Systems*. Cambridge, Mass.: MIT Press.

Chambliss, William J. 1973. "The Saints and the Roughnecks." *Society* 11:24–31.

Chirot, Daniel. 1985. "The Rise of the West." *American Sociological Review* 50:181–95.

Clark, C. 1990. "Emotions and Micropolitics in Everyday Life: Some Patterns and Paradoxes of 'Place.'" In T. D. Kemper, ed., *Research Agendas in the Sociology of Emotions*, pp. 305–34. Albany: State University of New York Press.

Clawson, Dan, Alan Neustadtl, and James Bearden. 1986. "The Logic of Business Unity: Corporate Contributions to the 1980 Congressional Elections." *American Sociological Review* 51:797–811.

Cloward, Richard A., and Lloyd E. Ohlin. 1960. *Delinquency and Opportunity: A Theory of Delinquent Gangs*. New York: Free Press.

Cohen, Bernard P. 1980. "The conditional nature of scientific knowledge." In Lee Freese, ed., *Theoretical Methods in Sociology*, pp. 71–110. Pittsburgh: University of Pittsburgh Press.

———. 1989. *Developing Sociological Knowledge: Theory and Method*. 2d ed. Chicago: Nelson-Hall.

———. Forthcoming. *Group Structure and Productivity in Innovative Work Teams*.

Cohen, Bernard P., Joseph Berger, and Morris Zelditch, Jr. 1972. "Status Conceptions and Interaction: A Case Study of the Problem of Developing Cumulative Knowledge." In Charles Graham McClintock, ed., *Experimental Social Psychology*, pp. 449–83. New York: Holt, Rinehart and Winston.

Cohen, Elizabeth G. 1982. "Expectation States and Interracial Interaction in School Settings." In R. H. Turner and J. F. Short, Jr., eds., *Annual Review of Sociology*, vol. 8, pp. 209–35. Palo Alto, Calif.: Annual Reviews.

———. 1984. "Talking and Working Together: Status, Interaction, and Learning." In P. Peterson and L. C. Wilkinson, eds., *The Social Context of Instruction: Group Organization and Processes*, pp. 171–87. New York: Academic Press.

———. 1990. "Teaching in Multiculturally Heterogeneous Classrooms: Findings from a Model Program." *McGill Journal of Education* 26:7–23.

———. 1993. "From Theory to Practice: The Development of an Applied Research Program." In Joseph Berger and Morris Zelditch, Jr., eds., *Theoretical Research Programs: Studies in the Growth of Theory*, pp. 385–415 and 488–91. Stanford, Calif.: Stanford University Press.

———. 1994. "Restructuring the Classroom: Conditions for Productive Small Groups." *Review of Educational Research* 64:1–35.

Cohen, E. G., and E. DeAvila. 1983. "Learning to Think in Math and Science: Improving Local Education for Minority Children." *A Final Report to the Johnson Foundation*. Stanford, Calif.: Stanford University School of Education.

Cohen, Elizabeth G., and Rachel A. Lotan. 1995. "Producing Equal-Status Interaction in the Heterogeneous Classroom." *American Educational Research Journal* 32:99–120.

Cohen, Elizabeth G., and Rachel A. Lotan, eds. Forthcoming. *Working for Equity in Heterogeneous Classrooms: Sociological Theory in Action*. New York: Teachers College Press.

Cohen, E. G., R. Lotan, and L. Catanzarite. 1988. "Can Expectations for Competence be Treated in the Classroom?" In M. Webster, Jr., and M. Foschi, eds., *Status Generalization: New Theory and Research*, pp. 27–54. Stanford, Calif.: Stanford University Press.

Cohen, E. G., R. Lotan, and C. Leechor. 1989. "Can Classrooms Learn?" *Sociology of Education* 62:75–94.

Cohen, E. G., and Susan Roper. 1972. "Modifications of Interracial Interaction Disability: An Application of Status Characteristics Theory." *American Sociological Review* 37:643–57.

———. 1985. "Modification of Interracial Interaction Disability." In Joseph Berger and

Morris Zelditch, Jr., eds., *Status, Rewards, and Influence: How Expectations Organize Behavior*, pp. 350–78. San Francisco: Jossey-Bass.

Cohen, E. G., and Shlomo Sharan. 1980. "Modifying Status Relations in Israeli Youth." *Journal of Cross-Cultural Psychology* 11:364–84.

Cohen, M. R., and E. Nagel. 1934. *An Introduction to Logic and Scientific Method*. New York: Harcourt, Brace.

Cohen, Percy. 1968. *Modern Social Theory*. London: Heinemann.

Cole, Stephen. 1994. "Why Sociology Doesn't Make Progress Like the Natural Sciences." *Sociological Forum* 9:133–54.

Coleman, James. 1964. *Introduction to Mathematical Sociology*. New York: Free Press.

———. 1972. "Systems of Social Exchange." *Journal of Mathematical Sociology* 2:145–63.

———. 1973. *The Mathematics of Collective Action*. London: Heinemann.

———. 1975. "Social Structure and a Theory of Action." In Peter M. Blau, ed., *Approaches to the Study of Social Structure*. New York: Free Press.

———. 1986a. *Individual Interests and Collective Action*. Cambridge, Eng.: Cambridge University Press.

———. 1986b. "Social Structure and the Emergence of Norms among Rational Actors." In *Paradoxical Effects of Social Behavior: Essays in Honor of Anatol Rapoport*, pp. 55–83. Heidelberg and Vienna: Physica-Verlag.

———. 1986c. "Social theory, social research, and a theory of action." *American Journal of Sociology* 91:1309–35.

———. 1988. *Theoretical Sociology*. San Diego: Harcourt Brace Jovanovich.

———. 1990. *Foundations of Social Theory*. Cambridge, Mass.: Harvard University Press.

Coleman, James, Elihu Katz, and Herbert Menzel. 1957. "The Diffusion of Innovation Among Physicians." *Sociometry* 20:253–70.

Collins, Randall. 1981. "On the Microfoundations of Macrosociology." *American Journal of Sociology* 86:984–1014.

———. 1984. "The Role of Emotion in Social Structure." In K. R. Scherer and P. Ekman, eds., *Approaches to Emotion*, pp. 385–96. Hillsdale, N.J.: Lawrence Erlbaum.

———. 1988. *Theoretical Sociology*. San Diego: Harcourt Brace Jovanovich.

———. 1989. "Toward a neo-Meadian Sociology of Mind." *Symbolic Interaction* 12:1–32.

———. 1994. "Why the Social Sciences Won't Become High-Consensus, Rapid-Discovery Science." *Sociological Forum* 9:155–77.

Cook, Karen S. 1975. "Expectations, Evaluations, and Equity." *American Sociological Review* 40:372–88.

Cook, Karen S., ed. 1987. *Social Exchange Theory*. Newbury Park, Calif.: Sage.

Cook, Karen S., and R. Emerson. 1978. "Power, Equity and Commitment in Exchange Networks." *American Sociological Review* 43:721–39.

———. 1984. "Exchange Networks and the Analysis of Complex Organizations." In S. B. Bacharach and E. J. Lawler, eds., *Research on the Sociology of Organizations*, vol. 3, pp. 1–30. Greenwich, Conn.: JAI Press.

Cook, Karen S., and Mary R. Gillmore. 1984. "Power Dependence and Coalitions." In Edward J. Lawler, ed., *Advances in Group Processes*, vol. 1, pp. 27–58. Greenwich, Conn.: JAI Press.

Cook, Karen S., and Karen A. Hegtvedt. 1983. "Distributive Justice, Equity, and Equality." *Annual Review of Sociology* 9:217–41.

———. 1986. "Justice and power: An exchange analysis." In Hans Werner Bierhoff, Ronald L. Cohen, and Jerald Greenberg, eds., *Justice in Social Relations*, pp. 19–41. New York: Plenum Press.

Cook, Karen S., and Joseph M. Whitmeyer. 1992. "Two Approaches to Social Structure: Exchange Theory and Network Analysis." *Annual Review of Sociology* 18:109–27.

Cook, Karen S., and Toshio Yamagishi. 1992. "Power in Exchange Networks: A Power-Dependence Formulation." *Social Networks* 14:245–65.

Cook, Karen S., Shawn Donnelly, and Toshio Yamagishi. 1992. "The Effect of Latent Paths on the Distribution of Power in Exchange Network Structures." Paper presented at the annual meeting of the American Sociological Association, Pittsburgh, August 20–24.

Cook, Karen S., Mary R. Gillmore, and Toshio Yamagishi. 1986. "Point and Line Vulnerability as Bases for Predicting the Distribution or Power in Exchange Networks: Reply to Willer." *American Journal of Sociology* 92:445–48.

Cook, Karen S., Linda D. Molm, and Toshio Yamagishi. 1993. "Exchange Relations and Exchange Networks: Recent Developments in Social Exchange Theory." In Joseph Berger and Morris Zelditch, Jr., eds., *Theoretical Research Programs: Studies in the Growth of Theory*, pp. 296–322 and 481–83. Stanford, Calif.: Stanford University Press.

Cook, Karen S., Robert M. Emerson, Mary R. Gillmore, and Toshio Yamagishi. 1983. "The Distribution of Power in Exchange Networks: Theory and Experimental Results." *American Journal of Sociology* 89:275–305.

Coser, Lewis. 1975. "Structure and Conflict." In Peter M. Blau, ed., *Approaches to the Study of Social Structure*, pp. 210–19. New York: Free Press.

Cowell, Frank Alan. 1977. *Measuring Inequality: Techniques for the Social Sciences.* New York: Halsted Press, Wiley.

Crews, F. 1987. "In the Big House of Theory." *New York Review*, May 29:36–42.

Crundall, Ian A., and Margaret Foddy. 1981. "Vicarious exposure to a task as a basis of evaluative competence." *Social Psychology Quarterly* 44:331–38.

Cutler, Anthony, Barry Hindess, Paul Hirst, and Athar Hussain. 1977. *Marx's Capital and Capitalism Today.* London: Routledge and Kegan Paul.

Dagum, Camilo. 1988. "Income Inequality Measures." In Samuel Kotz, Norman L. Johnson, and Campbell B. Read, eds., *Encyclopedia of Statistical Sciences*, vol. 4, pp. 34–40. New York: Wiley.

Daley, D. J., and D. G. Kendall. 1965. "Stochastic Rumors." *Journal of the Institute for Mathematical Applications* 1:42–45.

Davis, James A. 1994. "What's Wrong With Sociology?" *Sociological Forum* 9:179–97.

Davis, James A., and Samuel Leinhardt. 1972. "The Structure of Positive Interpersonal Relations in Small Groups." In Joseph Berger, Morris Zelditch, Jr., and Bo Anderson, eds., *Sociological Theories in Progress*, vol. 2, pp. 218–51. Boston: Houghton Mifflin.

Davis, Kingsley, and Wilbert Moore. 1945. "Some Principles of Stratification." *American Sociological Review* 10:242–49.

Deci, E. L. 1975. *Intrinsic Motivation.* New York: Plenum Press.

———. 1980. *The Psychology of Self-Determination.* Lexington, Mass.: Lexington Books.

Deutsch, Morton. 1985. *Distributive Justice: A Social-Psychological Perspective.* New Haven: Yale University Press.

Doise, W., G. Csepeli, H. D. Cann, C. Gouge, K. Larson, and A. Ostell. 1972. "An Experimental Investigation into the Formation of Intergroup Representations." *European Journal of Social Psychology* 2:202–4.

Dornbusch, Stanford M., and W. Richard Scott with the assistance of Bruce C. Busching and James D. Laing. 1975. *Evaluation and the Exercise of Authority.* San Francisco: Jossey-Bass.

Dovidio, J. F., C. E. Brown, K. Heltmann, S. L. Ellyson, and C. F. Keating. 1988. "Power

Displays Between Women and Men in Discussions of Gender-Linked Tasks: A Multi-channel Study." *Journal of Personality and Social Psychology* 55:580–87.

Driskell, J. E., Jr. 1982. "Personal Characteristics and Performance Expectations." *Social Psychology Quarterly* 45:229–37.

Driskell, J. E., Jr., and B. Mullen. 1988. "Expectations and Actions." In M. Webster, Jr., and M. Foschi, eds., *Status Generalization: New Theory and Research*, pp. 399–412 and 516–19. Stanford, Calif.: Stanford University Press.

———. 1990. "Status, Expectations, and Behavior: A Meta-analytic Review and Test of the Theory." *Personality and Social Psychology Bulletin* 16:541–53.

Duhem, P. 1954. *The Aim and Structure of Physical Theory*. Trans. Philip Wiener. Princeton, N.J.: Princeton University Press. Translated from *La Théorie physique—son objet—sa structure*, 2d ed., 1914.

Durkheim, Emile. 1951 [1897]. *Suicide: A Study in Sociology*. Trans. John A. Spaulding and George Simpson. Ed. George Simpson. New York: Free Press.

———. 1964 [1893]. *The Division of Labor in Society*. Trans. George Simpson. New York: Free Press.

———. 1982 [1901]. *The Rules of Sociological Method and Selected Texts on Sociology and its Method*. New York: Free Press.

Durkheim, Emile, and Marcel Mauss. 1963. *Primitive Classification*. Chicago: University of Chicago Press.

Easton, David. 1965. *A Systems Analysis of Political Life*. New York: John Wiley and Sons.

Eckstein, Harry, and Ted Robert Gurr. 1975. *Patterns of Authority: A Structural Basis for Political Inquiry*. New York: John Wiley and Sons.

Eisenstadt, S. N., and H. J. Helle, eds. 1985. *Micro-sociological Theory* (vol. 1) and *Macro-sociological Theory* (vol. 2). Beverly Hills, Calif.: Sage.

Elder, Joseph W. 1976. "Comparative Cross-National Methodology." In Alex Inkeles, ed., *Annual Review of Sociology*, vol. 2, pp. 209–30. Palo Alto, Calif.: Annual Reviews.

Elster, J. 1984. *Ulysses and the Sirens*. Cambridge, Eng.: Cambridge University Press.

———. 1986. "Introduction." In Jon Elster, ed., *Rational Choice*, pp. 1–33. New York: New York University Press.

Emerson, Richard M. 1962. "Power Dependence Relations." *American Sociological Review* 27:31–41.

———. 1972a. "Exchange Theory, Part I: A Psychological Basis for Social Exchange." In Joseph Berger, Morris Zelditch, Jr., and Bo Anderson, eds., *Sociological Theories in Progress*, vol. 2, pp. 38–57. Boston: Houghton Mifflin.

———. 1972b. "Exchange Theory, Part II: Exchange Relations and Networks." In Joseph Berger, Morris Zelditch, Jr., and Bo Anderson, eds., *Sociological Theories in Progress*, vol. 2, pp. 58–87. Boston: Houghton Mifflin.

———. 1981. "Social exchange theory." In M. Rosenberg and R. H. Turner, eds., *Social Psychology: Sociological Perspectives*, pp. 30–65. New York: Basic Books.

———. 1987. "Toward a Theory of Value in Social Exchange." In Karen S. Cook, ed., *Social Exchange Theory*, pp. 11–46. Newbury Park, Calif.: Sage.

Emerson, Richard M., Karen S. Cook, Mary R. Gillmore, and Toshio Yamagishi. 1983. "Valid Predictions from Invalid Comparisons: Response to Heckathorn." *Social Forces* 61:1232–47.

England, P., G. Farkas, B. Kilbourne, and T. Dou. 1988. "Sex Segregation and Wages." *American Sociological Review* 53:544–58.

Entwisle, Doris R., and Murray Webster, Jr. 1974. "Raising Children's Expectations for Their Own Performance: A Classroom Application." In Joseph Berger, Thomas L.

Conner, and M. Hamit Fisek, eds., *Expectation States Theory: A Theoretical Research Program*, pp. 211–43. Cambridge, Mass.: Winthrop. Reprinted Lanham, Md.: University Press of America, 1982.

Esses, V. M., G. Haddock, and M. P. Zanna. 1993. "Values, Stereotypes, and Emotions as Determinants of Intergroup Attitudes." In D. M. Mackie and D. L. Hamilton, eds., *Affect, Cognition, and Stereotyping: Interactive Processes in Group Perception*, pp. 137–66. San Diego, Calif.: Academic Press.

Eubank, Randall L. 1988. "Quantiles." In Samuel Kotz, Norman L. Johnson, and Campbell B. Read, eds., *Encyclopedia of Statistical Sciences*, vol. 7, pp. 424–32. New York: Wiley.

Evans, Merran, Nicholas Hastings, and Brian Peacock. 1993. *Statistical Distributions.* 2d ed. New York: Wiley.

Everett, Martin G. 1985. "Role Similarity and Role Complexity in Social Networks." *Social Networks* 7:353–59.

Fararo, Thomas J. 1973. *Mathematical Sociology.* New York: Wiley.

———. 1984. "Neoclassical Theorizing and Formalization in Sociology." *Journal of Mathematical Sociology* 10:361–394.

———. 1989. *The Meaning of General Theoretical Sociology.* New York: Cambridge University Press.

Fararo, Thomas J., and John Skvoretz. 1986. "E-State Structuralism: A Theoretical Method." *American Sociological Review* 51:591–602.

———. 1987. "Unification Research Programs: Integrating Two Structural Theories." *American Journal of Sociology* 92:1183–209.

———. 1989. "The Biased Net Theory of Social Structures and the Problem of Integration." In Joseph Berger, Morris Zelditch, Jr., and Bo Anderson, eds., *Sociological Theories in Progress: New Formulations*, pp. 212–55. Newbury Park, Calif.: Sage.

———. 1993. "Methods and Problems of Theoretical Integration and the Principle of Adaptively Rational Action." In Joseph Berger and Morris Zelditch, Jr., eds., *Theoretical Research Programs: Studies in the Growth of Theory*, pp. 416–50 and 491–94. Stanford, Calif.: Stanford University Press.

Feinberg, William E., and Norris R. Johnson. 1988. "'Outside Agitators' and Crowds: Results from a Computer Simulation Model." *Social Forces* 67:398–423.

———. 1989. "Crowd Structure and Process: Theoretical Framework and Computer Simulation Model." In E. J. Lawler and B. Markovsky, eds., *Advances in Group Processes*, vol. 6, pp. 49–86. Greenwich, Conn.: JAI Press.

Felson, R. B. 1993. "The (Somewhat) Social Self: How Others Affect Self-Appraisals." In J. Suls, ed., *Psychological Perspectives on the Self*, vol. 4, pp. 1–26. Hillsdale, N.J.: Lawrence Erlbaum.

Festinger, Leon. 1954. "A Theory of Social Comparison Processes." *Human Relations* 7: 117–40.

———. 1957. *A Theory of Cognitive Dissonance.* Stanford, Calif.: Stanford University Press.

Fisek, M. H. 1993. "The Combining of Status Information." Unpublished manuscript, Department of Psychology, Bogazici University, Istanbul, Turkey.

Fisek, M. Hamit, Joseph Berger, and Robert Z. Norman. 1991. "Participation in Heterogeneous and Homogeneous Groups: A Theoretical Integration." *American Journal of Sociology* 97:114–42.

Fisek, M. Hamit, Robert Z. Norman, and M. Nelson-Kilger. 1992. "Status Characteristics and Expectation States Theory: A Priori Model Parameters and Test." *Journal of Mathematical Sociology* 16:285–303.

Fisher, R. A. 1938. *Statistical Methods for Research Workers*. 7th ed. London: Oliver and Boyd.

Fiske, Susan T., and Shelley E. Taylor. 1991. *Social Cognition*. 2d ed. New York: McGraw-Hill.

Flament, Claude. 1963. *Applications of Graph Theory to Group Structure*. Englewood Cliffs, N.J.: Prentice-Hall.

Foddy, M., and H. Graham. 1987. "Sex and Double Standards in the Inference of Ability." Paper presented at the annual meeting of the Canadian Psychological Association, Vancouver, B.C., June.

Foddy, M., and M. Smithson. 1989. "Fuzzy Sets and Double Standards: Modeling the Process of Ability Inference." In Joseph Berger, Morris Zelditch, Jr., and Bo Anderson, eds., *Sociological Theories in Progress: New Formulations*, pp. 73–99. Newbury Park, Calif.: Sage.

Fogel, Robert W., and Stanley L. Engerman. 1974. *Time on the Cross*. New York: Norton.

Forgas, J. P. 1991. "Affect and Social Judgments: An Introductory Review." In J. P. Forgas, ed., *Emotion and Social Judgments*, pp. 1–29. Oxford: Pergamon.

Forgas, J. P., and G. H. Bower. 1987. "Mood Effects on Person-Perception Judgments." *Journal of Personality and Social Psychology* 53:53–60.

———. 1988. "Affect in Social and Personal Judgments." In K. Fiedler and J. P. Forgas, eds., *Affect, Cognition and Social Behavior*, pp. 183–208. Toronto: C. J. Hogrefe.

Foschi, Martha. 1971. "Contradiction and Change of Performance Expectations." *Canadian Review of Sociology and Anthropology* 8:205–22.

———. 1980. "Theory, Experimentation and Cross-Cultural Comparisons in Social Psychology." *Canadian Journal of Sociology* 5:91–102.

———. 1986. "Actors, observers, and performance expectations: A Bayesian model and an experimental study." *Advances of Group Processes* 3:181–208.

———. 1989. "Status Characteristics, Standards, and Attributions." In Joseph Berger, Morris Zelditch, Jr., and Bo Anderson, eds., *Sociological Theories in Progress: New Formulations*, pp. 58–72. Newbury Park, Calif.: Sage.

———. 1992. "Gender and Double Standards for Competence." In C. L. Ridgeway, ed., *Gender, Interaction, and Inequality*, pp. 181–207. New York: Springer-Verlag.

———. 1996. "Double Standards in the Evaluation of Men and Women." *Social Psychology Quarterly* 59: 237–54.

Foschi, Martha, and Shari Buchan. 1990. "Ethnicity, Gender, and Perceptions of Task Competence." *Canadian Journal of Sociology* 15:1–18.

Foschi, Martha, and M. Foddy. 1988. "Standards, Performances, and the Formation of Self-Other Expectations." In M. Webster, Jr., and M. Foschi, eds., *Status Generalization: New Theory and Research*, pp. 248–60 and 501–3. Stanford, Calif.: Stanford University Press.

Foschi, Martha, and Sabrina Freeman. 1991. "Inferior Performance, Standards, and Influence in Same-Sex Dyads." *Canadian Journal of Behavioural Science* 23:99–113.

Foschi, Martha, and William M. Hales. 1979. "The Theoretical Role of Cross-Cultural Comparisons in Experimental Social Psychology." In L. Eckensberger, W. Lonner, and Y. H. Poortinga, eds., *Cross-Cultural Contributions to Psychology*, pp. 244–54. Lisse, the Netherlands: Swets and Zeitlinger.

Foschi, Martha, and Edward J. Lawler, eds., 1994. *Group Processes: Sociological Analyses*. Chicago: Nelson-Hall.

Foschi, M., and J. Takagi. 1991. "Ethnicity, Task Outcome, and Attributions: A Theoretical Review and Assessment." In E. J. Lawler, B. Markovsky, C. L. Ridgeway, and H. A. Walker, eds., *Advances in Group Processes*, vol. 8, pp. 177–203. Greenwich, Conn.: JAI Press.

Foschi, Martha, L. Lai, and K. Sigerson. 1994. "Gender and Double Standards in the Assessment of Job Applicants." *Social Psychology Quarterly* 57:326–39.

Foschi, M., K. Sigerson, and M. Lembesis. 1995. "Assessing Job Applicants: The Relative Effects of Gender, Academic Record, and Decision Type." *Small Group Research* 26: 328–52.

Foschi, M., G. K. Warriner, and S. D. Hart. 1985. "Standards, Expectations, and Interpersonal Influence." *Social Psychology Quarterly* 48:108–17.

Foucault, Michel. 1972. *The Archeology of Knowledge.* New York: Pantheon.

———. 1979. *Discipline and Punish: The Birth of Prison.* Trans. Alan Sheridan. New York: Vintage Books.

Fox, J., and J. C. Moore, Jr. 1979. "Status Characteristics and Expectation States: Fitting and Testing a Recent Model." *Social Psychology Quarterly* 42:126–34.

Frank, R. H. 1988. *Passions within Reason.* New York: Norton.

———. 1990. "A Theory of Moral Sentiments." In J. J. Mansbridge, ed., *Beyond Self-Interest,* pp. 71–96. Chicago: University of Chicago Press.

Freeman, Linton C. 1979. "Centrality in Social Networks: Conceptual Clarification." *Social Networks* 1:215–39.

Freese, Lee. 1974. "Conditions for Status Equality in Formal Task Groups." *Sociometry* 37:174–88.

———. 1980a. "Formal Theorizing." *Annual Review of Sociology* 6:187–212.

———. 1980b. "The Problem of Cumulative Knowledge." In Lee Freese, ed., *Theoretical Methods in Sociology: Seven Essays,* pp. 13–69. Pittsburgh: University of Pittsburgh Press.

Freese, Lee, and Bernard P. Cohen. 1973. "Eliminating Status Generalization." *Sociometry* 36:177–93.

Freese, Lee, and Jane Sell. 1980. "Constructing Axiomatic Theories in Sociology." In Lee Freese, ed., *Theoretical Methods in Sociology: Seven Essays,* pp. 263–368. Pittsburgh: University of Pittsburgh Press.

Frey, B. 1992a. *Economics as a Science of Human Behavior: Toward a New Social Science Paradigm.* Boston: Kluwer Academic.

———. 1992b. "Tertium Datur: Pricing, Regulating, and Intrinsic Motivation." *Kyklos* 45:161–84.

Frey, K. S., and D. N. Ruble. 1990. "Strategies for Comparative Evaluation: Maintaining a Sense of Competence Across the Life Span." In R. J. Sternberg and J. Kolligian, Jr., eds., *Competence Considered,* pp. 167–89. New Haven: Yale University Press.

Friedkin, Noah E. 1992. "An Expected Value Model of Social Power: Predictions for Selected Exchange Networks." *Social Networks* 14:213–29.

———. 1993. "An Expected Value Model of Social Exchange Outcomes." In Edward J. Lawler, Barry Markovsky, Karen Heimer, and Jodi O'Brien, eds., *Advances in Group Processes,* vol. 10, pp. 163–93. Greenwich, Conn.: JAI Press.

Gecas, V. 1986. "The Motivational Significance of Self-Concept for Socialization Theory." In E. J. Lawler, ed., *Advances in Group Processes,* vol. 3, pp. 131–56. Greenwich, Conn.: JAI Press.

George, J. M. 1990. "Personality, Affect and Behavior in Groups." *Journal of Applied Psychology* 75:107–16.

Gerber, Gwendolyn L. 1992. "Instrumental and Expressive Personality Traits in Social Cognition: Parallels with Social Interaction." *Genetic, Social and General Psychology Monographs* 119 (1):99–123.

———. 1993. "Status in Same-Sex and Mixed-Sex Police Dyads: Its Impact on Personality." Paper presented in Panel, *Expectations States: Basic Concepts, Recent Developments and Future Directions*, Martha Foschi (Chair). Panel conducted at the Sixth Annual Group Processes Conference, Miami, August.

Gergen, K. J. 1973. "Social Psychology as History." *Journal of Personality and Social Psychology* 26:309–20.

———. 1976. "Social Psychology, Science and History." *Personality and Social Psychology Bulletin* 2:373–83.

———. 1982. *Toward Transformation in Social Knowledge.* New York: Springer-Verlag.

Gibbs, Jack P. 1975. *Crime, Punishment and Deterrence.* New York: Elsevier.

Giddens, Anthony. 1976. *New Rules of Sociological Method: A Positive Critique of Interpretive Sociologies.* London: Hutchinson.

———. 1984. *The Constitution of Society: Outline of the Theory of Structuration.* Berkeley: University of California Press.

Gilbert, D. T., E. E. Jones, and B. W. Pelham. 1987. "Influence and Inference: What the Active Perceiver Overlooks." *Journal of Personality and Social Psychology* 52:861–70.

Gilham, Steven A. 1981. "State, Law and Modern Economic Exchange." In David Willer and Bo Anderson, eds., *Networks, Exchange and Coercion*, pp. 129–51. New York: Elsevier-Greenwood.

Gillmore, Mary R. 1987. "Implications of General Versus Restricted Exchange." In Karen S. Cook, ed., *Social Exchange Theory*, pp. 170–89. Newbury Park, Calif.: Sage.

Gordon, S. L. 1981. "The Sociology of Sentiment and Emotions." In M. Rosenberg and R. H. Turner, eds., *Social Psychology: Sociological Perspectives*, pp. 562–92. New York: Basic Books.

Gottfredson, Michael R., and Travis Hirschi. 1990. *A General Theory of Crime.* Stanford, Calif.: Stanford University Press.

Gouldner, Alvin. 1960. "The Norm of Reciprocity." *American Sociological Review* 25:161–78.

Granovetter, Mark S. 1973. "The Strength of Weak Ties." *American Journal of Sociology* 83:1420–43.

Greenberg, J., and R. L. Cohen, eds. 1982. *Equity and Justice in Social Behavior.* New York: Academic Press.

Greenstein, Theodore N., and J. David Knottnerus. 1980. "The Effects of Differential Evaluations on Status Generalization." *Social Psychology Quarterly* 43:147–54.

Griswold, Wendy. 1983. "The Devil's Techniques: Cultural Legitimation and Social Change." *American Sociological Review* 48:668–80.

Hadar, Josef. 1971. *Mathematical Theory of Economic Behavior.* Reading, Mass.: Addison-Wesley.

Hamilton, David L. 1981. "Illusory Correlation as a Basis for Stereotyping." In D. Hamilton, ed., *Cognitive Processes in Stereotyping and Intergroup Behavior*, pp. 115–44. Hillsdale, N.J.: Erlbaum.

Hamilton, David L., Steven J. Stroessner, and Diane M. Mackie. 1993. "The Influence of Affect on Stereotyping: The Case of Illusory Correlations." In D. Mackie and D. Hamilton, eds., *Affect, Cognition, and Stereotyping*, pp. 39–62. New York: Academic Press.

Hammond, N. G. L. 1971. *A History of Greece to 322 B.C.* Oxford: Clarendon Press.

Hannan, Michael T. 1991. *Aggregation and Disaggregation in the Social Sciences.* Rev. ed. Lexington, Mass.: Lexington Books.

Hansen, R. D., and V. E. O'Leary. 1985. "Sex-Determined Attributions." In V. E. O'Leary, R. K. Unger, and B. S. Wallston, eds., *Women, Gender, and Social Psychology*, pp. 67–99. Hillsdale, N.J.: Lawrence Erlbaum.

Harary, Frank. 1969. *Graph Theory.* Reading, Mass.: Addison-Wesley.

Harary, Frank, Robert Z. Norman, and Dorwin Cartwright. 1965. *Structural Models: An Introduction to the Theory of Directed Graphs.* New York: Wiley.

Harris, R. J. 1983. "Pinning Down the Equity Formula." In D. M. Messick and K. S. Cook, eds., *Equity Theory: Psychological and Sociological Perspectives*, pp. 207–41. New York: Praeger.

Harrod, Wendy J. 1980. "Expectations from Unequal Rewards." *Social Psychology Quarterly* 43:126–30.

Harsanyi, John C. 1982. "Morality and the Theory of Rational Behavior." In A. Sen and B. Williams, eds., *Utilitarianism and Beyond*, pp. 39-63. Cambridge, Eng.: Cambridge University Press.

———. 1990. "Interpersonal Utility Comparisons." *The New Palgrave: Utility and Probability.* New York: Norton.

Hastings, N. A. J., and J. B. Peacock. 1974. *Statistical Distributions: A Handbook for Students and Practitioners.* London: Butterworth.

Hechter, Michael. 1987. *Principles of Group Solidarity.* Berkeley: University of California Press.

Hechter, Michael, ed. 1983. *The Microfoundations of Macrosociology.* Philadelphia: Temple University Press.

Hechter, M., K. Opp, and R. Whippler. 1990. *Social Institutions: Their Emergence, Maintenance, and Effects.* New York: Aldine de Gruyter.

Heckathorn, Douglas D. 1980. "A Unified Model for Bargaining and Conflict." *Behavioral Science* 25:261–84.

———. 1983a. "Extensions of Power-Dependence Theory: The Concept of Resistance." *Social Forces* 61:1206–31.

———. 1983b. "Valid and Invalid Interpersonal Comparisons: Response to Emerson, Cook, Gillmore and Yamagishi." *Social Forces* 61:1248–59.

———. 1988. "Collective sanctions and the creation of prisoner's dilemma norms." *American Journal of Sociology* 94:535–62.

———. 1989. "Collective action and the second-order free-rider problem." *Rationality and Society* 1:78–100.

———. 1990. "Collective sanctions and compliance norms: A formal theory of group-mediated social control." *American Sociological Review* 55:366–84.

Heckathorn, Douglas D., ed. 1993. *Rationality and Society* 5:157–293.

Hegtvedt, Karen A. 1988. "Social Determinants of Perception: Power, Equity, and Status Effects in an Exchange Situation." *Social Psychology Quarterly* 51:141–53.

———. 1990. "The Effects of Relationship Structure on Emotional Responses to Inequity." *Social Psychology Quarterly* 53:214–28.

Heider, Fritz. 1946. "Attitudes and Cognitive Organization." *Journal of Psychology* 21:107–12.

———. 1958. *Psychology of Interpersonal Relations.* New York: Wiley.

Heimer, Karen, and Ross L. Matsueda. 1994. "Role-taking, Role Commitment, and Delinquency: A Theory of Differential Social Control." *American Sociological Review* 59:365–90.

Heise, David. 1979. *Understanding Events: Affect and the Construction of Social Action.* Cambridge, Eng.: Cambridge University Press.

Hembroff, Larry A. 1982. "Resolving Status Inconsistency: An Expectation States Theory and Test." *Social Forces* 61:183–205.

Hembroff, Larry A., and David E. Myers. 1984. "Status Characteristics: Degrees of Task Relevance and Decision Processes." *Social Psychology Quarterly* 47:337–46.

Hembroff, Larry A., Michael W. Martin, and Jane Sell. 1981. "Total Performance Inconsistency and Status Generalization: An Expectation States Formulation." *Sociological Quarterly* 22:421–30.

Hempel, Carl G. 1965. *Aspects of Scientific Explanation*. New York: Free Press.

Hempel, Carl G., and P. Oppenheim. 1948. "Studies in the Logic of Explanation." *Philosophy of Science* 15:135–75.

Higgins, E. T., T. Strauman, and R. Klein. 1986. "Standards and the Process of Self-Evaluation: Multiple Affects from Multiple Stages." In R. M. Sorrentino and E. T. Higgins, eds., *Handbook of Motivation and Cognition: Foundations of Social Behavior*, vol. 1, pp. 23–63. New York: Guilford Press.

Hirschi, Travis. 1969. *Causes of Delinquency*. Berkeley: University of California Press.

Hobbes, Thomas. 1968 [1651]. *Leviathan*. New York: Penguin Books.

Hochschild, A. R. 1983. *The Managed Heart*. Berkeley: University of California Press.

Hoel, Paul G. 1971. *Introduction to Mathematical Statistics*. 4th ed. New York: Wiley.

Hoffman, M. L. 1986. "Affect, Cognition, and Motivation." In R. M. Sorrentino and E. T. Higgins, eds., *Handbook of Motivation and Cognition: Foundations of Social Behavior*, vol. 1, pp. 244–80. New York: Guilford Press.

Hogg, M. A., and D. Abrams. 1990. *Social Identifications*. London: Routledge.

Homans, George Caspar. 1950. *The Human Group*. London: Routledge and Kegan Paul.

———. 1958. "Social Behavior as Exchange." *American Journal of Sociology* 65:597–606.

———. 1974 [1961]. *Social Behavior: Its Elementary Forms*. Rev. ed. New York: Harcourt Brace Jovanovich.

———. 1975. "What Do We Mean by Social 'Structure'?" In Peter M. Blau, ed., *Approaches to the Study of Social Structure*, pp. 53–65. New York: Free Press.

Hopkins, Terence K., and Immanuel Wallerstein. 1967. "The Comparative Study of National Societies." *Social Science Information* 6:25–58.

Houser, Jeffrey A., and Michael J. Lovaglia. 1993. "Emotional Reactions, Status Characteristics and Social Interaction." Paper presented at the annual meeting of the American Sociological Association, Miami Beach, August 13–17.

———. 1994. "Compatible Emotions and Group Solidarity: An Expectation States Approach to the Ties that Bind Groups." Paper presented at the annual meeting of the American Sociological Association, Los Angeles, August 4-9.

Hummon, Norman P., and Thomas J. Fararo. 1995a. "Assessing Hierarchy and Balance in Dynamic Network Models." In David Heise, ed., *Sociological Algorithms: A Special Issue of the Journal of Mathematical Sociology* 20:145–59.

———. 1995b. "The Emergence of Computational Sociology." In David Heise, ed., *Sociological Algorithms: A Special Issue of the Journal of Mathematical Sociology* 20:79–87.

Huston, Ted L., and George Levinger. 1978. "Interpersonal Attraction and Relationships." *Annual Review of Psychology* 29:115–56.

Huber, Joan, ed. 1991. *Macro-Micro Linkages in Sociology*. Newbury Park, Calif.: Sage.

Humphreys, Paul, and Joseph Berger. 1981. "Theoretical Consequences of the Status Characteristics Formulation." *American Journal of Sociology* 86:958–83.

Hurwitz, J. I., A. F. Zander, and B. Hymovitch. 1960. "Some Effects of Power on the Relations among Group Members." In D. Cartwright and A. F. Zander, eds., *Group Dynamics*, pp. 448–56. New York: Harper and Row.

Isen, A. M. 1987. "Positive Affect, Cognitive Processes, and Social Behavior." In L. Berkowitz, ed., *Advances in Experimental Social Psychology*, vol. 20, pp. 203–53. New York: Academic Press.

Isen, A. M., M. Clark, and M. F. Schwartz. 1976. "Duration of the Effect of Good Mood on Helping: 'Footprints on the Sands of Time.'" *Journal of Personality and Social Psychology* 34:385–93.

Isen, A. M., and Stanley Simmonds. 1978. "The Effect of Feeling Good on a Helping Task That Is Incompatible with Good Mood." *Social Psychology* 41:346–49.

Izard, C. E. 1977. *Human Emotions*. New York: Plenum Press.

James, William. 1952 [1891]. *The Principles of Psychology*. Chicago: Britannica.

———. 1981 [1890]. *The Principles of Psychology*, vol. 1. Cambridge, Mass.: Harvard University Press.

Jankowski, Martin Sanchez. 1991. *Islands in the Street: Gangs and American Urban Society*. Berkeley: University of California Press.

Jasso, Guillermina. 1978. "On the Justice of Earnings: A New Specification of the Justice Evaluation Function." *American Journal of Sociology* 83:1398–419.

———. 1980. "A New Theory of Distributive Justice." *American Sociological Review* 45: 3–32.

———. 1982. "Measuring Inequality by the Ratio of the Geometric Mean to the Arithmetic Mean." *Sociological Methods and Research* 10:303–26.

———. 1986. "A New Representation of the Just Term in Distributive-Justice Theory: Its Properties and Operation in Theoretical Derivation and Empirical Estimation." *Journal of Mathematical Sociology* 12:251–74.

———. 1988. "Principles of Theoretical Analysis." *Sociological Theory* 6:1–20.

———. 1989. "The Theory of the Distributive-Justice Force in Human Affairs: Analyzing the Three Central Questions." In Joseph Berger, Morris Zelditch, Jr., and Bo Anderson, eds., *Sociological Theories in Progress: New Formulations*, pp. 354–87. Newbury Park, Calif.: Sage.

———. 1990. "Methods for the Theoretical and Empirical Analysis of Comparison Processes." In Clifford C. Clogg, ed., *Sociological Methodology 1990*, pp. 369–419. Washington, D.C.: American Sociological Association.

———. 1991. "Cloister and Society: Analyzing the Public Benefit of Monastic and Mendicant Institutions." *Journal of Mathematical Sociology* 16:109–36.

———. 1993a. "Building the Theory of Comparison Processes: Construction of Postulates and Derivation of Predictions." In Joseph Berger and Morris Zelditch, Jr., eds., *Theoretical Research Programs: Studies in the Growth of Theory*, pp. 213–64 and 474–78. Stanford, Calif.: Stanford University Press.

———. 1993b. "Analyzing Conflict Severity: Predictions of Distributive-Justice Theory for the Two-Subgroup Case." *Social Justice Research* 6:357–82.

Johnson, Norman L., and Samuel Kotz. 1969. *Distributions in Statistics: Discrete Distributions*. New York: Wiley.

———. 1970a. *Distributions in Statistics: Continuous Univariate Distributions—1*. New York: Wiley.

———. 1970b. *Distributions in Statistics: Continuous Univariate Distributions—2*. New York: Wiley.

Johnson, Norris R., and William E. Feinberg. 1977. "A Computer Simulation of the Emergence of Consensus in Crowds." *American Sociological Review* 42:505–21.

Johnston, J. R. 1988. "The Structure of Ex-Spousal Relations: An Exercise in Theoretical Integration and Application." In M. Webster, Jr., and M. Foschi, eds., *Status Generalization: New Theory and Research*, pp. 309–26 and 509–10. Stanford, Calif.: Stanford University Press.

Jones, E. E. 1986. "Interpreting Interpersonal Behavior: The Effects of Expectancies." *Science* 234:41–46.

Jones, E. E., and G. R. Goethals. 1971. "Order Effects in Impression Formation: Attribution Context and the Nature of the Entity." In E. E. Jones, D. E. Kanouse, H. H.

Kelly, R. E. Nisbett, S. Valins, and B. Weiner, eds., *Attribution: Perceiving the Causes of Behavior*, pp. 27–46. Morristown, N.J.: General Learning Press.

Kahneman, Daniel, and Amos Tversky. 1979. "Prospect Theory: An Analysis of Decision Under Risk." *Econometrica* 47:263–91.

Kalai, Ehud, and Meir Smorodinsky. 1975. "Other Solutions to Nash's Bargaining Problem." *Econometrica* 43:513–18.

Kalleberg, Arne L. 1989. "Linking macro and micro levels: Bringing the workers back into the sociology of work." *Social Forces* 67:582–92.

Kanter, R. M. 1968. "Commitment and Social Organization: A Study of Commitment Mechanisms in Utopian Communities." *American Sociological Review* 33:499–517.

———. 1972. *Commitment and Community: Communes and Utopias in Sociological Perspective.* Cambridge, Mass.: Harvard University Press.

Kauffmann, Stuart A. 1993. *The Origins of Order: Self-Organization and Selection in Evolution.* New York: Oxford University Press.

Kemeny, John G., and J. Laurie Snell. 1962. *Mathematical Models in the Social Sciences.* Boston: Ginn and Co.

Kemper, T. D. 1978. *A Social Interactionist Theory of Emotions.* New York: Wiley.

———. 1984. "Power, Status and Emotions: A Sociological Contribution to a Psychophysiological Domain." In K. R. Scherer and P. Ekman, eds., *Approaches to Emotion*, pp. 369–83. Hillsdale, N.J.: Lawrence Erlbaum.

———. 1987. "How many emotions are there? Wedding the social and autonomic structure." *American Journal of Sociology* 93:263–89.

———. 1991. "Predicting Emotions from Social Relations." *Social Psychology Quarterly* 54:330–42.

Knorr-Cetina, Karin D., and Aaron Cicourel. 1981. *Advances in Social Theory and Methodology: Towards an Integration of Micro- and Macro-Sociology.* London: Routledge and Kegan Paul.

Knottnerus, J. David. 1986. "The Relevance of Social Theory for Social Policy: The Expectation States Program." *Free Inquiry in Creative Sociology* 14:43–47.

———. 1988. "A Critique of Expectation States Theory: Theoretical Assumptions and Models of Social Cognition." *Sociological Perspectives* 31:420–45.

———. 1994a. "Expectation States Theory and the Analysis of Group Processes and Structures." In J. David Knottnerus and Christopher Prendergast, eds., *Recent Developments in the Theory of Social Structure*, pp. 49–74. Greenwich, Conn.: JAI Press.

———. 1994b. "Social Exchange Theory and Social Structure: A Critical Comparison of Two Traditions of Inquiry." In J. David Knottnerus and Christopher Prendergast, eds., *Recent Developments in the Theory of Social Structure*, pp. 29–48. Greenwich, Conn.: JAI Press.

Knottnerus, J. David, and Theodore N. Greenstein. 1981. "Status and Performance Characteristics in Social Interaction: A Theory of Status Validation." *Social Psychology Quarterly* 44:338–49.

Knottnerus, J. David, and Christopher Prendergast. 1992. "Exchange Theory and Social Structure: An Assessment with Synthetic Intent." *International Journal for Contemporary Sociology* 29:135–50.

Knottnerus, J. David, and Christopher Prendergast, eds. 1994. *Recent Developments in the Theory of Social Structure.* Greenwich, Conn.: JAI Press.

Kohn, Melvin L. 1987. "Cross-National Research as an Analytic Strategy. American Sociological Association, 1987 Presidential Address." *American Sociological Review* 52:713–31.

———. 1989a. "Cross-National Research as an Analytic Strategy." In Melvin L. Kohn, ed., *Cross-National Research in Sociology*, pp. 77–102. Newbury Park, Calif.: Sage.

———. 1989b. (Editor.) *Cross-National Research in Sociology*. Newbury Park, Calif.: Sage.

———. 1989c. "Introduction." In Melvin L. Kohn, ed., *Cross-National Research in Sociology*, pp. 17–31. Newbury Park, Calif.: Sage.

Kohn, M. L., and K. M. Słomczyński. 1990. *Social Structure and Self-Direction: A Comparative Analysis of the United States and Poland*. Cambridge, Mass.: Basil Blackwell.

Kontopoulos, Kyriakos M. 1993. *The Logics of Social Structure*. New York: Cambridge University Press.

Kornai, Janos. 1992. *The Socialist System: The Political Economy of Communism*. Princeton, N.J.: Princeton University Press.

Kotz, Samuel, Norman L. Johnson, and Campbell B. Read. 1982–1988. "Log-Laplace Distribution." In Samuel Kotz, Norman L. Johnson, and Campbell B. Read, eds., *Encyclopedia of Statistical Sciences*, vol. 5, pp. 133–34. New York: Wiley.

Kramer, R. 1993. "Cooperation and Organizational Identification." In J. K. Murnighan, ed., *Social Psychology in Organizations*, pp. 244–68. Englewood Cliffs, N.J.: Prentice-Hall.

Kristol, Irving. 1968. "Equality: Equality as an Ideal." In David L. Sills, ed., *International Encyclopedia of the Social Sciences*, vol. 5, pp. 108–11. New York: Macmillan.

Kuhn, Manfred, and Thomas McPartland. 1954. "An Empirical Investigation of Self-Attitudes." *American Sociological Review* 19:68–77.

Kuhn, Thomas S. 1962. *The Structure of Scientific Revolutions*. Chicago: University of Chicago Press.

———. 1970. *The Structure of Scientific Revolutions*. Chicago: University of Chicago Press.

Lakatos, Imre. 1968. "Criticism and the Methodology of Scientific Research Programs." *Proceedings of the Aristotelian Society* 69:149–86.

———. 1970. "Falsification and the Methodology of Scientific Research Programs." In Imre Lakatos and A. Musgrave, eds., *Criticism and the Growth of Knowledge*, pp. 91–195. Cambridge, Eng.: Cambridge University Press.

Lakatos, Imre, and A. Musgrave, eds. 1970. *Criticism and the Growth of Knowledge*. Cambridge, Eng.: Cambridge University Press.

Laudan, Larry. 1976. "Discussion: Two Dogmas of Methodology." *Philosophy of Science* 43:585–97.

———. 1977. *Progress and Its Problems: Towards a Theory of Scientific Growth*. Berkeley: University of California Press.

———. 1984. *Science and Values: The Aims of Science and Their Role in Scientific Debate*. Berkeley: University of California Press.

Lave, Charles A., and James G. March. 1975. *An Introduction to Models in the Social Sciences*. New York: Harper and Row.

Lawler, E. J. 1992. "Affective Attachments to Nested Groups: A Choice-Process Theory." *American Sociological Review* 57:327–39.

Lawler, E. J., and J. Yoon. 1993. "Power and the Emergence of Commitment Behavior in Negotiated Exchange." *American Sociological Review* 58:465–81.

———. 1995. "Power and Emotional Processes in Negotiations: A Social-Exchange Approach." In R. Kramer and D. Messick, eds., *The Social Contexts of Negotiation*, pp. 143–65. Newbury Park, Calif.: Sage.

———. 1996. "Commitment in Exchange Relations: Test of a Theory of Relational Cohesion." *American Sociological Review* 61:89–108.

Lawler, Edward J., Cecilia Ridgeway, and Barry Markovsky. 1993. "Structural Social Psychology and the Micro-macro Problem." *Sociological Theory* 11:268–90.

Lawler, E. J., J. Yoon, M. Baker, and M. Large. 1995. "Mutual Dependence and Gift Giving in Exchange Relations." In B. Markovsky, J. O'Brien, and K. Heimer, eds., *Advances in Group Processes*, vol. 12, pp. 271–98. Greenwich, Conn.: JAI Press.

Leal, A. 1985. "Sex Inequalities in Classroom Interaction: An Evaluation of an Intervention." Ph.D. diss., Stanford University.

Lee, Margaret T., and Richard Ofshe. 1981. "The Impact of Behavioral Style and Status Characteristics on Social Influence: A Test of Two Competing Theories." *Social Psychology Quarterly* 44:73–82.

Lee, T. W., E. A. Locke, and G. P. Latham. 1989. "Goal Setting Theory and Job Performance." In L. A. Pervin, ed., *Goal Concepts in Personality and Social Psychology*, pp. 291–326. Hillsdale, N.J.: Lawrence Erlbaum.

Leik, Robert K. 1992. "New Directions for Network Exchange Theory: Strategic Manipulation of Network Linkages." *Social Networks* 14:309–23.

Leik, Robert K., and Barbara F. Meeker. 1975. *Mathematical Sociology*. Englewood Cliffs, N.J.: Prentice-Hall.

———. 1993. "Interpersonal Competition and Cooperation: Group Process Interpretation of Arms Race and Population Ecology Models." Paper presented at Midwest Sociological Society, Chicago, April.

———. 1995. "Computer Simulation for Exploring Theories." *Sociological Perspectives* 38:463–82.

Lenski, Gerhard E. 1966. *Power and Privilege*. New York: McGraw-Hill.

———. 1975. "Social Structure in Evolutionary Perspective." In Peter M. Blau, ed., *Approaches to the Study of Social Structure*, pp. 135–53. New York: Free Press.

Lévi-Strauss, Claude. 1949. *Les Structures Elementaires de la Parente*. Paris: Presses Universitaires de France.

———. 1952. "Social Structure." In A. L. Kroeber, ed., *Anthropology Today: An Encyclopedic Inventory*, pp. 524–53. Chicago: University of Chicago Press.

———. 1963. *Structural Anthropology*. New York: Basic Books.

Lieberson, S. 1985. *Making It Count: The Improvement of Social Research and Theory*. Berkeley: University of California Press.

Lincoln, James, and Arne Kalleberg. 1985. "Work Organization and Workforce Commitment: A Study of Plants and Employees in the U.S. and Japan." *American Sociological Review* 50:738–60.

Lipset, Seymour M. 1975. "Social Structure and Social Change." In Peter M. Blau, ed., *Approaches to the Study of Social Structure*, pp. 172–209. New York: Free Press.

Locke, E. A., K. N. Shaw, L. M. Saari, and G. P. Latham. 1981. "Goal Setting and Task Performance: 1969–1980." *Psychological Bulletin* 90:125–52.

Lockheed, Marlaine E., A. Harris, and W. P. Nemceff. 1983. "Sex and Social Influence: Does Sex Function as a Status Characteristic in Mixed-Sex Groups of Children?" *Journal of Educational Psychology* 75:877–88.

Lovaglia, Michael J. 1992. "Power and Status: Exchange, Attribution, and Expectation States." Ph.D. diss., Sociology Department, Stanford University.

———. 1994. "Relating Power to Status." In E. Lawler, B. Markovsky, J. O'Brien, and K. Heimer, eds., *Advances in Group Processes*, vol. 11, pp. 87–111. Greenwich, Conn.: JAI Press.

———. 1995. "Status and Power: Exchange, Attribution and Expectation States." *Small Group Research* 26:400–426.

Lovaglia, M. J., and J. A. Houser. 1994. "*Noblesse Oblige*: Reciprocal Gift Exchange and Status Inequality." Paper presented at the annual meeting of the American Sociological Association, Los Angeles, August 4–9.

———. 1996. "Emotional Reactions and Status in Groups." *American Sociological Review* 61: forthcoming.

Lovaglia, Michael J., John Skvoretz, David Willer, and Barry Markovsky. 1995. "Negotiated Exchanges in Social Networks." *Social Forces* 74: 123–55.

Lucas, J., V. Wynn, and A. Vogt. 1995. "Emotion and Status in Face-to-Face Groups." Paper presented at the annual meeting of the American Sociological Association, Washington, D.C., August 19–23.

Luce, R. Duncan, and Howard Raiffa. 1958. *Games and Decisions.* New York: Wiley.

Lukes, Steven. 1974. *Power: A Radical View.* London: Macmillan.

———. 1978. "Power and Authority." In Tom Bottomore and Robert Nisbet, eds., *A History of Sociological Analysis*, pp. 633–76. New York: Basic Books.

Lyotard, J. F. 1984. *The Post-Modern Condition: A Report on Knowledge.* Trans. G. Bennington and B. Massumi. Minneapolis: University of Minnesota Press.

Mackie, D. M., and L. T. Worth. 1991. "Feeling Good, but Not Thinking Straight: The Impact of Positive Mood on Persuasion." In J. P. Forgas, ed., *Emotion and Social Judgments*, pp. 201–20. Oxford: Pergamon.

MacKinnon, Neil J., and David R. Heise. 1993. "Affect Control Theory: Delineation and Development." In Joseph Berger and Morris Zelditch, Jr., eds., *Theoretical Research Programs: Studies in the Growth of Theory*, pp. 64–103 and 463–65. Stanford, Calif.: Stanford University Press.

Macy, Michael. 1989. "Walking Out of Social Traps: A Stochastic Learning Model for Prisoner's Dilemma." *Rationality and Society* 1: 197–219.

———. 1990. "Learning Theory and the Logic of Critical Mass." *American Sociological Review* 55: 809–26.

———. 1991a. "Chains of Cooperation: Threshold Effects in Collective Action." *American Sociological Review* 56: 730–47.

———. 1991b. "Learning to Cooperate: Stochastic and Tacit Collusion in Social Exchange." *American Journal of Sociology* 97: 808–43.

Magala, Sławomir. 1980. *Simmel.* Warszawa: Wiedza Powszechna. In Polish.

Maines, David R., and Marjorie J. Molseed. 1986. "The Obsessive Discover's Complex and the 'Discovery' of Growth in Sociological Theory." *American Journal of Sociology* 92: 158–64.

Malinowski, Bronislaw. 1922. *Argonauts of the Western Pacific.* New York: Dutton.

Mann, Michael. 1986. *The Sources of Social Power.* Vol. 1. New York: Cambridge University Press.

Margolis, H. 1982. *Selfishness, Altruism, and Rationality.* Chicago: University of Chicago Press.

Markovsky, Barry. 1987. "Toward Multilevel Sociological Theories: Simulations of Actor and Network Effects." *Sociological Theory* 5: 101–17.

———. 1988a. "Anchoring Justice." *Social Psychology Quarterly* 51: 213–24.

———. 1988b. "From Expectation States to Macro Processes." In Murray Webster, Jr., and Martha Foschi, eds., *Status Generalization: New Theory and Research*, pp. 351–65. Stanford, Calif.: Stanford University Press.

———. 1992. "Network Exchange Outcomes: Limits of Predictability." *Social Networks* 14: 267–86.

———. 1993. "Evolution and Nebulousness in Theories." Paper presented at the Sixth Annual Small Groups Conference, Miami, August.

Markovsky, B., and Lawler, E. J. 1994. "A New Theory of Group Solidarity." In E. Lawler, B. Markovsky, J. O'Brien, and K. Heimer, eds., *Advances in Group Processes*, vol. 11, pp. 113–37. Greenwich, Conn.: JAI Press.

Markovsky, Barry, Le Roy F. Smith, and Joseph Berger. 1984. "Do Status Interventions Persist?" *American Sociological Review* 49 : 373 – 82.

Markovsky, Barry, David Willer, and Travis Patton. 1988. "Power Relations in Exchange Networks." *American Sociological Review* 53 : 220 – 36.

Markovsky, Barry, John Skvoretz, David Willer, Michael Lovaglia, and Jeffrey Erger. 1993. "The Seeds of Weak Power: An Extension of Network Exchange Theory." *American Sociological Review* 58 : 197 – 209.

Marsden, Peter V. 1983. "Restricted Access in Networks and Models of Power." *American Journal of Sociology* 53 : 686 – 717.

Marsden, Peter V., and N. Lin, eds. 1982. *Social Structure and Network Analysis.* Beverly Hills, Calif.: Sage.

Marsh, Robert M. 1967. *Comparative Sociology: A Codification of Cross-Societal Analysis.* New York: Harcourt, Brace and World.

Martin, Michael W., and Jane Sell. 1979. "The Role of the Experiment in the Social Sciences." *Sociological Quarterly* 20 : 581 – 90.

———. 1980. "The Marginal Utility of Information: Its Effects upon Decision-Making." *Sociological Quarterly* 21 : 233 – 42.

Marwell, Gerald, and Pamela Oliver. 1993. *The Critical Mass in Collective Action: A Micro-Social Theory.* Cambridge, Eng.: Cambridge University Press.

Marx, K. 1964. "Economic and Philosophical Manuscripts." In T. B. Bottomore, ed. and trans., *Karl Marx: Early Writings.* New York: McGraw-Hill.

———. 1967 [1867]. *Capital.* New York: International Publishers.

———. 1968 [1849]. "Wage Labour and Capital." In *Karl Marx and Frederick Engels: Selected Works*, pp. 74 – 97. New York: International Publishers.

———. 1973 [1857]. *Grundrisse.* New York: Vintage Books.

Matsueda, Ross L. 1992. "Reflected Appraisals, Parental Labeling, and Delinquency: Specifying a Symbolic Interactionist Theory." *American Journal of Sociology* 97 : 1577 – 611.

Maupin, Helen E., and Ronald J. Fischer. 1989. "The Effects of Superior Female Performance and Sex-Role Orientation on Gender Conformity." *Canadian Journal of Behavioural Science* 21 : 55 – 69.

Mauss, Marcel. 1954. *The Gift.* Trans. I. Cunnison. London: Cohen and West.

Mayhew, Bruce. 1980. "Structuralism vs. Individualism: Part I, Shadowboxing in the Dark." *Social Forces* 59 : 335 – 75.

Mazur, Allan. 1985. "A Biosocial Model of Status in Face-to-Face Primate Groups." *Social Forces* 64 : 377 – 402.

Mazur, Allan, Eugene A. Rosa, M. Faupel, J. Heller, R. Leen, and B. Thurman. 1980. "Physiological Aspects of Communication via Mutual Gaze." *American Journal of Sociology* 86 : 50 – 74.

Mazur, James E. 1994. "Effects of Intertrial Reinforcers on Self-Control Choice." *Journal of the Experimental Analysis of Behavior* 61 : 83 – 96.

McPherson, J. Miller, and Lynn Smith-Lovin. 1987. "Homophily in Voluntary Organizations: Status Distance and the Consequences of Face-to-Face Groups." *American Sociological Review* 52 : 370 – 79.

Mead, G. H. 1934. *Mind, Self and Society: From the Standpoint of a Social Behaviorist.* Chicago: University of Chicago Press.

Meeker, Barbara F. 1971. "Decisions and Exchange." *American Sociological Review* 36 : 485 – 95.

———. 1984. "Cooperative Orientation, Trust, and Reciprocity." *Human Relations* 37 : 225 – 43.

Meeker, Barbara F., and Robert K. Leik. 1994. "Conceptualizing Reciprocity, Satiation and Equity." Presentation at the MicroComputing Section of the American Sociological Association, Los Angeles, August.

———. 1996. "Describing 'Locking In' in Dyadic Interaction." Paper presented at the annual meeting of the American Sociological Association, New York, August.

Merton, Robert K. 1938. "Social Structure and Anomie." *American Sociological Review* 3: 672–82.

———. 1945. "Sociological Theory." *American Journal of Sociology* 50: 462–73.

———. 1949. "Manifest and Latent Functions." In Robert K. Merton, ed., *Social Theory and Social Structure*, pp. 21–81. Glencoe, Ill.: Free Press.

———. 1968. *Social Theory and Social Structure.* New York: Free Press.

———. 1975. "Structural Analysis in Sociology." In Peter M. Blau, ed., *Approaches to the Study of Social Structure*, pp. 21–52. New York: Free Press.

Merton, Robert K., and Alice S. Rossi. 1950. "Contributions to the Theory of Reference Group Behavior." In R. K. Merton and P. Lazarsfeld, eds., *Continuities in Social Research: Studies in the Scope and Method of "The American Soldier,"* pp. 40–105. New York: Free Press.

Messner, Steven F., Marvin D. Krohn, and Allen E. Liska, eds. 1989. *Theoretical Integration in the Study of Deviance and Crime: Problems and Prospects.* Albany: State University of New York Press.

Metropolis, Nicholas, and Gian-Carlo Rota, eds. 1993. *A New Era in Computation.* Cambridge, Mass.: MIT Press.

Mikula, Gerald. 1980. "On the Role of Justice in Allocation Decisions." In G. Mikula, ed., *Justice and Social Interaction*, pp. 127–65. New York: Springer-Verlag.

Mill, J. S. 1872. *A System of Logic, Ratiocinative and Inductive: Being a Connected View of the Principles of Evidence and the Methods of Scientific Investigation.* 8th ed. London: Longman, Green, Reader and Dyer.

———. 1893. *A System of Logic.* 8th ed. London: Harper.

Miller, Dale T., and W. Turnbull. 1986. "Expectancies and Interpersonal Processes." In M. R. Rosenzweig and L. W. Porter, eds., *Annual Review of Psychology*, vol. 37, pp. 233–56. Palo Alto, Calif.: Annual Review Press.

Molm, Linda D. 1985. "Gender and Power Use: An Experimental Analysis of Behavior and Perceptions." *Social Psychology Quarterly* 48: 285–300.

———. 1990. "The Dynamics of Power in Social Exchange." *American Sociological Review* 55: 427–47.

———. 1993. "When Coercive Power Fails: Incentive and Risk in Social Exchange." Paper presented at the annual meeting of the American Sociological Association, Miami, August.

Molotoch, Harvey. 1994. "Going Out." *Sociological Forum* 9: 221–39.

Monod, Jacques. 1971. *Chance and Necessity: An Essay on the Natural Philosophy of Modern Biology.* New York: Knopf.

Moore, B. S., and A. M. Isen. 1990. "Affect and Social Behavior." In B. S. Moore and A. M. Isen, eds., *Affect and Social Behavior*, pp. 1–21. Cambridge, Eng.: Cambridge University Press.

Moore, Barrington. 1966. *Social Origins of Dictatorship and Democracy: Lord and Peasant in the Making of the Modern World.* Boston: Beacon Press.

Moore, James C. 1985. "Role Enactment and Self-Identity." In Joseph Berger and Morris Zelditch, Jr., eds., *Status, Rewards, and Influence: How Expectations Organize Behavior*, pp. 262–316. San Francisco: Jossey-Bass.

Morris, Ann. 1981. "A Glossary of Terms of the Elementary Theory." In David Willer and Bo Anderson, eds., *Networks, Exchange and Coercion: The Elementary Theory and Its Applications*, pp. 225–33. New York: Elsevier-Greenwood.

Moses, Lincoln E. 1968. "Statistical Analysis: Truncation and Censorship." In David L. Sills, ed., *International Encyclopedia of the Social Sciences*, vol. 15, pp. 196–201. New York: Macmillan.

Mucha, Janusz, Grażyna Skąpska, Jacek Szmatka, and Izabella Uhl, eds. 1991. *Polish Society on the Verge of Changes*. Wrocław-Kraków: Ossolineum. In Polish.

Münch, Richard. 1994. *Sociological Theory: Development Since the 1960s*. Vol. 3. Chicago: Nelson-Hall.

Munroe, P., and R. K. Shelly. 1994. "Do Women Engage in Less Task Behavior than Men?" Paper presented at the Group Process Conference, American Sociological Association annual meeting, Los Angeles, August.

Myerson, Roger B. 1991. *Game Theory: Analysis of Conflict*. Cambridge, Mass.: Harvard University Press.

Nagel, Ernst. 1961. *The Structure of Science*. New York: Harcourt Brace.

Nash, John. 1950. "The Bargaining Problem." *Econometrica* 18:155–62.

———. 1953. "Two-Person Cooperative Games." *Econometrica* 21:128–40.

Norman, Robert Z., and Fred S. Roberts. 1972. "A Measure of Relative Balance for Social Structures." In Joseph Berger, Morris Zelditch, Jr., and Bo Anderson, eds., *Sociological Theories in Progress*, vol. 2, pp. 358–91. Boston: Houghton Mifflin.

Norman, Robert Z., Roy Smith, and Joseph Berger. 1988. "The Processing of Inconsistent Status Information." In M. Webster, Jr., and M. Foschi, eds., *Status Generalization: New Theory and Research*, pp. 169–87 and 493–95. Stanford, Calif.: Stanford University Press.

Nowak, Stefan. 1975. "Introduction." In Georg Simmel, *Sociology*. Warszawa: PWN. In Polish.

———. 1977. "The Strategy of Cross-National Survey Research for the Development of Social Theory." In Alexander Szalai and Riccardo Petrella, eds., *Cross-National Comparative Survey Research: Theory and Practice*, pp. 3–47. Oxford: Pergamon.

———. 1989. "Comparative Studies and Social Theory." In Melvin L. Kohn, ed., *Cross-National Research in Sociology*, pp. 34–56. Newbury Park, Calif.: Sage.

Nowakowska, Maria. 1973. *Language of Motivation and Language of Actions*. The Hague: Mouton.

Oliver, Pamela E., and Gerald Marwell. 1988a. "The paradox of group size in collective action: A theory of the critical mass. II." *American Sociological Review* 53:1–8.

———. 1988b. "Social networks and collective action: A theory of the critical mass. III." *American Journal of Sociology* 94:502–34.

Oliver, Pamela E., Gerald Marwell, and Ruy Teixeira. 1985. "A theory of the critical mass. I: Interdependence, group heterogeneity, and the production of collective action." *American Journal of Sociology* 91:522–56.

Oppenheim, Felix. 1968. "Equality: The Concept of Equality." In David L. Sills, ed., *International Encyclopedia of the Social Sciences*, vol. 5, pp. 102–8. New York: Macmillan.

Painter, Sidney. 1965. *A History of the Middle Ages: 284–1500*. New York: Knopf.

Palen, John J. 1987. *The Urban World*. New York: McGraw-Hill.

Parsons, Talcott. 1951. *The Social System*. Glencoe, Ill.: Free Press.

———. 1968 [1937]. *The Structure of Social Action: A Study in Social Theory with Special Reference to a Group of Recent European Writers*. Vol. 2. New York: Free Press.

———. 1975. "Social Structure and the Symbolic Media of Interchange." In Peter M. Blau, ed., *Approaches to the Study of Social Structure*, pp. 94–120. New York: Free Press.

Patton, Travis, and David Willer. 1990. "Connection and Power in Centralized Exchange Networks." *Journal of Mathematical Sociology* 16:31–49.

Pfeffer, Jeffrey, and Gerald R. Salancik. 1978. *The External Control of Organizations*. New York: Harper and Row.

Pierce, W. David, and Mary Sharon. 1982. "The Effects of Withdrawing Performance Feedback and Social Comparison Cues on Self and Other Performance Expectations." *Canadian Journal of Sociology* 7 : 181–99.

Plato. 1952 [4th century B.C.]. *The Dialogues of Plato.* Trans. Benjamin Jowett. Chicago: Britannica. Original work.

Polivy, J. 1981. "On the Induction of Emotion in the Laboratory: Discrete Moods or Multiple Affect States." *Journal of Personality and Social Psychology* 41 : 803–17.

Popper, K. R. 1959. *The Logic of Scientific Discovery.* New York: Basic Books.

———. 1982. *Realism and the Aim of Science.* Ed. W. W. Bartley. Totowa, N.J.: Rowman and Littlefield.

Powell, Walter W., and Paul J. DiMaggio, eds. 1991. *The New Institutionalism in Organizational Analysis.* Chicago: University of Chicago Press.

Prendergast, Christoper, and J. David Knottnerus. 1994. "Recent Developments in the Theory of Social Structure: Introduction and Overview." In J. David Knottnerus and Christopher Prendergast, eds., *Recent Developments in the Theory of Social Structure,* pp. 1–26. Greenwich, Conn.: JAI Press.

Przeworski, Adam, and Henry Teune. 1970. *The Logic of Comparative Social Inquiry.* New York: Wiley-Interscience.

Pugh, Meredith D., and Ralph Wahrman. 1983. "Neutralizing Sexism in Mixed-Sex Groups: Do Women Have to Be Better Than Men?" *American Journal of Sociology* 88 : 746–62.

Rabbie, J. M., and M. Horowitz. 1988. "Category Versus Group as Explanatory Concepts in Intergroup Relations." *European Journal of Social Psychology* 19 : 172–202.

Ragin, C. C. 1987. *The comparative method: Moving beyond qualitative and quantitative strategies.* Berkeley: University of California Press.

———. 1989. "New directions in comparative research." In Melvin L. Kohn, ed., *Cross-National Research in Sociology,* pp. 57–76. Newbury Park, Calif.: Sage.

Rawls, John. 1971. *A Theory of Justice.* Cambridge, Mass.: Harvard University Press.

Richardson, Lewis F. 1960. *Arms and Insecurity.* Pittsburgh: Boxwood.

Riches, Phoebe, and Margaret Foddy. 1988. "Ethnic Accent as a Status Cue." *Social Psychology Quarterly* 52 : 197–206.

Ridgeway, Cecilia L. 1982. "Status in Groups: The Importance of Motivation." *American Sociological Review* 47 : 76–88.

———. 1984. "Dominance, Performance, and Status in Groups: A Theoretical Analysis." In Edward J. Lawler, ed., *Advances in Group Processes,* vol. 1, pp. 59–93. Greenwich, Conn.: JAI Press.

———. 1987. "Nonverbal Behavior, Dominance, and the Basis of Status in Task Groups." *American Sociological Review* 52 : 683–94.

———. 1988. "Gender Differences in Task Groups: A Status and Legitimacy Account." In Murray Webster, Jr., and Martha Foschi, eds., *Status Generalization: New Theory and Research,* pp. 188–206 and 495–97. Stanford, Calif.: Stanford University Press.

———. 1989. "Understanding Legitimation in Informal Status Orders." In Joseph Berger, Morris Zelditch, Jr., and Bo Anderson, eds., *Sociological Theories in Progress: New Formulations,* pp. 131–59. Newbury Park, Calif.: Sage.

———. 1990. "The Social Construction of Status Value: Gender and Other Nominal Characteristics." Paper presented at the annual meeting of the American Sociological Association, Washington, D.C., August 11–15.

———. 1991. "The Social Construction of Status Value: Gender and Other Nominal Characteristics." *Social Forces* 70 : 367–86.

———. 1993. "Legitimacy, Status, and Dominance Behavior in Groups." In S. Worchel and J. Sempon, eds., *Conflict Between People and Groups*, pp. 110–27. Chicago: Nelson-Hall.

Ridgeway, Cecilia L., and James W. Balkwell. 1992. "Group Processes and the Diffusion of Status-Value Beliefs." Paper presented at the annual meeting of the American Sociological Association, Pittsburgh, August 20–24.

———. 1997. "Group Processes and the Diffusion of Status Value Beliefs." *Social Psychology Quarterly* 60: forthcoming.

Ridgeway, Cecilia L., and Joseph Berger. 1986. "Expectations, Legitimation, and Dominance Behavior in Task Groups." *American Sociological Review* 51 : 603–17.

———. 1988. "The Legitimation of Power and Prestige Orders in Task Groups." In Murray Webster, Jr., and Martha Foschi, eds., *Status Generalization: New Theory and Research*, pp. 207–31 and 497–501. Stanford, Calif.: Stanford University Press.

Ridgeway, Cecilia L., and David Diekema. 1989. "Dominance and Collective Hierarchy Formation in Male and Female Task Groups." *American Sociological Review* 54 : 79–93.

Ridgeway, Cecilia L., and Cathryn Johnson. 1990. "What Is the Relationship between Socioemotional Behavior and Status in Task Groups?" *American Journal of Sociology* 95 : 1189–212.

Ridgeway, Cecilia L., and Lynn Smith-Lovin. 1994. "Structure, Culture, and Interaction: Comparing Two Generative Theories." In E. Lawler, B. Markovsky, J. O'Brien, and K. Heimer, eds., *Advances in Group Processes*, vol. 11, pp. 213–39. Greenwich, Conn.: JAI Press.

Ridgeway, Cecilia, and Henry Walker. 1995. "Status Structures." In K. Cook, G. Fine, and J. House, eds., *Sociological Perspectives in Social Psychology*, pp. 281–310. Boston: Allyn and Bacon.

Ridgeway, Cecilia L., Joseph Berger, and LeRoy Smith. 1985. "Nonverbal Cues and Status: An Expectation States Approach." *American Journal of Sociology* 90 : 955–78.

Ridgeway, Cecilia L., David Diekema, and Cathryn Johnson. 1991. "Status, Legitimacy, and Compliance in Male and Female Groups." Paper presented at the annual meeting of the American Sociological Association, Cincinnati, August 23–27.

Ridgeway, Cecilia L., Cathryn Johnson, and David Diekema. 1994. "External Status, Legitimacy, and Compliance in Male and Female Groups." *Social Forces* 72 : 1051–77.

Rietman, Edward. 1989. *Exploring the Geometry of Nature.* Blue Ridge Summit, Pa.: Windcrest.

Ritzer, George. 1991. *Sociological Theory.* 3d ed. New York: McGraw-Hill.

———. 1992. *Contemporary Sociological Theory.* 3d ed. New York: McGraw-Hill.

Roberts, Karlene H., and Leigh Burstein. 1980. *Issues in Aggregation.* San Francisco: Jossey-Bass.

Rohner, Ronald P. 1977. "Why Cross-Cultural Research?" In Leonore Loeb Adler, ed., *Issues in Cross-Cultural Research*, pp. 3–12. New York: New York Academy of Sciences.

Rorty, Richard. 1979. *Philosophy and the Mirror of Nature.* Princeton, N.J.: Princeton University Press.

Rosenholtz, S. J. 1985. "Modifying Status Expectations in the Traditional Classroom." In J. Berger and M. Zelditch, Jr., eds., *Status, Rewards, and Influence: How Expectations Organize Behavior*, pp. 445–70. San Francisco: Jossey-Bass.

Ross, L. 1977. "The Intuitive Psychologist and His Shortcomings: Distortions in the Attribution Process." In Leonard Berkowitz, ed., *Advances in Experimental Social Psychology*, vol. 10, pp. 173–220. New York: Academic Press.

Ross, L., M. R. Lepper, and M. Hubbard. 1975. "Perseverance in Self-Perception and

Social Perception: Biased Attributional Processes in the Debriefing Paradigm." *Journal of Personality and Social Psychology* 32 : 880–92.

Ross, Michael, and Fiore Sicoly. 1979. "Egocentric Biases in Availability and Attribution." *Journal of Personality and Social Psychology* 37 : 322–37.

Rossi, Ino. 1981. "Transformational Structuralism: Lévi-Strauss's Definition of Social Structure." In Peter M. Blau and Robert K. Merton, eds., *Continuities in Structural Inquiry*, pp. 51–80. Beverly Hills, Calif.: Sage.

Roth, Guenther. 1968. "Introduction." In Max Weber, *Economy and Society: An Outline of Interpretive Sociology*, vol. 1, pp. 27–54. New York: Bedminister Press.

Rothbart, Myron, and Oliver P. John. 1986. "Social Categorization and Behavioral Episodes: A Cognitive Analysis of the Effects of Intergroup Contact." *Journal of Social Issues* 41 : 81–104.

Rubinstein, Ariel. 1982. "Perfect Equilibrium in a Bargaining Model." *Econometrica* 50 : 97–109.

Sachdev, Itesh, and Richard Y. Bourhis. 1985. "Social Categorization and Power Differentials in Group Relations." *European Journal of Social Psychology* 15 : 415–34.

Samuel, Y., and M. Zelditch, Jr. 1989. "Expectations, Shared Awareness, and Power." In Joseph Berger, Morris Zelditch, Jr., and Bo Anderson, eds., *Sociological Theories in Progress: New Formulations*, pp. 288–312. Newbury Park, Calif.: Sage.

Scheff, T. J. 1990. *Microsociology: Discourse, Emotion, and Social Structure*. Chicago: University of Chicago Press.

Schwarz, N. 1990. "Feelings as Information: Informational and Motivational Functions of Affective States." In E. T. Higgins and R. M. Sorrentino, eds., *Handbook of Motivation and Cognition: Foundations of Social Behavior*, vol. 2, pp. 527–61. New York: Guilford Press.

Schwarz, N., H. Bless, and G. Bohner. 1991. "Mood and Persuasion: Affective States Influence the Processing of Persuasive Communications." In Mark P. Zanna, ed., *Advances in Experimental Social Psychology*, vol. 24, pp. 161–99.

Scimecca, Joseph A. 1989. "The Philosophical Foundations of Humanist Sociology." *Current Perspectives in Social Theory* 9 : 223–38.

Seidman, Steven. 1991. "The End of Sociological Theory: The Postmodern Hope." *Sociological Theory* 9 : 131–46.

Sell, Jane, and Lee Freese. 1984. "The Process of Eliminating Status Generalization." *Social Forces* 63 : 538–54.

Sell, Jane, and Michael W. Martin. 1983. "An Acultural Perspective on Experimental Social Psychology." *Personality and Social Psychology Bulletin* 9 : 345–50.

Sen, A. K. 1973. "Behavior and the Concept of Preference." *Economica* 40 : 241–59.

———. 1977. "Rational Fools: A Critique of the Behavioral Foundations of Economic Theory." *Philosophy and Public Affairs* 6 : 317–44.

Sen, A. K., and B. Williams. 1982. "Introduction." In A. Sen and B. Williams, eds., *Utilitarianism and Beyond*, pp. 1–22. Cambridge, Eng.: Cambridge University Press.

Sev'er, Aysan. 1989. "Simultaneous Effects of Status and Task Cues: Combining, Eliminating, or Buffering?" *Social Psychology Quarterly* 52 : 327–35.

Sewell, William H., Jr. 1992. "A Theory of Structure: Duality, Agency, and Transformation." *American Journal of Sociology* 98 : 1–29.

Sewell, William H., Jr., and R. M. Hauser 1975. *Education, Occupation, and Earnings: Achievement in the Early Career*. New York: Academic Press.

Shelly, Robert K. 1988. "Social Differentiation and Social Integration." In M. Webster and M. Foschi, eds., *Status Generalization: New Theory and Research*, pp. 366–76 and 512–15. Stanford, Calif.: Stanford University Press.

———. 1993. "How Sentiments Organize Interaction." In E. J. Lawler, B. Markovsky,

K. Heimer, and J. O'Brien, eds., *Advances in Group Processes*, vol. 10, pp. 113–32. Greenwich, Conn.: JAI Press.

Simmel, Georg. 1964 [1917]. *The Sociology of Georg Simmel*. Trans. and ed. Kurt Wolff. New York: Free Press.

———. 1978. *The Philosophy of Money*. New York: Routledge and Kegan Paul.

Skocpol, Theda. 1979. *States and Social Revolutions*. Cambridge, Eng.: Cambridge University Press.

Skvoretz, John. 1983. "Salience, Heterogeneity and Consolidation of Parameters: Civilizing Blau's Primitive Theory." *American Sociological Review* 48:360–75.

Skvoretz, John, and Thomas J. Fararo. 1989. "Action Structures and Sociological Action Theory." *Journal of Mathematical Sociology* 14:111–37.

———. 1992. "Power and Network Exchange: An Essay Toward Theoretical Unification." *Social Networks* 14:325–44.

Skvoretz, John, and David Willer. 1991. "Power in Exchange Networks: Setting and Structure Variations." *Social Psychology Quarterly* 54:224–38.

———. 1993. "Exclusion and Power: A Test of Four Theories of Power in Exchange Networks." *American Sociological Review* 58:801–18.

Skvoretz, John, David Willer, and Thomas J. Fararo. 1993. "Toward Models of Power Development in Exchange Networks." *Sociological Perspectives* 36:95–115.

Słomczyński, Kazimierz M. 1989. *Social Structure and Mobility: Poland, Japan, the United States*. Warszawa: IFiS.

Słomczyński, Kazimierz M., Joanne Miller, and Melvin Kohn. 1981. "Stratification, Work, and Values: A Polish–United States Comparison." *American Sociological Review* 46:720–44.

Smith, E. R., and J. R. Kluegel. 1982. "Cognitive and Social Bases of Emotional Experience: Outcome, Attribution, and Affect." *Journal of Personality and Social Psychology* 43:1129–41.

Smith-Lovin, Lynn, and David R. Heise. 1987. *Analyzing Social Interaction: Advances in Affect Control Theory*. New York: Gordon and Breach. Special issue of *Journal of Mathematical Sociology* 13.

Sohn, D. 1982. "Sex Differences in Achievement Self-Attributions: An Effect-Size Analysis." *Sex Roles* 8:345–57.

Sozański, Tadeusz. 1986. "On the Notion of Structure in Sociology and Mathematics: Graph Models of Social Wholes." *Studia Socjologiczne* 2:111–34. In Polish.

———. 1992. "A Combinatorial Theory of Minimal Social Situations." *Journal of Mathematical Sociology* 17:105–25.

———. 1993a. "A Tentative Formalization of Network Exchange Theory." In Tadeusz Sozański, Jacek Szmatka, and Marian Kempny, eds., *Structure, Exchange and Power: Studies in Theoretical Sociology*, pp. 149–93. Warszawa: IFiS. In Polish.

———. 1993b. "Hierarchical Exchange Systems: A Replication of an Experiment of David Willer." In Tadeusz Sozański, Jacek Szmatka, and Marian Kempny, eds., *Structure, Exchange and Power: Studies in Theoretical Sociology*, pp. 233–71. Warszawa: IFiS. In Polish.

———. 1994. "Toward a Theory of Equilibrium in Network Exchange Systems: A Mathematical Development of Equal Dependence Formulation." Paper presented at the 13th World Congress of Sociology, Bielefeld, Germany, June.

Sozański, Tadeusz, Jacek Szmatka, and Marian Kempny, eds. 1993. *Structure, Exchange and Power: Studies in Theoretical Sociology*. Warszawa: IFiS. In Polish.

Spergel, David N., and Neil G. Turok. 1992. "Textures and cosmic structures." *Scientific American* 266 (3):52–59.

Staniszkis, Jadwiga. 1992. *The Ontology of Socialism*. Oxford: Clarendon Press.

Stark, Rodney. 1994. *Sociology*. 5th ed. Belmont, Calif.: Wadsworth.

Stewart, Penni. 1988. "Women and Men in Groups: A Status Characteristics Approach to Interaction." In Murray Webster, Jr., and Martha Foschi, eds., *Status Generalization: New Theory and Research*, pp. 69–85 and 484–86. Stanford, Calif.: Stanford University Press.

Stewart, Penni, and James C. Moore. 1992. "Wage Disparities and Performance Expectations." *Social Psychology Quarterly* 55:78–85.

Stinchcombe, Arthur L. 1968. *Constructing Social Theories*. New York: Harcourt Brace.

———. 1994. "Disintegrated Disciplines and the Future of Sociology." *Sociological Forum* 9:279–91.

Stolte, John. 1988. "Formation of Justice Norms." *American Sociological Review* 52:774–4.

Stolte, John, and Richard M. Emerson. 1977. "Structural Inequality: Position and Power in Exchange Structures." In Robert L. Hamblin and John H. Kunkel, eds., *Behavioral Theory in Sociology*, pp. 117–38. New Brunswick, N.J.: Transaction Books.

Stouffer, Samuel A., et al. 1949. *The American Soldier*. 2 vols. Studies in Social Psychology in World War II. Princeton, N.J.: Princeton University Press.

Strodtbeck, Fred L. and R. D. Mann. 1956. "Sex Role Differentiation in Jury Deliberations." *Sociometry* 19:3–11.

Strodtbeck, Fred L., R. M. James, and C. Hawkins. 1957. "Social Status in Jury Deliberations." *American Sociological Review* 22:713–19.

Stryker, Sheldon R. 1980. *Symbolic Interactionism: A Social Structural Version*. Menlo Park, Calif.: Benjamin Cummings.

———. 1987. "The Vitalization of Symbolic Interactionism." *Social Psychology Quarterly* 50:83–94.

Stuart, Alan, and J. Keith Ord. 1987. *Kendall's Advanced Theory of Statistics, Volume 1: Distribution Theory*. 5th ed. Originally by Sir Maurice Kendall. New York: Oxford University Press.

Such, Jan. 1972. *On Universality of Scientific Laws*. Warszawa: PWN. In Polish.

Suls, J. M., and R. L. Miller. 1978. "Ability Comparison and Its Effects on Affiliation Preferences." *Human Relations* 31:267–82.

Suls, J. M., and R. L. Miller, eds. 1977. *Social Comparison Processes: Theoretical and Empirical Perspectives*. Washington, D.C.: Hemisphere.

Sutherland, Edwin. 1924. *Criminology*. Philadelphia: Lippincott.

Szmatka, Jacek. 1994. "Elementary Theoretic Research Program: An Extension of Social Exchange Theory." Paper presented at the annual meeting of the American Sociological Association, Los Angeles, August 4–9.

Szmatka, Jacek, and Tadeusz Sozański. 1994. "On Four Myths of Sociology and Three Generations of Sociological Theories." *Polish Sociological Review* 107:219–33.

Szmatka, Jacek, and David Willer. 1993. "Towards a Theoretical Research Program of the Dynamics of Social Structure." In Tadeusz Sozański, Jacek Szmatka, and Marian Kempny, eds., *Structure, Exchange and Power: Studies in Theoretical Sociology*, pp. 29–71. Warszawa: IFiS. In Polish.

———. 1995. "Exclusion, Inclusion and Compound Connection in Exchange Networks." *Social Psychology Quarterly* 58:123–32.

Szmatka, Jacek, Zdzisław Mach, and Janusz Mucha, eds. 1993. *Eastern European Societies on the Threshold of Change*. New York: Edwin Mellen Press.

Tajfel, Henri. 1978. *Differentiation Between Social Groups: Studies in the Social Psychology of Intergroup Relations*. New York: Academic Press.

———. 1981. *Human Groups and Social Categories: Studies in Social Psychology*. New York: Cambridge University Press.

Tajfel, H., and J. C. Turner. 1985. "The Social Identity Theory of Intergroup Behavior." In S. Worchel and W. S. Austin, eds., *Psychology of Intergroup Relations*, pp. 7–24. Chicago: Nelson-Hall.

Tajfel, Henri, M. G. Billig, R. P. Bundy, and C. Flament. 1971. "Social Categorization and Intergroup Behavior." *European Journal of Social Psychology* 1:149–78.

Takahashi, N., and T. Yamagishi. 1993. "Power in Social Exchange Networks." *Sociological Theory and Methods* 8:251–69. In Japanese with an English abstract.

Tallman, I., L. Gray, and R. Leik. 1991. "Decisions, Dependency, and Commitment: An Exchange Based Theory of Group Development." In E. J. Lawler, B. Markovsky, C. Ridgeway, and H. Walker, eds., *Advances in Group Processes*, vol. 9. pp. 227–57. Greenwich, Conn.: JAI Press.

Taylor, M. 1987. *The Possibility of Cooperation*. Cambridge, Eng.: Cambridge University Press.

Thibaut, John W., and Harold H. Kelley. 1959. *The Social Psychology of Groups*. New York: Wiley.

Thomas, George M., Henry A. Walker, and Morris Zelditch, Jr. 1986. "Legitimacy and Collective Action." *Social Forces* 65:378–404.

Thomas, William I., and Dorothy S. Thomas. 1928. *The Child in America: Behavior Problems and Programs*. New York: Knopf.

Tilly, Charles. 1973. *The Vendée: A Social Analysis of the Counter-Revolution of 1793*. Cambridge, Mass.: Harvard University Press.

———. 1984. *Big Structures, Large Processes, Huge Comparisons*. New York: Russell Sage.

———. 1990. *Coercion, Capital, and European States, A.D. 900–1990*. Oxford: Basil Blackwell.

Treiman, D. J., and K. Yip. 1989. "Educational and Occupational Attainment in 21 Countries." In Melvin L. Kohn, ed., *Cross-National Research in Sociology*, pp. 373–94. Newbury Park, Calif.: Sage.

Turner, John C. 1985. "Social Categorization and the Self-Concept: A Social Cognitive Theory of Group Behavior." In E. J. Lawler, ed., *Advances in Group Process*, vol. 2, pp. 77–121. Greenwich, Conn.: JAI Press.

Turner, Jonathan H. 1989. "Introduction: Can Sociology Be a Cumulative Science?" In Jonathan H. Turner, ed., *Theory Building in Sociology: Assessing Theoretical Cumulation*, pp. 8–18. Newbury Park, Calif.: Sage.

———. 1991. *The Structure of Sociological Theory*. 5th ed. Belmont, Calif.: Wadsworth.

Turner, Stephen P. 1989. "Jasso's Principle." *Sociological Theory* 7:130–34.

Tuzlak, Aysan. 1988. "Boomerang Effects: Status and Demeanor Over Time." In Murray Webster, Jr., and Martha Foschi, eds., *Status Generalization: New Theory and Research*, pp. 261–74 and 503–5. Stanford, Calif.: Stanford University Press.

———. 1989. "Joint Effects of Race and Confidence on Perceptions and Influence: Implications for Blacks in Decision-Making Positions." *Canadian Ethnic Studies* 21:103–19.

Tuzlak, Aysan, and James C. Moore. 1984. "Status, Demeanor, and Influence: An Empirical Assessment." *Social Psychology Quarterly* 47:178–83.

Tversky, Amos, and Daniel Kahneman. 1986. "Rational Choice and the Framing of Decisions." In Robin M. Hogarth and Melvin W. Reder, eds., *Rational Choice: The Contrast between Economics and Psychology*, pp. 67–94. Chicago: University of Chicago Press.

Vila, Bryan J., and Lawrence E. Cohen. 1993. "Crime as Strategy: Testing an Evolutionary Ecological Theory of Expropriative Crime." *American Journal of Sociology* 98:873–912.

Volterra, V. 1931. *Leçon sur la théorie mathématique de la lutte pour la vie.* Paris: Gauthier-Villars.

Wagner, David G. 1984. *The Growth of Sociological Theories.* Beverly Hills, Calif.: Sage.

———. 1992a. "Gender Differences in Reward Preference: A Status-Based Account." Under review.

———. 1992b. "Status Inconsistency and Reward Preference." Under review.

Wagner, David, and Joseph Berger. 1985. "Do Sociological Theories Grow?" *American Journal of Sociology* 90:697–728.

———. 1986. "Programs, Theory, and Metatheory." *American Journal of Sociology* 92:168–82.

———. 1993a. "Status Characteristics Theory: The Growth of a Program." In Joseph Berger and Morris Zelditch, Jr., eds., *Theoretical Research Programs: Studies in the Growth of Theory*, pp. 23–63 and 454–63. Stanford, Calif.: Stanford University Press.

———. 1993b. "Gender and Interpersonal Behavior: Status Expectation Accounts." Paper presented at the meeting of the American Association for the Advancement of Science, Boston, February.

Wagner, David G., Rebecca S. Ford, and Thomas W. Ford. 1986. "Can Gender Inequalities Be Reduced?" *American Sociological Review* 51:47–61.

Walker, Henry A., and Bernard P. Cohen. 1985. "Scope Statements: Imperatives for Evaluating Theory." *American Sociological Review* 50:288–301.

Walker, Henry A., Larry Rogers, and Morris Zelditch, Jr. 1988. "Legitimacy and Collective Action: A Research Note." *Social Forces* 67:216–28.

Walker, Henry A., George M. Thomas, and Morris Zelditch, Jr. 1986. "Legitimation, Endorsement, and Stability." *Social Forces* 64:620–43.

Walker, Henry A., Larry Rogers, George M. Thomas, and Morris Zelditch, Jr. 1991. "Legitimating Collective Action: Theory and Experimental Results." *Research in Political Sociology* 5:1–25.

Walster, E., E. Berscheid, and G. Walster. 1976. "New Directions in Equity Research." In L. Berkowitz and E. Walster, eds., *Advances in Experimental Social Psychology*, vol. 9, pp. 1–42. New York: Academic Press.

Walton, John. 1986. *Sociology and Critical Inquiry.* Chicago: Dorsey Press.

Watson, James D. 1969. *The Double Helix.* New York: Penguin Books.

Weber, Max. 1963 [1919]. "The Social Causes of the Decay of Ancient Civilization." Trans. R. Frank. In Russell Kahl, ed., *Studies in Explanation*, pp. 339–55. Englewood Cliffs, N.J.: Prentice-Hall.

———. 1968 [1918]. *Economy and Society: An Outline of Interpretive Sociology.* New York: Bedminister Press.

Webster, Murray A., Jr. 1975. *Actions and Actors.* Cambridge, Mass.: Winthrop.

———. 1977. "Equating Characteristics and Social Interaction: Two Experiments." *Sociometry* 40:41–50.

———. 1982. "Moral Characteristics and Status Generalization." Research proposal funded by the National Science Foundation.

Webster, Murray, Jr., and James E. Driskell, Jr. 1979. "Status Generalization: A Review and Some New Data." *American Sociological Review* 43:220–36.

———. 1983. "Beauty as Status." *American Journal of Sociology* 89:140–65.

Webster, M., Jr., and M. Foschi. 1988. "Overview of Status Generalization." In Murray Webster, Jr., and Martha Foschi, eds., *Status Generalization: New Theory and Research*, pp. 1–20 and 477–78. Stanford, Calif.: Stanford University Press.

Webster, Murray A., Jr., and Martha Foschi, eds. 1988. *Status Generalization: New Theory and Research.* Stanford, Calif.: Stanford University Press.

Webster, M., Jr., and S. J. Hysom. Forthcoming. "Sexual Orientation as Status." MS available from the authors at Dept. of Sociology, UNCC, Charlotte, NC 28223.

Webster, Murray, and John Kervin. 1971. "Artificiality in Experimental Sociology." *Canadian Review of Sociology and Anthropology* 8:263–72.

Webster, Murray, Jr., and L. Smith. 1978. "Justice and Revolutionary Coalitions: A Test of Two Theories." *American Journal of Sociology* 84:267–92.

Webster, Murray, Jr., and Barbara Sobieszek. 1974. *Sources of Self-Evaluation: A Formal Theory of Significant Others*. New York: Wiley.

Weil, Frederick D. 1989. "The Sources and Structure of Legitimation in Democracies: A Consolidated Model Tested with Time-Series Data in Six Countries Since World War II." *American Sociological Review* 54:682–706.

Weiner, B., D. Russell, and D. Lerman. 1979. "The Cognition-Emotion Process in Achievement-Related Contexts." *Journal of Personality and Social Psychology* 37:1211–20.

Weinstein, Eugene, and P. Deutschberger. 1963. "Some Dimensions of Altercasting." *Sociometry* 26:454–66.

Wesołowski, Włodzimierz. 1979. *Classes, Strata, and Power*. London: Routledge.

Wesołowski, Włodzimierz, and Bogdan Mach. 1986. "Unfulfilled Systemic Functions of Social Mobility I: A Theoretical Scheme." *International Sociology* 1:19–35.

Westcott, M. R. 1988. *The Psychology of Human Freedom*. New York: Springer-Verlag.

White, R. W. 1959. "Motivation reconsidered: The concept of competence." *Psychological Review* 66:297–333.

Whitley, B. E., M. C. McHugh, and I. H. Frieze. 1986. "Assessing the Theoretical Models for Sex Differences in Causal Attributions of Success and Failure." In J. S. Hyde and M. C. Linn, eds., *The Psychology of Gender: Advances Through Meta-Analyses*, pp. 102–35. Baltimore: Johns Hopkins University Press.

Whyte, William F. 1943. *Street Corner Society*. Chicago: University of Chicago Press.

Wiggins, B., and D. R. Heise. 1987. "Expectations, Intentions, and Behavior: Some Tests of Affect Control Theory." In L. Smith-Lovin and D. R. Heise, eds., *Analyzing Social Interaction: Advances in Affect Control Theory*, pp. 153–69. New York: Gordon and Breach. Special issue of *Journal of Mathematical Sociology* 13.

Willer, David. 1967. *Scientific Sociology Theory and Method*. Englewood Cliffs, N.J.: Prentice-Hall.

———. 1981a. "The Basic Concepts of Elementary Theory." In David Willer and Bo Anderson, eds., *Networks, Exchange and Coercion: The Elementary Theory and Its Applications*, pp. 25–53. New York: Elsevier-Greenwood.

———. 1981b. "Quantity and Network Structure." In David Willer and Bo Anderson, eds., *Networks, Exchange and Coercion: The Elementary Theory and Its Applications*, pp. 109–24. New York: Elsevier-Greenwood.

———. 1984. "Analysis and Composition as Theoretic Procedures." *Journal of Mathematical Sociology* 10:241–70.

———. 1985. "Property and Social Exchange." In Edward J. Lawler, ed., *Advances in Group Processes*, vol. 2, pp. 123–42. Greenwich, Conn.: JAI Press.

———. 1986. "Vulnerability and the Location of Power Positions: Comment on Cook, Emerson, Gillmore, and Yamagishi." *American Journal of Sociology* 92:441–44.

———. 1987. *Theory and Experimental Investigation of Social Structures*. New York: Gordon and Breach.

———. 1992a. "Predicting Power in Exchange Networks: A Brief History and Introduction to the Issues." *Social Networks* 14:187–211.

———. 1992b. "The Principle of Rational Choice and the Problem of a Satisfactory

Theory." In J. S. Coleman and T. J. Fararo, eds., *Rational Choice Theory: Advocacy and Critique*, pp. 49–79. Newbury Park Calif.: Sage.

Willer, David, and Bo Anderson, eds. 1981. *Networks, Exchange and Coercion: The Elementary Theory and Its Applications*. New York: Elsevier-Greenwood.

Willer, David, and Barry Markovsky. 1993. "Elementary Theory: Its Development and Research Program." In Joseph Berger and Morris Zelditch, Jr., eds., *Theoretical Research Programs: Studies in the Growth of Theory*, pp. 323–63 and 483–86. Stanford Calif.: Stanford University Press.

Willer, David, and Travis Patton. 1987. "The Development of Network Exchange Theory." In E. J. Lawler and B. Markovsky, eds., *Advances in Group Processes*, vol. 4, pp. 199–242. Greenwich, Conn.: JAI Press.

Willer, David, and Jacek Szmatka. 1993. "Cross-National Experimental Investigations of Elementary Theory: Implications for the Generality of the Theory and the Autonomy of Social Structure." In Edward Lawler, Barry Markovsky, Karen Heimer, and Jodi O'Brien, eds., *Advances in Group Processes*, vol. 10, pp. 37–81. Greenwich, Conn.: JAI Press.

Willer, David, and Judith Willer. 1973. *Systematic Empiricism: Critique of a Pseudoscience*. Englewood Cliffs, N.J.: Prentice-Hall.

Willer, David, Barry Markovsky, and Travis Patton. 1989. "Power Structures: Derivations and Applications of Elementary Theory." In Joseph Berger, Morris Zelditch, Jr., and Bo Anderson, eds., *Sociological Theories in Progress: New Formulations*, pp. 313–53. Newbury Park, Calif.: Sage.

Wilson, B. 1979. "Classroom Instructional Features and Conceptions of Academic Ability." Ph.D. diss., Stanford University.

Wilson, James Q., and Richard J. Herrnstein. 1985. *Crime and Human Nature*. New York: Simon and Schuster.

Worth, L. T., and D. M. Mackie. 1987. "Cognitive Mediation of Positive Affect in Persuasion." *Social Cognition* 5:76–94.

Wuthnow, R. 1987. *Meaning and Moral Order*. Berkeley: University of California Press.

Yamagishi, Toshio. 1992. "Evolution of Norms Without Metanorms." Paper presented at the 5th International Conference on Social Dilemmas, Bielefeld, Germany, June.

Yamagishi, Toshio, and Karen S. Cook. 1993. "Generalized Exchange and Social Dilemmas." *Social Psychology Quarterly* 56:235–48.

Yamagishi, Toshio, Mary R. Gillmore, and Karen S. Cook. 1988. "Network Connection and the Distribution of Power in Exchange Networks." *American Journal of Sociology* 93:833–51.

Yamaguchi, Kazuo. 1996. "Power in Networks of Substitutable and Complementary Exchange." *American Sociological Review* 61:308–32.

Yogev, A., and R. Shapira. 1987. "Ethnicity, Meritocracy and Credentialism in Israel: Elaborating the Credential Society Thesis." In R. V. Robinson, ed., *Research in Social Stratification and Mobility*, vol. 6, pp. 187–212. Greenwich, Conn.: JAI Press.

Yoon, J. 1994. "An Empirical Test of a Commitment Model for Negotiated Exchange." Ph.D. diss., University of Iowa.

Zelditch, Morris, Jr. 1991a. "Levels in the Logic of Macro-historical Explanation." In Joan Huber, ed., *Macro-Micro Linkages in Sociology*. Newbury Park, Calif.: Sage.

———. 1991b. "Levels of Specificity Within Theoretical Strategies." *Sociological Perspectives* 34:303–12.

———. 1992. "Problems and Progress in Sociological Theory." *Sociological Perspectives* 35:415–31.

Zelditch, Morris, Jr., and Henry A. Walker. 1984. "Legitimacy and the Stability of Authority." In Edward J. Lawler, ed., *Advances in Group Processes*, vol. 1, pp. 1–25. Greenwich, Conn.: JAI Press.

Zelditch, Morris, Jr., Patrick Lauderdale, and Stephen Stublarec. 1975. "How Are Inconsistencies in Status and Ability Resolved?" Technical Report No. 54. Laboratory for Social Research, Stanford University.

———. 1980. "How are Inconsistencies Between Status and Ability Resolved?" *Social Forces* 50:1025–43.

Index

277, 282, 284, 287, 296, 298, 299,
303, 307, 309–11, 314–16, 318,
320–24, 326–30, 334, 336, 337, 347,
349–51, 369, 392, 400, 401, 406, 419;
operationalizing, 23, 25; testing of, 88,
115, 241
Multiple standards, 6, 7, 201, 202, 207–9,
212, 213, 216, 217, 220, 221

N-branch, 286
Negative heuristic, 48
Negotiation protocol, 314, 315, 317
Network exchange system, 307, 308, 312,
314, 319, 324, 348; formal modeling
of, 307
Network exchange theory, 96, 160, 303,
320, 324, 349
Network interaction theory, 305
Network model, 9, 362, 363
Networks, 4, 5, 7–9, 14, 23, 24, 32, 38,
53, 69, 96, 98, 103, 105, 120–22, 131,
137, 157–60, 177, 273, 285, 286,
293–98, 300–303, 307, 308, 312,
324–26, 331, 332, 337, 349, 351, 352,
354, 356, 358–61, 400, 408
Nominal distinction or characteristic (N):
definition of, 2, 22, 24, 25, 46, 77,
184, 206, 214, 299, 307, 308, 314,
319–21, 323, 324, 327, 328, 330, 337,
345–48, 385; salience of, 139, 197
Norms, 38, 51, 52, 58, 59, 120, 128, 129,
132, 133, 206, 280, 304, 365–67, 369,
379, 388, 397, 407

Objectivist, 120–22, 131, 132, 135
Observation statements, 78
Observation values, 71
Offer, 1, 2, 4, 73, 89, 96, 108, 150, 153,
165, 178, 180, 199, 203, 286, 299,
308, 313, 315–18, 325–27, 350, 351,
355, 360, 390; realistic, 316, 327, 351;
reliable, 16, 173, 180, 302, 316; socially approved, 316, 317
Operationalization, 16, 24, 75, 86, 298
Orienting strategies, 4, 29, 30, 35–37,
40–42, 46

Parallelism, 9, 362, 364, 367–69, 372,
383, 385
Pareto variate, 250, 253, 256, 263, 264,
266, 267, 269, 271

Peer status, 7, 222–24, 226, 229, 233,
234, 236, 238
Performance evaluations, 206; biased, 7,
35, 204, 410
Performance expectations, 43, 44, 124,
125, 129, 130, 141, 149, 165, 169,
176, 177, 181–88, 191–93, 195–98,
202, 204, 205, 217, 218, 281
Personality characteristics, 216
Philosophy of science, 73, 76, 81
Population ecology, 57, 121
Position in a network exchange system:
peripheral, 96, 104, 286, 292, 312,
317, 318, 346–50
Positions, 4, 5, 9, 14, 16, 24, 34, 36, 40–
44, 46, 53, 96, 98, 102, 104, 120, 122,
126, 128, 133, 135, 159, 165, 168,
178, 180, 183, 225, 275–78, 280, 281,
295–97, 308–19, 322, 324, 325, 331,
334, 336–39, 345–56, 358–60, 410;
social, 1–10, 13, 14, 18, 19, 22–24,
26, 32, 34–39, 41, 44, 45, 47–51, 55,
56, 58–62, 67–70, 78, 80, 87–90, 92,
94–96, 99, 100, 114, 119–23, 125–
39, 141, 144, 148–54, 156–60, 163,
164, 168, 169, 174, 179, 181, 195,
205–7, 213, 214, 222–25, 243, 253,
257, 273–81, 283–85, 288, 289, 293,
294, 296, 297, 303–6, 309, 312–14,
316, 317, 349, 351, 352, 358–60,
362–69, 371, 372, 374, 378, 379, 383,
385, 386, 388–96, 400, 402, 405, 406,
408, 410, 411, 419, 420
Positive heuristic, 48, 49, 70
Power, 5, 7–9, 18, 19, 26, 29, 31–34, 37,
38, 40, 43–45, 53, 82, 84, 90, 94–96,
98, 100, 101, 104, 112, 115, 122–24,
128, 129, 131, 133–35, 137, 148, 149,
151, 154, 159–69, 176–79, 181, 183,
187, 203, 204, 212, 218, 234, 238,
250, 252, 274, 273, 274, 276, 277,
281, 283, 284, 286–98, 300–302,
306, 307, 311, 317, 318, 320, 325,
334–39, 344–52, 356, 358, 365, 401,
402, 406, 407, 411, 414, 416–19, 421;
coercive, 5, 8, 96, 99, 100, 102–5,
109, 274, 277, 279, 281–84, 289–91;
exchange, 4–10, 32, 41, 43, 45, 53,
58–62, 67, 68, 91, 96, 98, 100–104,
106, 108, 109, 121, 131–34, 139,
159–65, 170, 172–74, 176–78, 185,

Library of Congress Cataloging-in-Publication Data

Status, network, and structure : theory development in group
processes / edited by Jacek Szmatka, John Skvoretz, and Joseph
Berger.

   p. cm.

Includes bibliographical references and index.

ISBN 0-8047-2844-5 (alk. paper)

1. Sociology—Philosophy.   I. Szmatka, Jacek.   II. Skvoretz,
John.   III. Berger, Joseph, 1924– .

HM24.S7425   1997

301'.01—dc21   97-2429
                                                          CIP

♾ This book is printed on acid-free, recycled paper.

Original printing 1997

Last figure below indicates year of this printing:

06   05   04   03   02   01   00   99   98   97

This book is to be returned on
or before the date stamped below